THE THREE LAWS OF
INVESTMENT

The Three Laws of International Investment

*National, Contractual, and International
Frameworks for Foreign Capital*

JESWALD W. SALACUSE

OXFORD
UNIVERSITY PRESS

OXFORD
UNIVERSITY PRESS

Great Clarendon Street, Oxford, OX2 6DP,
United Kingdom

Oxford University Press is a department of the University of Oxford.
It furthers the University's objective of excellence in research, scholarship,
and education by publishing worldwide. Oxford is a registered trade mark of
Oxford University Press in the UK and in certain other countries

First Edition published in 2013
First published in paperback 2014

Impression: 1

Published in the United States of America by Oxford University Press
198 Madison Avenue, New York, NY 10016, United States of America

British Library Cataloguing in Publication Data
Data available

Library of Congress in Publication Data
Data available

ISBN 978–0–19–965456–7 (Hbk.)
ISBN 978–0–19–872737–8 (Pbk.)

Printed in Great Britain by
Lightning Source (UK) Ltd.

Links to third party websites are provided by Oxford in good faith and
for information only. Oxford disclaims any responsibility for the materials
contained in any third party website referenced in this work.

In Memory of William L. Salacuse,
Attorney & Counselor at Law

Preface

International investment is an increasingly powerful force for economic growth and prosperity throughout the world. All countries, rich and poor, seek foreign capital and its associated technology and know-how as vital elements in their plans for national economic development. Accordingly, all governments have either explicitly or implicitly formulated policies about international investment and have incorporated them into their legal systems. At the same time, companies from both developed and developing countries are investing massive amounts of capital abroad in their search for markets, natural resources, production efficiencies, and knowledge. In connection with these efforts, investors and their legal counsel take great care in using a variety of legal devices to structure their investments in ways that will maximize investment returns and minimize investment risks.

While economic forces are the essential drivers of international investment, they are not the only factors that influence it. Legal rules and institutions also affect international investment flows. Law determines whether and how investments may be made in a particular country, the nature of the respective rights of investors and host country governments, the means by which governments and investors may adjust their legal relationships to changing circumstances, and the processes they may use to resolve their investment disputes.

The rules applicable to international investments are derived from three basic legal frameworks: (1) national laws, both of the host country and the investor's home country; (2) contracts, whether between investors and host governments or among investors; and (3) international law, consisting of applicable treaties, customs, and general legal principles developed by states. Any international investor must therefore understand the nature and complex interaction among these three legal frameworks—national, contractual, and international—in undertaking, managing and protecting a foreign investment. Thus, United Kingdom investors seeking to build a power plant in India to sell electricity to a state government's public utility must evaluate and use the Indian laws governing the ability of foreigners to enter the power sector, the state regulations concerning the production and sale of electricity to state power companies, the contract between the contemplated power company and the state corporation, and the international rules protecting investor rights embodied in a variety of sources, including treaties between India and the United Kingdom. For the UK investors, the economic success of the power project depends crucially on the content and application of the three frameworks. For the central government of India and the state government, the three frameworks are equally essential for securing and regulating a reliable and economical source of electricity so essential to their growth and development. In their operation, these frameworks are not isolated but interrelated. Thus, the content of the contractual framework is profoundly influenced by the applicable national law, and investor rights under international law are influenced by national legislation. For example, in the event of conflict with the Indian government, the ability of the UK investors to invoke treaty protection may require them first to avail themselves of remedies in the Indian courts, at least for a period of time.

This book examines the content of each of these three legal frameworks for international investment and explores how they influence the foreign investment process and the operation of international investment transactions, projects, and enterprises. The term "international investment law," so commonly used to describe the law applicable to foreign investments, contains an inherent ambiguity. It may refer either to the international law governing investments or to all the law applicable to international investments. Thus, while many excellent books exist on the subject of "international investment law," they focus primarily on the international law and thus tell only part of the legal story of foreign investment. Indeed, in their focus almost uniquely on the international law governing investment, one can say that such works tell only one-third of that story since they do not examine in depth the two other crucial legal frameworks—national laws and investment contracts. Consequently, they do not explain how host and home countries use their legal systems to encourage and regulate international investment, nor do they consider the various legal devices and techniques that investors and governments employ to structure investment projects and transactions. An understanding of both of these dimensions of the investment process is vital for lawyers, executives, and government officials working with foreign investment.

In taking a comprehensive view of the laws affecting foreign investment, this book is divided into five parts, each of which consists of three or more chapters. *Part I: International Investment and the Law*, after explaining the contemporary nature and significance of international investment, examines the theoretical and practical links between law and the investment process. It explores how and why law fosters or impedes investment and posits that the international investment process is influenced by the actions of three basic players: the host country, the investor, and the investor's home country. It examines the interests and policies of each player and how those interests and policies influence the content and application of the laws of foreign investment. Part I concludes with an overview of the nature of the three principal legal frameworks for international investment resulting from the interplay of these interests.

Part II: The National Legal Framework explores the nature of a country's national laws affecting foreign investment. It begins with a chapter examining the factors that influence national policies and laws on international investment, particularly governmental ideologies, popular attitudes, and accepted economic models of national development. Subsequent chapters explore state controls on the exit and entry of capital, national regulation of foreign investment, and the problem of legal and regulatory instability. Regardless of legal tradition and economic history, national regulatory systems are fundamentally influenced by two, often competing imperatives: the need to encourage the inflow and investment of foreign capital and the need to control that flow and its use once it has entered the country. The precise balance that the national legal framework strikes between these two imperatives varies from country to country and also changes over time.

Any foreign investment is basically a bargain between the foreign investor and the host country. Countries use their legal systems to maximize the perceived benefits and minimize the contemplated costs of that bargain. In doing so, all national regulatory frameworks must address four basic issues: (1) the nature of the foreign investment the country seeks or will accept; (2) the incentives that it is willing to grant to desired investments; (3) the regulatory controls to which desired investments will be subject; and (4) the governmental apparatus that will administer the foreign investment process. Part II considers each of these legal issues and their impact on foreign investments and investors. It then concludes with a consideration of the challenges of legal change and its impact on investors and governments.

In *Part III, The Contractual Framework*, the book explores the nature of the contractual framework for international investments, and the complex of rules that have been shaped by negotiated agreements between the parties. It begins by discussing the role of contracts in the investment process. Since any investment transaction is invariably the product of negotiation between the parties concerned and the host government, the following chapter explains the process by which agreements are negotiated and the techniques employed by the foreign investors and governments to advance their respective interests in the process. Part III then examines in detail particular types of investment contracts employed in international investment, especially joint venture agreements, project finance arrangements, and international loans. A separate chapter is devoted to a special kind of contract that is part of many international investment transactions: political risk insurance. Since investment contracts are invariably long-term transactions subject to the vicissitudes of changing circumstances, Part III concludes with a chapter on contractual stability and renegotiation, subjects of vital concern for both investors and host governments.

Part IV: The International Legal Framework explores the international rules and institutions for investment to be found in the complex of treaties, customs, and general legal principles that have emerged to protect investment from certain types of injurious actions by host country governments. The international legal framework developed primarily because foreign investors and their home governments judged that the national and contractual legal frameworks in host countries did not afford foreign investments sufficient protection. This part of the book first explores the historical development of the international legal framework, then examines its contemporary elements and principles, and finally considers its effectiveness and the various ways these international rules are applied and investment disputes settled.

To conclude the volume, *Part V* considers how the three legal frameworks interact with each other.

I have worked in the field of the law of international investment for nearly forty years as teacher, scholar, legal consultant, and arbitrator. During that time, I have benefited from invaluable conversations with countless lawyers, economists, government officials, business executives, scholars, arbitrators, and international experts in many disciplines. They are too numerous to list here by name but I am deeply grateful to all of them for helping me understand this important area of law and its relationship to economic growth and development.

In writing this book, various persons have provided invaluable assistance for which I am grateful. In that regard, I especially want to thank Gaurav Tiwari, Cecelia Vogel, and Hyejin Park for their research help.

Jeswald W. Salacuse

Medford, Massachusetts
August 2012

Preface to the Paperback Edition of The Three Laws of International Investment

I am very pleased that Oxford University Press is publishing a paperback edition of *The Three Laws of International Investment: National, Contractual, and International Frameworks for Foreign Capital*. In writing the book, I naturally hoped to reach as many professionals as possible working in the field of international investment. But I was also especially concerned to provide university students, whether in law, business, or international relations, a comprehensive, yet compact and accessible text for undertaking serious study of the legal aspects of international investment, an increasingly important area of economic activity. It is my hope that this paperback edition will provide students with that desired access.

I have used this book as a basic text on the law of international investment both at Harvard Law School and the Fletcher School of Law and Diplomacy, Tufts University, with gratifying results. The syllabus for the course at Harvard Law School, *International Investment, Development and the Law*, which consists of forty-eight hours of instruction, may be found on the OUP web site at http://ukcatalogue.oup.com/product/9780199654567.do, while the syllabus for the course at the Fletcher School, *International Investment Law*, extending over twenty-six hours of instruction, may be found on the Fletcher School website at http://fletcher.tufts.edu/

I would also be pleased to receive and respond to readers' comments, questions and criticisms about the book.

Jeswald W. Salacuse
Visiting Professor of Law, Harvard Law School
Henry J. Braker Professor of Law
The Fletcher School of Law and Diplomacy
Tufts University
Jeswald.Salacuse@Tufts.edu

Cambridge, Massachusetts
April 14, 2014

Contents

PART V: CONCLUSION

Table of Cases

Table of Legislation

Table of Agreements, Conventions, Rules, and Treaties

List of Abbreviations

AREAER	Annual Report on Exchange Arrangements and Exchange Restrictions
BATNA	Best Alternative to a Negotiated Agreement
BJP	Bharatiya Janata Party
BIT	bilateral investment treaty
BOO	build-operate-own
BOT	build-operate-transfer
BT	build-transfer
CAFTA-DR	Dominican Republic–Central America–United States Free Trade Agreement
CAO	contract, add and operate
CFIUS	Committee on Foreign Investment in the United States
COMESA	Common Market for Eastern and Southern Africa
DOT	develop, operate and transfer
ECGD	Export Credits Guarantee Department
ECT	Energy Charter Treaty
EPA	Economic Partnership Agreement
FCN	friendship, commerce and navigation
FDA	Food and Drug Administration
FDI	foreign direct investment
FIRB	Foreign Investment Review Board
FTA	free trade agreement
GATTS	General Agreement on Trade in Services
IAB	"Investing Across Borders"
ICC	International Chamber of Commerce
ICMA	International Capital Market Association
ICSID	International Centre for Settlement of Investment Disputes
IEEPA	International Emergency Economic Powers Act
IFC	International Finance Corporation
IIA	international investment agreement
ITO	International Trade Organization
LIBOR	London Interbank Offered Rate
MAI	Multilateral Agreement on Investment
MIGA	Multilateral Investment Guarantee Agency
MNC	multinational corporation
NAFTA	North American Free Trade Agreement
NIEO	New International Economic Order
OECD	Organization for Economic Cooperation and Development
OPIC	Overseas Private Investment Corporation
PPP	Public Private Partnership
PSI	pre-shipment inspection
QFI	"qualified foreign investors"
ROO	rehabilitate, own, and operate
ROT	rehabilitate, operate, and transfer
SEBI	Securities Exchange Board of India
SWF	Sovereign Wealth Fund
TEU	Treaty on European Union
TNC	transnational corporation
TRIMs	Trade-Related Investment Measures
UNCTAD	United Nations Conference on Trade and Development

UNCTC	United Nations Centre on Transnational Corporations
UNGA	United Nations General Assembly
UNCITRAL	United Nations Commission on International Trade Law
WAIPA	World Association of Investment Promotion Agencies
WTO	World Trade Organization

PART I

INTERNATIONAL INVESTMENT AND THE LAW

1

The Nature and Significance
of International Investment

1.1 The Meaning of Investment

The meaning of the term "investment" at its most basic level is the commitment of resources by a physical or legal person to a specific purpose in order to earn a profit or to gain a return. Etymologically, the word invest is derived from the Latin *investire*, which means "to clothe."[1] An investor is in effect "clothing" an enterprise with capital through the process of investment. In economic terms, investment, a form of savings, is the opposite of consumption. Investment is fundamental to economic growth and to the provision of needed goods and services in any society.

The term investment is generally used in two senses. One sense is the *process* or *transaction* by which a person or legal entity makes an investment. Thus, the act of purchasing 100 shares of stock on an exchange or buying a shop in which to sell goods is an investment. The second meaning refers to the *asset* acquired as a result of investing. In this sense, both the shares purchased and the shop acquired are considered investments. Discussions of investment and foreign investment sometimes emphasize their process or transactional dimensions and sometimes their asset dimensions.[2] This book will examine the legal rules governing both the processes by which international investments are made and the legal rights of investors and others in the assets acquired as a result of the investment transaction.

As we shall see, the term "investment" is a basic concept used in national legislation, contracts, and international treaties; consequently, it is important to understand its ramifications. Whether or not a particular asset or transaction is considered an investment in national law, a contract, or a treaty may have important consequences and may mean the difference between according and denying legal protection to that asset or transaction. It is also important to recognize at the outset that lawyers, arbitrators, economists, financiers, and business executives may define the concept of investment in different ways. As a result, a transaction that an entrepreneur may consider as an "investment" may not qualify as such under relevant legislation, regulations, contractual provisions, or treaties. For example, in one case that arose in the Democratic Republic of the Congo in 1999, the country's armed forces closed down a thriving law firm established by an

---

[1] *The Oxford English Dictionary* defines "to invest" as "to employ (money) in the purchase of anything from which a profit is expected..." See *The Oxford English Dictionary* (2nd edn 1989) vol VIII 46. *Webster's Third New International Dictionary of the English Language, Unabridged* defines the term as "to commit money for a long period in order to gain a return." *Webster's Third New International Dictionary of the English Language, Unabridged* (3rd edn 1981) 1189.

[2] For example, the *Encyclopedia of Public International Law* in defining foreign investment as "a transfer of funds or materials from one country (called capital exporting country) to another country (called host country) in return for a direct or indirect participation in the profits of that enterprise" focuses on the process of making the investment. *Encyclopedia of Public International Law* (1985) vol VIII 246. On the other hand, E Graham and P Krugman in their *Foreign Investment in the United States* focus primarily on the assets acquired as a result of that process when they define foreign investment in the following terms: "Foreign direct investment is formally defined as ownership of assets by foreign residents for purpose of controlling the use of those assets." E Graham and P Krugman, *Foreign Investment in the United States* (2nd edn 1991) 7.

American in Kinshasa, thereby effecting a total deprivation of the American's enterprise. When the American lawyer sought to bring a claim against the Congolese government before an international tribunal under the United States—Congo bilateral investment treaty, the arbitrators rejected his claim on the grounds that his firm did not constitute an "investment" under the treaty.[3] Similarly, the governing authorities in a country that has enacted legislation granting "investments" specified incentives and privileges may conclude that certain business arrangements, such as franchises, do not constitute investments under the national investment code and therefore are not entitled to receive special investment incentives and privileges, such as tax and customs exemptions.

1.2 The Forms of Investment

Investments can take many forms. Indeed, the great diversity of individual investment forms seems to be limited only by the creativity of investors seeking to meet their interests and those of the enterprise in which they are investing. As a result, new types and forms of investments are continually developing to meet new economic situations and achieve evolving financial objectives. An understanding of these diverse forms is important because the form an investment takes may influence the legal rights to which it and the investor are entitled under domestic legislation, relevant contracts, and international treaties. Three attributes of any investment form are particularly important: (a) the property and contractual rights resulting from the investment, (b) the control attributes of the investment, and (c) the enterprise form in which the investment is made.

(a) Property and Contractual Rights Resulting from Investments

Legally, when an investor makes an investment in an enterprise, the investor gains certain specified property and contractual rights in the investment as a result. Generally speaking, an investor's rights with respect to an investment fall into one of two basic categories: *equity* or *debt*. An equity investment, like shares of stock in a company or a property rights in a fixed asset like a shop, gives the investor an *ownership interest*. As an ownership interest, equity in company shares or a fixed asset entitles the investor to share in the profits (if any) of the enterprise, to participate to a greater or lesser extent in its management, and to hold that property interest until that investor transfers its interest to another person. On the other hand, an investment in the form of a debt, like a loan or a bond, gives the investor a *claim* to be repaid (rather than an ownership interest in assets), entitles the investor to fixed payments of principal and interest at specified times according to the investment agreement, and normally provides for a maturity date for full payment upon which the investor's claim will end. In most legal systems, debt has priority over equity in the event of the enterprise's bankruptcy and liquidation, which means that holders of debt are paid before holders of equity from whatever enterprise assets remain.[4]

---

[3] JD Mortenson, "The Meaning of 'Investment': ICSID's *Travaux* and the Domain of International Investment Law," 51 *Harvard International Law Journal* (2010) 257. See also *Mihaly International Corporation v. The Democratic Socialist Republic of Sri Lanka*, ICSID Case no ARB/00/02, Award, March 15, 2002, (2002) 12 *ICSID Review—Foreign Investment Law Journal* 142–60 in which the Tribunal determined that expenses incurred in the preparation of an investment project that never materialized did not constitute an investment either under the ICSID Convention or the United States–Sri Lanka bilateral investment treaty and that therefore the Tribunal had no jurisdiction over the claim.
[4] O Hart, "Different Approaches to Bankruptcy," 4(1) *CESifo DICE Report* (2006) 3–8.

Whether an investment in a given enterprise takes the form of debt or equity and the specific nature of the rights and liabilities attached to a particular equity or debt investment will depend on a host of variables. These include the prevailing law, projected interest rates, the financial goals and intentions of the parties involved in the enterprise, evaluations of the risks to be encountered, the projected revenues of the enterprise, and many other factors. In most instances, investments in specific enterprises will consist of a mixture of equity and debt. Financial analysts refer to that mixture as the enterprise's *capital structure*.[5]

An important element of the capital structure of any enterprise is the ratio of its debt-to-equity. In many investment projects, the amount of debt invested may far exceed the amount of equity. For instance, in the capital structure of the first phase of the Dabhol Power Company, an example of project finance in India to be discussed in Chapter 10,[6] the total amount of capital invested was US$932 million, which consisted of US$289 million in equity contributed by the three project partners and US$643 million in debt provided by a variety of foreign and domestic banks and financial institutions. The debt–equity ratio of the Dabhol Power Company was therefore more than two to one. In most industries, it is generally believed the higher the debt–equity ratio the greater the risk faced by the enterprise. The precise debt–equity ratio in a specific enterprise usually depends on the relative cost of debt and equity to the investors seeking to establish the enterprise, as well as the legal or regulatory requirements of the specific industries or countries in which the investment is made. Indeed, the usual investment to establish or rehabilitate an enterprise rarely takes the form of a contribution of equity alone, but also often involves a host of other complex legal arrangements, including loans (both short-term and long-term), credit arrangements to finance equipment purchases, loan guaranties, licensing agreements, management contracts, long-term sales and supply arrangements, and political risk insurance. Moreover, in addition to the more common forms of equity and debt, there are hybrid investments, such as preferred shares and convertible debentures, which possess some of the characteristics of both debt and equity securities.[7]

(b) Control Attributes of Investments

A second important question concerning an investment relates to the extent of the investor's legal rights to control the underlying enterprise or assets in which the investment is made. "Control" in this context means the ability of the investor to determine the actions and policies of that enterprise. An investor may have an ownership interest in an enterprise from which it gains certain financial benefits, but still may not be able to control it because the investor's ownership interest is not large enough. Thus, to take an extreme example, an investor who purchases 100 shares of Microsoft Corporation or Barclays PLC gains an equity interest in those enterprises but that interest is not large enough to allow the investor to determine the policies and actions of either company. On the other hand, if two companies each contribute 50 percent of the equity to form a joint venture to manufacture software and each elects members of the venture's board of directors, they each have an equity interest that allows them to participate in control of the enterprise.

Whether or not an investor has control of the enterprise in which it invests is a matter of importance both for the investor and for the government of the country in which the

---

[5] F Modigliani and MH Miller, "The Cost of Capital, Corporation Finance and the Theory of Investment," 48 *The American Economic Review* (1958) 261–97.

[6] See section 10.7.

[7] EF Brigham and MC Ehrhardt, *Financial Management: Theory and Practice* (10th edn 2002).

enterprise is located. For the investor, control not only enables the investor to determine the actions and policies of the enterprise, and therefore to pursue strategies that will bring benefits to the investor, but also allows individual investors to protect themselves from the potentially negative and self-serving actions of other investors and creditors. Since governments are also concerned about the actions of enterprises taken on their territories, they too are often vitally interested in who controls those enterprises. For example, if foreign persons seek to buy a controlling interest in certain enterprises, local law may require prior government approval or even forbid such foreign control altogether.

The issue of enterprise control requires a second categorization of investment forms that distinguishes *direct investment* from *portfolio investment*. A direct investment establishes or purchases some form of permanent enterprise or facility, such as a factory, mine, plantation, hotel, or power station, in whose control and management the investor will participate. A portfolio investment is one which gives the investor no right to participate in the control and management of the underlying enterprise. Whether or not an investor has such control and whether or not the investment therefore qualifies as direct or portfolio investment will depend, of course, on the specifics of the investment. For statistical purposes, governments and international organizations usually classify an equity investment of 10 percent or more as a direct investment.[8] An investment that gives the investor less than a 10 percent voting interest is considered a portfolio investment.

The International Monetary Fund distinguishes between direct and portfolio investments in similar terms. It provides that a direct investment consists of either equity capital or retained earnings between "affiliated enterprises." An enterprise is affiliated with another enterprise if the former has a voting interest of 10 percent or more in the latter.[9] The key difference between these two categories of investment is the right of the investor to exert control over the investment. Thus, as a general rule, a direct investment is an equity interest in an enterprise that gives the investor 10 percent or more voting power.

(c) Enterprise Forms

Yet a third way of categorizing investments relates to the legal form of the enterprise in which the investment is made. An enterprise is usually enclosed within a particular legal form of enterprise organization. Here, a fundamental distinction is whether the enterprise or asset is owned directly by the investor or owned by a separate legal entity in which the investor has an equity interest. If the asset is owned directly by a corporate investor, it is considered a *branch* of the investor. On the other hand, the asset or enterprise might be owned by a separate legal entity all of whose shares are in turn owned by the investor. In this case, the investment would take the form of a *subsidiary* of the investor. For example, a refrigerator manufacturer that wants to establish a factory to produce air conditioners

---

[8] eg, US Dept of Commerce, *Statistical Abstract of the United States 1995* (115th edn 1995) 806–7. See also International Investment Survey Act of 1976, 22 USC § 3102(10).

[9] The International Monetary Fund defines direct investment as follows: "A direct investment enterprise is defined as an incorporated or unincorporated enterprise in which a direct investor, who is resident in another economy, owns 10 percent or more of the ordinary shares or voting power (for an incorporated enterprise) or the equivalent (for an unincorporated enterprise). Direct investment enterprises comprise those entities that are subsidiaries (a nonresident investor owns more than 50 percent), associates (an investor owns 50 percent or less) and branches (wholly or jointly owned unincorporated enterprises) either directly or indirectly owned by the direct investor. Subsidiaries in this connotation also may be identified as majority owned affiliates. Foreign-controlled enterprises include subsidiaries and branches, but associates may be included or excluded by individual countries according to their qualitative assessments of foreign control. Also, a public enterprise may in some instances be a direct investment enterprise, as defined in this paragraph." International Monetary Fund, *IMF Balance of Payments Manual* (1993) 86 (BPM5).

might make the factory a branch of its existing operations or alternatively create a separate subsidiary to own the factory and produce the air conditioners. The decision on whether to make an international investment as a branch or a subsidiary involves numerous factors. For example, from the point of view of the investor a branch may make the efficient management of a foreign investment easier than would a subsidiary. On the other hand, a subsidiary in the form of a separate company or corporation enjoying limited liability will protect the parent company from liabilities incurred by the subsidiary.[10] The choice of whether to make a foreign investment in the form of a branch or a subsidiary is not always a matter to be decided by the investor alone. Host country laws may require that any direct investment take the form of a subsidiary organized under and subject to host country company laws and regulations.

Whether an enterprise is a branch or a subsidiary can have significant legal consequences for the investor and the operation of the enterprise. When the enterprise has a separate entity, other investors may take part through contribution of capital. In such cases, the investment, instead of being a wholly owned subsidiary, will take the form of a joint venture or consortium. If the investment receives capital from numerous shareholders who do not participate actively in the business of the enterprise, the enterprise may take the form of a publicly traded corporation. Depending on the legal system of the country concerned, the law may provide a variety of enterprise forms such as a sole proprietorship, partnership, limited partnership, closely held corporation, or publicly traded corporation. Each form has different legal attributes and is subject to different legal requirements. And if a state invests in an enterprise, that enterprise may take the form of a government corporation subject to laws and rules separate from those governing private companies.

1.3 The Nature of International Investors

Investment laws, contracts, and treaties govern not only investments, but also investors: the persons and organizations that make investments. As a result of globalization, growing numbers of individuals and organizations invest abroad and are therefore in a general sense to be considered "foreign investors." Thus the universe of potential foreign investors consists of literally millions of individuals, companies, and organizations, and that number continues to expand steadily. Each of these millions of individuals, companies, and organizations and their trillions of dollars of capital may potentially be affected by the laws of international investment.

There are many kinds of international investors. Depending on the nature of their owners, one can divide them into four basic categories: private, state, mixed, and international organizations.

(a) Private Investors

The first category consists of private investors, physical and legal persons that are not part of any government or state apparatus. Among private investors, the most important are those that take the form of corporations or companies.

It has been said that "[t]he most important organization in the world is the company: the basis of the prosperity in the West and the best hope for the rest of the world."[11] Companies

---

[10] See J Fiechter et al, "Subsidiaries or Branches: Does One Size Fit All?" *IMF Staff Discussion Note*, March 7, 2011 (SDN 11/04).

[11] J Mickelwait and A Wooldridge, *The Company: A Short History of a Revolutionary Idea* (2003) xv.

and corporations are the world's most significant depositories of assets and technology and a primary force for wealth creation and allocation. Indeed, although companies and corporations have been created under different domestic laws, they share many common features and have all been designed to encourage investment. For example:

1. Companies and corporations are legal entities that are separate and distinct from their investors and shareholders. Thus, they are said to have "legal personality." As a result, they may hold, acquire, and transfer property in their own names, make contracts, sue and be sued in their individual capacity, and engage in legal transactions just as physical persons can.

2. Shareholders in companies and corporations enjoy "limited liability." That is, they are not liable for the debts and obligations of the company in which they have invested, a factor that encourages investment by reducing investor risk. Since investors in the shares of corporations risk only their initial investment and are not personally liable for the debts and obligations incurred by the corporation itself, they are generally more willing to make investments than they would be if they were liable for such corporate obligations as well.

3. As entities existing apart from their investors, companies and corporations usually have an unlimited life under most domestic legal systems. This factor gives stability to enterprises in corporate form since their legal existence is unaffected by the entry and departure of individual managers or investors.

4. The corporate structure allows centralized control and management by a few managers of the assets and operations of a potentially diverse, vast, and widely dispersed enterprise. This structure facilitates the development of easily controlled groups of corporations, often located in many different countries. Indeed, the most discussed type of international investor, the "multinational corporation" (MNC), is legally not a single corporation at all but rather many corporations and companies linked together.

5. The domestic law of the country concerned usually allows ownership interest in the form of shares of stock to be easily transferred from one investor to another without affecting the legal structure of the underlying enterprise. This factor encourages investment by giving liquidity to investments in companies and allows for the easy entry and exit of shareholders.

The vast majority of the world's corporations are private corporations since their ownership and control are in the hands of private individuals and organizations. Nevertheless, they are each creatures of national law and are subject to the differing legislation and regulations of the countries of their creation and their operation.

Who exactly are *international* investors? Simply put, an international investor is a physical or legal person in one country who invests funds or capital in another country by means of an investment transaction, such as the earlier example. That bland definition masks the great diversity of individuals and organizations engaged in international investment and the broad variations in their economic objectives and activities. One of the principal types of international investor is the "multinational corporation" (MNC), also known as the "multinational enterprise" (MNE) and the "transnational corporation" (TNC). Basically, a multinational corporation is an enterprise that owns or has control over income-producing facilities in at least two countries.[12] Applying that definition, the

---

[12] "The nearly universally accepted definition of multinational corporation is one that owns outright, controls, or has direct managerial influence in income-generating, value-added facilities in at least two countries." SD

United Nations Conference on Trade and Development (UNCTAD) estimated that in 2009 there were 82,053 multinational corporations with 807,363 affiliates in the world.[13] That definition covers an extremely wide variety of enterprises, from global companies like Shell or General Motors with hundreds of subsidiaries around the world to small specialized enterprises with a single subsidiary affiliate in another country. Multinational corporations are by no means headquartered exclusively in developed countries. Increasingly, emerging market countries like China, India, Brazil, and certain Arabian Gulf States are developing their own multinational enterprises which are becoming active investors around the globe. For instance, India's Tata group has become a global brand with investments in technology, automobile, and manufacturing sectors.

Multinational corporations include a wide variety of business enterprises pursuing a diverse set of objectives. One way of trying to understand them is by the objectives they pursue. Companies invest abroad for different reasons. Some, which might be called "market seekers," invest in order to find and develop new markets for their products. Others, like petroleum or mineral companies, invest in order to find and obtain raw materials. They might therefore be called "raw-material seekers." Still others searching to reduce costs and improve efficiency of production by finding lower cost factors of production, like cheap labor or low-cost energy, might be called "efficiency seekers." And yet others, particularly in high-technology areas, invest abroad in order to obtain knowledge and might therefore be called "knowledge seekers."[14]

Regardless of their aim, for many years multinational corporations have been the subject of intense study and commentary by both scholars and the public and have engendered strong and opposing views. For some people, multinational corporations are important engines of economic development. For others, they are exploiters of labor and destroyers of the environment.[15] For some, their potential for economic development needs to be released from the strictures of onerous government policies and laws. For others, their potential for self-enrichment at the expense of national sovereignty, human rights, and the environment needs to be controlled by strict legislation, regulation, and international agreements. As a result, the role of the multinational corporation is central in international economic life, and as a result they are important subjects of all international investment laws, contracts, and treaties.

New types of multinational enterprises seem to be evolving constantly. Traditionally, multinational corporate investors have been engaged in manufacturing and production activities, but nonmanufacturing firms have also become important direct investors. Thus private equity firms are now actively engaged in direct foreign investment in foreign enterprises. Their goal is to take control of the enterprises, reorganize them to make them more efficient, and then sell them.

But multinational direct investors are by no means the entire universe of international investors. Banks and financial firms that extend loans and credits to governments, companies, and individuals in other countries are also foreign investors. These banks and firms control vast amounts of capital and devote significant funds to international investments.

Cohen, *Multinational Corporations and Foreign Direct Investment: Avoiding Simplicity, Embracing Complexity* (2007) 39.

[13] UNCTAD, *World Investment Report* (2009) at 223.

[14] D Eiteman and A Stonehill, *Multinational Business Finance* (12th edn 2009). Eiteman and Stonehill have thus categorized investors into four types: market seekers, raw-material seekers, production-efficiency seekers, and knowledge seekers.

[15] For a discussion of the history of multinational corporations and the various views concerning the role in the international economy, see generally SD Cohen (n 12).

Institutional investors, such as pension, endowment, and mutual funds, are increasingly committing their resources to both debt and equity investments in foreign countries to enhance their returns and manage their risks through diversification. And as a result of the development of capital markets around the world, improved communications, and more readily available financial information on a global scale, individual portfolio investors are also increasingly seeking to invest their funds in shares, credit instruments, and bonds issued by entities outside their home countries.

(b) State Investors

A second large and important category of investors consists of governments and governmental entities. Virtually all governments, to a greater or lesser extent, invest in enterprises designed to provide services or goods to the inhabitants of their countries. Thus, states may establish corporations to provide air and maritime transportation, telecommunications, mining, and steel production, to mention just a few. Such state entities, called state or government corporations, are usually subject to a separate legal regime that is distinct from that governing private companies and corporations. Moreover, these state entities may choose to invest at home or abroad for myriad financial or political reasons. For instance, since 2004, China's strategy of state intervention and private investment in Africa has raised questions over the geopolitical impact of the scale of such investments.[16]

The extent to which a government becomes an investor depends on a variety of factors, including the existence or lack thereof of private investors in a particular economic field or sector, the quality and cost of needed goods and services provided through private enterprise, the existing political situation, and the prevailing ideology in that country. Indeed, in many countries whether private enterprise or government should invest in a particular economic sector is an important public policy question having strong ideological and political implications.

The question of who invests in what is not a purely economic one. The identity of who owns and controls a country's enterprises has important political implications because assets and enterprises endow their owners with both political and economic power. As a result, the subject of investment by foreigners, as will be seen in Chapter 4, is a matter regulated by law in most countries.

The prevailing ideology in a country may significantly influence the respective roles accorded to private and state investors. For example, countries with a strong socialist orientation may choose to reserve to the state important areas of economic activity, such as the production of electricity, the provision of air and land transportation, and the pursuit of mineral development; consequently, the government may exclude private enterprise from these economic sectors. A government's nationalist ideology may severely limit foreign investment in economic sectors considered vital to preserving a country's sovereignty, economic independence, or national security. One of the consequences of the end of communism in Eastern Europe and the former Soviet Union and the elimination of socialism in many other countries was "privatization," or the transfer of state enterprises

---

[16] D Brautigam, "Africa's Eastern Promise: What the West Can Learn from Chinese Investment in Africa," *Foreign Affairs*, January 2010. Available at <http://www.foreignaffairs.com/articles/65916/deborah-brautigam/africa%E2%80%99s-eastern-promise> accessed on October 2, 2011.

and assets to private hands and the reduction of barriers to private investment throughout the economy.[17]

Today, despite the end of communism and the widespread and massive privatization of state assets throughout the world, governments remain important investors both domestically and internationally. In 2010, UNCTAD estimated that there were 650 state-owned multinational corporations with 8,500 foreign affiliates and that they accounted for 11 percent of global flows of direct foreign investment in that year.[18]

An increasingly important manifestation of governments as investors is the Sovereign Wealth Fund. Sovereign Wealth Funds (SWFs) are state agencies holding a portion of a country's foreign currency reserves. Established by such countries as Kuwait, Norway, Singapore, and China with the goal of maximizing returns, they are authorized to invest their assets in foreign investments of varying degrees of risk. Their investment capital is derived from their countries' growing foreign currency reserves resulting from revenues from their commodity exports and expanding international trade. In addition to formally established Sovereign Wealth Funds, other important sources of state funds for investment abroad are international reserves, public pension funds, and state-owned enterprises and development funds.[19] In 2011, it was estimated that the total amount of assets managed by Sovereign Wealth Funds was US$4.1 trillion and that other sovereign investment vehicles held an additional US$6.8 trillion.[20] Because of their potential economic power and the fact that they are controlled by governments with various political aims, the activities of these sovereign investors have raised concern in host countries and prompted calls for increased transparency and regulation of their activities.[21]

(c) International Organizations

A third important category of investor consists of international institutions and organizations created and owned by states. These international institutions and organizations have international legal personalities, and are subject to international law, primarily the treaties that created them. The World Bank, its affiliates such as the International Finance Corporation (IFC), and regional development banks such as the Asian Development Bank and the InterAmerican Development Bank, are all international institutions whose purpose is to invest funds secured from states and from private capital markets in order to promote economic development.[22] They invest billions of dollars each year through both loans and equity participations in order to simultaneously support economic development and earn a return on their invested capital. As will be seen later in this chapter, one of the

---

[17] JW Salacuse, "From Developing Countries to Emerging Markets: A New Role for Law in the Third World," 33 *The International Lawyer* (1999) 875. See Chapter 6, section 6.8, for a more detailed discussion of privatization and its relation to foreign investment.

[18] UNCTAD, *World Investment Report 2010* (2010) at x.

[19] R Kimmitt, "Public Footprints in Private Markets: Sovereign Wealth Funds and the World Economy," *Foreign Affairs* (January/February 2008) 119–30.

[20] The CityUK, *Sovereign Wealth Funds* (April 2011) 1.

[21] E Truman, "Sovereign Wealth Funds: Threat or Salvation?" Peterson Institute for International Economics, 2010. Available at <http://bookstore.piie.com/book-store/4983.html> accessed October 3, 2011. See also M Sornarajah, "Sovereign Wealth Funds and the Existing Structure of the Regulation of Investments," 1 *Asian Journal of International Law* (2011) 267–88; YCL Lee, "The Governance of Contemporary Sovereign Wealth Funds," 6 *Hastings Business Law Journal* (2010) 197–237.

[22] RD Fraser, *The World Financial System* (1st edn 1987) 363–450. See also statements about the mission of selected international financial institutions at <http://www.worldbank.org/> (for World Bank), <http://www.ifc .org/ (for International Financial Corporation), <http://www.adb.org/ (Asian Development Bank), and http:// www.iadb.org/> (for InterAmerican Development Bank).

distinguishing characteristics of loans from international organizations is that they often impose severe conditions on the governmental policies of debtor countries.

(d) Mixed Enterprises

Frequently, the various types of investors mentioned above invest together in particular enterprises. For example, it is common for private companies to form joint ventures with state corporations to undertake productive activities such as manufacturing machinery or operating an airline. In some countries, such mixed enterprises may be subject to a distinct legal regime. Often, an international organization like the World Bank or the International Finance Corporation is included as a party. Thus, a large infrastructure project such as an electrical generation and transmission system or a telecommunications network may involve a state corporation, a private company, and an international organization as investors within a single legal entity

1.4 Investors and the Role of Return and Risk

With the possible exception of certain subsidized government enterprises, all investors are concerned about two basic factors in making and managing their investments: return and risk. Indeed, one can say that return and risk are the driving factors behind all investment decisions. The reason investors invest is to gain a return, to make a profit. The ways in which an investor will gain a return from a particular investment will depend on the nature of the enterprise and the investment made in it. Investors may gain a return through sharing in the profits of the enterprise, through the receipt of interest paid on its loans to the investment enterprise, through capital gains made on the sale of an investment to a third party, as well as by a variety of other transactions, such as technology transfers and management contracts, associated with the investment.[23]

At the same time, all investors are also concerned about the risks affecting their proposed investments. One may define risk as the probability that expected returns from an investment will not be realized. Thus investments in which the probability is high that expected returns will not be achieved are said to present a high risk. Investors evaluate potential investments not just in terms of the absolute returns to be expected from a particular investment but on the basis of the expected returns measured against the projected levels of risk. In the calculation of most investors, a greater risk requires a higher rate of return to justify an investment.[24]

Investors analyze risk in various ways, but a basic distinction made by most investors is between commercial risk and political risk. Commercial risks are those possible negative effects derived from ordinary commercial activities affecting the enterprise. For example, market sales may be less than expected, management may be inefficient, or the enterprise's technology may prove more costly or less effective than planned. Political risks are negative events that derive from political actions, such as the expropriation of an enterprise by the government, the establishment of price controls by a regulatory authority, or a riot that damages investment assets. A fundamental purpose of investment treaties and political risk

---

[23] <http://www.worldbank.org/>(for World Bank), <http://www.ifc.org/(for International Financial Corporation), <http://www.adb.org/(Asian Development Bank), and http://www.iadb.org/>(for InterAmerican Development Bank).

[24] R Higgins, *Analysis for Financial Management* (9th edn 2009).

insurance, both of which are discussed in subsequent chapters of this book, is to provide foreign investors and their investments with a level of protection against political risk.[25]

If, upon evaluating the potential risk of a contemplated investment, an investor judges the risk to be unacceptably high, three possible courses of action present themselves: (1) to refuse to make the investment; (2) to secure an increased rate of return to compensate the investor for accepting the contemplated level of risk; or (3) to find ways to reduce the contemplated level of risk through legal and other means. In evaluating any proposed investment to determine political risk, as well as anticipated return, investors always take into account the applicable legal order.

All investors, private, state, mixed, and international, also seek to structure and operate their investments in ways that will enhance their returns and minimize their risks. To achieve this result, they use a variety of devices, including contracts, legislative provisions, and international treaties. From the point of view of the investor, the primary utility of an investment treaty is that it reduces the political risks of investing in a foreign country. Similarly, countries and communities seeking to attract or encourage investment will try to find ways to increase returns, for example by building roads or granting investors tax exemptions, or to reduce risk, for instance by making stabilization agreements promising not to increase the regulatory burden on the investment or by guaranteeing to purchase the product produced by the investment. In general, governmental actions that increase return or reduce risk encourage investment. Conversely, actions that reduce returns or increase risk discourage investment. Thus, for example, from the point of view of host countries, the primary utility of an investment treaty is to promote investment from the other signatory country. Reflecting these two goals, the title of most investment treaties states that they are "agreements to protect and promote investment."

1.5 The Nature of International Investment

This book is particularly concerned not just with investment but specifically with *international* investment. What is "international investment"?

Historically, investors and entrepreneurs have sought economic gain not only in their home countries but in other countries as well. Originally, the primary mechanism for seeking such gains was through foreign trade. Trade eventually led to early forms of international investment. Indeed, such international investment was originally focused on financing trade with other countries. Thus, for example, during the Renaissance, individual merchants formed limited partnerships or *commendas* with shipowners or sea captains to finance shipment of goods or trade in goods with other countries.[26] Later in connection with trade, merchants might acquire buildings or property within foreign countries to create trading establishments. For example, in 991 A.D., the Byzantine Emperors Basil II and Constantine VIII, in a document known in Latin as a *chrysobul*, granted the merchants of Venice the right to trade in the ports and other places of the Byzantine Empire without paying customs duties, as well as the right to a quarter in Constantinople, known as an *embolum*, for dwelling and trading.[27] The acquisition and development of such a trading

---

[25] NS Kinsella and ND Rubins, *International Investment, Political Risk, and Dispute Resolution: A Practitioner's Guide* (2005).

[26] J McCusker (ed), *History of World Trade Since 1450* (1st edn 2006) vol II, 557–8.

[27] P Fischer, "Some Recent Trends and Developments in the Law of Foreign Investment," in KH Boeckstiegel et al (eds), *Völkerrecht, Recht der internationalen Organisationen, Weltwirtschafatsrecht: Festschrift für Ignaz Seidl-Hohenveldern* (1988) 97. See also "Concessions granted to the Merchants of Venice, by the Byzantine Emperors Basilius and Constantinus, executed in March 991," in P Fischer, *A Collection of International Concessions and Related Instruments* (1976) vol I, 15–18.

and dwelling quarter in Constantinople was a form of direct foreign investment by Venetian merchants. In time, investors would undertake investments in other countries for other purposes, including acquiring natural resources and manufacturing.

In most cases, an international investment is *international* because it has two defining attributes: (1) the person or entity undertaking the investment is not a citizen, or at least not a resident, of the country in which the investment is made; and (2) the investment process includes the transfer of funds or capital from a foreign country to the country of investment, which results in a continuing legal relationship between the investor and the foreign enterprise. Thus, most "foreign investments" in a particular country are made by foreign corporations or foreign individuals, and they involve the transfer of money or capital from abroad to that country. For example, a corporation with headquarters in France wishing to establish a factory in Malaysia to manufacture refrigerators or computers would establish a wholly owned subsidiary in Malaysia and transfer to that subsidiary the necessary capital and technology to construct and operate the factory. In that situation, France would be considered the "home country" of the investor and Malaysia would be considered the "host country."

While the above description is the basic model for many, and probably most, direct foreign investment transactions, an investor of foreign nationality or residence and a physical transfer of capital from one country to another may not necessarily be present in all international investment transactions. For example, a foreign company could undertake an investment through the mobilization of capital within a host country by borrowing from local banks or raising funds on the local capital market. On the other hand, indigenous entrepreneurs owning funds held in banks abroad may transfer a portion of those funds to the investor's home country in order to undertake an investment. Do either of the above-described transactions qualify as "international" or "foreign" investments?

The answer depends upon who is characterizing the transaction and for what purpose. Economists and economic institutions may use one definition of foreign investment to gather statistics or analyze financial trends, but lawyers, regulatory authorities, and arbitration tribunals might use another when applying laws and treaties. Without engaging in a detailed discussion of this issue, it is worth noting that the definitions of foreign investor and foreign investment are important starting points in analyzing the coverage of foreign investment legislation, regulations, and treaties.

1.6 Forms of International Investment

Like purely domestic investment, foreign investment can take a variety of forms. The following are some of the most common:

(a) **Foreign Direct Investment**. Foreign direct investment (FDI), sometimes also called direct foreign investment (DFI), is an equity or ownership investment of more than 10 percent by an investor in one country (known as "the home country" or "capital-exporting country") in an enterprise located in another country (the "host country" or "capital-importing country").[28] Foreign direct investment is a growing feature of modern economic

---

[28] SD Cohen states: "Quantitatively, the nearly universally accepted definition of FDI is ownership of at least 10 percent of common (voting) stock of a business enterprise operating in a country other than one in which the investing company is headquartered." *Multinational Corporations and Foreign Direct Investment: Avoiding Simplicity* (2007) 38. See also n 9 for the definition used by the International Monetary Fund.

life. In 2010, global foreign direct investment (FDI) inflows amounted to US$1.24 trillion.[29] Of that amount, US$602 billion were invested in developed countries, approximately US$574 billion were invested in developing countries, and US$68 billion were invested in Southeast Europe and the Commonwealth of Independent States.[30] While most of the discussion concerning foreign investment and foreign investment law concerns investments by multinational corporations in developing countries, it must be remembered that most international investment is among *developed* countries.[31] It must also be recognized that certain developing countries are increasingly becoming a source of FDI for both the developed and developing world. For instance, in 2010 the FDI outflows from developing Asia grew by 20 percent to US$230 billion.[32]

In 2010, the total stock of foreign direct investment in the world was estimated to have reached US$19.1 trillion.[33] Foreign direct investment has the effect of giving investors in one country ownership rights in and control over economic assets in another country. As a result, foreign direct investment is a powerful force for integrating national economies and fostering the phenomenon of globalization. As governments and populations in host countries become concerned about the influence of foreigners on domestic politics, local economies, national security, and indigenous culture as a result of their direct investments, these same factors give foreign direct investment significant political overtones. In this regard, it is important to recognize that foreign direct investment in most instances involves more than the transfer of money or assets from one country to another. Its purpose is to create productive capacity. To achieve that goal, the foreign direct investor usually must also transfer know-how, skills, and management capability along with money, capital, and technology. Thus, in most cases, a foreign direct investment, like the one to create a factory to manufacture air conditioners, consists of a package of money, equipment, human skills, technology, and know-how.

(b) **Foreign Portfolio Equity Investment.** A foreign portfolio investment is an investment by a resident of one country in a company based in another country through the purchase of shares equaling less than 10 percent of the overall voting power in that company. Here too, the fundamental distinction between foreign direct investment and foreign portfolio investment lies not in the form of the investment (ie shares) but in the amount of control transferred. A direct foreign investment is large enough to enable the investor to participate in control of the enterprise, while a portfolio investment is not large enough to give such control.

---

[29] UNCTAD, *World Investment Report 2011* (2011). It should be noted that in 2010 FDI flows were still some 15 percent below their pre-crisis average and nearly 37 percent below their peak in 2007.

[30] UNCTAD, *World Investment Report 2011* (2011).

[31] For example, FDI inflows to developed countries in 2010 declined marginally to US$602 billion from the prior year. UNCTAD also found that the inflows to Europe were US$313 billion, a fall of 19 percent from 2009. Declining FDI flows were also registered in Japan, where net inflows turned negative (US$1.25 billion) due to large divestments by foreign transnational corporations. In contrast, inflows of FDI to North America showed a strong turnaround, with an increase of 44 percent to US$252 billion. FDI outflows from developed countries reversed their downward trend since 2008 with a 10 percent increase in 2010. UNCTAD, *World Investment Report 2011— Non-equity Modes of International Production and Development* (October 02, 2011) UNCTAD/WIR/2011. Available at <http://www.unctad.org/Templates/webflyer.asp?intDocItemID=22044&docid=15189&intItemID= 2068&lang=1&mode=press> accessed October 02, 2011.

[32] UNCTAD, *World Investment Report 2011* (2011), 8.

[33] In 2010, the inward stock of foreign direct investment was estimated to have reached US$19,141 billion and the outward stock was US$20,408 billion. UNCTAD, *World Investment Report 2011* (2011) at 24.

The purchase of shares of one country's companies by another country's residents has also grown significantly in recent years. The total value of portfolio investments of this type amounts to trillions of US dollars, and that total seems to be growing rapidly.[34] A variety of factors have driven this phenomenon, including the development of stock markets in many countries, the emergence of technologies to facilitate cross-border portfolio investment, the removal or reduction of legal restrictions on the investment by foreigners in local companies, and improved knowledge and information about foreign stock markets and foreign companies. Another factor has been the recognition by institutional investors throughout the world that exposure to foreign markets is an important element in increasing the returns earned by such institutions as mutual funds, pension funds, and endowment funds.

(c) **International Loans.** Loans by banks and other financial institutions based in one country to enterprises located in another country constitute yet another form of foreign investment. In many cases, in order to spread the risk, especially large loans are provided not by a single financial institution but by a syndicate of several banks located in different countries. International loans are not only made between unrelated entities. Corporations often make them to their subsidiaries and affiliates as a means of financing the latter's operations. In some cases, loans are often a substitute for an equity investment. Loans are usually subject to lengthy agreements that often impose conditions or "covenants" on the activities and operations of the borrower as a means of reducing the risk to the lender of the borrower's nonrepayment.

A particular type of international loan is the *sovereign* loan, that is, a loan made to a state or state agency. Sovereign loans are distinct from nonsovereign loans in at least two respects. First, the borrower, as a sovereign, is usually immune in varying degrees from judicial enforcement mechanisms such as bankruptcy and insolvency proceedings. Second, sovereigns usually refuse to accept the usual types of covenants or restrictive conditions that commercial lenders normally impose on private borrowers as a condition for the loan. On the other hand, loans made to sovereigns by international organizations often do contain significant restrictions on the sovereign debtor's governmental operations, a feature known as "conditionality." Indeed, loans from such institutions may be conditioned on the borrower's undertaking major policy changes or institutional reforms affecting the governance of the country concerned.[35]

---

[34] For example, foreign holdings of US securities as of June 30, 2010, were measured at US$10,691 billion, of which US$9,736 billion were holdings of US long-term securities (original term-to-maturity in excess of one year) and US$956 billion were holdings of US short-term securities. As of June 30, 2009, total foreign holdings amounted to US$9,641 billion. *Report on Foreign Portfolio Holdings of U.S. Securities as of June 30, 2010* (Dep't of Treasury April 2011).
　　Available at <http://www.treasury.gov/resource-center/data-chart-center/tic/Documents/shla2010r.pdf> accessed October 02, 2011.
　　US holdings of foreign securities in 2009 totaled US$5,977 billion, of which holdings of foreign equities amounted to US$3,995 billion and holdings of foreign debt—US$1,981 billion. Report on U.S. Portfolio Holdings of Foreign Securities as of December 31, 2009 (Dep't of Treasury October 2010).
　　Available at <http://www.treasury.gov/press-center/press-releases/Documents/claims%20report%2010_27_2010%20with%20appendix%20tables.pdf> accessed October 02, 2011.
[35] Article I(ii) of the Articles of Agreement of the International Bank for Reconstruction and Development states that the IBRD may provide financing based on "suitable conditions." See World Bank, *Review of World Bank Conditionality: Legal Aspects of Conditionality in Policy-Based Lending* (June 29, 2005, World Bank Legal Vice Presidency) which states at 3–4 that the conditions for lending to Bank's sovereign borrowers may require them to: (1) maintain an adequate macroeconomic framework, (2) implement the Bank financed program in a manner satisfactory to the Bank, and (3) comply with policy and institutional actions (ie "program conditions") which are critical to the program financed by the policy-based loan.

(d) International Bonds. Both governments and corporations raise some of the needed capital for their activities by issuing bonds, notes, and other negotiable instruments to investors in other countries. Once issued, such bonds, notes and other negotiable instruments are often traded among investors on capital markets. The value of new international bonds issued during 2006 was equivalent to US$3,114.945 million.[36] Normally such loans are denominated in dollars, euros, yen, or other readily convertible international currencies. However, with the development of local credit markets, foreign investors are increasingly investing in bonds and notes of foreign issuers denominated in other local currencies that are less easily convertible. Issuance of international bonds is also meant to serve as a signal to investors that a country is keen to join capital markets.

Bonds issued by states and state agencies and entities are known as "sovereign bonds." They present the same types of problems posed by sovereign loans, discussed above, with respect to judicial enforcement and the impositions of conditions on sovereign debtors.

(e) Suppliers' and Others' Credits. Companies in one country will often sell goods on credit to a company in another country. Many times that credit is supported by a guarantee from a financial or governmental institution. Such credit is also a type of investment by the supplier and often accrues interest until the amount of the purchase is fully paid. In such transaction, unlike a loan or the purchase of a bond from foreign issuer, no money crosses borders. Nevertheless, it is an investment because the supplier has committed capital in the form of goods to the transaction, and it expects a return in the form of repayment of the purchase price, plus an agreed upon amount of interest, for financing the sale.

(f) Other Contractual Arrangements. A variety of other contractual arrangements, particularly long-term arrangements between persons in different countries, may also qualify as investments to the extent that they require one party to commit capital or money to a venture with the expectation of receiving a return at a later time. Thus, concession contracts between persons and entities based in different countries to run public services, mineral exploration arrangements, development agreements, construction contracts, land purchase agreements, and innumerable other contractual devices may all be considered international investments. Exposure to sovereign risk and corruption can be significant obstacles even when contracts are in place.

International investment transactions and forms have been growing rapidly in size, frequency, and variety in recent decades as a result of the economic imperatives of globalization. The continuing drive for economic efficiency will propel this trend in the decades ahead. The above indicated forms of international investment are by no means an exclusive list. They are offered as illustrations of the principal ways in which international investments are made. In response to economic necessity and the creativity of business and financial entrepreneurs, new forms will no doubt arise in the future.

---

[36] The International Capital Market Association (ICMA) has found that the total of new international bond market issues for the first half of 2007 was US$1,814 billion. This figure shows a 13 percent increase in the value of new issuance compared with the figure for the first half of 2006. Total market size in terms of outstanding international bonds stood at over US$11 trillion as at June 30, 2007. International Capital Market Association Press Release (ICMA), "ICMA figures for first half 2007 bond market issuance," (July 17, 2007) ICMA/2007/20. For more information see the ICMA website <http://www.icmagroup.org>.

1.7 State and Investor Interests Shaping the Laws of International Investment

An international investment potentially involves the interests of three parties: (1) the host country where the investment takes place, (2) the investor, and (3) the home country of the investor. Each of these three players employs law and legal devices to advance its own particular interests. Since interests drive legal content, it is important to understand these interests as background to understanding the applicable law and legal arrangements that the three parties employ. This section will briefly examine their interests in a general fashion.

(a) Host Country Interests

Like foreign investors, host countries also view foreign investment in terms of its costs and its benefits, its risks and its rewards, and they enact laws and regulations accordingly so as to maximize the benefits and minimize the risks and costs of the investment to the host country concerned. It is important for foreign investors and their legal and business advisers to understand these host country interests in order to work with applicable host country legislation and regulations and to conduct useful negotiations with government officials.

(i) Benefits and Rewards of Foreign Investment

Host country governments, as a group, believe that the introduction of foreign capital and the establishment of foreign investment projects within their territories offer them numerous potential benefits. Under proper conditions, host governments expect foreign investment to bring to host countries a combination of resources, technologies, skills, and activities that will result in a surplus of output and real income beyond that which goes directly to the investor as profit. This surplus may take the form of one or several particular benefits to the host country.[37] These may include the creation of increased employment opportunities for its people, the development of natural resources that the government or local entrepreneurs have no means to develop, links to international markets and strengthened international trade opportunities, the provision of desired goods and services that domestic enterprises are unwilling or unable to provide, the improvement of balance of payments—especially when the investment project will yield export earnings—and increased taxes and public revenues resulting from the activities of the enterprise.[38] The importance that any single host country attaches to a specific benefit will normally depend on that country's particular situation. For example, an African country with a desperate shortage of foreign exchange may see the principal benefit of foreign investment as a means to improve its foreign currency reserves. On the other hand, an oil-producing state with a balance of payments surplus may invite foreign investment—not to obtain foreign exchange—but rather to acquire needed technology and know-how.

---

[37] See Committee for Economic Development, *Transnational Corporations and Developing Countries: New Policies for a Changing World Economy* 20 (1981) [hereafter cited as *Transnational Corporations and Developing Countries*].

[38] For a discussion of the potential benefits of foreign investment to the host country, see SH Robock, KR Simmonds and J Zwick, *International Business and Multinational Enterprises* (rev edn 1977) 173–98.

Ordinarily, a host country adopts investment laws, policies, and regulations in such a way as to encourage those special types of investment from which it thinks it will particularly benefit. As will be discussed in Chapter 6, the law may provide special incentives, such as tax exemptions, to attract particularly desirable investments and conversely may specifically prohibit certain types of investments, for example by excluding them from specified economic sectors, such as retail trade, in order to protect certain national interests or interest groups. In an effort to maximize the benefits from foreign investment, host country laws may include a variety of devices such as provisions to assure that the investor will bring only new resources into the country as part of the project and will not instead merely mobilize existing local resources, for example, by borrowing from local banks. At the same time, it should be noted that host countries sometimes face problems in identifying and evaluating the benefits to be derived from a particular foreign investment project: some effects are indirect and may not be felt for a long time, while others may be difficult to attribute to a foreign investor because domestic conditions or government action may be equally important in creating the effect.[39]

(ii) The Risks and Costs of Foreign Investment

Just as foreign investment presents certain risks and costs to the investor so too does it present risks and costs to the host country. Western business executives often claim that foreign equity investment provides unlimited benefits to the host country and that it costs the host country virtually nothing; consequently, they are surprised and sometimes even outraged when host country governments are reluctant to accept their investment proposals—a reaction viewed by local officials as either naive or disingenuous. It is therefore important that foreign investors and their legal counsel understand the perceived risks and costs to the host country so as to formulate proposals and to conduct negotiations in a manner that will lead to acceptance by host government officials and local joint venture partners. One must not assume that negative attitudes toward foreign investment are found only in developing countries with a socialist orientation. On the contrary, certain industrialized countries, depending on time and circumstance, have also become concerned about the impact of foreign investment on their economies and societies.

For the host country, the costs of foreign investment may take a variety of forms, and may be economic, political, and social in nature. For example, while in the short run a foreign investment project may improve the country's holdings of foreign exchange, it may in the long run have an adverse impact on balance of payments and drain off national resources through the repatriation of profits, the payment of royalties, and the servicing of foreign debt. Moreover, the presence of foreign capital in the country may be so substantial that the economy, or at least key portions of it, either in reality or appearance, becomes subject to the control of foreigners. A foreign direct investment usually results in foreign control of local assets, and that foreign control can raise a variety of concerns and anxieties within the host country. For example in 2006, DP World, a state-owned corporation based in the United Arab Emirates, proposed to acquire the port management business of six

---

[39] *Transnational Corporations and Developing Countries*, n 37, at 21–3.

major United States ports. Prompted by national security concerns, strong opposition to the acquisition in the US Congress led DP World to abandon the transaction.[40]

Shifting the focus of economic decision making from local business enterprises to parent corporation headquarters outside the host country may even be viewed as a threat to national independence. Inevitably, the real or imagined consequence of this phenomenon is that the economy—and indeed the country—exists not for the benefit of its own nationals, but for the benefit of foreign interests.[41] The perception within a host country by certain segments of the population that the investor's goals and those of the host government are in conflict is often at the base of local opposition to a foreign investment, either when it is proposed or after it has begun operation.

In addition to feared adverse economic influence, host governments and groups are often concerned that foreign investment may exert political influence in the affairs of the host country. As an example, one may cite the numerous allegations by developing countries against multinational companies which have either attempted to keep certain governments in power or to depose others, to support certain politicians they favored and oppose those they did not.[42] Political interference may also take place in other, more subtle ways, for example, when foreign investors lobby host governments for favorable changes in local laws and policies affecting the operation of their investment projects. Moreover, certain foreign investment projects may thwart the policies of the host country. For example, a host country pursuing a policy of social and economic equality for its people may discover that foreign investment will create a privileged class of its nationals who work for, or are in some way associated with, foreign investors and foreign investment projects. Most host countries are aware of the potential political risks posed by foreign investment in their territories, and their concern may be manifested in negotiations and dealings with the investor.

Host country governments perceive additional risks in that a foreign investment, instead of fostering and strengthening local enterprise, may actually stultify local business through destructive competition. Such competition is, of course, obvious when a foreign investment project operates in the same area of economic activity as an existing local enterprise; for instance, a foreign investor's battery plant might compete with a local battery plant in the local market. A foreign investor, often equipped with superior financial and technological resources, as well as with special privileges granted by the government itself, may easily dominate the local manufacturer of similar products. But the destructive effects may also be felt even when the foreign investor and local manufacturers operate in totally different economic domains. For example, a local foundry in a developing country may discover that it is in competition with a foreign battery manufacturing project, not for customers, but for human and financial resources in an economy of scarcity. Because of its power and special privileges, the foreign investment project can command foreign exchange for needed imports and can pay high salaries to attract skilled workers in a way that the foundry cannot. In countries where public sector corporations play an important role in the economy and follow policies of social welfare, rather than policies of pure maximization

---

[40] G Lyons, "How State Capitalism Could Change the World," *Financial Times,* July 2007. Available at <http://www.ft.com/cms/s/0/6eb8da08-1503-11dc-b48a-000b5df10621.html#axzz1YoTjqcWq> accessed on September 23, 2011.

[41] A Rotstein, "The Multinational Corporation in the Political Economy—A Matter of National Survival," in H Hahlo, J Smith, and R Wright (eds), *Nationalism and the Multinational Enterprise: Legal, Economic and Managerial Aspects* (1973) 187.

[42] P Drucker, "Multinationals: The Game and the Rules: Multinationals and Developing Countries: Myths and Realities," 53 *Foreign Affairs* (October 1974) 121–34.

of profit, host country officials fear that such public entities will become increasingly unprofitable and ultimately depend on government subsidies as they compete with foreign enterprises who are freed of such social obligations and have superior financial and technological capabilities.

While foreign investment may transfer needed technology to the host country, some governments may be concerned that such technology will be inappropriate to the conditions prevailing in the country and harmful to the environment. For example, the methods used by a foreign investor to conduct logging operations in a tropical country may encourage erosion in the areas worked. Or, the introduction of capital-intensive technology, such as a highly mechanized factory in an area of great unemployment, may result in further labor displacement and local resentment. In addition, the foreign investment project, accompanied by a sizeable presence of foreigners, may have an adverse impact upon the society. It may disrupt established values, change living patterns, and erode traditional authority. Thus, a large touristic complex in a small developing country may lead to undesirable behavior among local youths, and factories producing certain types of luxury consumer goods may create undesirable consumption patterns in the society as a whole.

In any given country, the perceived opportunities for national gains from foreign investment and the associated contemplated risks and costs are fundamental to shaping national investment policy and related laws and regulations. Some host countries convinced of the benefits of foreign capital develop a legal order to favor and encourage foreign investment, while others, concerned about the costs and risks, create more restrictive laws and regulations on foreign investment. But once enacted, such national laws and regulations are by no means permanent. They may change over time in response to local or international political and economic conditions. For example, whereas many developing countries created legal regimes that restricted foreign investment during the 1960s and 1970s, many of these same countries, in order to cope with new economic conditions of the late 1980s and the 1990s and in response to the "Washington Consensus,"[43] advanced by the World Bank, the International Monetary Fund, and other international financial institutions, modified their legal systems and entered into international legal arrangement so as to encourage foreign investment.[44]

(b) Investor Interests

As discussed earlier in this chapter, the foreign investor's two basic interests with respect to undertaking and managing a foreign investment are to maximize returns and minimize risks. The precise way in which the investor will attain these ends will depend on the nature of the investment, the political, economic and social conditions in the host country, the law and policy of the investor's home country, and prevailing international economic and political trends. Investors use and rely on law to maximize their benefits and minimize their risks. Indeed, they often take steps to shape laws, regulations, and legal arrangements to

[43] The term "Washington Consensus" was coined in a 1990 paper by John Williamson, which outlined ten policy reforms that Latin America should undertake: fiscal discipline, redirection of public expenditures toward high-yield areas such as health and education, tax reform, interest rate liberalization, competitive exchange rate, trade liberalization, liberalization of inflows of FDI, privatization, deregulation, and secure property rights. John Williamson, "What Washington Means by Policy Reform," in John Williamson (ed), *Latin American Adjustment: How Much Has Happened?* 5, 5–20 (1990).

[44] See generally, JW Salacuse, "From Developing Countries to Emerging Markets: A New Role for Law in the Third World," 33 *The International Lawyer* (1999) 875.

meet their interests. Thus, prior to undertaking a foreign investment, they may seek to obtain tax advantages under host country legislation or lobby the host government to adopt laws and regulations that will favor their interests. They may also make contracts with host governments that give their investments favorable treatment, encourage their home governments to make treaties and other international arrangements, such as bilateral investment treaties, to reduce their political risks within a country, and enter into legal arrangements in their home country, such as political risk insurance offered by home government agencies, to gain protection against expropriation of their investment. Thus, multinational corporations and other foreign investors take law very much into account in devising their business strategies.

(c) Investor Home Country Interests

Home country governments are the third important player in the foreign investment process. It is sometimes erroneously assumed that the interests of the home country government are identical to those of its investors abroad. While the interests of home countries and their foreign investors are aligned to a large extent, they also diverge in certain respects with regard to particular issues. Thus, home country governments may believe that their foreign investors bring the country certain national benefits such as increased trade opportunities in the countries in which they invest, increased remittances in the form of repatriated profits and royalty payments from their foreign enterprises, increased home country influence in host countries, and improved political and economic relationships with host countries. It is for this reason, for example, that many capital-exporting countries have established governmental agencies that offer their nationals and corporations political risk insurance to protect their nationals' investments abroad. Traditionally, capital-exporting governments have also been ready to offer their investors diplomatic protection in their investment disputes with host country governments in order to protect their investors' interests, as well as their own related interests.

On the other hand, there are instances in which the interests of the home government diverge from those of its investors. Home governments may therefore seek to limit or control the ability of their investors to invest capital abroad for a variety of reasons, including the desire to preserve capital for use at home, particularly in times of monetary stress or crisis, to preserve employment opportunities for their nationals at home when a foreign investment will result in the closure of a domestic enterprise, to prevent investments in countries that are actual or potential adversaries, and to be assured that the activities of their companies abroad do not have negative effects at home, for example, by violating its policies on competition or corruption. Most home countries have adopted legislation and regulations to further these particular interests. Companies contemplating investments abroad must conform to them or risk significant sanctions.

It is well to remember that for both the home and host states a foreign investment is not merely a commercial transaction between a foreign investor and the enterprise in which an investment is made, it is also an act of international relations between sovereign states. While investors' primary interest is protecting their investments from risk and maximizing their returns, states, their governments, and indeed the international community have other, broader interests that need to be considered and accounted for in developing a legal order for international investment.

National governments are concerned with achieving prosperity, economic development, security, and improving the general welfare of their people. To the extent that international investment in or from their territory facilitates the achievement of those goals, national governments will foster and encourage foreign investment. To the extent that a home or host government perceives the goals of foreign investors as contrary to its aims, its response will be less favorable. Indeed, it is in that circumstance of perceived conflicting interests and goals that investor–state disputes arise.

States view foreign investment as a form of international economic cooperation. As seen by states, its purpose is not just to assure legal rights to investors but also to achieve broader societal goals that individual investors often forget or ignore. For host countries, investment laws, regulations, contracts, and treaties are mechanisms to concretize and advance the economic cooperation between states that advances their individual economic development and prosperity.

1.8 Investment and Trade: What's the Difference?

While foreign investment is often associated with international trade or has trade as its objective, investment transactions and trade transactions are conceptually distinct. For one thing, the typical trade transaction is basically an exchange of goods or services for money. Once that exchange is made, the transaction is complete and usually no further legal relationship exists between buyer and seller. Investment transactions, on the other hand, are of a longer duration and once made result in a continuing legal relationship between the investor and the enterprise in which the investor has invested. Foreign investment also results in a continuing relationship between the investor and the foreign country where the investment is made because the investment is now subject to the sovereignty of that country. Because an asset owned by the investor is under the jurisdiction of foreign sovereign, the investor and its investment is subject to that sovereign's future actions. To the extent that those future actions have a negative impact on the investment, the investor and its investment face political risk emanating from that country. Normal trade transactions do not result in similar continuing relationships and so are not subject to the same kinds of political risks as foreign investment transactions.

While they are conceptually distinct, trade and investment are nonetheless often interrelated. Many foreign investments are undertaken to facilitate and foster trade. For example, the French company mentioned above may have established a subsidiary to manufacture refrigerators in Malaysia specifically in order to take account of lower production costs and gain the ability to sell its products throughout Asia. Because of the close connection between investment and trade activities, the World Trade Organization has adopted various rules through binding treaties that govern investments which have an impact on trade. One such treaty, to be discussed later in this volume, is the Agreement on Trade-Related Investment Measures (TRIMs).[45] Another is the General Agreement on Trade in Services (GATTS).[46] The provision of services, such as those related to insurance, telecommunications, construction, or law, often require that the provider of the service make an investment in the country in which it intends to provide the service.

---

[45] "Uruguay Round Agreement on Trade-Related Investment Measures," in *The Results of the Uruguay Round of Multilateral Trade Negotiations, the Legal Texts* (1994) 163. (TRIMs Agreement). Also available at <http://www.wto.org/english/docs_e/legal_e/legal_e.htm> accessed February 18, 2009.

[46] "General Agreement on Tariffs and Trade 1994 in *WTO Legal Texts*." Also available at <http://www.wto.org/english/docs_e/legal_e/ursum_e.htm#General> accessed September 23, 2011.

2

The Relationship between Law
and International Investment

2.1 Introduction

The general discussion in the previous chapter on the nature of international investment may lead one to ask a fundamental question: What relationship does international investment, a basically economic phenomenon, have to do with law and the legal system? The purpose of this chapter is to explore that question and to probe the theoretical and practical relationships between law and investment. The word "law" in this context does not refer to any specific legislation or legal rule, many of which will be discussed in great detail in subsequent chapters, but rather to legal systems or legal orders in general. "Law" in this context means an authoritative rule for human conduct accompanied by the potential application of a sanction for failure to respect that rule. Such rules may be found in a wide variety of sources, including legislation, regulations, treaties, and contracts.

The effectiveness of law in influencing human conduct requires more than legal rules written on a piece of paper. It requires institutions. "Institutions," according to Douglass C North, recipient of the Nobel Prize in Economics in 1993, "are the humanly devised constraints that structure political, economic and social interaction."[1] For North, institutions consist of both informal constraints, such as taboos and traditions, and formal rules, such as constitutions, laws, and property rights. This chapter, indeed, this entire book, focuses particularly on formal constraints, on what may be called legal institutions. With that definition in mind, this chapter asks the questions: Do law and legal institutions influence investment positively or negatively? How and why do laws and legal institutions influence investment? What particular elements of the legal order influence investment and in what way?

This inquiry begins with the proposition that international investors and host and home country governments, who together are the three primary participants in the international investment process, are concerned about the way in which contemplated and existing international investments affect their interests. Specifically, they assess the impact of investment on those interests in terms of the benefits and rewards they individually may gain on the one hand and the risks and costs they may incur on the other from international investments generally, as well as from specific international investment transactions in particular. Governments make policies to advance those interests. In reviewing the lessons of experience with respect to foreign investment around the world, the International Finance Corporation (IFC), an affiliate of the World Bank found that one lesson was: "The flow and direction of FDI flows respond to the national and international policy environment."[2]

The term "national policy environment" is a somewhat vague concept. But whatever else is included within in it, certainly the legal system is a vital part. Law and the legal system are the means by which policy is articulated, made real, and applied. Indeed, law is the most

---

[1] DC North, "Institutions," 5 *Journal of Economic Perspectives* (1991) 97.
[2] International Finance Corporation, *Foreign Direct Investment: Lessons of Experience (No. 5)* (1997) 20.

authoritative means that a government has to communicate policy to a society and to secure its respect and implementation by the members of that society. Policy without law to support it is often a mere academic exercise. In making investment laws and related legal institutions, governments are operating on the basis of a theory about the relationship of law to investment, about the way in which law influences the investment process.

While investors, unlike governments, do not make laws or regulations, they are able to shape the legal environment in which they operate through their negotiations with and lobbying of governments and through the contracts they make with states and private parties. Like governments, investors are acutely sensitive to the ways in which the legal environment affects their interests.

One way to understand and evaluate the link between law and international investment is to determine to what extent the applicable legal order may influence the distribution of the benefits and rewards, as well as the costs and risks, associated with the investment. As rational actors, investors and host and home country governments actively seek to increase their benefits and reduce their risks and costs from international investments. In pursuit of this goal, they use various devices, one of which is the applicable legal order. Accordingly, it is important to ask: What is it about the legal order that influences the distribution of an investment's costs and benefits? In response, one may advance the following propositions.

2.2 Law Enhances or Diminishes the Predictability of Investment Transactions

Human and government conduct is inherently unpredictable. An investor may promise to build a factory in a country but never build it. A host government may enact a low corporate tax rate in one year with a promise never to raise it, yet pass legislation to increase taxes drastically the day after an investor makes an investment. It is the inherent unpredictability of human and government conduct that creates perceived risk for a contemplated investment. As Chapter 1 defined the term, risk is the probability that expected benefits to be derived from an investment will not be received. Faced with significant risk to a contemplated investment, an investor may decide not to make the investment and a host or home government for its part may decide not to permit it. On the other hand, to the extent that the conduct of governments and investors may be rendered more predictable, the perceived risk may be diminished to the point that an investor will invest its capital and the host or home government may permit the investor to make the investment.

One of the purposes of law is to constrain human and governmental behavior and thereby make it more predictable and less risky to other persons. As North reminds us, "Throughout history, institutions have been devised by human beings to create order and reduce uncertainty in exchange."[3] Thus, the criminal law, by sanctioning conduct deemed illegal, seeks to prevent that conduct from happening, and administrative law, by regulating how governments may act, seeks to constrain governmental action to certain forms and procedures. To the extent that law and legal institutions effectively constrain governmental and human behavior, they thereby make it more predictable to other persons. By increasing predictability, law and legal institutions reduce the risk that unexpected conduct will occur.

On the other hand, laws that are unclear or that are applied inconsistently or arbitrarily reduce the predictability of investment transactions and may therefore have the effect of

---

[3] DC North, "Institutions," S *Journal of Economic Perspectives* (1991) 97.

inhibiting or reducing investment, both foreign and domestic. For example, at one point in the 1970's, Egypt had several exchange rates for its currency, including an "official rate" of US$2.50 to the Egyptian pound, and a "parallel rate" of US$1.44 to the pound. The Egyptian foreign investment law at the time provided that foreign investment capital entering the country would be converted at the official rate but also stated that capital repatriated from the country would be converted at "the prevailing rate." Uncertainty over the meaning of the term "prevailing rate," and whether it referred to the official rate, the parallel rate, or some other rate, led investors to slow the introduction of capital into Egypt until the uncertainty had been clarified by an amendment to the law.[4]

In underscoring the importance of the predictability engendered by law and its impact on the investment process, one may cite the work of the noted German scholar Max Weber in the late nineteenth and early twentieth centuries, who sought to understand why capitalism arose in Europe. Deeply knowledgeable in the disciplines of law, economics, and sociology, he argued that a rational capitalist economy required "a promptly and predictably functioning legal system," which only a modern state could provide. In particular, he concluded that one of the reasons for the rise of European capitalism was the nature of European law, which allowed what he called the "calculability" of transactions. Weber emphasized the role that law plays in raising the probability that contemplated actions will take place.[5] Calculability, according to Weber, encourages investment transactions.

For Weber three conditions were necessary for law to be calculable: (1) the legal text must lend itself to prediction; (2) the administration and application of the legal text must not be arbitrary; and (3) contracts must be enforced.[6] Thus, for example, the Egyptian investment law, referred to above, did not lend itself to prediction by investors on the crucial question of the applicable exchange rate to be applied to the repatriation capital. Even when the text of the law is clear, its application by government officials and courts in an inconsistent way, for example, on the basis of personal favoritism or the payment of bribes, reduces predictability and therefore the willingness of investors to invest their capital. Contracts are, of course, one of the principal instruments by which governments and businesses seek to control and therefore make future events more predictable. Indeed, one may say that the very existence of a capitalist economy is based on the notion that contracts made will be respected and enforced. So even if written law is clear and the courts and bureaucracy apply it consistently, the economic environment becomes unpredictable and therefore not calculable if the courts and governing authorities do not treat contracts as "the law between" the parties and therefore enforce them as such.[7]

In order to attract foreign investment, both host states and investors make various commitments and representations to each other. Some of these undertakings are embodied in formal bilateral agreements such as investment accords, development contracts, public service concessions, and tax stabilization agreements, to mention only a few. Others are found in unilateral acts like foreign investment legislation, licenses, and regulatory permissions. Still others consist of less formal governmental actions, such as oral statements by government officials and corporate executives, as well as promises about investment

---

[4] JW Salacuse and T Parnall, "Foreign Investment and Economic Openness in Egypt: Legal Problems and Legislative Adjustments of the First Three Years," 12 *The International Lawyer* (1978) 764, 772.

[5] M Weber, *Economy and Society* (1922) 161–2.

[6] R Swedberg, "Max Weber's Contribution to the Economic Sociology of Law," 2 *Annu Rev Law Soc Sci* (2001) 61, 69–70. See also DM Trubek, "Max Weber and the Rise of Capitalism," *Wis L Rev* (1972) 720.

[7] See, eg, Article 1134 of the French Civil Code: "Agreements legally entered into have the force of law for those who have made them." (*Les conventions légalement formées tiennent lieu de loi á ceux qui les ont faites*).

treatment published by the government in the press or by corporations in their promotional literature.

In varying degrees, investors and governments rely on such obligations and undertakings in making decisions related to a proposed investment and its operation once made. They usually consider the continued willingness of the host state to respect its commitments to be crucial to the profitability of an investment, and sometimes to its very survival. Since these arrangements are governed by the law of the host country and are subject to the actions of its institutions, their continued viability is premised on the assumption that the host government will not unilaterally modify or terminate them at some later time—a phenomenon that has in fact taken place on numerous occasions. Thus, a mineral development agreement made with a foreign investor by one government may be cancelled by a subsequent government as a result of a change in policy or economic conditions. A government may grant a foreign investor the right to operate a landfill one year and cancel it the next because of changes in environmental legislation. A host government's obligations to foreign investors are therefore, in the oft-quoted words of Raymond Vernon, "obsolescing bargains" between the investor and the host country.[8] In other words, they are subject to change, often on the initiative of the government concerned.

The cause of the obsolescence of the investment bargain has much to do with two important factors: (1) changing circumstances and (2) the decline in the investor's bargaining power after making the investment. With regard to the first factor, states, like rational private parties, will generally continue to respect their obligations to the extent that the perceived net benefits of performance exceed those of nonperformance. But when, for whatever reason, a state judges the net costs of continuing performance to exceed the perceived net benefits, the result will usually be rejection of the obligation or, at the very least, a demand to renegotiate the original undertaking.[9] For example, a developing country government may eagerly sign a mining agreement with a French minerals company because of the prospect of high revenues. But, if after a few years the revenues do not meet governmental expectations, or if another mining company promises higher income, the government will cancel the contract if it concludes that the cost of doing so will not exceed the benefits to be derived from a new arrangement. In making this calculation, the host government weighs the expected benefits from a new arrangement against such political and economic costs as defending against a lawsuit or arbitration claim brought by the French company, as well as any sanctions that the French government might impose, such as a reduction in foreign aid.

The concept of costs and benefits is not limited to purely economic factors. When states are involved, the costs and benefits of both political and social effects will weigh heavily in any decision to continue or end an investment undertaking.[10] For example, in one case involving a foreign investment project designed to build a luxury resort near the Giza pyramids in Egypt, the Egyptian government originally signed the agreement believing the economic benefits of the project would exceed its costs. But, when public and international opposition became strong and persistent because of fears of the project's negative effects on a treasured archeological site, the government cancelled the project. The government

---

[8] R Vernon, *Sovereignty at Bay: The Multinational Spread of U.S. Enterprises* (1971) 46. Vernon developed the concept of the obsolescing bargain within the context of investments in minerals, but it also has application to other types of investments in many cases.

[9] JW Salacuse, *The Global Negotiator* (2003) 223–7.

[10] L Wells and E Gleason, "Is Foreign Infrastructure Investment Still Risky?" *Harvard Business Review* (September–October 1995) 44–54.

judged that the project's political costs outweighed the economic benefits to be derived from its construction.[11]

A second factor that contributes to the obsolescence of state undertakings is the decline in an investor's bargaining power after making an investment. When proposing an investment, the investor has a certain amount of bargaining power to secure favorable treatment and conditions for its investment because of the government's desire to acquire the investment. However, once the investor has made the investment and thus placed its capital under the sovereignty of the host state, its bargaining power with the host state diminishes and the governmental commitment toward the project runs the risk of becoming obsolete in the eyes of the host government.[12]

All foreign investors therefore face a fundamental problem: How can they be certain that host states will continue to respect the commitments made at the time the investment was made? One approach is to employ legal devices that increase the perceived costs to the host state for failing to fulfil its undertakings. For example, the existence of an investment treaty between the host state and the investor's home state may subject the host government to investor–state arbitration before an international tribunal for its violation of treaty provisions concerning the treatment of protected investments.[13] As a consequence, a state deciding whether or not to continue to respect its obligations toward a particular investment would at least in theory have to include in its calculations the significant costs of defending and losing an investor–state arbitration. The state would also have to consider the resulting negative impact on its investment climate. Public knowledge of an investor–state dispute may dissuade other investors from investing in a host country that is alleged to have violated its investment commitments.

From a foreign investor's point of view, elevating such potential governmental costs through treaty provisions constitutes an inducement to host countries to fulfil their obligations in the face of opposing pressures. Moreover, by giving an individual investor the right to bring an investor–state arbitration and obtain compensation for the nonperformance of state obligations, such a treaty provision increases the bargaining power of the investors in their dealings with the host government and works to insure continued state compliance. It is for these reasons that a large number of investment treaties contain provisions, often referred to as "umbrella clauses," to achieve this result by making performance of state undertakings a part of the treatment owed to investors.[14]

Governments for their part are also concerned that investors will live up to the promises they make; consequently, governments too seek to raise the costs to the investor for its failure to perform as expected. Thus, for example, in a concession agreement whereby a foreign investor has agreed to operate a water or electricity system owned by a host government, the investor, as a precondition, may be required to secure a substantial letter of credit or bank guarantee payable to the host government in case of failure to operate the concession at the required level of performance.[15]

---

[11] See *SPP (Middle East), Ltd, and Southern Pacific Properties Ltd v. The Arab Republic of Egypt*, ICC Case No 3493 (ICC Award) (March 11, 1983) (1983) 22 ILM 752.

[12] M Sornarajah, *The International Law on Foreign Investment* (2010).

[13] See generally, JW Salacuse, *The Law of Investment Treaties* (2010) 359–92.

[14] For a discussion on Umbrella Clauses, see generally, K Yannaca-Small, "Interpretation of the Umbrella Clause in Investment Agreements," *OECD Working Paper on International Investments*, Number 2006/3. Available at <http://www.oecd.org/dataoecd/3/20/37579220.pdf> accessed October 19, 2011. See also JW Salacuse, *The Law of Investment Treaties* (2010) 271–84.

[15] See generally, K Gassner, A Popov and N Pushak, *An Empirical Assessment of Private Sector Participation in Electricity and Water Distribution in Developing and Transition Countries* (2007, World Bank: Washington, D.C.).

2.3 Law Increases or Reduces Associated Transaction Costs

As indicated above, both investors and governments are concerned about the costs they will incur as a result of undertaking or permitting a foreign investment. As rational actors, both governments and investors seek to reduce the costs they incur for the investment and to increase the benefits they may derive.[16] To a significant extent, the costs and benefits of an investment are determined by negotiation between the host government and the foreign investor. A foreign direct investment can be viewed as a bargain between the two parties in interest. That bargain may be incorporated in a detailed, complex contract between the investor and an agency of the host government. However, at least certain terms of the bargain are to be found in the prevailing host country legislation applicable to the investment. Thus, for example, the terms governing distribution of costs and benefits pertaining to a large agro-industrial project will be stipulated not only in the lengthy contract between the government and the foreign investor but also in such important national legislation as the tax code, environmental legislation, labor laws, and health and safety regulations, to name only a few.

Each of these individual laws, regulations, contractual provisions, and other legal elements embodied in that bargain will entail genuine costs and benefits for the parties concerned with the investment. Thus a high tax rate by the host government raises the costs of the investment to the investor but increases the benefits to be gained by the government. In addition, a tax rule by the investor's home country that income is taxable at the time earned by a foreign subsidiary may make investments more costly to the investor than a rule providing that income is taxable by the home government only when it is repatriated. An evaluation of the costs and benefits relating to an investment by each of the three parties in interest—foreign investor, host government, and home government—will affect their actions with respect to a contemplated or existing investment.[17] Thus, a high tax rate may dissuade a foreign investor from undertaking a project because the increased taxes to be paid render it insufficiently profitable or not profitable at all.

In addition to specific terms in investment contracts and relevant legislation, the legal and governmental system as a whole may also have an impact on the investment costs and benefits. For example, the failure of a government to provide security to an investor's assets from seizure by brigands, to protect its personnel from kidnapping by terrorists, or to enforce contracts in host country courts will require the investor to use other, often private means, to secure its assets, protect its personnel, and enforce its contracts; however, such other means will usually require the investor to incur substantial costs. Thus, the investor may have to hire its own security force or make contracts that provide for international arbitration. Such measures generally will be more costly to the investor than if an effective government assumed the tasks of security and contract enforcement. As Professor Ronald Coase, a recipient of the Nobel Prize in Economics, posited, an

Available at <http://siteresources.worldbank.org/INTSDNETWORK/Resources/2007_June_Impact_of_PSP_in _elec_and_water.pdf> accessed October 19, 2011.

[16] Professor James Buchanan, recipient of the 1986 Nobel Prize in Economics is known for his work in the field of public choice theory, which utilizes the economics framework to study the behavior of politicians and governments as self-interested agents. See generally, J Buchanan and G Tullock, *The Calculus of Content: Logical Foundations of Constitutional Democracy* (1962).

[17] See generally, T Irwin, "The Allocation of Three Risks," *Government Guarantees: Allocating and Valuing Risk in Privately Financed Infrastructure Projects*, Washington, D.C.: The World Bank, 2007, 71–101. Available at <http://siteresources.worldbank.org/INTSDNETWORK/Resources/Government_Guarantees.pdf> accessed October 19, 2011.

effective system of property rights can reduce the transaction costs of dealings.[18] Thus, when the investor's costs rise to the point of insufficient profitability it may abandon the investment or alter it in some way—for example, by removing its high value operations to another country—so as to reduce transaction costs.

Law and the legal system can also raise investment transaction costs. In dealing with a perceived social problem, for example the sale of counterfeit goods or the failure of street vendors to pay taxes, the immediate action of governments is to try to regulate the problem out of existence, for example by requiring all retail sellers to have a special license or by imposing the purchase of an annual tax stamp on street vendors. Such regulation may have the effect of reducing entrepreneurial activity and investment and thereby reduce social benefits. As Ronald Coase wrote in his seminal article, "The Problem of Social Cost,"

> All solutions have costs and there is no reason to suppose that government regulation is called for simply because the problem is not well handled by the market or the firm. Satisfactory views on policy can only come from a patient study of how in practice, the market, firms, and governments handle the problem of harmful effects.... It is my belief that economists, and policy-makers generally, have tended to over-estimate the advantages which come from governmental regulation.[19]

In a practical application of Coase's ideas, Peruvian scholar Hernando De Soto (without specifically citing Coase) later showed in his book *The Other Path*,[20] that governmental regulations imposed on businesses may be so burdensome and time-consuming that they have the effect of either preventing entrepreneurs from starting businesses or of driving them underground into the "informal economy" where they face other kinds of costs. Compliance with regulations entails costs. He argued that regulations have two kinds of costs: the costs of access to a specific activity and the costs of remaining in that activity. Foreign investors have similar sets of costs: the costs of making an investment and the costs of operating an investment once it is made. With respect to the former, De Soto reports on a research project undertaken by scholars in Peru in which they sought to document the exact cost both in time and money for an entrepreneur to meet all of the legal and regulatory requirements for establishing a small furniture factory. They concluded that a person of modest means would have to spend 289 days on bureaucratic procedures to fulfil the eleven requirements for setting up the factory. The total costs for fulfilling these procedures and thus gaining access to the activity of furniture making, including a ten-month delay, resulted in lost profits of US$1,231—32 times the monthly minimum wage in Peru. The researchers also found that once an enterprise had complied with regulations to gain access, it then had to expend considerable funds—as much as 11.3 percent of its production costs and 347 percent of its after-tax profits to remain compliant with the country's regulations.[21] When the costs of compliance exceed the benefits to be gained from the enterprise, entrepreneurs and investors will behave as De Soto revealed in his study of Peruvians: they will either refrain from undertaking an enterprise or engage in an illegal or informal enterprise. But operating as an illegal or informal enterprise also has significant costs, which inhibit achieving the full economic potential of the enterprise, thereby denying benefits not only to the entrepreneur but also to the economy as a whole.

---

[18] See generally, RH Coase, "The Problem of Social Cost," 3 *Journal of Law and Economics* (1960) 1–44.
[19] RH Coase, "The Problem of Social Cost," 3 *Journal of Law and Economics* (1960) 1, 10. (1960).
[20] See generally, H De Soto, *The Other Path: The Invisible Revolution in the Third World* (1989).
[21] H De Soto, *The Other Path: The Invisible Revolution in the Third World* (1989) 134 and 148.

Following the approach used by De Soto and his colleagues, other scholars and institutions have sought to evaluate the costs of national regulation on business activity based on the belief that regulations have cost to those who are regulated and that such costs diminish a country's investment climate and therefore the willingness of investors to invest. Of particular note in this regard is the World Bank's program and website "Investing Across Borders (IAB)," a World Bank Group initiative comparing the regulation of foreign direct investment in countries around the world. Through its publications and an on-line data base, it presents quantitative indicators on various economies' laws, regulations, and practices affecting how foreign companies invest across sectors, start businesses, access industrial land, and arbitrate commercial disputes.[22] Each year, it publishes a year book, *Investing Across Borders* that provides selected indicators of foreign direct investment regulation in a growing list of the world's economies. For example, *Investing Across Borders 2010* found that most of the 87 economies measured by IAB have FDI-specific restrictions that hinder foreign investment. Thus, a fifth of the countries surveyed require foreign companies to go through a foreign investment approval process before proceeding with investments in light manufacturing, a requirement adding, on average, nearly one month to the establishment process—and in some countries up to six months. Such requirements, of course, increase the transaction costs of investments with corresponding negative consequences for the investor. Although host governments may find that these requirements bring them benefits in assuring that new foreign investments meet the concerns of national policy, they should also be aware, as Coase points out, that such regulations entail costs in terms of delayed or lost investments; consequently, host governments must carefully evaluate the contemplated benefits against the costs that they pay for investment regulation.

2.4 Law is an Instrument to Direct, Control, and Encourage International Capital Flows

Governments rarely have a neutral position with regard to the capital flows into or out of the states they govern. On the contrary, because of the perceived significant economic, political, and social consequences to their populations of such flows, they normally have definite policies about the extent of foreign capital to allow into their territories, the specific economic sectors in which to allow foreign capital, legal conditions under which foreign capital may operate, and the incentives they are prepared to grant to foreign investors to encourage them to invest in their territories. Law is the instrument governments use to articulate, apply, and enforce such policies. Such law may be found in their national legislation and regulations, in the treaties and international agreements they sign, and in the contracts and agreements they make with specific foreign investors. For example, many countries, particularly in the developing world, have enacted foreign investment laws and foreign investment codes which define the types of investments the country is seeking, the controls to which such investments will be subject, the incentives they may grant to encourage desired investment, and the process by which investment may be undertaken.[23]

---

[22] See *Investing Across Borders*, World Bank: Washington, D.C. Available at <http://iab.worldbank.org/> accessed October 19, 2011.

[23] See, eg, Angola: Law Number 15/94, Foreign Investment Law, National Assembly, September 23, 1994, available at <http://www.un.int/wcm/webdav/site/angola/shared/documents/official%20documents/Foreign%20Investment%20Law.pdf>; Saudi Arabia Foreign Investment Law, 5/1/1421 (H) available at <http://www.saudia-online.com/txtinvestment.htm>; Democratic Republic of Congo: Law No. 004/2002 of February 21, 2000 On the Investment Code, available at <http://www.anapi.org/eng/IMG/pdf/investment_code.pdf>; Chile,

Similarly, because the outflow of capital from a state can have significant negative effects, governments may also enact capital and monetary controls to regulate the outward flow of funds from their territories.[24] For example, during the Asian financial crisis at the end of the twentieth century, Malaysia imposed capital controls to limit the amount of funds that investors might remove from the country so as to protect the value and stability of its currency.[25] Other countries may prevent the flow of capital to particular nations that they consider adversaries in an effort to weaken or at least not strengthen that adversary. Thus, the United States has legislation that prohibits US companies from investing in Iran.[26]

Laws that are not specifically aimed at international investment may nonetheless influence international capital flows. For example, in view of the crucial role that technology transfer plays in the success of any investment, legislation in the home country that prohibits the export of certain technology to particular countries may effectively prevent certain foreign investments in those countries from taking place. Similarly, host countries without effective legal protection of intellectual property may find themselves denied foreign investment that relies on such technologies.[27]

Numerous factors within individual legal systems may influence international investment flows, and subsequent chapters of this book will examine some of them in detail. For purposes of general analysis, one may identify them at three levels: (1) the level of individual legal provisions that encourage or discourage investment by increasing or reducing risks or costs of the investment transaction (the legislative level); (2) legal and administrative institutions which function in such a way as to increase or reduce risks and costs, for example a weak or strong judiciary (the institutional level); and (3) systemic factors—ie fundamental characteristics concerning the functioning of the legal system as a whole, such as the existence or lack of a strong rule of law (the systemic level).[28]

2.5 Law Defines and Regulates Investment Rights, Responsibilities, and Relationships

Investments are invariably defined and analyzed in terms of rights, obligations, and relationships—the language of the law. Thus, in a joint venture between a French company and a Malaysian company to manufacture air conditioners in Vietnam, the parties need to know the exact amount of capital they are obligated to contribute to the venture and when

---

Foreign Investment Statute Decree Law 600, Restated, Coordinated and Standardized Text of Decree-law No 600, as of 1974 of the Foreign Investment Statute (published in the Official Gazette en December 16, 1993), established by the Decree having force of law No 523 of the Ministry of Economy, Development and Reconstruction as of September 3, 1993. available at <http://www.cochilco.cl/english/normativa/descarga/DecreeLa_n600.pdf>; Republic of Korea, Foreign Investment Promotion Act. This Act was adopted on September 16, 1998 as Act No 5559, repealing the previously enforced Foreign Investment and Foreign Capital Inducement Act, in order to widely ease the regulations and restrictions on investment by foreigners, to expand investment tax incentives, and to reorganize institutions and systems related to foreign investment, such as foreign investment zones, available at <http://untreaty.un.org/cod/avl/pdf/ls/Shin_RelDocs.pdf>.

[24] See, eg, A Alesina, V Grilli and G Milesi-Ferretti, *The Political Economy of Capital Controls* (NBER Working Paper Series, vol w4353, May 1993).

[25] E Kaplan and D Rodrik, "Did the Malaysian Capital Controls Work?" in S Edwards and J Frankel (eds), *Managing Currency Crises in Emerging Markets* (2002).

[26] Iran Sanctions Act, US Department of Treasury. Available at <http://www.treasury.gov/resource-center/sanctions/Programs/pages/iran.aspx> accessed October 17, 2011.

[27] See generally, W Park and D Lippoldt, "Technology Transfer and the Economic Implications of the Strengthening of Intellectual Property Rights in Developing Countries," *OECD Trade Policy Working Paper No. 62*. Available at <http://www.oecd.org/officialdocuments/publicdisplaydocumentpdf/?cote=TAD/TC/WP%282007%2919/FINAL&docLanguage=En> accessed October 18, 2011.

[28] See JW Salacuse, "Direct Foreign Investment and the Law in Developing Countries," 15 *ICSID Review-Foreign Investment Law Journal* (2000) 382.

they will have to contribute it, their respective rights to withdraw profits and to dissolve the venture if it fails to make a profit, and the nature of the venture's relationship with the Vietnamese government, among many others issues. Indeed, the business relationship among the investors and between the investors and the government will usually be defined to the extent the parties are able to articulate it in terms of legal rights and obligations and then embodied in various legal documents, including a joint venture contract, the articles of incorporation of the joint venture company, and the permits and licenses received from the host government.

The rights, obligations, and relationships of the participants in the joint venture are not mere legal instruments to be invoked in the event of conflict; they also constitute the plan of the enterprise, the plan that the parties and the government are to carry out so that air conditioners may be manufactured and sold as originally contemplated. The fact that these rights, responsibilities and relationships are embodied in a legal document and given the force of law—that is, they constitute authoritative commands the failure of which will entail a sanction—gives greater assurance to the parties concerned that their plan will be respected and carried out. Without the force of the rule of law and the threat of sanction, any one of the participants may be tempted to defect from the agreed plan if its own particular interests at a given moment so dictate. Thus, for example, the Malaysian investor, having agreed in January to commit US$1 million in capital to the venture, may find a better of use for its funds in the following September and therefore decide not to invest in the joint venture. A legal obligation embodied in an enforceable contract will tend to prevent such defection. If defection were possible with ease and with no penalty for doing so, the French partner might not have agreed to the joint venture or taken steps to organize it. And the Vietnamese government, unsure of the intentions of the investors, might not have approved the venture and issued the license. Thus law is a mechanism to facilitate and assure collective action and cooperation necessary to undertake and operate an investment.

2.6 Law is a Means to Resolve Investment Disputes

The risk of conflict is inherent in any investment relationship. A foreign investor and a host government may become embroiled in a dispute over a change in governmental environmental regulations that are detrimental to the investor's interest or over the investor's inability or unwillingness to export the amount of its production promised in its feasibility study at the time it gained government approval of the project. Partners in a joint venture may fall into conflict over the ways in which profits of the enterprise are to be shared between them or over the failure of a partner to transfer technology to the project as promised in the joint venture contract. The existence of investment conflicts such as these can have a significant negative effect on the benefits that the participants had intended to derive from the project. It is therefore important that a mechanism exists for the settlement of such disputes, efficiently, fairly, expeditiously, and at least cost. To the extent that a state's judicial system has these characteristics, the parties may rely on it or specifically choose it to the exclusion of other court systems. Thus, for example, most international loans provide that in the event of a dispute the courts of the lender's location, usually a financial center such as New York, London or Frankfurt, will have exclusive jurisdiction to hear and decide such matters. In the event that no specific state system exists upon which the parties can agree, they will often choose alternative methods such as arbitration, international or local, as a means to resolve their disputes.

The function of dispute resolution institutions is not merely to resolve conflict between parties involved in an international investment. It is also to assure *enforcement* of related property and contractual rights. The prospect of a suit in court or in arbitration and its associated costs will presumably encourage both governments and private parties to respect and carry out the legal commitments that they have made with respect to the investment. Enforcement mechanisms are thus intended as constraints on human behavior that will assure predictability that is so vital to the international investment process. However, enforcement is always costly. In designing enforcement mechanisms, investors need to evaluate the costs of enforcement along with other costs and benefits to be accounted for in evaluating the desirability of any investment.[29]

---

[29] As Douglass C North has written, "...the structure of enforcement mechanisms and the frequency and severity of [their] imperfection plays a major role in the costs of transacting and in the forms that contracts take...Enforcement is costly. Indeed, it is frequently costly even to find out that a contract has been violated, more costly to measure the violation, and still more costly to apprehend and impose penalties on the violator." DC North, *Institutions, Institutional Change and Economic Performance* (1990) 54, 58.

3

Three Legal Frameworks for International Investment: National, Contractual, and International

3.1 The Investment Frameworks in General

Host states, international investors, and home states—the three parties with fundamental interests in international investment—have constructed rules to govern international investment transactions and have embodied them in a variety of legal instruments and institutions. The purpose of this complex of legal rules is to influence the conduct of the various parties with respect to investments in desired ways. The three interested parties have adopted legal rules and created institutions as a means to achieve their ends because they consider legal rules and instruments to be a more effective means of influencing behavior than other available methods, such as general statements of encouragement, recommended business plans, and general expressions of good will. These legal rules and instruments thus become the basic structure or framework within which the investment is undertaken and operated.

Upon examining this complex structure of rules applicable to individual international investments, one sees that it is composed of three linked legal frameworks: (1) the *national* legal framework consisting of the national laws and regulatory systems of the states having jurisdiction over the investment transaction and the related investors; (2) the *contractual* legal framework composed of the various agreements negotiated by the parties to govern the investment; and (3) the *international* law framework, the complex of treaties, customary laws, and international institutions that the nations of the world have agreed, either bilaterally or multilaterally, to put in place to regulate international investment. One of the principal factors that distinguish each of the legal frameworks is the differing basic *sources* from which they are derived. The national legal framework is derived from the law-making authorities of independent sovereign states in accordance with their prevailing constitutional arrangements. The contractual legal framework is the product of negotiation and bargaining among investors or between investors and a relevant government for the purpose of regulating the investment. The effectiveness and enforcement of such contracts and agreements depends crucially on the existence of some national legal system. And finally, the elements of the international framework are derived from agreements and arrangements among sovereign states, either in the form of specific treaties or embodied in generally accepted international customs. Let us now examine the nature of each of the three frameworks in detail.

3.2 The National Legal Framework

The national legal framework consists of the legislation, regulations, administrative acts, and judicial decisions of the governmental authorities of countries and their subdivisions having jurisdiction over the investment or the investor. National legal frameworks are exceptionally diverse. Since there were more than 200 sovereign states in the world in 2012, there were at that time more than 200 national frameworks for foreign investment, without counting subnational systems of law. No two national frameworks are exactly alike, although as will be seen they have many common characteristics.

National legal frameworks express and concretize the policies of states toward foreign capital. In general, national frameworks seek to do two things in varying degrees: to encourage foreign investment and to control foreign investment. They attempt to encourage foreign investment by granting foreign investors and investments increased freedom of action and by providing them with various incentives. National frameworks seek to control foreign investment by imposing rules and restrictions on foreign investors and foreign investment projects. Virtually all national legal systems contain some elements of investment encouragement and some elements of investment control. Thus, for example, host country legislation might offer tax exemptions and subsidized factors of production to encourage investment, but at the same time require that foreign investment projects be approved by a specific government department and restrict the sectors open to foreign capital or limit foreign equity participation to a minority position in certain types of enterprises.

The precise balance between the imperatives of investment encouragement and of investment control varies from country to country. The national legal frameworks of some countries are considered to be highly encouraging while others are found to be highly restrictive and therefore highly controlling.[1] The World Bank's *Investing Across Borders* initiative (IAB), which examines the degree to which national legal frameworks encourage or control foreign investment, has concluded:

> Countries with poor regulations and inefficient processes for foreign companies receive less FDI and have smaller accumulated stocks of FDI...Based on IAB results, countries tend to attract more FDI if they allow foreign ownership of companies in a variety of sectors, make start-up, land acquisition, and commercial arbitration procedures efficient and transparent, and have strong laws protecting investor interests.'

However, the IAB study also offers this important caveat:

> But this correlation does not imply existence or direction of a causal relationship. Many other variables—such as market size, political stability, infrastructure quality, or level of economic development—are likely to better explain the relationship.

The degree to which a national legal framework will encourage or restrict foreign direct investment (FDI) may change over time depending on a country's economic and political circumstances. For example, during the 1960s and 1970s, many developing countries seeking economic independence adopted policies of "self-reliance," expropriated foreign investments, promoted "import-substitution industries," restricted the inflow of foreign capital and technology through heavy regulation, and curtailed the import of foreign goods through high tariffs and rigorous exchange controls.[2] Thus, for example,

---

[1] See, eg, The World Bank Group, *Investing Across Borders 2010—Indicators of Foreign Investment Regulation in 87 Economies* (2010), and its related online database that offers "indicators measuring how countries around the world facilitate market access and operations of foreign companies. For each of the 87 countries surveyed, the report identifies sectors with restricted entry for foreign investors, defines roadmaps for companies seeking to create foreign subsidiaries and acquire real estate, assesses the strength of commercial arbitration systems, and presents dozens of other indicators on regulation of foreign direct investment." Available at <http://iab.worldbank .org/~/media/FPDKM/IAB/Documents/IAB-report.pdf>.

[2] For a discussion of legislation and regulation enacted by East African states in the 1970s to reduce foreign influence in their economies, see P Sebalu, "East African Community," 16 *Journal of African Law* (1972) 345, 360. "In the recent past, the most significant developments which have affected the growth of the community have

annual nationalizations of foreign-owned property grew steadily from 1960 and reached its peak in the mid-1970s.[3] Beginning in the mid-1980s, this trend was reversed as countries increasingly enacted legislation and regulations to encourage foreign investment and reduced those regulations that restricted and controlled foreign capital.[4] For example, in 2000 alone, seventy countries made a total of 150 legislative and regulatory changes affecting foreign investment, only three of which (ie 2 percent) were considered to be restrictive.[5] During the following decade, a new trend emerged in national legislation toward more restrictive provisions so that in 2010 74 countries adopted 149 measures affecting foreign investment, of which forty eight (ie 32 percent) were judged to be restrictive,[6] leading the United Nations Conference on Trade and Development (UNCTAD), a close observer of foreign capital movements, to identify a new "... long-term trend of investment policy becoming increasingly restrictive rather than liberalizing."[7]

As important as the restrictions and incentives set down in national laws and regulations are the extent to which national legal frameworks recognize and enforce the two funda-mental building blocks of the investment process, property rights and contractual rights. Both of these rights are the creation of some national legal system; both are legal constructs. How the national legal framework conceives of, defines, and enforces these two rights is fundamental to the process of undertaking and operating an investment project. As Nobel Prize-winner Douglass C. North has written:

> Property rights are the rights individuals appropriate over their own labor and the goods and services they possess. Appropriation is a function of legal rules, organizational forms, enforce-ment and norms of behavior–that is, the institutional framework.[8]

The purpose of property rights is to constrain the behavior of other persons and organiza-tions who would seek to appropriate another person's labor, goods or services for them-selves and against the will of that person. For foreign investors, the importance of effective property rights lies in the extent to which they effectively inhibit the host government, local cartels, business competitors, and criminal gangs, among others, from seizing or otherwise interfering with the investor's use and benefit of the physical and intangible things incorp-orated in its investment. In modern economies, and particularly in the realm of investment, the subject of property rights is not limited to physical things. Also important are intellec-tual property rights, the rights that the law granted to persons over creations of the mind, including inventions, literary and artistic works, designs, and artistic creations.

Countries have developed systems for the recognition and enforcement of property rights because they have come to believe that such systems will bring them economic benefits. Insecure or poorly enforced property rights are seen as inhibiting economic growth in at least four ways. First, insecure or poorly enforced property rights increases

---

been: (a) measures by the Partner States to remove the control of the economy from the hands of noncitizens and putting it into the hands of citizens or of the state by nationalisation [*sic*] or State trading Corporations; (b) exchange control..." See generally, AM Akimuni, "A Plea for the Harmonization of African Investment Laws," 19 *Journal of African Law* (1975) 134 (discussing numerous examples of governmental interference with foreign economic activity).

[3] United Nations, *World Investment Report* (1993) 17. The United Nations identified 875 distinct acts of governmental taking of foreign property in 62 countries in the period 1960–74. DL Piper, "New Directions in the Protection of American-Owned Property Abroad," 4 *International Trade Law Journal* (1979) 315.

[4] See JW Salacuse, "From Developing Countries to Emerging Markets: A Changing Role for Law in the Third World," 33 *The International Lawyer* (1999) 875, 885–9.

[5] UNCTAD, *World Investment Report 2011* (2011) at 94.

[6] UNCTAD, *World Investment Report 2011* (2011) at 94.

[7] UNCTAD, *World Investment Report 2011* (2011) at 94.

[8] DC North, *Institutions, Institutional Change, and Economic Performance* (1990) 33.

the risk of expropriation by governments or seizure by nongovernmental groups of an investor's assets and thereby reduce the incentive to invest and produce economically. Second, insecure property rights increase the costs of protecting the physical and intangible things in the investor's possession. Third, insecure property rights prevent or inhibit the most efficient use or deployment of economic resources. For example, an investor may be unwilling to deploy its most advanced technology in a country with inadequate legal protection of intellectual property but would be willing to risk a less advanced and less efficient technology. And finally, insecure property rights prevent or make more costly other useful economic transactions, such as securing financing through the provision of collateral.[9]

Because of the centrality of property rights to the economy and society, the national legal framework of countries often includes constitutional provisions that recognize and define property rights, thus establishing a foundation for their treatment in other parts of the national legal system. For example, the Fifth Amendment of the Constitution of the United States provides: "No person shall … be deprived of life, liberty or property without due process of law; nor shall private property be taken for public use, without just compensation."[10]

The effectiveness and security of property rights under national law depend on much more than constitutional provisions. Above all, it requires the resources and commitment of the political authorities and the courts to enforce and implement them. In this regard, countries throughout the world differ in their willingness and ability to recognize and enforce property rights, a factor that international investors consider in evaluating the political risk to be encountered in individual countries.[11]

Contractual rights are the second fundamental building block for international investment. For parties concerned with the investment process, two dimensions of contractual rights are particularly important: (1) the scope of contractual freedom and (2) the actual security and enforcement of contractual rights. The first deals with the matters over which individual parties may contract. Thus, certain rules relating to investment may by law be

---

[9] T Besley and M Ghatak, *Reforming Property Rights* (2009) available at <http://www.voxeu.org/index.php?q=node/3484>.
[10] Article 25 of the Constitution of South Africa, part of its Bill of Rights, treats the issue of property rights in a more detailed manner. It states in part:

    25. Property
    1) No one may be deprived of property except in terms of law of general application, and no law may permit arbitrary deprivation of property.
    2) Property may be expropriated only in terms of law of general application
        a) for a public purpose or in the public interest; and
        b) subject to compensation, the amount of which and the time and manner of payment of which have either been agreed to by those affected or decided or approved by a court.
    3) The amount of the compensation and the time and manner of payment must be just and equitable, reflecting an equitable balance between the public interest and the interests of those affected, having regard to all relevant circumstances, including
        a) the current use of the property;
        b) the history of the acquisition and use of the property;
        c) the market value of the property;
        d) the extent of direct state investment and subsidy in the acquisition and beneficial capital improvement of the property; and
        e) the purpose of the expropriation.
    …

[11] See, eg, the International Property Rights Index which seeks to evaluate individual countries with respect to the strength of their property rights regime. In 2010, out of 129 economies that were evaluated, the countries with the strongest property rights regimes were Sweden and Finland and the weakest were Zimbabwe and Venezuela. See *International Property Rights Index 2011 Report* available at <http://www.international propertyrightsindex.org/>.

subject to national law exclusively, not contractual arrangements. For example, some national legal frameworks may specify which economic sectors are open and which are closed to foreign investment, they may require investors to have a local partner, and may limit the maximum amount of equity that a foreign national may hold in an investment project. Other countries may leave these matters to whatever arrangements the parties to the investment may make.

The second dimension, the security and enforcement of contractual rights obtained by parties to the investment, also varies from country to country. Like property rights, contractual rights are crucially dependent on the willingness and resources of the political and judicial authorities of the countries concerned. Whereas property rights are threatened by the actions of others who seek to appropriate goods and services held by a person, contractual rights are threatened by the unwillingness of other persons to act in accordance with their contractual promises. Generally speaking, economically advanced countries provide effective means for the enforcement of contracts since contractual transactions have been key factors in their economic development and prosperity. Economically underdeveloped countries, on the other hand, often attach much less importance to them, a deficiency that has impeded their economic advancement. Douglass C. North has written that "...the inability of societies to develop effective, low-cost enforcement of contracts is the most important source of historical stagnation and contemporary under-development in the Third World."[12] Let us now examine the contractual legal framework for investment.

3.3 The Contractual Framework

An international investment is not only subject to the legal rules set down in national laws, but it is also governed by the rules contained in the provisions of one or more contracts. These contracts, which are given effect and made enforceable by some applicable system of national law, govern numerous important matters relating to the organization, structure, operation and functioning of the investment, and the respective rights and obligations of the investors. Together, they constitute the contractual legal framework of the investment.[13] They are also a source of law binding the parties to the investment. As a result, one cannot fully understand and evaluate an investment without examining and analyzing its contractual framework. But unlike the elements of the national legal framework, the provisions of the contractual framework are determined to a significant extent through negotiations of the parties concerned.

Not only is the enforceability of contracts dependent on national law, but the very ability of the parties to make their own rules for their investment is also dependent on that law. Thus, for investors and their lawyers planning an investment, a fundamental question is the extent to which national law will permit them to make rules by contract and the extent to which the national law prohibits such private law-making, a subject often referred to as "party autonomy." For host governments, the extent to which foreign investors will enjoy party autonomy to shape their own investment rules is an important public policy question. Investors must constantly ask to what extent will a particular facet of an investment be subject to public ordering and therefore be governed by the national legal framework and to what extent will aspects of the investment process be subject to private ordering and

---

[12] DC North, *Institutional Change, and Economic Performance* (1990) 54.

[13] See, eg, Article 1134 of the French Civil Code: "Agreements legally entered into have the force of law for those who have made them." (*Les conventions légalement formées tiennent lieu de loi á ceux qui les ont faites*).

therefore fall within the domain of the contractual legal framework. Governments seeking a greater role for state intervention in the economy often implement this goal by removing certain elements of ordering economic transactions from the realm of a country's contractual framework to the realm of its national legislative framework. Countries seeking to liberalize their economies, on the other hand, often do so by giving greater scope and freedom to the role of contract in ordering economic and investment transactions.

A case from Nigeria illustrates the problem of the interplay between a country's national and contractual framework. In an effort to indigenize the Nigerian economy, to encourage the development of Nigerian entrepreneurs, and to give Nigerian nationals greater control over the country's economic resources, the government of Nigeria adopted the Nigerian Enterprises Promotion Act (NEP) of 1977, which required that Nigerian ownership in certain types of enterprises be not less than 60 percent. At the same time, the Nigerian Companies Act gave the incorporators of companies significant scope—that is, contractual freedom—to allocate corporate decision making power according to their discretion and wishes. Following the passage of the NEP Act, a group of Nigerian investors entered into a joint venture with a Japanese company to establish an assembly plant. The Nigerians contributed 70 percent of the venture's capital and the Japanese 30 percent, thus satisfying the requirements of the NEP Act. However, since the Japanese were also providing technology and management to the enterprise they wanted to be in a position to influence, if not totally control, important decisions made by the joint venture company. The enterprise's articles of association therefore provided for two classes of shares, Class A Shares held by the Nigerians and Class B shares owned by the Japanese. The article further provided that every resolution of the company had to be supported by a majority of each class, thus giving the Japanese, despite their minority equity position, an effective veto over corporate actions. Furthermore, it also provided that in relation to "special matters," which included the appointment and terms of service of the managing and assistant managing director, directors elected by Class A shares, held by the Nigerians, would have one vote but that directors elected by Class B shares, held by the Japanese, would have three votes. Thus, by contract the joint venture partners sought to create a control structure for the firm that they believed best served their interests.

The Nigerian Companies Act required that the documents creating the new company be approved and recorded by the Nigerian Registrar of Companies. Upon reviewing the control structure created by the parties, the Registrar declined to register the new company on the grounds that it conflicted with the intent of the NEP Act, a decision that the investors proceeded to challenge in the courts. The court held that the joint venture, being 70 percent owned by Nigerians complied with the NEP Act, despite the control structure agreed by the parties; consequently, the Registrar of Companies could not refuse to register the joint venture company. The court therefore directed the Registrar of Companies to do so.[14]

Contracts are an inherent part of organizing and operating any foreign direct investment. Even a simple direct foreign investment, for example a joint venture between a United Kingdom company and a Thai firm to manufacture air conditioners in Thailand, will necessitate numerous contracts. Some of the principal types of such contracts, to be considered in subsequent chapters of this book include the following:

---

[14] *Kehinde v. Registrar of Companies* [1979] 3 LRN 213. See also OA Osunbur, "Nigeria's Investment Laws and the State's Control of Multinationals," 3 *ICSID Review—Foreign Investment Law Journal* (1988) 38–78.

a) **Investor Contracts**. Investor contracts include agreements among the investors and between the investors and the investment enterprise. Investors undertaking an investment must first negotiate contracts to set down their agreements as to their respective rights and obligations. Thus, in the case of the joint venture between the UK company and the Thai firm, the parties will conclude at a minimum a joint venture agreement, setting out their understanding of the proposed enterprise, the articles of incorporation and the statutes of the legal entity that is to operate the investment, and a shareholder agreement as to how they will vote their shares and conduct themselves in participating in the management of the company.

b) **Enterprise Supply, Finance, and Sales Contracts**. These are contracts between an investment entity, for example the Thai air conditioner manufacturing company, and various external parties that will provide the entity with resources and services where necessary. Thus, there may be loan agreements with banks to provide debt financing, licensing agreements with other companies to provide, for example, intellectual property or, technology, and components to support the manufacturing process, and long-term supply contracts with Thai and foreign companies for the necessary raw materials. Other contracts may govern the disposition and sale of the products and services of the investment enterprise. Certain of these contracts may require as a condition an additional contract in the form of a guarantee by one or more of the investors to guarantee the performance of the investment enterprise, for example that it will repay its loans to creditor banks as promised.

c) **Insurance Contracts**. The investors or the enterprise in which they have invested may enter into a variety of insurance contracts to protect against various risks faced by their investment. One important type is political risk insurance, which is the subject of Chapter 11. Political risk insurance is offered by three sources: national governments, private insurance companies, and international organizations. For example, many home governments offer foreign investment insurance to their nationals, and such insurance contracts, which are designed to protect the investor against political risks such as expropriation, currency inconvertibility and political violence, become an important part of the investment's contractual legal framework.

d) **State Contracts**. Contracts between the investors or the investment enterprise on the one hand and government entities of states having jurisdiction over the investment transaction, on the other, constitute a fourth important group of agreements that form the contractual legal framework. They take many different forms and bear many different names: investment accords, development contracts, public service concessions, and tax stabilization agreements, to mention only a few. Generally speaking, such contracts have one or both of two broad purposes: (1) to provide investors or their investments with certain desired guarantees and benefits; and (2) to regulate and control the conduct of the investors or their investment. As an example of the first, a host country government, in order to attract a desired foreign investment, might promise to exempt an investor or an investment enterprise from taxation for a fixed period of time. With regard to the second, a country which had granted a foreign investor a concession to operate a public service for a period of time would ordinarily require that investor to enter into an elaborate contract regulating in detail how that public service is be operated and imposing penalties on the investor for failure to meet its contractual obligations.

Investor–state contracts have been part of the foreign investment process for hundreds of years. Indeed, since the very inception of international investment, foreign investors have sought assurances from the sovereigns in whose territory they have invested that their interests would be protected from negative actions by the sovereign and local individuals and even that the sovereign would grant them certain privileges and benefits that nationals themselves did not enjoy. Often these assurances and grants of privilege would be embodied in some kind of document that the sovereign issued or agreed to. In the era before the formation of states that conducted foreign relations, traders and investors often formed themselves into associations and would negotiate directly with foreign sovereigns to obtain such assurances and grants. For example, in 991 AD, the Byzantine Emperors Basil II and Constantine VIII, in a document known in Latin as a *chrysobul*, granted directly to the merchants of Venice the rights to trade in the ports and other places of the Byzantine Empire without paying customs duties, as well as the right to a quarter in Constantinople, known as an *embolum*, for dwelling and trading.[15] Various other sovereigns also granted concessions and franchises to individuals or groups of traders and investors. Such developments were also taking place across Western, Northern, and Eastern Europe at the time. For example, King Henry II of England issued a grant, dated 1157 AD, guaranteeing protection to German merchants from Cologne and to their establishment in London.[16]

While these documents were not called agreements, but rather were designated as "grants" or "concessions," and usually took the form of a unilateral act by the sovereign, they were normally the product of negotiation to some degree between the sovereign or his representatives and the foreign traders who were their beneficiaries. Sovereigns were motivated to grant protection and privileges to foreign traders out of a desire to secure certain advantages for themselves, such as the promotion of foreign trade or the improvement of relations with other groups in foreign territories. Thus the basis of these early grants and concessions was reciprocity of benefits, a rationalization articulated, for example, by King Erik of Norway in 1296 AD when he granted the Hamburg merchants extensive privileges for the purpose of "*ad meliorandum terram nostram cum mercaturis*"—"for the amelioration of our territories through trade."[17]

3.4 The International Legal Framework

The international legal framework for investment consists of international law and international legal institutions. International law has traditionally been conceived as the law governing relations among states.[18] Strictly speaking, in former times, international law did not apply to individuals and private organizations. Thus, rules of international law applied directly only to sovereign states and were not enforceable against private parties except to

[15] P Fischer, "Some Recent Trends and Developments in the Law of Foreign Investment," in K-H Boeckstiegel et al (eds), *Völkerrecht, Recht der internationalen Organisationen, Weltwirtschafatsrecht: Festschrift für Ignaz Seidl-Hohenveldern* (1988) 97. See also "Concessions granted to the Merchants of Venice, by the Byzantine Emperors Basilius and Constantinus, executed in March 991," in P Fischer, *A Collection of International Concessions and Related Instruments* vol I, 15–18.

[16] "Concessions granted to the Merchants of Venice, by the Byzantine Emperors Basilius and Constantinus, executed in March 991," in P Fischer, *A Collection of International Concessions and Related Instruments* vol I, 97. Hansa societies worked to acquire special trade privileges for their members. For example, in 1157 AD the merchants of the Cologne (Köln) Hansa persuaded Henry II of England to grant them special trading privileges and market rights which freed them from all London tolls and allowed them to trade at fairs throughout England.

[17] P Fischer, *A Collection of International Concessions and Related Instruments* (1976) xix.

[18] "International law governs relations between independent States. The rules of law binding upon States therefore emanate from their own free will as expressed in conventions or by usages generally accepted as expressing principles of law and established in order to regulate relations between these co-existing independent communities or with a view to the achievement of common aims." *The Case of the S.S. Lotus (France v. Turkey)* (1927) PCIJ Series A No 10; 2 Hudson, World Ct Rep 20.

the extent that they were sanctioned by individual nations and states. In the contemporary era, however, international law has given a growing role to nonstate actors. One authoritative definition states: "International law...consists of the rules and principles of general application dealing with the conduct of states and of international organizations and with their relations *inter se*, as well as with some of their relations with persons, whether natural or juridical."[19] As will be seen, international law affects private international investment transactions in at least three ways. First, it influences domestic legislation affecting transactions. Many elements of national legislation and regulation governing international business have their origin in or are at least linked to the international system, and individual states enforce them because they are bound to do so by international agreement. Thus, for example, many national regulations on monetary matters or trade questions are determined by prevailing international treaties, such as the Articles of Agreement of the International Monetary Fund[20] and the General Agreement on Tariffs and Trade. Second, certain rules of international law apply directly to individuals and companies and may even afford them an international means of redress when a state fails to respect those rules. For example, bilateral investment treaties guarantee foreign investors a specific level of protection under international law and grant them the ability to invoke international arbitration when a host state fails to respect its treaty obligation. Third, international law creates international organizations and institutions, such as the International Centre for Settlement of Investment Disputes (ICSID), which play important roles in many areas of international investment.[21]

The world is organized on the basis of sovereign and equal states and has no supranational legislature or court with authority to make rules governing such states. As a result, the rules of international law are those that have been accepted as such by the international community. Where is one to find those rules? What are the sources of international law?

The most generally accepted statement of the sources of international law is found in Article 38(1) of the Statute of the International Court of Justice,[22] which provides:

1. The Court, whose function is to decide in accordance with international law such disputes as are submitted to it, shall apply:
   a. international conventions, whether general or particular, establishing rules expressly recognized by the contesting states;
   b. international custom, as evidence of a general practice accepted as law;
   c. the general principles of law recognized by civilized nations;
   d. subject to the provisions of Article 59, judicial decisions and the teachings of the most highly qualified publicists of the various nations, as subsidiary means for the determination of rules of law.[23]

According to this provision, there are three fundamental sources of international law: (1) international conventions; (2) international custom; and (3) general principles of law recognized by states. Judicial decisions and the writings of legal scholars are not in

---

[19] The American Law Institute, *Restatement of the Law, The Foreign Relations Law of the United States* (3rd edn 1987) vol I, § 101 at 22.

[20] Articles of Agreement of the International Monetary Fund (IMF Articles of Agreement) (Bretton Woods, July 22, 1944, 2 UNTS 39). The text of the Articles of Agreement, as amended, may be found on the IMF website at: <http://www.imf.org/external/pubs/ft/aa/index.htm>.

[21] Convention on the Settlement of Investment Disputes Between States and Nationals of Other States (March 18, 1965) 17 UST 1270, TIAS 6090, 575 UNTS 159 (ICSID Convention).

[22] Statute of the International Court of Justice (ICJ Statute) (San Francisco, June 26, 1945, 33 UNTS 993, 59 Stat 1055).

[23] ICJ Statute, Article 38(1).

themselves autonomous sources of international law. They are supplemental or secondary sources which are used by courts, tribunals, governments, and others to establish what a specific rule of international law is.[24] Since these three sources (in particularized form) constitute the foundations of international investment law, let us examine each briefly. Thereafter, we will also consider another important element of the international legal framework: international organizations.

(a) **International conventions** are binding agreements between or among states. International conventions have a variety of designations in their titles: treaty, agreement, protocol, pact, convention, and covenant, among others. Thus, in the field of international investment, important international sources of law include the North American Free Trade *Agreement*,[25] the Energy Charter *Treaty*,[26] and the *Convention* on the Settlement of Investment Disputes Between States and Nationals of Other States.[27] Despite their differences in name, each of these three documents has the same binding effect on the states that have consented to them. The particular name given to an international agreement has no consequence as to its legal force or the binding effect it has on its parties.[28]

The basic international law governing treaties and their interpretation and application is the Vienna Convention on the Law of Treaties.[29] Like contracts, treaties bind only the state parties which have consented to them. If a state's internal law is inconsistent with its obligations under a treaty, that state may not invoke that internal law as a justification for not performing its obligations under the treaty.[30] Thus, for example, if a state has entered into a treaty in which it promises not to expropriate property without payment of full compensation, it may not in an international proceeding use a domestic law that authorizes the taking of property without compensation as an excuse for failing to live up to its treaty obligations. On the other hand, states that are not signatories to an international agreement or treaty are usually not bound by its terms. But, if a treaty gains wide enough acceptance among states it will be deemed to constitute international customary law and will have binding effect even on nonsignatories.[31] Article 38 of the ICJ Statute cites international conventions first in its listing of the sources of international law, but it does not specifically state that they will have precedence over the other two sources, ie customary international and general principles of law.[32] It is generally agreed that should a custom of international

---

[24] I Brownlie, *The Principles of Public International Law* (6th edn 2003) 19, 23.

[25] North American Free Trade Agreement (NAFTA) (San Antonio, December 17, 1992, 32 ILM 289, 605).

[26] Energy Charter Treaty (ECT) (The Hague, December 17, 1994, 34 ILM 360).

[27] Convention on the Settlement of Investment Disputes Between States and the Nationals of Other States (ICSID Convention) (Washington, D.C., March 18, 1965, 575 UNTS 159, 17 UST 1270) available at <http://icsid.worldbank.org/ICSID/StaticFiles/basicdoc/CRR_English-final.pdf>.

[28] I Brownlie, *The Principles of Public International Law* (6th edn 2003) A Aust, *Modern Treaty Law and Practice* 15 (2000).

[29] Vienna Convention on the Law of Treaties (The Vienna Convention) (Vienna, May 23, 1969, 1155 UNTS 331; 8 ILM 679; 63 *AJIL* 875; UN Doc A/Conf.39/27).

[30] Vienna Convention on the Law of Treaties (The Vienna Convention) (Vienna, May 23, 1969, Article 27); A Aust, *Modern Treaty Law and Practice* (2000) 144.

[31] A McNair, *Law of Treaties* (1961) 5, 124, 749–52; RR Baxter, "Treaties and Custom," 129 *Rec des Cours* (1970-I) 25, 101; RR Baxter, "Multilateral Treaties as Evidence of Customary International Law," 41 *BYIL* (1965–66) 275.

[32] Brownlie notes that: "[Article 38] itself does not refer to 'sources' and, if looked at closely, cannot be regarded as a straightforward enumeration of the sources. They are not stated to represent a hierarchy, but the draftsmen intended to give an order and in one draft the word 'successively' appeared. In practice the Court may be expected to observe the order in which they appear: (a) and (b) are obviously the important sources, and the priority of (a) is explicable by the fact that this refers to a source of mutual obligation of the parties." I Brownlie, *The Principles of Public International Law* (6th edn 2003) 5. Lauterpacht has a similar view: "The rights and duties of States are determined in the first instance, by their agreement as expressed in treaties—just as the case of individuals their rights are specifically determined by any contract which is binding upon them. When a controversy arises between

law conflict with a treaty provision, the treaty provision will prevail unless the custom is determined to fall under Article 53 of the Vienna Convention which describes "peremptory norm[s] of general international law," sometimes referred to as *jus cogens*. A peremptory norm of international law is one that is ". . . accepted and recognized by the international community of States as a whole as a norm from which no derogation is permitted and which can be modified only by a subsequent norm of general international law having the same character."[33]

Just as national legislation and regulation have increasingly supplanted custom and common law to become the legal foundation of domestic economies, international treaties have increasingly become the foundation for international economic relations. As will be seen, this shift has been particularly clear in the area of international investment which as of 2011 embodied over 3,100 distinct international agreements.[34] Thus, one may say that the international legal framework for investment has undergone a significant *treatification* in the latter part of the twentieth and the first part of the twenty-first century.[35]

At the same time, the existence of a treaty does not mean that the other sources of international law, namely custom and general principles of law, are not relevant or applicable to international investment. Often treaties incorporate concepts whose full meaning cannot be understood without reference to customary international law. More-over, treaties may specifically declare that the other sources of international law are to supplement the treaty if its provisions are silent about a particular issue or problem. Thus, for example, if an investment treaty declares that an investor is to be given "full protection in accordance with international law," an arbitration tribunal would have to refer to customary international law to determine the extent of protection provided.[36]

(b) International Custom is a second source of international law under Article 38 of the ICJ Statute. International custom is defined simply as "a general practice accepted as law." Thus a customary rule of international law must meet two criteria: 1) it must be a general practice of states, and 2) states must engage in that practice out of a sense of a legal obligation.[37] With respect to the first criteria, the practice of states is what actions states undertake to carry out government business. These can include policy pronouncements, statements at international conferences, diplomatic communications and correspondence with other states, national legislation, decisions of domestic courts, and other actions taken

two or more States with regard to a matter regulated by a treaty, it is natural that the parties should invoke and the adjudicating agency should apply, in the first instance, the provisions of the treaty in question." H Lauterpacht, *International Law: Collected Papers* (1970) 86–7.

[33] Vienna Convention Article 53.

[34] As of the end of 2010, the UNCTAD reported that the nations of the world had concluded 2807 bilateral investment treaties and 309 free trade agreements (FTAs) with investment agreements. UNCTAD, *World Investment Report 2011*. To this number one must had the Energy Charter Treaty, the North American Free Trade Agreement, and various regional treaties, all of which have significant provisions governing international investment.

[35] JW Salacuse, "The Treatification of International Investment Law," 13 *Law and Business Review of the Americas* (2007) 155–66.

[36] For example, Article 1131 of the North American Free Trade Agreement empowers the Free Trade Commission of NAFTA to make binding interpretations of NAFTA provisions on investment arbitration tribunals. In the exercise of that power, the Commission issued an interpretation holding that Article 1105(1) of NAFTA "prescribes the customary international law minimum standard of treatment of aliens as the minimum standard of treatment to be afforded investments of investors of another Party" and that "the concepts of 'fair and equitable treatment' and 'full protection and security' do not require treatment in addition to or beyond that which is required by the customary international law minimum standard of treatment of aliens." NAFTA Free Trade Commission, "NAFTA Commission Notes of Interpretation of Certain Chapter 11 Provisions" (2001) <http://www.dfait-maeci.gc.ca/tna-nac/NAFTA-Interpr-en.asp>.

[37] The American Law Institute, *Restatement of the Law, The Foreign Relations Law of the United States* (3rd edn 1987) vol I, § 102(2) at 24.

by governments in respect of international matters.[38] To satisfy this first criterion, the practice, according to the ICJ, must be "both extensive and virtually uniform."[39] The practice need not be particularly long standing to be a custom, for as the Court has also stated "the passage of only a short period of time is not necessarily, or of itself, a bar to the formation of a new rule of customary international law . . . "[40]

Just because states act in a particular way does not mean that such actions automatically constitute customary international law. States must act in a particular way out of a sense of legal obligation. This is the second requirement under Article 38, the requirement of *opinio juris sive necessitatis*, that state practice should "occur[] in such a way as to show a general recognition that a rule of legal obligation is involved."[41]

These two requirements for international customary law can make it difficult to establish a particular rule of customary law even under the best of conditions. Where there is significant disagreement among states or significant differences in practice, finding a rule of customary international law may be next to impossible. As will be seen, the field of international investment law, for example, has generated significant disagreement among nations as to the nature and content of applicable international rules. As a result, in many forums the very existence of customary international investment law has been questioned, if not challenged outright, over the years.

(c) **General principles of law,** referred to in the ICJ statute as "general principles of law recognized by civilized nations," constitute the third and final source of international law.[42] This source of law refers to the legal principles that are common to the world's major legal systems.[43] These "general principles" are often seen as a source to help fill in gaps where no applicable treaty provision or international custom exists. While certain general principles, such as *pacta sunt servanda*, have emerged to become custom, tribunals will generally be hesitant to find such a general principle unless it is clear there is broad acceptance in the world's legal systems.[44]

(d) **International Organizations and Institutions.** In addition to the rules of international law, the international framework for investment also consists of international organizations. They consist of two types: (1) intergovernmental organizations, whose members are states, and (2) non-governmental organizations, whose members are essentially nonstate actors.

Intergovernmental international organizations are institutions, such as the World Bank, the International Centre for Settlement of Investment Disputes, and the International

---

[38] The American Law Institute, *Restatement of the Law, The Foreign Relations Law of the United States* § 102, comment b, at 25. See also I Brownlie, *The Principles of Public International Law* 6 (6th edn 2003).

[39] *North Sea Continental Shelf (FRG v. Den; FRG v. Neth)* [1969] ICJ Rep 3, 43.

[40] *North Sea Continental Shelf (FRG v. Den; FRG v. Neth)* [1969] ICJ Rep 3, 43.

[41] *North Sea Continental Shelf (FRG v. Den; FRG v. Neth)* [1969] ICJ Rep 3, 43.

[42] On their status as a source of law, Brownlie observes that they are "a source which comes after those depending more immediately on the consent of states and yet escapes classification as a 'subsidiary means.'" I Brownlie, *The Principles of Public International Law* (6th edn 2003) 15.

[43] O Schachter distinguishes five categories of general principles that have been invoked and applied in international law discourse and cases. O Schachter, *International Law in Theory and Practice* (1991) 50. Brownlie notes: "the view expressed in Oppenheim is to be preferred: 'The intention is to authorize the Court to apply the general principles of municipal jurisprudence, in particular of private law, in so far as they are applicable to relations of States.'" I Brownlie, *The Principles of Public International Law* (6th edn 2003) 16.

[44] Schachter, pp. 50–55.

Monetary Fund, by which sovereign states agree to cooperate with one another in a given area of international relations. International organizations are ordinarily created by international treaty and their powers are derived from the authority granted them by their membership. Through the conventions creating them and other acts of delegation of authority, such organizations make rules and decisions that can have an impact on international investment activities. Thus, for example, the World Bank, formally known as the International Bank for Reconstruction and Development,[45] along with its affiliates the International Finance Corporation[46] and the International Development Association,[47] are major investors in development projects throughout the world, and its other affiliate, the ICSID,[48] has become a leading forum for arbitrating investor–state disputes. Although many intergovernmental international organizations have a global focus, the scope activity of others, such as the European Investment Bank,[49] European Bank for Reconstruction and Development,[50] and the North American Free Trade Commission,[51] may be limited to particular regions.

International nongovernmental organizations are essentially organizations of private persons and organizations from diverse countries that have joined together to pursue activities that are international in scope. Thus, the International Chamber of Commerce (ICC) is a global institution composed of private business organizations that seeks to foster and strengthen international business activity in a variety of ways, including the development of common rules with respect to international business transactions and the provision of facilities for the settlement of international investment disputes.

3.5 The Interrelationships of the Three Legal Frameworks

The three legal frameworks for international investment, while conceptually distinct, are interrelated. Thus, the contractual framework is shaped and influenced by the national legal framework, and the international legal framework may constrain and influence the content of the national legal framework. For example, a purpose of investment treaty provisions prohibiting expropriation except on payment of just compensation or requiring that investment treatment be "fair and equitable" is to constrain the actions that national governments may take with respect to international investors. At the same time, the

---

[45] Articles of Agreement of the International Bank for Reconstruction and Development (IBRD Articles of Agreement) (Washington, D.C., December 27, 1945, 2 UNTS 134). The text of the Articles as amended effective February 16, 1989 may be found at <http://siteresources.worldbank.org/EXTABOUTUS/Resources/ibrd-article-sofagreement.pdf>.

[46] Articles of Agreement of the International Finance Corporation (IFC Articles of Agreement) (Washington, D.C., May 25, 1955, 264 UNTS 118, 2197 TIAS 3620). The text of the Articles as amended through June 27, 2012 may be found at <http://www1.ifc.org/wps/wcm/connect/corp_ext_content/ifc_external_corporate_site/about+ifc/articles+of+agreement>.

[47] Articles of Agreement of the International Development Association (IDA Articles of Agreement) (Washington, D.C., January 26, 1960, 439 UNTS 249). The text of the Articles as amended effective September 24, 1960 is available at: <http://web.worldbank.org/WBSITE/EXTERNAL/EXTABOUTUS/IDA/0,,contentMDK:20052323~menuPK:115747~pagePK:51236175~piPK:437394~theSitePK:73154,00.html>.

[48] ICSID Convention (n 27).

[49] Treaty on the Functioning of the European Union (Treaty of Rome) (Rome, March 25, 1957, 289 UNTS 11), Articles 3(j) and 129. The Treaty of Rome contains the Protocol on the Statute of the European Investment Bank (EIB Statute), annexed to the Treaty 289 UNTS 64. The current version of the EIB statute and other relevant governing provisions may be found at <http://www.eib.org/attachments/general/statute/eib_statute_2009_en.pdf>

[50] Agreement Establishing the European Bank for Reconstruction and Development (Paris, May 29, 1990, 29 ILM 1077), available at <http://www.ebrd.com/pages/research/publications/institutional/basicdocs.shtml>.

[51] NAFTA, Article 2001 available at <http://www.nafta-sec-alena.org/en/view.aspx?conID=590>.

applicability of an international treaty provision may depend on the nature of rights gained under national law. For example, if an investor engaged in a transaction that does not result in property rights under national law, treaty provisions on expropriation may be inapplicable since the investor had nothing that was expropriated. As a result of these interrelationships, investors, host government, and home governments must constantly bear in mind all three frameworks as they pursue their interests through the foreign investment process.

PART II

THE NATIONAL LEGAL FRAMEWORK

4

Factors Shaping National Legal Frameworks for International Investment

4.1 Introduction

All national legal systems implicitly or explicitly address two fundamental issues with respect to international investment: (1) the extent to which foreign capital in its various forms is permitted to enter and exit national territory and (2) the treatment to be given to foreign capital once it enters national territory. Chapter 5 will address the first of these issues and Chapter 6 will address the second.

The content of national laws and regulations on these two issues is shaped by the interests, attitudes, and ideologies of countries' governing authorities. At any particular time, governmental positions on questions relating to the entry, exit, and treatment of international investment are in turn influenced by domestic interest groups, such as labor unions and business associations, as well as by external forces such as diplomatic pressure from allies and from international institutions like the International Monetary Fund and the World Bank. Moreover, changes in countries' governing regimes can lead to abrupt and far reaching alterations in their national frameworks for international investment. For example, the October Revolution of 1917 in Russia and the subsequent establishment of the Dictatorship of the Proletariat brought to power a governing regime that was hostile to foreign private capital. The new Soviet government confiscated foreign private property on a vast scale[1] and refused to make restitution or pay compensation. It proceeded to create a national legal system that was extremely negative toward foreign private investment.[2] On the other hand, when Anwar Sadat became President of Egypt in 1971 upon the death of Gamal Abdel Nasser, he reversed many of his predecessor's policies opposing foreign investment and changed Egypt's national legal framework by instituting a series of measures known as "economic openness" (*infitah*) that encouraged international investment.[3]

Despite its economic implications, the subject of international investment is fundamentally political. It is political in the sense that governmental officials, community leaders, civic groups, and populations generally view it as having important consequences for the governance of their countries; therefore, they usually have strongly held positions and beliefs on its role in national life. Political attitudes in a particular country toward foreign investment depend on many factors, including general economic conditions, the kind of

---

[1] The Decree of October 26, 1917, adopted by the Second All-Russian Congress of Soviets, abolished private property in land without compensation. The Decrees of December 14, 1917 and January 26, 1918, socialized the banks "in order to liberate the workers and peasants and the whole population from the exploitation of the capitalist banks," and provided that the assets of the former private banks were to be confiscated. By June 1920 most industry had been socialized in the USSR. S Friedman, *Expropriation in International Law* (1953) 17–23; BA Wortley, *Expropriation in Public International Law* (1959) 61–2; Legislative Reference Service, Library of Congress for the Comm on Foreign Affairs 88th Cong 1st Sess, *Report on Expropriation of American-Owned Property by Foreign Governments in the Twentieth Century* (July 19, 1963) 8–10.

[2] For an historical study of the impact of these events on a particular foreign investment, see generally VV Veeder, "The Lena Goldfields Arbitration: The Historical Roots of Three Ideas," 47 *Int'l & Comp LQ* (1998) 747.

[3] See generally, JW Salacuse, "Egypt's New Law on Foreign Investment: The Framework for Economic Openness," 9 *The International Lawyer* (1975) 647–60; JW Salacuse, "Back to Contract: Implications of Peace and Openness for Egypt's Legal System," 28 *The American Journal of Comparative Law* (1980) 315–33.

investment projects being undertaken, and the nationality of the foreign investors in the particular case. Thus, for example, while certain developed countries such as the United States and Australia may be generally favorable to the inflow of foreign investment from other western countries, their populations often have deep misgivings about investment that will lead to foreign control of major companies and economic sectors or that comes from countries with which they have uneasy relations, such as China or the Arab world.[4]

This chapter examines some of the attitudinal, ideological, and conceptual factors shaping national laws on international investment. An appreciation of these factors is important for understanding the laws and regulations to which they have given rise. The chapter will first examine the four dominant attitudes—sometimes referred to as "theories," "schools of thought" or "approaches" about foreign investment, particularly direct foreign investment, and will then consider how resulting economic systems and development models adopted by countries influence their policies and laws toward foreign investment. At the same time, it should be emphasized that the prevailing attitudes, ideologies, and economic models in a particular country at a specific time are not permanent and may change over time, leading to alterations, sometimes minor but often profound, in national legal frameworks for international investment.

4.2 Four Dominant Attitudes toward International Investment

In examining the diversity of investment legislation and policy in the world, one may detect four basic theories—or perhaps, more accurately, four basic attitudes or approaches— about the relationship of foreign investment to economic growth, prosperity, and development.[5] These four theories, held by different governments, officials, and scholars, have shaped the provisions of particular investment laws, legal institutions, and individual investment projects and have also influenced investment relations among nations, governments, and investors. Let us examine briefly each of the four.

(a) Pro-international Investment Theories

The prevailing view among capital-exporting governments, multinational corporate executives, and counsel to foreign investors is that international investment is beneficial, fosters economic growth and prosperity, and yields significant benefits to capital-importing states (ie host countries), capital-exporting states (ie home countries) and foreign investors.[6] Proponents of this view invariably point to the benefits of international investment and its associated technology, including the creation of new industries and enterprises in the host country, the growth of employment opportunities for nationals, the transfer of new technologies, the introduction of management skills and other forms of know-how, the creation of export-oriented enterprises with the resulting advantages of international trade and improved balance of payments, the production of new and better goods and services in the host country, and the construction of needed infrastructure.

While proponents of pro-investment theories acknowledge that such investment may have costs for host countries, particularly in the form of repatriated profits, they argue that,

---

[4] See, eg, T Switzer, *Public Attitudes Toward Direct Foreign Investment* (2008 Australia's Open Investment Future) available at <http://www.ipa.org.au/library/publication/1229473321_document_switzer.pdf>.

[5] See generally, J Grieco, "Foreign Investment and Development: Theories and Evidence," in T Moran (ed), *Investing In Development: New Roles for Private Capital* (1986) 35–60.

[6] M Sornarajah, *The International Law on Foreign Investment* (2nd edn 2004) 50–7.

overall, the costs to the host country of using foreign direct investment in its development are less than other forms of finance. They point out that while international loans and bonds as a form of finance bring host countries only money, foreign direct investment yields them a package of vital elements for the creation of productive enterprises, including advanced technology, superior management skills and systems, and links to international markets. Moreover, foreign investment enables the host country to use its own capital for other needed purposes and thus expands the total amount of capital available for national economic development.

Pro-investment attitudes about the benefits of foreign investment have resulted in national legal frameworks that allow foreign capital relative freedom of entry, that avoid special restrictions on the activities of foreign investors, and that place foreign investments at least in a position of legal parity with national enterprises. The United States, for example, has adopted a pro-international investment attitude and an open-door policy toward foreign capital since its creation as a developing country at the end of the eighteenth century. Its first Secretary of the Treasury, Alexander Hamilton, who laid the foundations of the country's financial system, expressed a strong pro-international investment attitude when he wrote:

> Instead of being viewed as a rival, it [foreign investment] ought to be considered as a most valuable auxiliary, conducive to put into motion a greater quantity of productive labor, and a greater portion of useful enterprise than could exist without it.[7]

Pro-direct foreign investment attitudes are to be found not only among capital-exporting states and multinational corporations, but also within powerful international institutions such as the World Bank. The Bank has stressed the importance of improving "the investment climate" for achieving economic development and growth and has also devoted significant effort to helping countries achieve this goal.[8] For the Bank officials and many others, the investment climate is defined as "... the set of location specific factors shaping the opportunities and incentives for firms to invest productively, create jobs, and expand."[9] National laws and regulations, as well as government policies and behaviors, exert a strong influence in shaping that climate.

Pro-investment theories are imbedded in many legal institutions, including national laws of numerous countries that stress the importance of foreign investment for national development,[10] and in a multitude of international treaties. Such laws place relatively few

---

[7] Hamilton, "Report of the Secretary of the Treasury on the Subject of Manufactures," in F Taussig (ed), *State Papers and Speeches on the Tariff* (1895), quoted in Note, "An Evaluation of the Need for Further Statutory Controls on Foreign Direct Investment in the United States," 8 *Vanderbilt Journal of Transnational Law* (1974) 152, n. 24. See also RH Mundheim and DW Heleniak, "American Attitudes Toward Foreign Direct Investment in the United States," 2 *Journal of Comparative Corporate Law and Securities Regulation* (1979) 221–43.

[8] See, eg, International Bank for Reconstruction and Development,*World Bank Development Report 2005: A Better Investment Climate For Everyone* (2004), which states at 20: "The key message: for governments at all levels, a top priority should be to improve the investment climates of their societies. To do so, they need to understand how their policies and behaviors shape the opportunities and incentives facing firms of all types, domestic and foreign, formal and informal, small and large, urban and rural. The agenda is broad and challenging, but delivering on it is the key to reducing poverty, improving living standards, and creating a more inclusive, balanced, and stable world."

[9] IBRD, n 8.

[10] See, eg, Article 1 of Turkey's Law no 4875 of July 5, 2003, by which it introduced a new pro-international investment policy: "Article 1. The objective of this Law is to regulate the principles to encourage foreign direct investments; to protect the rights of foreign investors; to define investment and investor in line with international standards; to establish a notification-based system for foreign direct investments rather than screening and approval; and to increase foreign direct investments through established policies. This Law establishes the treatment to be applied to foreign direct investments." Available at <http://www.economy.gov.tr/upload/380BE181-C6CE-B8EF-37B940FAAD239BA2/FDI_Law.pdf>.

barriers to the entry of foreign capital and few restrictions on the operations of foreign investment once they enter the country. The preambles of most international investment treaties, international legal instruments designed to protect and promote foreign investment, also assert the common belief of the state contracting parties that foreign investment will encourage their economic development and prosperity.[11] Moreover the Articles of Agreement of the International Bank for Reconstruction and Development, the founding document of the World Bank, also embodies the pro–international investment theory in that the Bank's stated purposes are "(i) to assist in the reconstruction and development of the territories of members by facilitating the investment of capital for productive purposes ... (ii) to promote private foreign investment ... (iii) to promote the long-range balanced growth of international trade and the maintenance of equilibrium in balances of payments by encouraging international investment for the development of the productive resources of members ... (v) to conduct its operations with due regard to the effect of international investment on business conditions in the territories of members ... "[12] Thus, one of the reasons for the World Bank's prevailing pro–investment orientation is that its charter requires it.

(b) Anti-international Investment Theories

Some scholars, civic leaders, and government officials, unconvinced of the alleged benefits of international investment, have developed theories and approaches that challenge the pro–international investment view, particularly with respect to foreign direct equity investment. They argue that foreign investment, instead of promoting economic growth, actually inhibits real development and places host countries in a position of permanent dependence on multinational corporations and their home states. According to this view, multinational corporations, which for the most part are based in western capital-exporting states, devise their business strategies and conduct their operations so as to maximize their profits, preserve their economic dominance, and advance the interests of their home countries. Indeed, proponents of anti-foreign investment theories argue that multinationals have no real concern for the development of the countries in which they invest since it is usually in a multinational's interest to make every effort to keep developing host states in a permanent position of dependence on the multinational enterprise and on the multinational's home state.

Influenced by these views, certain scholars founded a school of thought known as "dependency theory" to justify this position.[13] Often referred to as "*dependencia*," dependency theory had its origins in the 1950s in Latin America, the first region to gain its independence from European colonialism and an area that historically has struggled to resist the powerful economic and political efforts of the United States to dominate that part of the world. Anti-foreign investment theories argue that foreign investors in developing countries harm host countries by mobilizing local capital for their activities, rather than transferring new resources, by introducing inappropriate technologies that reduce

---

[11] eg, the preamble to the bilateral investment treaty between the United Kingdom and Chile refers to the two governments as " ... recognizing the encouragement and reciprocal protection of such foreign investment will be conducive to the stimulation of individual business activity and will increase prosperity in both States." Agreement Between the Government of the United Kingdom of Great Britain and Northern Ireland and the Government of the Republic of Chile for the Promotion and Protection of Investments with Protocol, January 8, 1996.

[12] Article 1, Articles of Agreement of the International Bank for Reconstruction and Development, TIAS No 1507, 2 UNTS 134.

[13] J Grieco, "Foreign Investment and Development: Theories and Evidence," in T Moran (ed), *Investing In Development: New Roles for Private Capital* (1986) 37–9.

employment opportunities, and by driving local producers out of business through destructive and unfair methods of competition. Moreover, foreign investors form alliances with a small group of local elites in order to dominate the local political processes for purposes of protecting and advancing investor interests and those of their home countries.[14]

For proponents of the anti-international investment view, whatever benefits a state may gain from foreign investment are paid for at too high a cost, particularly in terms of repatriated profits, the destruction of local enterprises through unfair competitive actions by multinationals, environmental damage, exploitative labor practices, and in many cases human rights violations. The anti-foreign investment school of thought holds that international investment is invariably a bad thing and that it is not worth its substantial costs.

At various times and in various places, anti-foreign investment theories have influenced national legal frameworks through the adoption laws restricting the entry and operation of foreign capital. Such legislation has nationalized foreign enterprises, prohibited foreign capital from important sectors of the economy, and enacted rules requiring foreign investments to take the form of joint ventures with host state participation. Countries pursuing policies of "self-reliance" in its several variants, such as "*ujamaa*" in Tanzania under President Julius Nyerere in the 1960s and 1970s[15] and "*juche*" in North Korea under Kim Il Sung and his son Kim Jung Il[16] have all manifested an anti-foreign investment view and led these countries to adopt legislation that severely restricts the entry and operation of international investment in their territories.

From its independence in 1947, India adopted a cautious position with regard to foreign investment. Jawarhalal Nehru, its first prime minister and a dominant political leader in the Third World, expressed this cautious view in 1951: "It is better if we progress a little more slowly rather than allow ourselves in any way to depend on others, for I fear real progress does not come if we go about on crutches all the time."[17] India would subsequently enact a series of measures that gradually limited foreign investment in its territory and at the same time asserted the dominant role of the Indian state in the economy. This process culminated with the passage of the Foreign Exchange Regulation Act 1973, which restricted foreign equity ownership in domestic enterprises to a maximum of 40 percent and required foreign investors holding in excess of this amount to divest enough of their holdings to meet the new legal requirements. The effect of the law was essentially to end foreign investment in India until 1991 when the government took steps to reverse this restrictive policy.[18] In a more recent application of anti-foreign investment attitudes, Ecuador, in an

---

[14] See generally, E Cardoso and A Helwege, *Latin America's Economy: Diversity, Trends, Conflicts* (1992) 56–61. An intellectual and philosophical antecedent of *dependencia* may be found in the Calvo Doctrine, formulated by the Argentine jurist and foreign minister Carlos Calvo (1824–1906). The Calvo Doctrine held that that a sovereign independent state was entitled by reason of the principle of sovereign equality to complete freedom from interference in any form, whether by diplomacy or by force, by other states. Therefore, according to the Calvo doctrine, when an alien suffers an alleged injury his only remedies are local ones. Whereas capital-exporting countries claimed that host countries owed an international minimum standard of treatment to foreigners in their territory, the Calvo doctrine held that they owed foreigners only national treatment. Individual Latin American countries took significant measures to implement the Calvo doctrine through the inclusion of "Calvo clauses" in their constitutions, legislation, and contracts with foreign companies, which prohibited host governments from agreeing to submit disputes with foreign investors to international arbitration. See generally, DR Shea, *The Calvo Clause* (1955).

[15] See Z Ergas, "Why Did the Ujamaa Village Policy Fail?—Towards a Global Analysis," 18 *The Journal of Modern African Studies* (1980) 387–410.

[16] G Lee, "The Political Philosophy of Juche," 3 *Stanford Journal of East Asian Affairs* (2003) 105–12.

[17] M Kidron, *Foreign Investments in India* (1965) 100.

[18] PS Jha, *India & China: The Battle Between Soft and Hard Power* (2010) 168. See also N Bajpai and JD Sachs, *Foreign Direct Investment in India: Issues and Problems*, Development Discussion Papers, Harvard Institute for International Development. March 2000. Available at <http://www.earth.columbia.edu/sitefiles/file/about/director/pubs/759.pdf> accessed on November 21, 2011.

effort to establish greater control over its petroleum resources, passed a law in July 2010 authorizing the president to nationalize those foreign oil companies in the country that failed to follow Ecuadorian laws and government policies.[19]

(c) Negotiation Theories of International Investment

A third theory holds that international investment does not automatically result in net benefits or net losses to host countries and is therefore neither inherently good nor bad. Rather, proponents of this third view argue that whether or not foreign investment is beneficial to a particular country depends on the bargain that is negotiated between the investor and the host country with respect to the distribution of an investment's benefits and costs between the foreign investor and the host country.[20]

This theory is founded on two important insights. The first is that an international investment is not simply a transfer of assets from one country to another but is instead essentially a bargain, a "deal," between the investor and the host country, a bargain that allocates the benefits and costs of the transaction between the two sides. The ability of a host country to secure net positive gains from foreign capital therefore depends on its ability to negotiate a good deal with the investor. The terms of the deal are to be found in the investment legislation, regulatory framework, and contracts affecting that transaction. Proponents of this view argue that it is therefore important that the national legal framework of host countries for international investment set out specific provisions to assure that host countries receive a fair share of the investments benefits at least cost. Indeed for them, the goal of the national legal framework should be to maximize the benefits and minimize the costs to the host country of any foreign investment project. In order to achieve this goal, the national legal frameworks should establish a careful screening and monitoring system for all foreign investments and should specify in detail the contribution to the country that such projects must provide. For example, national investment laws and regulations influenced by the negotiation school of thought stipulate the required number and quality of employment opportunities for nationals; the degree to which the investor must transfer useful technology, management skills, and know-how; and the limitations on repatriation of profits and capital.[21] To further assure that they will receive a good bargain from foreign investments, many countries, in addition to passing foreign investment codes and laws, have established foreign investment agencies and authorities with the expert skills and capacity to seek out and negotiate good investments for the country.

A second important insight offered by negotiation theories of international investment is that negotiations between the investor and the host government do not end once the investor has made its investment. On the contrary, the relationship between the two sides thereafter is a continuing negotiation as each side seeks to gain greater advantages from the investment, often at the expense of the other. For example, the host government may increase taxes on the investor's enterprise or enact regulations requiring employees to receive higher benefits. In many instances, the host government is able to accomplish a redistribution of benefits to its advantage because of the fact that its bargaining power with

---

[19] At the time the law was adopted, President Rafael Correa stated: "With this law, any oil company that doesn't fulfil the policies of the state will see their fields nationalized and they will leave the country." *Bloomberg Businessweek*, "Ecuador President Imposes Oil Nationalization Law," July 24, 2010, available at <http://www.businessweek.com/ap/financialnews/D9H5LVA00.htm>.

[20] J Grieco, "Foreign Investment and Development: Theories and Evidence," in T Moran (ed), *Investing In Development: New Roles for Private Capital* (1986) 39–41.

[21] See generally, RE Gross, *Foreign Investment Codes and the Location of Foreign Investment* (1980).

the investor increases once the investor places its assets under the jurisdiction and sovereignty of the host country and cannot therefore easily remove them. In the words of Raymond Vernon, direct foreign investments, once made, are therefore "obsolescing bargains."[22]

(d) Structural Theories of International Investment

While acknowledging that the advantages of a foreign investment to host countries depends on the nature of the bargain they strike with foreign investors, certain scholars and officials argue that because of asymmetries of power many countries, particularly small developing countries, do not have the power to negotiate satisfactory investment bargains with foreign investors generally and multinational corporations in particular. In short, in their interactions with international investors, many countries suffer from a structural disadvantage. Advocates of this view also contend that the bargaining power does not always shift in favor of host governments once the investment is made so as to enable host governments to renegotiate the initial investment arrangement to gain a more favorable distribution of investment benefits. They point to the fact that multinational corporations are able to maintain their power advantage through the control of technology whose source is the investor's home country and through the alliances that they make with political and business elites in the host country.

As a result of these factors, many governments influenced by structural theories have adopted two basic strategies in an attempt to correct the perceived power imbalance in their relations with international investors. First, they are extremely cautious in negotiating foreign investment transactions and are alert to power differentials that might result in disadvantageous bargains. Second, they have sought ways to increase their negotiating power.

With regard to the first point, many countries have adopted investment laws that limit the kinds of investment that their governments may allow into the country and have also specified the sectors from which foreign investment is banned. With regard to the second, countries have sought to increase their bargaining by taking both national and international measures. National measures include improved training for officials involved in investment negotiations and the enactment of laws and regulations that require government approval of any investment or technology arrangements made by local entrepreneurs with foreign companies.[23] In such transactions, the foreign investor is in effect negotiating with the government as well as with a local entrepreneur.

International strategies consisted largely of efforts by developing countries to adopt international rules that would control and limit the actions of the perceived more powerful foreign investors and their home countries. The most notable manifestation of this approach was the developing countries' effort to establish a New International Economic Order (NIEO), primarily through the organs of the United Nations where they held a

---

[22] R Vernon, *Sovereignty at Bay: The Multinational Spread of U.S. Enterprises* (1971) 46.

[23] For example, Venezuelan legislation on technology transfer agreements achieved this goal by requiring all agreements to have a provision regarding the obligation of the supplier to train national personnel to implement the technology in the most efficient manner and to demonstrate a prepared training program. See Venezuelan Decree No 727 on Foreign Investment, Technology Licensing and Foreign Credit Regulations, Article 68 (January 18, 1990), (1990) 29 *International Legal Materials* 273. See generally, CM Correa, "Transfer of Technology in Latin America," 14 *Journal of World Trade Law* (1981) 388.

numerical majority.[24] Beginning in the 1960s and continuing through the 1970s, developing countries attempted to revise the established principles regarding foreign investor
rights and to bring about what they termed the "New International Economic Order"
(NIEO). They did this through a series of United Nations General Assembly resolutions
dealing with the issue of permanent sovereignty over natural resources and the economic
rights and duties of states. These resolutions included the United Nations General Assembly Resolution 1803 (XVII) in 1962, which contained the Declaration on Permanent
Sovereignty over Natural Resources,[25] Resolution 3201 containing the Declaration on the
Establishment of a New International Economic Order in 1974,[26] declaring the right of
each state to exercise control over and exploit its natural resources, "including the right to
nationalization or transfer of ownership to its nationals," and Resolution 3281, also in 1974,
containing the Charter of Economic Rights and Duties of States,[27] declaring inter alia, that
each state had the right " ... to regulate and exercise authority over foreign investment
within its national jurisdiction in accordance with its laws and regulations and in conformity with its national objectives and priorities ... " and that "no State shall be compelled to
grant preferential treatment to foreign investment." In 1974, the UN Economic and Social
Council also established at the United Nations Secretariat in New York City the UN Centre
on Transnational Corporations (UNCTC), one of whose functions was to consider proposals to regulate multinational corporations, the world's principal foreign investors. For
the next fifteen years, the Centre would work on a draft code of conduct for transnational
corporations but the code never became a reality and the UN Centre itself would ultimately
be absorbed by UNCTAD and moved to Geneva in 1993.[28] Part IV of this book, on the
international framework of international efforts, will examine these efforts in greater detail.
For the purpose of considering theories on foreign investment, they can be viewed as
heavily influenced by the structuralist school of thought and its underlying concept that
asymmetries of power between multinational corporations and developing countries
necessitated new international rules to govern the actions of international investors,
thereby redressing the power imbalance.

One may also note that the attempt to increase power through concerted international
action also took place at the regional level. For example, the countries of the Andean Pact
adopted Decision 22 in 1971, the so-called Andean Investment Code, which bound six
Latin American countries to adopt a highly restrictive set of foreign investment policies,
including forced divestment of certain existing foreign investment.[29] As will be seen, none
of these efforts succeeded in creating a new International Economic Order. Indeed, by 1990
the NIEO movement was basically dead.[30]

---

[24] See generally, SP Subedi, *International Investment Law: Reconciling Policy and Principle* (2008) 19–29. See
also RF Meagher, *An International Redistribution of Wealth and Power: A Study of the Charter of Economic Rights
and Duties of States* (1979).

[25] UNGA Res 1803 (XVII) (December 14, 1962) UN Doc A/RES/1803 (XVII) (1962) <http://www.un.org/
documents/ga/res/17/ares17.htm>.

[26] UNGA Res 3201 (S-VI) (May 1, 1974) UN Doc A/RES/3201 (S-VI) (1974), reprinted in 13 ILM 715 (1974).

[27] UNGA Res 3281 (XXIX) (December 12, 1974) UN Doc A/RES/3281 (XXIX) (1974) reprinted in 14 ILM 251
(1975). See RF Meagher, *An International Redistribution of Wealth and Power: A Study of the Charter of Economic
Rights and Duties of States* (1979).

[28] For a brief history of the UN Centre on Transnational Corporations, see <http://unctc.unctad.org/aspx/
index.aspx>.

[29] C Oliver, "A New Phase in the Quest for Normative Order as to Direct Foreign Investment," 66 *American
Journal of International Law* (1972) 763–84; PE Sigmund, *Multinationals in Latin America: The Politics of
Nationalization* (1980).

[30] See T Waelde, "Requiem for the "New International Economic Order,"" in Gerhard Hafner et al (eds),
Festschrift Fuer Ignaz Seidl-Hohenveldern (1998) 771.

4.3 National Economic Systems and Development Models

(a) In General

Attitudes and ideologies shape national economic systems which in turn are supported and enforced by appropriate legal frameworks. Whether a country has opted to base its economic system on private capitalism or socialism, whether it has chosen to rely on private entrepreneurs or state corporations, will have a profound effect on its laws, regulations, and legal institutions. An example of how economic systems and models can influence the shape and content of national legal frameworks may be seen in the experience of developing countries over the last half of the twentieth century and the beginning of the twenty-first as they have pursued their economic development. An examination of that experience sheds light on the relationship between economic models and systems on the one hand and national legal frameworks for international investment on the other.

(b) Models and Systems in the Developing World

For most of the second half of the twentieth century, the developing countries, sometimes called "the Third World," consisted of a disparate and amorphous group of over 120 African, Asian, and Latin American countries that together accounted for about seventy percent of the world's population.[31] Despite their enormous diversity in cultures, political systems, and ideologies, developing countries for more than six decades have shared a common declared national goal: "development." Their drive to achieve development has influenced broad areas of national life, including their laws and legal institutions relating to international investment.

The definition and focus of "development" has shifted and evolved over time. In the 1950s and 1960s, development meant simply economic growth as measured by gross national product per capita in individual developing countries.[32] Later, concerns about the equitable distribution of the results of economic growth and the needs of the Third World's poor would gain an increasing place on the development agenda.[33] In time, both policy makers and scholars came to see that development was not a purely economic phenomenon but that it also had social, political, and institutional dimensions, causes, and objectives.[34] Since the end of the 1980s, development has become increasingly linked to the protection of the environment. As a result, government policy makers, international organizations, and scholars now stress the need for "sustainable development," which one may define as development that does not take place at the expense of future generations.[35]

---

[31] M Mason, *Development and Disorder: A History of the Third World since 1945* (1997) 1. Alfred Sauvy, a French demographer, is credited with coining the term "Third World" in 1952, when he wrote in an article in *L'Observateur* (August 14, 1952) that the West and the communist countries were "struggling for the possession of the Third World (*tiers monde*), that is, the collectivity of those that were called in the language of the United Nations 'underdeveloped.'" Mason, at 30. With the end of communist regimes and thus the dissolution of the "second world," some persons would also include within the term "Third World" countries of eastern and central Europe and the former Soviet Union. Others chose to label them "countries in transition."

[32] eg, "A less developed country is simply one with real per capita income that is low relative to the present-day per capita income of such nations as Canada, the United States, Great Britain, and Western Europe." P Samuelson, *Economics* (9th edn 1973) 765.

[33] S Corbridge (ed), *Development Studies—A Reader* (1995) 4.

[34] See, eg, G Myrdal, *The Asian Drama* (3 vols), particularly Appendix 2, at 1859–78, "The Mechanism of Underdevelopment and Development and a Sketch for an Elementary Theory of Planning Development."

[35] The concept of sustainable development received particular impetus from the Brundtland Commission in 1987. Its report stated: "Sustainable development is development that meets the needs of the present without compromising the ability of future generations to meet their own needs. It contains two key concepts:

While the concept of development has been subject to change and evolution over time, it is important to note that throughout the last five decades government policy statements, academic discussions, and practitioners' conversations have tended to use the word development in two different ways: (1) development as a *set of goals* and (2) development as a *process* by which those goals might be attained. In fairly consistent fashion, development as a set of goals has generally included increased economic productivity, reduced poverty, improved health, and expanded education, among others. Development as process has concerned the *way* of achieving national economic and social goals. The development process has particularly preoccupied policy makers, foreign assistance agencies and academics as they have struggled to determine the interventions that would best achieve Third World development goals.

Until the 1980s, most developing country governments, with a few exceptions, as well as many international organizations, had in mind a similar model of the development process as they went about their work. That model of how development goals should be attained greatly influenced government policies and institutions, especially with respect to international investment. It also profoundly affected national legal systems and the way government officials, lawyers, and legal scholars thought about law and its role in development. Since the late 1980s, most developing countries, in varying degrees, have abandoned that first model of development (which one might call Development Model I) and have evolved a new model (which one might call Development Model II) that supersedes it. This fundamental change in development models was in many ways as significant a transformation for developing countries as was the movement in the 1950s and 1960s from dependent to independent political status. This transformation is partially reflected in the change of name used to describe the Third World: the "developing countries" of the 1960s became the "emerging markets" of the 1990s and beyond. The change in development models raised new challenges for law, lawyers, the courts, and legal education throughout the developing world. Just as Development Model I influenced the evolution of legal systems after independence, Development Model II also shaped and made new demands on national legal infrastructures. Developing countries are enormously diverse in culture, economics, politics, and law. They certainly have not marched in lock step as they have pursued economic development. Nonetheless, certain trends appear clear. The goal of the following sections is to sketch them.

(c) The Nature of Development Model I

Probably all developing countries became independent with a fundamental belief that their governments had the primary responsibility for bringing about economic development.[36] By government, of course, one meant the executive branch, for legislatures and judiciaries in most developing countries were generally considered weak and lacking the technical expertise to play a significant developmental role.

In the minds of most officials and scholars, the belief in government's dominant role evolved into a definite model about the nature of the development process. This model had

---

- the concept of 'needs', in particular the essential needs of the world's poor, to which overriding priority should be given; and
- the idea of limitations imposed by the state of technology and social organization on the environment's ability to meet present and future needs." Brundtland et al, *Our Common Future* (1987) 43. cf Sharachchandra Lele, "Sustainable Development: A Critical Review," 19 *World Development* (1991) 607–21.

[36] International Bank for Reconstruction and Development, *The State in a Changing World–World Development Report 1997* (1997) 1–2.

four basic elements: (1) public ordering and state planning of the economy and society; (2) reliance on state enterprises as economic actors; (3) restriction and regulation of private enterprise; and (4) limitation and control of the country's economic relations with the outside world. Let us consider each in turn.

(i) Public Ordering and State Planning

It was an article of faith throughout most of the Third World that development would not take place unless the state planned and directed economic and social life.[37] Policy makers might differ on the extent of such public ordering and the precise role to be accorded to private enterprise, but few persons denied the need for significant state intervention.[38] In their view, private enterprises, groups and organizations, left to their own devices, were incapable of bringing development to the Third World. It was up to the government, through planning, to guide and direct the various actions that would lead to development. The planning of economic and social development became a fundamental duty of the state, a duty that became enshrined in laws and constitutions.[39] Through planning, governments determined which economic sectors were to receive favorable treatment, how credit was to be allocated, where investments would be made, what economic targets the private sector was to attain, and even what prices were to be paid for commodities and products.[40] It also allowed governments to specify the role they would grant to foreign capital in the development process.

The nature of the planning process varied from country to country. In some, such as Algeria, state economic plans were highly directive and had the force of law;[41] in others, such as Mexico, development plans were merely indicative, general guides to decision making.[42] Whatever the nature of planning, all governments—Marxist and non-Marxist alike—seemed to agree that economic development could not take place without proper state planning. "The truth is," wrote W Arthur Lewis, who won the Nobel Prize for his work in development economics, "we are all planners now."[43] As a result of this belief, Third World governments created planning ministries, departments, and institutes, and they devoted significant material and human resources to the preparation, adoption, and supervision of planning documents, which in most cases took the form of multi-year development plans.[44]

---

[37] Professor ES Mason of Harvard University, a leading development economist of the day, summed up the prevailing attitude: "The plain fact is that throughout the underdeveloped world, the pressures for economic development are all but irresistible. A government that fails to seize the levers of economic development, or at least make the attempt, is probably not long for this world." ES Mason, *Economic Planning in Underdeveloped Areas: Government and Business* (1958) at x. See also International Bank for Reconstruction and Development, *The State in a Changing World–World Development Report 1997* (1997) 1–2.

[38] eg, "The state alone was credited with the ability to think and act in the long term interests of its citizens." S Corbridge, "Thinking about Development" in Corbridge (ed), *Development Studies: A Reader* (1995) 3.

[39] eg, the Constitution of Turkey of 1982, Article 166, provided: "The planning of economic, social and cultural development, in particular the speedy, balanced and harmonious development of industry and agriculture throughout the country, and the efficient use of natural resources on the basis of detailed analysis and assessment and the establishment of the necessary organization for this purpose are the duties of the state."

[40] See, eg, WA Lewis, *Development Planning—The Essentials of Economic Policy* (1966).

[41] For example, Article 2 of Ordinance no 70-10 of January 20, 1970 (*Journal Officiel de la République Algérienne*, January 20, 1970, 50), which adopted Algeria's 1970–73 Four-Year Plan, provided: "The four-year plan constitutes the fundamental law which governs the totality of the economic and social activity of the country during the period 1970–1973." See JW Salacuse, *An Introduction to Law in French-Speaking Africa, vol. II, North Africa* (1975) 167–90.

[42] MS Wionczek, "Incomplete Formal Planning: Mexico," in Hagen (ed) *Planning Economic Development* (1963) 150–82.

[43] WA Lewis, *The Principles of Economic Planning* (1949) 12.

[44] See generally, WA Lewis, *Development Planning* (1966); KB Griffin, *Planning Development* (1970); RL Meir, *Development Planning* (1965); J Tinbergen, *Central Planning* (1964).

Foreign aid agencies and international organizations provided large amounts of support in an effort to make development planning efficient and effective. Foreign investors looked to these plans for guidance on opportunities for investment in the countries concerned.

(ii) Reliance on Public Sector Enterprises

Not only was the economy to be shaped and controlled by government policies and actions, but government was also to be the primary economic actor in many sectors. In order to implement state economic plans, most countries vastly expanded their public sectors, creating numerous government corporations and public enterprises to carry out all sorts of economic activities from insurance and transportation to manufacturing and retail sales. Both officials and scholars judged this expansion necessary if development was to take place since the private sector in most developing countries was small, lacked adequate financial resources and technical expertise, was unresponsive to state needs, and in many cases was controlled by foreigners or government opponents. As Harvard University's Professor Edward Mason wrote in 1958, "... development plans in general evince little confidence in the capacity of private initiative and the free market to do the job."[45] In many cases, governments created completely new public enterprises; in others, they expropriated private companies, both national and foreign-owned, to establish them.[46]

The existence of state enterprises in a given economic sector usually meant that foreign private direct investment was excluded from that sector; however, that did not mean that other forms of capital were not welcome. For example, large sums in international bank loans from foreign commercial banks financed the development and expansion of state enterprises in many countries. Moreover, multinational corporations often entered into contractual arrangements whereby they provided state enterprises with technology and management skills and systems so that they might operate in sectors where the state had little or no experience or capacity. In some countries, the law required that direct foreign investments take the form of joint ventures with a public sector enterprise.

(iii) Restriction and Regulation of the Private Sector

A consequence of state planning and reliance on public sector enterprises was increased, pervasive regulation and restriction of the private sector.[47] In order to direct the private sector toward the achievement of predetermined developmental goals, developing country governments subjected private enterprises, both domestic and foreign, to regulation on such fundamental matters as investment, prices, currency exchange, trading operations, business formations, technology transfers, and wages and salaries of workers. The private sector could undertake few activities without first obtaining permission from a planning ministry or other government department.[48] The systems that emerged seemed based on a fundamental legal principle: no economic activity was to be permitted unless the state had

---

[45] ES Mason, *Economic Planning in Underdeveloped Areas: Government and Business* (1958) 43.

[46] P Guislain, *The Privatization Challenge* (1997) 6. See generally, International Legal Center, *Public Enterprises and Development in Arab Countries* (1977).

[47] With regard to this phenomenon in Latin America, see S Edwards, *Crisis and Reform in Latin America* (1975) 175. For Egypt, see JW Salacuse, "Back to Contract: Implications of Peace and Openness for Egypt's Legal System," 28 *American Journal of Comparative Law* (1980) 315.

[48] eg, with respect to Pakistan, see C Wilcox, "Pakistan," in EE Hagen (ed), *Planning Economic Development* (1963) 68.

specifically approved it. The pervasiveness of regulation was so great in India, for example, that business executives came to call the country the "License Raj."[49]

(iv) Restrictions on Foreign Investment and Influence in the Economy

Developing countries in the 1960s and 1970s not only sought political independence, but they also demanded economic independence. It was a time when dependence theories, discussed earlier in this chapter, had significant influence with policy makers, government officials, and scholars in developing countries. Accordingly, governments in varying degrees adopted policies of "self-reliance," expropriated foreign investments, promoted "import-substitution industries," restricted the inflow of foreign capital and technology through heavy regulation, and curtailed the import of foreign goods through high tariffs and rigorous exchange controls.[50] Much of this legislative effort was aimed at existing and future foreign investment. For example, the number of nationalizations of foreign-owned property grew steadily each year from 1960 and reached its peak in the mid-1970s.[51] The basic thrust of these measures was to restrict foreign influences on developing country economies and to control economic interactions with the outside world. The drive for economic independence also led many developing countries to create their own steel mills, automobile plants, and airlines, despite the fact that they did not have the markets, finances, or technical expertise to support them. The Third World became littered with inefficient and unprofitable public enterprises permanently dependent on government subsidies for their continued existence.

(d) Implications of Development Model I for National Legal Systems

The adoption of Development Model I by many countries not only affected their economies, but it also influenced their national legal systems. First, Development Model I, with its emphasis on state planning, public ordering, and heavy regulation relied heavily on public law to achieve its objectives and accorded private law only a limited role in the development process. More fundamentally, it led governments to see law's basic purpose as bringing about desired social and economic change, rather than merely setting down the rules within which persons and organizations would conduct their economic and social activities in accordance with their individual interests. Implicitly or explicitly, governments and scholars seemed to believe that law was a tool for social engineering; therefore they

---

[49] India's Industries (Development and Regulation) Act 1951 established the legal basis for the licensing system. It empowered the government to take the necessary steps for the development of industry, to regulate the patterns and direction of industrial development, and to control the activities, performance, and results of industrial undertakings in the public interest. For a discussion of the impact on Indian manufacturing output of dismantling the License Raj, see generally, P Aghion, R Burgess, SJ Redding, and F Zilibotti. "The Unequal Effects of Liberalization: Evidence from Dismantling the License Raj in India," 98 *American Economic Review* (2008) 1397–412.

[50] eg, for a discussion of legislation and regulation enacted by East African states to reduce foreign influence in their economies, see P Sebalu, "East African Community," 16 *Journal of African Law* (1972) 345, 360. "In the recent past, the most significant developments which have affected the growth of the community have been: (a) measures by Partner States to remove the control of the economy from the hands of noncitizens and putting it into the hands of citizens or of the state by nationalization or State trading corporations; (b) exchange control..." Sebalu, at 360. See generally, AM Akimuni, "A Plea For Harmonization of African Investment Laws," 19 *Journal of African Law* (1975) 134 discussing numerous examples of governmental interference with foreign economic activity.

[51] United Nations, *World Investment Report* (1993) 17. The United Nations identified 875 distinct acts of governmental taking of foreign property in 62 countries in the period 1960–1974. Piper, "New Directions in the Protection of American-Owned Property Abroad," 4 *International Trade Law Journal* (1979) 315.

embarked on programs of legal reform whose goal was to abolish certain social and economic practices and institute new ones in their place.

Even when governments undertook to reform private law, their goal was not usually to codify existing practice but rather to bring about change that accorded with developmental goals. The 1950s and 1960s witnessed the enactment of a spate of new codes and laws whose basic thrust was to change family structure and land tenure patterns, two areas seen as keys to social and economic change. For example, Tunisia in 1956, under its then President Habib Bourgiba introduced the Code of Personal Status,[52] which outlawed polygamy, granted new rights to women, and made judicial divorce the exclusive means to dissolve a marriage, leading one noted Islamic law scholar to label it as " . . . that most radical document of modern Islamic legislation."[53] Professor Rene David, an eminent French comparative law scholar who drafted a civil code for Ethiopia based on European law with little reference to the customs of the Ethiopian people, justified these legal experiments by declaring: "The African Revolution needs to be brightened by a program bestowing the order and rules of society that Africa wishes to install."[54] Nearly all Third World Countries had dualist legal systems consisting of traditional law based on indigenous institutions and practices and "modern law" derived from a former colonial ruler. During the era of Model I, Third World governments generally gave little role to indigenous law and traditional legal institutions in their development planning and in some cases sought to suppress them.[55] At best, governments of the day viewed traditional law as unimportant; at worst, they considered it an impediment to modernization and national unity since in most cases it was based on ethnicity, religion, or tribal custom.

Second, as a result of the growth of public law and regulation on everything from the price of rice to the ownership of land, the state increasingly limited the individual's freedom of contract. Development Model I generally called for restricting the private ordering of transactions, both domestic and foreign. In the middle of the nineteenth century, Sir Henry Maine, the great English legal historian, perceived the history of civilized society as a "movement from status to contract," as individuals' rights were determined less and less by the status of their birth and more and more by agreements which they made.[56] Viewing the growth of state economic regulation in the 1950s and 1960s, Professor Robert Seidman, a long-time observer of the Third World, saw a movement from "contract to plan,"[57] a shift from private ordering to public ordering of economic and social activity.[58]

Third, in order to implement Development Model I, many developing country governments enacted legislation to weaken the institutions of private property and to endow the state with increased power over land and natural resources. Unrestricted private property was seen as an obstacle to national development. In addition to expropriating foreign and national economic interests, developing country governments passed laws to limit the

---

[52] Decree of August 13, 1956, *Journal Officiel Tunisien*, December 28, 1956 at 1742. For an English translation, see 11 *Middle East Journal* (1957) 309–18. See generally, JW Salacuse, *An Introduction to Law in French-Speaking Africa, vol II, North Africa* (1975) 424–65.

[53] J Schacht, "Problems of Islamic Legislation," in Nolte (ed), *The Modern Middle East* (1963) 194–5.

[54] Rene David, "A Civil Code for Ethiopia: Considerations on the Codification of the Civil Law in African Countries," 37 *Tulane Law Review* (1963) 187, 203.

[55] See D Trubek and M Galanter, "Scholars in Self-Estrangement: Some Reflections on the Crisis in Law and Development Studies in the United States," *Wisconsin Law Review* (1974) 1062, 1079.

[56] H Maine, *Ancient Law* (4th American edn from 10th London edn 1906) 165.

[57] R Seidman, "Law and Economic Development in Independent, English-Speaking Africa," in Hutchison et al (eds), *Africa and Law* (1968).

[58] On the distinction between public and private ordering, see generally, A von Mehren and J Gordley, *The Civil Law System* (2nd edn 1977) 785–8.

rights of both their citizens and foreign investors to own and use land[59] and declared the state to be the ultimate owner of all lands and natural resources.[60] One of the reasons certain government took this action was to be able to assure foreign investors seeking rights in those lands and resources that the government and the government alone had the legal authority to grant them such investment rights.

Fourth, Model I led to the creation of special laws, often called "foreign investment codes," whose purpose was to strictly define the role of foreign investment in the economy and create an often rigid legal framework to regulate and control it.[61] As will be seen in subsequent chapters, such codes had four basic purposes: (1) to define the nature of desired foreign investments and specify those that were not desired; (2) to specify the incentives to which such desired investment might be entitled; (3) to establish the controls over the entry and operation of desired investments; and (4) to establish an administrative apparatus to administer and control the foreign investment process.[62]

During the era of Development Model I, a plethora of other new laws and regulations mushroomed where none had existed before. Public enterprise laws, joint venture investment codes, currency control regulations, nationalization decrees, land tenure and use legislation, and price regulations, to name just a few, filled the law books, and became the fundamental preoccupation not only of government officials, but of foreign investors and their counsel as well. This new public law, not the commercial code, became the basic law of economic and business activity in the developing world, including foreign investment transactions.

At the constitutional level, Model I required a strong national executive endowed with expanded powers and unfettered by the constraints of accountability to other branches of government.[63] Increasingly, developing countries expanded the powers of their presidents, instituted one-party systems, and relegated the roles of their legislatures to approving executive decisions. In many parts of the Third World, the military, in the name of development, swept aside civilian governments and seized virtually absolute power.[64]

Throughout the Third World, the courts had only a limited role in the legal orders shaped by Development Model I. Indeed, in a variety of ways both direct and indirect, developing country governments sought to weaken the independence of the judiciary and make it clear that the courts' basic function was to support the executive in its all-important task of pursuing development.[65] At the same time, the ranks of government lawyers

---

[59] In Egypt, shortly after the Free Officers' Revolution of 1952, the Nasser government expropriated and redistributed all land holdings in excess of 200 *feddans* (ie slightly more than 200 acres), prohibited any future ownership of land in excess of that amount, and set maximum rents and minimum terms on tenancies for agricultural land. SM Gadalla, *Land Reform in Relation to Social Development in Egypt* (1962) 31–45.

[60] Senegal, by Law no 64-46 of June 17, 1964 (*Journal Officiel de La République Senegalaise*, July 11, 1964, at 905), declared all unregistered lands, an area comprising over 95 percent of the country, to belong to the state.

[61] eg, R Grosse, "The Andean Foreign Investment Code's Impact on Multinational Enterprises," 14 *Journal of International Business Studies* (Winter, 1983) 121–33.

[62] See generally, OECD, *Foreign Direct Investment for Development: Maximizing Benefits, Minimizing Costs* (2002). Available at <http://www.oecd.org/dataoecd/47/51/1959815.pdf> accessed November 19, 2011. See also JW Salacuse, "The Emerging Regime for International Investment," 51 *Harvard International Law Journal* (2010) 427–71.

[63] See, eg, JC Jurgensmeyer, "African Presidentialism: A Comparison," 8 *Journal of African Law* (1964) 157. "Certainly there has been a striking movement toward presidentialism in the sense of vesting executive power, real and formal, in a monocephalus, irresponsible executive." Jurgensmeyer, at 174.

[64] See, eg, BO Nwabueze, *A Constitutional History of Nigeria* (1982).

[65] eg, in a speech to Algerian judges in 1969, President Houari Boumedienne declared that whereas the European judiciary had traditionally seen itself as the protector of the interests of the individual, the Algerian courts were to play a far different role. Instead of acting as the monitor and potential antagonist of the government, the Algerian judicial system was to be "an instrument for the realization of the revolution and for its consolidation." Speech of September 19, 1969, (1969) VI *Revue Algerienne des Sciences Juridiques, Economiques et*

increased substantially to draft, interpret, and apply the new law and regulations, while the private practice of law in some countries stagnated as a result of government opposition and the loss of private clients, both domestic and foreign, from nationalizations and expropriations.[66]

(e) The Emergence of Development Model II

By the mid-1980s, Development Model I was beginning to lose its hold on the minds and actions of policy makers, aid agencies, and international financial institutions. Several reasons explain this loss of influence.

First, Development Model I had quite simply failed to bring about development. By the 1980s, the economies of most developing countries were stagnant, burdened with enormous debt, and saddled with inefficient public enterprises requiring constant government subsidies. As one high-ranking Asian official who had formerly been a strong advocate of Development Model I explained: "We have painfully learned that the state cannot do everything. We cannot house everyone, feed everyone, or give everyone a job. We need to let other institutions in society do these things."[67] Whereas the perceived failures of the market in the 1950s and 1960s had argued for the strong state intervention implicit in Development Model I, by the 1980s the attention of practitioners and scholars was on the failures of the state.[68]

The second major reason for the abandonment of Development Model I was that powerful external forces were insisting upon fundamental changes in Third World economic policies, often as a condition to financial and developmental assistance. The World Bank, the International Monetary Fund, western bilateral aid agencies, and international commercial banks advocated a set of new policies, known as the "Washington Consensus," which required the elimination of budget deficits, strict control of the money supply, privatization of state-owned enterprises, and an openness to international trade and investment.[69] Together, these policies represented a new model of development, Development Model II.

Third, the end of communism in Eastern Europe and the Soviet Union in 1989 deprived many developing countries of sources of moral and material support for Development Model I. The Soviet and Eastern European systems had stood as examples of what many Third World countries hoped to achieve through state intervention, but the collapse of

---

Politiques 1239–145. The Nigerian Military Government took a more direct approach to controlling the judiciary by enacting the Federal Military Government (Supremacy and Enforcement of Powers) Decree, 1970, which provided: "Any decision, whether made before or after the commencement of this Decree by any court of law in the exercise or purported exercise of any powers under the Constitution...which has purported to declare the invalidity of any Decree or Edict...or the incompetence of any of the governments in the Federation to make the same is or shall be null and void and of no effect whatsoever as from the date of the making thereof." See Nwabueze, n 64, at 207.

[66] For a discussion of this phenomenon in Egypt after the Revolution of 1952, see F Ziadeh, *Lawyers, the Rule of Law and Liberalism in Modern Egypt* (1968) 159.

[67] Interview by the author, June 1993, Lao People's Democratic Republic.

[68] International Bank for Reconstruction and Development, *The State in a Changing World–World Development Report 1997* (1997) 23.

[69] The term "Washington Consensus" is said to have been coined by John Williamson, an economist in 1989. It consisted of ten broad reforms: (1) fiscal discipline; (2) reordering public spending priorities away from politically powerful groups, such as the military, and toward basic services and infrastructure; (3) tax reform; (4) financial liberalization; (5) competitive, stable exchange rates; (6) trade liberalization; (7) reduction in barriers to foreign investment; (8) privatization of state enterprises; (9) deregulation; and (10) property rights reform. Stephanie Flanders, "A New Washington Consensus," *The Financial Times*, March 14, 1997, at 2.

those systems in 1989 represented an undeniable failure of Development Model I.[70] After 1989, the states of Eastern and Central Europe, throwing off their own Model I, sought to build market economies and began calling themselves "emerging market countries," a label that many Third World nations would also adopt as they abandoned Development Model I for Development Model II.

Finally, the successful example of certain high-growth Asian states which had avoided many of the elements of Model I, particularly its restrictions on foreign capital and private enterprise, also prompted a search for a new approach. This search ultimately led to the formulation of a new model of development: Development Model II. The elements of Development Model II are in many ways the exact opposites of those in Development Model I. Let us consider the four most important.

(i) Reliance on Markets and Private Ordering

Acknowledging the failure of state planning, many developing countries, in varying degrees, turned to markets as mechanisms to allocate society's resources. Thus decisions on investments, commodity prices, and credit allocation were increasingly to be made by private actors in the market rather than by bureaucrats in government agencies and state planning departments. Whereas approximately 1 billion persons lived in market economies in 1985, by 1995 that number had quintupled to 5 billion people.[71]

Development Model II deemphasized state planning and heightened the role of markets in the economy. One symbolic manifestation of this change has been the fact that developing nations and eastern European countries in transition increasingly chose to call themselves "emerging markets" (a term originally coined within the international financial community), rather than developing countries. More concrete consequences of this change have been the elimination or political down-grading of planning ministries, the abolition of fixed rates of exchange and the adoption of floating currency exchange rates,[72] the allocation of credit and loans to businesses through the forces of supply and demand and credit worthiness (rather than by government decision and political influence), the elimination of price controls, and the growth of capital markets. This was also a first step in creating national climates favorable to international investment

(ii) Privatization

The developing countries' emphasis on the public sector to develop their economies resulted by the 1980s in a plethora of inefficient state enterprises whose existence depended on continued government subsidies. Their governments, prodded by international financial institutions, concluded that the only answer to the problems posed by public enterprises was to sell them either wholly or partially to local and foreign private investors. This

---

[70] For many developing countries, the example of their former colonial rulers may have been even more influential than the example of the Soviet Union in leading them to adopt Development Model I. The colonial system incorporated most of the elements of Model I. The new governing elites after independence took control of that system and adapted it to achieve development, their primary national goal.

[71] International Bank for Reconstruction and Development, *World Bank Annual Report* (1996) 11.

[72] In 1975, 87 percent of developing nations had some type of fixed exchange rate. By 1996, the proportion had fallen below 50 percent. F Caramazza and A Jahangir, *Fixed or Flexible? Getting the Exchange Rate Right in the 1990s* (IMF, Economic Issues No 13, 1998) 2–3. The authors point out that when one accounts for the relative size of economies the shift from fixed to flexible exchange rates is even more pronounced: "In 1975, countries with pegged rates accounted for 70 percent of the developing world's total trade; by 1996 this figure had dropped to about 20 percent," at 3.

transfer of assets from the public sector to the private sector, from the domain of public ordering to that of private ordering, became known as "privatization." Developing countries undertook privatization for a variety of reasons, including the elimination of state subsidies to inefficient government enterprises, the relief of governmental budget deficits through proceeds from the sale of public enterprises, the reduction of foreign debts (which in many instances had been caused by public sector growth), the improvement of inefficient state-owned enterprises by subjecting them to private sector management and discipline, and the desire to foster the development of a market-oriented private sector.[73]

The extent of privatization in the emerging market nations varied from country to country. In many nations, it has been rapid and massive. In other countries, internal political conflict has made the process slow and halting. Globally, the transfer of assets from the public to the private sector has been staggering. Between 1990 and 1994 alone, proceeds from privatization by developing countries as a group totaled over $100 billion.[74] By 1996, over a hundred countries had privatized some of their state-owned enterprises, and annual revenues received from the sale of these assets in 1994 and 1995 were running at a rate of approximate $80 billion.[75] This major transformation has led to the creation of vast numbers of new private enterprises, numerous publicly traded companies and many stock markets throughout the developing world. For example, whereas total capitalization of developing country stock markets in 1985 was less than $250 billion with fewer than 9,000 listed companies, by 1995 19,000 companies were listed on emerging market stock exchanges with a total capitalization of nearly US$2 trillion.[76] This trend has grown in strength into the twenty-first century, reaching a total of US$14 trillion by 2010 and expected to reach over US$80 trillion by 2030.[77] These stock markets and the new companies whose shares were traded on them gave foreign portfolio investors new opportunities to invest in developing economies.

At the same time, acts of expropriation, which had been so prevalent in the 1960s and 1970s in developing countries, diminished significantly. It should also be noted that significant privatization of public enterprises has taken place in developed countries as well and that this process offered significant additional opportunities for international investors.[78]

The privatization movement, which required major changes in national legal frameworks, became a major stimulus for international investment in many countries throughout the world. Multinational corporations were the principal, if not the only, organizations which had the capital, expertise, and technology necessary to reform and modernize inefficient and unprofitable state enterprises; consequently, developing countries had to create a legal framework that would attract them but that would at the same time protect important national interests. For example, the privatization of important public services such as electricity and telecommunications required a regulatory framework to assure that the privatized enterprise would furnish that service to the public at a satisfactory price and level of quality. In addition, the development of stock markets, on which many new

[73] P Guislain, *The Privatization Challenge* (1997) 16–20.

[74] *The Economist*, March 23, 1996, at 106.

[75] P Guislain, *The Privatization Challenge* (1997) 1.

[76] *The Economist*, July 27, 1996 at 66.

[77] S Wagstyl, "Goldman Forecasts Emerging Equities Bonanza," *Financial Times*, September 8, 2010. Available at <http://www.ft.com/cms/s/0/ca09873c-bb6c-11df-a136-00144feab49a.html#axzz1eHtBxDto> accessed on November 21, 2011.

[78] See generally, privatization of transportation services in developed and developing countries in J Gomez-Ibanez and JR Meyer, *Going Private: The International Experience with Transport Privatization* (The Brookings Institution, 1993).

privatized corporations were listed, gave new opportunities for foreign portfolio investors who were seeking to participate in profit-making ventures in the developing world. Chapter 6, section 6.8, considers the legal framework for privatization in detail.

(iii) Deregulation

The pervasive regulatory systems required by Model I eventually came to be seen not as means for directing economies toward growth, but as obstacles to economic activity and therefore development. For example, the Peruvian scholar Hernando De Soto examined the regulatory system in Peru and concluded that law was imposing such high costs on legitimate economic activity that economic actors were forced to operate outside the law in the "informal sector."[79] For De Soto and others who studied the problem, regulation in the Third World had become a brake on development. Not only did it thwart economic initiative, but it also permitted elites and oligarchies to exploit the poor and created significant opportunities for governmental corruption by bureaucrats who had gained a monopoly on awarding valuable permits, licenses, and authorizations.[80]

The abandonment of Model I, the consequent reduction in state planning, and the new reliance on private ordering and private actors in the economy necessitated a reduction in economic regulation. Developing countries eased or abolished many of the regulations enacted during the era of Development Model I. Mexico, for example, appointed a "deregulation czar," reporting directly to the President and Council of Ministers, and his efforts served to accelerate the process of Mexican reform.[81] Price controls, exchange controls, and business licensing requirements have become less pervasive under Development Model II than they were under Model Development I. Many countries, abandoning one of the fundamental principles of Model I, seemed in varying degrees to move toward a new basic legal norm: all economic activity is permitted unless specifically prohibited. Deregulation was another factor that fostered pro-investment climates in countries.

(iv) Opening Economies

The economies of developing countries in this new era exhibited a new openness to the rest of the world, particularly with regard to trade and investment. The failure of closed economies and economic self-reliance to bring about higher standards of living, improved health conditions, and other development goals, coupled with a need for new capital and advanced technology, led Third World countries to adopt a more open and outward orientation toward the rest of the world. Import substitution as a policy yielded to export orientation, and tariffs on imports were reduced. The result was an expanded role for foreign trade in the developing world. For example whereas exports and imports accounted for 33 percent of developing country gross domestic product in the mid-1980s, by the mid-1990s they amounted to 43 percent of GDP.[82] Although many, if not most Third World governments tended to emphasize the need to control foreign direct

---

[79] H de Soto, *The Other Path—The Invisible Revolution in the Third World* (1989) 131–87.

[80] RG Klitgaard, *Controlling Corruption* (1988). For a general discussion on impact of corruption and uncertain land rights on economic growth see also KW Dam, "Land, Law, and Economic Development," in JM Olin *Law & Economics Working Paper No. 472*, University of Chicago, January 2006.

[81] See International Bank for Reconstruction and Development, *The State in a Changing World–World Development Report 1997* (1997) 63.

[82] International Bank for Reconstruction and Development, *From Plan to Market: World Development Report 1996* (1996) 132.

investment in their laws and policies during the 1960s and 1970s, in the 1980s and 1990s nearly all moved in the direction of actively promoting foreign investment in their territories and of adopting legislation that would advance this goal. They came to see foreign investment not as a threat to their economic independence but as a means for obtaining the capital, technology, management skills and links to world markets which are necessary for development but which their countries often lack.[83] While direct foreign investment (valued in 1996 dollars) to developing countries amounted to less than $20 billion in 1987, developing countries received nearly $120 billion in 1996.[84] Foreign portfolio investment in Third World stock markets also grew dramatically.

The above-cited statistics do not fully reveal the new and enhanced role of private foreign capital as a source of development finance in the Third World. In 1982 foreign direct investment in developing countries accounted for only about 8 percent of total external flows (with portfolio investment at an insignificant 0.1 percent); in 1996, out of all external financial flows to developing countries, nearly 40 percent consisted of direct foreign investment, with portfolio investment accounting for an additional 16 percent.[85] Private direct foreign investment thus became the largest single source of external development finance for developing countries. By contrast, official development finance fell to only 14 percent of the total financial flows to the developing world in 1996.[86] By 2010, developing countries attracted over one half of the world's direct foreign investment flows (which amount to US$1.24 trillion) and many of their companies had become significant foreign investors. For example, FDI outflows from developing Asia grew by 20 percent to about $230 billion in 2010, compared to only $68 billion in 2006.[87] The late twentieth century and early twenty-first centuries thus witnessed a new willingness among developing countries to engage the rest of the world in new ways and to participate actively in the global economy. *Dependencia* as a theory to guide government policy had been discarded.

The change from Model I to Model II has by no means taken place uniformly and completely in all developing countries. Public enterprises, state planning agencies, and heavy regulation continue to exist in varying degrees. Models are, after all, merely intellectual constructs, simple theoretical patterns; they are not reality. Nonetheless, the last three decades have witnessed a significant policy reorientation throughout the developing nations, among countries in transition and indeed in most of the world. As a group, developing countries, by virtue of these major changes in policies, have made a significant shift in development models, a shift that may be represented as follows:

DEVELOPMENT MODEL I	DEVELOPMENT MODEL II
From:	To:
1. State Planning and Public Ordering	1. Markets and Private Ordering
2. Reliance on Public Enterprises	2. Privatization
3. Pervasive Regulation	3. Deregulation
4. Closed Economies	4. Opening Economies

---

[83] International Bank for Reconstruction and Development, *From Plan to Market: World Development Report 1996* (1996) at 63.

[84] International Finance Corporation, *Foreign Direct Investment: Lessons of Experience (No. 5)* (1997) at 10.

[85] International Bank for Reconstruction and Development, *From Plan to Market: World Development Report 1996* (1996) at 15.

[86] International Bank for Reconstruction and Development, *From Plan to Market: World Development Report 1996* (1996) at 15.

[87] UNCTAD, *World Investment Report 2011* (2011) 3.

This change in Models was not limited to developing countries. To a greater or lesser extent, developed countries' legal and economic systems also experienced (1) an increased reliance on markets and private ordering of economic transactions; (2) privatization of government enterprises; (3) deregulation; and (4) an increased openness to the global economy.

(f) Implications of Development Model II for National Legal Systems

The shift from Development Model I to Development Model II has had important implications for national legal systems and particularly the legal framework for international investment. First, the idea that law is a tool for social engineering and that legislation can bring about sweeping change in human behavior has been much less prevalent among developing country governments now than it was in the mid-twentieth century. Developing countries are no longer seeking to "brighten their revolutions" with radical codes and laws. Instead, law has become a set of rules within which persons and organizations conduct their affairs. Rather than rely on coercive pressure to bring about change, as was so common in the early days of the development era, the law now tends to employ incentives to influence behavior.[88]

A second major consequence of the shift is that Model II represents a movement from Plan back to Contract, from public ordering to private ordering of economic activity.[89] Organizations and individuals gained increased legal freedom to arrange transactions through contract. Conversely, the form and substance of economic transactions are less and less mandated by governmental regulations and directives. Of course, this new emphasis on markets and private ordering has meant a heightened role for private law in the economy, and the need for a private law system capable of sustaining sophisticated business and market transactions. Central to this process have been efforts to strengthen the recognition and enforcement of property rights and the enhancement and liberalization of the law of contract.[90] In the view of policy makers and officials pursuing Model II, an effective property rights system supports economic growth and wealth creation by rewarding effort and good economic judgment by actors in the market. A wide distribution of property rights within a society can also contribute to social stability by counteracting excessive concentrations of power in the political system.[91] For many emerging market countries that had either allowed private law to languish or had actively sought to limit its application during the era of Development Model I, the need for wide-ranging law reform and new legislation became paramount. With the advent of Development Model II, many developing countries, often with the help of foreign advisers, undertook legal reform programs to write new commercial codes, company laws, and land laws. They also worked to pass legislation on secured transactions, bankruptcy, stock exchanges, competition, taxation, and foreign investment laws.[92]

---

[88] International Bank for Reconstruction and Development, *World Development Report 1997—The State in a Changing World* (1997) 86–7.

[89] For an examination of Egypt's early movement in this direction, see generally, JW Salacuse, Back to Contract: Implications of Peace and Openness for Egypt's Legal System," 28 *The American Journal of Comparative Law* (1980) 315–33.

[90] RA Posner, "Creating a Legal Framework for Economic Development," 13 *The World Bank Research* (No 1) (February 1998) 1.

[91] International Bank for Reconstruction and Development, *World Development 1997—The State in a Changing World* (1997) 49.

[92] See, eg, TW Waelde and J Gunderson, "Legislative Reform in Transition Economies: Western Transplants— A Short-Cut to Social Market Economy Status?" 43 *International and Comparative Law Quarterly* (1994) 347–78.

In addition to an enhanced role for private law, Development Model II requires a new approach to regulation. While "deregulation" is one of its basic elements, Model II does not demand the end of all regulation. Regulation of markets and private transactions is necessary to be sure that the rules of the game are clear and that the private players abide by those rules and play fairly. The concern in many developing countries to enact anti-competition legislation and insider trading and stock market rules are examples of the kinds of regulation required by Development Model II.[93] Markets as a means of allocating society's resources require a minimum level of regulation not only to protect participants but also to maintain society's confidence in those markets as fair and efficient resource allocators. Whereas the role of regulation in Model I was essentially to *direct* transactions in particular ways that the government judged necessary, the role of regulation in Model II is to *protect* participants in the market from fraud, coercion, and abuse by other participants. Model II implies a shift in focus from directive regulation to protective regulation, from governmental marching orders to defensive governmental oversight. The shift from the closed economies of Development Model I to the new openness of Development Model II has also resulted in the participation by developing countries more than ever before in international legal arrangements, many of which they had previously avoided or resisted. Thus, the number of Third World countries participating in bilateral investment treaties,[94] the World Trade Organization,[95] the International Centre for Settlement of Investment Disputes,[96] and the Convention on the Recognition and Enforcement of Foreign Arbitral Awards,[97] to mention a few, has grown dramatically as a result of the new openness required by Development Model II.

New legislation and treaties alone are not sufficient to make the transition from Model I to Model II. Developing countries also require institutions capable of supporting and applying the new legislation. In particular, the judiciary, the neglected or suppressed institution of Model I, is crucial to making Model II work. In a market economy, the

[93] See, eg, MI Steinberg, "Emerging Capital Markets: Proposals and Recommendations for Implementation," 30 *The International Lawyer* (1996) 715–38.

[94] By the end of 2010, the total number of bilateral investment treaties that had been concluded amounted to 2,809 in addition to over 300 other economic agreements, such as free trade accords, with investment provisions. UNCTAD, *World Investment Report 2011* (2011) 100. Virtually all of these agreements included at least one emerging market country as a contracting party. This number compares with only 309 bilateral investment treaties in 1989. Pappas, "References on Bilateral Investment Treaties," 4 *ICSID Review- Foreign Investment Law Journal* (1989) 189, 194–203. The world has thus witnessed a remarkable amount of international law making in a relatively short time.

[95] As of July 2008, 153 states, the majority of which are developing countries, were members of the World Trade Organization. By contrast, at the time of the Kennedy Round of GATT negotiations (1964–67), only 62 countries participated in the GATT, the predecessor to the World Trade Organization. See WTO internet site <http://www.wto.org/>.

[96] Convention on the Settlement of Investment Disputes Between States and Nationals of Other States, done at Washington, March 18, 1965, [1965] 17 UST 1270, TIAS no 6090, 575 UNTS 159. As of October 2011, 157 states had signed the Convention and 147 had ratified it. <http://icsid.worldbank.org/ICSID/FrontServlet?requestType=CasesRH&actionVal=ShowHome&pageName=MemberStates_Home>. In 1984, by contrast, 90 countries had signed and 86 countries had ratified the Convention. ICSID, *1984 Annual Report* (1984) 6. The increase in membership is largely attributable to developing countries. Of particular interest is that the 1990s witnessed many Latin American countries, such as Argentina, Chile, Columbia, Peru and Venezuela join ICSID, thus overcoming the strictures of the Calvo doctrine (yet another manifestation of the drive for economic independence) which had previously caused them to refrain from participating in international arbitration arrangements.

[97] Convention on the Recognition and Enforcement of Foreign Arbitral Awards, June 10, 1958, 21 UST 2517, TIAS No 6997, 330 UNTS 3. As of February 10, 2012, 138 states had ratified the Convention. Institute of Transnational Arbitration, *Scoreboard of Adherence to Transnational Arbitration Treaties* (as of February 10, 2012) (1999), available at <http://www.cailaw.org/ita/publications/Scoreboard_Current.pdf>. By contrast, in 1987, only 77 countries had ratified the Convention. Institute of Transnational Arbitration, *Scoreboard of Adherence to Transnational Arbitration Treaties* (as of July 1, 1987) (1987). The increase in membership came largely from the ranks of Third World Countries.

courts become the final arbiters of conflict among private actors in the economy, a role played to a significant extent by bureaucratic institutions in a Model I economy dominated by public sector enterprises. Moreover, the courts also assure that government officials obey the law and stay within the bounds of discretion accorded them by legislation. The proper functioning of markets and the private sector necessitate the existence of clear rules that will be respected by government as well as private actors. In short, the effective and efficient markets envisaged by Model II require the Rule of Law,[98] and the courts are essential to its existence.

For courts to play the role required by Model II, many developing countries, often with foreign assistance, undertook judicial reform programs to strengthen the independence of the judiciary, improve the training of judges and court personnel, provide courts with the necessary material resources, modernize the judicial procedures, increase access to justice, and develop alternative methods of dispute resolution.[99] The specific goals of judicial reform efforts have included increased efficiency and dispatch in handling cases, depoliticizing the appointment and promotion of judges, a reduction in levels of corruption among judicial personnel, heightened technical knowledge of the sophisticated transactions of a Model II economy, and increased ability to judge disputes that may arise in connection with them. Similarly, private attorneys have had to assume new and expanded roles to serve the new players in the private sector. They need to have new skills to plan, negotiate, and structure transactions on behalf of their clients. The emphasis in training lawyers for Model II is less on social engineering and more on transaction engineering. Accordingly, legal education in the Third World has also needed to accommodate the shift from Development Model I to Development Model II in its curriculum and teaching methods.

More generally, the experience of the last six decades may reveal something about the nature of law in developing countries, or at least about the "modern law" that applies to modern economic transactions. Most developing countries have pluralistic legal systems consisting on the one hand of indigenous law and on the other of "modern" law which in most cases has its origin in a foreign country, often a former colonial power. While indigenous law has been relatively stable and persistent over the years, the imported element has been subject to sudden and major swings and shifts, from its wholesale importation during the colonial period, to its rapid readjustment during the era of Development Model I to its equally rapid and profound readaptation in the new-found enthusiasm for Model II. In each of these three phases, the shape and content of the law was driven by a prevailing economic ideology, whether it was French or British colonial mercantilism of the late nineteenth century, Arab or African socialism of the 1960s, or the Washington Consensus of the 1990s. In each of these three phases, government leaders and policy makers viewed law as a tool to achieve predetermined ends, and they readily borrowed those tools from foreign legal systems through legal transplants and foreign advisers. Rarely did they look to indigenous legal traditions for support in advancing the prevailing economic model of the day. Thus, just as the law of Model I did not arise organically out of the societies to which it was to apply, in many cases one may say the same thing about the new law that Third World governments have enacted to support Model II. Because the new law may not be sufficiently adapted to developing world societies, it too may in the end prove too weak a reed to support economic development.

---

[98] T Carrothers, "The Rule of Law Revival," 77 *Foreign Affairs* (March/April 1998) 95–106.
[99] IFI Shihata, 2 *The World Bank in a Changing World* (1995) 518–20. See also, M Dakolias, "A Strategy For Judicial Reform: The Experience in Latin America," 36 *Virginia Journal of International Law* (1995) 53–231.

(g) Conclusion: Future Models?

The shift from Model I to Model II among developing countries is not necessarily permanent. Just as the failure of Model I led to change, the same fate may happen to Model II. While Model II may indeed bring about increased productivity, it may do so at a cost that developing country societies ultimately judge unacceptable. What are those costs? They may be considerable. First, Model II, with its emphasis upon markets, may allocate social resources to areas which society ultimately judges inappropriate. Second, it may create unacceptable divisions between rich and poor and among classes and castes in societies which are politically explosive because of their social and ethnic pluralism. Third, corruption may grow to the point that markets are distorted and the public judges Model II to have created a system that is fundamentally unfair. Fourth, it may facilitate through market transactions the exploitation of the weak by the strong, the poor by the rich. Finally, the unrestrained application of Model II may lead to irreparable damage to the environment, the culture, and the social values of the countries concerned. The financial crisis that began in Asia in 1997, the Argentine crisis of 2000–2001, and the global crisis of 2008 have provoked concerns in some quarters about the fairness and effectiveness of market economies. Among the complex factors that led to these crises, one cause, according to some scholars, was inadequate systems of financial regulation and of corporate governance prevailing in many countries, resulting in insufficient disclosure, lack of transparency, over-investment in nonproductive activities, and management's inadequate concern for the rights of investors and other stakeholders.[100] The important task of the law in this new era must be to create a framework that will minimize the costs of Model II while maximizing its benefits. The failure to do so may mean a drift back toward Development Model I or perhaps a search for Development Model III.

[100] K Hurley et al, "Corporate Governance in Emerging Markets," 3 *EDI Forum* (Fall 1998) 14.

5

National Regulation of the Exit and Entry of Capital

5.1 Introduction

One may conceptually divide the making of an international investment into two phases: (1) the movement of investment capital from one country to another and (2) the commitment of that capital to a specific purpose in the latter country. Different rules of national law may govern each of these phases. This chapter will focus primarily on national laws governing capital movements while the following chapter will examine national laws regulating the commitment of capital to specific investment purposes.

In order to make an international investment, an investor must be able legally to remove the necessary capital, as well as any associated technology and personnel, from the jurisdiction of one country (often, but not always, the investor's home state) and then to transfer that capital to the jurisdiction of another country (the host state). Such investment capital consists of one of two types: (1) real capital (or real assets), which are physical goods, such as machinery and equipment, used by an enterprise to produce goods and services, and (2) financial capital (or financial assets) which consists of any liquid medium with purchasing power—most often funds—that can be employed in an enterprise's operations.[1] Virtually all international portfolio investments, including loans, are made through the medium of financial capital exclusively. Direct foreign investments, on the other hand, may consist of both types of capital. For example, a foreign investor establishing a sugar refinery in another country may transfer to that country machinery and equipment to be installed in the refinery, as well as funds in the form of convertible currency to purchase the land and finance the construction of the refinery buildings.

The movement of physical capital from one state to another requires the investor to ship capital goods by means of an appropriate form of international transportation, whether by sea, air, or land, and to comply with the export and import laws and regulations of the countries concerned. The transfer of financial capital, on the other hand, requires that the investor be able to make payments from one country to another, an operation that usually requires the exchange of one currency of one monetary system, for example the euro, for that of another, such as the United States dollar, and normally necessitates the use of the international banking system to effect the transfer. The exit of capital, whether real or financial, from one state and its subsequent entry to another is governed by the national legal frameworks of the concerned states. Some countries allow relatively free international movement of capital, while others may subject it to varying degrees of regulation. It is important for international investors to understand and comply with the legal frameworks of both the home and host states in making an investment.

---

[1] eg, according to Brazil's Foreign Capital Law, Law no 4.131, "foreign capital is considered to be any goods, machinery and equipment that enter Brazil with no initial disbursement of foreign exchange, and are intended for the production of goods and services, as well as any funds brought into the country to be used in economic activities, provided that they belong to individuals or companies resident or headquartered abroad." Brazil Foreign Relations Ministry, *Legal Guide for the Foreign Investor in Brazil* (2006) 25.

Foreign investors often fund their investments from several different sources. Thus, a multinational corporation with subsidiaries in several different countries may decide for business or tax reasons to draw on the funds of more than one subsidiary in order to amass the capital necessary for an international investment.[2] In such situations, investors have to comply with several national legal frameworks to effect the movement of the necessary capital.

The applicable regulations on the movement of real and financial capital from one country to another may be found in various parts of a national legal system and may bear differing labels—"capital controls," "exchange controls," "investment regulations" and "export and import regulations." Such controls and regulations have been shaped by national governments' perceived interests. Like many other issues relating to international investment, the question of the advisability and utility of national capital controls has been subject to significant debate, often prompted by financial and economic crises, changing governmental attitudes toward international investment, and pressure from international institutions like the International Monetary Fund. As a result, countries' legal provisions on the entry to and exit of capital from their territories demonstrate significant diversity throughout the world. This chapter examines the general ways in which national legal systems control the movement of capital into and out of their territories.

5.2 The Authority of States to Regulate International Capital Movements

A fundamental principle of the international system is that states are sovereign and equal.[3] As a result, states exercise sovereignty over their territories. Sovereignty in this sense means "the supreme and independent authority of the nation state within its own territory."[4] The consequence of a state's sovereignty is that a state has exclusive jurisdiction to prescribe, enforce, and adjudicate laws for its territory and the population living there. A corollary of the principle of sovereign equality of states is that a state also has a duty of nonintervention in the areas of exclusive jurisdiction of other states.[5]

The exit of capital from a state is subject to its exclusive sovereignty. Similarly, the entry of that capital to a second state is also subject to that state's sovereignty. It is well settled in international law that a state has the right to control the movement of capital into its territory, to regulate all matters pertaining to the acquisition and transfer of property within its national boundaries, to determine the conditions for the exercise of economic activity by natural or legal persons, and to control the entry and activities of aliens.[6] Thus, unless there is a specific treaty to the contrary, a home state may prevent or impose conditions on the exit of capital from its territory for purposes of foreign investment, and a host state may prohibit or impose conditions on the movement of that capital into its territory. Customary international law does not grant investors rights to move their capital from one country to another. In short, an investor does not have a right under customary international law to make an international investment or even to engage in the international movement of capital.

---

[2] For example, when the American International Group (AIG), the multinational insurance company, made its investment in a joint venture in Iran, it funded its investment from four separate subsidiaries, two located in Bermuda, one in the state of Connecticut and one in the state of Delaware. See Iran–US Claims Tribunal, "Case Concerning the American International Group, Inc./American Life Insurance Company & the Islamic Republic of Iran/Central Insurance of Iran," 23 *International Legal Materials* (1984) 1–23.

[3] I Brownlie, *Principles of Public International Law* (6th edn 2003) 287.

[4] TR Van Dervorty, *International Law and Organization* (1998) 12.

[5] I Brownlie, *Principles of Public International Law* (6th edn 2003) 287.

[6] A Fatouros, *Government Guarantees to Foreign Investors* (1962) 40–1.

A state may, however, agree by treaty with other states to permit all or certain types of investments to enter into or exit from their territories. In accordance with basic principles of international treaty law, the provisions of such treaties constitute international obligations that a contracting state must respect. Moreover, the existence of contrary national legislation or regulations does not relieve a contracting state of that responsibility.[7] For example, an investment treaty may grant the investor of one country "national treatment" in making investments in the other country, a provision that prevents a signatory host state from placing greater restrictions on the making of treaty-protected investments than on investments undertaken by host country nationals.[8] Similarly, individual trade treaties may affect the ability of governments to regulate the entry of capital goods from other treaty signatories. Part IV (of this volume) on the international legal framework for investment will consider various treaties that impose restrictions on the right of governments to regulate international capital and monetary flows into and out of their territories. Nonetheless, because the international rules governing monetary payments are so important to regulating the entry and exit of financial capital from states and are so global in scope, it is necessary to consider in this chapter the relevant international law applicable to the making of national law on the subject.

The basic international legal framework governing monetary relations among states is to be found in the Articles of Agreement of the International Monetary Fund (IMF),[9] an international organization that in 2010 included 187 member states.[10] Thus, nearly all countries of the world are subject to its provisions. One of the stated purposes of the IMF is to "... promote international monetary cooperation through a permanent institution which provides the machinery for consultation and collaboration on international monetary problems...."[11] and "... to maintain orderly exchange agreements..."[12] More specifically, IMF members, "[r]ecognizing that the essential purpose of the international monetary system is to provide a framework that facilitates the exchange of goods, services, and capital among countries," have an obligation "... to collaborate with the Fund and other members to assure orderly exchange arrangements..."[13] Each member state has an obligation to inform the IMF of its exchange arrangements, and the IMF has the power of surveillance over such exchange arrangements.[14] The Articles of Agreement do not define the meaning of "exchange arrangements;" therefore an authoritative, precise meaning is uncertain.[15] At a minimum, one can say that the term includes the rules and institutions governing the exchange of the currencies of one country for that of another.

---

[7] Articles 26 and 27 of the Vienna Convention on the Law of Treaties codifies these principles. Article 26 states: "Every treaty in force is binding upon the parties and must be performed by them in good faith." Article 27 provides in part: "A party may not invoke the provisions of its internal law as justification for its failure to perform a treaty." Vienna Convention on the Law of Treaties. (opened for signature May 23, 1969) 1155 UNTS 331; UN Doc A/Conf. 39/27; (1969) 8 ILM 679; (1969) 63 *AJIL* 875.

[8] See, eg, Article 1102(1), entitled "National Treatment," of The North American Free Trade Agreement between Canada, Mexico, and the United States which provides: "Each Party shall accord to investors of another Party treatment no less favorable than that it accords, in like circumstances, to its own investors with respect to the establishment, acquisition, expansion, management, conduct, operation, and sale or other disposition of investments." Available at <http://www.nafta-sec-alena.org/en/view.aspx?conID=590&mtpiID=142#A1102>.

[9] Articles of Agreement of the International Monetary Fund, 2 UNTS 39 (1947). The full text of the Articles as amended and in force may be found at <http://www.imf.org/external/pubs/ft/aa/index.htm>.

[10] For a listing of the current members of the IMF, see the website of the International Monetary Found at <http://www.imf.org/external/np/sec/memdir/memdate.htm>.

[11] Article I (i), Articles of Agreement of the International Monetary Fund.

[12] Article I (iii), IMF Articles of Agreement.

[13] Article IV, Section 1, IMF Articles of Agreement.

[14] Article IV, Sections 2 and 3, IMF Articles of Agreement.

[15] J Gold, *Exchange Rates in International Law and Organization* (1988) 102 ("What is meant by exchange arrangements is unclear.").

The IMF Articles govern two types of monetary transactions that may be affected by a member state's exchange arrangements: (1) capital movements and (2) and payments for current transactions. With respect to the former, the Articles specifically recognize the right of states to control capital movements. Article VI, Section 3 entitled "Controls of Capital Transfers," states:

> Members may exercise such controls as are necessary to regulate international capital movements, but no member may exercise these controls in a manner which will restrict payments for current transactions or which will unduly delay transfers of funds in settlement commitments, except as provided in Article VII, section 3(b) and in Article XIV, Section 2.[16]

This provision gives member states complete discretion to impose capital controls. Joseph Gold, long-time IMF General Counsel and a recognized expert on the IMF Articles of Agreement, has written that under Article VI, Section 3, " . . . inward and outward movements of capital are subject to the sovereign authority of members, provided that payments for current international transactions are not restricted as a by-product of capital controls. A member is free to impose, or to refrain from imposing, controls on the movement of capital."[17] The reason that the founders of the IMF included this provision in the Articles in 1944 was a concern to enable countries post-World War II to develop their economies without the threat of capital flight and the destabilizing effect of volatile currency movements. The Articles therefore specifically recognized a member state's right to regulate capital transfers.[18] A second reason that has been advanced was that negotiators of the IMF Articles viewed trade as vital to postwar reconstruction and therefore needed to be freed of monetary restrictions while foreign investment was seen as less important and more closely tied to a country's internal policies.[19]

The application of Article VI, Section 3, appears to be self judging. Thus, states in their sovereign discretion are free to regulate and control capital movements, a term that would seem to cover all forms of investment, both in and out of their territories. Article VI, Section 3 does, however, contain important provisos. First, IMF member states may not use their regulations on capital movements in ways that will restrict payments for current transactions. Whereas a state is free to control capital transactions, it may not control payments in connection with current transactions. The second proviso in Article VI, Section 3 is that a member state may not use capital controls to delay (as opposed to prohibiting outright) the transfer of funds in the settlement of commitments. Nor may a member state impose measures that restrict payments for such transaction on the pretext that they constitute capital transactions.

The application of these provisos raises a question as to the meaning of "payments for current transactions" and how they differ from "payments for capital transactions." Article XXX, "Explanation of Terms," provides a partial elucidation of the distinction between the two types of transactions in that its paragraph (d) states:

> (*d*) Payments for current transactions means payments which are not for the purpose of transferring capital, and includes, without limitation:

---

[16] Articles of Agreement of the International Monetary Fund, 2 UNTS 39 (1947). The full text of the Article as amended and in force may be found at <http://www.imf.org/external/pubs/ft/aa/index.htm>.

[17] J Gold, *The Fund Agreement in the Courts*, vol III (1986) 8–9.

[18] A Yianni and Carlos de Vera, "The Return of Capital Controls?" 73 *Law and Contemporary Problems* (2010) 357, 360; CJ Neely, "An Introduction to Capital Controls" *Review* (Federal Reserve Bank of St. Louis) 13 (November/December 1999).

[19] P Juillard, "Freedom of Establishment, Freedom of Capital Movements and Freedom of Investment," 15 *ICSID Review-Foreign Investment Law Journal* (2000) 322–39.

(1) all payments due in connection with foreign trade, other current business, including services, and normal short-term banking and credit facilities;

(2) payments due as interest on loans and as net income from other investments;

(3) payments of moderate amount for amortization of loans or for depreciation of direct investments; and

(4) moderate remittances for family living expenses.

The Fund may, after consultation with the members concerned, determine whether certain specific transactions are to be considered current transactions or capital transactions.[20]

The definition of current transactions is quite broad and may affect payments relating to various kinds of international investments. For example, whereas the making of international loans or direct foreign investments is a capital transaction and therefore legally subject to controls by states, the payment of interest on such loans or the repatriation of profits from a direct foreign investment is a current transaction subject to the IMF rules.[21] The definition set out in Article XXX, by its terms, is nonexclusive in that it clearly leaves scope that transactions not specifically mentioned as "current transactions" may nonetheless fall within that definition. It also allows the Fund and a member state to negotiate as to whether a particular transaction is or is not current.

The use of the terms "capital movements" and "current transactions" in the Articles and regulations influenced by them is a reflection of basic concepts applied in balance of payments accounting, the system by which each country measures its gains and losses in foreign exchange. This system also allows a country to determine its position relative to other countries in terms of an overall surplus or deficit in exchange due to all trade and capital transactions that have occurred over a period of time. The balance of payments accounting system of each country includes both a current account and a capital account. The current account, which is subdivided into a series of subaccounts, reflects primarily a country's trading in merchandise, plus the services it has bought and sold. The capital account shows the country's inflow and outflow of capital commitments, including all direct and portfolio investments, both short and long term.[22]

If a country has a surplus in its current account, it has a corresponding deficit in its capital account; if it has a surplus in its capital account, its current account is usually in deficit. Thus the capital account of a country is balanced by its current account. A less-developed country, for instance, often has a current account deficit since it usually must import more goods and services than it exports, but its capital account will show a surplus since the same factors that give it a current account deficit make it engage in inbound capital transactions, such as securing foreign loans and foreign investments, to finance its imports. In theory, a country's capital account should always equal its current account, although one number will be positive and the other negative; however, since it is difficult in practice to collect all relevant data on all transactions, current and capital accounts rarely

---

[20] Article XXX (d), Articles of Agreement of the International Monetary Fund.

[21] J Gold, *The Fund Agreement in the Courts*, vol III (1986) 9.

[22] A particularly useful source of statistics concerning the balance of payments is the *IMF Balance of Payments Yearbook* in which data are presented in a similar format for each country. The key accounts are: (A) Goods, Services and Unrequited Transfers (trade balance), (B) Long-Term Capital, and (C) Short-Term Capital. The Basic Balance (A + B) added to the Short-Term Capital Account (C) yields the "Deficit on a Reserve-Transactions Basis," which is often used as the overall balance of payments figure because it is the amount that must be financed by reserves. The meaning of the balance of payments does not have the same significance under the current floating exchange rates as it did under fixed exchange rates. Since rates are moving more freely, a deficit no longer reflects only the pressures on the exchange rate but also a variety of other factors. Although uses of the deficit have become more limited, long-term deficiencies still reveal underlying economic problems that may result in governmental intervention. For more information, see the IMF's website at <http://www.imf.org/external/>.

balance exactly. To deal with these discrepancies in data, the accounts usually include a balancing entry known as "errors and omissions" to ensure that the capital account is always balanced by the current account.

As indicated above, a country may impose controls on monetary exchanges and payments in connection with capital transactions. Thus, government authorities may require licenses for capital transfers and impose various taxes and restrictions to inhibit the exit of capital from their territories. Usually, the primary reason for employing such capital controls on the exit of capital is to correct balance of payments problems and to preserve capital for domestic purposes. A state is also free to restrict the *entry* of foreign capital for a variety of domestic policy reasons discussed later in this chapter.

While IMF members are thus free to impose capital controls, they have a basic obligation not to impose controls on payments for current transactions without the permission of the IMF. Article VIII sets out the "General Obligations of [IMF] Members." Section 2 (a) of Article VIII on "Avoidance of Restrictions on Current Payments" obliges member states not to impose restrictions on the making of payments and transfers for current international transactions "without the approval of the Fund . . . " Thus, although IMF members are subject to an obligation not to impose restrictions on the making of payments for current transactions, they may do so with the permission of the IMF. The Fund's policy has traditionally been to approve reasonable restrictions on current transactions.[23] Once the Fund has approved such regulations, the IMF Articles provide that exchange contracts that are contrary to such controls are unenforceable in the territories of any member of the IMF.[24] The purpose of this provision is to provide for the multinational enforcement of exchange controls that have been approved by the Fund and that support the implementation of member state's lawful policies relating to exchange arrangements.[25] This provision, however, has given rise to a significant amount of litigation in national courts, which have given it various interpretations, particularly with respect to the meaning of "exchange contracts." Some national courts have given it a broad meaning to the effect that it covers "any contract which in any way affects a country's exchange resources" while others have given it a narrow definition limited to contracts whose purpose is to exchange the currency of one country or the currency of another country.[26]

The prohibitions against restrictions on payments for current transactions in Article VIII are subject to four major exceptions. Members may impose foreign exchange restrictions (1) on transactions with non-IMF members,[27] (2) for security reasons,[28] (3) if the nation's local currency has been declared scarce by the Fund,[29] and (4) under Article XIV, when the nation has requested permission to engage in exchange controls as a "transitional

---

[23] J Gold, "Exchange Contracts," Exchange Control and the IMF Articles of Agreement Some Animadversions on Wilson, Smithett & Cope Ltd v. Terruzzi," 33 *International & Comparative Law Quarterly* (1984) 777, 779.

[24] Article VIII, Section 2(b) states: "(*b*) Exchange contracts which involve the currency of any member and which are contrary to the exchange control regulations of that member maintained or imposed consistently with this Agreement shall be unenforceable in the territories of any member. In addition, members may, by mutual accord, cooperate in measures for the purpose of making the exchange control regulations of either member more effective, provided that such measures and regulations are consistent with this Agreement." See A Yianni and C de Vera, "The Return of Capital Controls?" 73 *Law and Contemporary Problems* (2010) 357, 361–4.

[25] C Bamford, *Principles of International Financial Law* (2011) 38.

[26] C Bamford, *Principles of International Financial Law* (2011) 38–9; A Yianni and C de Vera, "The Return of Capital Controls?" 73 *Law and Contemporary Problems* (2010) 357, 361–4.

[27] Article XI, § 2, *IMF Articles*. ("Nothing in this Agreement shall affect the right of any member to impose restrictions on exchange transactions with nonmembers or with persons in their territories unless the Fund finds that such restrictions prejudice the interests of members and are contrary to the purposes of the Fund.")

[28] Executive Board Decision No 144-(52/51) of August 14, 1952, reprinted in III *The International Monetary Fund 1945–1965* (1969) 257.

[29] Article XIV, § 2, *IMF Articles*.

arrangement."[30] The last-mentioned transitional exception was originally instituted to facilitate the postwar recovery following World War II; however, it later became an important device to permit developing nations to establish the foreign exchange controls they believed were essential for fostering their economic development and correcting deficits in their balance of payments.

When a country joins the IMF, it is expected to declare its willingness to abide by Article VIII restrictions or to request Article XIV transitional status. Article VIII countries are not necessarily free of all controls—few nations are—for they may have special capital controls, as well as certain current payment controls that have been approved by the IMF as nonrestrictive and therefore permissible.[31]

Although the long-range goal of the IMF has been the eventual reduction of exchange controls throughout the world,[32] the Fund reported in 1986 that in some countries exchange controls had intensified significantly due to protectionist pressures for trade restrictions.[33] The worsening debt position of many developing countries also led to strengthened controls. In 1992, the IMF Board determined that many members had availed themselves of the Article XIV transition procedures for too long and concluded that they should take appropriate steps to remove the remaining restrictions. The Board therefore resolved to intensify its efforts to encourage countries to accept the Article VIII obligations. Overall, the goals set out in the 1992 report were met and substantial progress had been made by the early part of the twenty-first century. As of 2010, 165 out of 187 members had notified the IMF that they accepted Article VIII obligations—95 of those acceptances were made between 1992 and 2005.

Notification of the acceptance of Article VIII obligations, often a byproduct of underlying economic changes, reflects a Fund member's efforts to liberalize its legal framework and administrative practices in the area of foreign exchange regulation. Most countries that have notified acceptance of Article VIII obligations have also significantly simplified their exchange control regimes. This trend has also led certain countries to liberalize controls on capital movements because of what they consider to have been their positive experience

---

[30] Article XIV, § 2, *IMF Articles.* ("A member that has notified the Fund that it intends to avail itself of transitional arrangements under this provision may, notwithstanding the provisions of any other articles of this Agreement, maintain and adapt to changing circumstances the restrictions on payments and transfers for current international transactions that were in effect on the date on which it became a member. Members shall, however, have continuous regard in their foreign exchange policies to the purposes of the Fund, and, as soon as conditions permit, they shall take all possible measures to develop such commercial and financial arrangements with other members as will facilitate international payments and the promotion of a stable system of exchange rates. In particular, members shall withdraw restrictions maintained under this Section as soon as they are satisfied that they will be able, in the absence of such restrictions, to settle their balance of payments in a manner which will not unduly encumber their access to the general resources of the Fund.")

[31] The IMF reports each year extensively on its member states' various measures affecting international payments in its *Annual Report on Exchange Arrangements and Exchange Restrictions* (AREAER). Published since 1950, this authoritative, annual reference is based on the IMF database that tracks exchange and trade arrangements for all 186 IMF member countries, along with Hong Kong SAR, Aruba, and the Netherlands Antilles. The *Report* draws together information available to the IMF from a number of sources, including during official IMF staff visits to member countries. A separate chapter is devoted to each of the 189 countries included in the *Report*, outlining exchange measures in place, the structure and setting of exchange rates, arrangements for payments and receipts, procedures for resident and nonresident accounts, mechanisms for import and export payments and receipts, controls on capital transactions, and provisions specific to the financial sector. The report also provides detailed information on the operations of foreign exchange markets and exchange rate mechanisms and describes the regulatory framework for current and capital account transactions. The *Report* Analytical Appendix lists each member country's Article VIII or Article XIV status and summarizes the main features of each nation's restrictive exchange practices. See <http://www.imf.org/external/pubs/cat/longres.cfm?sk=23953.0>.

[32] Under Article I(iv) of the Articles of Agreement, a stated purpose of the IMF is to "...assist in the establishment of a multilateral system of payments in respect of current transaction between members and in the elimination of foreign exchange restrictions which hamper the growth of world trade...."

[33] IMF, *Annual Report on Exchange Arrangements and Exchange Restrictions, 1986,* at 5.

with removing restrictions on current international payments and transfers.[34] On the other hand, a country that has accepted Article VIII obligations may request approval from the IMF to impose transitional measures on payments for current transactions in the event of financial crises or other exceptional circumstances. Thus in 2008, Iceland, faced with the collapse of its banking system and its foreign exchange market, requested and received approval from the Fund to enact restrictions on payments relating to certain current international transactions, in addition to controls on capital transactions over which it had full sovereignty under the IMF Articles of Agreement, as well as under customary international law.[35] It should be recalled, however, that other international agreements, such as investment treaties, may limit the ability of a state to impose regulations on inward and outward movements of funds,[36] a subject that will be treated at greater length in Part IV of this book.

Despite the global movement to reduce exchange controls, certain countries nonetheless maintain them on a semi-permanent or temporary basis, for example, as a response to financial crisis, as was the case of Iceland. Because such controls can be very comprehensive, complex, and subject to frequent amendment, it is important for international investors and their legal counsel to consider them carefully in planning any international investment and in managing its operations once the investment is made. The remainder of this chapter will survey the nature and purpose of national regulations on investment outflows and inflows.

5.3 Regulation of Capital Outflows

Through their national legal systems, countries impose a variety of measures for different purposes to control the outflow of capital, both real and financial, from their territories. The type of instrument employed will depend on the situation the country confronts and its goals in trying to deal with that situation.

With respect to the export of real assets, governments may levy export taxes as a means to raise revenues, impose quantitative restrictions to make sure that the domestic market is adequately served, and require the issuance of an export license as a means to prevent strategic technology from falling into the hands of an adversary.[37] In some cases, a country may ban completely an investment or capital transfer as a means to pressure changes in another state's policies or to bring about a complete change of regime in that country. Thus during the apartheid era in South Africa, many countries that opposed South African racial policies forbade their nationals and corporations from making investments in South Africa. There was also pressure on foreign corporations with existing interests in that country to *disinvest.*[38]

---

[34] See *Article VII Acceptance by IMF Members: Recent Trends and Implications for the Fund*, prepared by the Monetary and Financial Systems and Legal Departments and approved by Ulrich Baumgartner and Sean Hagah, May, 2006. Accessible at <http://www.imf.org/external/np/pp/eng/2006/052606.pdf>.

[35] Letter of Intent and Technical Memorandum of Understanding from David Oddsson, Chairman of the Central Bank, and Arni M. Mathiesen, Minister of Finance, to Dominique Strauss-Kahn, Managing Director, International Monetary Fund, November 15, 2008, available at <http://www.imf.org/external/np/loi/2008/isl/111508.pdf>.

[36] See, eg, KP Gallagher, "Losing Control: Policy Space to Prevent and Mitigate Financial Crises in Trade and Investment Agreements," 29 *Development Policy Review* (2011) 387–413.

[37] For example, the United States maintains an elaborate export control system established by the Export Administration Act of 1979 (Pub L No 96–72, 93 Stat 503 (codified as amended at 50 USC app §§ 2401–20) and the related Export Administration Regulations (15 CFR §§ 730–774 (2010). See generally, WP Streng and JW Salacuse, *International Business Planning: Law and Taxation* (revised edn 2011) §§ 7.01–7.10.

[38] See generally, P Levy, *Sanctions in South Africa: What Did They Do?* (Yale University Economic Growth Center, Discussion Paper no 796, February 1999).

States also control the outward flow of financial assets, both with regard to capital transactions and often, with IMF approval, payments in connection with current transactions. Three of the most used types of instruments of control that states employ are (1) taxes, (2) price or quantity controls, and (3) outright prohibitions.[39] In employing restrictions on the outward flow of funds, whether in the form of capital controls or controls on current transactions, states are motivated to attain one or more goals: (a) to preserve savings for domestic use; (b) to generate revenue so as to finance an important national task such as a war; (c) to manage and direct the allocation of credit within a country; (d) to correct a balance of payments deficit; and (e) to achieve certain foreign policy purposes. Like any type of national regulations, these measures require substantial resources and costs for effective implementation. In addition, various actors in the economy often find ways to circumvent them.

(a) Controls to Preserve Domestic Savings for Domestic Use

With respect to the first goal, many developing countries experiencing shortages of investment capital have implemented measures to restrict or prohibit transfers of funds abroad out of a concern to preserve the savings of their nationals for domestic purposes and thereby advance national economic development. Governments have devised various regulatory schemes to achieve this purpose. Many possible methods of exchange control exist and national systems vary widely. A basic scheme of exchange control requires that all foreign exchange entering a country be funneled into a central agent or banking facility as an initial step. Thus, the law may prohibit residents of the country from holding foreign exchange, either in the country or abroad, and require them to convert such exchange at specified banks or with the country's central bank. Government regulations often state how individuals in the country may purchase foreign exchange, including provisions on permitted purposes, acceptable limits, and the necessity of obtaining a license. In addition, they may require that certain currencies—local or foreign—be used for transactions with or for payments to specified countries with which the nation has special bilateral payment agreements. There may be differing controls for imports and exports, and for enumerated categories of payments such as personal transfers, remittances of profits or capital movements. To enforce the exchange control system, legislation will usually designate a central authority for exchange control administration, such as a central bank, a monetary agency, or ministry of finance

In order to achieve the purpose of its exchange control system, the government must make decisions on how the foreign exchange it owns is to be used. These decisions, in turn, lead to the promulgation of regulations governing the purchase of foreign exchange by private individuals and companies from authorized agents and banks. Accordingly, regulations may stipulate priorities, prohibitions, and quotas for certain purposes; they may require licensing and advance deposits for imports; and they may impose surcharges, taxes, restrictions on financing and on arrangements for payments. Moreover, they may provide for a system of multiple exchange rates which sets down more favorable rates for especially desired transactions. Thus, for example, a country seeking to promote tourism may allow tourists to convert their currency at a rate that is more favorable than that applicable to other foreigners.

---

[39] CJ Neely, "An Introduction to Capital Controls" *Review* (Federal Reserve Bank of St. Louis) (November/December 1999) 13, 15.

To complete the system, controls of export proceeds may include export licensing, quotas and prohibitions, guarantee requirements, and surrender of export receipts to a central authority. To encourage desirable exporting practices, the government may offer incentives, including rebates, preferential financing, and the availability of risk insurance or exchange guarantees. Other areas in which exchange controls may operate include the conditions on nonresident accounts; on payments and proceeds of "invisibles"; and on payments related to personal income, travel, education and personal transfers such as gifts.[40]

Exchange controls vary significantly among countries. The specific rules are often highly technical and detailed, subject to change depending on a country's economic circumstances, and may also be subject to varying interpretations by officials charged with their application. It is therefore important to examine with care the exchange control regulations of countries in which an investor is operating or proposes to operate. One of the best global sources for understanding the basic exchange rules of individual countries and for tracking changes from year to year is the International Monetary Fund's *Annual Report on Exchange Arrangements and Exchange Restrictions*.

Persons engaged in an international business transaction subject to foreign exchange controls may be tempted to evade them, often on the assumption that the government concerned is unable to enforce such controls either within or outside its territory. Many methods of evasion seem possible: an importer may pay dollars directly to a foreign exporter who then trades the currency on an illegal exchange market at advantageous rates; the parties may privately exchange large amounts of foreign currency that exceed government quotas; an exporter may receive payment in hard currency from foreign importers for prohibited merchandise; parties may make private payment arrangements that do not comply with government guidelines; and currency may be paid into bank accounts in third countries to avoid all regulation by the countries of the parties involved.

While such maneuvers may seem to be difficult to detect, it must be remembered that violations of exchange controls normally constitute criminal offenses in the foreign country concerned and often result in severe penalties including fines and imprisonment or both. Even persons outside the territorial jurisdiction of an enforcing country may find themselves affected by its exchange controls since courts outside the enforcing country may give effect in certain cases to the exchange control laws and regulations issued by foreign governments. In this connection, as mentioned above, Article VIII, Section 2(b) of the Article of Agreement provides: "(*b*) Exchange contracts which involve the currency of any member and which are contrary to the exchange control regulations of that member maintained or imposed consistently with this Agreement shall be unenforceable in the territories of any member..."

(b) Controls to Generate Government Revenue

During times of war, countries often impose capital controls on outflows so as to prevent capital flight and thus preserve their tax base for financing the war. Most belligerents in both World War I and World War II followed this course of action. Such controls achieve governmental goals in various ways. First, it holds capital in the domestic economy and therefore facilitates its taxation and the collection of government revenues. Second, it often

---

[40] *International Monetary Fund: Annual Report of the Executive Board for the Financial Year Ended April 30, 2009* (2009) [hereinafter *IMF Annual Report*] at 16–17, and individual country surveys; S Robuck, K Simmonds and J Zwick, *International Business and Multinational Enterprises* (rev edn 1977) 209–12.

leads to a higher inflation rate, which also contributes to the growth of government revenues. And finally capital controls may reduce interest rates, which in turn lower government borrowing costs.[41]

(c) Controls to Manage and Allocate Credit

An example of the third purpose is to be found in the policy actions of Malaysia at the time of the Asian financial crisis in 1998. The devaluation of the Thai baht in that year caused significant capital outflows from Southeast Asia, which in turn caused a drop in the price of local equities and a sharp fall in exchange rates. To deal with this situation, the IMF urged governments in the region to increase interest rates so as to make their securities more attractive to foreign investors and therefore reverse the flight of capital. Concerned that a rise in interest rates would slow its domestic economy drastically, Malaysia chose another course of action. It imposed capital controls which prohibited transfers between domestic and foreign accounts, eliminated credit facilities to offshore enterprises, and prevented the repatriation of investments until March 1, 1999. In February, 1999, it adopted a system of taxes on outflows to replace the ban on repatriation.[42]

(d) Controls to Correct a Balance of Payments Deficit

An example of the fourth purpose—correcting a balance of payments deficit—is to be found in the Interest Equalization Tax maintained by the United States from 1963 to 1974. At that time, the United States maintained a fixed exchange rate for the dollar. Since interest rates in the other parts of the world, particularly Europe, were higher than in the United States, this factor made foreign assets seem more attractive to US residents and prompted them to invest increasing amounts of capital outside the United States, thus putting severe pressure on the US balance of payments deficit. In response, from the late 1960s until 1974 the US implemented a capital outflow control system comprising three mechanisms: (1) the interest equalization tax (begun in 1963); (2) foreign direct investment regulations; and (3) the Federal Reserve Board's voluntary foreign credit restraint program. The interest equalization tax was a federal excise tax designed to discourage portfolio investments (less than 10 percent ownership) in foreign equity and debt securities. Established as a counterpart of the interest equalization tax, the foreign direct investment regulations were imposed on foreign investments when the interest acquired was 10 percent or more. The regulations restricted the amount of capital sent abroad and the amount of foreign profits reinvested. The Federal Reserve Board's voluntary foreign credit restraint program restricted US bank credit available to foreign borrowers by setting ceilings on the amounts allowable.[43]

---

[41] CJ Neely, "An Introduction to Capital Controls," *Review* (Federal Reserve Bank of St. Louis) (November/December 1999) 13, 15.

[42] CJ Neely, "An Introduction to Capital Controls," *Review* (Federal Reserve Bank of St. Louis) (November/December 1999) 13, 22.

[43] Practicing Law Institute, *International Transactions Under the New Controls* (1972); McDermott, "The Foreign Direct Investment Controls," 11 *Harvard International Law Journal* (1970) 490; Comment, "Governmental Regulation of Foreign Investment," 47 *Texas Law Review* (1969) 421.

(e) Controls for Foreign Policy Purposes

And finally, a state may institute controls on the outward flow of investment funds so as to achieve certain foreign policy goals that may have little to do with that state's economy or finances. Generally, the aim of controls of this type is to put pressure on a foreign policy adversary. The United States has used such controls on several occasions. For example, in 1979, President Carter, under the International Emergency Economic Powers Act (IEEPA),[44] in response to an Iranian threat to withdraw all funds from US banks, issued an Executive Order[45] that blocked Iranian assets in the US. The President authorized the Secretary of the Treasury to promulgate appropriate regulations which resulted in a requirement that transfers of any Iranian assets had to be licensed by the Department of the Treasury, and that clearance had to be obtained for any transfers that were in process when the order was issued.[46]

The effectiveness of exchange controls in attaining any of the five above-stated governmental purposes varies. In any event they invariably entail costs for countries using them. No regulation is without costs. First, while controlling capital flows, they may also create undesirable and often unexpected distortions in the economy. While exchange controls may conserve domestic savings for domestic use, they may also discourage nationals with income abroad from repatriating that income and cause them to invest disproportionately overseas. Second, over time, firms subject to exchange controls find various ways to evade them or avoid some of their more detrimental consequences. For example, importers may pay early for imports in return for a discounted price. Exporters in that same country may allow delayed payments in exchange for a higher price. In both instances, the importer and the exporter are engaged in making short-term loans to international counterparts in violation of capital controls. And third, foreign exchange controls may also bring about other undesirable results. For example, since governmental officials are given wide powers of discretion in granting licenses, and since their decisions are not usually open to public scrutiny, corruption and bribery may flourish—or at least business morality may suffer—as a result of implementing such systems. Frequently the monetary effect of their actions on the transaction may be great. Illegal markets in both foreign exchange and import licenses may develop and the degree to which authorities tolerate them may vary from country to country.

While some countries have enacted laws and regulations that restrict or inhibit outward flows of capital, many other countries have adopted laws and created legal institutions to encourage their nationals to invest abroad. For example, countries that have created state-sponsored entities that offer political risk insurance to their nationals, such as the Overseas Private Insurance Corporation in the United States and the Export Credits Guarantee Department (ECGD) in the United Kingdom, to be discussed in Chapter 11, represent examples of pro-foreign investment policies that encourage outward flows of capital. The Chinese government in 1998 adopted the "Going Global Strategy" to encourage Chinese private and state-owned enterprises to invest overseas and announced a variety of legal and institutional initiatives to achieve this result.[47] Similarly, the countries that have active

---

[44] 50 USC §§ 1701–1706 (Supp III 1979).

[45] Exec Order No 12,170, 3 CFR 457 (1980), reprinted in 50 USC § 1701, at 1596 (Supp III 1979). See Note, "Asset Freeze-United States Blocks Iranian Assets, Exec Order No 12,170, 44 Fed Reg 65,729 (1979)," 21 *Harvard International Law Journal* (1980) 523–8.

[46] Treas Reg § 535.502, 31 CFR Part 535 (1980).

[47] The official Chinese language version of the "Going Global Strategy" (sometimes referred to as "the Going Out Strategy" is to be found on the official website of The Central People's Government of the People's Republic of

programs to negotiate by bilateral investment treaties to protect the rights of their investors abroad are also pursuing policies that encourage the outward flow of capital. These and other laws to encourage international investment will be discussed in subsequent sections of this book.

5.4　Regulation of Capital Inflows

Despite the proclaimed need for capital and the recognition of its importance for economic prosperity, probably no country in the world allows foreign capital to enter its territory with total freedom and be invested in any area of economic activity. In short, a true "open-door policy," a self-proclaimed label used by some countries, probably does not exist. Virtually all countries have regulations concerning the transfer of capital goods and funds to their territory, the economic sectors in which such funds may be invested, or both. Conceptually, such regulations and controls are of two types: (1) regulations concerning the entry of foreign real and financial assets into the territory of the host state, and (2) regulations concerning the purposes to which such assets may be devoted once they have entered the country. The first may be called "international capital controls," while the second may be considered "internal capital controls." This section will consider "international controls," while the following chapter will discuss the internal controls that countries use to encourage foreign investors to undertake certain kinds of enterprises and activities while denying them access to others. The freedom to transfer capital into a country must be distinguished from two other freedoms often discussed in connection with foreign investment: the freedom of investment and the freedom of establishment.[48] The freedom of investment is the freedom to commit capital to a specific purpose, while the freedom of establishment is the freedom to create some sort of permanent presence, such as branch or subsidiary, to carry out a particular economic activity. Both of these freedoms will be considered in subsequent chapters of this book.

The importation of capital goods to be used in connection with an investment enterprise is generally subject to the national system of import regulations and tariffs. Thus, an investor importing those goods must follow existing clearance and customs procedure and pay the applicable import duties, unless the national government of the host country has otherwise agreed. As will be seen, often foreign investors and the host government negotiate special rules relating to the importation of capital goods, for example that they may be allowed into the country without payment of customs duties. Similarly, if an investor's home country has a trade treaty with the host country, such as the North American Free Trade Agreement, the investor is entitled to the treaty benefits with respect to capital goods that are offered to other goods not intended as investment capital.

With respect to the transfer of financial capital, Article VI, section 3 of the IMF Articles of Association dealing with capital controls, discussed earlier, applies equally whether a country is seeking to limit inflows or outflows of capital from its territory. Thus, an IMF member state country has sovereign rights to limit the entry of capital to its territory subject to its obligation to notify the Fund of the content of such controls. While countries have generally welcomed flows of foreign capital as a means to finance productive investment

China at <http://www.gov.cn/node_11140/2006-03/15/content_227686.htm>. An English summary of the policy, *Going Out: An Overview of China's Outward Foreign Direct Investment* (March 30, 2011), is available on the website of US–China Economic & Security Review Commission <http://www.uscc.gov>.

[48] See generally, P Juilliard, "Freedom of Establishment, Freedom of Capital Investment and Freedom of Investment," 15 *ICSID Review—Foreign Investment Law Journal* (2000) 322–39.

projects, to create employment and to strengthen their economies, some states have been concerned that sudden surges in capital inflows may have a destabilizing effect, for example, by leading to sharp increases in their currency exchange rates, exaggerated inflation of asset prices, and harmful volatility in their financial systems. Accordingly, they have sought to slow and control the inflow of capital, particularly short-term investments in their territories. Toward this end, they have used their regulatory powers in a variety of ways, including the taxation of certain types of short-term, particularly volatile investments, imposing a minimum time limit for investments to remain in the country, and requiring foreign portfolio investors to make an interest-free deposit with the central bank of a fixed percentage of the investment made, with a penalty for early withdrawal of the investment. While capital controls on outflows have been subject to a variety of criticism as noted above, controls on inflows have generally been found to be more effective in achieving their purposes and have therefore been subject to less criticism.[49]

One example of capital controls imposed by the national legal system was Chile's *encaje* ("strong box") system, which existed in that country from 1991 to 1998. In the late 1980s and early 1990s, foreign capital, drawn by Chile's good economic prospects and sound fiscal system, began to return to that country. While the Chilean government viewed the prospect of foreign capital as an important driver of economic development, it was also concerned that the sudden influx of foreign capital would cause appreciation in the country's exchange rate and therefore make its exports less competitive, and that the growth of short-term foreign debt presented an increased risk of destabilizing volatility should investors withdraw their funds suddenly. To counter such unwelcome consequences, Chile imposed a requirement in 1991 that all direct investment was required to stay in the country for three years, a time period later reduced to one year in 1993. It also subjected all portfolio investments to the *encaje*, which was a one-year mandatory non-interest bearing deposit with the central bank. Initially, the amount of the deposit was 20 percent of the amount of the portfolio investment, an amount that was increased to 30 percent in 1991. If investors withdrew their investments before the one-year period, they were liable to pay an early withdrawal penalty of 3 percent. The effect of the *encaje* was to reduce somewhat the entry of capital, but its greatest effect was in changing the composition of international investment flows toward those of longer duration.[50]

---

[49] See generally, International Monetary Fund, *Capital Inflows: The Role of Controls* (IMF Staff Position Note, March 19, 2010, SPN/10/044).

[50] For a description of the *encaje*, see CJ Neely, "An Introduction to Capital Controls," *Review* (Federal Reserve Bank of St. Louis) (November/December 1999) 13, 25.

6

National Regulation of Foreign Investment

6.1 National Foreign Investment Policy and Law

The ability of a foreign investor to commit capital to a particular purpose in a given country depends on the laws and regulations of that country. As indicated in Chapter 5, unless a treaty provides otherwise, each state has complete sovereignty to control the movement of capital into its territory, to regulate all matters pertaining to the acquisition and transfer of property within its national boundaries, to determine the conditions for the exercise of economic activity by natural or legal persons, and to control the entry and activities of aliens.[1] For the reasons discussed in Chapter 4, national laws and policies toward foreign investment demonstrate extreme diversity throughout the world. On the one hand, some countries—particularly those with a strong statist or socialist orientation—severely limit equity investment by foreigners in their economies while allowing significant international borrowing by governmental agencies and corporations. On the other hand, numerous other countries have structured their legislation and policies to encourage the entry of direct foreign investment and even to provide it with special incentives not normally available to local investors. Moreover, foreign investment policies and laws may change significantly over time. For example, the outbreak of the Third World debt crisis of 1982, the end of Communist rule in Eastern and Central Europe in 1989, and the Asian financial crisis of 1997–98 led countries that had previously restricted or even curtailed foreign direct investment to adopt laws and policies that actively promoted it.[2]

The aim of this chapter is to consider basic approaches employed by national legal systems to regulate the principal forms of international investment, namely foreign direct investment, foreign portfolio investment, and foreign debt investments. A final section will consider the related issue of debt-to-equity conversions.

6.2 Regulation of Foreign Direct Investment

A foreign direct investment usually seeks to create or acquire a productive enterprise in a host country. Within individual countries, numerous laws and regulations may have an impact on the feasibility of undertaking a particular investment transaction by a given foreign investor. Such laws and regulations include those governing taxation, commodity price controls, antitrust and competition, securities and corporations, environmental protection, and labor and working conditions, all of which may either expressly or implicitly offer advantages or disadvantages to a contemplated transaction. Equally relevant to investors are constitutional provisions on private property rights, the ability of foreigners to secure legal rights in land, and foreign investors' freedom to make and enforce contracts. The effectiveness of such provisions depends to a significant extent on the country's general political stability, the honesty and effectiveness of its government, the competence and independence of its judiciary, its relevant national policies, both written

---

[1] See Chapter 5, section 5.2.
[2] See JW Salacuse, "From Developing Countries to Emerging Markets," 33 *The International Lawyer* (1999) 875–90.

and unwritten, and the attitudes of government officials toward private investment in general and the specific investment transaction in question in particular.

The national legal systems of virtually all countries have special legal rules that apply to foreign direct investments within their territories. Known variously as "investment laws,"[3] "investment promotion statutes,"[4] "joint venture laws"[5] and "foreign investment codes,"[6] such legislation now seems to be a basic element in the legal systems of almost every developing country in the world. One may also find similar foreign investment laws in such developed countries as Canada[7], Australia[8], and Japan.[9] Moreover, even when a country does not have a specific law covering "foreign investment," national legislation governing foreign exchange transactions, restrictive business practices, and mergers and acquisitions may serve to regulate foreign investment activity in its territory.[10] In addition to a general foreign investment law—or sometimes instead of it—some countries have separate laws regulating foreign investment in particular economic sectors such as petroleum, agriculture, tourism, or other areas to which a host government particularly wishes to attract foreign capital or about which it has special concerns. Because of the exceptional diversity of the world's foreign investment laws, one can do no more than summarize their general principles in the limited space available in the present chapter.[11]

Basically, all host country legislation governing direct foreign investment has two general purposes: to *control* and to *encourage* foreign investment within its territory.[12] In countries actively seeking foreign investment because of a shortage of local capital and technology, the investment codes or laws tend to emphasize the promotion or encouragement function. But, in countries skeptical of the benefits of foreign investment by reason of ideology or historical experience, the law at times has tended to emphasize control rather than promotion. In examining any national legal framework for direct foreign investment, one can usually identify certain provisions designed to encourage

---

[3] eg, Turkey: Foreign Direct Investment Law, Law no 4875 of June 5, 2003, available at <http://www.economy.gov.tr/upload/380BE181-C6CE-B8EF-37B940FAAD239BA2/FDI_Law.pdf>.

[4] eg, Ghana: Ghana Investment Promotion Centre Act (Act no 478) available at <http://ghanalegal.com/?id=3&law=144&t=ghana-laws>.

[5] eg, China: Law of the People's Republic of China on Chinese-Foreign Equity Joint Ventures, adopted on July 1, 1979 at the Second Session of the Fifth National People's Congress, and amended by the 4th Session of the Standing Committee of the 9th National People's Congress on March 15, 2000, available at <http://english.sohu.com/2004/07/04/78/article220847835.shtml>.

[6] Senegal: *Code des Investissements*, Law no 2004 of February 6, 2004, available in French at <http://www.droit-afrique.com/images/textes/Senegal/Senegal%20-%20Code%20des%20investissements.pdf>. English translation available at <http://www.investinsenegal.com/IMG/pdf/investment_code.pdf>.

[7] Investment Canada Act (RSC, 1985, c 28 (1st Supp)) available at <http://laws-lois.justice.gc.ca/eng/acts/I-21.8/index.html>.

[8] Foreign Acquisitions and Takeovers Act 1975, Act no 92 of 1975, as amended, available at <http://www.comlaw.gov.au/Details/C2010C00074/Html/Text#param1>. See also Foreign Acquisitions and Takeovers Regulations 1989, available at <http://www.comlaw.gov.au/Series/F1996B00559>.

[9] Foreign Exchange and Foreign Trade Control Law, Law no 228 of 1949, as amended,

[10] K Grewlich, *Direct Investment in the OECD Countries* (1978)49.

[11] Until June 2011, a useful source of information on the national laws and regulations affecting foreign investment was fdi.net, a database maintained by the Multilateral Investment Guarantee Agency (MIGA), an affiliate of the World Bank, available at <http://www.fdi.net/country/index.cfm>. It has now been discontinued but its information has been warehoused. MIGA has now focused its efforts on pri-center.com, a website devoted to political risk issues, available at <http://www.pri-center.com/>. This site also provides information on foreign investment rules of countries throughout the world. Another source of useful information on the subject is *Investing Across Borders*, a website maintained by the World Bank Group, which compares regulation of foreign direct investment around the world. It presents quantitative indicators on economies' laws, regulations, and practices affecting how foreign companies invest across sectors, start businesses, access industrial land, and arbitrate commercial disputes. See <http://iab.worldbank.org/>.

[12] See generally, S Guisinger, "Host-Country Policies to Attract and Control Foreign Investment," in T Moran (ed), *Investing in Development: New Roles for Private Capital* (1986) 157–72.

foreign investment and other provisions intended to control it. With the increased importance given by governments throughout much of the world to private enterprise and market economies since the 1980s, nearly all national legal systems have de-emphasized controls and significantly increased foreign investment promotion and liberalization.[13] Thus between 1992 and 2009, an UNCTAD study found that countries had introduced 2,748 legal and regulatory changes with respect to foreign direct invest-ment and that 89 percent of such changes favored encouraging foreign investors.[14] However, as the second decade of the twenty-first century began, some observers noted increased investment restrictions and controls in certain countries.[15]

A country's foreign direct investment law normally constitutes the basic legal framework for undertaking and operating foreign investment projects. It is not, however, the exclusive applicable legislation, since foreign investment projects also have to deal with and be subject to a host of other laws, rules and regulations. It sometimes happens that incentives granted by the foreign investment law are diminished by the impact of other legislation, such as those governing land, taxes, exchange controls, and labor relations.

The foreign direct investment law is normally a country's most authoritative, complete, and detailed statement of government policy toward foreign investment. Indeed, it is often the *only* statement of policy readily available to the investor, as well as to government officials with whom the investor must deal. At the same time, a country's investment law may appear quite general—even vague—to the investor. In most cases, the host govern-ment promulgates regulations or other subordinate legislation to complete the general investment law. Relevant governmental agencies may also provide other information of varying degrees of helpfulness and authority in a wide variety of forms, booklets, and brochures.[16]

Direct foreign investment, as noted in Chapter 4, has both benefits and costs for host countries. One of the fundamental purposes of foreign direct investment legislation is to create a legal framework that will maximize those potential benefits and minimize the potential costs to the host country. To put the matter in another way, the investment law is an effort to structure the bargain between the host country and the foreign investor with respect to sharing benefits and costs of foreign investment projects.

In creating a legal framework for foreign investment, national foreign investment laws almost always treat four major issues:

---

[13] The G20, a group consisting of nineteen countries and the European Union, was established in 1999, in the wake of the 1997 Asian Financial Crisis, to bring together major advanced and emerging economies to stabilize the global financial market and to foster global economic development. It made a commitment at its 2009 Summit Meeting in London to forego protectionism in matters of foreign investment and requested quarterly reports on members' adherence to this principle. In response the Organization for Economic Cooperation and Development (OECD) and the United Nations Conference on Trade and Development (UNCTAD) jointly prepare a regular report on G20 countries investment policy measures. Their *Sixth Report on G20 Investment Policy Measures* (October 25, 2011) concluded at 4: "On the whole, G20 members have continued to honour their pledge not to retreat into investment protectionism. Most of the few investment policy measures taken during the reporting period represent continued moves toward eliminating restrictions to international capital flows and improving clarity for investors. However, there have been a few instances of new restrictions." Available at <http://www.unctad.org/en/docs/unctad_oecd2011d6_en.pdf>.

[14] UNCTAD, *World Investment Report 2010* (2010) 76–7.

[15] KP Sauvant, "The Regulatory Framework for Investment: Where Are We Headed?" 15 *Research in Global in Global Strategic Management* (2011) 407–33.

[16] One such publication that is considered very authoritative and seems to have the effect of law is China's National Development and Reform Commission's *Catalog for the Guidance of Foreign Invested Enterprises*, revised from time to time, which divides investments into "encouraged," "restricted" and "prohibited" categories. For a listing in English of the principal Chinese laws governing foreign investment, see the website of the Chinese Government at <http://www.gov.cn/english/2005-08/30/content_27397.htm>.

(1) the definition of permitted foreign investment transactions;
(2) the incentives and guarantees offered to desired foreign investment;
(3) the controls applicable to foreign investment; and
(4) the system for administering the foreign investment process.[17]

This chapter will examine how national legal frameworks treat each one of these issues. Thereafter, it will consider certain special areas of regulatory concern, including privatization of state assets and enterprises and the regulation of foreign portfolio equity and debt investments.

6.3 The Definition of Permitted Investments

(a) In General

Foreign investment laws usually define the kinds of investments that foreigners are permitted or encouraged to undertake in the country concerned. They often also specify the investments that foreign nationals and corporations are forbidden to make. Despite the occasional proclaimed "open-door policies" by governments, probably no country allows foreign nationals to invest in any and all types of economic activity. In defining the types of foreign investments permitted or desired, national laws rely on some or all of the following devices: (1) sector prohibitions and restrictions; (2) specification of favored sectors; (3) provisions on desired substantive contributions to the economy; (4) joint venture requirements; (5) performance requirements; and (6) rules on the acquisition of land and natural resources. The following sections consider each of these devices.

(b) Sector Prohibitions and Limitations

Most national legal frameworks prohibit foreign investment in certain specified economic sectors or at least subject the entry and operation of foreign capital in those sectors to varying degrees of restriction. Indeed, sector controls seem to be the most common type of legal restriction on foreign investment. National laws demonstrate differing approaches to sector controls, including: (a) outright prohibition of foreign capital; (b) limiting equity investment to a specified maximum percentage of voting control in an enterprise in a given sector; (c) permitting equity investment without maximum limitation while restricting the activities in that sector that the enterprise may undertake; (d) allowing foreign investment in a sector only after evaluation and approval by a government agency; and (e) permitting foreign investment in a sector but requiring formal disclosure about the nature of the investment to a designated government agency.

The policy assumptions behind such regulations is that government control of the entry by foreign investment in particular sectors is necessary to protect important national interests, such as national security or strategic economic industries. On the other hand, the fact that some countries protect one sector while others do not leads to the conclusion that different countries perceive the need to protect specific economic sectors differently. It also leads to the implication that such sector limitations on foreign investment may actually be intended to protect various domestic interest groups from competition by foreign investors. For example, Article XVI, Section 11(1) the Constitution of the Philippines

---

[17] For a somewhat different approach to specifying the key issues in foreign investment legislation, see generally J Voss, "Basic Elements for Foreign Investment Legislation in the New Independent States," 16 *ICSID Review– Foreign Investment Law* (2001) 67–106.

prohibits any foreign ownership in the mass media sector,[18] while India limits foreign equity ownership of publishing companies and newspapers to a maximum of 26 percent.[19] On the other hand, Chile allows up to 100 percent foreign equity ownership of newspapers and radio and television companies.[20] While United States law does not completely exclude foreign investment from any sector, it does regulate foreign investment in specific sectors in three principal ways: (1) restricting the amount of foreign investment in certain sectors (for example no foreign investor may hold more than 25 percent voting equity interest in any US airline); (2) restricting the activities of a foreign-owned firm or a foreign parent once the investment is made (for example, commercial sailing vessels that are more than 25 percent owned by non-Americans may not carry cargo or passengers between US ports); and (3) requiring disclosure to the US government of specific types of investment, while limiting the nature and amount of investment. For example, under the Agriculture Foreign Disclosure Act of 1978,[21] any foreign person or entity that acquires more than ten acres of US agricultural land must report the acquisition to the US Secretary of Agriculture.[22]

Individual countries pursue various goals and policies by means of these legal prohibitions and restrictions. For some, concerns about national security and defense dictate that particularly sensitive industries—such as armaments or telecommunications—be firmly controlled by nationals of the host country, if not by the state itself. For other countries, the concept of "national security" extends beyond the protection of defense industries to assuring a country's "economic security" by preventing foreign control of important sectors of the economy, such as power generation and distribution, transportation, and the exploitation of petroleum and natural resources.

For still other countries, national security restrictions on foreign investment are not prompted by a general opposition to all foreign investment but rather by foreign investment in particular industries by investors from specific countries considered potential adversaries. This approach is reflected in United States legislation, notably the Exxon-Florio Amendment of 1988 and the Foreign Investment and National Security Act of 2007 (FINSA). Concerned about the possible acquisition by state-controlled investors from countries whose interests may conflict with those of the United States, the US Congress enacted and President Reagan subsequently signed the Exxon-Florio Amendment as part of the Omnibus Foreign Trade and Competitiveness Act of 1988.[23] This legislation established a process for screening "... any merger, acquisition, or takeover that is proposed or pending after August 23, 1988, by or with any foreign person which could result in foreign control of any person engaged in interstate commerce in the United States."[24] The Act authorizes the President of the United States, assisted by the Committee on Foreign Investment in the United States (CFIUS), consisting of government officials, to review such covered transaction "... to determine the effects of the transaction on the national security

---

[18] Article XVI, Section 11(1) of the 1987 Constitution of the Republic of the Philippines states: "The ownership and management of mass media shall be limited to citizens of the Philippines, or to corporations, cooperatives or associations, wholly-owned and managed by such citizens." Available at <http://www.gov.ph/the-philippine-constitutions/the-1987-constitution-of-the-republic-of-the-philippines/the-1987-constitution-of-the-republic-of-the-philippines-article-xvi/>.

[19] <http://iab.worldbank.org/Data/Explore%20Economies/India>.

[20] <http://iab.worldbank.org/Data/Explore%20Economies/Chile>.

[21] Pub L No 95–460, § 2, 92 Stat 1263 (codified as amended at 7 USC §§ 3501–08; 7 CFR pt 781 (2011).

[22] United States Government Accountability Office, *Sovereign Wealth Funds: Laws Limiting Foreign Investment Affect Certain U.S. Assets, and Agencies Have Various Enforcement Processes*, United States Government Accountability Office Report to the Committee on Banking, Housing, and Urban Affairs, US Senate, GAO-09-608 (May 2009) 14–15.

[23] Pub L No 100–418, United States Statutes at Large 102(1988): 1107; 50 USC Appendix 2170.

[24] 50 USC § 2170(a)(3).

of the United States."[25] The law specifies the various factors to be considered in making this determination, one of the most important of which is that the proposed merger, acquisition, or takeover is "a foreign-government controlled transaction." After appropriate review by the Committee, with the assistance of US national intelligence organizations, the President "... may take such action for such time as the President considers appropriate to suspend or prohibit any covered transaction that threatens to impair the national security of the United States."[26] In 2007, as a result of increased security concerns in the United States, as well as the growth of foreign sovereign wealth funds with the potential to invest in and control important US companies, the screening process was strengthened with the enactment of the Foreign Investment and National Security Act of 2007 (FINSA).[27]

On the other hand, probably no country today imposes an outright ban on the entry of all foreign investment.[28] Nonetheless, one can find throughout the world a variety of lesser restrictions on foreign investment entry. Some of these bans are sector based, that is, legislation limits or prohibits foreign investment from acquiring interests in certain sectors, such as retail trade, electrical power generation, or shipping. The justifications for the sector bans are often stated in grandiose, but vague terms: "national security," "protection of strategic industries," or the need to control the "commanding heights of the economy." Upon close analysis, one often finds that such justifications are pretexts for protecting the interests of certain national elites, rather than the public interest in general. On the other hand, as a result of market forces and international pressure, sector restrictions and prohibitions on foreign investment are being reduced in many countries. India, for example, which had made electrical power generation a virtual state monopoly since the 1950s, lifted the ban in the early 1990s in order to encourage foreign direct investment to enter this sector as a means to alleviate the country's desperate shortage of electricity.[29]

Instead of banning foreign capital outright in a particular economic sector, national legislation may limit the percentage of equity ownership that foreign nationals may hold in a company operating in such sectors. Canada, for example, among the twelve high-income OECD countries, has some of the more stringent restrictions on foreign equity ownership. It imposes specific statutory ownership restrictions on a number of service sectors. For example, foreign capital participation in the domestic and international air transportation sectors is limited to a maximum share of 49 percent. Moreover, under the Canadian telecommunications and broadcasting regime, foreign investors may own no more than

---

[25] 50 USC § 2170(b)(1)(A).

[26] 50 USC § 2170(d)(1).

[27] Pub L 110–49, 121 Stat 246, enacted July 26, 2007.

[28] For example, the Republic of Cuba, whose 1992 Constitution declares that it is a "socialist state of workers" and that it is "guided by the political and social ideas of Marx, Engels and Lenin," has nonetheless enacted a foreign investment law. Its Law 77 of 1995 on Foreign Investment has the stated purpose in Article 1 of "... promoting and encouraging foreign investment in the territory of the Republic of Cuba in order to carry out profitable activities that contribute to the country's economic capacity and sustainable development, on the basis of the respect for the country's sovereignty and independence and the protection and rational use of natural resources, and of establishing for that purpose, the basic legal regulations under which this should be realized." Available at <http://www.gov.cn/english/2005-08/30/content_27397.htm>. In addition, The Democratic People's Republic of Korea ("North Korea"), while strongly committed to a socialist state and to its self-reliance ideology of "juche" philosophy, has also promulgated extensive laws and regulations that are designed to encourage foreign investment, including the Foreign Investment Law, the Free Economic and Trade Zone Law, the Foreign Enterprises Law, the Equity Joint Venture Law, and the Contractual Joint Venture Law. See P Morely, *Legal Framework for Foreign Direct Investment in the Democratic People's Republic of Korea* (July 2011), available at <http://chosonexchange .org/wp-content/uploads/2011/07/Choson-Exchange-Report-on-Foreign-Investment-Laws-of-the-DPRK.pdf>.

[29] See, eg, RP Teisch and WA Stoever, "Enron in India—Lessons From a Renegotiation," 35 *The Mid-Atlantic Journal of Business* (1991) 51–62.

20 percent of the shares of a Canadian operating company directly, plus an additional 33 percent of the shares of a holding company. In aggregate, total direct and indirect foreign ownership in the telecommunications sector (fixed-line and mobile/wireless infrastructure and services) and in the television broadcasting sectors is limited to 46.67 percent. The health care sector is de facto closed to foreign direct investment because private hospitals and clinics may not receive payments from provincial health insurance funds, thereby depriving them of a vital source of income.[30]

On the other hand, Costa Rican legislation provides for equal treatment of domestic and foreign investors with respect to ownership of local companies. As a result, most economic sectors in that country are fully open to foreign equity ownership, except the electricity sector, which is state-owned and state-run.[31]

Investing Across Borders, a project of the World Bank, has found that out of 87 countries surveyed in 2010 only slightly more than a quarter had few or no sector-specific restrictions on foreign ownership and that smaller countries had fewer, while large countries such as China, Mexico, and Thailand were among those with the most. It also found that worldwide, restrictions on foreign ownership are strictest in media, transportation, electricity, and telecommunications industries. On the other hand, most countries allow foreign ownership in alternative energy, a field that nearly all governments seek to encourage in light of growing energy needs and increased environmental concerns.[32]

Countries have reduced their sector bans through careful reevaluation by asking the following questions: Precisely what national interests are being advanced by prohibiting or restricting foreign investment in specified sectors? What has been the record of national capital, public and private, in developing those sectors? What positive contribution could foreign investment make to such sectors in the current circumstances? New devices, such as the Build-Operate-Transfer (BOT) projects, to be discussed in a Chapter 10, have enabled certain countries to avoid specific sector restrictions while still permitting governments to assert that they have not turned over vital sectors permanently to foreign interests.

(c) Specification of Desired Investments

To provide guidance to potential investors, national legislation often affirmatively specifies those areas of economic activity in which foreign capital is particularly desired. Often, the law will define such areas in rather general terms similar to the following: "foreign capital shall be permitted to invest in industrialization, mining, energy, tourism, transportation, and other fields." For example, Egypt's Law on Investment Guarantees and Incentives (Law no 8 of 1997) lists 18 separate fields of activity, such as computer production, land reclamation, and tourism, in which foreign investment is specifically encouraged and offered investment incentives and guarantees. In addition, it authorizes the Council of Ministers to add other activities to the list of desired investments.[33] Sometimes the host country will enact separate investment laws for each economic sector to which it is trying to attract foreign capital; consequently, its applicable legislation might consist of an agricultural investment law, an industrial investment law, and a tourism investment law.[34]

---

[30] See *Investing Across Borders*, available at <http://iab.worldbank.org/Data/Explore%20Economies/Canada>.
[31] See *Investing Across Borders*, available at <http://iab.worldbank.org/Data/Explore%20Economies/Costa-Rica>.
[32] See *Investing Across Borders*, available at <http://iab.worldbank.org/Data/Interesting%20Facts#Investing>.
[33] "Egypt: The New Law on Investment Incentives," 13 *Arab Law Quarterly* (1998) 75–82.
[34] eg, the Tourism Incentive Investment Law of the Republic of Panama, Law no 8 of June 14, 1994, available at <http://www.fenixpanama.com/panama-tourism-incentive-law.html>.

Since general legislative provisions are of limited usefulness in guiding investors, many countries formulate, either by regulation or other administrative act, a list of specific permitted activities that foreign investment may undertake within given economic sectors. In addition, investment promotion agencies may prepare actual project proposals to be undertaken by foreign capital. Consequently, the foreign investment law itself represents only a general framework within which particular project activities are to be defined. The investor must therefore obtain further details and guidance from other regulations and governmental directives. Sometimes the precise fields to be promoted for foreign investment are linked to national development plans that give priority to specific sectors judged particularly important for economic growth.

(d) Defined Contributions to the National Economy

Under many national legal frameworks, sector specification for permitted investment is only a preliminary condition that the investor must satisfy. Legislation may also stipulate the required contribution that a foreign investment must make to the economy. That contribution may be measured in a variety of ways, including the number of jobs created, the additional export earnings gained, the foreign exchange saved or earned, the effect on hard currency reserves, the development of local managerial skills, and the real and effective transfer of useable technology to the country.

The law may therefore define permitted investments in such a way as to allow only those kinds of projects that have real potential for making the desired contributions to the economy. In addition to the fields of permitted investment activity, the investment law may specify the kinds of capital and other resources that may be invested. In order to insure a net inflow of new resources to the host country, the law may require that any invested capital emanate from a foreign source; in addition, it may limit the ability of the foreign investor to mobilize and use local capital and resources. The definition of permitted investments may also extend to the type of technology that the project is allowed to use. For example, the 1974 Egyptian law provided that approved projects may only incorporate machinery and equipment "compatible with modern technological developments and [that] have not been previously used...."[35] Such a provision could of course prevent a multinational corporation from transferring to a developing country the machinery and equipment already being used by one of its subsidiaries in an industrialized country, a commonly used strategy to extend the life of equipment and technology that has become outmoded in a developed economy. Other legal provisions may require the project to be located in particular parts of the country–often in those areas that the government particularly wants to develop economically–or may even specify the kind of products the project is to produce.

Often host country governments, in order to increase foreign exchange earnings, want foreign investment projects to produce only for export; therefore, they incorporate provisions in the law, making it difficult or virtually impossible for foreign investment enterprises to sell in the local market. The issue of whether permitted investment projects must

---

[35] Law No 43 of 1974, as amended by Law No 32 of 1977. I *Investment Laws of the World* (Arab Republic of Egypt, Text of Law) Article 2, §§ ii, at 4. See JW Salacuse, "Egypt's New Law on Foreign Investment: The Framework for Economic Openness," 9 *Int'l Law* (1975) 647, 650–1. The Egyptian law allowed the foreign investor to obtain an exemption from the requirement of new machinery and equipment.

be "export-oriented" or may instead serve the local market ("import substitution")[36] has often provoked controversy between host country official investors and foreign investors, who ordinarily prefer to serve the local market.

Finally, either the law or policy of the host country may require that permitted projects be a minimum size or that the foreign investor invest a minimum amount of capital. Such requirements are probably based on the assumption that certain projects may be so small as to offer no real benefit to the host country. Conversely, it is important for investors and their advisers to remember that if a project is sufficiently large, the host country government may be willing to grant it special privileges or concessions not ordinarily available to other investments entering the country.

(e) Joint Venture Requirements

Joint venture requirements, sometimes referred to as equity restrictions, provide that foreign investment may not undertake a direct investment project without the participation of local capital, either public or private. Laws often limit the permissible amount of foreign equity participation in a project to a maximum percentage, sometimes to less than 50 percent. The joint venture requirement faces the investor with a decision as to whether or not to include a partner in its proposed project and, if so, how and where to find an appropriate partner.[37]

Host governments offer several justifications for the joint venture requirement. First, requiring local and particularly state participation in the venture prevents important economic sectors or enterprises from coming under the control of foreigners. Second, the presence of local investors and managers in the venture facilitates the transfer of technology and management skills to host country nationals and thus fosters the development of national capital. Third, the presence of local investors in the project will increase the likelihood that the project will be managed in accordance with national interests. It is not clear that these justifications are always valid or realistic. Moreover, experience with the joint venture requirement does not seem to show that host countries have always derived the expected benefits or that the benefits achieved have outweighed the costs incurred by the host country.

Strong arguments exist that these restrictions raise the cost of private capital to the host country and may prevent it from using the investment received to maximum advantage. For example, there is evidence that foreign investors in joint ventures tend to transfer less advanced technology to joint ventures than to wholly owned subsidiaries which give them a greater ability to protect their technology from appropriation by local partners and others. Also, in such imposed joint ventures, the investor's commitment to the future development of the project may be less than optimal; consequently, it may focus on gaining revenues through its contractual arrangements with the project (for example as a supplier of technology) rather than as a project owner. Further, the project's potential for growth may be limited by the joint venture requirement because the foreign investor is saddled with a local partner who does not have the financial or managerial resources to build and develop the enterprise or take advantage of new opportunities after it has been established.

---

[36] "Import substitution" results when companies within the host country produce items for local consumption that were previously imported, thus saving the host country foreign exchange that was previously needed to pay for the imports.

[37] Chapter 10, sections 10.3 and 10.4, treat joint ventures in greater detail, particularly with regard to their contractual elements.

(f) Performance Requirements

Performance requirements are conditions imposed by law or regulation mandating that the foreign investment project operate in a particular way, for example that it export a minimum percentage of its production or that it purchase a minimum amount of locally produced inputs. Rather than let market factors determine such production decisions, host countries seek to compel them by law, sometimes with perverse results. Performance requirements generally raise the cost of production, which in turn increases the price of goods sold to consumers in the host country and the level of return required by the investor. The World Trade Organization (WTO) Agreement on Trade Related Investment Measures,[38] which emerged from the Uruguay GATT Negotiations, has made many of these performance requirements illegal when applied by one WTO member against another. Certain other treaties, such as the North American Free Trade Agreement (NAFTA),[39] also limit their use among treaty partners.

(g) Restrictions on the Acquisition of Land and Natural Resources

Many investments, such as agricultural and mining ventures, require the investors to acquire or obtain rights in land or other natural resources in the host country. Concerned to protect against foreign control of natural resources, many national legal frameworks restrict or prohibit foreign investors from acquiring such rights and thereby effectively limit foreign investments in those types of activities. The acquisition by foreigners of rights in land and natural resources is in many countries a sensitive and emotional issue. Even in the United States, which has traditionally had an open-door policy to foreign investment, large foreign investments in land, for example the purchase by Arab interests of agricultural land in the west and mid-west and the acquisition by the Japanese of the Rockefeller Center in New York, provoked outcries about the need to protect the national patrimony from foreigners.

In response, many countries have adopted restrictions that prevent foreigners from acquiring rights in land and other natural resources. In 2010 the World Bank's Project *Investing Across Borders* found that out of 87 countries surveyed 25 percent prohibited foreigners from owning land,[40] sometimes as a result of a constitutional provision.[41]

---

[38] Available at <http://www.wto.org/english/docs_e/legal_e/18-trims_e.htm>.

[39] Article 1146, North American Free Trade Agreement provides that none of the three contracting states may impose any of the following requirements in connection with the establishment of an investment by an investor: "(a) to export a given level or percentage of goods or services; (b) to achieve a given level or percentage of domestic content; (c) to purchase, use or accord a preference to goods produced or services provided in its territory, or to purchase goods or services from persons in its territory; (d) to relate in any way the volume or value of imports to the volume or value of exports or to the amount of foreign exchange inflows associated with such investment; (e) to restrict sales of goods or services in its territory that such investment produces or provides by relating such sales in any way to the volume or value of its exports or foreign exchange earnings; (f) to transfer technology, a production process or other proprietary knowledge to a person in its territory, except when the requirement is imposed or the commitment or undertaking is enforced by a court, administrative tribunal or competition authority to remedy an alleged violation of competition laws or to act in a manner not inconsistent with other provisions of this Agreement; or (g) to act as the exclusive supplier of the goods it produces or services it provides to a specific region or world market." Available at <http://www.nafta-sec-alena.org/en/view.aspx?x=343&mtpiID=ALL#mtpi120>.

[40] See *Investing Across Borders 2010* available at <http://iab.worldbank.org/~/media/FPDKM/IAB/Documents/IAB-report.pdf>.

[41] eg, the Constitution of the Republic of Philippines prohibits foreigners from owning land. Article XII, Section 7 provides: "Save in cases of hereditary succession, no private lands shall be transferred or conveyed except to individuals, corporations, or associations qualified to acquire or hold lands of the public domain." Under section 2 of Article XII the only persons qualified to acquire or hold lands in the public domain are Filipino citizens and corporations 60 percent of whose capital is owned by Filipino citizens.

Unable to obtain ownership of land or needed natural resources by law, an investor will usually seek to obtain some form of long-term lease. In other countries, the land law system may be so insecure that it cannot assure investors of clear defensible rights in the land or the natural resources necessary for their operations. No firm wants to invest without secure tenure of the land on which its facilities are located or required natural resources are to be found. Faced with the increased risks entailed by inadequate or insecure tenure, the investor will either avoid the investment or demand a high rate of return to compensate for the added risk. For example, Indonesia had traditionally allowed foreigners investing in the production of tropical tree products to obtain a long-term lease on land for that purpose. In 1980, a presidential decree provided that a foreign company or a joint venture in which a foreign company was a partner could no longer hold such a long-term lease. Instead, the Indonesian partner could obtain the lease and convey a right of use to the joint venture. Foreign investment in the sector virtually ceased as a result. No investor was willing to commit substantial funds to a venture to plant trees requiring at least eight years to mature without long term control of the land on which those trees were planted.[42]

6.4 Incentives and Guarantees Offered to Foreign Investment

(a) In General

In order to attract foreign investment, countries offer foreign investors certain incentives and guarantees. Such incentives and guarantees arise from three sources: (1) the economic and political attributes of the country; (2) the strength and quality of the host country's legal system; and (3) special provisions in the legal framework designed to encourage foreign investment directly.

The first group includes such factors as the country's political stability, the quality of its workforce, the condition of its infrastructure, and its geographic location. It is these factors that lead a particular foreign investor to a given country in the first instance. Thus, a country with a modern and efficient transportation infrastructure and a low-cost, well-educated workforce offers incentives for investment that a similar country without these attributes does not.

The second includes the respect for property rights and the sanctity of contracts, the enforcement of the rule of law, and the ability to control corruption within the government. Private property rights and the enforcement of contracts are legal elements that underlie the market system and foreign investment. To the extent that they are strengthened, the legal system creates a more favorable investment climate.[43] Similarly, the strength of the rule of law[44] varies from country to country.[45] All other things being equal, countries with a strong rule of law offer a greater incentive to invest than countries which do not. The rule of law is of course vital for democracy, but it is equally important for investment because it

---

[42] International Finance Corporation, *Foreign Direct Investment: Lessons from Experience (No. 5)* (1997) 35–6.

[43] See, eg, *The International Property Rights Index*, which annually ranks countries with respect to the degree of protection which they afford to rights in private and intellectual property. <http://www.internationalpropertyrightsindex.org/ATR_2011%20INDEX_Web.pdf>. See also the *Index of Economic Freedom* which also evaluates countries with respect to the strength of property rights: <http://www.heritage.org/index/pdf/2011/Index2011_ExecutiveHighlights.pdf>.

[44] See generally, T Carothers, "The Rule of Law Revival," 77 *Foreign Affairs* (March/April 1998) 95–106.

[45] For a quantitative evaluation of the strength of the rule of law in countries, see the World Bank database *Worldwide Governance Indicators*, which evaluates six governance indicators, one of which is the rule of law. Available at <http://info.worldbank.org/governance/wgi/mc_countries.asp>.

reduces risks—the risk of arbitrary governmental action. For foreign investors, the rule of law in the host country is a risk-reduction device and it saves on transaction costs.

The third group of incentives includes those that host countries devise and offer directly through their legal systems to encourage foreign investors. In an effort to attract foreign capital to their territories, the governments of many countries offer special incentives and guarantees to foreign investors. The nature of these incentives and guarantees varies from country to country, and as a group they demonstrate exceptional diversity. They include tax and customs duty exemptions, promises not to expropriate investors, government agreement to arbitrate investor disputes before international tribunals, direct subsidies, government agreements to purchase a share of production, government guarantees of the project's debts, customs duties exemptions, and priority in the use of government facilities such as railroads and ports. The remainder of this section will consider the nature of these incentives and the way they work.

(b) A General Theory of Investment Incentives

In considering the role of incentives in the foreign investment process, one begins with a fundamental question: Why do host countries offer foreign investors incentives? The simple answer to this question is that host governments assume that potential foreign investors do not find the host country sufficiently attractive for a direct investment because prevailing conditions either prevent them from earning adequate returns or confront them with unacceptable risks. Host governments further assume that granting potential investors certain guarantees and benefits will change their perceptions of anticipated risks and returns in that country and cause them to make investments that they would not otherwise make. Moreover, believing that they are in a competition for capital with other countries, host governments use incentives to make the investment climate in their countries appear superior to that of the countries with which they compete. For their part, investors capitalize on this perception and dynamic by creating competitions or "tournaments" among potential investment sites to determine which country will grant them the richest package of incentives.[46]

A second and related question is: How do incentives and guarantees offered by government actually influence investor decisions? Because of the fundamental importance of the investor's evaluation of risk and return in making an investment decision, the basic thrust of host country incentives and guarantees is either to raise the expected rate of return that the investor would otherwise earn or reduce the risk to which it would be otherwise subjected to the point that the investor judges that the project with the promised incentive affords it a satisfactory rate of return at an acceptable level of risk. Thus, for example, a host state that is prepared to grant a tax exemption on a foreign investment project income is hoping to influence the initial investment decision by increasing the anticipated rate of return to the investor, and a host government's proposed agreement to arbitrate any disputes with the investor before an international tribunal has the effect of reducing the perceived political risk of the project.

Accordingly, one can group incentives and guarantees into two categories: (1) those that seek to increase investment returns, such as tax exemptions, subsidies, and agreements to purchase products at a minimum price; and (2) those that reduce investment risks, such as guarantees to provide foreign exchange for debt servicing, agreements for the settlement of

---

[46] See generally, KP Thomas, *Investment Incentives and the Global Competition for Capital* (2011).

any eventual disputes by an international forum, and guarantees against nationalization or expropriation except upon prompt, adequate, and effective compensation.

(c) Types of Investment Incentives and Guarantees

A review of the incentives and guarantees offered by national legal frameworks reveals a significant diversity in type and a marked variation among countries. Nearly all host countries manipulate their tax and fiscal systems in order to attract foreign investment. One of the most common incentives is the "tax holiday," which exempts the investment enterprise—and sometimes the investor—from local income and other taxation for a specified period of years. The host country may also grant exemptions from taxes on dividends, royalty payments, interest payments, property taxes, and numerous other charges and fees for which the project, its investors, creditors and contractors would otherwise be liable. Yet another important tax benefit is the grant of a tax exemption to the project's foreign employees.

A variation on the tax holiday is "tax stabilization," which guarantees that the approved enterprise will pay no more than a specified maximum tax rate for a determined period of time. Host governments may enter into "tax stabilization agreements" or other types of stabilization agreements that commit the host government, for a fixed period of time, not to impose more onerous taxes or other regulations than exist at the time the agreement is made. It has been claimed that the growth in foreign investment in Peru has resulted from its policy of entering into stabilization agreements with investors.[47] An approved project may often obtain the privilege to import capital goods, spare parts, and sometimes raw materials at reduced tariff rates or without the payment of any customs duty whatsoever. Due to the high customs duties prevailing in some countries, such customs exemptions may be extremely important to the profitability of a foreign investment project.

One institutionalized form of incentive used by many countries is the "free zone," "industrial export zones" or "export processing zone." Despite differences in name, such zones are essentially areas designated by law[48] and supported with appropriate infrastructure and services within which approved enterprises may import goods without payment of duties, process and use them in manufacturing, and then export those processed and manufactured goods duty free and without the intervention of the customs authorities. Depending on the country concerned, the law may grant a variety of other financial and bureaucratic incentives to projects in such zones,[49] which are a form of manufacturing enclave.[50] Only when the goods are moved to consumers within the country in which the zone is located do they become subject to the prevailing customs duties. However, some countries, as an added incentive to investors, allow a portion of such goods to be sold without duty to the local market. Free-trade zones are usually located near major seaports, international airports, and national frontiers, areas that are geographically advantageous for international trade and transportation. Countries that create them pursue one or more of the following goals: (1) to secure foreign exchange earnings through the development of nontraditional exports; (2) to create employment and raise incomes of local workers; and

---

[47] L Sotelo, "Peru Economy, Foreign Investment Thriving under Stabilization Agreements" (March 23, 2010) available at <http://www.dlapiper.com/latinamerica/publications/detail.aspx?pub=4849>.

[48] See, eg, Kenya's Export Processing Zones Act (Cap 517).

[49] See, eg, Article 29 of the Kenya Export Processing Zones Act, granting a long list of fiscal exemptions to enterprises located within an export processing zone.

[50] PG Warr, "Export Processing Zones; The Economics of Enclave Manufacturing," 4 *The World Bank Research Observer* (1989, no 1) 65–88.

(3) to attract foreign investment and its associated benefits of transferring technology, know-how, and management skills.[51]

In many countries, particularly those with a socialist or statist orientation, both public and private enterprises are required to operate within a restrictive set of rules and regulations governing financial management, labor, prices, and numerous other matters. In an effort to attract foreign investment, some governments have been willing to exempt foreign investors from many of these rules and regulations. The exemption from various taxes and laws is one of the most prevalent forms of incentive, particularly in developing countries, where governments seem to find them attractive primarily because they appear to cost nothing to the host government, at least in the short run.

Competition from other actors in the market is always a risk for investors. Some host countries, in appropriate cases, are prepared to grant foreign investors a virtual monopoly over the local market by agreeing either (1) to prohibit other similar investments for a specific period of time, and/or (2) to limit the importation of competing goods by either a high tariff or an import quota.

The investment laws of some countries may grant incentives in proportion to the size of the project, its importance to the economy, or its geographic location in an underdeveloped area. Thus a project of $5 million might obtain a tax holiday of five years, while one of $20 million might receive an exemption of ten years. But regardless of what the law may say with respect to incentives, in some countries it is always possible, because of the size or importance of the project, to negotiate a special agreement with the government to obtain additional incentives and privileges beyond those specified in the law. As a result, the investor with a particularly important project may be able, through negotiation of a special investment agreement or concession agreement, to obtain a wide range of incentives and privileges not specifically granted in the law.

(d) The Effectiveness of Investment Incentives and Guarantees

Host countries that employ incentives as an investment promotion tool need to evaluate them carefully. In doing so, they should ask three basic questions.

1) **Do the incentives actually encourage desired investment?** In particular, if the foreign investor would have invested without the incentive, it would seem pointless and costly to grant an incentive. The problem is that countries seeking to attract investment are at an informational disadvantage about the expected benefits to be derived from the proposed investment, a type of information asymmetry similar to that faced by a potential used car buyer who because of insufficient information risks paying the car dealer too much for the car. Unable to accurately determine the investor's capabilities, intentions, and goals, such information asymmetry often leads host governments to pay too much for an investment project by granting "redundant" investment incentives, that is, incentives that do not really influence the investor's decision to invest. The investor knows what rate of return from an investment will meet its expectations, whether the expected rate of return in a particular host country meets or exceeds company goals, and how that expectation compares with investment opportunities in other countries. The host government, on the other hand, usually can only make an educated guess at best about each of these matters. As a result, a host country government may underestimate its attractiveness to the investor with respect to a particular project or overestimate the attractiveness of countries with

---

[51] The World Bank, "Export Processing Zones," *Premnotes Economic Policy* 1 (no 11, December 1998).

which it competes for investment. It may also overestimate the persuasive power of its available incentives, particularly tax and fiscal benefits.

Host countries spend significant funds on investment incentives. According to one study, the Philippines spent 1 percent of its GDP on redundant investments and Vietnam granted investment incentives equal to 0.7 percent of GDP in 2002. Another World Bank study found that the government of Yemen spent $6,000 in incentives for each of 8,000 jobs created by foreign investments, an amount more than six times the country's GDP per capita.[52] The granting of investment incentives is by no means limited to developing countries. The local and state governments in the United States grant incentives worth nearly US$50 billion each year.[53] Funds spent on incentives might more effectively have been used to improve a country's investment climate or infrastructure.[54] On their own, investment incentives should be used to address market failures and to generate multiplier effects.[55] In particular, fiscal incentives seem ineffective in attracting investments where countries suffer from a poor investment climate. A country's state of good governance and low tax rate are probably more effective than fiscal incentives in attracting foreign direct investment.

2) Are the benefits to be gained by the host country from the investment worth the cost of the incentives? Host governments often assume that incentives, especially tax incentives, are costless since the country is giving up something, ie tax revenues, which they do not now have. Host governments may be undervaluing the costs of incentives; consequently, they must analyze carefully the full extent of costs they are paying for this form of investment promotion.

3) Are incentives encouraging undesirable behavior in the investor? Investment incentives may encourage investment but the nature of the incentive may cause the investor to act in undesirable ways in operating its investment. For example government subsidies on inputs, such as water and electricity, may cause the investor to operate in ways or employ technologies that do not make the most efficient use of these factors of production.[56]

6.5 Controls over Foreign Investment Operations

(a) In General

In an effort to minimize the costs to the host country of a foreign investment as well as to maximize the benefits, national legal frameworks impose certain controls on investment projects and on investors themselves. The nature of those controls varies from country to country and usually reflects the peculiarities of the host country economy, its development objectives, and the government's social and political policies. Such controls are also dictated

---

[52] World Bank Group, *Report of Rationalization of Tax Incentives and Consolidation of Sub-National Taxes, Fees and Charges in Yemen (Yemen Tax Simplification Project)*. See also S James (2009), "Tax and Non-Tax Incentives and Investments: Evidence and Policy Implications," FIAS, The World Bank Group, 2009. Available at SSRN: <http://ssrn.com/abstract=1540074>.

[53] KP Thomas, *Investment Incentives and the Global Competition for Capital* (2011).

[54] A World Bank study has concluded that incentives have limited effects on investments and that it is more important for countries to improve their investment climate. S James, "Tax and Non-Tax Incentives and Investments: Evidence and Policy Implications." FIAS, The World Bank Group, 2009. Available at SSRN: <http://ssrn.com/abstract=1540074>.

[55] S James, "Tax and Non-Tax Incentives and Investments: Evidence and Policy Implications." FIAS, The World Bank Group, 2009. Available at SSRN: <http://ssrn.com/abstract=1540074>.

[56] See generally, "Tax Effects on Foreign Direct Investment," *OECD Policy Brief*, February 2008. Web: <http://www.oecd.org/dataoecd/62/61/40152903.pdf>.

by the nature of the investment project and may touch virtually every facet of its operation, including the prices it charges for its products, its ability to secure foreign exchange, the nationality of its managers, its expansion and reinvestment plans, as well as the requirement of "disinvestment," that is, the sale of participation in the project to local investors or to the government, over a specified period of time. Investment laws often specify various sanctions for failure to respect the controls imposed on the project, including loss of incentives and privileges, and fines and revocation of the approval to operate; however, some laws are silent as to the consequences for failing to respect controls. This section considers some of the more common types of investment controls.

(b) Price Controls

In cases in which the investor by virtue of its investment has obtained a monopoly over the provision of an important product, such as food or a public service like water, electricity, or communications, the prices it may charge the public for such product or service will invariably be subject to some type of governmental regulation so as to prevent the investor from abusing its monopolistic position in the economy. Ordinarily, the maximum price to be charged is fixed by an order of a government ministry or some designated administrative agency. Normally, such investments will be subject to an elaborate regulatory framework that specifies the conditions under which prices may be increased and the criteria for evaluating the quality of the product or service provided to the public. Over time, as costs of labor, materials, and overheads rise, the project may periodically have to seek an increase in the maximum selling price in order to maintain the profitability of its operations; consequently, foreign investors often find themselves in a process of virtually constant negotiation with relevant ministry officials or regulators over these issues. Even when the project is formally exempt from price controls, such controls may nevertheless affect operations if they apply to a competitor. It sometimes happens that the competitor is a public sector enterprise required to sell its products or services at a low price, the effect of which is to erode the competitive position of the foreign investment project and prevent it from selling its own products at a profitable price. In such cases, the foreign investor may find itself in the paradoxical position of supporting a competitor's request to the government to raise the applicable price controls on the competitor's products.

Transfer pricing—that is, prices charged between affiliates for commodities or services—may be another subject of host country regulation.[57] In view of the fact that such intra-corporate dealings cannot be considered arm's-length transactions, since the parent may manipulate the price to its subsidiary so as to avoid taxation, the host country government may consider it important to regulate, or at least monitor, such prices. Accordingly, it may institute a system of examination to make sure that the prices represent fair value on the world market. In cases where the foreign investment project is selling commodities to the parent, the host country government may require that such sales be done at its own government "posted price," and it may refuse to accept the price agreed upon by the two affiliates concerned.

---

[57] Several countries, including Uganda, Kenya, Egypt, Tanzania, and Namibia, have implemented transfer pricing regulations following the OECD's Guidelines on Transfer Pricing. See TP Analytics at <http://www.tpanalytics.com/uganda-new-transfer-pricing-regulation/>.

(c) Foreign Exchange Controls

In countries where foreign exchange is often in short supply, controls on the acquisition and use of foreign exchange by the investment project often constitute one of the most powerful means of regulating and influencing its activities. Thus, limitations on the availability of foreign exchange for foreign debt servicing, repatriation of profits, and acquisition of spare parts and raw materials can significantly affect, and indeed ultimately curtail, the operations of the project itself. Normally, the rules on these matters are set down in the host country's foreign exchange laws and regulations; however, the investment law will ordinarily include special provisions for foreign investment projects. In addition, among the incentives granted to the investment project the appropriate governmental ministry or the Central Bank may enter into a separate agreement or issue a license specifying the particular privileges and controls applicable to the project in question.

(d) Management Controls

Another area of control concerns the nationality of the managers and other employees of the project. In view of the host country's general objective of obtaining new skills and technology and of creating employment for its nationals, it will normally wish to maximize the employment of host country nationals; therefore, it may require, by quota or other means, that the project shape its employment policies accordingly. In order to achieve this goal, host governments may also require the project to create and implement a training plan for the development of local personnel so that over time indigenous employees will come to occupy virtually all positions in the project. A further type of related control is to be found in the joint venture requirement (discussed earlier in this chapter), which permits the investor to undertake a project only in association with local public or private capital. For certain especially important projects, the government may also insist that a designated official serve on the project company's board of directors.

(e) Financial Controls

In an effort to ease the financial burden on the local economy or extract additional benefits, host countries sometimes choose to impose on the project a variety of financing restrictions, including minimum equity requirements, prescribed debt-equity ratios, limitations on profit repatriation, requirements on the reinvestment of profits, and prohibitions on financing from local sources. Some developing countries also impose restrictions on payments for technology, royalties for trademarks, and technical services.

(f) Changing Controls

Since the late 1980s, many countries have eased investment controls as they have shifted from command to market economies and recognized a growing need to attract foreign investment to their territories. Consequently, foreign exchange controls have been reduced or eliminated in many parts of the world, and most countries instead of insisting on divestment by foreign investment have themselves been divesting their state-owned enterprises through privatization. Moreover, while host country governments originally imposed investment controls in an effort to minimize the costs and maximize the rewards from foreign investment, many have come to realize that in practice because of misconceived controls, bureaucratic inertia, corruption, or distortions in the economy, such restrictions often failed to achieve their objectives. They often simply increased the difficulties of undertaking and operating the project, while failing to yield the benefits desired by the host country.

6.6 Administration of Direct Foreign Investment Regulations

(a) In general

The implementation of a system to regulate foreign investment requires some kind of administrative apparatus; consequently, virtually all host countries have created governmental agencies for this purpose. Foreign investors and their counsel spend much time with such agencies to work out the arrangements for undertaking and implementing international investment projects and transactions. The specific body charged with administering the investment law varies from country to country; however, three basic organizational patterns have emerged. First, in some countries, a specific ministry or governmental department, such as the ministry of planning, has full responsibility for administering the foreign investment law. A variation on this approach is to give specific ministries the authority to regulate investments within their particular sectors of activity. Thus, the ministry of tourism might have the exclusive right to regulate a hotel or other touristic project, while the ministry of industry might approve proposals for new factories. In a second approach, national legislation entrusts the process of regulating investment to an inter-ministerial committee composed of representatives from concerned ministries. For example, from 1954 until 2003, Turkey adopted this approach by entrusting the administration of its system to "The Encouragement of Foreign Capital Committee" chaired by the Director General of the Turkish Central Bank and consisting of representatives of the Ministry of Finance, the Treasury, the Ministry of Industry and Trade, and the Chambers of Turkish Trade and Industry. To become effective, decisions of the committee approving foreign investment and international loans also had to be approved by Turkey's Council of Ministers.[58]

A third approach is to create an independent agency, separate from individual ministries but responsible to the President or the Prime Minister, with full powers to approve foreign investments and regulate the activities of investors. Conceived as a means of expediting investment, a single agency grants the investors all approvals and clearances necessary for a project, a concept known as "one-stop shopping." The Economic Development Board of Singapore, the Malaysian Industrial Development Authority, and the Industrial Development Authority of Ireland have been among the most successful administrative agencies following this model.[59] The experience of other countries adopting this model has often been less successful. While special inter-ministerial agencies may hold themselves out as "super ministries" capable of providing "one-stop shopping" and of issuing all necessary approvals, in practice the investor has found that even though it has secured approval from the investment agency, it must nonetheless obtain additional permits and licenses from other governmental ministries. For example, despite the fact that an investment agency has approved a project calling for the construction of a factory, the foreign investor may still

---

[58] Article 8, Law Concerning the Encouragement of Capital no 8224 of January 18, 1954, Official Gazette, January 24, 1954, available at <http://www.fdi.net/documents/WorldBank/databases/turkey/fdilaw_turkey.pdf>.

[59] F Sader, "Do One-Stop Shops Work?," Foreign Investment Advisory Service, International Finance Corporation, available at <http://www.ifc.org/ifcext/fias.nsf/AttachmentsByTitle/doonestopshopswork/$FILE/Do±One±Stop±Shops±Work.pdf>.

need to obtain the requisite building permits from the relevant unit of local government before beginning construction. Moreover, host government laws and regulations may require that technology transfer agreements and foreign loans be subjected to an additional screening and approval procedure by the central bank or ministry of finance.

In general, ministries, committees, and agencies responsible for regulating foreign direct investment are responsible for carrying out one or more of the following functions: (1) foreign investment screening or registration; (2) foreign investment promotion; and (3) foreign investment monitoring.

(b) Foreign Investment Screening or Registration

The primary reason for the agency's importance in most countries resides in the fact that host country regulations require that a proposed investment project be screened and approved by the responsible agency *before* the investment is undertaken. In an attempt to facilitate the inflow of capital, some countries have abandoned such screening in favor of simply requiring the investor to notify a government agency that it is undertaking a direct foreign investment. In a sweeping reform of its system of foreign investment regulation in 2003, Turkey changed from a screening system to a notification system, while abandoning its former Encouragement of Foreign Capital Committee in favor of entrusting full responsibility for administering the direct foreign investment law to the Under-secretariat of the Treasury.[60] However, in countries permitting investment without such screening, prior screening will be required if the project is to receive incentives, such as tax exemptions and other privileges; consequently, for all practical purposes, the investor in such countries needs approval of the investment before actually undertaking it.

Concerns about terrorism and national security in recent years seem to have intensified the concern of some governments to screen foreign investments, particularly if a state-owned foreign entity is involved in a project as an investor. The United States, which has traditionally been relatively open to foreign investment and did not have a fixed screening procedure or agency appeared to deviate from its traditional policy when it enacted the Foreign Investment and National Security Act of 2007 (FINSA),[61] along with subsequent implementing regulations.[62] This legislation strengthened the role of the previously existing Committee on Foreign Investment in the United States (CFIUS) as a screening body for incoming foreign investment for national security purposes. Chaired by the US Secretary of the Treasury, CFIUS has the authority to investigate all covered transactions and to negotiate and enforce conditions necessary to mitigate any risk to national security posed by such transactions. If, after conducting its investigation, CFIUS finds that a covered transaction presents national security risks and that other provisions of law do not provide adequate authority to address the risks, then CFIUS may enter into an agreement with, or impose conditions on, the parties to mitigate such risks or may refer the case to the President for action.[63] Like the United States, Australia has a similar agency in the form of the Foreign Investment Review Board (FIRB), which advises the government on

---

[60] Law no 4875 of June 5, 2003, Official Gazette, June 4, 2003, available at <http://www.economy.gov.tr/upload/380BE181-C6CE-B8EF-37B940FAAD239BA2/FDI_Law.pdf>. Article 1 states: "The objective of this law is . . . to establish a notification-based system for foreign direct investments rather than screening and approval . . ."

[61] PL 110–49, 50 USC app. 2061. Available at <http://www.gpo.gov/fdsys/pkg/PLAW-110publ49/pdf/PLAW-110publ49.pdf>.

[62] Regulations Pertaining to Mergers, Acquisitions and Takeovers by Foreign Persons 73 Fed Reg 70,702 (November 21, 2008).

[63] For further information on CFIUS, see the website of the Department of the Treasury at <http://www.treasury.gov/resource-center/international/Pages/Committee-on-Foreign-Investment-in-US.aspx>.

the application in specific cases of the country's Foreign Acquisitions and Takeovers Act 1975.[64]

During the approval process, a foreign investor may also encounter obstructive conflicts and jealousies between the investment agency on the one hand and the functional ministries on the other, or among several competing ministries—factors which may hinder undertaking the project. For example, in one country which had a separate law for investment in industry, administered by the Ministry of Industry, and another law for investment in agriculture, administered by the Ministry of Agriculture, foreign investors proposing to undertake integrated agro-industrial projects found themselves caught squarely in the middle of an intense jurisdictional rivalry between the two ministries.

Normally, the investment agency or the relevant ministry will have developed special procedures and forms which the investor must complete in order to obtain approval, often at significant expense. For example, many investment agencies will require the submission of a feasibility study, or at least a prefeasibility study, either of which may be costly. In addition, host country environmental legislation may require an environmental impact statement. Further expense is often caused by the long delays between the time the application is submitted and the time the approval is granted, a period during which the investor's executives and counsel devote considerable time in negotiations with host country officials. While some countries may give such approvals in a very expeditious fashion, others may take a long time, either because of lack of sufficient staff or because of political reasons.

Normally, the investment law constitutes a basic framework which grants authority, in varying degrees, to the investment organization to negotiate the particular terms to be accorded the individual foreign investor on such matters as foreign exchange allocation, tax holidays, customs duties exemptions, and other essential matters relating to the establishment and operation of the project. In most instances, obtaining approval for an investment is not automatic, but rather is a matter of negotiation, a process of give and take. Thus, to obtain desirable incentives, the investor may have to alter the project to satisfy governmental authorities.

(c) Foreign Investment Promotion

In addition to adopting foreign investment legislation and establishing an organization to screen proposed foreign investment transactions, most countries also engage to a greater or lesser extent in actively encouraging foreign companies and persons to invest in their territories. Such investment promotion activities are generally of three types: (1) image-building efforts to demonstrate that the country in question is a good place to invest; (2) investment-generating activities that are designed to encourage specific kinds of investments; and (3) the provision of services to prospective and current investors.

The organization charged with investment promotion varies.[65] Often, in addition to screening project proposals, the investment agency or ministry is supposed to promote and encourage foreign investment in the host country. It may execute this mandate in numerous ways, with varying degrees of effectiveness. Some do virtually nothing, viewing their primary function, regardless of the language of the law, as one of controlling foreign capital.

---

[64] The website of FIRB may be found at <http://www.firb.gov.au/content/default.asp>.

[65] The World Association of Investment Promotion Agencies (WAIPA), established in 1995, is an organization of 244 national and subnational agencies from 162 different countries. Its website lists each of the member agencies with email addresses and information about their activities. See <http://www2.waipa.org/cms/Waipa>.

Others provide information on investment opportunities, hold conferences for prospective investors, conduct road shows to principal financial centers in the world to acquaint potential foreign investors with opportunities in host countries, assist potential investors in finding local partners, and in general play an active role in bringing a proposed investment project to fruition. Still others may develop specific project ideas and actively seek out investors to undertake them. Investment promotion is essentially a process of marketing the host country to investors around the world.[66] Rather than entrust investment promotion to a government agency that is to screen investment, some countries create specialized organizations, often with personnel having substantial private sector experience, whose exclusive task is to promote foreign investment.[67]

(d) Foreign Investment Monitoring

Once the project has been approved, the agency may have a continuing role in monitoring its development and, once it begins operation, making sure that it meets the obligations and conditions specified in the investment approval or other document. Host country governments are by no means uniformly effective in monitoring investments. Due to problems of inadequate manpower, insufficient resources, and inexact accounting standards, to name just a few, some countries merely give lip service to this concept; however, a few do effectively supervise projects once they have been approved to make sure that investors respect all relevant conditions and restrictions.

6.7 Host Government Investment Approvals

Having decided to approve a particular investment proposal, the relevant host country agency will then authorize the project in a written instrument issued to the investor. Such instruments vary from country to country, and take different forms and names, including "investment agreement," "approval decree," "investment license," and "investment permit." Some may entail a detailed contract, while others may merely be a letter from the investment organization to the investor. In a few instances, notably those concerning particularly important projects, the approval for the project may take the form of a decree of the Council of Ministers or the President, or even an act of the legislature.

Despite variations, most host country authorizations may be analyzed as being either (1) an administrative act by the host country government concerned, or (2) a contract or agreement between the host country and the investor. Whether a particular authorization is analyzed as a contract or an administrative act may have implications for the enforceability of its provisions under local law. Often, investment agreements contain provisions for international arbitration, or for dispute resolution by the International Centre for Settlement of Investment Disputes (ICSID), an affiliate of the World Bank; consequently, such agreements may give the foreign investor greater assurance that the host country government will respect its provisions than would an authorization in the form of a "license" or "permit," which may, under local law, be modified or even abrogated at the will of the government. In other jurisdictions, investment approvals in the form of administrative acts may nonetheless afford the investor vested rights that are enforceable in the courts of law.

---

[66] See generally, LT Wells and AG Wint, *Marketing a Country: Promotion as a Tool for Attracting Foreign Investment* (rev edn 2000).

[67] See, eg, the Foreign Investment Promotion Agency of Tunisia (FIPA-Tunisia) <http://www.investintunisia.tn/site/en/article.php?id_article=820>.

In any event, counsel for the investor should seek to determine the precise legal effect of any investment authorization under local law. In appropriate cases, counsel may wish to cast the results of their negotiations with the government in the form of an investment contract with reference to appropriate governing law and to international arbitration so as to limit the ability of the government to modify the terms of an agreement once made.

Normally the investment authorization, whether in the form of a contract or an administrative act, will contain, at the very minimum, provisions on repatriation of capital and income, foreign currency allocation for debt service and other foreign expenditures, a time schedule for the implementation of the project, permission for the project to import goods without payment of duty, the nature and extent of tax holidays and tax exemptions, requirements for submitting reports to the government, and other pertinent matters. More detailed investment agreements will also address such matters as training programs for employees, the number of permitted foreign employees, the ability of the government to use the project's facilities, and project procurement policies.

Ordinarily, the host government wants an approved project to be established as quickly as possible. The investor, on the other hand, usually wishes to implement the project at its own pace. Most investment agreements and approvals include schedules that set deadlines for the implementation of the project. Failure to implement the project within the specified deadline may result in a revocation or cancellation of the authorization to undertake the investment; however, most investment laws permit the investor to seek extensions of such deadlines.

Some countries provide a procedure whereby a project may obtain provisional approval until such time as the feasibility study is completed and the necessary capital secured. Once the investor has definitely decided to undertake the project, it then applies for a permanent approval from the appropriate host country agency.

6.8 Privatization of State Assets as a Means to Encourage Foreign Equity Investment

(a) Background

The mid-1980s witnessed the beginning of a powerful movement that would have far-reaching consequences for international investment: the privatization of state assets and enterprises. Privatization is essentially a complex process by which governments transfer state assets or functions from the public or governmental sector to the private sector. In many if not most cases, foreign private investors have purchased such assets or assumed such functions.

The process of privatization, according to two scholars, can follow one of three basic models: (1) *formal privatization* which transforms an administrative public entity into a private law company, usually in the form of a corporation, but one in which the public sector remains the sole shareholder; (2) *functional privatization* which transfers functions (but not assets), previously performed by the public sector, to a private company, an arrangement sometimes referred as a Public Private Partnership (PPP); and (3) *material privatization*, which transfers both assets and functions into private hands.[68] It is the latter two models that have particularly involved foreign investors.

---

[68] B Weber and HW Alfen, *Infrastructure as an Asset Class: Investment Strategies, Project Finance and PPP* (2010) 56.

A specific form of privatization has been the sale or transfer of state assets or interests therein to private investors.[69] These state assets have included state-owned enterprises operating in virtually every economic sector, from agriculture and manufacturing to transportation and communications. Governments in countries that once had been eager to establish national airlines and government steel mills became just as eager to sell those same airlines and steel mills to private investors, both domestic and foreign. Indeed, in many, if not most cases, the foreign investors were either the most desired buyer or the most able to effectively manage the privatized assets.

The phenomenon of privatization began principally in developed countries in the early 1980s, especially when the British government privatized British Telecom through the sale to the public of US$4.9 billion worth of its shares in 1984. Other European countries would follow suit. Among developing countries, Chile, an early leader, began the process of selling its state-owned enterprises in 1974.[70] The trend developed with increased force in both developed and developing countries. Worldwide receipts from the sale of state assets exceeded US$25 billion in both 1989 and 1990, and reached nearly US$50 billion in 1991. Between 1984 and 1991, total receipts from privatization transactions amounted to approximately US$250 billion.[71] The process of privatization continued and accelerated into the twenty-first century so that by the year 2000 approximately a trillion US dollars-worth of state-owned assets in over 100 countries had been privatized with the result that virtually all countries had drastically reduced their share of state ownership of the economy.[72]

Countries as different in political structure and social system as Mongolia, the United Kingdom, Tunisia, Mexico, and Malaysia have adopted privatization programs; however, the individual reasons for doing so have varied from country to country. Many experts and policy makers believe that privatization is crucial to economic liberalization and reform, both in industrialized countries and in the Third World. Equally important, the World Bank, the International Monetary Fund, and other international financial institutions have actively encouraged the privatization movement and have often made it a condition for their financial assistance and support.

The existence of privatization programs in so many countries created new opportunities for foreign investors. Indeed, a privatization program, if appropriately structured, may be seen as yet another method of encouraging direct foreign investment and the national legislation governing the process as a specialized investment promotion statute. As a result, foreign investors have provided much capital and technology to the process of privatization throughout the world since the trend began. Rather than establish new enterprises, many foreign investors have chosen to purchase or assume control of existing state-owned enterprises or their assets, reorganize and improve them, and then attempt to operate them on a profitable basis. In many countries lacking sufficient local capital, technology, and management skills, the governments concerned aim their privatization program primarily at foreign investors and multinational corporations who have those crucial resources. Consequently, countries once reluctant to admit foreign capital have created

---

[69] R Hemming and AM Munsoor, *Privatization and Public Enterprises* 1 (International Monetary Fund, Occasional Paper 56, January 1988).

[70] HB Nankani, "Lessons of Privatization in Developing Countries," 27 *Fin & Dev* (March 1990) 43. Between 1974 and 1990, Chile privatized approximately 400 state-owned enterprises.

[71] "Escaping the Heavy Hand of the State," *The Economist*, 73 (June 13, 1992).

[72] OECD, *Privatizing State-Owned Enterprises: An Overview of an Overview of Policies and Practices in OECD Countries* (2003) 3.

incentives and opportunities for direct foreign investment in their countries through their privatization laws and programs.

In addition to direct foreign investment, privatization programs present multinational companies with two other types of business opportunities. First, certain types of privatization create possibilities of foreign portfolio investment by individuals, firms, and institutional investors located abroad. Some countries have chosen to make international public offerings of shares in their formerly state-owned enterprises, thereby enabling investors in many countries to obtain equity interests in those enterprises. In effect, international stock offerings tied to privatization programs in particular countries, such as Malaysia and Singapore, are contributing to the integration of global equity markets.

A second type of business opportunity relates to the services that multinational firms can provide to governments and their state enterprises in executing the privatization process itself. In order to privatize successfully, many governments have had to seek the help of foreign investment bankers, law firms, accounting firms, and other types of consulting organizations to plan privatization programs and to carry out the various transactions needed to complete those programs successfully. These services include the identification and reorganization of enterprises appropriate for privatization, valuation of those enterprises, preparation of offering circulars, introduction of new, internationally recognized accounting systems, financial restructuring, identifying possible foreign investors, and negotiating and drafting contracts to execute individual privatization transactions.

In addition to creating opportunities for multinational companies and other foreign investors, privatization also presents them with new challenges. For example, an uncompetitive state enterprise, as a result of the introduction of new capital, management, and technology, may become new and aggressive competitors in the international market. Moreover, a multinational company's existing competitors may use the privatization process to gain a foothold or a dominant position in a given country's market by buying a formerly state-owned enterprise.

(b) Reasons for and Objectives of Privatization Programs

Governments have launched privatization programs for a variety of reasons.[73] The countries of Eastern and Central Europe have undertaken privatization in an attempt to dismantle state-controlled, Communist economies that failed to give a satisfactory life to their people. Other countries have embarked on privatization to raise much-needed government revenues. Over 100 governments have undertaken privatization programs of some sort in the last two decades. In doing so, they have pursued a variety of objectives, depending on the particular situation of the country concerned. These varied objectives have in turn shaped the nature of the privatization process, defined the opportunities offered to foreign investors, and determined the mechanisms used to transfer public assets into private hands. As a result, it is important to understand clearly the objectives pursued by particular governments in undertaking privatization in specific countries. Such governmental objectives include the following or some combination thereof.

---

[73] For a comprehensive discussion of privatization see C Vuylsteke, *Techniques of Privatization of State-Owned Enterprises, Volume I Methods and Implementation* (World Bank Technical Paper Number 88, 1988). See also R Ramamurti, "Why Are Developing Countries Privatizing?" 23 *J Int'l Bus Stud* (1992) 225.

(i) Relief of Governmental Budget Deficits

The 1960s and the 1970s witnessed a great expansion in state-owned enterprises, particularly in developing countries.[74] For the most part, these state-owned enterprises proved inefficient and unprofitable. Governments were able to maintain them only by providing subsidies from the state budget. Such subsidies, when combined with other adverse economic circumstances, led to increasing governmental budgetary deficits. Also, many governments also found that the management of state-owned enterprises was a heavy and expensive administrative burden. To obtain relief from these burdens and to reduce budget deficits, many governments decided to sell inefficient state-owned enterprises to private investors, both foreign and domestic.

(ii) Relief from Indebtedness

Many governments financed the development of their public sector enterprises through heavy foreign borrowing. As a result of the debt crisis of the 1980s, these same governments found themselves unable to service these debts. In order to reduce the debt burden, many governments decided to sell off the indebted private enterprises. Later, in the aftermath of other crises and as a means to relieve foreign indebtedness and placate international lenders and international financial institutions such as the International Monetary Fund, countries undertook to privatize many if not most of their state-owned enterprises. Thus in 2011, during the euro crisis, Greece was forced by other European states to undertake a program of privatization in order to obtain financial assistance for its difficulties. Privatization is a condition often favored by international financial institutions in return for the provision of financial assistance during a financial crisis.[75]

(iii) Improvement of Enterprise Efficiency

Many of the state-owned enterprises were inefficient and poorly managed. Protected by subsidies, high tariffs, and government regulations, they often had no incentive to develop efficient, profitable operations. Governments also used state-owned enterprises to absorb unemployment; consequently, they often had too many workers to operate at a profit. In order to improve the efficiency of state-owned enterprises, many governments privatized them so as to place them under effective private management and subject them to the competitive discipline of market economic forces.

(iv) Increased Competition

Many state-owned enterprises had a virtual monopoly over specific products or economic sectors in the countries concerned. Inevitably, such monopolies produced goods and services of low quality and high prices. In the 1980s, governments became convinced of the benefits of economic competition as a way to improve the quality of goods and services, to make operations more efficient, and to lower prices. These governments embarked on policies of breaking up large state-owned enterprises and selling them off in small groups in

---

[74] In Chile, for example, the number of public enterprises grew from 46 in 1970 to 600 by the end of 1973. HB Nankani, "Lessons of Privatization in Developing Countries," 27 *Fin & Dev* (March 1990) 43.

[75] See OECD, *Privatizing State-Owned Enterprises: An Overview of an Overview of Policies and Practices in OECD Countries* (2003) 22.

order to foster a competitive environment in particular economic sectors or the economy as a whole.

(v) Development of Private Enterprises

Many governments, convinced of the value of an active private sector, undertook privatization programs in order to improve business conditions by fostering the development of private enterprises. In the face of large state-owned enterprises that were dominating specific economic sectors, private entrepreneurs found it very difficult to enter the market. Privatization was the means to encourage the growth of private enterprise.

(vi) Development of Wider Business Ownership

Many governments also wanted to bring about a wider public ownership of business and to mobilize public savings for economic development purposes through distribution of ownership interests in their state-owned enterprises. The fostering of stock markets and public equity markets necessitated wide ownership by the public of business enterprises, a goal that was pursued through the privatization of state-owned enterprises.

(vii) Implementation of Pre-existing Policies

Many governments established state-owned enterprises or purchased failing private companies with a declared purpose of simply launching a national industry or playing a catalytic role in the economy. In short, their stated purpose at the time was not to make the government the permanent owner or manager of business enterprises, but rather just to get them underway. Some governments have evoked these policies to justify privatization programs of state enterprises that were purchased or created at an earlier time.

(viii) Conditionality Imposed by International Financial Institutions

International financial institutions such as the World Bank and the International Monetary Fund have encouraged the privatization process. Indeed, they have often conditioned their assistance on a government commitment to undertake a privatization program. These international agencies have favored privatization since they felt that the state-owned enterprises had resulted in big budget deficits and large external indebtedness, both of which prevented governments from attaining fiscal soundness. In order to obtain needed financial assistance from these international agencies, the governments have been led to adopt privatization programs.[76]

Often, the decision in a particular country to undertake privatization has been prompted by a combination of two or more of the objectives stated above. For example, Tunisia, which has had what is considered by many the most successful privatization program in Africa, sought both to open up its market to international competition and to attract more foreign investment into the country. Mongolia, like the economies of Eastern and Central Europe, has used privatization as a tool to move from a centrally planned economy to a market economy. The preamble to Senegal's 1987 law on privatization lists four main

---

[76] eg, K Elborgh-Woytek and M Lewis, *Privatization in Ukraine: Challenges of Assessment and Coverage in Fund Conditionality* (IMF Policy Discussion Paper, 2002) available at <https://www.imf.org/external/pubs/ft/pdp/2002/pdp07.pdf>.

objectives: autonomy and accountability of enterprise management; mobilization of public and private savings into productive investments; reduction of subsidies to state-owned enterprises; and encouragement of widespread share ownership.[77]

(c) The Legal Basis of Privatization

Privatization is the transfer of state assets or functions into private hands, a serious matter in any nation. It therefore requires an appropriate legal authorization and structure. Such legal authorization may take many forms, depending on the country's constitutional and legal structure.

The constitution itself may require amendment of its provisions that prevent or impede privatization. For example, a constitution may stipulate that state-owned enterprises may not be transferred to private interests or that certain sectors, such as petroleum or energy, which the government now wants to privatize, may only be exploited by the state.[78] Even if the constitution does not prohibit privatization, many countries require an act of the legislature to authorize privatization, either because:

1) the constitution, as in many French-speaking African countries, requires a law to transfer assets from the public domain to the private sector; or
2) the state-owned enterprise itself was created by a legislative act and therefore only a similar type of act can legally authorize its privatization.

Moreover, in many countries privatization represents such a departure from the existing situation that a law is necessary to establish a permanent structure for the privatization process, to assure investors of the security of rights obtained in privatized property, to give clear authority to specific agencies to enter into privatization transactions, and to prevent courts and administrative agencies from subsequently canceling rights granted to investors. On the other hand, there are certain cases where no specific privatization law is necessary because the relevant administrative agency or executive department already has full legal power to dispose of state assets under its control. This is often the case with government holding companies, such as Italy's *Instituto per la Ricostruzione Industriale* (IRI), that want to sell their subsidiaries.

The legislative act authorizing privatization may either:

1) establish a general framework law for the sale or transfer of all state–owned enterprises; or
2) designate a particular group or class of state-owned enterprises, either by specific reference to identified companies or to companies in particular economic sectors.

Poland adopted the first approach in its law on privatization of state-owned enterprises,[79] but France's law authorized the privatization of 65 specified state-owned organizations. In a few countries, however, such as the United Kingdom, a third approach is found: a law is enacted for each state enterprise that is privatized.

---

[77] La loi n 87–23 du 18 août 1987 portant privatisation d'entreprises publiques. See C Vuylsteke, *Techniques of Privatization of State-Owned Enterprises, vol. I, Methods and Implementation* (1988) at 58. See also République du Senegal, *Bilan des Politiques du Privatisation des Entreprises Publiques au Senegal* (April 2007). The 1987 law was amended in 2004 by Loi n 2004–08 du 6 février 2004 modifiant l'annexe de la loi n 87–23 du 18 août 1987 sur la privatisation des entreprises publiques (*Journal Officiel* no 6152 of March 13, 2004), while retaining the stated objectives in its preamble. Available at <http://www.jo.gouv.sn/spip.php?article240>.

[78] WB Berenson, "Legal Considerations and the Role of Lawyers in the Privatization Process: An Overview," 37 *Fed B News & J* (March/April 1990) 159, 160.

[79] Law on Privatization of State-Owned Enterprises of July 13, 1990, (1990) 29 *Int'l Legal Mats* 226.

In addition to authorizing privatization, these laws also specify the agency that is to carry out the privatization program, the procedures to be followed, and the conditions and terms that are applicable to privatization transactions. Some countries have created a new department or ministry to implement the privatization program; others have entrusted this responsibility to an existing governmental department.

The transfer of public assets into private hands obviously has risks of abuse. One of the principal purposes of privatization procedures and guidelines is to protect the public interest, which includes securing a fair price to the state and assuring that the purchaser is capable of operating the enterprise efficiently. The law may also specify the interest or link, if any, that the state must maintain or preserve in the privatized enterprise. It should be noted, however, that foreigners may not necessarily be given unfettered opportunities to participate in a privatization program. Some countries, continuing to be concerned about foreign domination of their economies, may retain restrictions on foreign investment even though they seek to privatize many public enterprises. Other countries, recognizing that their nationals do not have sufficient capital to purchase privatized enterprises or sufficient expertise to run them, do not restrict the participation of foreigners in privatization programs.

On the other hand, whether the purchaser is local or foreign, most governments continue to be concerned about the operation of the enterprise after the sale. In this respect, the government in a privatization sale is unlike the ordinary private party who sells a business. The reasons for this continued governmental concern are numerous, including the privatized enterprise's impact on the national economy, the resulting condition of its workers, and in appropriate cases assuring the effective provision of an important public service. The government may manifest its concern by seeking in some way to influence or control the privatized company after the sale. In addition to using its regulatory power, a government may seek to influence a privatized enterprise by retaining some interest in it. For example, the government, after privatization, might continue to hold a majority interest, a minority interest, a special class of shares with increased voting rights, or a "special share" (sometimes called a "golden share"), which, while giving the government no right to participate in capital or profits, does enable it to send representatives to shareholder meetings, to veto certain important decisions, and even to appoint a number of directors.

In addition to the issue of the authority to privatize is the equally important question of the nature of the property or other rights that are transferred to the investor by virtue of the privatization process. The problem is particularly important in countries such as those of the former Soviet Union and Eastern Europe, whose previous Communist systems did not recognize the right of private property and whose public enterprises did not "own" assets, land and natural resources in the same sense as that term is used in western legal systems. Often the nature of public enterprises' rights in such assets was merely a leasehold or a right of management. Moreover, since those assets were in many cases obtained by former communist governments through expropriation, foreign investors also need to determine the nature of their exposure to possible restitution claims by the former private owners.

(d) The Privatization Process

The precise way in which government assets are privatized will depend on numerous factors, including the goals pursued by the government, the financial and physical condition of the state-owned enterprise, the nature of the local economy and capital markets, and the country's existing relationships with foreign lenders, multinational corporations, and international aid agencies.

Before engaging in a specific privatization transaction, a government usually takes steps to prepare the enterprise for the privatization. Often the legislation authorizing the privatization program will specify the necessary preliminary measures, as well as the procedures to be followed in actually carrying out the privatization transaction. First, the government must determine what existing legal requirements must be satisfied to privatize the enterprise. For example, the enterprise may have existing loan agreements and guarantee agreements with commercial banks and international aid agencies, which prohibit the government from selling its interest in or giving up its control over a state-owned enterprise. As a result, before it can privatize the enterprise, the government may have to pay off creditors, negotiate a release, or in some way involve them in the privatization transaction. Even if no such provision exists in loan agreements, the fact that a creditor holds a mortgage, lien, or other security interest in the assets of the enterprise may prevent the transfer of assets to private parties without the creditor's approval. It should be noted that governments often guarantee loans to state-owned enterprises by banks and international lending agencies. This fact raises the question of the continuing force of that guarantee if the enterprise is privatized. In most cases, the guarantee will continue after privatization unless the creditor agrees otherwise. As a result, the government is placed in the difficult position of guaranteeing the debts of an enterprise over which it no longer has control.

Another important set of legal considerations involves the internal organization of the state enterprise that is to be privatized. For one thing, the legal form of a state enterprise may have to be converted into a private company. This may require the formation of a company under private law and the transfer of all the assets of the state enterprise to the newly created entity. For example, the Polish law on privatization provided for a two-stage privatization process. In the first stage, state-owned enterprises were legally transformed into private law corporations whose shares were wholly owned by the Polish State Treasury. In the second stage, the shares are sold to private investors, foreign or domestic, and the enterprise thus becomes privatized. Even if this step is not required, the articles of association or other fundamental document of the enterprise normally require amendment before privatization can take place.

A third set of legal challenges relates to the general legal and regulatory framework within which the state-owned enterprise had operated. For example, if the law provided that only state-owned enterprises could operate in certain economic sectors, that legislation would have to be amended if the government hopes to privatize successfully enterprises operating in those sectors. Similarly price controls, credit regulations, and tax laws may need to be changed in order to create a business climate that is appropriate to private enterprise.

Other actions that governments take before privatizing an enterprise include recapitalization, valuation of the enterprise, the introduction of realistic accounting methods, elimination of debt, and write-down of assets. Having done these things, the government then has a wide variety of techniques to choose from in structuring the privatization transaction.

And finally, the privatization laws and regulations specify the process by which designated governmental agencies are to accomplish the desired privatization transaction. For example, there may be strict requirements on publicizing the privatization opportunity, on establishing a competitive bidding process, on determining the types of investors that may participate in bidding or negotiations, and on selecting the specific investor or investors to be awarded the privatization transaction.

(e) Types of Privatization Transaction[80]

(i) Public Offering of Shares

One important method of privatizing a public enterprise is to sell all or a portion of its shares to the general public through a public offering. The mechanics of the transaction may be similar to an initial public offering of shares in a company in a market economy, and would involve investment bankers, the preparation of a prospectus offering circular, and a stock distribution network. For a public offering to be successful, the following conditions have to be present:

   (1) the enterprise must be of substantial size with a reasonable earnings record and potential;

   (2) complete information on the firm must be prepared and made available to the investing public;

   (3) a local capital market of sufficient size and liquidity must exist;

   (4) mechanisms and institutions must exist to inform and attract the investing public.

Such conditions, however, exist in only a few developing countries. The main advantages of a public offering are that it allows widespread shareholding, is able to target the broad savings of the investing public, and is usually characterized by transparency and openness.

In some countries, such as Poland and the Czech Republic, governments have sought to achieve mass ownership of shares through the distribution to the public of vouchers or other certificates or book entry subscription rights for their citizens to use in acquiring shares in privatized enterprises. Often these rights are acquired for a relatively low sum. The voucher schemes have been criticized on the grounds that they fail to attract significant amounts of fresh capital either to the state treasury or to public enterprises. On the other hand, they do give a broad segment of the public a vested interest in privatization and the country's emerging market economy.

(ii) Private Sale of Shares

In many countries and for many enterprises, a public offering of shares is not feasible. In such circumstances, the government concerned may decide to sell all or part of its shares in a state enterprise to a purchaser or group of purchasers through a privately negotiated transaction. Most privatization programs in developing countries have been done through a private sale of shares, rather than a public offering.

Often, the privatization law will specify how such transactions may be effected. Generally, they provide either for a competitive bidding process with publicity or for direct negotiation with identified potential purchasers. Such private sales do not have the openness and transparency of public offerings and may therefore be subject to abuse. As a result, the privatization law may specify special procedures to assure the government a fair price for the sale. The law will therefore state the methods of valuation, the procedures for competitive bidding, the criteria for selecting the winning bidders, and the process of negotiation to be conducted thereafter. Because the government's goal in most cases is to form a privatized company that continues to operate, the contract of sale may include

---

[80] For a discussion of the various transactions employed in privatizations, see generally OECD, *Privatization in the 21st Century: A Summary of Recent Experience* (2010) available at <http://www.oecd.org/dataoecd/44/58/43449100.pdf>; OECD, *Privatizing State-owned Enterprises, an Overview of Policies and Practices in OECD Countries* (2003).

conditions on the enterprise's continuing operations, as well as prohibitions against dismantling and selling its assets after privatization.

(iii) Sale of State Assets

Rather than sell the whole enterprise, the government may decide to sell only some of its assets. The sale of assets can be based on open competitive bidding, an auction, or negotiation with an interested investor. For example, a state-owned airline may seek to focus exclusively on its core business and therefore sell off ancillary businesses, such as hotels, to private investors. Unlike the sale of shares in a going concern, an enterprise's assets are often sold without the related liabilities.

(iv) Reorganization into Component Parts

Rather than merely sell assets, the state enterprise may divide itself into several component parts, incorporate them into separate companies, and then sell them either by public offering or private sale of shares. This method permits privatization of an enterprise to take place at different times and under different conditions, to be determined by the government

(v) New Private Investment into an Existing State Enterprise

Rather than sell a state enterprise to private interests, the government may instead seek to introduce private capital into the existing enterprise, usually for purposes of modernization and expansion. In this type of transaction, the government is not selling its interest in the state-owned enterprise. Instead, its equity (and usually its control) is being diluted. The resulting enterprise is a "mixed" public–private company or joint venture. The continued presence of the government raises issues about the control structure so that the private investor can be assured that the enterprise will be managed in an efficient way that will maximize profits.

(vi) Management and/or Employee Buyout

Often, the managers and/or employees of a state-owned enterprise are the most appropriate or, indeed, the only potential buyers of the enterprise or its assets. In this instance, the privatization of an enterprise is effected by selling its assets or a controlling interest to a group of its managers and/or employees. This type of transaction usually requires external financing, which is then secured by the assets of the enterprise itself. Normally, the managers or workers first form a private company and then the shares or assets of the state enterprise are transferred to that company. Usually, this technique is used where the enterprise or its assets are not of interest to other investors. This type of transaction allows the government to avoid, at least temporarily, liquidations and the resulting employee lay-offs and dislocations.

(vii) Leases

Instead of selling the assets or shares of a state enterprise to private investors, a government may privatize an enterprise by leasing its assets to private operators for a specified period in return for a fixed fee or rental. Although no transfer of ownership takes place in these transactions, the assets are placed under private management, which hopefully will operate them with increased efficiency and profitability. For example, a government which was unable to operate a state-owned steel mill profitably, leased it to a foreign investor for a fee, and the investor thereafter had the commercial risk of running it on a profitable basis. Sometimes such leases also give the lessee the option to purchase the assets under specified conditions.

(viii) Concessions and Management Contracts

Rather than sell or lease state assets, which would give the investor property rights in them, a government may instead decide to grant the investor a concession contract or a management contract to operate them. Since the state retains ownership of the underlying assets, concessions are a means to privatize a previously state function without privatizing related state assets. Under a concession contract, which is often used in connection with the privatization of public utilities, such as water, sewerage, electricity and telecommunications services, the investor agrees to improve through investment and operate the public service in question for an extended period of time, which may be as long as 30 years, and to be compensated from the cash flow derived from the payments made by consumers for the service. In theory, the amount of the investor profits will depend on its ability to manage the service efficiently. Normally, because a public service is involved, the concessionaire must operate the concession within a state regulatory framework governing pricing and service quality.[81]

Under a management contract, a private manager agrees to manage the state enterprise or assets in return for a fee. Unlike a lease or a concession, the state retains the commercial risk of the enterprise's operations. If the managed enterprise sustains a loss, the state must bear it. The individual terms of leases and management contracts may blur the traditional distinction between these types of arrangements. For example, a manager's fee may be tied to the profitability of the enterprise and a lessee may be required to make an equity investment in the enterprise whose assets it has leased.

(f) Postprivatization Control Devices

Rather than lose all influence over former state enterprises that have been privatized, some governments have adopted control devices to assure that the newly privatized enterprise will be managed in the public interest. Such devises have consisted of three types: (1) golden shares; (2) insuring a stable body of investors; and (3) government retention of a controlling stake in the privatized enterprise.[82]

While not providing a substantial continuing financial stake in the enterprise, the gold shares held by the government give it certain special powers or veto rights to prevent hostile takeovers and to assure that the key decisions of the new private management will be in the interests of the public. Another approach to insuring management in the government's interest is to arrange for a group of national investors to gain a controlling interest in the privatized enterprise and to require them to agree to retain their interest for a specific period of time. And finally, the government itself may retain a controlling stake in the company while privatizing the remaining minority interest. All of these devices may enable the government to pursue what it considers valid policy aims but they may interject political elements into the management of the company and thereby thwart the principal goals of privatization discussed earlier.

---

[81] See JL Guasch, *Granting and Renegotiating Infrastructure Concessions: Doing it Right* (World Bank 2004).

[82] See generally, B Bortolotti and M Faccio, "Government Control of Privatized Firms," 22 *The Review of Financial Studies* (2009) 2918.

6.9 National Regulation of Foreign Portfolio Equity Investment

Portfolio equity investments are those that gain an investor less than a 10 percent voting interest in the underlying enterprise. As discussed in Chapter 1, the distinction between a direct foreign investment and a portfolio foreign investment is that the former gives the investor a voice in control over the enterprise while the latter is considered too small to permit control. In addition to equity investments, portfolio investments also include debt investments, a subject that will be treated at length in the following section of this chapter. Debt investments, unlike equity investments, generally do not give investors voting rights in the enterprise.

Equity portfolio investments usually consist of shares in a company or corporation. In virtually all cases, the company or corporation in which the portfolio investment is made is created by and subject to the company law of the host country concerned. The rights which the investor gains through an equity portfolio investment is determined by the governing company law, the company statutes and bylaws, and any agreements made among share-holders as to how they will vote, sell, or dispose of their shares. For example, if a Malaysian company invests US$800,000 to acquire voting common shares in a Vietnamese air conditioner manufacturing company with a capitalization of US$10,000,000 in outstanding voting shares, that investment would constitute a portfolio investment since the investor has less than 10 percent voting interest. In making that investment, the Malaysian investor might have agreed with the other shareholders that in the event it wishes to sell its shares it would give the other shareholders a right, known as a "right of first refusal" to purchase them at price equal to or greater than the offer it has received from an outsider.

The making of an equity portfolio investment may be subject to both the regulatory framework of the home country of the investor as well as to that of the country that receives the invested capital. Thus, in order to invest in the Vietnamese air conditioner manufac-turer, the Malaysian company would have to satisfy Malaysian law with respect to international payments and exchange controls. It would also have to comply with and be aware of Vietnamese law on purchasing, holding, and eventually selling its shares.

Equity portfolio investments consist of two basic types: (1) company shares that are publicly traded and listed on a stock or securities exchange; (2) company shares that are not publicly traded. The Malaysian investment in the case mentioned above falls into the second category since the shares of the Vietnamese company are not publicly traded or listed on a stock exchange, and since the specific transaction by which the Malaysian company acquired the shares was privately negotiated among the organizers of the company. It was therefore a private transaction not subject to the regulations governing sales of shares to the public.

The law of the host country usually distinguishes between these two types of share and imposes special regulations on publicly traded or publicly solicited shares in order to protect the public from fraud and other types of financial abuse. For example, in Brazil, Law no 6.404/76 (also known as the Brazilian Corporations Law) makes a distinction between "closed" and "open" companies. Open (or publicly held) companies must necessarily take the form of a corporation and their securities are admitted for trading on the securities market, allowing them to raise funds from the public. But because publicly held companies are permitted to raise funds through public offerings of their securities, they are subject to a series of specific obligations imposed by law and by regulations issued principally by the Brazilian Securities and Exchange Commission (*Commissar de Valor's Mobilizations*—the "CVM"). The CVM, created by Law no 6.385/86, is a federal agency linked to the Treasury.

The purpose of the CVM is to regulate, develop, control and supervise securities markets in Brazil.[83]

The purchase of shares by foreigners in an enterprise in the host country may nonetheless be subject to various special laws, such as capital and exchange control laws and foreign investments codes, like those discussed in previous sections on the making of foreign investment. For example, any investment made in Brazil by means of foreign currency must be registered with the Central Bank.[84] As indicated in Chapter 5, concerned about the volatility of substantial inflows and outflows in connection with short-term foreign investments in local capital and securities markets, certain countries have imposed restrictions and taxes to moderate the risk of harmful volatility, which can have negative impacts on currency exchange rates.

The great growth in privatization, market economies, and domestic and foreign investment has led to the significant development in many countries of stock and securities markets and a significant expansion of ownership of shares in their companies by both domestic and foreign private institutions and persons. While the opening of their markets to foreign investors presents significant economic and financial advantages to the countries concerned, some governments also perceived that increased share ownership by foreigners posed certain risks. First, governments, often prompted by local entrepreneurs and the managers of domestic companies, have been concerned to prevent foreign investors from using local stock markets to purchase large blocks of stock that would give them control of important national companies. To prevent such an occurrence, countries passed regulations limiting the amount of foreign equity ownership in all national companies or companies in designated sectors. In Korea, for example, stock market investment by nonresidents was prohibited until 1992 and then subject to stringent quantitative ceilings.[85] At the time of the 1997 financial crisis, foreign ownership of listed companies was limited to 20 percent of capital, with individual stakes limited to 5 percent.[86] The crisis and Korea's need for financial assistance from the International Monetary Fund would lead to strong pressure to liberalize foreign investment in Korean shares.

An alternative method of regulating foreign ownership of shares is to allow individual companies to create a class of shares reserved to foreign investors. Legislation may provide that foreigners may only purchase certain classes of shares, and that share classes reserved for foreigners would not give them sufficient voting rights to control the company concerned.[87]

Another method of preventing foreigners from using the local market to gain control of national companies and for limiting harmful speculation in their securities is to allow foreign investment through the local stock market only by means of approved financial institutions. Thus, in India, for example, only foreign institutional investors approved by the Securities Exchange Board of India (SEBI), the government agency charged with regulating public trading of securities, as well as nonresident Indians, were allowed to

---

[83] Foreign Relations Ministry of Brazil, *Legal Guide for the Foreign Investor in Brazil* (2008) 47.

[84] Foreign Relations Ministry of Brazil, *Legal Guide for the Foreign Investor in Brazil* (2008) 27.

[85] M Noland, *South Korea's Experience with International Capital Flows* (Institute for International Economics Working Paper No WP 05-4 (June 2005).

[86] M Noland, *South Korea's Experience with International Capital Flows* (Institute for International Economics Working Paper No WP 05-4 (June 2005).

[87] eg, Korea. According to Securities & Exchange Act and Regulation on Supervision of Securities Business in Korea, there is a foreign ownership limit for certain stocks of public corporations, including Korea Electric Power Corporation (KEPCO), Korea Telecom (KT), SK Telecom, Korean Airline, etc. For those shares, transactions between foreigners are possible, but between foreigners and residents are prohibited. As of March 2005, 24 listed companies had foreign ownership limits.

invest directly in local shares.[88] Foreign individuals and companies could not invest directly in Indian equities. However, in 2012, with capital inflows drying up, the regulation was relaxed to allow "qualified foreign investors" (QFIs) to invest in Indian capital markets, but limited to 10 percent of the equity of the company in which they are investing.[89]

Beyond specific legal rules aimed at portfolio investments by foreigners, countries in varying degrees have developed a regulatory framework to govern trading in portfolio equity investments as well as the markets on which such shares are bought and sold. This securities legislation varies in detail considerably across the world; however, it can be discerned as having four basic purposes: (1) *investor protection*—to protect investors from loss caused by fraud, deceit, and other forms of financial abuse; (2) *fair and orderly markets*—to enable both the primary and secondary markets for securities to operate in a fair and orderly manner, assuring that investors are provided with sufficient information to make investment decisions and that markets function in a transparent and open manner, not subject to manipulation; (3) *control of systemic risk*—to assure that the participants in the market effectively settle their transaction and that the failure of settlement does not cause other failures; and (4) *market competition*—to assure that markets for shares are competitive and fair, thus facilitating cost efficiency and effective capital formation through the market.[90]

6.10 National Regulation of International Debt Investments

(a) International Debt Investments in General

In purely quantitative terms, the largest amount of international investment takes the form of debt, rather than equity. For example, while direct foreign investments undertaken in 2010 amounted to US$1.24 trillion, international bonds alone in 2006 totaled US$3.1 trillion. Whereas direct and portfolio equity investment gives the investor an ownership interest in an asset or enterprise, debt investments result in the investor having a legal claim to be repaid the principal amount of the debt plus agreed upon interest on that principal.[91] Debt investors have a right to be paid money by their debtors, but they do not have an ownership interest in the entity to which they have provided debt financing.

Debt investments take two basic forms: loans and bonds. In a loan transaction, the lender, such as a bank, will make a loan of its funds to the debtor for a fixed period of time at a determined rate of interest, which may either be a fixed rate or a variable rate tied to certain agreed-upon indices, such as the London Interbank Offered Rate (LIBOR). If the amount of the loan is especially large, several banks or financial institutions may form a group or "syndicate" to provide the needed funding in a transaction that is usually called a "syndicated loan." Each member of the syndicate lends its separate portion of the loan to the debtor under the terms of single loan agreement. The syndicate will designate a specific bank to organize and administer the syndicated loan.[92]

Bonds, like loans, are debt instruments; however, they are a type of lending that takes the form of readily transferable debt securities that are sold to numerous investors, are usually listed on an exchange market, and thereafter are normally traded among investors once

---

[88] Securities and Exchange Board of India, *Circular CIR/IMD/FII&C/2012* (January 12, 2012), available at <http://www.sebi.gov.in/cms/sebi_data/attachdocs/1326453304731.pdf>.

[89] Securities and Exchange Board of India, *Circular CIR/IMD/FII&C/2012* (January 12, 2012), available at <http://www.sebi.gov.in/cms/sebi_data/attachdocs/1326453304731.pdf>.

[90] PS Collins, *Regulation of Securities, Markets, and Transactions* (2011) 19–23.

[91] See Chapter 1, section 1.2, for a discussion of the difference between debt and equity investments.

[92] PR Wood, *International Notes, Bonds, and Securities Regulation* (1995) 5.

they are issued. The debtor or "issuer" of the bond, such as a corporation or government, does not itself seek potential individual investors to buy the bonds. Instead, the bond issuance is usually organized by one or more investment banks which, through their network of contacts and relationships, sell the bonds initially to investors—usually financially sophisticated individuals and institutions—in what is known as the "primary market." Unlike a bank making a loan, an investment bank does not provide its own funds as long-term financing to the issuer of the bond. Rather, its principal function is to sell the bonds to investors. As freely transferable financial instruments, they are readily bought and sold in the "secondary market."

The debtor, through an administering bank, must make the required payments of principal and interest to the holders of the bonds at the time such payment is due as specified in the bond agreement. Individual bonds are usually denominated in relatively small amounts, for example US$1,000 each, so as to facilitate their sale from one investor to another in the secondary market. In order for bonds to trade easily in the secondary market and thereby give these instruments liquidity, a bond must be readily transferable. Bonds fall into two basic groups: bearer bonds and registered bonds. Bearer bonds are negotiable instruments, transferable by delivery. A holder of such bearer bonds in due course owns the instrument and is therefore entitled to trade it and to receive all payments by the debtor at the appropriate times. Registered bonds, on the other hand, are transferable only by written instrument and ownership is recorded on the register maintained by the registration agent appointed by the issuer.[93]

Loans and bonds are of course common financial instruments in purely domestic transactions and settings. Loans and bonds take on an international dimension because of one of three factors: (1) the lender and the borrower are located in different national jurisdictions; (2) the lender is providing funds in a foreign, not the national, currency of the borrower; or (3) the bonds are sold to investors by an international syndicate of financial institutions.

International debt investments, both bonds and loans, fall into two further categories: (1) "sovereign" debt in which a state or a state-owned entity is the debtor and (2) nonsovereign debt in which the debtor is not a state or a state-owned entity, but rather a private person or organization, such as a multinational corporation.[94] The distinction between the two types of debt investments lies essentially in the fact that the effectiveness of legal protection of creditors is less with respect to sovereign debt than with respect to nonsovereign debt. Effectiveness of creditor rights has two dimensions: (1) the ability of the creditor to impose conditions on the conduct of the debtor and (2) the effectiveness of creditor remedies in the event the debtor fails to make agreed-upon payments.

With regard to the first, it will be seen, in Part III on the Contractual Framework, that creditors use their bargaining power at the time that a debt is contracted to require that the private debtor, such as a corporation, abide by various "covenants" and conditions concerning its internal operations, its financial standings, and the use of loan funds. The purpose of these covenants is to reduce the risk to the creditor of nonpayment by the debtor. The failure to meet such conditions is usually considered an "event of default" under the debt instrument, which may result in the creditors' right to accelerate payment or to take various forms of legal actions. Such intrusive covenants are generally absent from sovereign loans. Sovereign states are jealous of their prerogatives and sensitive to negative

[93] PR Wood, *International Notes, Bonds, and Securities Regulation* (1995) 130–3.
[94] See generally, O Lienau, "Who's 'Sovereign' in Sovereign Debt?: Reinterpreting a Rule-of-Law Framework from the Early Twentieth Century," 33 *The Yale Journal of International Law* (2008) 63–111.

public reactions to any undue foreign intrusion into governmental operations. They therefore usually refuse to accept debt covenants imposed by foreign private lenders that might interfere with their ability to make and execute policy in the public interest.[95] It should be noted, however, that loans by international financial institutions, such as the International Monetary Fund and the World Bank, routinely do impose conditions on governmental operations, a phenomenon known as "conditionality."[96]

Second, and perhaps more important, national legal systems usually provide a legal mechanism to allow unpaid creditors to enforce their rights against delinquent private debtors by seizing debtor assets and in appropriate cases compelling the indebted enterprise to submit to judicial bankruptcy and eventual liquidation. Such mechanisms are available to both foreign and domestic creditors in countries where the debtor resides, and they are also available in other countries where the delinquent debtor has attachable assets. Similar processes are not usually available to the creditors of states and state-owned enterprises. No legal mechanism exists to allow creditors to drive sovereigns into bankruptcy, let alone to force them to liquidate. Within their own legal national systems, sovereigns enjoy a variety of immunities and privileges that make judicial enforcement of their debts difficult or impossible. In addition, the assets owned by sovereigns in other countries may be protected from their creditors' claims by a variety of legal principles, including sovereign immunity, the act of state doctrine, and principles of international comity. Although the strength of this protection has somewhat diminished in recent times due to legislative changes and notably the adoption of the restrictive theory of sovereign immunity holding that the issuance of sovereign bonds is a commercial act not subject to sovereign immunity, the effectiveness of enforcement provisions against sovereign debtors remains much more problematic than against private debtors. As a result, a continuing question in the theoretical literature of international economics is how a market in sovereign debt can exist in the absence of effective legal enforcement processes and why sovereign states do not always default on their loans and bonds.[97]

This section will first consider the general regulatory framework applicable to all international debt investment. Next, because of this fundamental distinction between sovereign and nonsovereign debt investments, the section will examine the regulation of sovereign international debt investments. It should be noted, however, that the bulk of the legal rules governing both sovereign and nonsovereign debt investments are shaped through the negotiations between debtor and creditor and is to be found in the contract that governs their relationship. This contractual aspect of the legal framework of international debt investments will be considered in Chapter 10 on the Contractual Framework.

(b) Regulatory Frameworks for International Debt Investments

A consideration of the regulatory framework of debt investments must take account of the regulations in the country that is the source of the capital—ie the creditor country—and the national regulations in the country that is to receive the capital, that is, the debtor country. National regulation in the source country may pursue a variety of policy goals, some of which were discussed in Chapter 5 on capital and exchange controls. A country that is concerned to preserve its financial resources for domestic development or is worried

---

[95] PR Wood, *Law and Practice of International Finance* (1980) 144.
[96] World Bank, *Review of World Bank Conditionality: Issues Note* (2005).
[97] See generally, U Panizza et al, "The Economics and Law of Sovereign Debt and Default," 47 *Journal of Economic Literature* (no 3 2009) 1–47.

about the negative impact on its balance of payments of loans to foreign countries may seek to inhibit foreign debt investments through a variety of means. For example, in the 1960s the United States imposed a tax on foreign investment so as to maintain low domestic interest rates. The result was the development of the eurocurrency market and euro loans as a new form of international finance.

The sources of loans are banks. The basic function of a bank is to receive the deposit of funds from a variety of depositors, usually on a short-term basis, and to lend those funds for longer terms to finance the activities of borrowers. This process carried out by banks is known as financial intermediation. Because of the important role that banks play in any society, they are ordinarily subject to significant banking regulation in the countries in which they operate. One of the purposes of bank regulation is to assure the safety and soundness of bank operations so that the funds deposited by the public are protected. The regulator is usually the central bank or a special purpose institution. In either event, the regulator will be concerned about the adequacy of bank capital to handle the risk, the nature of the bank's exposures, particularly with regard to the loans it has made, its system of controls, its ownership and management, and its foreign exchange risk.[98] Thus the ability of a bank to provide a foreign loan will depend on the size of the loan, the country for which it is destined, uses of the funds, the foreign exchange issues, and the risks of nonrepayment, to mention just a few.

The funds from a bond issue come not from banks, but from individual investors. Thus bank regulations are usually inapplicable to the issuance of bonds. Instead, bonds, which are considered a security in most countries, are subject to the securities regulation of the countries in which they are sold and traded.

(c) The Special Nature and Problems of Sovereign Debt Investments

Governments borrow from foreign creditors for many reasons, including the need to finance specific projects and to meet general budget deficits which for one reason or another cannot be filled by tax revenues. Individual countries often have complex laws and regulations to govern the borrowing process. This section will first examine some general issues applicable to that process and it will then consider the role of government regulation in the repayment of sovereign debts.

(i) Making Sovereign Debt Obligations

A sovereign debt is incurred by a particular government or government agency. An initial question for any investor in foreign sovereign debt is therefore to determine whether the state represented by that government or government agency will be legally liable for the debt once the investor has transferred its funds to that government or government agency. In incurring the debt obligation on behalf of the state, that government or government agency is acting as an agent of the state, which is its principal. Like any agent, a government can only obligate a principal if it is authorized to do so. A threshold issue is therefore to determine whether the government or agency is authorized to incur the debt obligation on behalf of the state. A country's constitution or its laws will almost always determine the rules by which such authority is determined. In some countries, the constitution may entrust authority to borrow to the legislature; in others, the government may have such

---

[98] PR Wood, *International Loans, Bonds and Securities Regulation* (1995) 377–99.

authority subject to approval by the legislature.[99] In addition, national law will usually specify which particular government department or agency may borrow on behalf of the government.

Related to the issue of the authority to borrow is the authority of governmental units to guarantee obligations incurred by others. As part of the investment process, investors may seek and obtain from governments guarantees of contractual obligations made to the investors by other governmental units. For example, in 1995, when a group of American investors proposing to build the Dabhol Power plant, located in the State of Maharashtra, entered into a power purchase agreement with the Maharashtra State Electricity Board (MSEB) to purchase all of the electricity produced by the power plant for a period of 30 years, the fulfilment of which was essential to the financial success of the project, the investors obtained a guarantee from the Indian central government of the payment obligation of the MSEB. When the MSEB failed to make promised payments a few years later, the investors sought payment of the guarantee.[100]

To prevent abuse of the ability to borrow or to guarantee, national law may impose a variety of restrictions, both substantive and procedural on its exercise. These may range from caps on the maximum amount of debt that the government may incur to limitations on the types of activities that may be financed through sovereign borrowings.[101] Because of the importance of determining authority to borrow or guarantee and of complying with all procedural and substantive restriction, creditors and investment banks will require at the time of the making of the obligation a legal opinion to the effect that the agreement supporting the obligation has been "duly authorized in accordance with the law," and that "the agreement will be treated by the courts of the country of the borrower as 'a legally binding obligation of the borrower enforceable in accordance with its terms.'"[102]

The lack of governmental authority or the failure by a governmental department to comply with all legal restrictions and limitations on borrowings and guarantees may mean that a state can avoid liability for the debt or guarantees made by its alleged agents. A state may try to avoid liability for its sovereign debts and obligations in two situations: (1) on grounds that the contracting governmental agency or department did not have the necessary authority under national law or did not follow required procedures, and (2) when a subsequent government seeks to avoid a prior government's legal commitments on grounds that the prior government was in some way illegitimate. For example, when a country has experienced a radical change of regime, as was the case in Iraq in 2003 when the government of Saddam Hussein was driven from power by the US invasion, a question sometimes arises as to whether the obligations incurred by the defunct regime, particularly if it was of a despotic nature, should bind the new government.[103] In response to such situation, certain scholars have developed the doctrine of "odious debt," which holds that a sovereign debt is "odious" and therefore not transferable to a successor government if the

---

[99] International Monetary Fund & World Bank Group, *Developing Government Bond Markets* (2001) 34. eg, Article 135 (a) of the Constitution of Spain provides: "The Government must be authorized by law to contract a Public Debt or obtain loans."

[100] PJ Anthony, "Company News; Dabhol, Enron Unit in India, Invokes Payment Guarantee" *New York Times*, February 7, 2002, <http://www.nytimes.com/2001/02/07/business/company-news-dabhol-enron-unit-in-india-invokes-payment-guarantee.html?src=pm>.

[101] See, eg, Article 216 (Government Guarantees) of the South African Constitution which provides: "1. The national government, a provincial government or a municipality may guarantee a loan only if the guarantee complies with any conditions set out in national legislation."

[102] PR Wood, *International Loans, Bonds and Securities Regulation* (1995) 226–48.

[103] See *Iraq's Debt*, Financial Times, June 16, 2003 at 20 available at <http://www.odiousdebts.org/odiousdebts/index.cfm?DSP=content&ContentID=7670>.

debt was incurred by a "despotic" regime and if it does not benefit the people of the country concerned.[104] One of the bases of the doctrine is that the "sovereign" in sovereign debt transactions is the people of the country and that they should not be liable for such obligations after the departure of a despotic regime if they have not consented and benefited from the debt. On the other hand, the traditional view is that the debtor in sovereign debt is not the people but the state, the juridical body having control over a specific people and territory.

A graphic example of the issue raised by government succession to sovereign debt obligations is the *Tinoco* case,[105] an international arbitration between Great Britain and Costa Rica concerning the refusal of the Costa Rican government to perform certain financial obligations that it had allegedly incurred in the early twentieth century. While the case concerns international law, it demonstrates that the application of international legal principles, in particular international investment transactions, is directly affected by the nature of the applicable national legal framework.

The case arose as a result of a coup in January 1917 by Frederico Tinoco, the Costa Rican Secretary of War, against Alfredo González Flores, who had been elected President by the Costa Rican Congress in 1913 in accordance with the country's Constitution of 1871. Upon seizing power, Tinoco organized elections that resulted in his election as president, a situation that seemed to win some support from certain segments of the population and also secured the adoption of a new constitution in 1917, supplanting the Constitution of 1879. Several countries recognized the Tinoco government, although the United States and Great Britain, among others, did not. Tinoco's administration established effective control over the country's territory and entered into various transactions with foreign companies, including the sale of an oil exploration concession to a British company and the securing of a line of credit from the Royal Bank of Canada. Within two years, Tinoco was forced from power. The previous constitution was restored, elections were held, and a Constitutional Congress began to function. In 1922, the Constitutional Congress adopted Law of Nullities no. 41, which invalidated all contracts made between the executive power and private persons, with or without the approval of the country's legislative power, during the period of the Tinoco regime. The effect of this action was to invalidate the oil concession to the British company and the loan obligations to the Royal Bank of Canada. Since the shareholders in both entities were British subjects, the government of Great Britain vigorously brought a claim against Costa Rica, which, under significant pressure, agreed to arbitrate the British claims and to accept the United States Chief Justice William Howard Taft, the former American president, as sole arbitrator.

At the outset, it should be noted that the *Tinoco* case concerned the issue of the succession of a subsequent *government* to the obligations incurred by a previous *government*, not the succession of subsequent *state* to the obligations incurred by a previous *state*. It is generally recognized, as indicated in the Restatement of the Foreign Relations Law of the United States, that "[i]nternational law sharply distinguishes the succession of states, which may create a discontinuity in statehood from a succession of governments which

---

[104] O Lienau, "Who is the 'Sovereign' in Sovereign Debt?: Reinterpreting a Rule-of-Law Framework from the Early Twentieth Century," 33 *The Yale Journal of International Law* (2008) 63, 65 The doctrine has its origins in the work of AN Sack, *Les Effets Des Transformations des Etats Sur Leurs Dettes Publiques et Autres Obligations Financières* (1927). See also P Adams, *Odious Debts: Loose Lending, Corruption, and the Third World's Environmental Legacy* (1991).

[105] *Tinoco* Case (*Gr Brit v. Costa Rica*) 1 R Int'l Arb Awards 369, 375–85 (1923), available at 18 *American Journal of International Law* (1924) 147. See generally, O Lienau, "Who is the 'Sovereign' in Sovereign Debt?: Reinterpreting a Rule-of-Law Framework from the Early Twentieth Century," 33 *The Yale Journal of International Law* (2008) 63–111.

leaves statehood unaffected."[106] While the international law on succession of states is unsettled and the subject of significant debate as to whether and under what conditions a successor state is liable for the debts of a predecessor state,[107] the position with regard to government succession is much clearer. A change of government or a regime of a state does not change that state's obligations; consequently; a subsequent government succeeds to state obligations incurred by a previous government. In his award in the *Tinoco case*, Chief Justice Taft adopted this principle as well established, citing the commentary of John Bassett Moore, a leading international scholar of the time:

> Changes in the government or the internal policy of a state do not as rule affect its position in international law. A monarchy may be transformed into a republic and or a republic into a monarchy; absolute principles may be substituted for constitutional, or the reverse; but, though the government changes, the nation remains with rights and obligations unimpaired... The principle of continuity of states has important results. The state is bound by engagements entered into by governments that have ceased to exist... [108]

In order to apply that principle, Taft next had to determine whether the Tinoco regime, which had made the concession contract and the loan agreement, was in fact and in law the sovereign government of Costa Rica at the time. Drawing on Moore, Taft asserted that the test of whether the Tinoco government was a sovereign government was whether it had de facto control over the territory of the Costa Rican state and that its method of coming to power and the fact that certain foreign countries including the United States and Great Britain did not recognize the Tinoco, government was irrelevant to that determination. After closely examining the history of the 30 months' existence of the Tinoco administration, he determined that the Tinoco government did have de facto control of the state of Costa Rica and it was therefore "an actual sovereign government"[109] during that time.

Having made that determination, Taft did not directly proceed to hold that Costa Rica was liable for the two contracts made by the Tinoco administration. Instead, he next made an inquiry into Costa Rica's national legal framework governing the making of such obligations. With regard to the oil concession agreement, that inquiry led him to conclude that the Tinoco government had not followed the applicable constitutional provisions and law and that therefore the concession was invalid and unenforceable. Specifically, one of the essential elements of the concession was a grant of a tax exemption for 50 years. The Tinoco Constitution required that only the country's Chamber of Deputies and Chamber of Senators, *meeting together as a single power*, had "to approve or disapprove laws, fixing, enforcing, or changing, direct or indirect taxes." Finding that the oil concession had been approved only by the Chamber of Deputies without the Senate, Taft concluded that the agreement was invalid and not binding on Costa Rica.[110] The important lesson of this holding is that even a government sovereign must respect its own laws in entering into obligations with foreign creditors and that failure to do so enables subsequent governments to escape liability for such obligations. It therefore behooves legal counsel involved in

---

[106] American Law Institute, *Restatement of the Foreign Relations Law of the United States (Third)* Reporters' Notes to section 208 (1987).

[107] I Brownlie, *Principles of Public International Law* (6th edn 2003) 625–6. See also JA King, "Odious Debt: The Terms of the Debate," 32 *North Carolina Journal of International Law and Commercial Regulation* (2007) 605, 609.

[108] *Tinoco Case*, at 150, quoting John Bassett Moore, *Digest of International Law*, vol I (1906) 249.

[109] *Tinoco case*, at 152. ("I must hold that from the evidence that the Tinoco government was an actual sovereign government.")

[110] *Tinoco Case*, 172. ("The result is that the Tinoco government could have defeated this concession on the ground of lack of power in the Chamber of Deputies to approve it.")

international sovereign loans to be sure that all existing legal provisions are respected at the time of entering into sovereign debt arrangements. One may also justify Taft's decision concerning the oil concession on the basis of agency law and theory. The government is the agent of the state. Its authority to bind the state is specified in the state's law and constitution. Failure to respect the laws in attempting to execute state obligations means that the government is without authority and therefore the purported obligation is void.

The Tinoco Award also found that the loan extended by the Royal Bank of Canada was not binding on Costa Rica. An examination of the facts of the transaction revealed that the loan proceeds were used not for governmental purposes but to defray the personal expenses of individual members of the Tinoco government and that the Bank was aware of their intended use. Concluding that "[t]he whole transaction here was full of irregularities," Taft stated:

> The case of the Royal Bank depends not on the mere form of the transaction but upon the good faith of the bank in the payment of money for the real use of the Costa Rican government under the Tinoco régime. It must make out its case of actually furnishing of money to the government for its legitimate use. It has not done so. The bank knew that this money was to be used by the retiring president, F. Tinoco, for his personal support after he had taken refuge in a foreign country. It could not hold his own government for the money paid to him for this purpose.[111]

This portion of the case also holds a lesson for investors and lawyers involved in sovereign lending, particularly with governments where corruption is rampant. If the creditor is aware that loan proceeds will be used for personal, rather than governmental purposes, the creditor risks the possibility that a future government may deny liability on the debt. Such a result can also be based on agency law and theory. Agents have authority to act on behalf of a principal and to bind that principal; however, a third party dealing with an agent cannot rely on the agency powers of an agent if the third party knows that the agent is not acting on behalf of the principal but for his own account. In that situation, the agent has neither actual nor apparent authority to bind the principal.

(ii) Performing Sovereign Debt Obligations

Sovereign debt obligations are not governed by international law but by the law of a particular national jurisdiction. In most instances, the underlying contract will specify the law applicable to the transaction. In most situations, the chosen law will be that of the country that is the source of the funds. While the governing laws provide for the enforcement of the contract, the specifics of its performance are normally determined by detailed and elaborate agreements negotiated between debtor and creditor representatives. The section on the contractual framework will consider some of the basic provisions found in such documents.

Also relevant to international debt investment is the ability of the borrowing state to intervene through legislation to restrict or prohibit outright the ability of the debtor, whether a state or a private person or corporation, to make scheduled repayments on its debt obligations. States will often take these measures when faced with balance of payments difficulties or a shortage of foreign exchange. Argentina is a case in point. In 1991 in order to attract foreign capital and reduce inflation, the Argentine government had enacted a law to tie or "peg" the Argentine peso to the United States dollar on a one-to-one basis.[112] Ten years later, faced with a financial crisis, Argentina enacted legislation to limit the amount of

---

[111] *Tinoco* Case, at 168.   [112] Law No 23,928 of March 27, 1991.

funds that persons might withdraw from bank accounts and abolished the link between the dollar and the peso.[113]

6.11 Debt-to-Equity Conversions

(a) Background

It sometimes happens that debtors, particularly sovereigns, who are having difficulty repaying their debts, enter into transactions with their creditors or others with the intent of converting debt investments into equity investment. One may look at the privatizations that took place in many countries as a form of debt-to-equity conversion: the indebted government, unable to pay its debt, sells off assets, in order to obtain the funds to repay its debt obligations to its creditors. Another approach is to trade debt directly with creditors for equity investments. Often national legislation is necessary to accomplish this result. During the last quarter of the twentieth century, this practice gained currency. As sovereign debt problems break out in the future, as they seem to do regularly, this approach may again be useful.

(b) History

In the wake of the dramatic oil price rises of the 1970s, many developing countries responded to severe balance of payments deficits by borrowing funds abroad from international commercial banks. Even countries with petroleum resources chose this approach because it offered a means of financing development at a quickened pace. As a result, the nations of the Third World accumulated a substantial burden of debt, which by 1987 amounted to nearly $800 billion.[114]

These developing country loans were basically of two types: (1) credits extended to private sector enterprises, and (2) sovereign debt in the form of loans to national governments, central banks, and state-owned enterprises, as well as private debt that had been assumed by governments as a result of a public guarantee. Sovereign debts constituted by far the largest portion of developing country obligations.

By 1982, it had become clear that many developing countries were unable to service their debts in a timely way and that the creditworthiness of their obligations was questionable. The developing countries were suffering from the combined effects of (1) rising debt service costs due to higher interest rates, (2) reduced commodity exports due to an economic recession in many parts of the world, and (3) increased payments abroad due to sharply higher oil prices. All of these factors provoked a debt crisis, which began in August 1982 when Mexico announced that it was unable to make payments on its $80 billion in foreign loans.

Since sovereign governments and state entities are not subject to bankruptcy or forced liquidation of assets, the inability of developing countries to make payments of principal and interest as they became due left the international commercial banks no alternative but to begin a process of "rescheduling" debt payments—that is, of negotiating an extension of the period over which payments would be made. The major banks dominated this rescheduling process, and the smaller banks involved in the loan syndications felt obligated to participate. The effect of the failure of developing countries to make payments in a timely

---

[113] Decree No 1,570/01 of December 3, 2001; Emergency Law no 25,561 of January 7, 2002.
[114] International Monetary Fund, *World Economic Outlook* (1986) 247.

fashion, when coupled with the rescheduling process, raised the question of the value of the loans that the banks held in their portfolios, and this concern placed pressure on many banks to try to relieve or adjust their exposure in developing countries.

These factors led to the creation of a secondary market among the banks for developing country debt obligations. Banks began to trade or "swap" obligations on a discounted basis among themselves, an activity that became known as "debt swaps." The banks would trade debt among themselves for a variety of reasons. The smaller banks with limited exposure in a particular developing country might seek to eliminate that exposure completely by selling or swapping the debt. Large banks, on the other hand, might enter the loan-swap market to balance or adjust their portfolios. For example, a bank with significant Latin American debt might agree with another bank to exchange a portion of that debt for eastern European debt which the second bank was holding, in order to give its loan portfolio a more balanced geographic exposure.[115] Other banks, to reduce the administrative costs of rescheduling debt in numerous countries, used the debt-swap market to consolidate their Third World exposure to a few countries, thereby allowing them to concentrate their rescheduling efforts. For whatever reason a bank might enter this market, such swaps were also advantageous because the pure barter of one debt obligation for another did not require the banks to recognize a loss for accounting purposes. This new secondary market in developing country debt gave banks greater flexibility in managing their portfolios than in the past, when their only option had been merely to hold the loan to maturity.

For the first few years, loan swaps were purely an interbank matter. Once in a while, however, a speculator might purchase a loan at a significant discount in hopes of making a profit if the loan were paid in full at maturity. In 1985, changes in the laws and policies of certain developing countries led to the creation of a new group of buyers who entered the secondary market in order to purchase loans at a discount and then convert them to equity investments in the developing country that owed the debt.[116] Chile was the first to act in this area. Beginning in 1985, it allowed persons holding Chilean external debt, which was selling at a significant discount, to exchange it for local currency at or near the face value of the obligation and to use the proceeds for certain specified investment purposes within Chile. Thus, through this process, debt was swapped or converted into equity investment in Chile itself. Over time, other countries, including Mexico, the Philippines, and Brazil, adopted similar laws and policies to permit debt-to-equity conversions, thereby creating a new mechanism for encouraging foreign investment in their territories. By the end of 1987, it was estimated that nearly $10 billion in developing country debt had been converted to equity investment through this process.[117] In addition to those countries which have established formal debt-to-equity conversion programs, others have engaged in this process on an ad hoc basis, depending on the degree of financial difficulty in which they find themselves. Once a country resolves its debt problems, it usually suspends or repeals its debt-for-equity program. Thus by the year 2000, most conversion programs had

---

[115] See W Ollard, *The Debt Swappers, Euromoney* (August 1986) 67, 74–5 (swap of Nicaraguan for Venezuelan debt proved successful for bank); J Newman, "LDC Debt: The Secondary Market, the Banks, and New Investment in the Developing Countries," *Colum J World Bus* (Fall 1986) at 69, 69–70 (discussing portfolio management).

[116] See, eg, World Bank, *Report on Chilean Debt Conversion*, September 24, 1986, reprinted at 26 *Int'l Legal Mat* (1987) 819; *Philippines: Explanatory Memorandum on Philippine Investment Notes*, 26 *Int'l Legal Mat* (1987) 808; *Decree No. 1521, Gaceta Oficial de la Republica de Venezuela*, April 14, 1987, at 1, translated at 26 *Int' l Legal Mat* (1987) 801; Schubert, "Trading Debt for Equity," *Banker*, February 1987, at 18, 20 (Mexican rules). See generally "Recent Development," 28 *Harv Int'l LJ* (1987) 507 (discussing programs in Chile, Mexico, and the Philippines).

[117] *Wall Street Journal*, August 13, 1987, at 3, col 2.

been terminated or suspended.[118] In view of the fact that the risks of over-indebtedness and financial crises are always present, both host governments and investors should be aware that debt-equity conversion is always one option to help alleviate, though probably not solve, the problem.

(c) Types of Conversion Transactions

Debt conversions generally cover three types of transactions: debt capitalizations; debt-for-equity investments; and debt-for-local-currency conversions. All three are referred to commonly as "debt-swaps." All three usually require authorization by the host state's national legal framework.

(i) Debt Capitalization Transactions

In debt capitalizations, the holder of a loan to a developing country obligor converts it into an equity interest in the same obligor, usually without an intervening transaction. The holder of the obligation might be either the original lender to the enterprise or a person who has acquired the obligation, usually at a significant discount, in the secondary market. The impetus for the transaction is often the inability of the enterprise to make payment on its loan. Generally, debt capitalization is not applicable in the case of sovereign debt. Many developing country investment laws contain provisions which permit or encourage the conversion of a loan to an enterprise into an equity investment in the same enterprise.

(ii) Debt-for-Equity Transactions

The laws of some indebted countries may provide a mechanism whereby the investor may convert the debt of one obligor into an equity investment in a totally different entity. Such debt-for-equity conversion is normally carried out in a series of steps. First, the investor wishing to make an investment in a particular developing country purchases the debt obligations of that country at a significant discount in the secondary market. Second, the authorities in that country agree to convert the obligation at or near its face value in local currency if the investor agrees to invest such proceeds in a project approved by the host country authorities. Third, the host country government or the central bank provides the investor with local currency or its equivalent, and the investor proceeds to make the investment under conditions stipulated by the host country authorities. It is this type of transaction, aimed at stimulating new investment by foreigners, that has been the subject of greatest attention by developing countries.

(iii) Debt-for-Local-Currency Transactions

In order to attract the foreign currency holdings of their own nationals, some developing countries have facilitated the purchase of foreign debt by their nationals and its subsequent conversion into local currency at or near face value. Their nationals may then use the local currency in their home country, but not necessarily for investment alone. Debt for local currency conversion is basically a mechanism to facilitate the repatriation of capital that was previously taken out of the country by its own citizens.

---

[118] See generally, M Moye, *Overview of Debt Conversion* (2001) available at <http://www.dri.org.uk/pdfs/EngPub4_DebtConv.pdf>.

(d) Reasons for the Development of Debt-Equity Conversions

As can be seen, no debt-equity conversion transaction can take place without the approval—indeed the active encouragement—of the host country government. The conversion of a foreign obligation selling at a large discount abroad into local currency at the obligation's face value requires the cooperation of the Central Bank, the Ministry of Finance, and national monetary authorities. Further, the investment of those funds will necessitate the approval of the agencies responsible for regulating foreign investment. Certain countries have chosen to adopt laws and regulations to facilitate this process. A variety of reasons have prompted this action. First, the debt-for-equity conversion process is viewed as a means of reducing—albeit in a limited way—the country's foreign debt and therefore its payments of foreign exchange for debt servicing. Second, to the extent that debt-equity conversion leads to new foreign investment, the country will benefit from increased productive capacity, employment, technology transfers, tax revenues, and economic activity. In those countries whose political climate may not permit changes in existing foreign investment laws and policies, a debt-for-equity conversion program may allow a government to encourage foreign investment indirectly when it could not do so directly. Similarly, it may also be a politically acceptable way of reattracting capital that its own nationals have previously taken from the country by questionable means.

For the foreign investor, debt-to-equity conversion offers an opportunity to make an investment more cheaply than would be possible by a direct infusion of foreign currency which would be converted at the official rate of exchange. In effect, the host country is subsidizing such investment by allowing the foreign investor, through the use of external debt purchased at a discount, to obtain local currency at a highly advantageous exchange rate. For example, if the foreign investor is able to buy host country foreign debt in the secondary market at a 50 percent discount and then to convert it to local currency at face value, the host government is, in effect, giving the investor a special exchange rate that will yield twice the amount of local currency that would have been received had the investor merely undertaken an investment by a direct infusion of foreign funds. In order to relate the size of the subsidy to the magnitude of the benefit to be derived from the investor, Mexico redeemed its debt at varying percentages of the face value, depending on the importance of the investment to be undertaken. In addition to the problem of subsidizing investments unnecessarily, debt–equity conversions are criticized on the grounds that through this approach developing countries are needlessly prepaying their debts to the international banks.

For international commercial banks, debt-for-equity conversion offers a means of reducing developing country exposure, since the purchase of the debt by an investor removes it from a bank's portfolio. Moreover, it allows banks to earn fees for arranging or brokering debt-equity transactions.

All of these factors gave significant impetus to the debt-for-equity approach to investment in some developing countries. Many countries, however, resisted the trend at the time because of perceived difficulties.[119] First, they fear that this approach in many cases merely gives an unnecessary subsidy to foreign investment that would have taken place in any event without a debt-for-equity program. Thus, many governments seek assurance that the debt–equity approach will bring them new investment that they would not otherwise have obtained. Second, host countries fear that this mechanism will in the end merely facilitate

---

[119] See generally, "Recent Development," 28 *Harv Int'l LJ* (1987) 507, 513.

the outflow of capital through eventual repatriation of the investment and through the payment of fees and dividends abroad. To deal with this problem, countries adopting the debt–equity approach often imposed conditions on how the local currency, once converted, may be used. Chile, for example, provided that the capital from investments made through this mechanism may not be repatriated abroad for a period of ten years and that profits must accumulate during the first four years after the investment is made and may be repatriated only thereafter.

A further concern is that the increase in local currency pumped into the economy to extinguish the foreign debt may have serious inflationary effects within the host country. In some cases, instead of issuing currency, host government chose to issue obligations; but this method may have the effect of enlarging national budgetary deficits. In formulating their laws and regulations on debt–equity conversion programs, developing countries have tried to blunt the potential inflationary and negative budgetary consequences. One approach is to limit the amount to be converted. Chile, for example, determined the total amount it will convert each month and then allocated this quota by holding an auction of conversion rights among interested persons.

Beyond the direct impact of this debt–equity conversion on the local economy is the question of its effect on debtor countries' relationships with the international banks and other creditors. On the one hand, it may be argued that this process allows banks to lessen their exposure (albeit at a cost) in a given country while rehabilitating the credit of that country in the international economic community. On the other hand, by reducing pressure on the banks, debt–equity swaps weaken the ability of debtor countries to attain their fundamental objective—outright debt relief.

(e) The Structure of Debt–Equity Transactions

The laws and regulations governing debt-for-equity conversions are generally complex and vary significantly from country to country. Structuring a debt-to-equity transaction requires careful attention to the relevant legislation, as well as to the underlying loan agreement. With regard to the latter, it is important to structure the transaction so that it does not violate the *pari passu* clauses in most loan agreements prohibiting payments to one creditor in preference to another. Such clauses are intended to assure lenders equality of treatment. Rescheduling agreements between developing countries and their principal bank creditors typically contained provisions permitting debt–equity conversion provided that the investor's rights of repatriation are limited, at least for a period of time.

To illustrate the nature of such a transaction, the following is a step-by-step example of structuring a debt-to-equity under the Chilean program in accordance with Chile's Central Bank regulations then applicable.[120]

1. The foreign investor, wishing to make an investment in Chile, contacts a foreign broker dealing in sovereign debt in order to locate a Chilean foreign debt instrument available for prepayment at a discount. The foreign investor agrees to purchase the debt and pay the broker a fee for completing the transaction upon the completion of certain conditions.

2. Once the broker finds an appropriate debt instrument, the foreign investor obtains the agreement of the Chilean debtor to redenominate the debt at its face value into local currency at the official exchange rate.

---

[120] World Bank, *Report on Chilean Debt Conversion*, at 834–6.

3. The foreign investor then applies to the Central Bank to obtain permission to make an investment in Chile with the local currency proceeds of the debt capitalization transaction. The application describes the project in detail and identifies all parties involved. The investor also accepts restrictions on its ability to repatriate capital and profits. Moreover, the Central Bank may require the investor to waive the free repatriation provisions applicable to its prior investments and even to make a portion of the new investment in foreign exchange, in addition to the proceeds of the debt–equity swap.

4. Having obtained the necessary authorizations, the foreign investor actually purchases the debt instrument at a discount through its broker and pays the broker's fee. Normally, a debt rescheduling agreement between the country's creditor banks and its central Bank will have authorized the assignment of such debt.

5. The investor delivers the note to a Chilean bank along with an irrevocable mandate to collect in cash the face value of the redenominated note or to exchange it for a new instrument payable in local currency.

6. The Chilean bank, with the prior approval of the foreign creditor bank and the Chilean debtor, redenominates the debt in local currency equal to the face value of the foreign obligation converted at the official exchange rate, thus transforming the foreign exchange obligation.

7. The Chilean bank creates a new local currency debt instrument with the Chilean debtor as the direct obligor payable to bearer and denominated in Chilean currency and payable, for example, over 15 years. The foreign debt instrument (now denominated in local currency) is canceled and the new instrument is delivered to the Chilean broker.

8. The Chilean broker places the debt instrument in the domestic financial market and delivers the local currency proceeds to the Chilean bank with a mandate to disburse the funds directly for the purchase of the approved equity shares or other form of investment.

9. The equity shares or other evidence of the investment are delivered to the foreign investor.

7

The Challenges of Legal Change

7.1 The Nature of Legal Change

By virtue of their sovereignty, states not only have the power to make laws but they also have the power to change the laws that they have made. This power to effect legal change creates challenges for both foreign investors and host country governments.

On the one hand, host governments seek to assure foreigner investors, as a means to encourage inward capital flows, of the stability of the existing national legal framework for investment. They know that legal stability, predictability, and "calculability" encourage investment while legal *instability* discourages it. On the other hand, governments also recognize that, because the future is always uncertain, it may be necessary to alter the existing legal framework at some time in order to advance the government's and the public's interests. Thus, while giving all sorts of assurance to the world at large and to investors in particular of their commitment to legal stability, governments try hard to avoid all formal constraints, beyond national constitutional limitations, on their powers to change laws and regulations when necessary since they know that at some future time in particular circumstances they will have to use that power. The "right to regulate in the public interest"[1] is an inherent element of state sovereignty; it includes both the right to make new laws and regulations and to change the elements of the existing national legal framework.

Foreign investors, for their part, make their investment decisions on the basis of an evaluation of the national legal framework in existence at the time they commit their capital to the host country. That evaluation not only considers the benefits and costs of the existing national legal framework but also evaluates the degree to which it is *stable*— that is, the likelihood that the host state will continue to respect commitments in national law and regulations after the foreign investment has been made. An evaluation of the stability of the national legal framework is therefore an important step in arriving at a decision as to whether or not to invest in a particular country. For investors, any significant change to that framework that negatively affects profitability frustrates their legitimate expectations created by the national legal framework at the time of making the investment. They therefore consider such legal changes unfair and a violation of their rights.[2] In their interactions with governments, foreign investors therefore stress the need for legal stability, and they naturally oppose any legal change negatively affecting their investments. On the other hand, foreign investors do not resist all changes to the national legal framework. Indeed, once they have made an investment in a particular

---

[1] See, eg, the Ministerial Declaration adopted November 14, 2001 by World Trade Organization Ministerial Conference (Doha, November 9–14, 2001), in which the WTO members agreed to negotiate "a multilateral framework to secure transparent, stable and predictable conditions for long-term cross-border investment, particularly foreign direct investment" (Para 20) but that "Any framework should reflect in a balanced manner the interests of home and host countries, and take due account of the development policies and objectives of host governments as well as their right to regulate in the public interest." (para 22). Available at <http://www.wto .org/english/thewto_e/minist_e/min01_e/mindecl_e.htm>.

[2] An important strand of jurisprudence in investor–state arbitration holds that changes in the legal framework which frustrate investors' "legitimate expectations" violate investment treaty clauses that promise investors "fair and equitable treatment" of foreign investments. See JW Salacuse, *The Law of Investment Treaties* (2010) 231–7.

host country, they invariably seek to effect various legal and regulatory changes in ways that favor their interests through lobbying, negotiation, and other means. While investors may vigorously object to new environmental legislation that increases the costs of their operations, they may advocate equally vigorously for a legal change to reduce the corporate tax rate.

Every international investment, whether in the form of equity or debt, is based on a bargain, a "deal" between the foreign investor and the host government of the country in which the investment is made. For the foreign investor, the terms of that bargain are to be found in three basic sources: (1) the national legal framework of host country laws and regulations; (2) contracts that the investor has specifically entered into with the host government and other relevant parties; and (3) international obligations of the host country, usually found in treaties that it has made. Of the three sources, the national legal framework is the principal pillar of the investment bargain, for to a significant extent it influences that bargain's other elements. For one thing, investor property and contractual rights, the basic legal building blocks of their investments, are creatures of national law. National law not only creates rights, but it may also modify or cancel them. For another, all the basic rules governing the operations of the investment, from taxation to environmental protection, from labor relations to the importation of raw materials, are matters subject almost exclusively to national regulation.

Should future events lead a government to believe that an increase in the tax rate, a strengthening of environmental standards, or modification of the intellectual property regime is necessary to improve the lives of its citizens, it will normally proceed to make such changes despite the fact that investors—whether foreign or domestic—have relied on the previous national laws in making their investments. To counter objections from investors, host governments argue with justification that the existence of a particular law or regulation by no means implies that such law or regulation will not be modified or repealed if the need arises and that, absent a contrary undertaking, the host country has made no such specific commitment of legal permanence to the investor. Indeed, they would also point out that foreign investors would not expect their home country laws to be frozen in time; consequently, they should not expect unchanged laws in the host country. Changes in laws and regulations are a normal fact of business life in any country, and foreign investors need to deal with legislative and regulatory change in the normal course of doing business. It is a risk of doing business anywhere.

Most, if not nearly all, disputes between investors and host governments are fundamentally about the legitimacy of legal change. The host government asserts its right to make a legal change in the national framework to advance the public interest while the investor considers such change a deprivation of its existing rights. The argument between them is essentially a conflict between the investor's property rights and the government's right to regulate in the public interest.

The nature and severity of postinvestment legal changes to the national legal framework has a wide range of variations. Outright confiscation by virtue of a host government's legislative or executive act is probably the most extreme form of interference. Thus, for example, a host country seeking to take control of a particular industry might enact a law declaring that as of a certain date all assets within that industry are to become the property of the state, a specified state agency, or a government corporation. Instead of such a generalized taking of property, which is often referred to as "nationalization," the host country government may merely seize specific properties belonging to particular investors, an action which is known as "expropriation."[3] Regardless of whether a governmental interference with an investment occurs as a general nationalization or as a specific expropriation, the effect of such action is, or course, the same: the compulsory transfer of title and control of assets from the investor to the government. Thus, by virtue of legal change, the property rights of the investor previously recognized by the national legal framework are canceled.

Other significant changes in the national legal framework may not involve the actual taking of physical assets, but rather consist of an interference with established contractual relations. Thus, for example, governments that have made contracts with foreign companies to engage in mineral exploration, to develop a resort, or to construct and operate a power plant may subsequently take legal measures to cancel those contracts or drastically change their terms, thereby abolishing or greatly diminishing the investors' contractual rights. For the host government, such contract cancellation or modification is in the public interest, but for the investor the canceled or modified contract, previously recognized and enforced by the national legal framework, results in the loss of funds spent on the project up to the time of cancelation or modification, as well as deprivation or diminution of expected future profits.

Instead of actually expropriating assets, a host country government, seeking to stimulate national ownership of a particular area of business activity, might require, as Nigeria did in the 1970s,[4] that as of a specified date ownership of majority interests in all enterprises in designated industries must be in the hands of nationals of the host country. As a result, foreign investors in those industries now have a legal obligation, which did not exist under the legal framework at the time they made their investment, to negotiate sales of interests in their enterprises to host country nationals. As an alternative approach to forcing divestment, the host country government may instead declare its intention to purchase a certain percentage of a foreign-owned industry and thereafter enter into negotiations with foreign investors for the purchase of all or a portion of such foreign-owned properties. Venezuela employed this technique in 1976 to take control of the Venezuelan petroleum industry, which at that time was primarily owned by Americans.[5] Thirty years later, at the beginning of the twenty-first century, as a result of an increase in oil prices, the Venezuelan government would use the same approach by forcing the renegotiation of operating agreements with foreign oil companies under a threat of contract cancelation.[6]

Instead of adopting any of the overt, direct approaches indicated above, a host country government may choose to gain control over an investment project through "creeping expropriation," a process whereby the government increasingly imposes controls and restrictions upon the investment project, or denies its benefits granted to locally owned enterprises. The result of such actions is to make it difficult, or impossible,

---

[3] JF Truitt, *Expropriation of Private Foreign Investment* (1974) 5. Governments sometimes refer to such acts of interference as a "requisition," a term which connotes a temporary seizure as opposed to a permanent taking. The 1989 International Court of Justice case between the United States and Italy involved the "requisition" for an initial period of six months by the Mayor of Palermo, Italy, of the plant and assets of an Italian subsidiary of an American corporation in an effort to prevent the closing of the plant and the dismissal of its employees. See *Elettronica Sicula SpA* (*ELSI*), Judgment, *ICJ Reports* 1989, at 15, reprinted in (1989) 28 *Int'l Legal Mat* 1109.

[4] The Nigerian Enterprises Promotion Decree, No 4 of 1972. See MI Jegede, "The Nigerian Enterprises Promotion Decree No. 4 of 1972," (1973) *The Nig LJ* (1973) 153–9.

[5] See FP Rossi-Guerrero, "The Transition from Private to Public Control in the Venezuelan Petroleum Industry," 9 *Vand J Transnat'l L* (1976) 475.

[6] J Cárdena García, "Rebalancing Oil Contracts in Venezuela," 33 *Houston Journal of International Law* (2011) 235–301.

for the foreign investor to continue to do business at a profit, thereby ultimately leading it to "sell" its property to the government or local investors—usually at a bargain price.[7] Although the ultimate disposition of the property may appear to be a legitimate sale in form, such "sale" has been concluded only as the result of governmental pressure and therefore in substance may be little different from an outright expropriation. Following World War II, "creeping expropriation" became an increasingly prevalent type of host country interference with foreign investment through changes in the national legal framework.[8]

And finally, even though the host country government has no intention of actually acquiring the investment, it may nonetheless, through the exercise of its legislative or executive powers, so change conditions as to alter radically the profitability of the project. Thus, for example, the host government may amend the tax to increase the tax rate or impose exchange controls to prevent or limit repatriation of profits. Such interference may effectively inhibit the operation of the project; however, it would not ordinarily constitute a "taking" under international law and therefore constitute expropriation. As will be seen in Chapter 15, determining whether a host government's action amounts to expropriation of the investment or merely a legitimate regulation is not always easy; however, that determination has vital significance for a variety of important issues, including the ability of the investor to secure assistance from its government, to receive compensation under foreign investment insurance, to obtain favorable tax treatment for the loss, and to pursue a claim against the host government in international arbitration under a bilateral investment treaty.

The methods by which governments seek to modify investor property rights have evolved over time. Whereas outright expropriation and contract cancelation through government seizure were common until the 1980s, it became an increasingly rare phenomenon thereafter. In the twenty-first century, governments dissatisfied with the original bargains made with foreign investors rarely send their troops to seize a factory or occupy a mine. Instead, they use their legislative and regulatory power in more subtle ways to alter the benefits flowing to the investor from the investment. Thus, a government may impose new regulations on the way the investment is operated, raise taxes on the investment substantially, or unilaterally change a contract to reduce the revenues flowing to a concessionaire. The investor remains in possession of the investment, and its title and control is not usually affected; however, the amount and nature of the benefits originally contemplated are significantly reduced. In legal terms, these regulatory actions diminish the nature of the investor's property rights over the investment, as originally established by the national legal system, and, if sufficiently extreme, may constitute a form of expropriation or dispossession. Such actions may rise to the level of an "indirect" expropriation, sometimes referred to as "regulatory taking."[9] They have become the most common type of intervention with foreign investments by host governments in the twenty-first century.

---

[7] See DVagts, "Coercion and Foreign Investment Rearrangements," 72 *Am J Int'l L* (1978) 17. See also LJ Creel, Jr, "Mexicanization: A Case of Creeping Expropriation," 22 *Sw L J* (1968) 281.

[8] For background on creeping expropriation, see generally, US Dep't of State, Bureau of Intelligence and Research, *U.S. Department of State Report on Nationalization, Expropriation, and Other Takings of U.S. and Certain Foreign Property Since 1960*, Study RECS-14, November 30, 1971, reproduced in 11 *Int'l Legal Mat* (1972) 84–118.

[9] SR Ratner, "Regulatory Takings in the Institutional Context Beyond the Fear of Fragmented International Law," 102 *AJIL* (2008) 475.

7.2 The Forces for Legal Change

(a) In General

An analysis of the stability of a national legal framework and the likelihood of legal change negatively affecting foreign investment must take account of the forces that prompt host governments to alter their legal and regulatory systems to the detriment of foreign investments As indicated above, a foreign investment rests on a bargain between the foreign investor and the host country government. The terms of that bargain are largely based on the national legal framework and the investment's contractual framework. By virtue of its legislative and regulatory authority, a host government has the power to change the terms of that bargain virtually at will once the investment is made. As a result, all foreign investments are in the oft-quoted words of Raymond Vernon, "obsolescing bargains" between the investor and the host country.[10]

The investment bargain's obsolescence has much to do with two important factors: (1) changing circumstances and (2) the decline in the investor's bargaining power after making the investment. With regard to the first factor, states, like rational private parties, will generally continue to respect their obligations to the extent that the perceived net benefits exceed those of nonperformance. But when, for whatever reason, a state judges that the net benefits of continuing performance are less than the net benefits of not performing, the result will usually be rejection of the obligation or, at the very least, a demand to renegotiate the original undertaking.[11] For example, a developing country that is attracted to a mining project proposed by a French mining company by the prospect of high revenues may eagerly enter into a mineral development contract with that company. But, if after a few years revenues do not meet governmental expectations, or if another mining company promises higher income, the government will cancel the contract if it concludes that the cost of doing so will not exceed the benefits to be derived from a new arrangement. In making this calculation, the host government weighs the expected benefits from a new arrangement against such political and economic costs as defending against a lawsuit or arbitration brought by the French company, as well as any sanctions that the French government might impose, such as a reduction in foreign aid.

The concept of costs and benefits is not limited to purely economic factors. When states are involved, the costs and benefits of both political and social effects will weigh heavily in any decision to continue or end an undertaking. For example, in one case involving a foreign investment project designed to build a luxury resort near the Giza pyramids in Egypt, the Egyptian government originally signed the agreement believing the economic benefits of the project would exceed its costs. But, when public and international opposition became strong and persistent, the government canceled the project. The government judged that the project's political costs outweighed the economic benefits to be derived from its construction.[12]

A second factor that contributes to the obsolescence of state undertakings is the decline in an investor's bargaining power after making an investment. When proposing an investment, the investor has a certain amount of bargaining power to secure favorable treatment and

---

[10] R Vernon, *Sovereignty at Bay: The Multinational Spread of U.S. Enterprises* (1971) 46.

[11] The prevailing system of governance in the host country may also affect the degree to which the investment bargain becomes "obsolete." An UNCTAD study has found that the lack of democracy and of constraints of executive action increases the likelihood of obsolescing bargains. See J Jakobsen, "Does Democracy Moderate the Obsolescing Bargain Mechanism? An Empirical Analysis, 1983–2001" 15 *Transnational Corporations* (2001) 67–106, available at <http://www.unctad.org/en/docs/iteiit20063a3_en.pdf>.

[12] *SPP (Middle East), Ltd, and Southern Pacific Properties Ltd v. The Arab Republic of Egypt*, ICC Case No 3493 (Award) (March 11, 1983), (1983) 22 ILM (1983) 752.

conditions for its investment because of the government's desire to acquire the investment. However, once the investor has invested and so placed its capital under the sovereignty of the host state, its bargaining power with the host state diminishes and the original investment bargain runs the risk of becoming obsolete in the eyes of the host government since the investor no longer has the bargaining power to maintain the original bargain.

Various forces or factors lead to the changed circumstances and diminished bargaining power that result in legal change. Those among the more significant follow.

(b) Financial and Political Crises

In the face of financial and political crises, host governments often feel compelled to take extraordinary measures which, while not specifically directed at foreign investments, nonetheless may have a significant negative effect on their operations or profitability. A case in point concerns Argentina. In 1991, in an effort to curb inflation and attract foreign investment, the Argentine government enacted what was known as "the Convertibility Law,"[13] which tied or "pegged" the exchange rate of Argentine currency to the US dollar by guaranteeing that the Central Bank of Argentina would exchange a fixed amount of Argentine currency for a fixed amount of US dollars. Ultimately the Argentine peso was pegged to the US dollar at a rate of one peso per dollar. By 2001, Argentina had exhausted its supply of dollars and other convertible currency, plunging the country into an economic crisis. To cope with the crisis, the government felt compelled to change the existing national legal framework through several drastic measures. They included a decree[14] imposing a "*corralito*" or "little fence" upon bank accounts so as to limit the amounts of cash withdrawals by account holders, the imposition of new taxes, and most drastic of all the adoption of the Emergency Law,[15] which (i) abolished the link between the Argentine peso and the US dollar, resulting in a significant depreciation of the Argentine peso; (ii) abolished the adjustment of public service contracts according to previously agreed indexations; and (iii) authorized the Executive branch of government to renegotiate all public service contracts. The consequences of these measures was a radical transformation of the national and contractual legal frameworks upon which foreign investors had relied in making their investments, causing substantial financial losses to foreign investors who subsequently brought numerous claims against the Argentine government for compensation.

(c) Changes in Government or Prevailing Ideology

A radical change in government, may ultimately lead to acts of expropriation, contract cancelations or other alterations of an investment's legal framework. Thus, the coming to power of a nationalist or socialist government may signal the expropriation of foreign investments invited into the country by a more conservative, previous regime. For example, when a nationalist government was elected to power in the Indian state of Maharashtra in 1993, it proceeded to cancel a massive electric power development agreement that its predecessor government had signed with an American corporation a few years before.[16] Similarly, the attainment of the Venezuela Presidency by Hugo Chavez, who had a strong

---

[13] Law No 23,928 (*Ley de la Convertibilidad del Austral*) of March 28, 1991.
[14] Decree No 1570/01 of December 3, 2001.
[15] Law No 25, 561 of January 6, 2002.
[16] RP Teisch and WA Stoever, "Enron in India: Lessons from a Renegotiation," 35 *Mid-Atlantic J Bus* (1999) 51–62.

populist ideology, led to measures to renegotiate arrangements with foreign investors in the petroleum sector.[17]

(d) Perceived Economic and Political Necessity

In many cases, changes in the legal framework for foreign investment are motivated not by ideology, but by perceived economic and political necessity. Thus, the perception that the country's economy, as a result of foreign investment, has become excessively dependent on outsiders, that the foreign investment project is exploiting the country and taking a disproportionate share of national resources, and that it brings the economy under the undue influence of foreigners are all factors that may ultimately prompt the host country government to correct the situation through legislative or regulatory intervention. Moreover, the host government may decide that its plans for economic development make such interference a necessity. With the emergence of infant industries that compete with foreign firms, the host country government may decide that it is in the best interests of the national economy to curtail, through expropriation or regulation, the competition offered by the foreign enterprises. In addition, negative host government actions against foreign investment may be tied to its foreign policy. For example, Cuba and Libya expropriated American property in retaliation against allegedly hostile US actions. Also, it sometimes happens that in order to forestall the closing of a foreign-owned plant or the termination of a foreign investment project—with the resulting detrimental consequences to the economy—the host country government may nationalize the plant in order to assure that it continues to operate and that its workers remain employed.[18]

(e) Governmental Desire to Improve the Investment Bargain

Having observed the performance of a foreign investment for a period of time, a host government may conclude that the original bargain between the government and the investor is no longer fair or in the best interests of the country because of a change in circumstances. Through the use of its legislative and regulatory powers, it will seek to alter the bargain so as to increase the benefits flowing to the host country with a corresponding diminution in benefits going to the investors. Thus, a substantial rise in commodity prices may cause governments to raise the royalty rates or taxes being paid by foreign investors producing those commodities.

(f) The Advancement of Public Welfare

Host governments, like governments in any country, will change national law in order to advance public welfare. Thus a government may adopt legislation to strengthen environmental standards, provide for greater consumer protection, or improve the health and safety of its citizens. Such legislation may also impose costs on investors and therefore reduce contemplated returns on the investment they have made. For example, in 2006, Uruguay, in an effort to reduce smoking among its population, passed new legislation to

---

[17] J Cárdena García, "Rebalancing Oil Contracts in Venezuela," 33 *Houston Journal of International Law* (2011) 235–301.
[18] See, eg, *Elettronica Sicula SpA* (*ELSI*), Judgment, *ICJ Reports* 1989, at 15, reprinted in 28 *Int'l Legal Mat* (1989) 1109, in which the Mayor of Palermo, Italy, "requisitioned" a plant owned by a foreign investor who had decided to close it.

limit cigarette advertising and to require large visible warnings on cigarette packaging with respect to the dangers of smoking. In opposition to these measures, a major foreign investor brought an arbitration case against Uruguay on the grounds that these legal changes violated the country's commitments to it under a relevant bilateral investment treaty.[19]

7.3 Investor Strategies for Coping with the Risk of Legal Change

Aware of the risk of legal instability to their investments, foreign investors in host countries employ a variety of strategies to protect against or at least mitigate the negative effects of changing laws and regulations after they have made an investment commitment. Such strategies fall into five broad categories: (a) international law strategies; (b) diplomatic strategies; (c) management strategies; (d) third-party insurance strategies; and (e) contract strategies. This chapter examines each strategy briefly; subsequent chapters will discuss particular applications in greater depth.

(a) International Law Strategies

Western capital-exporting states have taken the position for many years that international law places certain constraints upon host countries' rights to regulate foreign investments and investors. Beginning in the nineteenth century, western governments asserted that customary international law required that host states grant investors a "minimum standard of treatment." Legislative and regulatory acts violating this minimum standard gave rise to host states' international responsibility and a resulting obligation to compensate the investor for any injury which such acts caused. Capital-importing countries, however, denied that such a rule of international law existed. They contended that they owed foreign investors merely "national treatment," that is, treatment no less favorable than they afforded their own nationals. The implication of their position was clear: international law placed no limits on their ability to regulate foreign investors in their territory.

In response, capital-exporting states adopted a new strategy to protect their investors against harmful legal change in host countries: Following the end of World War II, they began to negotiate treaties governing the treatment owed by host governments to foreign investors. Investment treaties, often referred to as "international investment agreements" (IIAs), are essentially instruments of international law by which states (1) make commitments to other states with respect to the treatment they will accord to investors and investments from those other states and (2) agree on some mechanism for the enforcement of those commitments. Three basic types of investment agreements have evolved during that period: (1) bilateral investment treaties, commonly known as "BITs," (2) bilateral economic agreements with investment provisions, and (3) other investment-related agreements involving more than two states. As a result of the surge in treaty making undertaken by states since the end of World War II, the total number of treaties with meaningful provisions relating to foreign investment as of the beginning of 2010 exceeded 3,100.[20] By entering into an investment treaty, a state makes promises about the actions and behaviors—that is, the treatment—it will give to investments and investors of its treaty partners

---

[19] *Philip Morris Brand Sàrl (Switzerland), Philip Morris Products SA (Switzerland) and Abal Hermanos SA (Uruguay) v. Oriental Republic of Uruguay*, (ICSID Case No ARB/10/7).

[20] UNCTAD, *World Investment Report 2011* (2011) 100, reporting that there were 2,807 BITs and 309 "other IIAs."

in the future.[21] The treaty provisions on investor and investment treatment are intended to restrain host country government behavior and to impose a discipline on governmental actions, particularly its regulatory actions affecting foreign investments. They seek to achieve this goal by defining a *standard* to which host countries' governments must conform in their treatment of investors and investments. State actions that fail to meet the defined standard constitute treaty violations that engage the offending state's international responsibility and render it potentially liable to pay compensation for the injury it has caused.

International investment agreements can be viewed as devices to restrain host governments from engaging in illegitimate legal change. The standards of treatment employed to achieve this result bear a remarkable similarity in language and concept. Thus, nearly all investment treaties require host states to respect the norms of "fair and equitable treatment," "full protection and security," "most-favored-national treatment," "national treatment," and "nondiscriminatory treatment" with respect to protected investors and their investments. As of 2011, aggrieved investors relying on alleged treaty rights had brought more than three hundred investor-arbitration cases, many of which challenged legal changes that host governments sought to make in a foreign investment's legal framework. About one-third of the cases have resulted in substantial damage awards against governments. In other cases, the threat of suit has led to a negotiated settlement and revision of the challenged legal change.[22] In general, the existence of investment treaties appears to have imposed a restraint to some extent on the ability of host governments to effect certain legal changes in the national legal framework governing foreign investments. Chapters 14 and 15 will examine in detail the nature and evolution of this emerging international investment law regime.[23]

(b) Diplomatic Strategies

Foreign investors have traditionally relied on their home governments to protect their interests through diplomacy with host governments. Their home governments, for their part, have taken the position that customary international law gives them the right to pursue claims against foreign countries that illegally injure their nationals, a process that is known as "diplomatic protection."[24] Thus, investors threatened with the prospect of undesirable changes in the legal framework for their investments often urge their home governments to make various representations to host governments to dissuade them from

---

[21] In the ICSID case of *Suez, Sociedad General de Aguas de Barcelona SA, and Vivendi Universal SA v. The Argentine Republic* (ICSID case no ARB/O3/19), the tribunal defined "treatment" as follows: "The word 'treatment' is not defined in the treaty text. However, the ordinary meaning of that term within the context of investment includes the rights and privileges granted and the obligations and burdens imposed by a Contracting State on investments made by investors covered by the treaty." *Suez, Sociedad General de Aguas de Barcelona SA, and Vivendi Universal SA v. The Argentine Republic* (ICSID case no ARB/O3/19), Decision on Jurisdiction, August 3, 2006, para 55.

[22] For example, in the face of the arbitration claim brought by Phillip Morris against Uruguay because of its new regulations on cigarette advertising, mentioned in n 19, the Uruguay government indicated a willingness to modify the new legislation. R Carroll, "Uruguay Bows to Pressure Over Anti-Smoking Law Amendment," *The Guardian*, July 27, 2010, available at <http://www.guardian.co.uk/world/2010/jul/27/uruguay-tobacco-smoking-philip-morris>.

[23] See generally, JW Salacuse, "The Emerging Global Regime for Investment," 51 *Harvard International Law Journal* (2010) 427–73.

[24] "In precise language, diplomatic protection can be defined as a procedure for giving effect to State responsibility involving breaches of international law arising out of legal injuries to the person or property of the citizen of a State. With the expansion of economic and commercial intercourse between nations, diplomatic protection evolved into a rule of customary international law." J Cuthbert, *Nationality and Diplomatic Protection* (1969) 1.

making such changes and, in cases where such changes have actually taken place, to persuade them to reconsider. The assumption behind the use of diplomatic strategies is that the multifaceted relationship between host country and home country is sufficiently valuable to the host state that the threat of injuring that relationship would serve to restrain host governments from making injurious precipitous legal changes in the investment framework.

(c) Protective Business Strategies

Foreign investors incorporate into the organization and management of their investments various techniques designed to protect their investments from undesirable changes in their legal frameworks. Generally speaking, such techniques focus on one of two areas: (i) public and governmental relations and (ii) asset protection.

(i) *Governmental and Public Relations*

Foreign investors often manage their operations on the assumption that if the government, important local interest groups, and the public in general view the investment project favorably the government is less likely to enact negative changes in the investment legal framework. Such perception is dependent on the belief that the government, important local interest groups and the public in general are deriving benefits from the project. The foreign investor may therefore attempt to give its investment project as much of a local or national identity as possible so as to convince the host government and the public that the enterprise is managed in a way that is consistent with national goals and policies.

Foreign investors engage in this strategy in a variety of ways. One common way is take a local entrepreneur or company as a partner in the investment. Another is to appoint host country nationals to management positions. Yet another is to designate nationals, particularly those who are especially acceptable to governmental officials in the host country, as consultants to the investment project or to serve on the project company's board of directors. On the other hand, given the political volatility of many countries, local persons who were once in favor with the government can easily fall out of favor and thus bring governmental disapproval to investment projects in which they are involved. If a local public securities market exists and the foreign investment project is sufficiently mature, a portion of the equity in the project might be sold to the public. A wide distribution of shares enhances the national image of the investment project and gives host country nationals a vested interest in its economic success, while still permitting the foreign investor to retain a controlling position. Other devices to give the project a national image include training local personnel to assume skilled positions in the investment enterprise and developing commercial relations with host country businesses so as to integrate the project as much as possible into the local economy, while making strong efforts to communicate these facts to the government and the public.[25]

(ii) *Asset Protection*

Foreign investors adopt a variety of structural devices to protect their assets from adverse changes in the investment legal framework. Such structural devices may include

---

[25] JF Truitt, *Expropriation of Private Foreign Investment* (1974) 50.

participation in the investment project of investors from more than one foreign country. This technique is based on the theory that a host country government is less likely to expropriate or interfere with a project in which numerous foreign nationals are involved since multinational participation would lead to diplomatic difficulties with numerous foreign countries, while the expropriation of a project owned by persons having a single foreign nationality would result in conflict with only a single foreign government. The risk of expropriation is also reduced by spreading the equity ownership among participants from several foreign countries.

Segregating assets into separate legal entities may allow the investor to minimize the loss resulting from expropriation and nationalization. For example, if the host country is interested in certain types of assets, such as mineral deposits, but not particularly concerned about other property, such as office buildings and equipment, the investor might consider segregating the two types of assets into separate legal entities. Then too, to reduce financial exposure, it might seek to keep inventories of components, raw materials, and supplies to a minimum necessary to maintain production at an appropriate level. And in order to further minimize the net tangible assets of the project, investors often seek to lease or finance such assets from local sources, without of course providing guarantees from the foreign investor's corporation or other external entity. In addition, the investor engaged in the production of raw materials might as a protective measure establish his processing operations outside the jurisdiction of the host country. A further option is to operate the investment project as a branch, rather than as a subsidiary, if such is permitted by local law. It has been argued that such an approach establishes a basis for claiming that any assets of the project outside the host country are not subject to expropriation by the host government.[26]

When nationalization, expropriation, changes in exchange control laws, or other forms of governmental interference appear likely, some investors may become cautious about returning hard currency proceeds of foreign sales to the host country. For example, the project might deposit export earnings in a foreign bank or use them to make advance deposits on external purchases or to make loans to affiliated entities. Moreover, it might extend lengthy credit terms to certain of its recognized customers to delay the repatriation of foreign exchange earnings to the host country. Occasionally, more elaborate structural devices are used. For example, Mexicana de Cobre, SA (Mexcobre), a Mexican copper producer, negotiated to obtain a $210 million three-year loan from a syndicate of international banks led by Banque Paribas at an attractive interest rate. Although Mexcobre was a profitable company, the banks were concerned about the risk of governmental controls that might prevent payment of principal and interest, which amounted to $8 million a month for 36 months. To deal with this problem, Mexcobre entered into a long-term copper sales contract with SOGEM, a European copper buyer, whereby SOGEM would make its monthly payments for the copper into Mexcobre's escrow account with the Banque Paribas branch in New York. Banque Paribas would automatically deduct Mexcobre's payments on the loan each month from the account.[27]

Other strategies to reduce the risks of expropriation and negative legal changes include organizing the investment project in such a way that it is dependent upon the supply of technology, spare parts, components, and raw materials from one of the investor's other subsidiaries outside the host country. Not only may such a dependency dissuade the host

---

[26] PR Stansbury, "Planning Against Expropriation," 24 *Int'l Law* (1990) 677, 679.
[27] L Jacque and G Hawamini, "Myths and Realities of the Global Capital Market: Lessons for Financial Managers," *Journal of Applied Corporate Finance* (Fall 1993) 81, 89–90.

government from expropriatory action—since the enterprise may not be able to function without the continued cooperation of the investor—but it may also place the investor in a position, if the project is expropriated, to negotiate adequate compensation, as well as lucrative technology transfer and supply agreements, due to its possession of the necessary technology and components.

(d) Third-Party Insurance Strategies

A fourth important strategy to protect investments against the risks posed by certain changes in law and regulations is to secure insurance against that risk from a third party. In such transactions, the insurer, for consideration, agrees to bear the risk and to compensate the insured should the risk come to pass.

Traditionally, a foreign investor has been able to obtain protection from some, but not all, of the risks of legislative instability by securing political risk insurance. Political risk insurance does not protect the investor or the project against all possible risks; it only protects against certain specified political risks. Under most insurance programs, an investor may purchase protection against one or more of the following three political risks: (1) inconvertibility of local currency into convertible foreign exchange; (2) expropriation and measures affecting contractual rights; and (3) damage from political violence such as war, revolution, insurrection, and civil strife.

Political risk insurance is available from private companies, governmental agencies in capital-exporting countries, and an international organization, the Multilateral Investment Guarantee Agency (MIGA), an affiliate of the World Bank. Coverage by private companies is generally more expensive and less comprehensive than insurance offered by governmental programs and by MIGA. As a result, the latter two have become the primary sources of such protection. In the United States, the Overseas Private Investment Corporation (OPIC) is the principal institution from which an American investor may obtain insurance against the political risks to its investments in foreign countries. Chapter 11 treats OPIC, MIGA, and other types of political risk insurance in detail.

In addition to traditional foreign investment insurance, there exist specialized types of insurance on certain investment transactions. For example, investors in foreign sovereign bonds may purchase "credit default swaps," which are agreements with an insurer to compensate the purchaser of a debt instrument in the event of a loan or bond default.

(e) Contractual Strategies

In an effort to minimize the risks of legal instability, foreign investors enter into specific agreements with host country governments, stipulating in detail the rights and privileges of the investors and their investment. Variously called "economic development agreements,"[28] "state contracts," or "foreign investment contracts," such agreements often contain provisions that seek to protect the investor and the investment from adverse changes in the national legal framework, as well as to assure them of special governmental privileges and benefits. For example, they may contain commitments not to expropriate except upon payment of just compensation, guarantees on repatriation of profits and capital, and stabilization clauses ensuring that future changes in legislation will not impose

---

[28] See generally, J Hyde, "Economic Development Agreements," 105 *Hague Recueil* (1992) 271; CT Curtis, "The Legal Security of Economic Development Agreements," 29 *Harv Int'l L J* (1989) 317; and I Pogany, "Economic Development Agreements," 7 *ICSID Review* (1992) 1.

more onerous conditions on the project than those that existed at the time it was undertaken. In more recent times, the privatizations of important public services, such as the provision of water, sewerage, electricity, and telecommunications, by governments have also taken the form of concession contracts between the government and the foreign investor which stipulate precise rules governing the pricing system to be used by the investor to assure an adequate cash flow over ten, twenty or even thirty years in the future.

Despite the existence of strong contractual language, investors are concerned about the effectiveness of such contractual arrangements in restraining adverse governmental action in the future. An initial and basic problem with respect to such agreements is whether a sovereign state can bind itself in a contract not to use its sovereign powers. From a theoretical point of view, a state cannot effectively bind itself not to expropriate property or to amend its laws in the future since the power to expropriate and to legislate stems from its power of eminent domain and is an inherent part of its sovereignty. Since its purpose as a sovereign state is to secure the public interest of its citizens and to safeguard their welfare, the state must remain free to exercise its right of eminent domain when circumstances so require.[29] To give up the power to expropriate private property or to legislate on other matters would be to give up its status as a sovereign state.

Moreover, if a contract is a creature of the host country law, the host country should be able to alter that contract by a subsequent law. It is often held that the legislative power of a sovereign state cannot be limited by a contractual provision, particularly where such legislation is for the public benefit.[30] Indeed, many legal systems in the industrialized world allow the government under certain conditions to interfere with contracts in the public interest in certain situations.[31] The breach of state contracts and other obligations to investors is not ordinarily considered a breach of international law. The Permanent Court of International Justice in the *Serbian Loans* case[32] stated that "any contract which is not a contract between States in their capacity as subjects of international law is based on the domestic law of some country." More recently, in *Noble Ventures v. Romania*,[33] a case involving alleged breaches of an agreement to privatize a Romanian steel enterprise made by Romanian authorities, an ICSID tribunal stated:

> . . . the well established rule of general international law that in normal circumstances *per se* a breach of a contract by the State does not give rise to direct international responsibility on the part of the State. This derives from the clear distinction between municipal law on the one hand and international law on the other, two separate legal systems (or orders) . . . .[34]

In order to meet these theoretical and practical limitations on the use of contractual provisions to protect investments, foreign investors have sought to develop devices to "internationalize" such contracts, to remove them from the purview of host country law and make them subject to a body of law over which the host government has no control. In short, they have sought to use contracts and international law to restrain the legislative

---

[29] I Delupis, *Finance and Protection of Investments in Developing Countries* (1973) 31.

[30] M Sornarajah, The *International Law on Foreign Investment* (2nd edn 2004) 410.

[31] PM Norton, "A Law of the Future or A Law of The Past? Modern Tribunals and the International Law of Expropriation," 85 *American J Int'l L* (1991) 474, 493. See also M Sornarajah, *The International Law on Foreign Investment* (2nd edn 2004) 422–3, who argues that state contracts with private parties are universally recognized as defeasible in the public interest and that no illegality can be attached to its breach by the state if such breach is for a public purpose.

[32] (1929) PCIJ Rep Series A No 20, 41.

[33] *Noble Ventures, Inc v. Romania*, ICSID Case No ARB/01/11 (Award) (October 12, 2005).

[34] *Noble Ventures, Inc v. Romania*, ICSID Case No ARB/01/11 (Award) (October 12, 2005), 53.

power of sovereign states as a means to protect their investments abroad. Investment agreements with governments are designed and negotiated to apply to a specific investment in a particular country; consequently, they demonstrate great diversity in content. Nonetheless, investors attempt to rely on four clauses in particular for protection from undesirable legal change. They include the following.

(i) Choice-of-Law Provisions

In order to isolate the contract from future undesirable changes in the law of the host country, the investor may seek to include a provision in the contract which subjects the agreement to a body of law other than that of the host country.[35] Although the validity of this approach was challenged at one time on the assumption that a contract between a state and a foreign national had to be governed by the state's municipal law, it is now generally agreed that the parties to the agreement may choose another law to govern its provisions.[36] Theoretically, the range of choices open to the parties is broad and may include: the domestic law of the investor's home country; the domestic law of a third country; international law; "general principles of law"; legal principles common to the legal systems of both parties; and some combination of any of the preceding choices.[37]

Despite the breadth of the *theoretical* range of choices concerning the law applicable to an investment or economic development agreement, the foreign investor has relatively few real choices in practice. Although a foreign investor in former days might have been able to impose a foreign law on the contract, in today's world of heightened economic and political nationalism few host country governments would accept a foreign law provision. As a result, the vast majority of choice of law provisions in economic development and investment agreements provides that the applicable law shall be that of the host country.[38] International loan agreements, however, invariably opt for the law of the creditor or of one of the principal international financial centers, such as London or New York.

While a host country may categorically refuse to accept a provision applying foreign law, it may, under certain circumstances, agree to the application of international law or general international principles to the agreement. Although international law may be vague on many points, an investor may consider that it offers protection superior to that offered by the legal system of the host country. For one thing, the maxim *pacta sunt servanda*—that contracts are to be performed—is generally considered a fundamental principle of

---

[35] For a detailed discussion of choice-of-law provisions, see Chapter 8, section 8.2(a). See also R Brown, "Choice of Law in Concession and Related Contracts," (1976) 39 *Mod L Rev* 625. See also GA Bermann, "Contracts Between States and Foreign Nationals: A Reassessment," in Smit, Galston and Levitsky (eds), *International Contracts* (1981) 183–95. See CN Brower, "International Legal Protection of United States Investment Abroad," in W Surrey and D Wallace (eds), *A Lawyer's Guide to International Business Transactions* 3, (2nd edn 1981) 30–4. In earlier times, another reason for choosing foreign law to govern the concession agreement was that the law of the host country was vague, uncertain, or unfavorable with respect to important questions affecting the investment project.

[36] G Bermann, "Contracts Between States and Foreign Nationals: A Reassessment," in Smit, Galston and Levitsky (eds), *International Contracts* (1981) 187–9. But see M Sornarajah, *The International Law on Foreign Investment* (2nd edn 2004) 410–13 for a contrary view. It may be noted that Article 42(l) of the World Bank Convention on the Settlement of Investment Disputes between States and Nationals of Other States, 17 UST 1270, TIAS No 6090, 575 UNTS 159, provides as follows: "The tribunal shall decide a dispute in accordance with such rules of law as may be agreed by the parties. In the absence of such agreement, the tribunal shall apply the law of the contracting state party to the dispute (including its rules on the conflict of laws) and such rules of international law as may be applicable."

[37] G van Hecke, "Contracts Subject to International or Transnational Law," in Smit, Galston and Levitsky (eds), *International Contracts* (1981) 26–8.

[38] GR Delaume, "State Contracts and Transnational Arbitration," 75 *Am J Int'l L* (1981) 784, 796.

international law.[39] This principle may be applied to require a state to respect its contractual obligations to a foreign national where such obligations are embodied in agreements specifically subjected to international law. For example, in arbitrations rising out of Libya's nationalization of foreign oil interests and its repudiation of related obligations embodied in deeds and concessions with the nationalized parties, three separate international arbitrations applied the principle of *pacta sunt servanda* to the Libyan agreements and held Libya liable for its failure to respect its commitments.[40]

Choice of law provisions which seek to "internationalize" investment contracts between the host country and the foreign investor may refer only to international law, or "the general principles of law," or they may provide for the application of some combination of domestic and international law. For example, the choice of law provision applied in the Libyan arbitration cases provided that the applicable law was to be the "principles of law of Libya common to the principles of international law and in the absence of such common principles then by and in accordance with the general principles of law, including such of those principles as may have been applied by international tribunals."[41]

(ii) Dispute Settlement Provisions

In order to provide additional protection for an investment, foreign investors seek to obtain an agreement from the host country government that any dispute with the government relating to the investment shall be resolved in a forum outside the host country, rather than in host country courts. The purpose of such a provision is to assure the investor of a neutral tribunal that will not be biased in favor of or influenced by the host government. While it is theoretically possible to select a court of a foreign country to decide such matters, investment agreements, with the exception of international loans, rarely provide for this option, if only because of national sensitivities of the host country government to subjecting itself to the jurisdiction of another sovereign state. Instead, if the host country government is willing to yield the jurisdiction of its own courts, the parties will generally agree that any disputes relating to the investment are to be submitted to some form of international arbitration. And, in fact, an international arbitration clause is a common feature in many investment agreements.

Numerous reasons justify a foreign investor's choice of arbitration as a means for resolving investment disputes. First and foremost, of course, arbitration removes the dispute from the jurisdiction of the host country courts, which may be subject to undue influence by the host country government—the opposing party in the dispute. Even if the government does not actively seek to influence the courts, judges in many countries may be loath to rule against their own governments. Moreover, since the parties to an arbitration ordinarily participate in the selection of the members of the arbitral tribunal, it is within their power to bring persons of expertise in matters of foreign investment to the dispute resolution process, whereas judges of comparable ability may not be found in an ordinary court case. In addition, since the arbitral proceeding is ordinarily confidential and not subject to publicity, the host country government does not have the problems of "saving face" which it would have as a participant in a public judicial proceeding, and the foreign

---

[39] See, eg, Gormley, "The Codification of Pacta Sunt Servanda by the International Law Commission," 14 *St. Louis ULJ* (1970) 367, 371–5. See generally H Wehberg, "Pact Sunt Servanda," 53 *Am J Int'l L* (1959) 775–86.

[40] See RB von Mehren and N Kourides, "International Arbitrations Between States and Foreign Private Parties: The Libyan Nationalization Cases," 75 *Am J Int'l L* (1981) 476, 513–15.

[41] RB von Mehren and N Kourides, "International Arbitrations Between States and Foreign Private Parties: The Libyan Nationalization Cases," 75 *Am J Int'l L* (1981) 497–500.

investor may be no less concerned about the proceeding's impact on its reputation or maintenance of business secrets. As a result of confidentiality, the parties may be more willing to compromise or to comply with any eventual arbitral award. Finally, the existence of international treaties, particularly the New York Convention of the Recognition and Enforcement of Arbitral Awards[42] and the Convention on the Settlement of Investment Disputes between States and Nationals of Other States,[43] give heightened assurance that arbitration agreements and awards can be enforced.

Generally speaking, the parties are free to shape the arbitral process according to their agreement. International arbitration may be divided into two types: institutional and ad hoc. If the parties opt for ad hoc arbitration, they themselves administer the process. If they choose institutional arbitration, they elect to have the arbitration conducted under the auspices of an established body, such as the International Chamber of Commerce or the American Arbitration Association. In this respect, it should also be noted that a special international institution, the International Centre for the Settlement of Investment Disputes, an affiliate of the World Bank Group, exists to resolve investment disputes between states and the nationals of other states. Established and governed by the Convention on the Settlement of Investment Disputes between States and Nationals of Other States,[44] the Centre has become the principal body to arbitrate disputes between foreign investors and host states. As of 2010, over 140 states had ratified the Convention to become members, and reference to ICSID is increasingly found in investment contracts and legislation. In addition, many international investment treaties provide that disputes between investors of signatory countries and the other signatory government are to be settled under ICSID auspices.

(iii) Sovereign Immunity Waivers

Both public international law and the municipal law of virtually every country in the world provide, in varying degrees, for the immunity of states from suit in the courts. The precise extent of such immunity varies from country to country. Some follow the absolute theory of sovereign immunity according to which a sovereign is immune from suit for all of its acts. Many others, including the United States, have adopted the restrictive theory of sovereign immunity which, generally speaking, limits the ability of the state to assert immunity as a defense only to those claims arising out of a state's sovereign or public acts. The Foreign Sovereign Immunities Act of 1976,[45] for example, governs the extent of immunity of foreign states in US courts. Many other countries have similar legislation.[46]

The possibility that the host country may raise the defense of sovereign immunity in any eventual investment dispute increases the risk that an injured foreign investor may not receive redress for injuries arising out of interference by the host government with the investment. On the other hand, the concept of sovereign immunity permits a state, if it

---

[42] New York Convention: Convention on the Recognition and Enforcement of Foreign Arbitral Award (June 10, 1958), 330 UNTS 3.

[43] Convention on the Settlement of Investment Disputes between States and Nationals of Other States, 17 UST 1270, TIAS No 6090, 575 UNTS 159.

[44] Convention on the Settlement of Investment Disputes between States and Nationals of Other States, done at Washington, D.C., March 18, 1965, 17 UST 1270, TIAS No 6090, 575 UNTS 159.

[45] 28 USC §§ 1330, 1391, 1602–11.

[46] eg, United Kingdom: State Immunity Act of 1978, SI 1978, No 1572, reprinted in 17 *Int'l Legal Mat* 1123 (1978); Canada: Canadian State Immunity Act, Act to Provide for State Immunity in Canadian Courts, ch 95, 1980–81–82 Can. Stat. See also European Convention on State Immunity and Additional Protocol, done May 16, 1972, 11 *Int'l Legal Mat* 470 (1972).

wishes, to submit itself to the jurisdiction of the court; consequently, a foreign investor may avoid the problems inherent in sovereign immunity if it can secure from the host country a waiver of sovereign immunity in disputes arising out of the foreign investment. The United States Foreign Sovereign Immunities Act specifically provides for such waiver,[47] and most legal systems of the world also recognize the possibility of waiver.

A waiver of sovereign immunity may be either explicit or implicit. An explicit waiver of sovereign immunity will be embodied in a provision in the investment agreement by which the host country agrees not to claim sovereign immunity in respect of a suit, jurisdiction of a court, attachment, or execution in connection with any dispute arising out of the agreement. A foreign state may also *implicitly* waive its sovereign immunity by various acts. Thus, even though the agreement does *not* contain an express provision for waiver of sovereign immunity, the fact that the parties have agreed to international arbitration will generally be interpreted as an implicit waiver of sovereign immunity.[48]

(iv) Stabilization Clauses

Concerned about the potential instability of the host country's national legal and regulatory framework upon which the initial investment decision was made, potential foreign investors insist on contractual provisions that in various ways will "stabilize" a country's legal and regulatory situation. Such provisions are particularly frequent in large natural resource, energy, and infrastructure projects which require a significant capital investment at the outset of the project to be repaid through project cash flows over a long period of time in the future, frequently as long as 20 or 30 years.[49] The amount and certainty of that cash flow depends crucially on the absence of significant changes in the prevailing legal framework. In effect, this method of investor protection seeks to inhibit the host country's legislative discretion by providing that the investment project is to be governed, in whole or in part, by the host country's laws and regulations *as of a certain date*—normally the date of the execution of the contract itself.[50] The effect of such provisions, it is often said, is to "stabilize" or "freeze" host country law with respect to the particular investment in question. As a result, these provisions are known generally as "stabilization clauses."

The specific content of stabilization clauses depends on the nature of the investment project concerned and the respective bargaining powers of the investor on the one hand and the host government on the other. The principal variations in stabilizations include the following:

- *Intangibility clauses,* which provide that changes in the investment contract can only be made with the consent of the parties and in which the government expressly promises not to nationalize the investment project.

---

[47] 28 USC § 1605(a)(1).

[48] See GR Delaume, "State Contracts and Transnational Arbitration," 75 *Am J Int'l L* (1981) 784, 786 and the authority cited therein.

[49] L Cotula, "Briefing 4: Foreign Investment Contracts," *Sustainable Market Investment Briefings* 2 (International Institute for Environment and Development, August 2007). See also L Cotula, "Reconciling regulatory stability and evolution of environmental standards in investment contracts: Towards a rethink of stabilization clauses," 1 *Journal of World Energy Law* (2008) 158–79. See also R Dolzer and C Schreuer, *Principles of International Investment Law* (2008) 75–7; T Walde and G Ndi, "'Satbilizing International Investment Commitments': International Law versus Contract Integration," 31 *Texas International Law Journal* (1996) 215.

[50] *Amoco International Finance v. Islamic Republic of Iran*, 15 Iran-US CTR at 239. See also E Paasivirta, "Internationalization and Stabilization of Contracts Versus State Sovereignty," 50 *British Yearbook of International Law* (1989) 315; DE Vielleville and BS Vasani, "Sovereignty Over Natural Resources Versus Rights Under Investment Contracts: Which One Prevails?" 5 *Transnational Dispute Management*, vol 5, issue 2, April 2008.

- *Consistency clauses*, which provide that the laws and regulation of the host country will only apply to the investment if they are consistent with the investment contract.

- *Freezing clauses*, which provide that the laws and regulation applicable to the project will be those in effect at a specific date and that subsequent legislation that is inconsistent with the "frozen" law will not be applicable to the project.

- *Issue stabilization clauses*, which stabilize the application of domestic law in specific areas, such as the tax or customs duty regime.

- *Economic equilibrium clauses*, which seek to preserve the economic balance of the investment project by tying any alteration of law that negatively affects that balance to an obligation on the part of the government either to renegotiate the contract to restore the balance or pay the investor appropriate compensation.[51]

Some investment contracts include two or more of these clauses in an effort to protect investors against the hazards of legislative and regulatory instability.[52] In most, the stabilization clause, included in an investment contract, is concluded by a duly authorized representative of the host government concerned. In order to give such stabilization clauses even greater legal effect, certain countries, particularly in Latin America, have enacted laws specifically granting or authorizing the conclusion of stabilization agreements. Such laws, referred to as "legal stability agreements laws," generally grant legal stability to all investors. The country which was the first and has been the most effective to use legal stability agreements has been Peru.[53]

One may ask about the durability of such agreements and the ability of the state that has agreed to a stabilization clause to cancel or refuse to respect it later on. In short, can one argue that a state that enters into a stabilization agreement is engaging in an impermissible attempt to limit its sovereignty? Although some scholars have argued that legally the power of the state to legislate cannot be restrained by a simple contract,[54] arbitral tribunals have generally held such stabilization clauses to be valid and enforceable.[55] Their basic reasoning is that when the state in a valid exercise of its sovereignty makes a stabilization agreement with an investor, it cannot thereafter invoke its sovereignty to disregard obligations it has

---

[51] L Cotula, "Briefing 4: Foreign Investment Contracts," *Sustainable Market Investment Briefings* 2 (International Institute for Environment and Development, August 2007).

[52] See, eg, Article 21.1 of the Host Government Agreement between the Government of Turkey and the MEP Participants (October 19, 2000), governing the Baku–Tbilisi–Ceyhan (BTC) oil pipeline, which states: "The Parties hereby acknowledge that it is their mutual intention that no Turkish law now or hereafter existing (including the interpretation and application procedures thereof) that is contrary to the terms of this Agreement or any other Project Agreement shall limit, abridge or affect adversely the rights granted to the MEP Participants or any other Project Participants in this or any other Project Agreement or otherwise amend, repeal or take precedence over the whole or any part of this or any other Project Agreement." Article 7.2 provides: "If any domestic or international agreement or treaty; any legislation, promulgation, enactment, decree, accession or allowance; any other form of commitment, policy or pronouncement of permission has the effect of impairing, conflicting or interfering with the implementation of the Project, or limiting, abridging or adversely affecting the value of the Project or any of the rights, privileges, exemptions, waivers, indemnifications or protection granted or arising under this Agreement or any other Project Agreement it shall be deemed a Change in Law under Article 7.2 (xi)." The latter article also states that any changes in the law that affect the economic equilibrium of the project require the government of Turkey to "take all actions available to [it] to restore the Economic Equilibrium" of the project. If such equilibrium is not restored, the Turkish government must pay compensation (Article 10.1(iii)). Similar provisions are contained in Articles 7.2, 9 and 20 of the 2000 BTC–Georgia and BTC–Azerbaijan Host Government Agreements.

[53] Legislative Decree no 662 of 1991, Published in the Official Gazette "El Peruano" on August 29, 1991. An English translation is available at <http://www.lexadin.nl/wlg/legis/nofr/oeur/arch/per/D.L.%2520662tradrev.pdf>.

[54] M Sornarajah, *The International Law on Foreign Investment* (2nd edn 2004) 406–10.

[55] See, eg, *Kuwait v. American Independent Oil (AMINOIL)* 21 ILM (1982) 976.

obtained with respect to foreign investors.[56] Thus in *AGIP v. Government of the Popular Republic of Congo*,[57] the ICSID tribunal stated:

> These stabilization clauses, freely accepted by the Government, do not affect the principle of its sovereign legislative and regulatory powers, since it retains both in relation to those, whether national or foreigners, with whom it has not entered into such obligations, and that in the present case, changes in the legislative and regulatory agreements stipulated in the agreement simply cannot be invoked against the other contracting party.[58]

The following chapters on the contractual framework will consider in greater detail stabilization clauses and other provisions common to investment agreements.

---

[56] A Faruque, "Validity and Efficacy of Stabilization Clauses—Legal Protection vs Functional Value," 23 *Journal of International Arbitration* (2003) 317, 322.

[57] Award of November 20, 1979, (ICSID), (1982) 21 *Int'l Legal Mat* (1982) 726.

[58] Award of November 20, 1979, (ICSID), (1982) 21 *Int'l Legal Mat* (1982) 736.

PART III

THE CONTRACTUAL LEGAL FRAMEWORK

8

The Nature and Functions of the Contractual Framework for Investments

8.1 In General

All international investment transactions are shaped by contracts. A contract under virtually all systems of law is an agreement between two or more persons that creates legally enforceable obligations.[1] An "investment contract," for the purposes of this volume, is any contract that governs or relates to an international investment.[2] In some cases, for example a portfolio investment in shares of a publicly traded company, the related contract may be relatively simple; however, other investment transactions, such as the construction and operation of a project-financed power plant, may require a complex network of contracts covering among other things the legal relationships among the sponsors of the project, the arrangements for the construction of the power plant, the government's obligation to buy the electricity produced, the financing mechanisms with various lenders, and investment insurance against political risk, to mention just a few. Together the applicable contracts constitute the contractual legal framework of the investment.

An international investment's contractual framework differs from its national legal framework in several important respects. First, unlike the national legal framework, which is a manifestation of the will of the governing authorities of the state, contracts are a reflection of and a function of the will of the parties to the investment. Second, whereas the national legal framework results from the legislative and regulatory processes of a specific country, the contractual framework is a product of bargaining—of negotiation—between and among interested parties, including the governing authorities of the country in which the investment is to take place and the foreign investors providing the capital and technology. The contractual legal framework therefore reflects the relative bargaining power of the parties to the investment transaction. Third, whereas the national legal framework contains rules of a certain degree of generality so as to cover a class of transactions, the contractual framework, having been designed to govern a particular transaction, has a high degree of specificity and detail, and indeed may be unique, if not idiosyncratic.

Investment contracts are legal instruments in that they are created by law and have legal consequences, but they also have very definite economic and social functions. This chapter examines both of these dimensions.

---

[1] eg, the American Law Institute's *Restatement (2nd) of Contract*, section 1, defines a contract as follows: "A contract is a promise or set of promises for the breach of which the law gives a remedy or the performance of which the law in some way recognizes as a duty." Article 1101 of the French Civil Code states: "A contract is an agreement by which one or more persons become bound toward one or more other persons to give, to do, or not to do something." *"Le contrat est une convention par laquelle une ou plusiers personnes s'obligent, envers une ou plusieurs autres, à donner, à faire, ou à ne pas faire quelque chose".*

[2] The terms "international investment contract" and "foreign investment contract" are sometimes used to refer only to contracts and agreements between foreign investors and host country governments. See, eg, L Cotula, "Foreign Investment Contracts" *Sustainable Markets Investment Briefings* 4, International Institute for Environment and Development, August 2007, available at <http://pubs.iied.org/17015IIED.html>.

8.2 Investment Contracts as Legal Instruments

(a) The Legal Basis

The contractual legal framework consists of the legal rules that the parties to an investment have made to govern the investment transaction and their relationship with one another. They have chosen to use contracts to structure their investment transaction because they have judged that contracts are the most effective instrument available to them to achieve their purposes. A contract, in Sir Frederick Pollock's succinct definition, is "a set of promises that the law will enforce."[3] Thus despite occasional suggestions to the contrary that certain kinds of state contracts constitute "an independent legal order,"[4] agreements concerning international investments require the application of some national legal order to give them obligatory, enforceable effect. As FA Mann has written, "... every legal relationship in general and every contract in particular must be governed by a system of law and is otherwise unthinkable."[5] Mann's statement echoes that of the Permanent Court of International Justice in the *Serbian Loans case* that "any contract which is not a contract between States in their capacity as subjects of international law is based on the domestic law of some country."[6] Thus if an agreement between two parties creates legally binding rules, it fundamentally is not because their agreement says so but because the applicable national law of contracts requires it.[7] Contracts therefore do not simply hover in the air, unconnected to a national legal system. On the contrary, all contracts must be based on a particular body of law. It is that body of law that gives force to the rules that the parties have devised to govern one another's conduct. Moreover, even if a state is a party to an agreement with a foreign investor, that fact does not transform their agreement into treaty governed by international law. A treaty, according to Article 2(a) the Vienna Convention on the Law of Treaties, is defined as "an international agreement concluded between States in written form and governed by international law ... "[8] Treaties are forms of agreement that are reserved to states, and to states alone.

If international investment contracts are created by and subject to a system of law, how does one determine the particular body of law that governs a specific contract? Contemporary international investment contracts almost always contain a "choice-of-law clause" or "governing law clause" by which the parties select the law that is to govern their contract.[9] Although this practice, known as "party autonomy," was often rejected by the courts in earlier times on the grounds that it allowed the parties to "legislate" and thereby avoid the public policy of the state, today courts will generally enforce choice-of-law provisions, subject to certain limitations, in order to protect the justified expectations of

---

[3] F Pollock, *Principles of Contract* (12th edn 1941) 1.

[4] A Von Verdross, "Quasi International Agreements and International Economic Transactions," 27 *Year-Book of World Affairs* (1964) 230.

[5] FA Mann, "The Proper Law of Contracts Concluded by International Person," 35 *The British Year Book of International Law* (1959) 49.

[6] (1929) PCIJ Rep Series A No 20, 41.

[7] See, eg, Article 1134 of the French Civil Code: "Agreements legally entered into have the force of law for those who have made them." (*Les conventions légalement formées tiennent lieu de loi à ceux qui les ont faites*). A similar principle is to be found in other civil codes. For example Article 196 of the Kuwait Civil Code, adopted by Law no 67 of 1980, provides: "The contract is the law of the contracting parties. It is prohibited for each of the contracting parties to unilaterally abrogate or modify its provisions, unless in the bounds of what the contract or the law allow." M Al-Saeed, "Legal Protection of Economic Development Agreements" 17 *Arab Law Quarterly* (2002) 150, 164. See also M Sornarajah, *The International Law on Foreign Investment* (2nd edn 2004) 417–29.

[8] Vienna Convention on the Law of Treaties (May 22, 1969); UN Doc A/Conf. 39/27; 1155 UNTS 331; 8 ILM 679 (1969); 63 *AJIL* (1969) 875 (VCLT).

[9] For a discussion of the strategic considerations of choice-of-law provisions, see Chapter 7, section 7.3(e)(i).

the parties and foster predictability in business dealings. Indeed in 1974, the United States Supreme Court stated that a choice-of-law provision is "... an almost indispensable precondition to the achievement of the orderliness and predictability essential to any international business transaction."[10]

The principle of party autonomy is almost universally recognized by courts in all countries except with regard to transactions that are purely domestic,[11] a factor which is never present in an international investment agreement. Indeed, it has been said that "... the principle of party autonomy in the matters of choice of law is also a principle of public international law as it's a universally accepted principle of private international law."[12]

In choosing a particular law to govern an investment contract, the parties may seek other goals in addition to predictability. The specific reason for selecting a particular law may vary from contract to contract. In certain cases, the parties may choose the law of a particular jurisdiction because such law is highly developed and is capable of providing clear answers in any future dispute. Their choice may also be influenced by a desire to avoid jurisdictions whose law is undeveloped and unclear. For both of these reasons, international loan agreements usually provide that the governing law is to be that of the lender—ie New York, England, or France—rather than that of the country of the borrower.[13] Indeed, as the world's most important money centers, England and New York are the most common choices for the governing law in international loan agreements.[14] Their laws are highly developed and capable of supplying answers to complex financial problems.[15] Lenders particularly seek their application, since New York and English law probably are more protective of banking interests than would be the law of a borrower's country. But probably the most important reason for choosing an external law is to isolate the investment contract or loan agreement from legal changes in the borrowing country or the country of investment.[16] In loan agreements, the most common legal changes made by local governments to protect local borrowers include moratoria on foreign obligations, reductions in applicable interest rates, requirements that repayment be made in local currency to a local custodian, and exchange controls.[17] Moreover, in any investment transactions in which a government or state agency is a party, foreign investors may also wish to avoid the applicable law since it is subject to change by the host government at any time.

In certain cases, the parties may choose in their governing law clause from more than one body of law, a process known as *dépeçage*, a French word which means to slice thinly,

---

[10] *Scherk v. Alberto-Culver*, 417 US 506, 516 (1974).

[11] PJ Borchers, "Choice of Law in the American Courts in 1992: Observations and Reflections," 42 *American Journal of International Law* (1994) 125, 135. See also RJ Weintraub, "Functional Developments in Choice of Law for Contracts," 187 *Recueil des Cours* (1984) 239, 271; G Ruhl, "Party Autonomy in the Private International Law of Contracts: Transatlantic Convergence and Economic Efficiency" CLPE Research Paper 4/2007 Vol 03 No. 01 (2007) available at <http://papers.ssrn.com/sol3/papers.cfm?abstract_id=921842>.

[12] AFM Maniruzzaman, "State Contracts in Contemporary International Law: Monist versus Dualist Controversies," (2001) 12 *European Journal of International Law* 309, 322. (citing RY Jennings, "State Contracts in International Law," 37 *British Yearbook of International Law* (1961) 156, 178.)

[13] See M Gruson, "Governing Law Clauses in International and Interstate Loan Agreements—New York's Approach," *U Ill L Rev* (1982) 207, 208.

[14] PR Wood, *International Loans, Bonds, and Securities Regulation* (1995) 62.

[15] M Gruson, "Governing Law Clauses in Commercial Agreements—New York's Approach," 18 *Colum J Transnat'l L* (1979) 323, 325.

[16] PR Wood, *International Loans, Bonds, and Securities Regulation* (1995) 62 ("It does not matter which law, so long as it is external.").

[17] PR Wood, *International Loans, Bonds, and Securities Regulation* (1995) 62.

referred to in English as "splitting."[18] For example, they may stipulate that the law of country X is to govern the interpretation of certain contractual terms and the law of country Y is to govern others.[19]

Occasionally, in formulating a choice-of-law provision, the parties select a body of legal principles that is not tied to a specific national legal system—particularly if the dispute is to be resolved by arbitration rather than by a court of law. For example, they may agree that the rules of a trade association or established international commercial customs are to govern their contract. They may also opt to be governed by such non-national legal standards as "general principles of international trade law" or "general principles of law." While such choice may suffer from a certain degree of vagueness and lack of predictability, both parties may conclude that there are overriding considerations for making it, particularly in situations where neither side will accept the law of the other's country. The government, for reasons of national pride and prestige, may wish to avoid subjecting itself to the application of the law of a foreign state, while the foreign national may believe it is preferable to rely on general principles of law, rather than on the host country law whose application and very substance may be influenced by the host government. The selection of "general principles of law" avoids both of these obstacles.

The precise extent to which national courts and arbitral tribunals will recognize and apply the law chosen by the parties for their investment contracts will depend on the law applied by the particular court or tribunal. Generally speaking, there is a general tendency throughout the world in favor of party autonomy, although the specific application of that principle varies from country to country. In the states of the European Union, by virtue of the 1980 Rome Convention on the Law Applicable to Contractual Obligations, now embodied in Regulation (EC) No 593/2008 of the European Parliament and of the Council of June 17, 2008 on the law applicable to contractual obligations (Rome I)[20] member states are to recognize and enforce party autonomy with respect to the law applicable to contracts. Article 3 (Freedom of Choice) of the Convention states:

'1. A contract shall be governed by the law chosen by the parties. The choice shall be made expressly or clearly demonstrated by the terms of the contract or the circumstances of the case. By their choice the parties can select the law applicable to the whole or to part only of the contract.

2. The parties may at any time agree to subject the contract to a law other than that which previously governed it, whether as a result of an earlier choice made under this Article or of other provisions of this Regulation. Any change in the law to be applied that is made after the conclusion of the contract shall not prejudice its formal validity under Article 11 or adversely affect.'

In most of the 50 states of the United States, despite the effort to foster predictability, party autonomy does have certain limits, since parties to a contract are not totally free to choose any law for whatever reason they desire. In defining these limits, American courts have made a distinction between (1) applying the chosen law for purposes of interpreting and construing contractual terms, and (2) applying the chosen law to issues of validity of contractual provisions. With regard to the former, it is generally agreed that the parties are free to choose any law whatever to govern issues which they could have resolved by an

---

[18] ML Moses, *The Principles and Practice of International Commercial Arbitration* (2008) 72–3.

[19] *Restatement (Second) of Conflict of Laws* § 187 Reporter's Note, subsection (1) at 570 (1971).

[20] *Official Journal (Legislation)* 177, 4.7.2008, 6–16, available at <http://eur-lex.europa.eu/smartapi/cgi/sga_doc?smartapi!celexplus!prod!DocNumber&lg=en&type_doc=Regulation&an_doc=2008&nu_doc=593>.

express provision in their contract on that issue.[21] As Comment c to the *Restatement (Second) of Conflict of Laws* § 187 points out, an agreement as to choice of law in such a case is merely a short-hand expression of their intent with respect to the detailed matters affecting their agreement. The courts will apply the chosen law in such cases despite the fact that the chosen law may have no other relationship to the transaction. For example, if the parties chose English law to govern a contract for the shipment of wheat from the United States to Pakistan by a Greek ship, despite the fact that England has no connection whatsoever with the transaction, a court would apply English law to determine the parties' duties to take delivery since the parties could have defined these duties specifically in the contract itself.[22]

With respect to contractual issues which the parties could not have resolved by stipulation in the contract, US law places two fundamental limitations on enforcement of the choice-of-law clause: (1) the jurisdiction whose law is chosen must have a "reasonable" or (in some cases) "substantial" relationship to the transaction; and (2) the application of the chosen law must not be contrary to a fundamental policy of the forum state or a state having a materially greater interest in the transaction. Section 187(2) of the *Restatement (Second) of Conflicts of Law* states the general rule:

> The law of the state chosen by the parties to govern their contractual rights and duties will be applied, even if the particular issue is one which the parties could not have resolved by an explicit provision in their agreement directed to that issue, unless either:
> (a) the chosen state has no substantial relationship to the parties or the transaction and there is no other reasonable basis for the parties' choice, or
> (b) application of the law of the chosen state would be contrary to a fundamental policy of a state which has a materially greater interest than the chosen state in the determination of the particular issue and which, under the rule of § 188 [relating to the most significant contact] would be the state of the applicable law in the absence of an effective choice by the parties.

The state of New York, an important center for international investment and finance, on the other hand, has enacted legislation to enforce unlimited party autonomy in large commercial transactions. Under § 5–1401 of the New York General Obligations Law, the parties' governing law clause must be enforced, regardless of whether the underlying transaction bears a reasonable relationship to New York State, whenever the amount of the transaction exceeds $250,000.

Courts interpreting governing law provision are sometimes faced with the question of whether they should apply the chosen law as of the time of the contract or as of the time of the dispute, an issue of importance if the law has changed between the time the contract was signed and the time the dispute occurred. Generally speaking, unless the agreement specifically provides otherwise, the courts will apply the law in force as of the time of the dispute, rather than the law as it existed at the time of formation.[23] To insure this result, the parties might specifically provide that the law of country X "for the time being in force" or "as from time to time in force" is the law to be applied. On the other hand, it is sometimes advantageous, particularly in long-term contracts with foreign governments, to "stabilize" the applicable law by providing that the law in effect as of a particular date is to govern the rights and duties of the parties throughout the duration of their agreement.

---

[21] American Law Institute, *Restatement (Second) of Conflict of Laws* § 187(1) (1971).
[22] *Hellenic Lines, Ltd v. Embassy of Pakistan*, 307 F Supp 947, 954 (SDNY 1969).
[23] See G Delaume, "State Contracts and Transnational Arbitration," 75 *Am J Int'l L* (1981) 784, 805.

If the parties fail expressly or implicitly to choose a governing law, then a court or arbitral tribunal applying the investment contract will refer to its own choice-of-law principles in order to determine the applicable law. In view of the variations and uncertainties in the diverse conflict of law systems prevailing throughout the world, such a result may not give the transaction the degree of predictability desired by the parties. For example, in the absence of a choice of law clause, most courts in the United States, as illustrated by § 188 of the *Restatement (Second) of Conflict of Laws*, would undertake an analysis of the contract to determine the state having the most significant relationship with the transaction and the parties.[24] While such an approach may result in an equitable solution in most cases, it is hardly designed to foster predictability in the interpretation and application of the specific contract in question.

(b) State Contracts

While investment contracts between governments and private parties are ordinarily subject to the domestic law of a particular state, they are nonetheless different from contracts between purely private parties because of the special powers that governments exercise in making and applying such contracts. It is for this reason that they constitute a distinct class of investment contracts, known generally as "state contracts."[25] The special nature of state contracts is derived from a variety of factors which distinguish them from ordinary business and investment contracts between private parties. First, their purpose, from the point of view of the government concerned, is to carry out an activity or function of the state, not simply to achieve a commercial profit. Second, because of such distinct purpose and function, the process of making state contracts is usually subject to special legal rules and regulations that do not apply in purely commercial transactions. For example, national legislation may require that before entering into any significant investment contract, such as the development of a power plant, the government engage in a publicly transparent bidding process among potentially interested parties. Thus the law prevents government agencies from simply selecting a foreign investor and negotiating an investment contract on a confidential basis as usually occurs among private joint venture partners. Third, for the ostensible purpose of protecting the public welfare, national law may impose specific terms that state contracts must embody on a wide range of matters, such as the ability to have recourse to international arbitration for dispute settlement or to select foreign auditing firms to verify the accounts of the transaction in which the state is a party. As a result, negotiators of state contracts may have considerably less latitude in shaping the terms of an investment transaction than they would in the case of a similar transaction without government involvement. And finally, once the contract has been

---

[24] American Law Institute, *Restatement (Second) of Conflict of Laws* § 188(1) (1971): "The rights and duties of the parties with respect to an issue in a contract are determined by the local law of the state which, with respect to that issue, has the most significant relationship to the transaction and the parties..." Among the factors to be considered in making a determination of the state with the most significant relation to the transaction are the following: (a) the place of contracting, (b) the place of negotiation of the contract, (c) the place of performance, (d) the location of the subject matter of the contract, and (e) the domicile, residence, nationality, place of incorporation and place of business of the parties. The *Restatement* also provides: "These contracts are to be evaluated according to their relative importance with respect to the particular issue."

[25] The literature on state contracts is extensive. See, eg, AF Maniruzzaman, "State Contracts in Contemporary International Law," 12 *European Journal of International Law* (2001) 309–28; J Hyde, "Economic Development Agreements," 105 *Hague Receuil* (1992) 271; CT Curtis, "The Legal Security of Economic Development Agreements," 29 *Harvard International Law Journal* (1989) 317; I Pogany, "Economic Development Agreements," 7 *ICSID Revue* (1992) 1.

concluded, governments either by law or by political power feel they have the right to change terms in state contracts in order to protect public welfare and state interests.

A specific type of state contract that has gained significant attention from scholars and arbitrators is the "economic development agreement," which has its origins in the 1950's with the emergence of developing countries from their colonial status to political independence.[26] Many developing countries entered into long-term contractual arrangements with foreign corporations to obtain the capital and technology that they deemed necessary to further their economic development. The growth of these arrangements and their increasing frequency throughout the developing world led some scholars to consider them a special category of state contract.[27] According to one noted commentator, the characteristics of economic development agreements that justified their classification as a special type of state contracts are the following: (1) the contract is between a government and a foreign corporation whose legal existence depends on the law of a foreign country; (2) the contract is not for a single transaction but for a long-term economic relationship between the two parties; (3) the contract grants the foreign corporation rights of quasi political nature, such as duty-free status or exoneration from paying certain taxes or being subject to certain national laws and regulations; (4) the rights granted to the investor because of their long-term nature are akin to property rights; (5) economic development contracts in many countries are governed by public, rather than private law; and 6) by agreement of the parties, disputes under economic development agreements are subject to international arbitration rather than local courts.[28]

While economic development agreements may be considered functionally different from other kinds of investment contracts, an important question is whether they should be considered *legally* different and entitled to a different *legal* treatment. A few scholars and arbitrators argued that economic development agreements should be "internationalized," that is they should be subject to international law, a condition which would prevent national governments from invoking their legislative powers to subsequently modify economic development agreements which they had accepted. Some arbitration cases have taken the position that by their nature such agreements are governed by international law even if there was no specific provision in the agreement calling for its application. Thus in three frequently cited early cases[29] involving oil concession agreements made by western oil companies with Middle Eastern governments, arbitrators determined that international law applied to such investment contracts on the dubious grounds that Islamic law, the contract law of the countries in question, was not sufficiently developed to be applicable to such sophisticated undertakings. A few arbitrations found that international law applied to economic development agreements implicitly by virtue of the fact that the parties had opted for international arbitration[30] or because it was determined that the national law applicable to the contract included international law.[31] The effect of these rulings was to "internationalize" or "delocalize" the investment contracts involved in the cases, thereby

---

[26] See J Hyde, "Economic Development Agreements," 105 *Receuil Des Cours, Hague Academy of International Law* (1962) 271.

[27] SI Pogany, "Economic Development Agreements," 7 *ICSID Review* (1992) 1.

[28] McNair, "The General Principles of Law Recognized by Civilized Nations," 33 *British Year Book of International Law* (1957) 1–19.

[29] *Petroleum Development Ltd v. Sheikh of Abu Dhabi*, 18 ILR (1951) 144; *Ruler of Qatar v. International Maritime Oil Company* 20 ILR (1953) 535; *Saudi Arabia v. Arabian American Oil Company* (Aramco Case) 27 ILR (1963) 116. See generally, KM Al-Jumah, "Arab State Contract Disputes: Lessons from the Past," 17 *Arab Law Quarterly* (2002) 215–40.

[30] *Texaco Overseas Petroleum Ltd v. Libya* 53 ILR (1975) 389.

[31] *Southern Pacific Properties v. Egypt* (1983) 23 ILM 572.

removing the agreement from host country law so as to prevent the host government from using its legislative power to change the bargain after it has been made. If the contract is subject to host country law and thereafter the host government authorities change the contract by law, the host government can assert that breach of contract has not taken place.[32]

In response to rulings internationalizing economic development agreements, state practice in the 1970s developed whereby host governments insisted on including provisions in economic development agreements specifically stating that the national law of the host country governed the contract to the exclusion of other laws. Indeed, for many countries the application of national law to state contracts is such an important policy that they have adopted legislation requiring its application to some or all state contracts and prohibiting governmental authorities from agreeing to the application of foreign law in their negotiations with foreign investors. By the 1990s, one commentator, after reviewing arbitration awards involving economic agreements concluded that the paucity of arbitral awards recognizing economic development agreements as a category of state contracts that is automatically internationalized was a strong indication that the internationalization doctrine had little foundation in international law.[33]

Nonetheless, a state party is still free to agree that international law, or some variant thereof, is to govern an investment agreement. Faced with an insistent foreign investor holding out the prospect of a particularly valuable project, host governments may be willing to do so. Thus, in addition to specifying the law of the host state as governing the investment agreement, an approach which now appears to be dominant, one can also find state contracts that provide for "general principles of law recognized by civilized nations," international law, or some combination of national and foreign law.[34]

In the event that the parties to a state contract fail to specify a governing law, arbitrators would generally hold that host country law governs the contract. However, it should be noted that Article 42(1) of the Convention[35] governing the functioning of the Centre for Settlement of Investment Disputes (ICSID), the leading arbitral body deciding investor–states disputes provides the following choice of law rule for ICSID arbitrators to follow:

(1) The Tribunal shall decide a dispute in accordance with such rules of law as may be agreed by the parties. In the absence of such agreement, the Tribunal shall apply the law of the Contracting State party to the dispute (including its rules on the conflict of laws) and *such rules of international law as may be applicable.*
(Emphasis added.)

The language of this provision would enable a tribunal to find in appropriate cases that international law applied to a state investment contract by virtue of the facts and circumstances of the case under consideration. For example, a tribunal might conclude that the law of the host state (ie "the Contracting State party") included international law or the nature of the investment transaction made international law "applicable."

---

[32] AFM Maniruzzaman, "State Contracts in Contemporary International Law: Monist versus Dualist Controversies," 12 *European Journal of International Law* (2001) 309, 320.

[33] SI Pagony, "Economic Development Agreements," 7 *ICSID Revue* (1992) 1, 13.

[34] CT Curtis, "The Legal Security of Economic Development Agreements," 29 *Harvard International Law Journal* (1998) 317, 320–1.

[35] Convention on the Settlement of Investment Disputes Between States and the Nationals of Other States, March 18, 1965, 17 UST 1270, 575 UNTS 159.

8.3 The Economic and Social Functions of Investment Contracts

Investment contracts are not only legal instruments that specify the rights and obligations of the parties. They are also social arrangements among persons engaged in economic activities.[36] The purpose of any contract, according to one noted scholar, is to secure "cooperation to achieve social purposes by use of promises given in exchanges arrived at through bargain..."[37] Investors make contracts in order to secure the cooperation ie desired behavior by other parties, whether private enterprises or government agencies, in order to achieve desired ends, such as the construction and operation of a power plant in India, a loan at a profitable rate of interest to a government agency in Peru, or the purchase of privatized assets in Poland. The promises exchanged in the contract are usually expressed in the form of rules to govern the conduct of the parties. The rules of the contractual framework are thus the crystallization of the promises that the parties have made to one another. From the point of view of the national legal system, the contract grants the parties legal rights and imposes upon them legal obligations that they must fulfil.

From an economic point of view, an investment contract is more than merely a statement of legal rights and duties. It also serves important economic functions that are fundamental in achieving the purposes of the investment and in assuring the cooperation that is so necessary for economic activity. Five of the most important economic functions serviced by investment contracts are: (a) risk allocation; (b) investment planning; (c) investment control; (d) benefit extraction; and (e) regulation and governance. Let us look at each one briefly.

(a) Risk Allocation

In view of the fact that human conduct is fundamentally unpredictable and indeterminate, any agreed upon cooperation between different persons has risks for both sides. In this context, the notion of risk means for each party that the expected cooperative action expected from the other party will not take place. Every investment transaction therefore embodies risks because every investment is a prediction and a wager on an unknown and indeterminate future behavior. In general terms, the risks include the likelihood that one side will not conform its conduct to the specified terms of the agreement, or that some third party or intervening force will make cooperative action between the contracting sides impossible or unexpectedly costly.

An important function of the contractual framework is to allocate the risks and costs arising out of their cooperative venture specifically to individual parties. All contracts, including investment contracts, can therefore be considered *risk allocation devices*. As a general matter, the contracting parties have two general approaches to dealing with specific risks in the investment transaction. They may agree that one or both of the parties may bear the risk or instead shift the risk to a third party insurer. For example, a foreign investment serving the local market, such as an auto assembly plant, faces currency risks of two types. Its earnings in local currency may depreciate against its home country currency with the result that its expected earnings in its home currency are less than expected. In addition, the host country government may impose currency controls that restrict the investor's

---

[36] For an early inquiry into the role of contract in the social order, see generally KN Llewellyn, "What Price Contract? An Essay in Perspective," 40 *Yale L J* (1931) 704–51.

[37] EA Farnsworth, "The Past of Promise: An Historical Introduction to Contract," 69 *Columbia Law Review* (1969) 576, 578.

ability to repatriate its earnings. In order to protect itself against either or both of these risks, the foreign investor may enter into a variety of contractual arrangements, such as securing political risk insurance against inconvertibility of currency from a third-party insurer and making currency futures contracts with currency traders as protection against devaluation. Similarly, in order to mitigate the risks of exchange controls, it might negotiate exemptions from such controls with the host country central bank, or by contract hold a portion of its export earnings in a foreign currency account in an offshore bank.

(b) Investment Planning

A second important function of a contract is as a *planning device* that specifies the tasks to be accomplished by the parties to the investment. Every investment contract has within it a plan of cooperation envisaged by the contracting parties to achieve their ends. Thus a joint venture contract between a foreign multinational and local entrepreneur to manufacture refrigerators will specify what assets, factors of production, and technologies each will provide and how the parties will manage them once the venture is in operation. Similarly, a state contract with a foreign investor governing a concession to operate a public service, such as a water and sewerage system or telecommunications network, will specify in some detail the precise nature of the investments that the investor must make and the standards of quality to which it must adhere in delivering the service to the public.[38]

(c) Investment Control

In order to assure the desired cooperation on which the success of any investment depends, investors seek ways to control the behavior of those persons and organizations whose actions may affect the investment. Contracts are important devices to assure such control. Contractual investment controls demonstrate great diversity. The extent and nature of control that an investor gains through contracts depends on the type of investment made and the bargaining power of the investor.

One may divide them into two basic groups: (1) investment controls directed at the conduct of participants in the investment and (2) investment controls that seek in some way to limit the action of the host government and the investor when government is not formally an enterprise participant. The former include joint venture and shareholder contracts that assure the investor of control of or at least meaningful participation in the enterprise's decision-making processes, covenants in loans agreements that seek to prevent conduct by the debtor which threatens the interests of the creditor, and concession agreements by which governments seek to assure that the foreign concessionaire operating a public service such as a water or electrical system will do so in a way that provides high quality service to the public at least cost. Even if the government is not part of the investment, various contracts may seek to control the behavior of either or both. Thus, for example, through stabilization clauses, discussed in Chapter 7[39] investors seek to restrain governments from exercising their regulatory powers in ways that will negatively affect investor interests, and economic development agreements endeavor to control investor behavior in ways that will benefit the host country.

---

[38] For a detailed description of the terms of a water and sewerage concession as a planning document, see Decision on Liability of the ICSID case of *Suez et al v. The Argentine Republic* (ICSID Case no Arb/03/19) of July 30, 2010, paras 34–44, available at <http://italaw.com/documents/SuezVivendiAWGDecisiononLiability.pdf>.
[39] See section 7.3 (e) (iv).

(d) Benefit Extraction

The goal of investors and governments that engage in the foreign investment process is to obtain a return, a gain, a benefit. Contracts are important devices for extracting that benefit from the investment. The precise nature of the benefit sought depends on the business objectives of the investor and the policy goals of the host country. Investors may benefit from their investments in a variety of ways. Thus, for example, as will be seen in Chapters 9 and 10, a multinational firm that establishes a manufacturing subsidiary in Kenya may benefit not only from profits made by the subsidiary, but also from the sale of components by the parent to the subsidiary, from royalties received for technology and intellectual property rights transferred and ultimately from the sale of the subsidiary to a foreign or Kenyan firm at a profit. Each of those conduits for extracting benefits from the investment will be governed by contracts. Thus, the parent and the subsidiary will enter into separate contracts for the purchase of components, the licensing of technology, the provision of management to the subsidiary, and ultimately the sale of the subsidiary to other investors. Host governments, to extract their desired benefits from the investor, may require investors to enter into investment or development agreements by which they commit to hire a minimum number of local residents, to purchase a minimum amount of locally produced goods and services, to invest a minimum amount of capital by a specific date in the approved foreign investment project, and to undertake training programs to transfer to nationals technical knowledge and management skills.

(e) Regulation and Governance

Investment contracts may also be instruments of regulation and governance in the host country in two fundamental respects. First, they may be the means by which the host government regulates the activities of the investor in carrying out various activities related to its investment. For example, the contracts applicable to the purchase by a foreign investor of privatized assets or the concession to a multinational corporation for the operation of a public service will usually contain detailed rules as to how the investor is to conduct itself in using the privatized assets or in operating the concession in order to protect the public interest. Second, a state investment contract may grant the investor certain administrative roles, powers, or functions normally exercised by governments. For example, a host government may grant a large agro-industrial project located in a remote area of an under-developed country the authority to establish and manage settlements, hospitals, and roads for workers and local residents. Thus rather than creating governmental institutions by law, the government opts to govern by contract.

(f) Conclusion

No matter how detailed the investment contracts, it is well to remember that they are only frameworks for behavior of the parties and that the economic and social necessities of life may intervene to affect fulfilment of contractual obligations. In all investment contracts, there is therefore a continuing struggle between the legal structures of the contract and the demands of life. In 1931, the noted American scholar Karl Llewellyn made a thoughtful inquiry into the role of contract in the social order and concluded: "One turns from the contemplation of the work of contract as from the experience of a Greek tragedy. Life struggling against form."[40] With respect to contracts, he concluded:

> To sum up, the major importance of a legal contract is to provide a frame-work for well-nigh every type of group organization and for well-nigh every type of passing or permanent relation between individuals and groups, up to and including states—a frame-work highly adjustable, a frame-work which almost never accurately indicates real working relations, but which affords a rough indication around which such relations vary, an occasional guide in cases of doubt, and a norm of final appeal when the relations cease in fact to work.[41]

---

[40] KN Llewellyn, "What Price Contract? An Essay in Perspective," 40 *Yale L J* (1931) 704, 751.
[41] KN Llewellyn, "What Price Contract? An Essay in Perspective," 40 *Yale L J* (1931) 736–7.

9

The Negotiation of International Investment Contracts

9.1 The Role of Negotiation in the Investment Process

International investment contracts do not suddenly and miraculously spring into existence on their own initiative. They are always the product of negotiation between foreign investors and other interested parties, including governments. Some investment contracts, such as those governing the purchase of a hundred shares of stock on the Mumbai stock exchange, can be made easily and cheaply. Others, for example the contracts to undertake a major infrastructure project, may entail lengthy and costly discussions among numerous parties with no guarantee at the end that the contractual frameworks necessary for the project will ever receive all the necessary approvals by the parties or their governments.[1] It is safe to say that all investment transactions require negotiation by concerned parties. This chapter will therefore examine the nature of the investment negotiation process, the principal obstacles to be encountered in conducting such negotiations, and, in view of the crucial role actually or potentially played by governments, the special challenges that investors face in negotiating with foreign governments.

9.2 The Nature of the Negotiation Process

Negotiation is basically *a process of communication by which two or more parties seek to advance their individual interests or those of the persons they represent through an agreement on a desired future course of action.* The parties to a negotiation are involved in that communication because at least one side has decided that it can improve its situation in some way if both sides agree on some act that requires the participation of both sides, such as the creation of a strategic alliance to manufacture cell phones in Vietnam or the establishment of a power plant in Sri Lanka. In the case of an investment negotiation, the interests that the parties seek to advance are essentially the economic benefits to be gained from the investment. That communication process can happen through a variety of means, including a meeting between executives in a conference room, a telephone call in the middle of the night, an exchange of e-mails between companies located on opposite sides of the world, or conversations with government officials in a ministry office. Indeed, the final investment transaction may be the result of all these types of communication. Whatever the context, those communications will usually culminate in some form of written contract or agreement.

The negotiation of investment transactions has both *substantive* and *process* dimensions. The substantive dimensions relate to the specific terms to be found in the contracts, such as the amount of capital to be paid by the investor, the covenants and guarantees made by the

---

[1] For a description of the lengthy, and ultimately fruitless, negotiation during more than two years in 1992–1994 between a foreign investor and the government of Sri Lanka concerning a possible electricity generation project, see the award in the ICSID arbitration of *Mihaly International Corporation v. Democratic Socialist Republic of Sri Lanka* (ICSID Case no ARB/00/2) Award, March 15, 2002, paras 36–48, 17 *ICSID Review- Foreign Investment Law Journal* (2002) 140–65.

debtor, and the dates when specified actions must be taken. The process dimensions relate to the ways in which the parties conduct themselves in order to reach agreement. Effective negotiation requires a mastery of both substance and process.

Like other processes, negotiations tend to go through distinct phases. The effective negotiator understands those phases and recognizes that each calls for special skills, approaches, and resources. There are three basic phases to an investment negotiation: (a) prenegotiation, (b) conceptualization, and (c) detail arrangement.

(a) Prenegotiation

In the first phase, which can be called prenegotiation, the parties to a potential investment transaction determine whether they want to negotiate at all and, if so, what they will talk about, and how, when, and where they will do it. Either the investor or the host country government may launch the prenegotiation phase leading to a possible foreign investment project. For example, a country seeking to build its electrical generation capacity may publicize in international publications its desire to receive "expressions of interest" from possible foreign investors and may also create a website with additional information about the nature of the power generation projects it is seeking and the specific kinds of data it desires from potential investors.[2]

Rather than leave the negotiation process to the discretion of a government agency, national laws and regulation may also seek to establish a formal bidding process or auction in order to be assured of selecting the best potential investors with which to negotiate, that is, the most technically and financially advanced foreign companies that appear ready to undertake the project at the most advantageous economic terms to the country. Thus, host country legislation may establish the minimum qualifications for companies to participate in the bidding, specify the means for publicizing the bidding opportunity, determine the standards to be applied in evaluating expressions of interests or bids, and set out the process of judging qualified companies with which to negotiate a final contract. To control the prenegotiation process even further, countries may adopt specific bidding rules that specify in detail how bids are to be presented and what information they must contain.[3] After an evaluation of the submissions received from investors, the host government will decide the foreign companies with which to negotiate.

Much prenegotiation may happen in letters, telephone calls, and e-mails even before the parties sit down together, but the process may continue for many meetings and months thereafter. Information gathering and efforts by each of the parties to evaluate the other characterize the prenegotiation phase. It ends when both sides make a decision to negotiate a deal together, or when one informs the other, directly or indirectly, that it no longer wishes to continue discussions. If the parties do decide to enter into negotiations, their transition to the next stage of deal making may be evidenced by making an agenda for their talks and even signing a confidentiality agreement in which they promise not to divulge or to use for profit information that is exchanged during their substantive discussions.

---

[2] See, eg, the advertisement by the Bangladesh Power Development Board, "Notice of Expression of Interest from the Interested Sponsors for the Establishment of a Minimum 200 MW LNG Power Plant," *The Economist*, January 21, 2011, at 80.

[3] For an example of such a legislative and regulatory framework for a privatization, see the discussion of the bidding process that accompanied the privatization of the water and sewerage system of Buenos Aires, Argentina, in the ICSID case *of Suez, Sociedad General de Aguas de Barcelona SA, and Vivendi Universal SA v. The Argentine Republic* (Case no ARB/03/17), Decision on Liability, July 30, 2010, paras 72–97.

Differing cultural or business backgrounds may affect the way that investors and their counsel approach and conduct prenegotiation. As a general rule, executives from certain Asian countries, such as Japan, tend to devote more time and attention to the prenegotiation phase than do Americans. Whereas Americans generally want to "dispense with the preliminaries" and to "get down to cases," many Asians view prenegotiation as an essential foundation to any business relationship; consequently they recognize the need to conduct prenegotiation with care before actually making a decision to undertake substantive negotiations. One of the consequences of this difference in approach is that Americans sometimes assume that discussions with Asian counterparts have passed from prenegotiation to a subsequent stage when in fact they have not.

Neither party may be able to make a decision to enter into negotiations with the other without exchanging confidential information relating to their respective technologies, business plans, financial resources, and other sensitive matters. This imperative creates a problem for both sides. On the one hand, the information disclosed should be sufficiently explicit to allow the parties to decide whether they want to enter into an investment relationship. On the other hand, it should not be so extensive as to give the parties a valuable resource to use other than for intended purposes. Should negotiations fail, the use of such exchanged information by one of the parties thereafter could be damaging to the other. Once a potential negotiating partner has been identified, it is therefore common for the parties to enter into an "Information Exchange Agreement" or a "Confidentiality Agreement" to protect information that may be exchanged during the course of the negotiation. Such an agreement obligates each of the parties to preserve the confidentiality of information exchanged, not to disclose it to any third party without the written consent of the party originally providing it, and binds the receiving party to use care in limiting, selecting and contractually binding the personnel to whom it gives access to such confidential information.

(b) Conceptualization

In the second phase of the process, which might be called conceptualization, the parties seek to agree on a basic concept or set of fundamental principles upon which to build their investment transactions. For example, in negotiating an agro-industrial project, the foreign investor and the government will need to decide whether the project will take the form of a wholly-owned subsidiary of the investor or a joint venture and, if the latter, whether the government will be a party. Even if the parties have agreed on the basic nature of their transaction, they will then need to find an acceptable formula for its structure. For example, in one case involving the renegotiation of a long-term contract for the sale at a fixed price of electricity between a state power company in Ghana and a foreign-owned aluminum smelter, the parties, who were stymied on the question of price, only made progress when they agreed on the principle that the price of electricity under the contract would be "linked to the international price of energy."[4]

The conceptualization phase of negotiations is marked by the definition of the parties' interests, the advancement of proposals and counterproposals, and the exploration of options. In this phase, the creativity of negotiators comes into play, as they seek to shape a basic concept and to find the precepts for their transaction that will allow both sides to

---

[4] A Sawyer, "Redoing an Old Deal: Case Study of the Renegotiation of the Valco Agreement," (unpublished paper, 1991). See also FS Tsikata (ed), *Essays from the Ghana-Valco Renegotiations: 1982–85* (1986).

satisfy their interests. Once the parties have agreed, they may sign a letter of intent, memorandum of understanding, or similar document to record their understanding.

Neither a letter of intent nor a memorandum of understanding is a legal requirement for a formal investment contract. These documents serve basically to record the intentions of the parties and their fundamental understanding up to that point in the negotiations. They may also enable each of the potential participants in the investment to obtain the necessary internal corporate or governmental authorizations to pursue subsequent phases of the investment negotiations. Psychologically, they also serve to provide momentum by giving negotiators a sense of accomplishment. Normally, they set out the general structure of the proposed venture; however, they also make clear that the stated intentions or understandings are nothing more than a basis for further negotiations and, in the event the parties do not reach agreement, for whatever reason, neither party will be liable to the other. In some cases, a letter of intent or memorandum of understanding may provide for some degree of liability (eg, for expenses incurred in the negotiation process), but strictly limit the extent of that liability. When timing is important, the memorandum or letter will state a deadline for completing the negotiations or the various actions needed to launch the joint venture. And finally, the letter or agreement may include an "exclusivity provision," providing that neither party will conduct negotiations with any third party for a similar investment without notice to the other.

(c) Detail Arrangement

The final phase in the negotiation process is devoted to working out the details and implications of the agreed-upon concept. This phase relies heavily on technical expertise as the parties explore the problems of implementation. Here, negotiators come to understand the full meaning of the old saying "the devil is in the details." For example, it is one thing to agree that the price of electricity should be linked to the international price of energy, but it is quite another to turn that concept into a formula for an effective pricing system that can be accurately and efficiently applied day-to-day throughout the life of the transaction. This phase usually concludes with the signature of a detailed contract documenting the parties' understanding on the various issues concerned with their investment transaction. Chapter 10 considers the content of investment agreements.

No negotiation is as neat and simple as this three-phase model suggests.[5] In the heat of discussion, the precise boundaries between the different phases may be unclear. Sometimes when the parties are unable to find an acceptable concept, they may try to agree on certain details in order to build confidence in one another and to give their talks the appearance, and perhaps the reality, of having momentum. Nonetheless, the above description of the phases of the investment negotiation process may serve as a road map to give negotiators a sense of where they are in the deal-making process and what resources they need to make each phase a success.

9.3 Barriers to Negotiating an International Investment

Negotiating any investment may encounter barriers that hinder or stop the process dead in its tracks. One side gets locked into a position and refuses to look at other options. The

---

[5] For a discussion of this tripartite analysis within the context of diplomatic negotiations, see IW Zartman and MR Berman, *The Practical Negotiator* (1982). See also JW Salacuse, *The Global Negotiator: Making, Managing, and Mending Deals Around the World in the Twenty-first Century* (2003) 17–20.

negotiators come to dislike each other and let their personal feelings interfere with the talks. One team thinks the other is hiding information or lying. The members of both teams start bickering among themselves. Negotiators meet these obstacles whether they are proposing to build a factory in their hometown or to create a timbering joint venture in Indonesia. But when executives negotiate international investments, they also face other, special barriers that they do not usually encounter in making purely domestic transactions.

To illustrate the point, let us take a simple example. Houston Glue Company, a manufacturer located in Houston, Texas, USA, makes and distributes a powerful adhesive under the trademark MegaGlue. A few years ago, because of the growth in its business, it acquired for US$10 million Dallas Adhesive Company, a family-owned business located in Dallas, Texas, which Houston Glue now operates as a separate subsidiary. Since then, the market demand for MegaGlue has expanded rapidly so Houston Glue began looking for additional production capabilities and has identified Budapest Adhesive Co., a recently privatized enterprise in Budapest, Hungary, as a possible acquisition with an initial asking price of 25 billion Hungarian forints. Superficially, these two investment transactions may seem similar. They each involve the acquisition at roughly the same cost of similar assets producing similar products; however, the process of negotiating and making these two investment transactions raises distinctly different problems. Specifically, in negotiating the proposed Budapest transaction, the Houston Glue negotiators will encounter special negotiation barriers that were not present in making the Dallas investment. Seven such barriers are particularly important: (1) the negotiating environment; (2) foreign laws and governments; (3) ideological differences; (4) foreign organizations and bureaucracies; (5) multiple currencies; (6) political instability and sudden change; and (7) cultural differences. The following sections briefly examine each one.

9.4 The Barrier of the Negotiating Environment

Negotiations do not happen in a vacuum. They take place in a specific environment, and the elements of that environment—place, time, surroundings, and people—can influence the discussions profoundly. In international deal making, the negotiating environment can be a particular barrier because for one of the parties that environment is distinctly foreign. Thus, while Houston Glue Co's negotiators would not be especially concerned about the negotiating environment in Dallas, they would most definitely have to plan for and study carefully the negotiating environment in Budapest, an environment with which they are probably not familiar. At the very least, an encounter with a foreign negotiating environment places pressures on the foreign investor to learn about the local context, to cope with a foreign language, to understand local business practices and laws, and to incur the expenses of travel to and maintenance in a foreign country. In deciding on a site for negotiations, negotiators have four basic options: (1) their home territory, (2) the other side's territory; (3) a third place, and (4) thanks to electronic communications, no place at all. Each option has distinct advantages and disadvantages. The conclusion of a specific investment contract may involve some or all four of these options.

Like athletes seeking the "home field advantage," most people perceive many benefits in negotiating on their own territory. First, they have the advantage of familiarity with the negotiating environment, a factor that usually gives them increased confidence at the bargaining table. Their opponents, on the other hand, run the risk of unfamiliarity and, if they come from abroad, even culture shock. Negotiating at home also allows a negotiator to control the environment, including the selection and arrangement of the meeting room, the seating of participants at the bargaining table, and the nature and timing of hospitality and social events, while giving them easy access to experts for advice and to superiors for consultation. Finally, negotiating at home is cheaper, eliminating travel costs and saving time. Negotiating at home also spares them the pressures of being away from family and daily activities, pressures that sometimes causes visiting negotiators to make a deal or break off talks more quickly than if they were negotiating on their own turf—often to their disadvantage.

At first blush, negotiating on the other person's territory seems to offer only disadvantages. But for a company seeking an investment in a foreign country, the only way to make that investment is to go to that country. The choice of a negotiating site also has symbolic value. It demonstrates a foreign investor's serious intent and strong desire to make a deal—factors that can be invaluable in persuading them to sign a contract. The most important reason of all for negotiating on the other side's territory is that it gives an investor an opportunity to *learn*. A vital purpose of any negotiation is to allow both sides to learn about each other, their organizations, and the conditions in which they must operate. In this respect, the home field *doesn't* hold an advantage.

When talks are ongoing and when relationship building is an important consideration, it often makes sense to alternate rounds of negotiation between the two parties' territories, a format that is particularly appropriate if the negotiations will stretch over a long period of time and the parties hope for a long-term business relationship such as a joint venture.

Choosing a neutral, third place for negotiation has a certain superficial attraction: the location gives neither side a special advantage or disadvantage. But neutral territory can be the worst of both worlds, as it limits the ability of each side to learn much about each other.

When negotiators come from different countries, the choice of a third country for talks may be useful if additional learning is not necessary to advance the transaction and if other advantages, such as reduced cost or time, can be achieved. Negotiating in a third country also removes both teams from their daily preoccupations and allows them to focus on the task at hand.

Then, too, if parties are attempting to settle a serious dispute, for example a conflict with a sovereign government over its treatment of a foreign investment, a neutral location, away from each side's supporters, may indeed be the best place to hold discussions.

With increasing frequency, negotiators are avoiding face-to-face meetings entirely and instead relying on communication technologies. E-mail, satellite telephone, and videoconferencing offer low-cost and convenient means of making deals. Some negotiators facing particularly important talks have also created secure websites where documents and other information can be stored for easy consultation by both sides.

While communication technologies are important supports for negotiations, they are not always a satisfactory substitute for face-to-face meetings. Their principal defect is that they prevent parties from learning as much about each other as they would at a bargaining table. Videoconferencing, e-mails, and telephone calls convey non-verbal cues poorly, if at all. Moreover, there is evidence that, when used alone, they may encourage lying and impetuous and insensitive messages. Then too, electronic communications do not convey valuable information about the other side's working environment, and they eliminate completely the opportunities for productive socializing and relationship building that often lead to successful transactions. That said, electronic negotiation can work well in two circumstances: (1) relatively simple transactions, such as the sale of a standard commodity, in which two sides gain sufficient knowledge via computer, telephone, or video; and (2) negotiations in which parties already know each other well and have agreed on a set of rules for using electronic communications in their deal making.

9.5 The Barrier of Foreign Laws and Governments

The special problems posed by foreign laws and governments create a second major barrier in negotiating international investment transactions. The most obvious dimension of the problem is that laws of the site of the investment are usually different from those of the investor's home country and that the investor must therefore spend time and money learning the law that will apply to the proposed investment. The barrier of foreign laws and government also has three other significant dimensions that affect negotiation: the black box, the squeeze, and hometown justice.

The problem of the black box resides in the fact that there may be no law or it may be impossible to find it on a particularly important subject. For example, in the mid-1990s, Laos launched a program to privatize public enterprises and attract foreign investment without a basic corporation law on its books. It may be equally difficult to try to understand the decision-making process of foreign government departments, decisions which seem to emanate from a mysterious black box.

The problem of the squeeze resides in the fact that the same transaction may be governed by the laws of two or more countries and taxed by two or more authorities. Thus legal pluralism always creates the risk that the negotiation and the deal itself will be squeezed between two or more laws, state authorities, and national jurisdictions. And finally, executives and lawyers working in any foreign legal system must be concerned about unfair discrimination—the problem of hometown justice—and must try to build mechanisms in their transactions to cope with this risk, such as international arbitration or linkage to the protective provisions of bilateral investment treaties and trade agreements.

In view of the significant role that foreign governments play in international investment transactions, section 9.11 of this chapter will treat that subject in depth and endeavor to offer advice on effective ways to deal with governments.

9.6 The Barrier of Ideological Differences

Consciously or unconsciously, negotiators bring their ideologies to the negotiating table, and differences in ideologies between negotiators can create yet another barrier in the deal-making process. An ideology is a more or less systematic body of beliefs that explains how society should function and what programs of action it ought to follow. It is different from culture in that while culture is assimilated by a person over time as a member of a community, ideology is more a consciously learned set of political ideals and beliefs. Thus while the Chinese in Hong Kong and the Chinese in the People's Republic of China share the same culture, they may have very different ideologies. Indeed, overseas Chinese themselves often fail to appreciate the impact of communist ideology on business practice in mainland China. Ideologies may be particularly salient in investment transactions because, as noted in Chapter 4, foreign investment for many people has definite political and ideological connotations.

Although it is sometimes claimed that the end of the Cold War also put an end to international ideological differences, ideology is still very much alive today. The ideologies of nationalism, Islamic fundamentalism, and state capitalism remain strong and can serve to complicate a negotiation in several ways. First, ideologies can give an adversarial quality to the discussion. Ideologies have their heroes and their villains, their friends and their foes, their good guys and their bad guys, factors which may lead negotiators to see themselves as engaged in combat rather in a task of joint problem solving. Second, ideologies often complicate communications between negotiators. Words like "profit," "human rights," "free enterprise" and even "the state" can have strong positive or negative implications for a negotiator, depending on his or her ideology. And finally, ideologies may lead parties to take hard-and-fast positions, prevent flexibility and inhibit the search for an accommodation of interests at the bargaining table. Whereas the lawyer or executive for Houston Glue Company probably shared a similar ideology with his or her counterpart in Dallas, he or she must be sensitive to the possibility of ideological differences that may be encountered abroad and must seek ways to avoid them in the course of the negotiation.

9.7 The Barrier of Foreign Organizations and Bureaucracies

In most cases, international investment creates a link between and among organizations. Although negotiation is an intensely personal activity driven by the personality, skill, and experience of the individual negotiators involved in the process, it is also a bureaucratic activity influenced by the nature of their respective organizations. As a result, a negotiator not only has to be concerned about the person sitting across the table but he or she must also constantly think about the organizations and bureaucracies behind each of them. While negotiating with the person across the table, it is important to remember that there are internal negotiations occurring in his or her organization about the proposed deal just as there are similar internal negotiations happening in your own organization. Thus, deal making always involves at least three separate but linked negotiations: the external discussions with a counterpart and the internal discussions in each of the two organizations. What happens in each of the three can influence the deal-making process profoundly; consequently, an international investment negotiator must take account of all three in planning and executing strategy. For example, even though two negotiators have reached agreement, they both may now face the challenge of convincing their respective organizations to approve that agreement. Sometime negotiators have to find ways to help each other in the process of securing such approvals.

The variety of bureaucracies is endless. Before plunging into a negotiation, it is important for negotiators to try to understand the bureaucracy with which they are dealing, to learn how it makes decisions, to determine if other organizations should be involved in the discussions, and to decide the most effective way to approach and penetrate the organizations with which they hope to negotiate an investment transaction.

9.8 The Barrier of Multiple Currencies

Unlike purely domestic investments, international investment transactions take place in a world of many currencies and monetary systems. This factor creates yet another special barrier to the international negotiating process, a barrier that is unknown in a purely domestic deal, such as Houston Glue Company might make with Dallas Adhesives Company. The world of multiple currencies creates three problems that the international negotiator must constantly think about. First, as one saw in the Mexican peso crisis of 1994 and the Asian financial crisis of 1998, the world's currencies are constantly changing in value in relation to one another, a factor which injects significant currency risk into any transaction. The negotiator must therefore seek ways to cope with the risk so as to maintain the value of the transaction. Basically, there are four approaches to resolving the problem: accept the risk, give it to the other side, share the risk, or put the risk on to a third party through some form of insurance or hedging transaction. Second, many countries' currencies are not freely convertible so that the actions of governments or central banks become part of the negotiator's calculations in the deal-making process. The great challenge for the international deal maker in these situations is to find mechanisms that will assure payment in freely convertible currency or its equivalent. In some countries, for example, a foreign investor may have no choice but to structure a countertrade transaction in goods as a means of repatriating profits from an investment. And a third aspect of the world of multiple currencies is simply the required mechanics, such as letters of credit and currency conversion, for making payment from one monetary system to another. These mechanisms serve to increase the transaction risks and costs to the parties.

9.9 The Barrier of Political Instability and Sudden Change

Change, of course, is a fact of life. Sudden changes in circumstances can happen in both domestic and international business transactions. Nonetheless, the risk of change in an international investment transaction is generally far greater than in the purely domestic transaction. War, revolution, closed trade routes, currency devaluations, and sudden changes in government are just a few of the types of events that can have severe and widespread consequences for any international investment. Even apparently minor governmental changes can threaten the existence of a lawful deal. In Indonesia, for example, a US insurance company formed a joint venture with an Indonesian firm and developed a profitable business. A few years later, the prime minister appointed a new minister with authority over insurance, and he began to pressure the Americans to find a new local partner because for some reason he found their current partner to be unacceptable. To protect themselves against such eventualities, some international investors specifically provide in their joint venture agreements that if the local partner becomes unacceptable to the host government, the foreign firm would have the right to dissolve the joint venture or buy out the local partner's interest.

Experienced deal makers know that the challenge of international business is not just "getting to yes," but also staying there. International investment agreements, solemnly signed and sealed after hard bargaining, often break down because of changes in circumstances or attitudes of the parties. When a change in circumstances means that the cost of respecting the contract for one of the parties is greater than the cost of abandoning it, the result is usually rejection and renegotiation. The two sides either walk away from each other for good or walk back to the negotiating table to restructure their deal. A traditional theme in international business circles is the lament over the "unstable contract," the profitable agreement that the other side refuses to respect. The risk of instability and sudden change, then, is yet another barrier to the international deal-making process. Chapter 12, devoted to the renegotiation of investment contracts, will consider these issues in depth.

9.10 The Barrier of Cultural Differences

(a) In General

International investment transactions not only cross borders, but they also cross cultures. Culture profoundly influences how people think, communicate and behave, and it also affects the kinds of transactions they make and the way they make them. Differences in culture among business executives, for example between a Chinese public sector plant manager in Shanghai and an American division head of a family company in Cleveland, can create negotiating barriers that impede or completely stymie the negotiating process. For executives and lawyers negotiating investment transactions in various parts of the world, cultural differences with their foreign counterparts are often difficult obstacles to overcome.

(b) The Meaning of Culture

What is meant by culture? Definitions of culture are as numerous and often as vague as definitions of negotiation itself. Some scholars would confine the concept of culture to the realm of ideas, feeling, and thoughts. For example, one working definition offered by two negotiation experts is that "Culture is a set of shared and enduring meanings, values, and beliefs that characterize national, ethnic, and other groups and orient their behavior."[6] Others would have culture also encompass behavior patterns and institutions common to a given group or community. E. Adamson Hoebel, a noted anthropologist, defined culture as "the integrated system of learned behavior patterns which are characteristic of the members of a society and which are not the result of biological inheritance."[7] While the essence of culture may reside in the mind, it must be pointed out that persons gain their understanding of their and others' cultures primarily, if not exclusively, from observing the behavior and institutions of a particular group.

For purposes of this section, one may define culture as the socially transmitted behavior patterns, norms, beliefs, and values of a given community. Persons from that community use the elements of their culture to interpret their surroundings and guide their interactions with other persons. So when an executive from a corporation in Dallas, Texas, sits down to negotiate a business deal with a manager from a Houston company, the two negotiators rely on their common culture to interpret each other's statements and actions. But when persons from two different cultures—for example an executive from Houston and a manager from Budapest—meet for the first time, they usually do not share a common pool of information and assumptions to interpret each others' statements, actions, and intentions. Culture can therefore be seen as a language, a "silent language" which the parties need in addition to the language they are speaking if they are truly to communicate and arrive at a genuine understanding.[8] Like any language, the elements of culture form a system, which has been variously characterized as a "system for creating, sending, storing, and processing information,"[9] and "group problem-solving tool that enables individuals to survive in a particular environment."[10] Culture serves as a kind of glue—a social adhesive—that binds a group of people together and gives them a distinct identity as a community. It may also give them a sense that they are a community different and separate from other communities.

This section is concerned primarily with national cultures, cultures identified with a particular country. But culture and nationality are not always the same thing. Within Nigeria, for example, the culture of the Ibos of the largely Christian southeastern part of the country and the Hausas of the mainly Muslim north are different and distinct. Similarly, individual corporations and professions may have their own distinct organizational or professional cultures whose norms and behavior patterns may predominate in certain respects over the ethnic or national cultures of their profession's members. For example, a continuing concern in purely domestic mergers and acquisitions is the problem of

---

[6] GO Faure and JZ Rubin (eds), *Culture and Negotiation* (1993) 3.
[7] EA Hoebel, *Anthropology: The Study of Man* (4th edn 1972) 7.
[8] E Hall, *The Silent Language* (1959).
[9] ET Hall and MR Hall, *Understanding Cultural Differences* (1990) 179.
[10] RT Moran and WG Stripp, *Successful International Business Negotiations* (1991) 143.

blending the cultures of the organizations concerned. But while cultural values, attitudes, and behavior patterns may appear permanently embedded in a group, particularly in the context of an encounter between two different cultures, in fact culture is dynamic. It is constantly changing.

And finally, in considering the role of culture in international investment negotiation and relationships, it is important to remember that the world has a staggering diversity of cultures. For example, while certain observers speak of "Asian culture" as if it were a homogeneous set of values, beliefs and behavior patterns followed by all Asians, in reality Asia has many different and distinct cultures from India to Laos, from Korea to Indonesia. Each has its own values and practices that may differ markedly from those prevailing in another country—or indeed in another part of the same country. The negotiating style of Koreans, for example, is not the same as that of the Lao. And even within countries that from outward appearances seem to have a fairly uniform cultural identity, like the French and the Germans, significant differences may nonetheless exist between regions, for example the difference between the business community in Paris and that of the *midi* in southern France.

(c) The Elements of Culture

One may conceive of the four cultural elements mentioned in the earlier definition— behavior, attitudes, norms and values—as forming a series of concentric circles, like the layers of an onion.[11] The process of understanding the culture of a counterpart in a negotiation is similar to peeling an onion. The outer-most layer of the onion is behavior, the words and actions of one's counterpart. It is this layer which a negotiator first perceives in an intercultural negotiation. A second, inner layer consists of attitudes of persons from that culture toward specific events and phenomena, for example attitudes about beginning meetings punctually or the appropriate format of presentations. Attitudes may become evident to a counterpart in an intercultural negotiation only after protracted discussions. Next are norms, the rules to be followed in specific situations. Here, for example, a negotiator may come to realize that his or her counterpart's seemingly rigid insistence on punctuality is not merely a personal idiosyncrasy but is based on a firm rule derived from his or her culture.

The inner-most layer—the core—consists of values. Norms about the way meetings are conducted, representatives chosen, or persons rewarded are usually based on certain values that are important to that culture. Such differences in values are often the most difficult for negotiators to detect and understand. Indeed, the parties to an international negotiation may discover their value differences only after they have signed a joint venture contract and begun to work together. Such differences in cultural values between partners may lead to severe conflict and ultimately the failure of their enterprise, a factor which may explain why many international joint ventures have a short life.

In their valuable book *The Seven Cultures of Capitalism* (1993), based on extensive survey research among thousands of executives from throughout the world, Hampden-Turner and Trompenaars found sharp differences that could only be explained by different cultural values to such basic management tasks as group decision making, hiring, rewarding employees, and making and applying rules. For example, with respect to

---

[11] See generally, JW Salacuse, *The Global Negotiator* (2003) 89–115.

group decision making, wide variations among cultural groups existed in answering the following question:

> What is the better way to choose a person to represent a group?
> A. All members of the group should meet and discuss candidates until almost everybody agrees on the same person; or
> B. The group members should meet, nominate persons, vote and choose the person with a majority of the votes even if several people are against the person.

In this question, according to the authors, the values of adversarial democracy and consensual democracy were in tension. While 84.4 percent of the Japanese opted for Answer A (consensual democracy), only 37.7 percent of the Americans did so. It is interesting to note that there were differences among Asians on this question. For example, unlike the Japanese, only 39.4 percent of the Singaporeans chose Answer A, exhibiting an aversion to consensual democracy that is perhaps reflected in Singapore's authoritarian political system. One can imagine that this difference in cultural values about decision making between Japanese and American executives in a joint venture might lead to serious conflict between the joint venture partners.

Other kinds of value conflicts may arise, for example between individualism prized by Americans and communitarianism embodied in many Asian cultures, about whether in hiring an employee it is more important to consider individual talent or the ability to fit into the organization, about whether to reward persons on the basis of group performance or by individual achievement only.

Differences in cultural values can present themselves in international investment transactions and relationships time after time and day after day, and they may ultimately turn what appeared to be a harmonious negotiation or business relationship into a continuing source of conflict between the parties. Once the conflict surfaces, it may be exacerbated by the way the parties try to cope with it. One unfortunate tendency is for each of the parties to extol their own cultural values but to denigrate those of their business or negotiating partner. For example, Americans, with their high store on individualism, will tend to see their value system positively: as supporting individual rights and human freedom; as putting the individual above the tyranny of the group; as knowing that a group prospers only when individuals prosper; and as efficient. Persons coming from cultures where communitarian values are prized will see themselves as: unselfish, humane, for group interests and rights, and knowing that individuals prosper only when the group prospers. Yet, Americans, when confronted with a communitarian culture, may tend to ascribe to it only negative characteristics. So Americans, reacting to Japanese values in a decision to retain an employee of 15 years whose performance has declined, might consider their Japanese counterparts as: tolerant of free loaders; giving in to the tyranny of the group; weak; and inefficient. On the other hand, the Japanese would probably characterize the Americans as ignoring the contributions and needs of the group; lacking in loyalty; inhumane; and selfish.It is important therefore for business executives in a negotiation to understand the values inherent in the culture of their counterparts and not to characterize those values in a negative way.

(d) Culture's Effect on Investment Negotiation

Differences in culture between investment negotiators can obstruct negotiations in many ways. First, they can create misunderstandings in communication. If one UK executive responds to another UK executive's proposal by saying, "That's difficult," the response, interpreted against UK culture and business practice, probably means that the door is still open for further discussion, that perhaps the other side should improve its offer. In some other cultures, for example in Asia, persons may be reluctant to say a direct and emphatic "no," even when that is their intention. So when a Japanese negotiator, in response to a proposal says, "That is difficult," he is clearly indicating that the proposal is unacceptable. "It is difficult," means "no" to the Japanese, but to the UK executive it means "perhaps."

Second, cultural differences create difficulties not only in understanding words, but also in interpreting actions. For example, while Americans and Canadians may find it perfectly appropriate to conduct business discussions at lunch, Brazilian and Japanese executives may consider serious business negotiations to be totally out of place in that setting. Thus there can be sharp cultural differences as to when and where deal making is appropriate.

Most westerners expect a prompt answer when they make a statement or ask a question. The Japanese, on the other hand, tend to take longer to respond. As a result, negotiations with Japanese are sometimes punctuated with periods of silence that seem excruciating to an American. For the Japanese, the period of silence is normal, an appropriate time to reflect on what has been said. The fact that they are not speaking in their native language lengthens even more the time needed to respond.

From their own cultural perspective, Americans may interpret Japanese silence as rudeness, lack of understanding, or a cunning tactic to get the Americans to reveal themselves. Rather than wait for a response, the American tendency is to fill the void with words by asking questions, offering further explanations, or merely repeating what they have already said. This response to silence may confuse the Japanese, who are made to feel that they are being bombarded by questions and proposals without being given adequate time to respond to any of them.

On the other hand, Latin Americans, who place a high value on verbal agility, have a tendency to respond quickly. Indeed, they may answer a point once they have understood it even though the other side has not finished speaking. While inexperienced American negotiators are sometimes confused by Japanese delays in responding, they can become equally agitated in negotiations with Brazilians by what Americans consider constant interruptions.

Third, cultural considerations also influence the form and substance of the deal you are trying to make. For example, in many parts of the Muslim world, where Islamic law prohibits the taking of interest on loans, it may be necessary to restructure or relabel finance charges in a transaction as "administrative fees" in order to gain acceptance at the negotiating table.

More substantively, differences in culture will invariably require changes in products, management systems, and personnel practices. For example in Thailand, the relationship between manager and employee is more hierarchical than in many western countries. Workers are motivated by a desire to please the manager, but they in turn expect and want their manager to sense their personal problems and be ready to help with them. In other cultures, for example in Australia, employees neither expect nor want managers to become involved with employees' personal problems. Thus an Australian investment project in Thailand would need to change its concept and management of employee relations because of the local culture.

And finally, culture can influence "negotiating style," the way persons from different cultures conduct themselves in negotiating sessions. Research indicates fairly clearly that negotiation practices differ from culture to culture. Indeed, culture may influence how persons conceive of the very nature and function of negotiation itself. Studies of negotiating styles are abundant.[12] Some seek to focus on describing and analyzing the negotiating styles of particular groups. Indeed, the practitioner's fascination with cultural negotiating styles seems to have spawned a distinct literary genre: the "Negotiating With…" literature. Numerous books and articles bearing such titles as "Negotiating with the Japanese," "Negotiating with the Arabs," and Negotiating with the Chinese," seek to lead the novice through the intricacies of negotiating in specific cultures.[13]

9.11 Negotiating Investment Contracts with Foreign Governments

(a) In General

Despite the powerful forces of privatization, deregulation, and globalization that have swept the world since the 1980s,[14] foreign governments are still important players in international business. Indeed, with the rise of sovereign wealth funds potentially holding trillions of dollars in assets and the renationalization of key industries in certain countries, their role has heightened in recent years. As a result, governments are an actual or potential presence in the negotiation of nearly all significant international investments.

Foreign governments may play many different roles in the negotiation of an international investment. They may be parties to the transaction as investors, borrowers, guarantors, buyers, suppliers, financiers, or partners, whose representatives are active participants at the bargaining table. In other transactions, their role is that of regulator whose permission or authorization is necessary if an investment is to go forward, a factor necessitating negotiations with one or more government departments or agencies to obtain the authorizations needed. In still other cases, even when a government entity is not physically present at the negotiating table and has no specific authority to regulate the transaction, it nonetheless may be lurking in the wings as a "ghost negotiator" exerting a powerful influence on local parties to assure that governmental interests are protected. So even if a foreign investor is not negotiating directly with a government in those situations, it still eventually may have to deal indirectly with one or more governmental units in order to make the transaction it wants. And finally, if the public becomes concerned about an investment that a foreign company is trying to negotiate, that company should be prepared for the government to make its presence felt at the negotiating table.

In approaching any significant international investment, executives and lawyers should always ask three important questions:

1. To what extent does a government have an actual or potential interest in this transaction?
2. How and to what extent will that government be involved in the negotiation?
3. If a government is not directly involved, how might it nonetheless intervene in the negotiation or the resulting transaction to protect its interests?

The purpose of this section is to examine the role played by governments in negotiating international investment and to provide some general guidance on negotiating with them.

---

[12] For a detailed discussion of the effect of culture on negotiating style, see generally JW Salacuse, *The Global Negotiator: Making, Managing, and Mending Deals Around the World in the Twenty-first Century* (2003) 89–115. See also JW Salacuse, "Ten Ways that Culture Affects Negotiating Style: Some Survey Results," 14 *Negotiation Journal* (1998) 221–40.

[13] For a bibliography of such literature, see JW Salacuse, *The Global Negotiator: Making, Managing, and Mending Deals Around the World in the Twenty-first Century* (2003) 291–8.

[14] See JW Salacuse, "From Developing Countries to Emerging Markets: A New Role for Law in the Third World," 33 *International Lawyer* (1999) 875.

The reader should bear in mind that no two governments are alike and that effective negotiation with any government requires a thorough knowledge of its particular political history, culture, and bureaucratic traditions.[15]

(b) Government Attitudes toward Negotiation

At the outset, it is important to recognize that government officials often have a different attitude toward the process of negotiation with private parties than do individuals and companies. Whereas corporate executives usually consider business negotiation as a free-wheeling process to make deals and solve problems, many government officials in their interactions with private parties often view themselves as merely carrying out the laws and regulations they are obligated to apply. They are *dispensers* of the transactions that the law allows, not negotiators. As one official from the Mexican Central Bank told the author, "For government officials, negotiation is not proper. Law is a not a negotiable thing when you are in charge of applying it."

Despite the Mexican official's protestations, few governmental systems in reality make automatic, mechanical decisions. Because legislators do not have perfect foresight, they cannot make laws or regulation that provide for all possible eventualities that may happen in the future. As a result, all governmental systems require in varying degrees that their operators exercise some degree of *discretion* in making their decisions, whether it is granting a concession to operate a public service, issuing a building permit, or purchasing a weapons system. Discretion in this context means the ability to make a decision involving a choice among various options. The existence of discretion is the opening to negotiation, and the goal of an investment negotiator is to persuade the government official across the table to exercise that discretion in a desired way. It is therefore important for business negotiators to determine precisely how much discretion the officials with whom they are dealing have.

Despite the widespread prevalence of negotiations between government departments on the one hand and foreign companies and individuals on the other, many government officials, like the one from the Mexican Central Bank, strongly resist the idea that when they do their jobs they are engaged in "negotiation." An understanding of the reason for this attitude provides some useful insights into government officials as negotiators and indeed into the whole process of negotiating with governments.

First, many officials take comfort in the fiction that their decisions are made according to rules, automatically applied. Thus, their decisions are not their responsibility, but that of the institution that made the rules. If a private party does not like that decision, he or she should blame the institution—the legislature or the ministry that made the rule, not the public official who merely applied it. This rationalization protects officials from complaints and criticism by various interest groups and individuals. For an official to acknowledge that the issuance of a contract or permit resulted from a negotiation, which implies a back-and-forth exchange of proposals and counterproposals, is to admit that the decision did not result from an automatic application of the rules, thus opening government officials to questions, challenges, and even threats that might undermine their positions and injure their careers.

Second, for many people, compromise is implicit in the notion of negotiation. Although the public accepts compromise in certain contexts, it may consider compromise inappropriate in others. For example, while it is one thing for a business executive to acknowledge

---

[15] See generally, JW Salacuse, *Seven Secrets for Negotiating with Government* (2008).

engaging in compromise when negotiating a merger with another private company, it is quite another thing for a public official to admit compromising in granting a permit or making a state contract. In the public's view, the application of public policy, law, and regulations should not to be subject to compromise. Rather, the public expects governments to apply law, regulations, and policies uniformly to all persons. It is this attitude, for example, that has caused public opposition in certain countries to negotiated infrastructure and public service contracts as opposed to those arrived at by a strict competitive bidding process.

To accept that the application of laws and regulations is the product of negotiation and that therefore some persons benefit from them and others do not is seen as an affront to basic notions of democracy and equality before the law. For most officials and regulators, a model government decision with respect to a company or individual is objective, impersonal, and uniform. A negotiated decision, on the other hand, implies just the opposite. A negotiated decision is subjective, personal, and special to the party concerned.

These considerations have certain important implications for conducting negotiations with governments. First, it is important to find a justification for the transaction in the law, regulations, or objective standards that are defensible to the public, civic groups, and the government's political opponents. Second, the process by which the deal was negotiated must also be defensible, and this may require business negotiators to abandon certain cherished precepts of business deal making. For example openness and transparency may be more important than confidentiality. And third, in many investor interactions with governments, it is often best to avoid the word "negotiation" in referring to the process in which the investor is engaged. To respect governmental sensitivities, refer to your negotiations with government officials by other names: "discussions," "conversations," "requests," or "interactions."

(c) Governments Feel Different

"Governments feel different," an experienced corporate dealmaker once told the author in reflecting on his years of negotiating international investment transactions. What he meant was that governments as negotiators are not like private parties. They approach, prepare for, conduct, and conclude negotiations in ways that are different from those used by individuals and corporations. In order to deal with governments effectively, private persons and companies must understand these differences and develop strategies to cope with them.

If governments as negotiating counterparts feel different from private organizations, it is particularly because of two factors: the special *powers* that governments wield and the special *constraints* to which they are subject at the bargaining table. The nature and extent of government powers and constraints will of course vary from country to country and from government department to government department. But in preparing to negotiate with any foreign government, negotiators should seek to understand its special powers, as well as the special constraints affecting a government's ability to use those powers.

(d) The Special Negotiating Powers of Foreign Governments

Within the context of any negotiation, "power" means the ability to influence the decisions of another party in a desired way.[16] In addition to the negotiating power gained as a result

---

[16] See generally, IW Zartman and JZ Rubin (eds), *Power and Negotiation* (2000); and JW Salacuse, "How Should The Lamb Negotiate With The Lion?: Power In International Negotiations," in D Kolb (ed), *Negotiation Eclectics* (1999) 87–99.

of such natural attributes as wealth, resources, and physical location, all governments derive special powers in investment negotiations from: (1) their monopoly position; (2) their special governmental privileges and immunities; (3) their role as defenders of the public interest and welfare; and (4) their special protocols and forms. Let's examine each one.

(i) Power No 1: The Power of Monopoly

Most of the time, when a private company negotiates with other private individuals and organizations it has alternative courses of action if the negotiations fail. If it is negotiating to establish an auto assembly plant in a particular country, it usually has the option of locating the plant in another country if it can't reach a satisfactory agreement in the first country. If it is negotiating to acquire another company as part of its strategy of corporate growth, it usually has yet another company in mind as a possible target for acquisition. These alternatives may be good or bad, but other options do exist. The nature and extent of a negotiator's other options affect his or her bargaining power in a negotiation. If you have other good options, you have a position of strength in negotiation. If your alternatives are poor, you have less power.

In most negotiations with governments, the particular government department in question has a monopoly over what the investment negotiator is seeking. As a result, negotiators in such cases feel that they have few other options to satisfy our interests. That realization has the effect of giving negotiators a sense that they are in a weak bargaining position when they negotiate with a government department because alternatives for making a deal are usually not very good. For instance, if a pharmaceutical company wants to sell a drug in the United States, it has to obtain approval from the Food and Drug Administration (FDA), and the Food and Drug Administration alone. No other department can give that approval. The FDA's monopoly position gives it a position of power in its negotiations with pharmaceutical companies

Companies often have to negotiate with other organizations that have a dominant position in the market, like Microsoft or Wal-Mart, a position that seems close to a monopoly. The difference between negotiating with a Microsoft or a Wal-Mart on the one hand and a government on the other is that a government usually has a *legal* monopoly over what the negotiator seeks. That legal monopoly makes it impervious to various market factors, such as share price or technological change, that strongly influence a Wal-Mart or Microsoft, no matter how dominant it is for the time being. Governments' legal monopoly makes them impervious to market forces and gives them a sense of permanence that few companies in the private sector enjoy. Also, unlike a company that has a dominant market position, a government department has the ability to use force to maintain its legal monopoly. So if a company tries to sell a drug without FDA approval, federal authorities will close down its plant and charge its executives with a crime.

On the other hand, a government's monopoly rarely extends beyond its territory. One way of countering the power of a governmental monopoly is to develop other options in other territories beyond its reach and to make the government aware of your efforts. Thus, for example, Japanese auto manufacturers seeking to establish car plants in the United States engaged in a process of simultaneously negotiating benefits from several different state and local governments before making a decision on the precise locality in which to build a plant.

(ii) Power No 2: The Power of Privilege and Immunity

Governments also feel different from other negotiators because they enjoy many legal privileges and immunities that private companies and persons do not. Not only do they have the power to regulate how businesses operate, they also have the ability to seize property, cancel contracts, threaten force and, if need be, actually use it to obtain their objectives. Moreover, in many countries, a private party cannot sue the government in a court of law no matter how arbitrary its actions, nor can it force the government to respect the contracts it has signed. Even if a suit is legally possible, governments nonetheless often benefit from judicial bias in their favor. National legal systems give governments an array of privileges and immunities in order to allow them to perform their basic task of governing.

These extensive privileges and immunities also give governments special power at the negotiating table. The implicit or explicit threat by a government to exercise its special powers against a counterpart has influenced the results of many negotiations between government units and private corporations. Multinational corporations, while having a vast pool of capital and technology at their command, do not have these kinds of powers. The result, as a senior executive at a giant global pharmaceutical company once said, is that even "the smallest governments can jerk you around."

Many times, a government's explicit or implicit threat to use this power causes private negotiators to make concessions that they would not normally make in a negotiation with another private company. It is the exercise of this power that often forces companies with advantageous government contracts to renegotiate them and thereby give a government more favorable terms.

One way to reduce this power differential is for a private party to enlist the assistance of another government or organization as an equalizer. For example, to avoid the problems of a judicial partiality toward the government, investment contracts might provide for all disputes to be settled by international arbitration in a neutral country. And if a foreign investor is having a problem with a local government in a host country, it might seek help from its own government.

(iii) Power No 3: The Power of Representing the Public Interest

Governments justify all of their actions, legal or not, on grounds that they are acting in the public interest rather than for private gain. Thus, they claim that they are acting in the interests of "national security," "public welfare," or "the good of the people." In many negotiations, government officials often take the moral high ground in order to justify their demands and obtain concessions from the other side. After all, they are altruistically seeking to achieve the public good in the negotiation, while the representatives of a private company are merely looking to make a selfish profit. The government's role as representative of the public interest also gives it the ability to mobilize popular support for its negotiating positions and to use political influence to gain advantages that no private corporation ever could. For example, during its financial crisis in 2001, the Argentine government refused to pay its international debts, declaring that to do so would threaten the basic welfare of the Argentine people. It portrayed foreign creditors and investors as imperiling the very survival of the country, a tactic that gained the government great popular support and foreign banks widespread hostility. African governments have used a similar tactic in their negotiations with international pharmaceutical companies to obtain low prices on HIV drugs and other medicines essential to public health.

As a result of the power of governments to represent the public interest, companies engaged in negotiations with governments often find that they must conduct two related but separate negotiations to achieve their objectives: one inside the negotiating room with government representatives and the other outside in the media and in public relations. Almost any negotiation with a government has the potential to become a public issue in which civic organizations, nongovernmental organizations, and the public in general take an active, vocal part, thus turning what foreign investors thought was a private, bilateral negotiation into a public, multilateral negotiation.

(iv) Power No 4: The Power of Protocol and Form

Governments and their representatives are usually acutely sensitive to matters concerning their status, prestige, and dignity, since these elements are essential to carrying out their primary task: governing. All other things being equal, a government that is respected by its people and by other nations will find it easier to govern than a government that does not.

One of the ways in which governments seek to preserve and enhance their status and power is through their use of various forms and protocols, particularly those that relate to how private persons and companies are to communicate and interact with the government and its officials. Governments usually have express or implicit rules about the way private persons are to approach them, what form of address they are to use, and where they are to sit or stand in relation to government representatives. Officials consider the failure to respect these forms as a sign of disrespect or, worse, a challenge to their authority.

Governments also use these forms in order to enhance their power in a negotiation, and their officials therefore frequently bring to the negotiating table attitudes and approaches that seem to introduce rigidity into the deal-making process. By virtue of their governmental status, negotiators for government departments, ministries, and state corporations often behave differently in negotiations from the way private company executives and lawyers would. For one thing, government officials resist being considered as equals to the private businesspeople on the other side of the table. Indeed, any suggestion that the two sides are equals may be considered an insult. Government officials represent the "the state," "the nation," and "the people," and a sovereign country, no matter how small, is superior in status to a private business firm, no matter how large. Any slight to a government official may be considered an affront to the dignity of the nation.

In one instance, an African minister asked for a meeting with the head of a foreign mining company that had operations in his country. The meeting took place in the office of the minister of mines and was attended by nine other government ministers. The minister of mines said that the government wanted to renegotiate its concession agreement with the company to obtain a greater share of mineral revenues, and he listed the points that needed to be discussed. In response, the chairman of the mining company reviewed each item, but at one point he flatly said, "We cannot entertain that." To emphasize his position, he struck the table with his hand. The minister immediately adjourned the meeting and refused to continue the discussions.

While the response of the mining company chairman might have been acceptable in a negotiation between two private companies, it was inappropriate in a discussion with what amounted to nearly the entire government of a sovereign state. Instead of an outright rebuff, the chairman should have shown a willingness to listen and to discuss all of the government's concerns. Such flexibility, of course, does not mean that a company has to give in on every point. In this case, it took nearly nine months to get the negotiations going again, and during that time the government made operations difficult for the company. Ultimately, the two sides did renegotiate the mining concession.

African government officials are by no means the only ones to look unkindly upon challenges to their authority. Indeed, one can find similar example of such sensitivities throughout all governments. The lesson they teach is very clear. In negotiations with government officials, negotiators should avoid challenging their authority. As one experienced government affairs professional told the author, "You need to give people the respect due their office." A government department's basic capital is its authority, and it is authority that enables it to function. If you challenge its authority, either directly or indirectly, you are in effect challenging the ability of that department to perform its basic tasks. When their authority is challenged, the instinct of government officials, like the African ministers, is to rebuff the challenge in the clearest possible and most forceful terms. Moreover, having been challenged once by an organization, a government official will continue to remember that challenge in future dealings for a long time to come, much to the cost of that organization. Wise negotiators learn the established protocols and forms for dealing with a particular government, and they respect them scrupulously.

(e) Governments' Special Negotiating Constraints

A government's monopoly position, its array of privileges and immunities, its role as defender of the public interest, and its forms and protocols give it a clear position of power in its negotiations with private parties. On the other hand, few governments are free to use that power in any way they wish. In one respect or another, they all are subject to constraints on its use. An understanding of those constraints may allow negotiators to mobilize them to their advantage and thereby reduce the power differential of government officials with whom you are negotiating.

(i) *Constraint No 1: Negotiating Rules*

Government bureaucracies exist to apply laws, regulations, and rules. Rules govern all their operations, including their negotiations with private persons and companies. As a result, negotiating with governments is very much a rule-driven process, not the freewheeling interaction that usually characterizes deal making between purely private parties. Rules and regulations affect not only the kinds of deals governments make but also the way they make them.

The rules incorporated in these laws and regulations state the ways negotiators are to engage the government office concerned, what kind of documentation they must present to it, the precise terms that will need to appear in the final contract, and much, much more. The effect of these rules is to limit the freedom of contract of governmental departments, agencies and state corporations, as well as investment negotiators' interactions with them. Government officials may be required to use standard form contracts that include mandatory clauses on payment terms, insurance, and guarantees, to mention just a few. They may also be required to favor certain kinds of business over others, for example by giving preference to national companies over foreign companies.

Like an elaborate ballet, the entire negotiation process may follow a strict choreography to its completion. Thus, making a transaction to build a power plant in a country with a government partner often requires the foreign investor to engage in distinct, intricate phases—tendering, evaluation, selection, and challenge—each of which is governed by detailed rules. The first phase is *tendering*, whereby the government announces its needs and requests interested and qualified persons to make an offer of the services or goods to be procured. Often, the tendering phases provides for a sealed bidding process in which the bidding investor is to present two envelopes: one setting out the technical details of its proposal and the second specifying the financial aspects. Next, the bids are subjected to evaluation, using criteria that have been decided upon and made public. Once the evaluation is completed, the government agency makes a selection and proceeds to enter into a formal agreement. But before such agreement is finalized, a process of challenge is possible, whereby disappointed bidders are given an opportunity to contest the selection decision. The whole process is time-consuming, costly, and complicated, often requiring the services of specialists in this domain.

Few companies in the private sector would conduct negotiations in this fashion, for the simple reason that it would not be "efficient" in the sense of achieving the maximum output for a given input. Here then is a further major difference between negotiations with governments and negotiations between purely private parties. Whereas ostensible "efficiency" is the highest goal sought by private negotiators, ostensible "fairness" is the goal sought by governments in their negotiations. One of the reasons that purely private negotiations value efficiency so highly is that the participants' organizations will directly benefit from any savings or gains achieved in the negotiations. A win-win solution that allows both companies to save money or create new wealth in a particular transaction will have the result that both companies have increased earnings for investment in other projects and for possible distribution to shareholders.

A gain secured for a government in a negotiation, on the other hand, does not benefit the department concerned but usually passes directly to the state budget, without having a positive impact on the department's own resources. The inability of a government department to capture gains may influence the government negotiator's reluctance to try innovative solutions to problems, particularly if those innovative solutions are not specifically authorized by the rules and might be challenged by third parties as "unfair."

To say that the purpose of such rules and regulations is to assure that negotiations are "fair" does not just mean that they are fair to the government or fair to the private party that gets the contract; rather, they must also be "fair" to those who did not succeed in making a contract with the government—and to the public as well. In order to protect itself from accusations of unfairness, arbitrariness, or corruption, the government department must show that it has followed the rules in all respects, not by demonstrating that the deal is economically efficient. As a result, the process of conducting a negotiation according to the rules often becomes an end in itself. Because the rules on negotiations have such a central place in negotiations with governments, it is important for negotiators representing private individuals and companies to understand them. In any negotiation with a government, the power to convince an official will almost always depend on a negotiator's ability to find a rule to justify his or her position.

The fact that no rule prohibits what a foreign investor is asking may not be enough to convince the officials sitting across the table. If a government department is presented with two possible courses of action, one which is clearly authorized by the prevailing law or regulation and the other only vaguely permitted, that department will almost always favor the first and look dubiously on the second. For example, during the late 1970s, when Egypt began to open its doors to foreign investment after they had been closed for over 20 years, President Sadat gave glowing speeches about Egypt's openness to and need for foreign investment and warmly urged investors to establish their operations in the country. Drawn by this rhetoric, investors were disappointed to find that the Egyptian bureaucracy was slow to approve their investment proposals. When investors pointed to the speeches that Sadat had been giving as justification for expediting approvals in their negotiations with the Egyptian Investment Authority, Egyptian bureaucrats replied that their job was to apply the law and rules governing investment, not the speeches of the president. The Egyptian laws and regulations on foreign investment were clear about the approval process for investment projects, and so the Egyptian bureaucracy applied them strictly, as it felt bound to do. The process of approving foreign investment proposals would become easier for investors only with the adoption of new regulations that abolished the old requirements and enabled the Egyptian bureaucracy to facilitate approvals.

(ii) Constraint No 2: Constituents

Just because a particular government department or agency has a monopoly over what an investor is seeking does not mean that department or agency is omnipotent. Inevitably, any governmental unit relies on some constituency for resources and support, and that constituency can therefore influence the way that particular unit behaves. Depending on the country, state, or locality, government departments and officials rely on a wide variety of constituents and supporters—political parties, labor unions, the military, the media, and civic organizations—from which they derive power and authority. So, in negotiating with any government department, a foreign investor needs to understand its particular constituents and the levers they command to influence government action.

The key constituents of a government department are not always readily apparent. Like cultures, each of the world's governmental systems is distinct and different. The French government does not make policy the way the German government does. And an American lawyer or executive cannot assume that governments abroad work the way the US government does at home. As a result, negotiators may be tempted to think that government and bureaucratic decision making is some kind of a mysterious black box, whose workings are impossible for an outsider to fathom. One way of beginning to understand government decision making is to look to the influence of constituents and opponents of the unit making the decision.

Raytheon, a major US defense contractor, learned this lesson several years ago when it tried to put together a consortium of European companies to produce for NATO a weapons system that it had already built successfully for the US military. Knowing the capabilities of various European firms, Raytheon selected those it thought would do the best job and began negotiating with them. These conversations were abruptly cut short when individual NATO governments told Raytheon that they, not the American manufacturer, would choose the European participants in the consortium. Recognizing political realities, Raytheon ended discussions with the firms it had selected, began negotiations with those chosen by individual governments, and ultimately put together a consortium that successfully produced the weapons systems for NATO.

A few years later, at the urging of the American government, Raytheon sought to produce a version of the same weapons system for Japan. Having learned what it thought was a useful lesson from its earlier experience in Europe, it opened talks directly with the Japanese government, expecting the government to indicate the Japanese companies with which the US manufacturer was to work. No such indication was forthcoming. Japanese officials studiously avoided suggesting appropriate Japanese partners. Finally, in a private conversation with a Raytheon senior executive, the Japanese deputy minister of defense made it clear that Raytheon, not the Japanese government, should decide on the Japanese companies to participate in producing the weapons system. The reason was that two very powerful Japanese electronics firms were the primary contenders for participation, and the

Japanese government did not want to incur the wrath and political antagonism of either one by choosing the other.[17] The Japanese Ministry of Defense needed the continuing support of both of these constituents if it was to preserve its influence, budget, and status.

In both the European and Japanese cases, the black box of government processed a political decision, but each came out with a different result. In Europe, in matters of national defense and the allocation of contracts among companies in different countries, there was a dominant supplier, often a government or government-financed entity itself, in each country, which had significant influence over the government departments concerned with the production of weapons systems. In Japan, the government, when faced with two competing Japanese electronics giants, recognized that if it favored one over the other, the losing company through its political and financial clout could make life difficult for the government.

Chrysler also used its knowledge of government constituents to good advantage several years ago in negotiations to sell its money-losing plants in the United Kingdom to the British government. It reacted to the government's low initial offer by threatening to liquidate its factories one by one, beginning with a plant located in an important electoral district in Scotland. The British Labour government at the time had a very slim majority and depended on Scotland to maintain its hold on power. In response to Chrysler's threat, Labour leaders in Scotland put strong pressure on the government to keep the plant open. In the end, the government increased its offer significantly and made a deal with Chrysler.[18]

(iii) Constraint No 3: The Political Imperative

An understanding of interests, both yours and the other side's, is fundamental to success in any negotiation.[19] All negotiators, governmental or private, are driven by their interests. Those interests are often multiple and complex; consequently, one has to probe deeply to uncover them in order to succeed.

Because of their special interests, government officials and politicians perceive and act on negotiating issues and problems in ways that are often different from the way private parties would in similar situations. Part of the reason for this is that whereas corporate negotiators usually respond to economic incentives—the need to make a profit, to increase share price, or to assure a fat bonus for the year—government officials respond to "political imperatives"—the need to protect departmental budgets, to preserve areas of authority, to defend themselves against political opponents, to support the interests of constituents, to enhance departmental prestige, and to ward off competition from other governmental agencies.

All government negotiators are agents, that is, they are negotiating on behalf of the state or its subdivisions, not for themselves.[20] In practice, as agents they also have their own personal and bureaucratic interests to advance and they will certainly do so in their dealings and negotiations. An understanding of these undeclared interests is vital in dealing with any government department. A constant question in the mind of any government official involved in an investment negotiation is: How will this negotiation affect my career?

---

[17] Author's interview with the late Charles Francis Adams, former chairman of Raytheon.

[18] D Lax and J Sebenius, *The Manager as Negotiator: Bargaining for Cooperation and Competitive Gain* (1986) 354–5.

[19] On the importance of interests in negotiation, see, eg, R Fisher, W Ury and B Patton, *Getting to YES: Negotiating Agreement Without Giving In* (2nd edn 1991).

[20] See generally, R Mnookin and L Susskind (eds), *Negotiating on Behalf of Others* (1999).

Concerned about "career-enhancing activities" and "career-destroying activities," bureaucrats eagerly seek the former and assiduously try to avoid the latter. The question weighs more heavily on some officials than on others, but it is always there. For example, in one negotiation over mineral rights in a Middle Eastern developing country, the representative of the American company and the deputy minister of mineral resources developed a strong, friendly relationship but the negotiations seemed to be going nowhere. After dinner one evening, the American executive asked what the problem was, and the deputy minister replied: "I have to be frank with you. If I make a deal with your competitor who is well known to the government ministers, the deal will be approved with no problems. If I make a deal with your company that has never operated in our country before, any deal that I make will be questioned. Even though your company will probably do a better job for us because your technology is more effective, I just can't take the chance. I have two years to go before retirement and I need to protect my position in government and my pension. Also, my wife and son both work for the government, so I can't do anything that will put them in danger, either." Then he added, apparently sensitive to the American negotiator's own bureaucratic interests, "But if it will help you with your company, we can continue to negotiate, if you want to."

Generally speaking, the power of political imperatives in a given negotiation will vary inversely to the sense of security that government negotiators feel in their bureaucratic position. Politically insecure officials are usually more influenced by political imperatives than are politically secure officials.

One strategy that officials often use to defend their career interests is to follow the rules assiduously. The rules, which have usually been set down by some higher authority, function to protect that official from career-damaging criticism and censure. An investment negotiator seeking to achieve an innovative transaction that is not specifically authorized by the rules is likely to encounter an attitude characterized by the old bureaucratic maxim: "Never do anything for the first time." Negotiators therefore need to find a tactic to blunt bureaucratic aversion to innovation.

In any negotiation with a government official, it is important to understand the political and bureaucratic interests at work and to find ways to satisfy them. It is also important to make transactions that are politically defensible for the government making them. Finding an appropriate precedent is one way of doing that.

(iv) Constraint No 4: Operational Norms

Government departments normally operate according to norms that one rarely finds in private business.[21] In particular, these norms affect a government department's revenues, resources, and objectives. They not only influence how government departments act but also affect how they negotiate.

1. Revenue norms. A first important norm concerns departmental revenues. Part of the reason that governments are not influenced by commercial incentives to the same extent as are private sector companies is that the government departments negotiating the deal usually cannot retain the commercial and financial benefits of the deals they make. Whereas a company in negotiating with a supplier will increase its earnings by a dollar

---

[21] See JQ Wilson, *Bureaucracy: What Governments Do and Why They Do It* (2000) 197.

for every dollar it saves at the negotiating table, a government department that saves a dollar in negotiating with a supplier will not increase its budget by an equal amount. Rather, that dollar goes to the general state budget. In fact, the government department may be penalized next year, when its budget is reduced because of the savings it made the preceding year in its negotiations. This may have some perverse effects. For one thing, it often leads to a flurry of negotiating activity as the end of a particular fiscal year approaches when government departments seeks to spend all of their annual budget, a factor sometimes used by private negotiators to their advantage in order to close a deal. Understanding the budgetary cycle of bureaucracies can work to the advantage of private negotiators as deadlines approach.

2. **Resource allocation norms.** The second important operational norm is that most governments are not free to allocate the various factors of production, such as capital, labor, and technology, the way that the managers and negotiators in that department judge best. Whereas private companies will decide whom to hire and whom to fire, and what equipment to buy or not to buy according to their view of that decision's impact on the profitability of their company, government departments often have to make similar decisions according to politically imposed rules. Since government entities in business are usually subsidized by the state treasury and are controlled by government officials, their principal goal may not be the maximization of profit, as is the case with private firms, but the advancement of social and political ends. For example, if a manufacturing joint venture between a US company and a foreign state-owned corporation were to be faced with a decline in product demand, the reaction of the US partner might be to lay off workers. However, the state corporation under government control, despite reduced profitability, might reject that solution to prevent an increase in unemployment in the country. In negotiating a transaction, it is often important to recognize and discuss at the table divergences in goals, rather than be surprised by them later on.

3. **Objectives norms.** The third normative constraint is that government agencies and departments must pursue the objectives that the legislator has specified for them. They may not seek the goals that they themselves judge important. Companies change products and strategies in accordance with the market demands. Government departments and agencies cannot change objectives as easily. When the Ford Motor Company realized that the Edsel automobile, which it introduced in 1957, was a loser in the marketplace, it stopped making it in 1959. Had Ford been a government department, it might still be manufacturing Edsels today.[22]

(f) A Government Deal is Never Done

One of the risks of government negotiations is that governments tend to see any deal they make as always being open to reconsideration and renegotiation, even after the contract has been signed, when it suits that government's interests. In this regard, it is well to remember the British Prime Minister Benjamin Disraeli's remark to the House of Commons: "Finality is not the language of politics."

Despite lengthy negotiations, skilled drafting, and strict enforcement mechanisms, parties to solemnly signed and sealed agreements with governments often find themselves

---

[22] Wilson, *Bureaucracy*, at 115 et seq.

returning to the bargaining table later on to renegotiate their agreements. So a key challenge in negotiating with foreign governments is not just getting to yes, but also staying there. Thus, the world has witnessed the renegotiation of state mineral and petroleum agreements in the 1960s and 1970s, often in the face of threatened host country nationalizations and expropriations; the loan reschedulings of the 1980s following the debt crisis in developing countries; the restructuring of government infrastructure projects as a result of the Asian financial crisis of the late 1990s; and the renegotiation of a host of transactions as a result of the Argentine collapse at the beginning of the current century.

The risk of renegotiation of apparently definitive agreements is particularly present in dealings with governments for a variety of reasons. Governments often reserve to themselves the right to unilaterally change contracts on grounds of protecting national sovereignty, national security, or the public welfare. Moreover, the usual remedies in court for breach of contract may be unavailable or ineffectual against governments who take such actions. As we have seen, governments are particularly susceptible to political forces in their negotiations with private persons and companies. The changing nature of the political imperatives under which governments labor can cause them to change their position on agreements that they have previously made. Throughout the world, from Albania to Zambia, when political opposition develops toward agreements that governments have made, at some point, when the pressure becomes too great to resist, those governments will look for ways to cancel or redo those agreements in order to satisfy their political constituents. As a result, it is important for foreign investors to incorporate into their negotiation strategies mechanisms to deal with this risk. Because of its prevalence in dealings with governments, negotiators need to understand the forces that give rise to renegotiation, the nature of the renegotiation process, and the best ways to renegotiate deals that they thought were done.

(g) Coping with Corruption in Government Negotiations

Although many public officials throughout the world work diligently for their governments, corruption is a particular risk in negotiations with governments. While corruption has many legal definitions, it is basically the abuse of a public office for private gain. Corruption arises in negotiations with governments when government negotiators employ their discretion to advance their own personal interests, instead of the interests of the government and the public they are supposed to represent. It can take many forms: cash payments to an official to secure a government contract, gifts to a politician's spouse to gain that politician's endorsement of a permit, or an interest-free "loan" to the brother of an official reviewing your company's tax returns.

The subject of government corruption is complex, and a full treatment is beyond the scope of this chapter. Its potential to affect a negotiation is influenced by a variety of intricate factors, including the legal or business traditions of the country or industry concerned, the strength of the bureaucracy concerned, the nature of the persons sitting across the table, and a company's own internal policies, culture, and controls, to mention just a few. In nearly all countries, the payment of a bribe to a government official to secure a favorable contract or action in a negotiation is a crime by law; however, the readiness of a particular legal system to enforce those laws varies from country to country, from state to state, and even town to town. From an institutional point of view, corruption, as Robert Klitgaard has pointed out, is a function of three factors: discretion, monopoly, and accountability.[23] The likelihood of corruption rises when government officials have great discretion, when they have monopoly power of what investors are seeking, and when mechanisms for holding officials accountable for their decisions are weak.

(h) Guidelines for Negotiating with Governments

Governments "feel" different in international business negotiations because they are different. As this chapter has shown, governments require a different approach in negotiation. The following seven guidelines may be helpful:

- **Guideline No 1.** In approaching negotiations with any government, it is important to recognize that the government possesses powers and is subject to constraints different from those to be found in negotiating with private persons and organizations. Investment negotiators should seek to understand how one may incorporate these factors into negotiating strategies and tactics. As a result of these powers and constraints, government negotiators will often behave differently from their private sector counterparts at the negotiating table.

- **Guideline No 2.** All governments and their officials jealously guard their authority because authority is what allows them to govern. Never challenge the authority of a government department or agency and avoid any action that might be interpreted as a challenge. Respect and deference should guide all negotiations with any government.

- **Guideline No 3.** Learn the rules governing the negotiation process and the protocols and forms expected of nongovernmental negotiators. To gain that knowledge, negotiators should seek the advice of consultants, people in the particular community concerned, and those persons who have had experience in negotiating with a particular governmental unit.

- **Guideline No 4.** All governments enjoy to a greater or lesser extent certain privileges and immunities. Learn what they are in the case of the particular government with which you are negotiating.

- **Guideline No 5.** The "public interest" is always an actual or potential factor in any negotiation with any government. It can turn any seemingly bilateral negotiation between an investor and a government department into a multilateral negotiation involving uninvited members of the public, civic groups, and the media. Negotiators should always plan their negotiations accordingly.

- **Guideline No 6.** Nearly three hundred years ago, François de Callières, a distinguished French diplomat who wrote one of the first practical manuals[24] on negotiating with governments, stressed "the necessity of continual negotiation" between states through their permanent representatives as the basis of modern diplomacy—a novel idea in its time but one that modern diplomats take for granted today. Twenty-first-century investment negotiators must also recognize that a productive relationship with a government is a constant process of negotiation. Just as negotiations do not stop

---

[23] R Klitgaard, *Controlling Corruption* (1988) 7.

[24] F de Callières, *De La Manière de négocier avec les souverains. De l'utilité des négociations, du choix des ambassadeurs et des envoyés et des qualités nécessaires pour réussir dans ces emplois* (Amsterdam: Pour la Compagnie, 1716). The book has been published in many languages since it was written. The most recent English language version is François de Callières, *On the Manner of Negotiating with Princes*, trans AF Whyte, with introduction by Charles Handy (2000).

when two countries seal a treaty, negotiations do not end when a company signs a contract with a government department or agency.

- **Guideline No 7** Always search for the political imperatives driving governmental counterparts in a negotiation and find ways to satisfy them while attaining your interests. Remember a good deal to government officials is a deal that is defensible to their superiors, political opponents, and the public.

9.12 Negotiating Long-Term Investment Contracts

Virtually all direct foreign investments, as well as many portfolio investments, are intended by the parties, at least at the outset, as long-term transactions and arrangements. The negotiation of long-term international business transactions and arrangements raises special problems for the international negotiator. As a result of globalization, businesses are increasingly entering into long-term relationships with companies and organizations abroad. Rather than merely engaging in separate foreign trade transactions or establishing foreign branches and wholly-owned subsidiaries to pursue their objectives, companies are joining with businesses from around the world in all sorts of long-term, ongoing relationships—joint ventures, strategic alliances, global franchising arrangements, 50-year production sharing agreements, construction consortia, and build-operate-transfer infrastructure deals, among others. An important result of this trend is that international investors in growing numbers are becoming *partners* in substance, if not in name, with foreign enterprises throughout the globe. Indeed, the essence of international business success today and for the foreseeable future in all countries is very much a matter of working effectively with foreign partners. Even when investors make cross-border acquisitions of other companies, they will usually find that they also face the challenge of working with foreign partners—the personnel, management, and organizations that they have acquired.

If it is true that working with foreign partners has become the essence of international business today, it is also true that many international managers and their lawyers are unprepared for this challenge. Working with foreign partners in an international business relationship presents problems and obstacles that executives do not ordinarily encounter in purely domestic dealings. In particular, these kinds of arrangement require international lawyers and business executives to develop a new approach to international business negotiation.[25]

Although the parties to alliances, joint ventures, and mergers usually announce them with great fanfare at the start, they often become disappointed within a short time and in many cases terminate them earlier than expected. One study by a private consulting firm concluded that at least a third of all joint ventures fail to meet the expectations of the companies involved. Another found that the average international alliance ended after 3.4 years.[26]

The challenges of working effectively with foreign partners present themselves in many forms. Some are external to the partnership; some are internal to the relationship between the parties. Here are a few examples drawn from experience around the world:

- A UK investor's foreign partner, a small emerging market company, feels that it is much weaker than the UK company and is constantly fearful that it will be taken

---

[25] See JW Salacuse, *The Global Negotiator* (2003) 193–204.
[26] BJ Gomes-Casseres, "Joint Venture Instability: Is It a Problem?" 22 *Columbia Journal of World Business* (1997) 97.

advantage of. Consequently, in all dealings with the UK company, it is extremely guarded and slow to reach agreement, an attitude that is hampering the development of the venture.

- A US investor has created a pharmaceutical joint venture in Russia. It wants to confine it to narrow and specific areas, but its Russian partner wants to expand into activities unrelated to the US company's competence, like the production of television programs. Disagreement over this question is causing tension in the relationship.

- A French company and a Chinese enterprise have established a joint venture that has clear mutual benefits, but both parties are very cautious about sharing information. The Chinese partner withholds information about customer problems with products and requests for new product features. In response, the French have slowed the transfer of technology badly needed by the venture. The two sides are also in conflict over advertising expenses. The French want to spend heavily on advertising while the Chinese oppose these expenditures as unnecessary.

- A Canadian pharmaceutical firm with a long tradition of strong presidents and top-down management, has acquired a Swedish firm with a management style that entails getting the whole management group's approval before making big decisions, rather than handing down orders—*alla aer I baten*, "getting everybody in the boat," according to the Swedes. The difference in style is causing severe internal conflict and the possible loss of talented managers and scientists.

None of these problems can be solved by contractual provisions alone. None can be settled by invoking arbitration or other dispute settlement clauses. One may argue therefore that these issues are management problems or personnel questions, matters that have nothing to do with law or the lawyer's work in negotiating and structuring international transactions. On the other hand, if the lawyer's fundamental task is to help the client establish the best possible basis for an international transaction, not just to draft a contract, then these issues should be of concern from the very start of negotiations.

Rather than view the basic objective in an international business negotiation as securing an advantageous contract for the client, an international lawyer ought to strive for the goal of establishing a basis for the client to work productively with a foreign partner. Had the negotiators in the deals mentioned above kept that aim in mind, perhaps their clients would have avoided the problems they later encountered in working with their foreign partners. Throughout negotiations, international business lawyers must keep asking themselves a basic first question: After the contract, what?

To negotiate productive working relationships with potential foreign partners, international investors should bear in mind the following principles.

1. A Signed Contract Does Not Necessarily Create an International Business Relationship. In long-term transactions, the parties are seeking to create a business relationship, a complex set of interactions characterized by cooperation and a maximum degree of trust. A relationship implies a connection between the parties. Just as a map is not a country, but only an imperfect description thereof, a contract is not a business relationship. A contract may be a necessary condition for a business relationship in some, but not all countries; however, it is never a sufficient condition for a business relationship in any country. A business negotiator, while necessarily concerned about contractual provisions, should also be concerned that a solid foundation for a business relationship is in place. Accordingly, a negotiator should also ask a variety of non-legal and non-contractual questions: How well do the parties know one another? What mechanisms are in place to foster communications between the two sides after the contract is signed? Is the deal balanced and advantageous for both sides? Do the parties understand and respect each others' interests, values and cultures?

While a contract may seem the essence of a business relationship in North America, other cultures often give it far less importance. Indeed, different cultures may tend to view the very purpose of a negotiation differently. For North Americans, the goal of a business negotiation, first and foremost, is usually to arrive at a signed contract between the parties. They consider a signed contract as a definitive set of rights and duties that strictly binds the two sides, an attitude succinctly summed up in the statement "a deal is a deal."

Japanese and other cultural groups in Asia, on the other hand, often consider that the goal of a negotiation is not a signed contract, but the creation of a relationship between the two sides. Although the written contact expresses the relationship, the essence of the deal is the relationship itself. For Americans, signing a contract is closing a deal; for many Asians signing a contract might more appropriately be called opening a relationship. This difference in view may explain why Asians tend to give more time to negotiation preliminaries, while Americans want to rush through this first phase in deal making. Negotiation preliminaries, whereby the parties seek to get to know one another thoroughly, are a crucial foundation for a good business relationship. They may seem less important when the goal is merely a contract.

2. An International Deal is a Continuing Negotiation. Some lawyers think that the negotiation process ends when all the details are resolved and the contract is signed. In fact, this view is hardly ever a reflection of reality. In truth, an international deal is a *continuing negotiation* between the parties to the transactions as they seek to adjust their relationship to the rapidly changing international environment of civil strife, political upheavals, military interventions, monetary fluctuations, and technological change in which they must work together.

No negotiation can predict all eventualities that the parties may encounter, nor can any negotiation achieve perfect understanding between the parties, especially when they come from differing cultures. If they do encounter changes in circumstances, misunderstandings, or problems not contemplated by their contract, the parties need to resort to negotiation to handle their difficulties. In short, negotiation is a fundamental tool for *managing* their deal. And when the parties to a deal are embroiled in genuine conflict—for example, the failure to perform in accordance with one side's expectations or interpretation of the contract— negotiation may be the only realistic tool to resolve the controversy, particularly if the parties want to preserve a business relationship. Thus when the deal is broken, negotiations may be the only means to mend it. So in the life of any deal, one may encounter three types of negotiation: deal making, deal managing, and deal mending.

If the risk of change and uncertainty is constant in international business, how should deal makers cope with it? They should approach the problem of renegotiation before, rather than after, they sign their contract. Both sides should recognize at the outset that the risk of changed circumstances is high in any long-term relationship and that at some time in the future either side may seek to renegotiate or adjust the contract accordingly.

Most modern contracts deny the possibility of change. They therefore rarely provide for adjustments to meet changing circumstances. This assumption of contractual stability has proven false time and time again. For example, most mineral development contracts assume that the agreement will last for 50 to 99 years, but they rarely remain unchanged beyond a fraction of that time. One method of dealing with this problem is to provide specifically in the contract for renegotiation at defined periods for specific issues that are particularly susceptible to changing circumstances. Rather than dismiss the possibility of renegotiation and then be forced to consider review of the entire contract at a later time in an atmosphere of hostility between the partners, it is better to recognize the possibility of renegotiation at the outset and set down a clear framework within which to conduct the process. In short, recognize the possibility of redoing the deal, but control the process.[27]

3. Don't Rush Prenegotiation. The initial phase of any international business negotiation is prenegotiation, a phase in which the parties to a potential deal determine whether they want to negotiate at all and, if they do, what they will negotiate about, and how, when, and where they will go about it. This phase is vital if the parties are to know one another well. The prenegotiation phase is characterized by information gathering and efforts by each of the parties to evaluate the other. It ends when both sides make a decision to negotiate a deal with the other, or when one informs the other, directly or indirectly, that it no longer wishes to continue discussions.

4. Consider a Role for Mediation or Conciliation in the Deal. Third parties, whether formally called mediators, conciliators, advisers, or something else, can often help the two sides in deal making, deal managing, and deal mending negotiations and in building and preserving partnership relations. For example, when some companies contemplate long-term international business relationships requiring a high degree of cooperation, they may hire a consultant to develop and guide a program of relationship building that might include joint workshops, get-acquainted sessions, and executive retreats, all of which take place before the parties actually sit down to negotiate the terms of their contract. The consultant will facilitate and perhaps chair these meetings, conduct discussions of the negotiating process, make the parties recognize potential pitfalls, and discuss with them ways to avoid possible problems. Once negotiations start, the consultant may continue to observe the process and be ready to intervene when the deal-making process encounters difficulties.[28]

Once the deal has been signed, consultants, lawyers, and advisers may continue their association with one or both parties and informally assist as mediators in managing conflict that may arise in the execution of the transaction. In some cases, the parties to a complex or long-term transaction, seeking to minimize the risk of conflict, may include specific provisions in their contract stipulating a process to manage conflict and prevent it from causing a total breakdown of the deal. For example, the contract may provide that in the event a conflict cannot be settled at the operational level, senior management of the two sides will engage in negotiations to resolve it. Generally, top management, not directly embroiled in the conflict and with a broad view of the transaction and its relationship to the company's overall strategy, may be in a better position to settle a dispute than persons at the operating level, who have come to feel that they have a personal stake in "winning" the dispute. Once top management of the two sides has reached an understanding, they may

---

[27] See JW Salacuse, *The Global Negotiator: Making, Managing, and Mending Deals Around the World in the Twenty-First Century* (2003) 229–55. See also SR Salbu and R Brahm, "Planning Versus Contracting for International Joint Venture Success: The Case for Replacing Contract With Strategy," 31 *Colum J of Transnat'l L* (1993) 283–317.

[28] C Buhring-Uhle, *Arbitration and Mediation in International Business* (1996) 318–19.

have to serve as mediators with their subordinates to get them to change behavior and attitudes with respect to interactions at the operational level.[29]

The international construction industry has developed an important form of deal-managing mediation that employs a designated third person, often a consulting engineer, to resolve disputes that may arise in the course of a major construction project, like a dam or a power plant. International construction projects typically include many parties, involve highly technical complexities, and take a long time to complete. The possibilities for conflict among the participants are virtually endless, yet it is essential for all concerned that their disputes do not impede the progress of the project. The construction contract will therefore usually designate a consulting engineer, review board, permanent referee, or dispute adviser, with varying powers, to handle disputes as they arise in a way that will allow the construction work to continue. Sometimes, as in the case of a consulting engineer, the third person will have the power to make a decision which may later be challenged in arbitration or the courts; sometimes as in the case of a dispute adviser, the third person plays the role of a mediator by engaging in fact finding or facilitating communication among the disputants.[30]

The use of such dispute review boards or dispute advisers in construction contracts has proved to be a cost-effective means of settling disputes while permitting a continuation of the construction project in an expeditious manner. This mechanism would seem to have application in other areas of international business. For example, in a complex multi-party strategic alliance, the participants might designate a person or organization to serve as a permanent mediator to assist the parties in managing conflicts that may arise in the course of their business relationship. Thus far, however, this device does not appear to have reached much beyond the construction industry.

The dispute resolution mechanism of choice in most international business transactions is international commercial arbitration. The parties invoke arbitration in much the same circumstances where in a domestic transaction they would resort to litigation: when they judge the deal to be broken. International commercial arbitration is much like litigation in that it is expensive, adversarial, and in most cases lengthy. It usually results in dissolution of the business relationship, not in its reconstruction.

Traditionally, companies engaged in an international business dispute have not actively sought the help of mediators or other third parties. They have first tried to resolve the matter themselves through negotiation, but when they judged that to have failed, they have immediately proceeded to arbitration. Various factors explain their failure to try mediation: their lack of knowledge about mediation and the availability of mediation services, the fact that companies tend to give control of their disputes to lawyers whose professional inclination is to litigate, and the belief among many lawyers and executives that mediation is merely a stalling tactic that only delays the inevitability of an arbitration proceeding.

---

[29] C Buhring-Uhle, *Arbitration and Mediation in International Business* (1996) 318–19.

[30] One particular type of mediator worthy of note is the Dispute Review Board, which was used in the construction of both the Channel Tunnel between England and France and the new Hong Kong Airport and is now required by the World Bank in any Bank-financed construction project having a cost of more than $50 million. Under this procedure a Board, consisting of three members, is created at the start of the project. One member of the board is appointed by the project owner and a second by the lead contractor. The third member is then selected either by the other two members or by mutual agreement between the owner and the contractor. The Board functions according to rules set down in the construction contract. Generally, it is empowered to examine all disputes and to make recommendations to the parties concerning settlement. If the parties to a dispute do not object to a recommendation, it becomes binding. If, however, they are dissatisfied, they may proceed to arbitration, litigation or other form of mandatory dispute settlement. NG Bunni, "Major Project Dispute Review Boards," in *House Counsel International* (June–July 1997) 13–15.

With increasing recognition of the disadvantages of arbitration, a few companies are beginning to turn to more explicit forms of mediation and third-party intervention to resolve business disputes. When a dispute can be quantified, for example the extent of damage to an asset by a partner's action or the amount of a royalty fee owed to a licensor, the disputants sometimes engage an independent third party such as an international accounting or consulting firm to examine the matter and give an opinion. The opinion is not binding on the two sides but it has the effect of allowing them to make a more realistic prediction of what may happen in an arbitration proceeding.

Recognizing the terminal effect of arbitration on the business relationship, some parties to a business transaction agree in their contract to attempt *conciliation* before invoking arbitration. Many arbitration institutions, such as the International Chamber of Commerce and the International Centre for Settlement of Investment Disputes, offer a service known as conciliation, which is normally governed by a set of rules.[31] In addition, the United Nations Commission on International Trade Law has prepared a set of conciliation rules which parties may use without reference to an institution.[32] Generally, in institutional conciliation, a party to a dispute may address a request for conciliation to the institution. If the institution concerned secures the agreement of the other disputant, it will appoint a conciliator. While the conciliator has broad discretion to conduct the process, in practice he or she will invite both sides to state their views of the dispute and will then make a report proposing an appropriate settlement. The parties may reject the report and proceed to arbitration, or they may accept it. In many cases, they will use it as a basis for a negotiated settlement. Conciliation is thus a kind of non-binding arbitration. Its function is predictive. It tends to be rights-based in its approach, affording the parties a third person's evaluation of their respective rights and obligations. Conciliators do not usually adopt a problem-solving or relationship building approach to resolving the conflict between the parties.

---

[31] eg, ICC, *International Chamber of Commerce Rules of Optional Conciliation*, (1995) reprinted in 10 *ICSID Review* (1995) 158–61.

[32] UNCITRAL Conciliation Rules, 35 UN GOAR Supp. (No 17) at 32, UN Doc. A/35/17 (1980). See Eisemann, "Conciliation as a Means of Settlement of International Business Disputes: The UNCITRAL Rules as Compared with the ICC System," in Schultz and van den Berg (eds), *The Art of Arbitration* (1982) 121.

10

The Nature and Content of International Investment Contracts

10.1 Introduction

International investors use contracts to structure their investments in ways that will allow them to achieve their goals. As a result, the specific provisions of the contractual framework governing an international investment are subject to great diversity and depend on a host of factors, including the law and politics of the countries concerned, the nature of the investment project, investor bargaining power, and expected developments in the international economic and political context. It would be extremely difficult, if not impossible, to catalogue the diverse provisions of the contractual frameworks for the multitude of investments made in the world. Instead, this chapter will focus on the contractual frameworks of four of the most common types of international investments: (1) wholly owned direct foreign investments; (2) international joint ventures; (3) international project finance transactions; and (4) international loans.

10.2 Wholly Owned Foreign Direct Investments

In undertaking a wholly owned, direct foreign investment, a single investor, either a physical or legal person, acquires a productive asset in a foreign country and controls and operates that asset for the purpose of making a profit. In order to acquire that asset, the investor must make a contract or series of contracts with other persons and may also have to enter agreements with host state entities for permission to operate the investment or to obtain desired incentives, such as tax exemptions. For example, a French investor wishing to manufacture air conditioners in Senegal would need to conclude contracts to acquire the rights in land on which to build a factory, to construct manufacturing facilities, to purchase the needed machinery, and to obtain utility services, such as water, electricity, and telecommunications.

Undertaking a wholly owned, direct investment in a foreign country also requires an investor to make a fundamental strategic decision on the legal form that the investment project is to take: whether the project will be a *branch* or an independent *subsidiary*. A branch is an integral part of the company or entity undertaking the investment, and it usually constitutes a presence by such foreign company in the host country. A subsidiary, on the other hand, is legally independent of the parent and is organized as a separate entity, normally as a company under the laws of the host country.

Numerous factors influence an investor's decision on whether to establish an investment project as a branch or a subsidiary. Among the most important are the tax consequences of the choice under the laws of both the host country and the investor's home country.[1] For

---

[1] P Luiki, "Joint Ventures: Definitions and Legal Issues," in DA Prescott and SA Swartz (eds), *Joint Ventures in the International Arena* (2nd edn 2010) 4. For example, throughout the 1980s, China preferred joint ventures over wholly owned subsidiaries, taxing joint ventures at a preferable rate than wholly owned subsidiaries. JP Engel, "Foreign Direct Investment and Tax Incentives in China," 20 *J Int'l Tax'n* (2009) 48, 54.

example, the home country law may tax the income of a branch as it accrues but tax the income of a subsidiary only if it is repatriated to the investor's home country. Host country law may have a major influence on the decision in other respects. For example, the legislation of the host country may specifically forbid the use of a branch in establishing a foreign investment project, or it may indirectly make a subsidiary the only realistic organizational form available to the investor, as in the case, for example, where its investment code grants incentives only to companies incorporated under local law. Moreover, if local law requires that investment projects take the form of a joint venture, the use of a separately incorporated subsidiary may be the only possible means of satisfying that requirement. Since a branch constitutes the presence of the investor in the host country and thereby potentially exposes all of its assets to host country jurisdiction, many investors may prefer to avoid such a result by incorporating the investment project as a separate subsidiary under the law of the host country, which in most instances grants shareholders limited liability. In addition, incorporating an investment project in the form of a subsidiary under local law may reduce somewhat the foreign image of the investment project and give it a more local appearance. A further factor affecting the decision will be the cost and formalities required for conducting business in the two forms. Traditionally, branches could be established with a minimum of cost; however, today the establishment of a branch in many countries may require expense and formalities as onerous as those needed for organizing a separately incorporated subsidiary.

10.3 International Joint Ventures

In making a direct investment abroad, a company must make another strategic decision: whether to undertake the project alone or in association with other investors. Prior to World War II, direct foreign investment normally took the form of a wholly owned subsidiary in the host country. With the enormous expansion of international business in the postwar era, foreign investment has increasingly been cast in another form: the joint venture.[2] Particularly since the 1970s, the number, magnitude, and geographical dispersion of international joint ventures have increased exponentially.[3] Indeed, today, the joint venture is one of the most prevalent vehicles for undertaking direct investments abroad.

The term "joint venture" is used in a variety of ways and appears to have both general and specific definitions.[4] In its most general sense, the joint venture is an association of two

---

[2] Several studies have analyzed the factors that influence multinational corporations' mode of entry into foreign markets as wholly owned subsidiaries or joint ventures, specifically examining the host country's political, cultural, and legal environment as determinants in the decision to seek more control through a wholly owned subsidiary or to leverage local advantages. See A Arslan, "Impacts of Institutional Pressures and the Strength of Market Supporting Institutions in the Host Country on the Ownership Strategy of Multinational Enterprises: Theoretical Discussion and Propositions," 16 *J Mgmt and Governance* (2010) 107 (discussing the host country institutional environment as a factor in ownership strategy); see generally, Yi-C Chang et al, "How Cultural Distance Influences Entry Mode Choice: The Contingent Role of Host Country's Governance Quality," *J Bus Res* (2011); see also C Lopez-Duarte and MM Vidal-Suarez, "Culture Distance and the Choice Between Wholly-Owned Subsidiaries and Joint Ventures," *J Bus Res* (2012); see also C Williams et al, *Legal Legitimacy, Political Stability and MNE Entry into Developing Countries: The Role of BIT Design (2012)* available at <http://business.umsl.edu/seminar_series/Spring2012/UMSL_PoliticalStabilityBITs_Williams_et_al_Jan_2012.pdf>; see also JP Roy and C Oliver, "International Joint Venture Partner Selection: The Role of the Host Country Legal Environment," 40 *J Int'l Bus Stud* (2009) 779.

[3] JP Roy and C Oliver, "International Joint Venture Partner Selection: The Role of the Host Country Legal Environment," 40 *J Int'l Bus Stud* (2009) 779.

[4] PD Ehrenhaft, "International Joint Ventures: Setting Them Up, Taking Them Apart," 27 *No 2 Corp Counsel's Art.* (2011) 1; *Transnational Joint Ventures*, Executive Legal Summary 347 (2011); P Luiki, "Joint Ventures: Definitions and Legal Issues," in DA Prescott and SA Swartz (eds), *Joint Ventures in the International Arena* (2nd edn 2010).

or more persons to undertake a relatively limited and well-defined business activity.[5] In the realm of international business, the term "joint venture" has a variety of meanings. For some, it implies that the partners in a project have nationalities different from one another or different from the country in which the joint venture is to operate. For example, the creation of a manufacturing facility in Canada by a French firm and an American corporation would qualify as an "international joint venture." For many developing countries, the term has yet another meaning: it refers to an investment project in a host country by one or more foreigners and one or more *local* partners from the host country itself. Among a few developing nations, it is used in an even more limited sense to mean a joint investment project in which at least one joint venture partner comes from abroad and at least one other partner is a local *state enterprise* from the host country itself. As was indicated earlier, some host country laws require that a foreign investment project take the form of a joint venture, rather than a wholly owned subsidiary.

Whereas the term "joint venture" under United States law refers to a legal form of business enterprise either identical to or derived from a partnership,[6] its use within the context of international business does not connote a particular legal form of enterprise.[7] Rather, the international joint venture is essentially an economic or financial relationship which may be cast into a variety of legal forms, depending upon the laws of the host country in question.

Analytically, international joint ventures can be divided into two categories: equity joint ventures and contractual joint ventures. The most common type, the equity joint venture, usually entails the creation of a separate joint venture legal entity in which each partner contributes capital to the venture and owns a portion of the resulting enterprise, while participating in its control and sharing its risks.[8] In a contractual joint venture, the foreign partner, either by preference or because of the restrictions of local law, has no equity interest in an enterprise in the host country, but is merely obligated to provide certain services or operations on a long-term basis.[9]

The variations on the contractual joint venture are numerous, but in most instances the parties agree to undertake a particular business activity in which they may share profits and risks, while individually retaining ownership of any capital or assets necessary for the operation of the enterprise. For example, a United Kingdom automobile manufacturer and a Hungarian enterprise might agree to undertake jointly the manufacture of engines in Hungary at the Hungarian's plant, with the UK company providing the needed technology and marketing expertise, the Hungarians providing the factory, and both parties sharing expenses, as well as any profits, according to specified ratios.

In many instances, a foreign investor would prefer an equity, as opposed to a contractual joint venture, so as to obtain a long term ownership interest in a profitable enterprise; however, where the profitability of the venture is questionable, a foreign investor may

---

[5] FH O'Neal and RB Thompson, *Close Corp and LLCs: Law and Practice* § 1:7 (Rev 3rd edn 2011) 1.

[6] The joint venture was not recognized in English common law as a distinct legal entity, but began to be recognized as such in American courts in the latter half of the nineteenth century. American judges and lawyers have often referred to it as a "joint adventure." See generally, FL Mechem, "The Law of Joint Adventures," 15 *Minn L Rev.* (1931) 644. See also WHE Jaeger, "Joint Ventures: Origin, Nature and Development," (1960) 9 *Am UL Rev* 1; R Flannigan, "The Joint Venture Fable," (2010) 50 *Am J Legal Hist* (2010); JD Cox and TL Hazen, *Treatise on the Law of Corporations* § 1:8 (3rd edn 2011) 1; A Bromberg, *Crane and Bromberg on Partnership* § 35 (1968).

[7] See W Friedmann and J Beguin, *Joint International Business Ventures in Developing Countries* (1971) 3.

[8] *Transnational Joint Ventures*, Executive Legal Summary (2011) 347; P Luiki, "Joint Ventures: Definitions and Legal Issues," in DA Prescott and SA Swartz (eds), *Joint Ventures in the International Arena* (2nd edn 2010) 1.

[9] See DA Prescott and SA Swartz (eds), *Joint Ventures in the International Arena* (2nd edn 2010) 2. See also United Nations Industrial Development Organization (UNIDO), *Manual on the Establishment of Industrial Joint-Venture Agreements in Developing Countries* (1971) 3.

instead opt for a contractual, as opposed to an equity, joint venture, so as to avoid the risk of loss of capital.[10] On the other hand, some countries may prohibit foreign investors from engaging in equity joint ventures altogether. Such may be the case in certain state-dominated economies whose laws require that the state own all means of production, or in mining and natural resource projects in developing countries, where the law vests ownership of all such resources exclusively in the state.

Numerous factors explain the enormous growth in joint ventures since World War II. One reason is that some host countries have required that foreign investment in their territories take this form rather than the form of a wholly owned subsidiary. The degree and scope of this requirement vary from country to country. Some countries have adopted an absolute rule that prohibits all foreign investment unless it takes the form of a joint venture in which local investors—either public or private—own a majority of the equity and hold a controlling position. Others impose this requirement only in particularly important segments of the economy, such as agriculture, mining, or natural resource development.[11] Still others may require joint ventures as a general rule, but are willing to grant exceptions in appropriate cases.

Several motives have prompted host countries to favor or require joint ventures. One of the most important is the desire to integrate the investment project into the economy of the country. Host government officials believe that with significant local participation, such integration is more likely to succeed than if the project is wholly owned by foreigners. In addition, developing country governments consider that joint ventures facilitate the creation of local management skills and the transfer of technology, while mitigating the real or apparent foreign domination of the economy or important economic sectors.[12] Joint ventures may also facilitate access by the local partner to the foreign partner's international marketing network. Moreover, it is argued that a joint venture, as opposed to a wholly owned subsidiary, will be more responsive to government policies and conduct its operations in the best interests of the country as a whole. Finally, a joint venture places the host country government and the local investor in a position to take over the entire project through nationalization or negotiated purchase; consequently, its use is viewed as contributing to the formation of nationally owned industries and economic activities.[13]

---

[10] *Transnational Joint Ventures*, Executive Legal Summary (2011) 347. See also SK Kapur, "Comment: Structuring and Negotiating International Joint Ventures: Anecdotal Evidence from A Large Law Firm Practice," 53 *Case W Res L Rev* (2003) 937, 938 (discussing common reasons to prefer equity joint ventures). See generally RC Sampson, "The Role of Lawyers in Strategic Alliances," 53 *Case W Res L Rev* (2003) 909 (discussing the choice between equity and contractual joint ventures).

[11] For example, a 2008 Russian law restricted foreign investment in 42 strategic economic sectors, primarily covering minerals and oil. Significant ownership of a Russian company in one of those sectors by a foreign investor requires the approval of a prime-ministerial commission. Without approval, foreign investors are limited to a 10 percent share of any Russian company owning more than 70 million tons of oil, 50 billion cubic meters of gas, 1.6 million ounces of gold, or 500,000 tons of copper. I Bremmer, *The End of the Free Market* (Portfolio 2010) 109. China, on the other hand, imposes no ceiling on foreign ownership share in a joint venture generally; however, it does have ceilings preventing majority foreign ownership in life insurance companies, securities firms, investment fund management companies, and civil aviation companies. H Huang, "The Regulation of Foreign Investment in Post-WTO China: A Political Economy Analysis," 23 *Colum J Asian L* (2003) 185, 190. See also PD Ehrenhaft, "International Joint Ventures: Setting Them Up, Taking Them Apart," 27 No 2 *Corp Counsel's Art* (2011) 1.

[12] For example, the Law on Chinese-Foreign Equity Joint Ventures actually requires foreign investors in a joint venture to contribute advanced technology that will contribute to China's economic development. G Wang, "China's Practice in International Investment Law: From Participation to Leadership in the World Economy," 34 *Yale J Int'l L* (2009) 575, 578.

[13] See PD Ehrenhaft, "International Joint Ventures: Setting Them Up, Taking Them Apart," 27 No 2 *Corp Counsel's Art* (2011) 1, (discussing joint ventures as a means to developing industry sectors through technology transfer and foreign capital and host country requirements to transfer the joint venture to local ownership).

Generally, investors have not shown great enthusiasm for the joint venture requirement due to their reluctance to share a potentially profitable venture, their fear of the difficulties that can arise from the divided management of an enterprise, and their unwillingness to reveal valuable technology and business secrets which, in the end, may be used in competition against them.[14] For this reason and in an effort to encourage foreign investment more actively, many countries have eliminated or eased the joint venture requirements since the late 1980s as they undertook the process of transformation from command to market economies and became more active in their pursuit of foreign capital.

At the same time, one finds that multinational corporations on their own initiative have turned to joint ventures or "strategic alliances" as an important tool of international business activity when it suits their purposes. They have preferred the joint venture to the wholly owned subsidiary in numerous situations—when they seek to share the risks of a venture, to obtain needed capital which they are unable or unwilling to contribute, to penetrate the markets by using the expertise and marketing organization of the partner, or to obtain needed technology and know-how which they do not possess.[15] Moreover, when local interests are involved in a project, a joint venture may present fewer political risks and be less susceptible to nationalization than would a company owned entirely by foreigners.[16] Often, multinational corporations will purport to enter into a joint venture as a means of selling their technology and products to the host country. In such cases, the western firm makes a small contribution to capital—often in the form of capitalized technology—and then enters into long-term, lucrative contracts to sell its equipment, technology, management services, and technical assistance to the joint venture in question, which is almost wholly financed by the host country government or local entrepreneurs.

The organization of a joint venture will ordinarily require the expenditure of more time and funds than does the organization of a wholly owned subsidiary, since the foreign investor must first engage in a sometimes lengthy search for an appropriate partner and then undertake protracted negotiations in order to define the relationship that is to exist among the parties to the joint venture. Partner selection is crucially important because it determines a joint venture's mix of skills, knowledge, resources, vulnerability to indigenous conditions, and competitiveness.[17] In many countries—often, ironically, those which require joint ventures as a condition for investment—the foreign investor may find that few, if any, local enterprises have the necessary experience and financial resources to become useful and reliable joint venture partners. Studies have shown that perceptions of the host country legal environment, such as the strength of the rule of law and the level of corruption, are a significant factor in international joint venture partner selection, influencing the types of desired qualities in a partner.[18]

[14] VD Travaglini, *Foreign Licensing and Joint Venture Arrangements*, in *Foreign Business Practices* 83 (US Dept of Commerce, 1981). See also P Luiki, "Joint Ventures: Definitions and Legal Issues," in DA Prescott and SA Swartz (eds), *Joint Ventures in the International Arena* (2nd edn 2010) 3.

[15] DA Prescott and SA Swartz (eds), *Joint Ventures in the International Arena* (American Bar Association 2nd edn 2010) 3. See PD Ehrenhaft, "International Joint Ventures: Setting Them Up, Taking Them Apart," 27 No 2 *Corp Counsel's Art* (2011) 1.

[16] On occasion, certain foreign investors have actually advocated joint ventures as a way of doing business. For example, at the height of the petro-dollar surplus in the oil-producing states of the Middle East during the mid- and late 1970s, numerous western firms were actively seeking to organize "trilateral ventures" in developing countries, a form of joint venture which would bring together western technology, Arab capital, and local resources and manpower in a single project. JW Salacuse, "Arab Capital and Trilateral Ventures in the Middle East: Is Three a Crowd?" in Kerr and Yassine (eds), *Rich and Poor States in the Middle East* (1982) 129–63.

[17] JP Roy and C Oliver, "International Joint Venture Partner Selection: The Role of the Host Country Legal Environment," 40 *J Int'l Bus Stud* (2009) 779.

[18] See JP Roy and C Oliver, "International Joint Venture Partner Selection: The Role of the Host Country Legal Environment," 40 *J Int'l Bus Stud* (2009) 779.

Yet, in many countries where the private sector is underdeveloped, or indeed non-existent, a government-owned enterprise, a ministry, or a publicly financed development bank may afford the investor the only realistic possibilities for finding a local joint venture partner in the host country. Sometimes, international business relationships with such entities may present peculiar problems. For example, whereas the goal of a foreign, private investor is usually the maximization of profit, a public enterprise may pursue social or public welfare objectives. This divergence of basic objectives may eventually provoke conflict within the joint venture; for example, in times of slow demand, the foreign partner might seek to reduce the labor force to cut costs, while the public enterprise partner might insist on retaining idle labor so as not to increase unemployment in the country. Additional conflict may be engendered by decisions on pricing the venture's products and services, allocating contracts for the supply of materials from local or foreign contractors, and training host country personnel. In addition to such business problems, joint ventures with foreign public entities may pose certain special legal issues, such as possible claims of sovereign immunity in the event of a legal dispute. Normally, counsel to the investor may avoid this problem by securing a waiver of foreign sovereign immunity from the public enterprise and by providing for the arbitration of disputes under the auspices of some neutral international body.

On occasion, a public entity may prove to be an effective joint venture partner by virtue of its political power. For example, a public enterprise may be better equipped than a private sector partner to secure local financing, necessary government approvals, and needed foreign exchange allocations from the Central Bank.

In addition to local partners, whether public or private, certain international organizations and agencies may participate in the joint venture with a private foreign investor. The International Finance Corporation, the Arab Investment Company, and the InterAmerican Development Bank, among others, may provide financing or contribute equity to ventures in which foreign businesses are involved. These agencies also have their own particular objectives and methods of operation.

10.4 International Joint Venture Contracts

(a) In General

In virtually every case, the participants in a joint venture will seek to embody their relationship in a written joint venture contract. Because of the divergence of objectives and perspectives among the potential partners—local, foreign, and international—the negotiation of the joint venture agreement may take considerable time and demand great negotiating skill from all parties concerned.[19] The joint venture agreement may be embodied in a single document; however, in many instances, it consists of several agreements—a basic joint venture contract sometimes called a "founders agreement," and individual, auxiliary agreements covering such matters as management services, patent and trademark licensing, technical services, loans, and long term sales arrangements. It may also be preceded by a preliminary joint venture agreement covering the exploratory phase of the venture.

---

[19] For a discussion of the negotiation of international investment agreements, see generally Chapter 9.

(b) Preliminary Joint Venture Agreements: The Case of the Kenana Sugar Company (Phase I)

Joint venture agreements are by no means standard, and their provisions vary according to the intentions and needs of the parties. While one cannot set down in these pages a definite formula for determining the content of joint venture agreements, it should be noted that the legislation or regulations of the host country may require that the agreement treat particular issues in a prescribed fashion.

The preparation of the final joint venture agreement may proceed in stages. Before binding themselves to a definitive joint venture contract, the parties might first conclude a preliminary agreement to undertake a feasibility study of the proposed project, to explore modes of financing it, and to determine other essential issues within a fixed period of time. A feasibility study is usually the first crucial step in transforming an investment idea into the reality of an investment project. Its purpose is to make an objective examination of the strengths and weaknesses of a proposed venture, the needed resources to achieve it, its likelihood of success, and its expected profitability. Two reasons make a feasibility study the subject of a preliminary joint venture agreement. First the cooperation of various potential joint venture partners, as well as the host government, is often required to make a useful feasibility study and one of the purposes of the preliminary joint venture agreement is to define and assure that cooperation. Second, having expended the resources necessary to make a feasibility study, often a costly exercise, the project sponsor wants some assurance that the potential partners will participate in the project if the study concludes that it is feasible. The preliminary joint venture often includes such conditional commitments. If, upon satisfaction of these conditions, the parties remain convinced of the desirability of the project, they may then proceed to negotiate and conclude a definitive joint venture agreement, along with other necessary contracts.

An example of this phased approach to joint venture development is the Kenana Sugar Company of Sudan, one of the largest integrated sugar production projects in the world.[20] In 1972, Lonrho Limited, a UK company with major investments in Africa, came to believe in Sudan's potential to grow significant amounts of sugar cheaply because of its abundant land and water resources. It therefore proposed the idea to the Sudanese government of jointly developing a project to grow sugar cane and refine it into sugar. As a first step, Lonrho and the Sudanese government entered into an agreement, known as the "Sugar Agreement" on June 9, 1972,[21] by which Lonrho was to prepare "in cooperation with the Government, a feasibility study on a project for the growing, cultivation, production, manufacture and marketing of sugar and the construction and establishment of sugar mills for the production and manufacture of sufficient quantities of raw and white sugar in the Sudan, so as to meet, together with existing and other currently projected sources of supply, the internal requirements of the Sudan and to allow the substantial export thereof and the industrial utilization of by-products of sugar manufacture . . ."[22]

In order to allow the feasibility study to proceed, the Sudanese government was to designate three alternatives sites of approximately 100,000 acres from which Lonrho was to choose one on which to conduct a study at its own expense to determine the technical, commercial, and financial feasibility of a project to grow and refine sugar under

---

[20] See the website of the Kenana Sugar Company at <http://www.kenana.com/>.
[21] Agreement made the ninth day of June 1972 between the Government of the Democratic Republic of the Sudan and Lonrho Limited (hereinafter "The Sugar Agreement").
[22] Sugar Agreement, Preamble, at 1.

irrigated conditions.[23] In the event that Lonrho determined that the development of "a site as a sugar estate was to be economically and commercially viable to it," the government and Lonrho were to establish a limited company under Sudanese law with sufficient capital, as proposed in the feasibility study, to carry out the project. The government was to own 51 percent of the shares and Lonrho would hold 49 percent.[24] To help the Government finance the purchase of its shares in the proposed company, Lonrho agreed to provide a five-year loan.[25] For its part, the government agreed to lease the land to the company for the amount of 10 piastres (approximately US$0.25 at the time) a *feddan*, to provide adequate water rights, to allow duty-free importation of all machinery and equipment, and to grant other tax and fiscal benefits under the country's Organisation and Promotion of Investments Act "or any other benefits contained in any amendments thereto or in any other Investment or Promotion Act, whether existing or future, . . . "[26] The Sugar Agreement further provided that it was to be governed by the "laws of the Democratic Republic of the Sudan" and that disputes concerning the agreement and its implementation, if not resolved amicably by negotiation, would be settled by a panel of three arbitrators under the rules of the International Chamber of Commerce.[27]

The feasibility study confirmed the economic and technical potential of the sugar project: however, its projected costs were much greater than Lonrho and the Sudanese government had originally contemplated and beyond what they alone could provide. Consequently, there was a need to bring other participants into the joint venture to secure the needed capital, a requirement that led to the negotiation and conclusion of a second, definitive joint venture agreement.[28]

(c) The Structure of Joint Venture Agreements

The purpose of a definitive joint venture agreement is three-fold: (1) to define the legal relations among the participants in the venture; (2) to commit the participants to provide agreed upon resources to the venture; and (3) to assure that the participants will cooperate in allowing the venture to achieve agreed upon purposes and actions. It is in a real sense a legal constitution for the joint venture.

For a joint venture to become a reality as a functioning business, it must secure various resources and services, many of which will be provided by the parties to the joint venture itself. Normally individual contracts between a specific joint venture partner and the joint venture entity will govern the provision of these resources and services. In order to give legal certainty to the commitments to provide the necessary resources and services, the joint venture partners will ordinarily prepare these contracts at the time the joint venture agreement is negotiated and stipulate in the joint venture agreement that the partners, as shareholders in the joint venture company, will take all appropriate action to cause the joint venture company once it is formed to enter into these contracts, which are usually annexed to the joint venture agreement. The agreement between the joint venture partners may be called by various names: "joint venture agreement," "preincorporation contract," or "founders' agreement."

---

[23] Sugar Agreement, Article 1.
[24] Sugar Agreement, Article 5.
[25] Sugar Agreement, Article 6.
[26] Sugar Agreement, Articles 10, 11, and 17.
[27] Sugar Agreement, Articles 35 and 36.
[28] For background on the events leading to the creation of the Kenana Sugar Company, see "Kenana: Exit Lonrho," *Sudanow*, August 1977, at 23–5. See also J Waterbury, *Hydropolitics of the Nile Valley* (1979) 189–95.

For example, suppose that American Air Conditioners, Inc., a New York corporation, decides to form a joint venture with Agraria Refrigerators Corporation, a family-owned company, to manufacture air conditioners in Agraria, a developing country. American Air Conditioners, Inc. will contribute 40 percent of the capital and Agraria Refrigerators will contribute 60 percent to form the joint venture company, Agraria Air Conditioners, Ltd. The business plan negotiated by the two partners provides that Agraria Air Conditioners, Ltd. will build a manufacturing facility on land to be purchased from Agraria Refrigerators Corporation and employ used manufacturing equipment and machinery to be bought from American Air Conditioners, Inc. The manufacturing process will employ American Air Conditioner's patented technology, and the air conditioners will bear the trademark "MultiCool," also owned by American. In the initial stages of production, Agraria Air Conditioners will use components purchased from American Air Conditioners. American will also provide the joint venture with management and marketing expertise. In order to protect American as a minority partner, it is also agreed that American will appoint the General Manager of Agraria Air Conditioners and that the joint venture company will make no major policy decision over American's opposition.

In order to give legal certainty to these various understandings, the parties to the joint venture would prepare the following agreements:

1. **Company Statutes**, stating the rules by which the joint venture company would be run, including special provisions to protect American Air Conditioners, Inc. as a minority shareholder.

2. **Management Structure Description,** outlining the internal management organization of the joint venture company.

3. **Land Purchase Agreement**, by which the joint venture company is to obtain the land for its factory from Agraria Refrigerators Corporation.

4. **General Assistance Agreement**, by which American Air Conditioners will provide technical assistance and advice to the joint venture company.

5. **Components Supply Agreement**, by which the joint venture company agrees to purchase components from American Air Conditioners for a specified time period.

6. **Machinery and Equipment Purchase Agreement**, by which the joint venture company agrees to buy from American Air Conditioners, Inc. the necessary used equipment and machinery to manufacture air conditioners.

7. **Technical License Agreement**, by which American agrees to license its patented technology to the joint venture company for use in manufacturing air conditioners.

8. **Trademark License Agreement**, by which American Air Conditioners Inc. agrees to license its trademark "MultiCool" to the joint venture for use in marketing the air conditioners.

9. **Shareholder Agreement**, by which the two partners agree to vote their shares in the joint venture company to carry out specified policies and agreements.

10. **Marketing Policy**, by which the two partners agree that the joint venture company will carry out a predetermined marketing policy.[29]

At the time the two partners sign their joint venture agreement, the joint venture company is not yet in existence. The process of forming the company can take considerable time, depending on the legal and bureaucratic environment of the country concerned. Therefore to be certain that once formed the joint venture company will enter into contracts

---

[29] For a similar joint venture with full documentation, see DN Goldsweig and RH Cummings (eds), *International Joint Ventures: A Practical Approach to Working With Foreign Investors in the U.S. and Abroad* (1990).

containing terms agreed upon, the parties in their joint venture agreement commit themselves to vote their shares and to take all necessary actions to cause the Board of Director of Agraria Air Conditioners, Ltd. to enter into all of the specified contracts, which are ordinarily annexed to and made an integral part of the joint venture agreement.

10.5 The Content of International Joint Venture Agreements

(a) In General

The structure of the Kenana Sugar Project's joint venture agreement would follow a similar pattern. In that case, the enlarged projected integrated sugar project, the need for significant amounts of additional capital, and the change in economic circumstances led the participants to conclude a definitive joint venture agreement, known as "Founders Agreement" on February 17, 1975, among six participants in the joint venture to establish a major new enterprise in Sudan: (1) the Sudanese Government, (2) the Arab Investment Company, a joint stock company owned by Arab states,[30] (3) Lonrho, (4) the Sudan Development Corporation, a Sudanese state institution, (5) Gulf Fisheries Company, a Kuwaiti company with Kuwaiti and Sudanese private investors, and (6) Nissho-Iwai Co Ltd, a Japanese trading company.[31] In general, the Founders Agreement set out the basic structure of the proposed Kenana Sugar Company that was to be organized, the principles for its governance and the management of the project, the various commitments made by the six participants to provide funds and other needed resources and benefits required by the project, and a firm commitment by the participants to cause the company, once established, to enter into five annexed agreements: (1) Memorandum and Articles of Association of the Company; (2) a lease agreement between the Government of Sudan and the Company with respect to approximately 150,000 *feddans*[32] of land for a period of 30 years, renewable for an additional 20 years, at a rental of 10 piastres (ie approximately US$0.25) per year for each *feddan* of land; (3) a management services agreement between the Company and Lonrho which appointed Lonrho as "Manager of the Company" for a period of 10 years; (4) a Sugar Sales Agreement entitling the Arab Investment Company to purchase specified quantities of sugar produced by the Company, and (5) a Memorandum of Understanding of December 22, 2012. Together these documents established the contractual framework for the project. The following sections will examine some of the more salient provisions of joint venture agreements, with specific examples drawn from the Kenana joint venture in Sudan.

(b) Preambles and Recitals

A joint venture contract will ordinarily begin with a preamble or recital by the parties of their past dealings with one another, their intentions in undertaking the project, and the circumstances under which they have reached their agreement. In the event of any future

---

[30] With headquarters in Riyadh, Saudi Arabia, the Arab Investment Company was established in 1974 by the governments of seven Arab countries: Saudi Arabia, Kuwait, Sudan, Egypt, Qatar, Abu Dhabi, and Bahrain. Other Arab states would join it later. Its purpose was to encourage economic development in the Arab states. For background on the development of Arab investment at the time, see JW Salacuse, "Arab Capital and Middle Eastern Development Finance: The Emerging Institutional Framework," 14 *Journal of World Trade Law* (1980) 283, 304.

[31] Founders Agreement, Kenana Sugar Company Limited, February 17, 1975 (hereinafter Founders Agreement).

[32] A *feddan* is equivalent to slightly more than one acre.

conflict on matters not specifically covered in the agreement itself, the preamble or recitals may be useful, as statements of intention, in negotiations or in arbitration aimed at resolving such dispute. For example, the preamble in the Founders Agreement for the Kenana Joint venture continues for two single-spaced pages, recounting the important understandings and undertakings of the parties up to the point of executing their joint venture.

(c) Organization and Capitalization

A joint venture agreement will normally specify in some detail the capital to be contributed by each of the participants and the steps to be taken to establish the contemplated joint venture company. Normally, it will provide for the type of legal form to be used, the law under which it is to be organized, and the party or parties who will have the responsibility for fulfilling the legal requirements of the organization and for obtaining other necessary government approvals. It will also stipulate the authorized capital, how the shares are to be allocated among the parties, and the time when each party is to make its capital contribution. It should be recalled, however, that host country legislation may impose a maximum limitation on the percentage of ownership allowed to foreigners. For example, the 1975 Kenana Founders Agreement provided the incorporation of a company under Sudanese law with an authorized capital "...ten million Pounds, to be divided into 10 million ordinary shares of one pound each...," with the shares being allotted to the venture participants as follows: 51 percent to the Sudanese government, 17 percent to the Arab Investment Company, 12 percent to Lonrho, 10 percent to the Sudan Development Corporation, 5 percent to Gulf Fisheries, and 5 percent to Nissho-Iwai.[33]

In addition, if other forms of financing are contemplated, such as loans or export credits, and the parties have an obligation either to provide, guarantee, or procure them from other persons, the joint venture agreement usually also states those responsibilities. For example, the Kenana Founders Agreement obligated the Sudanese government to provide a loan of US$50 million to the company and the Arab Investment Company to provide or syndicate loan funds of US$15.75 million.[34] If the contributions to capital are to be paid in cash, the agreement specifies the amount and type of currency in which payment is to be made. Normally, both the foreign and local partners will want to limit their capital exposure by holding cash equity payments to a minimum; consequently, debt–equity ratios of joint ventures are often high. If the contributions are to be made in property or technology, the agreement will contain specific provisions concerning the valuation of such non-cash contributions. Difficult problems concerning the relative value of contributions by foreign and local partners can arise when the government maintains an artificially high exchange rate which has the effect of overvaluing host country currency and assets.

Yet another problem which the parties address at this stage concerns capital contribution for future expansion of the project. Sometimes the local partner will be unwilling or unable to make such contribution at the appropriate time, and the entire burden will fall on the foreign partner, in which case the parties will be forced to resolve the difficult issues of adjusting the relative ownership shares and control to correspond fairly to total capital contributions.

---

[33] Founders Agreement, Articles 2–4.   [34] Founders Agreement, Articles 10 and 11.

(d) Control and Management

In view of the potential differences in the objectives and attitudes of joint venture partners, the creation of a satisfactory control structure for the venture is imperative. Toward this end, the joint venture agreement contains various control provisions which will also be included in the articles of incorporation or the bylaws of the proposed company. Among the issues to be treated in the agreement are the size of the board of directors, the manner in which the various parties will be represented thereon, the election of directors, the procedures of the board, and the selection of officers. If the board of directors is large, the joint participants may find it appropriate to create a special executive committee to which the board may delegate powers concerning the ongoing execution of the project. Such a device may be particularly convenient to obviate the need for extensive foreign travel by numerous persons to attend regular meetings of the full board of directors. Thus, for example, the Kenana Founders Agreement provided for the creation of a company board of directors of 12 persons and specified the number of directors to be nominated by each joint venture partners. Accordingly, six directors were to be named by the Sudanese government, two by the Arab Investment Company, and one each by the remaining four partners. In addition, Lonrho, which would have a contract to manage the project, had the right to appoint the company's Managing Director, who was entitled to attend board meetings but had no voting rights.[35] In addition, the Founders Agreement committed the parties to amend the Articles of Association of the Company to constitute a four-person Executive Committee, consisting of two representatives of the government and one representative each from Lonrho and the Arab Investment Company with authority to procure equipment, and approve all consulting contracts and loans.[36]

Control is often a particularly difficult issue to resolve in formulating the joint venture agreement. The minority partner is normally unwilling to leave its fate entirely to the will of the majority, and it will therefore seek to write special protective provisions into the agreement. The thrust of such provisions is to give the minority partner a veto over major decisions with which it may not agree. This result is most often achieved by requiring a super-majority, or even unanimity, for board action over especially important issues. The danger of such an approach is, of course, that the enterprise may be thrown into a state of paralysis in the event of a protracted conflict among the partners.

Whether or not a separate management contract is concluded, the joint venture agreement must treat in detail the appointment and removal of the executive officers and those charged with the general management of the project. In joint ventures in which the partners are equal participants, it is common for one partner to appoint the chairman of the board of directors and the other to designate the president or chief executive officer. The provisions on these matters must be coordinated with any special management services agreement between the joint venture company and an outside manager. It is essential to define the relationship between the Board and the outside manager since the potential for conflict between them is great. And finally, since one of the host country's

---

[35] Founders Agreement, Article 19. Within a few years, before the completion of project construction, Lonhro would be terminated as manager of the project and would eventually leave the joint venture entirely. The Kenana Project, with eventual total capital costs of US$1.1 billion, would begin processing sugar in 1981 and commence exporting its production in 1991. As of 2012, the Kenana Sugar Company, operating on 165,000 acres of irrigated land in Sudan, was owned by eleven shareholders, with the Sudanese Government holding 35 percent of the equity, the General Investment Authority of Kuwait holding 30.6 percent, the Government of Saudi Arabia holding 10.97 percent and the Arab Investment Company 7 percent. See <http://www.Kenana.com>.

[36] Founders Agreement, Article 20.

objectives in entering into a joint venture is to facilitate the transfer of management skills, the joint venture agreement may also include a definite schedule for the development of local managerial expertise, as well as a statement of the obligations of the foreign partner to train local persons.

In many joint ventures, shares are evenly divided between the partners. Here, depending on the original will and foresight of the parties, the control structure may be organized in such a way as to insure deadlock and inaction in the event of disagreement, or preferably to provide a means by which the deadlock may ultimately be broken, as through the use of various devices such as granting a tie-breaking vote to an independent member of the board, informal dispute resolution procedures, arbitration, delegation of ultimate authority on certain specified issues, and buy–sell options.

In a joint venture with host country partners, the foreign partner, even though contributing only a small portion of the capital, will ordinarily seek to assure itself a position from which it will be able to "run" the joint venture. Since it is ordinarily supplying technology, management, and marketing, the foreign partner usually believes that it cannot provide these elements effectively or protect its proprietary technology adequately unless it dominates the operation of the enterprise. One means of divorcing management from ownership to achieve this result is for the joint venture to enter into a long term management contract with the foreign partner, who will then have responsibility for the day-to-day operation of the venture. The Kenana Sugar Company adopted this approach by concluding a management contract with Lonrho.

(e) Reimbursement of Preincorporation Expenses

Certain participants in the joint venture may have incurred significant preincorporation expenses for such matters as feasibility studies, engineering designs, legal fees, and travel. The joint venture agreement will often stipulate how those preincorporation expenses are to be borne. One possibility is, of course, that the contemplated joint venture company, once formed, reimburse the parties in cash for those expenses. Another possibility is to capitalize the expenses and include them as the party's contribution to capital for which it will receive shares. On the other hand, the parties may agree that each will bear its own costs, as is reasonable for any investor to do in investigating a possible investment. The Kenana Founders Agreement provided that "Lonrho shall be entitled to be reimbursed by the Company for all reasonable costs and expenses incurred by it in connection with the Project prior to the commencement of Lonrho's duties as Manager under the Management Services Agreement," while stipulating the types of expenses to be included in such designation.[37]

(f) Financial Policies

Parties to a joint venture also seek to reach agreement on the financial principles governing the joint venture. While this subject covers numerous issues, perhaps one of the most difficult concerns the distribution of profits. If the venture becomes profitable, conflict may arise over whether profits should be distributed to the partners or retained for the expansion of the enterprise. Often foreign partners seek the latter, while local partners desire the former. Consequently, to avoid serious conflicts over this issue, the joint venture agreement

---

[37] Founders Agreement, Article 7.

stipulates some basic principles to govern the distribution of profits. For example, it may provide that before any profits of the joint venture company are distributed as dividends to the shareholders, a stipulated percentage of each year's net after-tax profits is to be set aside to meet the capital and other requirements of the joint venture company. In negotiating this provision, the local partner will, of course, be fully aware that the foreign partner has numerous means besides dividend payments to extract profits from the enterprise, including management contracts and technology transfer agreements.[38]

(g) Other Partner Obligations and Guarantees

Joint venture agreements normally state explicitly any obligations and guarantees that the partners in their individual capacities have agreed to undertake for, or on behalf of, the joint venture. For example, in the Kenana Founders Agreement, Nissho-Iwai, a Japanese trading company, is to procure from Japanese manufacturers equipment and machinery up to US$75 million in value and to use its "best endeavors" to procure loans and guarantee facilities in respect of such equipment from Japanese export finance agencies.[39]

If the government is a party to the agreement and has agreed to provide tax incentives, assistance in the construction of infrastructure, subsidized loans, and other privileges and immunities, the agreement should clearly state the nature of such obligations. In the Kenana Founders Agreement, the Sudanese government undertook to secure for the benefit of the company (i) all necessary licenses and permits; (ii) the maximum advantages and concessions " . . . under the Development and Encouragement of Industrial Investment Act of 1974 or any similar legislation whether already in force or hereafter to be enacted including the maximum exemption from customs duties which can be granted to the Company"; and (iii) "[t]otal exemption from the Income Tax Act 1971 from all taxes for the Company, its foreign sub-contractors, foreign lenders, foreign suppliers of goods and services, and the expatriate employees of the foregoing."[40] If the government is not a party to the contract, the partners, in appropriate cases, may seek to have it recognized or acknowledged by the government, so as to have some assurance that the government will not interfere with it at some time in the future.

On the other hand, the local partner may seek, and local law may require, that the foreign partner, especially if it is supplying technology and know-how, guarantee its quality, and even the results to be achieved. In such cases, the foreign party may be able to negotiate limits to such liability and perhaps obtain insurance locally to cover the risk.[41]

(h) Accounting and Auditors

The agreement should stipulate basic provisions with respect to auditing the joint venture's operations—provisions essential to the protection of the interests of the parties and to the preservation of harmony in their continuing relationships. Since the accounting profession in certain countries may not be developed nor fully capable of working on the complex

---

[38] For an illustration of a conflict among joint venture partners concerning the use of accumulated profits, involving an American company, see the case of Tesoro Petroleum Corporation, and the government of Trinidad and Tobago, which was ultimately resolved through conciliation. See L Nurick and SJ Schnably, "The First ICSID Conciliation: Tesoro Petroleum v. Trinidad and Tobago," *ICSID Review-Foreign Investment Law Journal* 1 (1986), 340–53.

[39] Founders Agreement, Article 13.

[40] Founders Agreement, Article 28.

[41] Flynn, "Anatomy of a Yugoslav Joint Venture," *Int'l Fin L Rev* (August 1982) 7, 9.

audits of such enterprises, joint venture agreements often provide that the auditor must be acceptable to all the partners and be an internationally recognized accounting firm. In the alternative, the agreement may specifically appoint a named firm of auditors in order to limit future discretion with regard to this important matter.

(i) Transfer of Shares

Because the relationships among joint venture partners are usually crucial to the success of the enterprise, the agreement will normally contain provisions governing the transfer of shares to third persons, as well as changes in the relative equity positions of the parties. In most cases, such shares will not be freely transferable, but instead, transfers will be subject to the approval of the other joint venture participants. Moreover, the agreement may provide for some sort of buy–sell arrangement to enable the parties to liquidate their investment under certain conditions, for example, only after a period of years, or only if the venture attains a certain level of profitability. Valuation provisions are, of course, essential to such an arrangement.

(j) Applicable Law and Dispute Settlement

As in most international business agreements, the joint venture agreement usually stipulates the governing law, which will normally be the law of the host country, and provide for the settlement of disputes—usually by international arbitration. In view of the fact that preservation of cordial relationships among the partners is ordinarily essential to the enterprise, it is often provided that parties must engage in good faith negotiation and conciliation before invoking formal arbitration. The Kenana Founders Agreement provided for governing law and dispute settlement in the following terms:

> This agreement and the provisions hereof shall be construed and governed by Sudanese Law and all disputes arising in connection therewith shall be finally settled under the rules of conciliation and arbitration of the International Chamber of Commerce by three arbitrators appointed in accordance with the Rules. The Arbitration shall be held in Paris and shall be conducted in the English Language.[42]

(k) Termination

Joint ventures are sometimes unstable, and they may terminate for many reasons, including achievement of the purposes for which they were formed, fundamental disagreement among the parties, basic changes in the law or business conditions that make continuation unfeasible or illegal, management deadlock, or a change in control of one of the partners, or bankruptcy. Joint venture contracts therefore often specify the events that will trigger termination and the consequences flowing therefrom. A termination provision may provide for the liquidation and dissolution of the joint venture entity or for its continuation by one or more of the joint venture partners. In either case, the joint venture agreement will specify the consequences of termination with respect to division of assets and liabilities of the joint venture, indemnifications, discharges, payment of outstanding loans that have been guaranteed by joint venture partners, the return of all confidential information and

---

[42] Founders Agreement, Article 27.

materials and the continuation of confidentiality obligations, and arrangements with respect to licensing or assignment of technology rights.

10.6 International Investment in Infrastructure

(a) Background

Until the late 1980s, many countries did not permit direct foreign investment to play any significant role in infrastructure development. For strategic, nationalistic, and ideological reasons, their governments strongly believed that providing roads, ports, power, water, communications, and other vital infrastructure services should not be done by foreigners but should be carried out only by national governmental entities. Governments, particularly in developing countries, feared that foreign control of infrastructure would lead to foreign domination of their economies and would ultimately impede their economic development and independence.

Since the late 1980s, however, this traditional resistance to foreign private infrastructure development has changed dramatically as more and more countries have adopted laws, regulations, and policies to allow foreign private investors to undertake all sorts of infrastructure projects, from roads and power plants to telecommunications systems and bridges. The reasons for this dramatic change are largely the same as the reasons that caused governments to privatize their public sector industries. Large governmental fiscal deficits, heavy foreign indebtedness, inefficient government agencies, and the need for massive amounts of capital to undertake large infrastructure projects vital to national economic development have made public financing of infrastructure projects difficult, and in some cases impossible, to meet the rising demand for infrastructure services. These factors have led governments to turn to the private sector—particularly foreign private investors—for help in the construction, maintenance, and operation of infrastructure projects that traditionally had been the sole responsibility of the government.

In recent years, significant changes in host country laws and policies have created new opportunities for foreign investors in infrastructure through project structures that have had a variety of names, including build-operate-transfer (BOT), build-operate-own (BOO), and public–private partnerships (PPP). The purpose of this section is to examine these contractual arrangements. Host countries employ the build-operate-transfer (BOT) model of project financing for new construction projects in which a sponsoring foreign investor or consortium of investors and lenders supervises the construction and operation of an infrastructure facility, such as a road or power plant, for a determined length of time, and subsequently transfers ownership and control of the facility to the host government. Under the build-operate-own (BOO) method, on the other hand, a sponsor or sponsoring consortium constructs and owns the infrastructure project, without a subsequent transfer of project assets to a host government. Both models, used primarily within the telecommunications, transportation, and power generation industries, are in effect privatization techniques, and have become increasingly popular in developing countries as a method of infrastructure project financing.[43]

The basic distinction between the BOT and BOO models is the possibility in the former of future ownership by the state of the project. Eventual state ownership of the infrastructure

---

[43] CJ Sozzi, "Comment: Project Finance and Facilitating Telecommunications Infrastructure Development in Newly-Industrializing Countries," 12 *Santa Clara Computer & High Tech L J* (1996) 435, 442. See generally, International Finance Corporation, *Financing Private Infrastructure* (1996).

facility may be important if the host government for ideological or political reasons believes it necessary to control sensitive economic activities that have strategic significance. In such cases, a host country will require a reversion of ownership to the government and therefore opt for a BOT model, rather than a BOO model, of project financing.[44] Other variations on the BOT and BOO models include: build-transfer (BT); build, lease and transfer (BLT); build, transfer and operate (BTO); contract, add and operate (CAO); develop, operate and transfer (DOT); rehabilitate, operate and transfer (ROT); and rehabilitate, own and operate (ROO).

Despite the differences in name, these foreign investment projects have certain common characteristics. First, they involve the participation of foreign capital and management in the development and operation of what is usually considered a public service, with all of the attendant public sensitivities common to that economic sector. Second, there is usually some governmental involvement in the project, either in the form of participation in the project or as a regulator of the service being provided. Third, they almost always take the form of project finance.

(b) Project Finance Transactions

Because of the large amounts of capital required for the construction of infrastructure, project finance transactions typically entail not only equity investment but also significant debt of a particular kind. In project finance lending, the lender relies on the assets and revenues of the project, rather than on the credit of the project sponsor, for repayment of loans. Loans in project financings are made on a "nonrecourse" basis, which means that project sponsors and investors have no liability to lenders for repayment of project loans. International commercial banks are the primary source of loans in project finance transactions. The capital structure of the project relies generally heavily on debt, which may be several times the amount of equity capital contributed by the project promoters.

For host governments, this factor is also an important advantage since the infrastructure development in the form of project finance, unlike governmental infrastructure financings in the past, has no impact on the government's level of outstanding indebtedness and does not make demands on its annual budget. At the heart of the BOT arrangement is a concession agreement by which the host government permits a private party or parties to provide a service to the public in return for payment, while at the same time allowing the government to avoid managerial participation in, financial commitments to, or operating and administrative costs associated with projects.[45] The private sector participants in a BOT or BOO arrangement organize a special project company and, after obtaining a concession agreement from the government, which is in effect permission to collect revenue for delivering what had previously been a public service, proceed to construct and operate a facility for a determined period of time, usually between 15 and 25 years, depending on the nature of the project. The precise length of the concession is determined by the estimated time required to obtain sufficient revenue to pay back accrued debt and provide a reasonable return on equity to the investors in the project company. At the end of that period, the private sector participants transfer to the host government the project company or the project assets along with the managerial expertise and technological

---

[44] Andrew D Cao, "Infrastructure Financing Methods: Paving the Way for Privatization in Latin America," *Latin Finance*, January 1993, at 22.

[45] M L Hemsley and EP White, "The Privatization Experience in Malaysia: Integrating Build-Operate-Own and BOT Techniques within the National Privatization Strategy," 28 *Colum J World Bus* (1993) 70, 89.

capability to enable the host government to assume control and effectively operate the project thereafter.

In a variation, some infrastructure projects rather than being based on a concession contract are based on a "take-or-pay contract," a binding contract obligating the government or some other credit-worthy entity to purchase the product or service, such as electricity, produced by the project company on a long-term basis. These purchasers would be required to purchase the output even though, for example, the purchases may not be economical. Thus, the financial stability and integrity of the ultimate purchaser(s) of the venture's production may provide the essential ingredient for this type of financing package, particularly if such purchasers have entered into long-term output purchase contracts. The ability of the project company to secure the necessary financing from banks will depend on strong assurance of long-term cash flow to service the debt. Thus, the strength and creditworthiness of the concession agreement or take-or-pay contract becomes a vital element in persuading banks to provide the necessary non recourse financing.

(c) The Advantages and Risks of International Infrastructure Investments

Foreign investment infrastructure projects have increased rapidly in number and size since the early 1990s because of the advantages they offer to both investors and host country governments. However, experience since that time has shown that they also pose certain risks.

(i) For Host Countries

A key advantage of BOTs and other infrastructure investments for host country governments is that these arrangements facilitate the acquisition and efficient operation of modern infrastructure without the need for the host country to provide or raise the necessary capital. Since such projects are based upon nonrecourse project financing, they do not increase government indebtedness, divert government funds from other needed purposes, or require a government guarantee of loans to the project as was usual for infrastructure development in the past. At the same time, they enable the government to control the development and operation of the project through the concession agreement and take-or-pay contract, as well as an appropriate regulatory regime. Because many of these arrangements do not make the foreign investor the permanent owner of the facility, some host governments may allow foreign investment in certain sectors only on a BOT basis. China, for example, has a policy which prohibits foreign investors from exclusive operation and control of infrastructure projects that closely affect the daily lives of the Chinese people.[46] In the power industry, the Chinese government passed legislation stating that with the exception of build-operate-transfer projects, "a foreign investor generally is not permitted to take more than a 30 percent equity interest in a power plant."[47]

International infrastructure investment projects also hold out the prospect to host governments of reducing overall project costs. Since a single private firm or consortium acts as owner, designer, and builder of the project, it has strong incentives to design and construct the facility for efficient, low cost operations. Because the investors' interest in the project is often for only a limited period, they will be motivated to provide quality services

---

[46] AC Lam, "Infrastructure Investment Tips," *China Bus Rev* (September 1994) at 44.
[47] AC Lam, "Infrastructure Investment Tips," *China Bus Rev* (September 1994) at 44.

and run an efficient operation from the outset of the project in order to recover costs and make a profit as rapidly as possible through consumer revenue. For the same reason, the investor also has a strong interest in transferring management skills and technology effectively to the project to achieve these ends. The same kind of incentives for efficiency and effective technology transfer did not exist under traditional infrastructure development arrangements where the host country contracted with an international construction firm to design and construct the project and then turn it over to the government which would operate it.

Infrastructure project finance also holds certain risks for host countries. The limited liability of project financing poses the risk that it may encourage investors to pursue risky practices at the potential expense of the public. The nonrecourse nature of project financing means that no investor will be subjected to unlimited liability in the event of loan default. Thus, in a telecommunications project, for instance, any problems the investors encounter may be passed on to users and subscribers in the form of long delays in repairing lines, poor line quality, relatively high communication fees, and network mismanagement. Since a BOT or similar arrangement enables private firms to have control of important infrastructure services for long periods of time, they may continually increase the price of their services so that the public ends up paying more than they would have if the government had provided the same service from the outset.

(ii) For Foreign Investors

International infrastructure investments are attractive to private investors for several reasons. First, they allow entry to economic sectors, such as power, telecommunications, and transportation that were formerly closed to foreign investors. Because the demand for infrastructure services is so strong and is predicted to grow dramatically in the years ahead in developing countries, appropriately designed projects in the right countries offer the prospect of significant revenues for years to come. While BOTs and similar transactions are in essence a type of contractual joint venture with the host country government, it may be more suitable for foreign market penetration than traditional joint ventures in certain circumstances since the BOT model affords parties the predictability and security of a limited timeframe, while maintaining most of the beneficial elements of traditional joint ventures.

The risks faced by private investors in undertaking an infrastructure project are considerable. Project completion risk, operation risk, political risk, market risk, currency risk, and the limited liability nature of non recourse financing are factors that potential investors must evaluate carefully. Completion risk, or the risk of whether the construction of the project can be completed and brought into operation, is affected by a variety of factors including possible cost overruns, delays, labor problems, technical setbacks, accidents, and natural disasters. Operation risk will be affected by the availability of needed inputs such as fuel, the management expertise of the operator, the competence of the workforce, and the project's susceptibility to breakdown and environmental degradation. Conflicts of interest among and between investors and host governments can potentially lead to the breakdown of the working relationship between the parties to an infrastructure project and ultimately reduce the efficiency of operations.

Political risks arising under an infrastructure transactions include the threat of nationalization of project facilities during the concession period and the host government's arbitrary action in changing the terms of the concession agreement or "the take-or-pay contract." For example, in a project for the development of electrical generation, the concession agreement usually specifies the tariff rate for the sale of electricity to users, a factor that is crucial to shaping the project's financing. If the government later intervenes to lower the tariff, the project could easily become a losing operation. Other forms of political risk include damage to the project due to war, revolution or civil disorder; overt expropriations without compensation; and covert expropriation actions such as the imposition of confiscatory taxes or royalties, the cancellation of construction licenses or licenses to import project equipment, and the imposition of export prohibitions, price controls, and exchange control regulations.

Market risk refers to the probability that a project will have an assured, stable market for its services. For example, in developing countries, it sometimes happens that the anticipated customers for a toll road or cellular telephone service are not as numerous as the project sponsors expected because low incomes in the country prevent most people from using the infrastructure services to the level the project proponent anticipated originally. Currency risk occurs when the currency of the project's revenue differs from the currency in which the project has been financed. The relative value of the revenue currency to the financing currency may change unfavorably, or the government through exchange control regulations may restrict the ability of the project company to convert its holdings of local currency into foreign currency necessary to pay foreign expenses, service foreign loans, or repatriate profits to investors.

(d) Parties to International Infrastructure Investments

The two indispensable parties to an international infrastructure investment contract are the appropriate government agency, on the one hand, and private sector entities on the other.[48] The government entity may be a national government agency, such as a host nation's Ministry of Transportation, a government-owned or controlled corporation, or a local government unit, such as a province or municipality. The government agency determines the need for a project and then invites the private sector either partially or wholly to undertake it. The private sector party may consist of several different elements participating in various capacities within a BOT or other infrastructure arrangement. In most cases, the private sector parties include the project proponent, the contractor, and the facility operator. In addition, lenders such as international commercial banks and financial institutions usually provide the bulk of the capital necessary to construct the facility. Through their loans, they have a contractual relationship with the project.

The project proponent or project sponsor is normally the only entity with which the host government has a contractual relationship in connection with the project. The project proponent has the contractual responsibility for the construction and operation of the project, and must make separate contracts with suppliers, contractors, and facility operators. In order to carry out its responsibilities, it must also have adequate financial resources and commitments from financial institutions to cover the estimated project costs. Since many projects are often too large and complex for a single company to handle, several interested private investors may create a joint venture or consortium to undertake it.[49] Generally, the investor or investors form a locally incorporated project company to hold project assets and be legally responsible for the project. Such a local project company also serves to isolate project investors from the risks of project liability, and facilitates

---

[48] AAG Quirino, "Implementing and Financing BOT Projects: The Philippine Experience," in CJ Holgren (ed), *Symposium, Private Investments Abroad–Problems and Solutions* (1993) 5-1, 5–11 (1995).
[49] P Wood, *Law and Practice of International Finance* (1990) 14.02[1].

subsequent transfer of project assets to the host government. Host governments normally require local incorporation in any event since they feel that such incorporation gives them increased ability to control and tax the project. A host government may restrict foreign participation in the project company by requiring a certain percentage of the company to be owned by its own nationals. In the Philippines, for example, projects that require a public utility franchise must have at least 60 percent Filipino ownership.

The contractor may or may not be the project proponent, but must be accredited under the laws of the host government to undertake construction and supply equipment for the project. Some host governments may place special conditions on foreign contractors, for example by requiring that local labor be employed in the construction process. Before entering into a concession agreement, the host government may require the project proponent to identify the contractor who will undertake project construction.

The facility operator may or may not be the project proponent, and is responsible for all aspects of operation and maintenance of the infrastructure, including the collection of payments from users. As with the contractor and project company, the host government may require the facility operator to have a certain percentage of local equity ownership.

(e) The Infrastructure Approval Process

Because infrastructure projects involve the provision of a public service and may entail a monopoly over that service, they always require government approval and are usually subject to some form of governmental regulation upon their completion. After identifying areas in need of development, the concerned government agency will normally publicize and request bids for its infrastructure project needs, often by publication in national or international newspapers or magazines. Foreign investors may obtain government approval of an infrastructure project in one of three ways:

1. by international competitive bidding, which accounts for the majority of project approvals;

2. by competitive negotiation, where the government following the announcement of its interest, selects several short-listed bidders using particular criteria and then negotiates with each; and

3. by direct negotiation, which may be initiated by the government or by an investor with an unsolicited proposal.[50]

The process of public bidding is usually begun with the publication by the host government of a notice or invitation to prequalify and bid upon a designated project. The notice states the deadline for submission of prequalification statements and the qualifications that project participants, such as the contractor or facility operator, must be preidentified for prequalification purposes.[51] The government agency overseeing the approval process makes available to interested investors the bid/tender documents to serve as guidelines for the preparation of prequalification applications and bid proposals. These documents may include: instructions to bidders, minimum design and performance standards and specifications, economic parameters, draft contracts, bid forms, forms of bid and performance securities, and any other materials considered necessary by the government

---

[50] International Finance Corporation, *Financing Private Infrastructure* (1996) 48–50.
[51] AAG Quirino, "Implementing and Financing BOT Projects: The Philippine Experience, in CJ Holgren (ed), *Symposium, Private Investments Abroad–Problems and Solutions* (1993) 5–15.

agency. Prospective bidders are given a specified period of time from the last date of publication of the notice to prepare and submit these documents to the host government. Among other things, they should state the bidder's compliance with legal requirements, experience and technological expertise, and financial credibility. After possible prebid conferences with the host government agency to clarify any provisions of the bid documents, private investors typically submit both a "technical proposal" and a "financial proposal."

Under some bidding procedures, the government employs a two-envelope/two-stage evaluation system. In the first stage, only the "technical proposals" submitted in the first envelopes are opened to ascertain whether they are complete with all necessary data and bid securities. The second envelopes, containing "financial proposals," are returned unopened to bidders disqualified because of incomplete data. In the second stage, the second envelopes of bidders who passed the first stage are to be opened for further consideration. Infrastructure projects are generally awarded to the bidder who has submitted the lowest bid and the most favorable terms for the project. Unsolicited proposals may be accepted by the host government agency on a negotiated basis under certain circumstances. These circumstances may include the existence of new technology or a concept that the host government had not identified as a priority project; a proposal not requiring a direct government guarantee, subsidy or equity; or a situation where the host government receives an attractive proposal after failing to receive any bids in response to its original published invitation. A host government may also engage in direct negotiations with a potential investor in cases where the government has only one qualifying bidder for the designated project, either because it received no other bids or because all other bids did not meet the prequalification or proposal requirements. In some countries, a disqualified bidder may be able to appeal the decision of disqualification to the head of the government agency.[52] After the winning bidder is notified, the parties are given a short period of time to execute the concession or "take-or-pay contract". In the event of refusal, inability or failure by the winning bidder to execute the contract, it forfeits its bid security. The next lowest complying and qualified evaluated bid is then considered. The project may be subject to rebidding if either the government or the bidder refuses to execute a contract.[53]

(f) Financing International Infrastructure Projects

After securing governmental approval of the project and execution of the concession agreement or take-or-pay contract, the project company will then make contracts with equipment suppliers, a construction contractor, and an operations and maintenance contractor. Normally, the project company or consortium has the responsibility of securing the necessary financing for construction of the project. In addition to the equity contributed by investors in the project company, sources of finance include loans from commercial banks, leasing companies, insurance companies, pension funds, governmental bond authorities, and bilateral and multilateral lending institutions. Export credit agencies often provide credit guarantees. Like most project financing schemes, financing is predicated on the merits of a project rather than the credit of the project sponsor. Thus, lenders to the project base their credit appraisal on the expected cash flow from the contemplated revenues of the project, independent of the credit worthiness of the project sponsor. Moreover, the debt is nonrecourse, so that the project sponsor has no direct legal obligation

---

[52] eg, Philippine Republic Act No 7718 s. 5-A, Implementing R & Regs R. 10.
[53] AAQ Quirino, "Implementing and Financing BOT Projects: The Philippine Experience," in CJ Holgren (ed), *Symposium, Private Investments Abroad-Problems and Solutions* (1995) 5-1, 5–18.

to repay the project loans or make interest payments if the cash flows prove inadequate to service debt.[54] Such "project specific" lending often enables developing countries to receive more favorable credit terms than they might otherwise obtain in circumstances where political upheaval or a history of debt default has caused lenders to view such countries as high credit risks.

Because the ability of the project sponsor to produce revenue from project operations is the foundation of project financing, the project's legal and contractual framework has an important impact on project viability and the allocation of risks. Project financing also requires a predictable regulatory and political environment and a stable market to produce dependable cash flow. To the extent this predictability is questionable, lenders may require credit enhancement to protect them from external uncertainties and changes in law. Thus lenders may demand and receive security in the form of guarantees by investors or others of loans to the project company, the pledge of shares in the project company, an assignment of rights from the project agreement, and the mortgage of assets. The lenders must be persuaded that for the term of project contract, project cash flow will be sufficient to cover costs and repay the loans on schedule and before transfer of the facility to the host government. The concession agreement or take-or-pay contract provides the basis for revenues payable to the project company. The project company may be repaid in the form of tolls and fees, a share in revenues, or nonmonetary payments, such as a portion of the land reclaimed by the government. The tolls and fees that may be charged are set at levels that allow the project proponent to recover its total investments and the costs of operations and maintenance and to obtain a reasonable rate of return on investments and operating and maintenance costs. They are subject to adjustment during the life of the contract, based on predetermined formulas in the contract or the regulatory framework.

(g) The Legal and Contractual Framework for Infrastructure Investments

The legal framework for international infrastructure investments consists of the relevant host country legislation, its system of regulations, the concession agreement or take-or-pay contract between the host country agency and the project company, and the various contracts between the project company and its lenders, contractors, suppliers, and other organizations necessary for the project. Although the concession agreement or take-or-pay contract stipulates key provisions governing the relationship between the host country and the project company, the source of many of those concession provisions is set out in the law and regulations of the host country. For example, the law may place maximum limits on the rate of return permitted to the project company. National legislation may also specify certain privileges and guarantees to be enjoyed by infrastructure projects and provide a framework for the enforcement of contractual obligations. One important issue is the existence of a reliable mechanism ensuring that earnings in local currency can be converted into foreign currency and repatriated.[55] For example, Vietnam's BOT Regulation stated:

> The government shall guarantee that the revenue received by the BOT company during this period of operation be converted from Vietnamese currency into foreign currencies in accordance with the contract for the purposes of repaying loan capital and interest, paying all

---

[54] SL Hoffman, "A Practical Guide to Transactional Project Finance: Basic Concepts, Risk Identification, and Contractual Considerations," 45 *Bus Law* (1989) 181, 182–3.

[55] I Arstall and D Platt, "Project Finance," *Int'l Fin L Rev* (February 1995) 27.

expenditure requiring foreign currency and paying to foreign investors their share of profits which are transferred abroad.[56]

A host government may regulate project concession agreements or take-or-pay contracts either through special legislation or through ordinary contract and administrative law. Turkey, for example, passed legislation in 1994 attempting to ensure the effective implementation of infrastructure investment arrangements by delineating the process for awarding contracts to local joint stock and foreign companies that want to provide capital investment or services under such arrangements. It also articulated the governmental approval process and the required characteristics of companies seeking to participate in infrastructure projects, including technical qualifications and investment and capitalization ratios.[57] This legislation also sought to remove Turkish infrastructure investment projects from the realm of concession agreements, since aggrieved private parties to concessions under Turkish law can only adjudicate their claims in Turkish courts and may not have recourse to international arbitration. The 1994 law declared BOT agreements to be commercial contracts, which can be arbitrated internationally and which therefore would give investors greater assurance of a neutral and impartial dispute resolution process in any dispute with the Turkish government in connection with a BOT arrangement. However, the Turkish Constitutional Court decided in a 1996 case that BOT projects are concessions, not commercial contracts, and therefore fall under the laws and regulations governing concessions. The effect of this ruling is to give Turkish administrative courts exclusive jurisdiction over BOT disputes.[58]

Several countries have also enacted codes governing concessions within particular industries and sectors. These codes may establish requirements concerning ownership of resources, state participation in the operation of the project, taxation of project revenues, regulation of project operations, maximum rates of return, and bidding procedures for the award of infrastructure projects.[59] An important issue with respect to the infrastructure investment legal framework concerns the status of concession agreements under host country law. A concession agreement has a dual nature as both contract and an act of the sovereign. The world's legal systems view concession agreements in different ways. Most countries based on the common law tradition distinguish between private and government contracts. Traditionally, under such legal regimes, contractual and tort remedies are available only for breaches of private contracts. A private party to a government contract may not sue the government if the government breaches the contract, unless the law expressly allows such suits. Thus, a host government might permit suits either explicitly in the concession agreement or in the law.

The two main branches of the civil law tradition, the French and German legal systems, treat concessions differently. French civil law considers a concession agreement as a *"contrat administratif,"* rather than private law agreement. French administrative law, with a well-developed body of jurisprudence, treats the parties to administrative contracts unequally and allows the state or its contracting instrumentality to alter the provisions of an administrative contract unilaterally.[60]

---

[56] I Arstall and D Platt, "Project Finance," *Int'l Fin L Rev* (February 1995) 27.

[57] CJ Sozzi, "Comment: Project Finance and Facilitating Telecommunications Infrastructure Development in Newly-Industrializing Countries," 12 *Santa Clara Computer & High Tech L J* (1996) 465–6.

[58] CJ Sozzi, "Comment: Project Finance and Facilitating Telecommunications Infrastructure Development in Newly-Industrializing Countries," 12 *Santa Clara Computer & High Tech L J* (1996) 465–6.

[59] V Soloveytchik, "New Perspectives for Concession Agreements," 16 *Hous J Int'l L* (1993) 261, 267.

[60] V Soloveytchik, "New Perspectives for Concession Agreements," 16 *Hous J Int'l L* (1993) at 264–5.

German civil law considers the grant of a concession or license as a unilateral administrative act and makes no distinction between private and government contracts. The contract merely describes the relationship between the concessionaire and the government. The German legal system, therefore, considers a concession agreement's binding power as predicated "upon the existence of a valid administrative act."[61]

For the foreign investor in a BOT or other infrastructure arrangement, a key concern is the stability and enforceability of the concession agreement. Once having entered into a concession agreement, the investor is concerned with a basic question: To what extent can the host government change the concession's terms by unilateral action or by enacting laws that obstruct the operation of the project or place more onerous burdens on it than were contemplated at the time of the concession agreement's execution? In order to protect themselves against such eventuality, foreign investors often insist that concession agreements contain special commitments not to expropriate the project, guarantees on repatriation of profits and convertibility of project revenues, choice-of-law clauses making the agreement subject to foreign law, the selection of international arbitration for the settlement of all disputes, and stabilization clauses stipulating that future changes in legislation will not impose more onerous conditions on the project than those that existed at the time the concession agreement was executed. The purpose of these provisions is to shield the project agreement from the unilateral acts of the host government. The efficacy of these contractual techniques are subject to two basic questions: (1) the willingness of the host country government to agree to them; and (2) the binding effect of these techniques on a sovereign state even if the host government agrees to some or all of them. Chapter 7, section 7.3 Investor Strategies for Dealing with the Risk of Legal Change discusses both questions in detail.

(h) Concession Contract Provisions

The concession or project agreement between the host government and the project company is the legal heart of any international infrastructure investment. It establishes the respective legal rights and obligations of the parties and provides the license for construction and operation of the project. It will also influence the kinds of other agreement, such as construction contracts, project loans, company charters, and operating contracts that project companies will have to negotiate with other parties in order to construct and operate an infrastructure facility. Among the issues normally treated in a concession agreement are the following.

(i) Concession Rights and Obligations

The contract defines what is required of the project operator, what precisely the operator will be permitted to do, and the length of time for which the concession is granted.[62] This section of the agreement states the general rights and obligations granted to the concessionaire and usually that the concessionaire has the responsibility to undertake them at its own expense and risk, without government financial credits or guarantees. The provision may also deal with concession fees to be paid to the government, land

---

[61] V Soloveytchik, "New Perspectives for Concession Agreements," 16 *Hous J Int'l L* (1993) at 264–5.

[62] CJ Sozzi, "Comment: Project Finance and Facilitating Telecommunications Infrastructure Development in Newly-Industrializing Countries," 12 *Santa Clara Computer & High Tech L J* (1996) 435, 471.

ownership arrangements, and any related works that the government may be required to provide in the area to support the project.

(ii) The Project Company

The concession agreement often stipulates the capital and other requirements of the project company, and may even set out its corporate charter, including provisions on capital structure, restrictions on foreign ownership and control, internal organization and management, and the structure of the board of directors.

(iii) Timing

Since the development of a large infrastructure facility is a complex and lengthy process, the concession agreement will usually stipulate dates for the completion of various phases in making the project a reality. It may also provide for penalties in the event the investor fails to meet the agreed schedule.

(iv) Land Acquisition

Often the government has the responsibility to acquire the land for the infrastructure project. The concession agreement will specify the government's obligations in this regard and the nature of the rights to be transferred to the project company under the concession.

(v) Appointment of an Independent Engineer

The concession usually provides for the appointment of an independent engineer during the construction phase, and possibly thereafter, to report to the government, the concession company and the lenders on the work being done. The independent engineer has the responsibility to inspect the facility upon completion of construction and to certify that it meets construction contract specifications.

(vi) Fees, Tariffs, Tolls, and Compensation

The agreement will specify the fees and tolls to be charged by the project company for the service provided to the users or the consumers' facility and will usually incorporate a formula or set of principles governing fee and toll increases in the future. To assure that the project company operates the facility in an efficient manner, concession agreements often link payments to required performance levels, such as minimum power availability, the number of new water or telephone connections, toll road and bridge capacity, and fault repair times. The agreement may state that if the project company fails to meet specified performance criteria it will have to pay certain penalties to the host government.

(vii) Operation and Maintenance

This provision specifies the nature of the project company's obligations in connection with the operation and maintenance of the facility.

(viii) Profit Sharing and Other Payments to the Government

Often the project agreement will stipulate payment of a portion of the profits or revenues from the project to the government. Additional issues that may arise in negotiating the agreement include: whether the host government is to be compensated through royalty payments and taxation or by an equity share in the project company; whether the project company will be subject to existing price controls or mandatory local sale requirements; and whether the company will be permitted to import foreign materials and equipment supplies free of customs duties. It may also be necessary to include renewal provisions to facilitate future restructuring if the parties decide to extend the concession period in the future.

(ix) Termination

The contract normally includes provisions on termination. Because the project usually has important consequences for public service, the government will retain the right to terminate the contract due to the faulty performance of the project operator. If as a result, the infrastructure facility passes to the ownership of the government, it is important to determine what compensation if any is due to the project company or the investors.

(x) Governing Law and Dispute Settlement

Concession contracts usually include provisions on governing law and the settlement of disputes between the project company and the government concerned. In most cases the governing law will be that of the host country and often dispute resolution will be in local courts, although many investors may seek international arbitration instead.

(xi) Other Provisions

The investors in the project may seek additional legal security through provisions on force majeure, tax reassessments, government guarantees on convertibility of local currency for repatriation of capital and profits, and payment of debt service and purchase of needed imports, and the right of the project company to freely manage the project without government interference. Project sponsors, as discussed earlier, also seek stabilization clauses and specific provisions against the expropriation and nationalization of the project prior to its natural termination. Such provisions should clearly define the activities that will constitute a "nationalization" by the government. In Thailand in 1995, for example, a highway project encountered this issue when the parties failed to agree as to whether the Thai government's forcing open of a toll road, prior to completing a specific agreement on revenue-sharing and other matters, constituted a "nationalization" of the project. Since a project company requires a 20 to 30 year concession period in which to recover its costs and repay its lenders, the earlier the termination by governmental action the greater would be the government's liability in damages in the event of such a breach of the concession agreement.[63] In addition to these key provisions, concession agreements may contain a variety of annexes on such matters as project design procedures, principal terms to be

---

[63] PA Sherer, "Mass-Transit Mystery: Bangkok Begins Building As-Yet Unfunded Railway," *Asian Wall St. J Wkly*, May 1, 1995, at 1.

included in the construction contract, guarantee bonds, and environmental permits and requirements.[64]

(i) Other Project Contracts

The project sponsor enters into a variety of other contracts in order to construct, develop, and operate the infrastructure facility contemplated by the concession agreement. These agreements include the following.

(i) Consortium Agreements

The project company may be controlled by a consortium, comprising investors, construction companies, consultants, financiers, and equipment suppliers, as well as the host government if it chooses to participate in the project company through ownership of a portion of the equity. In the event such a consortium of participants exists, they will usually conclude a consortium agreement, similar to the joint venture agreements discussed at the beginning of this chapter, to determine their respective rights and obligations, to regulate the relationship among them, and to guide the day-to-day management of the company. The consortium contract states funding responsibilities and levels of shareholding, as well as any restrictions on share transfer. It may also include a detailed liquidation procedure in the event the project fails prior to its transfer to the host government. The consortium's charter documents also address issues such as share capital, number and appointment of directors, requirements regarding loan finance, appointment of financial and legal advisers, access to accounting records, confidentiality, dividend policy, share transfers, debt servicing, governing law, service of process, and resolution of disputes.[65]

(ii) The Project Company

The project company may take one of several legal organizational forms: a wholly owned subsidiary, general partnership, limited partnership, joint venture or limited liability company. The choice as to which form to use will depend on an analysis of many factors including taxation, local law requirements, demands of lenders, operating convenience, and business objectives of the parties, among others. For example, some countries may not allow complete foreign ownership of corporate entities or may restrict foreigners from owning certain common carrier facilities. Moreover, the host government may seek to retain some control over the company during the concession operation, but at the same time may not be able or willing to be an equity participant in the project. In such cases, a partnership or contractual joint venture may be an appropriate legal form. On the other hand, a limited partnership, under which each "limited partner" shares in the project profits while enjoying limited liability, may permit capital contributions by passive project investors, such as contractors and equipment suppliers, while giving them certain tax advantages.

---

[64] For an outline of basic terms in toll road concession agreements and power purchase agreements, see International Finance Corporation, *Financing Private Infrastructure* (1996) 112–26.

[65] CJ Sozzi, "Comment" (1996) at 474.

(iii) The Construction Contract

The project company will generally seek to enter into a fixed-price, lump-sum turnkey contract for the construction of the facility so as to fix an important portion of project costs and hedge completion risks. Completion delays, cost overruns, and failure of the completed facility to perform according to expectations are some of the main uncertainties associated with construction risk. The construction contract will seek to deal with these problems by clearly specifying dates and performance standards, and it will include liquidated damages provisions for late completion or failure to meet guaranteed performance. The construction contractor will also be required to provide a project completion performance bond from a reliable bonding company to compensate the project company and the host country for failure to complete the project on time because of bankruptcy, default, labor strikes, or natural disasters. In some cases, where completion bonds are unavailable, the contractor may be required to provide a standby letter of credit from a recognized international commercial bank. Other construction risks considered in the contract are price changes caused by currency fluctuations or inflation, material shortages, design changes required by law, and labor disputes.[66]

(iv) Operations and Management Agreement

The project company may entrust management of the facility to another party, in which case the companies will enter into an operations and management agreement. In addition to receiving fixed operations/management fees from incoming revenues, the operator may be remunerated through incentive payments designed to encourage superior levels of performance and may also be obligated to pay penalties if performance does not meet stipulated standards.

The host government may seek to retain some control over the project to ensure efficient operation of the facilities. Toward this end, the contract may provide for the assignability of an operator's obligations and rights by the government so as to allow the removal of ineffective operators in the event of certain predetermined contingencies, such as inadequate revenue, failing technology, or poor service quality. Another relevant issue treated in the operations and management contract is indemnification. The contracting agency or the host government will usually wish to be protected against all liabilities and claims resulting from the project company's operation of the project.

(v) Loan Agreements

A major portion of the funding for infrastructure projects comes from lenders of varying sorts. These loans are of course supported by loan agreements. In order to protect themselves from the considerable risks entailed by infrastructure projects, lenders normally require their loan documents to include numerous loan covenants stipulating how the borrower (ie the project company) will use the funds and manage the project. Such loan covenants may include provisions on minimum debt service ratio, a measure of a project's debt service obligations relative to its cash flow. Covenants may also prohibit the payment of dividends to investors if the current ratio falls below a stated amount, and limit capital expenditures to a maximum amount per year. To assure payment of debt service, the loan

---

[66] CJ Sozzi, at 482. See also International Finance Corporation, *Financing Private Infrastructure* (1996) 69–70.

agreement may require the establishment of debt reserve accounts of a fixed amount to ensure that debt servicing will continue uninterrupted if there is a fall in project revenues. Lenders may even require that debt reserve accounts be held off-shore in an established financial institution, to avoid the risk of possible intervention by the host government to prevent its use.

10.7 A Case Study of Infrastructure Investment: The Dabhol Power Company in India

(a) Background

One may gain an understanding of the dynamics at work in shaping a contractual framework for an international infrastructure investment by examining a specific case, the negotiations involved in Enron's Dabhol Electricity Power Project in India,[67] a project that subsequently encountered difficulties and received significant media attention.[68]

India, the largest democracy in the world, had a population exceeding 920 million people in 1995, which was increasing at an annual rate of 2.3 percent. A poor country with a per capita income of US$370 a year, it also had a growing middle class of 250 million people located primarily in the cities. The former jewel in the crown of the British Empire, India gained its independence in 1947 and is a federation consisting of twenty-six states and six union territories. It has a strong central government with a 600-member Parliament that is elected every five years. Following the British parliamentary model, the political party with the majority in Parliament forms the executive government and that party's leader becomes the Indian Prime Minister. Each Indian state has its own legislature and an executive consisting of a Chief Minister and cabinet of state ministers chosen from the elected members of the state assembly. State elections are held every five years but not necessarily at the same time as central government elections.[69]

From its independence in 1947 until the early 1990s, India based its economic policies on self-sufficiency, import substitution, and state control of basic industry and infrastructure. Historically, the country was wary of foreign investment and its policies in that area were extremely restrictive, particularly under Prime Minister Indira Gandhi in the 1970s. With broad popular support, Gandhi had forced Coca-Cola, IBM, and other multinational firms out of India, thereby driving away foreign investment for a generation.[70] After that, much of India's trade was with the Soviet Union, whose collapse had severe consequences for the Indian economy.[71]

India's economic policies of self-sufficiency, state control of basic industry and infra-structure, and restriction on foreign investment were probably no more apparent than in its

[67] For background, see RP Teisch and WA Stoever, "Enron in India: Lessons From a Renegotiation," 35 *Mid-Atlantic J Bus* 1999) 51–62; Harvard Business School, *Enron Development Corporation: The Dabhol Power Project in Maharashtra, India* (A) (HBS Case no 9-596-099, March 25, 1997) [hereinafter *Harvard Study (A)*]; Harvard Business School, *Enron Development Corporation: The Dabhol Power Project in Maharashtra, India (B)* (HBS Case no 9-596-100, December 16, 1996) [hereinafter *Harvard Study (B)*]; Harvard Business School, *Enron Development Corporation: The Dabhol Power project in Maharashtra, India (C)* (HBS Case no 9-596-101, December 16, 1996) [hereinafter *Harvard Study (C)*].

[68] See, eg, JF Burns, "Indian Politics Derail a Big Power Project," *NY Times*, July 5, 1995, at D1; M Nicholson, "Survey—Maharashtra 1996: U-Turn that Saved the Project," *Fin Times*, July 11, 1996, at 3; "The Mugging of Enron," *Euromoney*, October 1995, at 33; G McWilliams and S Moshavi, "Enron: Maybe Megadeals Mean Megarisk," *Bus Week*, January 22, 1996, at 62; R Rao, "Enron's Power Outage in India," *Fortune*, October 2, 1995, at 35–6. The subsequent difficulties of the Dabhol Project are discussed in detail in Chapter 12, section 12.6.

[69] See Burns, n 68 at D1.

[70] Burns, n 68 at D1.

[71] See V Kanwarpal, "Power Shift," *Independent Energy*, July/August, 1996.

electric power sector. The generation and distribution of electricity was the exclusive domain of the central and state governments, and political factors, rather than market forces, were primary considerations in the operation of the Indian electrical power system. The Indian Energy Supply Act of 1948[72] initiated this monopoly, establishing state electricity boards to develop the power sector at the state level and the Central Electricity Authority to set policy at the national level. Under this regime, total electricity generating capacity amounted to approximately 81,000 megawatts (MW) in 1995, of which state agencies accounted for 65 percent; the national government, 31 percent; and private enterprise, a mere 4 percent.[73]

As India entered the 1990s, the country's demand for electrical power greatly exceeded its ability to supply it. In 1993–1994, for example, demand for electricity exceeded supply by 22.5 billion kilowatt hours (kWh).[74] As a result, the country was experiencing serious power outages with significant negative impact on industrial production. Furthermore, many rural areas received little electricity and some 95,000 Indian villages had none at all. Experts predicted that the situation would only grow worse in the years ahead. One source estimated that India would need to create an additional generating capacity of 62,000MW by 2005 at an estimated cost of US$165 billion.[75] The US Energy Department estimated that by the same year India would need a staggering 140,000MW of additional capacity.[76] The Indian government identified the country's lack of power resources as a fundamental obstacle to economic development.[77]

Neither the Indian central government nor the various state electricity boards had the necessary capital to develop the capacity to meet the nation's growing demand for electricity. Indeed, most state electricity boards were insolvent or nearly so due to the inefficiency of their operations. Power losses from their distribution grids were as much as 40 percent. Electricity was stolen from the system and in many cases pricing for certain privileged groups, such as farmers, resulted in it being sold for less than the cost of production. The entire system of electricity generation and distribution was beset by high costs, entrenched subsidies, and bloated employment rolls. The state electricity boards were selling electricity for as much as 50 percent below cost and the agricultural sector was paying as little as 20 percent of the rates charged to industrial users. As a result, the accumulated losses of the public power sector amounted to US$6.4 billion in 1996.

One of the consequences of the subsidies and method of operation was the existence of entrenched constituencies opposed to reform of the power sector and especially privatization. Attempts to raise electricity rates in the state of Haryana, for example, resulted in riots and several deaths. At the same time, growing public demand for increased electricity and the resolution of a power deficit that was increasingly viewed as a crisis became an important political issue in the country. In 1991, the Congress Party narrowly won an election victory with promises to address the problem.[78] The Prime Minister PV Rao, an advocate of market reforms, appointed as his finance minister Manmohan Singh, who began a series of reforms, similar to those being adopted elsewhere in developing countries that sought to transform the economy from one based on state control to one

[72] See *Harvard Study (A)* at 6.
[73] See "Survey: Business in Asia—Underpowered," *Economist*, March 9, 1996, at 6.
[74] *Harvard Study (A)* at 6.
[75] R Sarathy, *Enron: Supplying Electric Power in India* Case 16.4 (7th edn 1997).
[76] Teisch and Stoever, n 67, at 53.
[77] *Int'l Private Power Quarterly*, 3rd Quart, 1996, at 140.
[78] See Teisch and Stoever, n 67, at 54.

based on market forces.[79] A central focus of this package of reforms was the encouragement of private and foreign investment in India.

To address the entrenched problems of the power sector, the new Indian government secured the adoption of the Electricity Laws Act of 1991,[80] which represented an historic shift in policy. This legislation allowed private sector companies with 100 percent foreign ownership to build, own, and operate power plants, mandated a minimum rate of return of 16 percent on equity, allowed foreign investors to repatriate profits entirely, permitted new projects to have a debt-to-equity ratio of 4:1, outlined procedures by which private and foreign-owned projects could sell electricity to state electricity boards, and specified how electrical tariff rates should be set.

Despite these substantial reforms, foreign power companies did not immediately rush to India to develop new projects.[81] In May of 1992, the Indian government therefore took the initiative of sending its Power Secretary, S Rajgopal, to the United States in an effort to attract US companies to invest in the Indian power sector. One company that responded positively to Mr. Rajgopal's overtures was Enron Corporation, based in Houston, Texas.

(b) Negotiating the Dabhol Project

Enron Corporation was a diversified energy company that earned a net income of US$453 million on revenues of approximately US$9 billion in 1995. Facing the problem of slow growth in the US energy market, it made a strategic decision to focus heavily on the demand for power in foreign countries, a demand that was expected to grow to 560,000MW. In order to pursue this strategy, it created Enron Development Corporation, a wholly owned subsidiary, to exploit the growing worldwide demand for energy, particularly in high growth, emerging market countries.[82] The visit to Enron by the Indian Power Secretary persuaded the company's leadership that India offered the kind of opportunities that fit Enron's worldwide strategy. The following month, on June 15, 1992, a team of Enron executives arrived in Delhi, the capital of India, to continue discussions with central government officials and to explore concrete opportunities for power projects.[83]

Under the guidance of central government officials, the Enron team identified the state of Maharashtra as the most advantageous site from which to begin to serve the Indian electricity market. With a population of nearly 79 million people, Maharashtra was India's third largest state and the home of its commercial capital, Bombay (later to be Mumbai). Moreover, as the country's most important industrial state, Maharashtra had the highest gross national product per capita in India. At the time of the Enron visit, the Congress Party, which controlled the central government and was the dominant force in Indian politics since before the country's independence, also controlled the Maharashtra state government.

In discussions with officials of the Maharashtra state government and the Maharashtra State Electricity Board (MSEB), Enron proposed the construction of a 2015MW power plant at a cost of nearly US$3 billion, which would make it the largest foreign investment

---

[79] See JW Salacuse, "From Developing Countries to Emerging Markets: A Changing Role For Law in the Third World," 33 *Int'l Law* (1999) 875, 890.

[80] See Teisch and Stoever, n 67, at 52.

[81] Teisch and Stoever, n 67, at 52.

[82] See *Harvard Study (A)* at 6.

[83] See Government of Maharashtra, *Report of the Cabinet Sub-Committee to Review the Dabhol Power Project*, available at <http://www.hrw.org/reports/1999/enron/enron-b-htm> (giving chronology of events leading up to agreement on Dabhol Project).

project ever undertaken in India. A plant of that size requires a large reliable source of fuel. Enron believed that liquefied natural gas would be the most cost efficient fuel. A dependable source of natural gas lay across the Indian Ocean in the Arabian Peninsula 1,200 miles away; specifically, in the country of Qatar with which Enron had already entered into a joint venture for liquefied natural gas development. In view of the substantial time and capital needed to develop facilities to liquefy, handle, and ship natural gas, Enron proposed to divide the electricity project into two phases: a first phase of 695MW using locally produced fuel and a second phase of 1,320MW using imported liquefied natural gas. Dividing the project into two phases also permitted Enron to test India's credibility and allowed India to determine Enron's ability to deliver a reliable source of electricity. Enron decided that the best location for its power plant was the town of Dabhol, located on the Indian Ocean approximately 120 miles south of Bombay.

An essential requirement for the financial success of the proposed Dabhol project was the existence of a credible, long-term purchaser of the electricity it would generate. A commitment from such a buyer was necessary to enable the project company to secure long-term debt financing and to assure the equity investors an adequate return on their investment. For the Dabhol Project to become a reality, it was therefore necessary for the Maharashtra State Electricity Board, the only potential buyer in the state, to enter into a long-term power purchase agreement with the Dabhol Power Project Company. In order to assure the necessary cash flow to finance the project, the project promoters envisaged the power purchase agreement as a "take-or-pay contract." On June 20, 1992, just three days after the Enron team's arrival in Bombay and only five days after entering the country for the first time, Enron and the MSEB signed a memorandum of understanding outlining the project as described above and proposing a power purchase agreement, which stipulated that the price to be charged by the Dabhol Power Project would be no more than 2.40 rupees (7.3 US cents) per kWh.

Over the course of the next year, Enron, the Maharashtra State Electricity Board, and various concerned Indian central and state government departments negotiated the precise arrangements under which the proposed Dabhol Power Project would come into existence and sell electricity in Maharashtra. At the same time, Enron persuaded two other US companies, General Electric, a manufacturer of power equipment, and Bechtel International, a global construction firm, to join it in forming a consortium to carry out the project.

The negotiation encountered three major problems. First, the World Bank, which served as a consultant to the central government, wrote a report claiming that the Dabhol project was too large and would create excess capacity for years to come. It also asserted that the proposed project was too expensive when compared with electricity generated by more traditional fuels such as coal. In response, Enron, stressing the environmental benefits of the Dabhol project and the long term power needs of India, undertook a lobbying campaign in key departments of the Indian government and succeeded in countering the negative effects of the World Bank's report.[84]

The second and more difficult problem concerned the project's expected rate of return. Enron projected a rate of return to equity holders of 26.52 percent, which the government of Maharashtra as well as the central government's Foreign Investment Promotion Board considered too high. The Indian side felt that 20 percent was much more reasonable. Enron

---

[84] Government of Maharashtra, *Report of the Cabinet Sub-Committee to Review the Dabhol Power Project*, available at <http://www.hrw.org/reports/1999/enron/enron-b-htm>; see also M Palnitkar and KS Nayar, "Enron Decision: Shockwaves," *India Abroad* (August 11, 1995) 4.

insisted that given the risks involved and prevailing market expectations for similar projects, the projected rate of return on the Dabhol project was reasonable and that even 30 percent would be appropriate. Although the negotiations nearly collapsed over the issue, the two sides finally agreed on a rate of return of 25.22 percent, although various government officials still considered the agreed upon rate of return as too high. Other difficult issues concerned the project's capital costs, the government guarantees, the pricing escalation factor in the power purchase agreement, and the provisions on monetary exchange rate fluctuations.

The third problem that surfaced during the negotiations was a growing negative view of the project among certain segments of the Indian public. Opponents of the project strongly criticized its high rate of return, the high electricity tariff that Indians would ultimately have to bear, and the government's failure to engage in competitive bidding, as had been standard practice with other power plants constructed in the country. Accusations were made that Indian officials had been bribed to approve the project. Public demonstrations against the project took place and at one point a bomb exploded in the hotel in which the Enron team was staying.[85] Despite these manifestations of public opposition, negotiations continued.

To undertake the project, Enron, with its two US minority partners, General Electric and Bechtel, each of which held 10 percent of the equity, formed the Dabhol Power Company in April 1993. On December 8, 1993, some twenty months after the Indian Power Secretary's first contact with Enron, the Dabhol Power Company and the Maharashtra State Electricity Board signed the Power Purchase Agreement, formally launching the Dabhol Project, the biggest foreign investment project ever undertaken in India.

(c) The Contractual Framework of the Dabhol Project

The central contractual support of the Dabhol Power Project was the Power Purchase Agreement. It was an example of a "take-or-pay contract," discussed earlier in this chapter. The basic provisions of the Power Purchase Agreement were as follows:

- The Dabhol Power Company agreed to design, finance, and build within thirty-three months an electrical generating plant with a baseload capacity of 625MW and additional peak load capacity of 70MW. Failure to provide commercial service within 33 months of the deadline would result in penalty payments by the Company to the MSEB of US$14,000 per day. Moreover, if the Company failed to reach baseload capacity of 625MW within one year after the beginning of commercial service it would be required to pay US$100 for each kilowatt below the required 625MW requirement.

- The Maharashtra State Electricity Board and the government of the State of Maharashtra agreed to provide the land and the necessary infrastructure, including roads to the site, communications, and transmission lines from the power plant to the MSEB grid.

- The Maharashtra State Electricity Board agreed to purchase what amounted to at least 90 percent of the Dabhol plant's output, thus making the Power Purchase Agreement a "take-or-pay contract." The MSEB was obligated to pay for electricity from the Dabhol Power Company under a complex payment formula for an initial period of 20 years. The formula consisted of two parts: (1) a capacity payment determined by the

---

[85] See *Harvard Study (A)* at 6.

baseload and peak capacities, regardless of the amount of power actually used by the MSEB and (2) an energy payment based on the actual amount of power produced. The result of the formula was that the estimated cost of power to the MSEB would be 7.05 US cents per kWh at the commencement of commercial operations. The tariff was indexed to Indian inflation rates and was expected to rise to 11.34 US cents per kWh by 2015.

- Although the MSEB's payments were to be made in rupees, it also had the responsibility of bearing any changes in the dollar-rupee exchange rate over time.

- The Maharashtra State government guaranteed the MSEB payment obligations to the Dabhol Power Company, and the central government issued a counter-guarantee.

- Although Indian Law governed the Power Purchase Agreement, the parties agreed to settle any disputes arising under the agreement by binding arbitration in London under UNCITRAL arbitration rules.

- At the end of 20 years, MSEB had the option to extend the Power Purchase Agreement for an additional five or ten years. If it chose not to renew the Agreement, the MSEB would be required to purchase the plant at 50 percent of its then depreciated replacement value.

Enron then moved rapidly to finance and implement the project. In addition to the equity contribution of US$279[86] million from the three project partners, it ultimately secured loan commitments of US$643 million from banks, export credit agencies, and lending agencies.[87] The specific loan commitment were as follows: (1) a bank syndicate led by Bank of America and ABN Amro—US$150 million; (2) Overseas Private Investment Corporation—US$100 million; (3) Industrial Development Bank of India and other Indian financial institutions—rupee loans equivalent to US$96 million; and 4) the United States Export-Import Bank of the United States—US$298 million. Construction on Phase I began almost immediately thereafter and was completed, despite the difficulties to be described in Chapter 12, in May 1999, when it began commercial operations.

The construction of Phase II, which would treble the plant's capacity to 2,184 megawatts, also began in 1999, and was scheduled for completion in 2001. In total, to finance two phases of the project Enron raised US$1.9 billion in project debt from a variety of sources, which included a syndicate of international commercial banks, Indian government-owned banks, export credit agencies, and the United States Overseas Private Investment Corporation (OPIC), a provider of foreign investment insurance and developmental finance, which is discussed in the following chapter. OPIC was the single largest supplier of loans to the Project. In addition to loans of US$160 million, it also provided US$200 million in political risk insurance to cover the investments of Enron, Bechtel, and General Electric, as well as approximately US$32 million to one of the commercial lenders.[88] The key element that allowed the Project sponsors to raise this level of funding was the Power Purchase Agreement, which promised a cash flow to the project for at least 20 years, an amount, it was assumed, sufficient to pay off the lenders and provide the equity investors with a satisfactory profit. Without the legal assurance of the stream of payments provided by that

---

[86] Enron Power Corporation, which had the responsibility for construction management, operations, maintenance, and fuel management, contributed US$233 million; Bechtel Enterprises, a construction contractor on the project, contributed equity of US$28 million; and General Electric also had an equity interest of US$28 million.

[87] Enron, *Press Release: Dabhol Project Achieves Financial Close: Resumes Construction,* available at <http://www.enron.com/india/Newsroom/Press_Release02.htm> (December 10, 1996) [hereinafter Dabhol Resumes Construction].

[88] K Hanson, RC O'Sullivan and WG Anderrson, "The Dabhol Power Settlement: How it Happened. Why?" in <http://www.infrastructurejournal.com>.

investment contract, as well as the guarantee of MSEB payments made by the Indian central government, neither the project sponsors not the project lenders would have invested in the Dabhol Power Company. As will be seen in Chapter 12, that promise of a flow of payments would eventually fail by the year 2001, resulting in litigation and negotiations as the various investors sought to salvage as best they could their investments in what was then India's largest foreign investment project.

10.8 International Loan Contracts

(a) Introduction

Vast amounts of international investment take the form of loans which, like other international investment forms, have a specific contractual framework. One may define an "international loan" as a loan where the lender and borrower are located in different countries or where the loan is denominated in a currency other than that of the country of the lender or the borrower. Much of such lending is done by banks, but other entities, such as multinational corporations and international development agencies, also make international loans. The borrowers in international loans include a wide variety of entities including governments, governmental agencies and corporations, multinational corporations, domestic private companies, such as the Kanana Sugar Company, and specific purpose project vehicles, such as the Dabhol Power Company, both of which are discussed earlier in this chapter.

An important source of funding for international loans are "eurodollars," a deposit liability, denominated in US dollars, of a bank outside the United States, even though that bank may be a subsidiary of a US bank.[89] The bank holding that deposit may be a foreign branch of a US bank or a foreign bank. This international financial market is not, however, limited to US dollars. It is therefore sometimes referred to as the eurocurrency market. Accordingly, other currencies also exist in "euro" form. As such, those currencies are also on deposit outside their country of origin. Therefore, the euro market can involve euro-sterling (UK pounds located outside the UK), Euro-euros (euros on deposit outside the euro area), and euro-yen (yen on deposit outside Japan). The assumption in using this "euro" designation is that this funding is coming from a European source (including from the United Kingdom) but it could be sourced from an Asian bank or some other location outside the United States. With the expansion in international banking has come the growth of deposits of other currencies outside their countries of origin and these "euro-currency" deposits have also become funding sources for international loans. For example, the deposit of Japanese yen in a Singapore bank would be considered a euro-yen deposit and a deposit of European euros in a United Kingdom bank would be a "euro-euro" deposit, both of which might fund an international loan.[90]

Banks may also make multicurrency loans by extending a eurocurrency loan which gives the borrower the opportunity to specify the particular currency of the loan as of the time the borrower draws down the loan. This type of multicurrency arrangement enables a multinational enterprise to draw funds where and when needed. Such loans may also be structured to enable the currency of the loan to be changed periodically at the loan's interim maturity or "rollover" dates. Other variations exist in this context, partly to enable the borrower to spread the currency devaluation risk over a number of currencies.

---

[89] C Bamford, *Principles of International Finance* (2011) 146–8.
[90] HS Scott, *International Finance* (14th edn 2007) 501.

Unlike joint venture and project finance contracts, which demonstrate a relatively high degree of diversity because of the diverse nature of the underlying projects they govern, international loan contracts exhibit a high degree of uniformity as a result of the evolution of common practices by banks and their lawyers over the years. The purpose of this section is simply to outline the general contractual structure that international loans take, the basics of the international lending process, and some of the common provisions to be found in international loan agreements.[91]

Virtually all international loans are term loans, that is, they provide for the loan of funds for a specific period of time, at the end of which the borrower must repay the lender in full the principal amount of the loan. There are nonetheless three important subcategories of international loans: (1) individual bank loans and syndicated bank loans; (2) fixed interest rate and floating interest rate loans; and (3) secured and unsecured loans.

An individual bank loan consists of a single bank negotiating a loan agreement with the borrower and providing it with the required loan funds. Especially large loans, however, are usually accomplished by a syndicate of banks, as was the case with the Dabhol Project discussed earlier in this chapter. Syndication is a means of spreading the credit risk among a group of banks which lend separate portions of the needed funds to the borrower under the terms of a single loan agreement that is organized and administered by an agent bank.[92] One of the principal goals of the syndication agreement is to assure the participating banks equality of treatment.

Lenders are compensated for making loans through the payment of interest by the borrower. The interest rate on the loan is therefore a key contractual provision. The interest rate may be fixed for the term of the loan, but a more common practice in international lending is the use of a floating rate. The reason for this is that where the lender is a bank the source of its funding is short-term deposits, a factor that creates a considerable risk for a bank that lends those deposits for a long-term period. To protect themselves against such risks, banks lend those funds on a floating interest rate basis, which means that the borrower's interest payment for each specified period during the duration of the loan is an amount that is calculated on the index for short-term interest rates that banks must pay to borrow money, such as the London Interbank Offered Rate (LIBOR), plus a margin which is a fixed percentage of the outstanding loan. Thus the interest obligation for a given loan might be LIBOR plus a margin of 1 percent. The LIBOR amount represents the lending bank's cost of funds and the margin is its profit. The specified interest rate for the loan is thus pegged at a specified percentage over the London Interbank Offered Rate (LIBOR). The total interest rate percentage will depend on various factors including (1) the length of the loan maturity and (2) the creditworthiness of the borrower. For other than short-term loans, that interest rate will normally be adjusted periodically to take into account the variations in the lender's cost of funds for the money provided to the borrower. Such floating rate loans thereby protect bank profits against increases in the interest rate on eurodollar deposits (and provide corresponding benefits to the borrower when that rate declines).

A third distinguishing feature among loans is whether they are unsecured or secured. In an unsecured loan transaction, the lender relies on the creditworthiness of the borrower for repayment. A secured loan on the other hand, grants the lender some sort or property

---

[91] For a more detailed treatment of this subject, see generally, PR Wood, *International Loans, Bonds, and Securities Regulation* (1995); C Proctor, *The Law and Practice of International Banking* (2010); and C Bamford, *Principles of International Finance* (2011).

[92] PR Wood, *International Loans, Bonds, and Securities Regulation* (1995) 5–6.

interest, such as a mortgage, in the assets of the borrower in the event of failure to repay the loans. For example, loan agreements to allow the purchase of aircraft usually grant the lender a security interest in the aircraft financed through the loan.[93]

(b) The International Lending Process

(i) Commitment Letter

After initial discussion with a prospective borrower, the lender that has tentatively decided to go forward with a loan often will provide the borrower with a commitment letter, sometimes called a "term sheet." This letter or memorandum will outline the basic terms of the anticipated loan. However, the letter is structured so as not to constitute a binding commitment and not to foreclose any future negotiations of specific points not precisely enumerated in the letter. The basic terms identified in the term sheet will include: (1) the amount and currency of the loan; (2) the interest rate and interest payment schedule; (3) the amortization schedule for the loan payments; (4) additional fees, eg, a loan commitment fee; (5) anticipated and permitted use of the loan proceeds; (6) representations and warranties to be required; (7) potential covenants to be required and the identification of possible loan default events; (8) the reimbursement (or gross-up) of the amounts payable for local country taxes; and (9) the identification of any potential or required guarantors of this debt.

(ii) Mandate Letter

If the loan is to be syndicated, the proposed borrower will normally issue a "mandate letter." The purpose of this letter is to designate one or more financial institutions to be the managers or co-managers of the proposed financing that will be syndicated among various other financial institutions. Through this letter, the borrower secures the services of a specific institution to act as the borrower's agent in placing and, thereafter, administering the loan. The manager for the borrower is often an investment bank that specializes in forming loan syndicates on behalf of various prospective borrowers. The mandate is normally stated as a nonlegally binding commitment that is subject to the negotiation and conclusion of a contract.[94]

(iii) Syndicate Manager

The functions of the manager of a loan syndication (sometimes called the "bookrunner") will include:

(i) advising and negotiating with the borrower as to the terms on which the manager considers it will be able to place portions of the entire credit in the financial market;

(ii) obtaining a mandate from the borrower authorizing the manager to arrange the financing on the borrower's behalf;

(iii) preparing and assisting in the preparation of an Information (or Offering) Memorandum, which is used in the participation of other financial institutions in the proposed syndicate.;

---

[93] C Proctor, *The Law and Practice of International Banking* (2010) 579–90.
[94] PR Wood, *International Loans, Bonds, and Securities Regulation* (1995) 90–1.

    (iv) seeking banks to participate in the financing and allocating shares to these banks as the syndicate is being formed;

    (v) supervising the preparation and negotiation of loan documentation; and

    (vi) arranging the closing of the loan arrangements.

(iv) Offering Memoranda

The syndicate manager will prepare an offering memorandum on behalf of the borrower to provide prospective lenders with relevant information concerning the prospective borrower and the loan transaction itself. This memorandum usually includes the following information: (a) an analysis of the financial position of the borrower; (b) the purpose of the loan transaction; (c) the anticipated repayment method for the principal and the payment of interest, plus the sources of funds anticipated to be available to the borrower to support these projected payment methods; (d) relevant information concerning the anticipated application of the loan funds when received by the borrower, the background of the borrower, the borrower's country (and, particularly, if a developing country, that foreign country's current and projected future balance of payments positions); (e) an identification of the guarantor (if any), and an analysis of the guarantor's financial position; and (f) an identification of any specific collateral to be pledged in support of the repayment commitment for this loan.

(v) Conclusion of a Definitive Loan Agreement

The final stage in the loan process is the conclusion of a definitive agreement covering the loan. The loan agreement will be the definitive document describing the rights and obligations of (1) the borrower, (2) the lender(s), (3) the agent bank(s), (4) the guarantor and (5) any other parties to that agreement. That agreement may have attached to it as exhibits specific agreed forms for ancillary documents such as: promissory notes, guarantee agreements, security documents, corporate resolutions, governmental authorizations, and other types of certificates.

(c) The Provisions of the Loan Agreement

International loan agreements tend to follow a common pattern that has been polished and developed over the years by banks and their legal counsel. Loan agreements normally include the following provisions:[95]

    (i) *Representations and Warranties.* These paragraphs confirm the fundamental premises concerning the status and condition of the borrower and upon which the lender is relying in funding the loan.

    (ii) *Conditions Precedent.* Conditions are enumerated which must be satisfied before the loan will be funded. These might include that, if adverse changes occur to the borrower before loan funding, the obligations of the lender will be modified.

    (iii) *Covenants.* Stated both in affirmative and negative terms, the covenants will specify those conditions which must be satisfied during the entire period that the loan is outstanding.

---

[95] For an example of the text of an international loan agreement, see PR Wood, *International Loans, Bonds, and Securities Regulation* (1995) 413–56.

(iv) *Events of Default.* Those events which trigger a "default" and, therefore, an acceleration of the repayment obligation are enumerated in this paragraph. Events of default will ordinarily include significant violations of one or more of the conditions agreed to in the loan agreement. Often this provision will include a cross-default clause which specifies that, if the borrower fails to pay any debt when it becomes payable to any other lender and the party to that debt has the right to accelerate the maturity of that debt, then the payment of the amount owing to the lender in the current lending project shall also be accelerated.

(v) *Interest Rate.* Nearly all international loans provide for a floating interest rate that is tied to an interest rate index, the most common of which is the London Interbank Offered Rate (LIBOR). The loan agreement will define in precise terms the specific meaning of LIBOR as the arithmetic mean of the interest rates supplied to the Agent of the loan syndicate quoted by certain designated "Reference Banks" (named in the loan agreement) to leading banks in a particular loan market as of a particular date for a specific interest period. The interest period is usually one, two, three, or six months. The interest to be paid by the borrower for that period under its loan will be the LIBOR rate plus a fixed interest margin. The interest on the loan is payable at the end of each interest period.

(vi) *Loan Repayment.* The loan agreement specifies when payments of principal are due. Normally, such payments are payable in equal installments annually or semi-annually. Thus, a ten-year loan might normally provide that the borrower is to repay the principal amount of the loan in ten equal semi-annual installments beginning 60 months after the effective date of the loan agreement, thereby delaying the commencement of principal payments for five years.

(vii) *Local Taxation.* The taxation provision will specify who bears the economic burden for currently imposed and subsequently imposed withholding and other income and transaction taxes in the destination country. Often the loan agreement will require the borrower to "gross-up" the interest payment so that the lender receives the agreed interest amount net of all applicable taxes. However, the lender will want to have the availability of those taxes as being paid by the lender and as available for use by the lender as a foreign tax credit against the home country (presumably US) income tax liability. The ultimate impact of this burden can be partially dependent upon the availability of a foreign tax credit to the lender in its home country (eg, the US, where a foreign tax credit system is quite important).

(viii) *Governing Law and Jurisdiction.* This provision will specify the choice of governing law and, additionally, the selection of the forum, location, and manner of resolving disputes and enforcing rights in connection with the loan transaction. Normally, the law selected will be that of a leading international money center, such as England, New York, or Japan, and the court selected to hear disputes relating to the loan will be the courts of those money centers. Unlike joint venture agreements, international loan agreements rarely provide for international commercial arbitration as a method of resolving disputes related to the transaction.

(ix) *Restrictions on Funds and Profits.* The loan agreement will include indemnification provisions if the lender's anticipated yield on the loan is restricted due to taxes, reserve or regulatory requirements, changes in applicable laws, and similar occurrences.

(x) *Rate Limitations.* Usury and similar rate limitations where floating interest rates are specified in the agreement (providing protection against illegality in both the lender's and the borrower's jurisdictions) will be specified.

(xi) *Agency Provision.* In a multi-lender loan arrangement, the agent for the lender will be identified and its responsibilities described.

(d) Other Related Agreements

(i) Security Agreements

A security agreement may provide for the commitment of collateral to further assure the loan repayment by the foreign borrower. That collateral could include (1) real property located in the lender's or the borrower's jurisdiction, (2) liquid securities, including such assets which might be located in a third country financial institution which acts as the agent for holding this collateral, or (3) the segregation of an income stream into a "lock-box" arrangement with a financial institution in the borrower's country. In this context, many local law questions will arise as to both (1) the perfectibility and (2) the enforceability of that security in the borrower's jurisdiction; consequently, the parties to the loan transaction will need to address these issues to assure the probability that the security will be available to the lender, if necessary.

(ii) Guarantees

A parent corporation or third party may provide guarantees as to the repayment of the loan by the borrower. Such an arrangement necessitates a definitive guarantee agreement between the lender and the guarantor, stipulating such terms as (1) when the obligations under the guarantee will be triggered, (2) how those obligations will be enforced, and (3) what will be the governing law and jurisdiction for the enforcement of the guarantee.

(iii) Inter-creditor Agreements

Separate lenders or separate syndicates may have previously loaned or may be contemporaneously lending funds to the same overseas based borrower. The lenders may desire to agree among themselves as to the coordination of various matters, such as their separate rights to available cash flow, sharing of collateral, methods of triggering acceleration of payment provisions when default occurs on any one of these loans, and, generally, harmonizing their mutual objectives of assuring repayment. This last-mentioned objective would be accomplished through the inclusion of an appropriate cross-default payment acceleration provision in the several loan agreements.

11

Political Risk Insurance

11.1 Political Risk

Risk, which one may define as the probability that expected benefits will not be received, is inherent in any investment. Traditionally, business analysts have divided the risks faced by international investments into two categories: commercial risks and political risks. Commercial risks are those associated with normal economic activities, such as fluctuations in commodity prices, the failure of a new technology to perform as expected, or the advent of a new competing product that makes the investor's product obsolete. Political risks, on the other hand, are those which arise out of governmental actions or political developments. The World Bank Group's Multilateral Investment Guarantee Agency (MIGA) offers the following definition of political risk:

> Political risks are associated with government actions which deny or restrict the right of an investor/owner (i) to use or benefit from his/her assets; or (ii) which reduce the value of the firm. Political risks include war, revolutions, government seizure of property and actions to restrict the movement of profits or other revenues from within a country.[1]

Whenever a foreign investor places its assets in a foreign territory, it thereby subjects them to the jurisdiction of the host country government. Those assets then become susceptible to host country legislative and administrative acts, including expropriation, nationalization, dispossession, and alteration of property rights. Such uncertainty over the security of property rights is the essence of political risk.[2]

In contemplating an investment in a foreign country, investors always calculate the degree to which their assets, both tangible and intangible, will be subject to political risk. That calculation is invariably rendered difficult by the fact that investments are long-term transactions, often projected to extend over many years and even decades into an always uncertain future. While conditions may appear safe for investment property at the time the investment is made, those conditions can change rapidly and dramatically as a result of shifting political and economic dynamics in host countries, the regions in which they are located, and indeed the world itself. Popular uprisings, wars, regime changes, coups, economic crises, insurrections, and the outbreak of terrorist activity are just a few of the events that can place investor property and contractual rights in jeopardy. In response to such events, governments may use their legislative and administrative powers to revise investors' legal rights in ways that it considers to be in the public interest but that investors judge prejudicial to their interests.

One may view an investment at the time it is made as a bargain between the investor and the host country government regarding their respective rights to benefit from that investment. In response to subsequent political and economic realities, governments often seek to change the terms of that bargain unilaterally by altering investors' legal and contractual

---

[1] See <http://www.pri-center.com/directories/glossary.cfm>, sponsored by MIGA's Political Risk Insurance Center.

[2] N Rubins and NS Kinsella, *International Investment, Political Risk and Dispute Resolution: A Practitioner's Guide* (2005) 1–29.

rights in ways that increase the government's benefits from the investment and decrease the investor's.

The most dramatic way in which governments can change that bargain is by seizing an investment and thereby canceling the investor's property rights. Thus, for example, governments can simply seize factories, mines, plantations, and other physical assets owned and controlled by foreign investors. Such direct expropriations were a constant concern throughout the nineteenth and twentieth centuries as numerous incidents of expropriation and dispossession of investors took place during that period in Latin America, the Soviet Union, the Middle East, Africa, and Eastern Europe. In many of those cases, the governments asserted their legal rights to take the property and denied any obligation to compensate investors for what they had taken. Where governments did pay compensation, the amount was often less than the dispossessed owners considered adequate or fair.

Just as the forms of international investment have evolved over time so, too, have the methods by which governments seek to modify or interfere with investor property rights. Whereas outright expropriation through government seizure was common until the 1980s, it became increasingly rare thereafter. In the twenty-first century, governments dissatisfied with the original bargains made with foreign investors rarely send their troops to seize a factory or occupy a mine. Instead, they use their legislative and regulatory power in more subtle ways to alter the benefits flowing to the investor from the investment. Thus, a government may impose new regulations on the way the investment is operated, raise taxes on the investment substantially, or unilaterally change a contract to reduce the revenues flowing to an investor. The investor remains in possession of the investment, but the amount and nature of the benefits originally contemplated are significantly reduced. In legal terms, these regulatory actions diminish the nature of the investor's property rights over the investment and, if sufficiently extreme, may constitute a form of expropriation or dispossession. Such actions may rise to the level of an "indirect" expropriation, sometimes referred to as "regulatory taking."[3] They have become the most common type of intervention with foreign investments by host governments in the twenty-first century.

11.2 Political Risk Insurance

In order to protect themselves from political risk, investors not only evaluate political risk at the time they are contemplating an investment but they also build into the management of that investment once made a process of continuing political risk analysis and will also structure and manage the investment in a way that reduces political risk.[4] For example, structuring a direct foreign investment as a joint venture with a local partner is a way of reducing the investment's political risk, as is implementing investment plans gradually and monitoring political developments in the country closely.[5] Another technique of political risk management is to protect an investment asset from specified political risks by securing political risk insurance on that asset.

Insurance is essentially a contract by which one party (the insurer) for a stipulated consideration or "premium" agrees to compensate another party (the insured) for loss on a specified subject by the happening of specified perils. The essential function of any

---

[3] S R Ratner, "Regulatory Takings in the Institutional Context Beyond the Fear of Fragmented International Law," 102 *AJIL* (2008) 475.

[4] See, eg, TH Moran (ed), *International Political Risk Management: The Brave New World* (2004). See also Chapter 7, section 7.3 "Investor Strategies for Coping with the Risk of Legal Change."

[5] Multilateral Investment Guarantee Agency, *2011 World Investment and Political Risk* (2011) 46–7.

insurance is to shift the risk of financial loss from the insured to the insurer. Accordingly, political risk insurance is an agreement between an investor and an insurer to compensate the investor wholly or partially for the financial loss sustained to the investment by reason of the happening of a specified event of political risk, such as expropriation or physical damage to an asset because of war or terrorism. The essential function of foreign investment insurance is to shift the burden of political risk, wholly or partially, from the investor to a financial institution. As part of its investment planning, international investors often decide to secure political risk insurance on their investments abroad. During the period 2003–2005, for example, it is estimated that 3 percent of all direct foreign investment flows and 30 percent of all foreign direct investment flowing to a developing country were covered to some extent by political risk insurance of some sort.[6] Such agreements become part of the contractual framework of the investment.[7] For example, the US investors in the Dabhol Power Company in India, discussed in the preceding chapter, secured political risk insurance contracts from the Overseas Private Investment Corporation, a United States governmental agency, against certain political risks, including expropriation. When the Maharashtra Board, which had entered into a power purchase agreement from the Dabhol Power Company repudiated the power purchase agreement and the Indian government failed to honor its guarantee of the Electricity Board's payments to the company, the investors brought a claim against OPIC under the insurance contract and ultimately received more than US$57,000,000 as compensation.[8]

Largely the product of the post-World War II era, foreign investment insurance was originally developed primarily by governments and governmental agencies in capital-exporting countries to encourage their nationals to invest abroad. Later private companies and multilateral international organizations would also emerge to provide insurance for foreign investments.[9] One may therefore begin an analysis of foreign investment political risk insurance by examining the three sources from which it may be obtained: (1) national governmental entities; (2) multilateral international organizations; and (3) private companies. In making this analysis, this chapter will focus for purposes of illustration on two important sources, the Overseas Private Investment Corporation, a national program of the United States, and the Multilateral Investment Guarantee Agency, an international organization affiliated with the World Bank.

11.3 National Governmental Programs

Nearly all of the major capital exporting countries have established or supported programs and entities to provide political risk insurance to their nationals and companies investing abroad. In addition, certain large developing countries, such as China, India, and South

---

[6] K Gordon, *Investment Guarantees and Political Risk Insurance: Institutions, Incentives and Development* (2009) 2.

[7] A foreign investment enterprise is also often covered by the usual kinds of business insurance, including insurance against property damage from accidents and natural disasters and liability insurance against accidental injuries to other persons and enterprises. Such arrangements are also part of the investment's contractual framework.

[8] *Bechtel Enterprises International (Bermuda) Ltd; BEn Dabhol Holdings, Ltd; and Capital India Power Mauritius I, (Claimants) against Overseas Private Investment Corporation, (Respondent)*, September 3, 2003, at 29, available at <http://www.opic.gov/sites/default/files/docs/2294171_1.pdf>. For background on this case, see K Hanson et al, "The Dabhol Power Project Settlement: What Happened? And How," *infrastructurejournal.com*.

[9] For a comparison of these various programs, see generally K Gordon, *Investment Guarantees and Political Risk Insurance: Institutions, Incentives and Development* (2009) 2. For earlier comparisons, see also MD Rowat, "Multilateral Approaches to the Improving Investment Climate of Developing Countries: The Cases of ICSID and MIGA," 33 *Harv Int'l LJ* (1992) 103, 119–44 and T Meron, *Investment Insurance in International Law* (1976) 39.

Africa, whose nationals undertake significant foreign investments, have established similar programs.[10] Some offer only political risk insurance on investment while others combine this service with credit insurance on exports.

The primary stated goal of these programs to strengthen the economic performance of the countries concerned since foreign investment by their nationals and companies is seen as contributing to national economic growth. Other stated objectives include the desire to assist in the development of host countries, to fill the gap created by incomplete coverage through purely private insurance sources, and to advance a country's diplomatic relations.[11]

Governments foster the provision of political risk insurance in basically one of four ways: (1) through a governmental department financed by the regular government budget; (2) through a separate, self-financed agency that nonetheless functions with the full faith and credit of the government concerned; (3) through a public limited company that is state owned; and (4) through a private company that is publicly sponsored. Despite differences in structure, the various national programs tend to offer coverage on four basic political risks: (1) currency inconvertibility and transfer risks; (2) confiscation, expropriation, and nationalization; (3) losses from political violence; and (4) default on obligations such as contracts, arbitral claims and loans. An investor may choose to insure its investment against one or more of these risks for a period of time, which may extend as long as 20 years. The premium to be paid by the investor for such coverage depends on the nature of the risks insured and the length of time it wishes to secure insurance coverage. Coverage is generally limited to investors who are nationals and companies of the country offering the insurance, or to investors having close ties to that country. In all cases, the insured investor must enter into a formal contract of insurance governed by the national law of the insurance provider. The insurance contract may impose certain obligations on the insured in the management of its investment so as to be eligible for compensation in the event that an insured risk should occur. The specific provisions of such contracts are normally determined by applicable law and regulations, as is the method for resolving disputes between the insurer and the insured with respect to their application.

Most national programs will not insure investments in countries whose governments have not entered into an agreement permitting such programs to operate in that country and agreeing to abide by certain principles including the right of the insurer, if it has paid compensation to an insured investor under an insurance contract, to seek reimbursement from the host government. That right under general principles of insurance law is known as subrogation. Certain insuring countries also require that the host country have concluded a bilateral investment treaty (BIT) with them before they will provide political risk insurance to investments in those countries. Moreover, such BIT may specifically recognize the right of the insurer country to be subrogated to the rights of the insured and to seek reimbursement from the offending host country.[12] Such agreements are normally governed by international law and provide for state-to-state international arbitration in the event of

---

[10] For a list of political risk insurance providers, both public and private, see the website pri-center. com maintained by the Multilateral Investment Guarantee Agency at <http://www.pri-center.com/directories/sub_index.cfm?typenum=661,681>. Only three OECD governments, Ireland, Mexico, and New Zealand, do not provide some form of political risk insurance. K Gordon, *Investment Guarantees and Political Risk Insurance: Institutions, Incentives and Development* (2009) 6.

[11] K Gordon, *Investment Guarantees and Political Risk Insurance: Institutions, Incentives and Development* (2009) 6.

[12] Germany's BITs make such provision. See, eg, Article 6, Treaty between the Federal Republic of Germany and Jamaica concerning the Reciprocal Encouragement and Protection of Investments, September 24, 1992, available at <http://www.unctad.org/sections/dite/iia/docs/bits/germany_jamaica_gr_eng.pdf>.

dispute about their application. As a result of the subrogation provisions in such agreements, disputes, which began as controversies between investors and host governments subject to national law, are converted into diplomatic disputes between states, with all the attendant international law consequences. There are of course many variations among national programs of political risk insurance available to investors. To examine in detail, one such program, a major insurer of foreign investment, this chapter will now consider the United States Overseas Private Investment Corporation (OPIC).

11.4 The United States Overseas Private Investment Corporation (OPIC)

(a) Background

The oldest and most geographically diverse program of foreign investment insurance is conducted by the United States and has its origins in the US Investment Guarantee Program, which was part of the Marshall Plan and American efforts to rebuild Western Europe after World War II. In order to encourage new US investment in Europe, the Economic Cooperation Act of 1948,[13] which established the Marshall Plan, guaranteed US investors in Europe against the risk that they would be unable to repatriate investment capital or income due to the inconvertibility of host country currency. Shortly thereafter, the Program was expanded to cover the risks of expropriation and confiscation and to make it applicable to countries outside Europe. With the rapid economic recovery of Europe, an investment guarantee program for that part of the world was no longer necessary; consequently, the United States reorganized the program to make it applicable only to developing countries. The Investment Guarantee Program became a part of the US foreign aid effort and was administered within the State Department by the Agency for International Development.[14]

Ten years later, however, the US Congress concluded that an autonomous government corporation, rather than a department within the United States government, would be a more effective vehicle for the issuance of foreign investment insurance and the mobilization of private US capital and technology in the economic development of Third World countries. It therefore established the Overseas Private Investment Corporation (OPIC) by an amendment to the Foreign Assistance Act of 1961.[15] Although its governing legislation has been the subject of several amendments since that time and the organization is subject

---

See also Article 7, Agreement between the People's Republic of China and the Federal Republic of Germany on the Encouragement and Reciprocal Protection of Investments, December 1, 2003, which provides as follows:

> Article 7
> Subrogation
> If one Contracting Party or its designated agency makes a payment to its investor under a guarantee given in respect of an investment made in the territory of the other Contracting Party, the latter Contracting Party shall recognize the assignment of all the rights and claims of the indemnified investor to the former Contracting Party or its designated agency, by law or by legal transactions, and the right of the former Contracting Party or its designated agency to exercise by virtue of subrogation any such right to same extent as the investor. As regards the transfer of payments made by virtue of such assigned claims, Article 6 shall apply mutatis mutandis.

Available at <http://www.unctad.org/sections/dite/iia/docs/bits/china_germany.pdf>.

[13] Pub L No 80–472, 62 Stat 137.
[14] For a discussion of the history of the investment guarantee program, see T Meron, *Investment Insurance in International Law* (1976) 49–51.
[15] Pub L No 91–175, 83 Stat 807 (codified at 22 USCA §§ 2191–2193, 2199 (1970)).

to periodic Congressional reauthorization, OPIC remains today the primary source of foreign investment insurance for US investors abroad.[16]

(b) Objectives

The United States Congress created the Overseas Private Investment Corporation (OPIC) as "... an agency of the United States under the policy guidance of the Secretary of State..." in order "... to mobilize and facilitate the participation of United States private capital and skills in the economic and social development of less developed countries and areas, and countries in transition from nonmarket to market economies, thereby complementing the development assistance objectives of the United States." To carry out this mandate, the Corporation is authorized to engage in several different types of activity, including investment insurance, investment guarantees, investment finance, investment encouragement, and the provision of technical assistance. While OPIC carries out all of these functions, its most important activity is its program of foreign investment insurance. From its establishment in 1971 until 2009, OPIC has supported through investment insurance or finance more than 4,000 projects involving $188 billion of investment in emerging markets. OPIC-supported transactions are estimated to have generated $74 billion in US exports and to have supported more than 274,000 US jobs. In 2009, OPIC managed a $13 billion portfolio of projects in more than 150 countries.[17]

By virtue of a lengthy, detailed, and sometimes seemingly contradictory statement of purposes in the law, the US Congress sought to circumscribe OPIC's activities in order to assure its responsiveness to US policy. OPIC is, first of all, an agency designed to assist developing countries and those in transition from nonmarket to market economies. To assure that OPIC will devote its primary effort to the poorest of the less-developed countries, the law specifically states that OPIC is to "give preferential consideration to investment projects in less developed countries that have per capita incomes of $984 or less in 1986 United States dollars and restrict its activities with respect to investment projects in less developed countries that have per capita incomes of $4,269 or more in 1986 U.S. dollars..." (other than countries designated as beneficiary countries under section 2702 of Title 19, Ireland, and Northern Ireland).[18] In addition to these basic quantitative criteria, OPIC, in deciding whether to provide insurance, financing, or reinsurance for a project, is to be "... guided by the economic and social development impact and benefits of such a project and the ways in which such a project complements, or is incompatible with, other developmental assistance programs or projects of the United States or other donors."[19] On the other hand, it should be noted that the statute does not specifically require OPIC, in carrying out its activities, to take into account the benefits to be gained by the US investor.

The lengthy Congressional statement of purpose in the law also sets down numerous other policy guidelines for OPIC operations. In addition to considering the benefits to be gained by the host country, it must also "... conduct its insurance operations with due regard to the principles of risk management..." and "... further to the greatest degree

---

[16] The Overseas Private Investment Corporation Amendments Act of 2003, Pub L 108–58, December 3, 2003, 117 Stat 1949 extended the authority of OPIC until September 30, 2007. Subsequently, Pub L 111–117, Div F, Title VII, § 7079(c), December 16, 2009, 123 Stat 3396, provided that: "Notwithstanding section 235(a)(2) of the Foreign Assistance Act of 1961 (22 USC 2195(a)(2)), the authority of subsections (a) through (c) of section 234 of such Act [subsecs (a) to (c) of this section] shall remain in effect through September 30, 2010."

[17] *OPIC 2009 Annual Report* 5. OPIC annual reports are available online at <http://www.opic.gov/publications/reports-handbooks>.

[18] 22 USCA § 2191(2).

[19] 22 USCA § 2191(1).

possible, in a manner consistent with its goals, the balance of payments and employment objectives of the United States."[20] Indeed, the law specifically requires OPIC to decline to insure, guarantee, or finance any project which significantly reduces the number of the investors' employees in the United States, or even any project which is likely to cause a significant reduction in the number of employees, whether of the insured or other enterprise, in the United States. Moreover, as a result of a 1981 amendment to the law, OPIC must also refuse to insure, reinsure, or finance any investment subject to "performance requirements which would reduce substantially the positive trade benefits likely to accrue to the United States from the investment."[21] Although the meaning of "performance requirements" is not defined in the statute, the term refers to requirements imposed by host country governments on foreign investment projects with respect to their operations, for example, that the investment project export a specified percentage of its production or purchase a specified amount of local goods and services. The United States government has increasingly opposed the imposition of performance requirements on US investments abroad, and the World Trade Organization has sought to limit them through a multilateral Agreement on Trade Related Investment Measures.[22]

Congressional concern to protect the environment, public health, and workers' rights in host countries led to the addition of yet another prohibition in the 1985 amendment to the OPIC legislation. As a result, OPIC may not insure, reinsure, or finance any project that poses an "unreasonable or major environmental, health, or safety hazard" or that results in significant degradation of national parks or similar protected areas.[23] Moreover, projects may be insured, reinsured, or financed only in countries that take steps to implement internationally recognized worker rights (as defined by section 2463(a)(4) of the Title 19) of workers in that country.[24] In furtherance of this objective, a 1992 amendment to the law now requires all OPIC contracts with investors not to use forced labor, not to take actions to prevent employees of the covered foreign enterprise from lawfully exercising their right of association and their right to organize and bargain collectively, and to respect applicable laws relating to minimum wages, hours of work, and occupational health and safety.[25]

(c) Organizational Structure

The organizational structure of OPIC consists of a Board of Directors, a President, an Executive Vice President, and such officers and staff as the Board of Directors determines. The powers of the Corporation are vested in and exercised by or under the authority of the Board of Directors, which is composed of 15 persons.[26] The Administrator of the United States Agency for International Development (USAID) is the Chairman of the Board *ex officio*, and the United States Trade Representative is its Vice Chairman *ex officio*. Eight directors, who may not be officials or employees of the United States government, are appointed by the President of the United States, with the advice and consent of the Senate. They serve for a term of no more than three years, and at least two of the eight members must have experience in small business, one in organized labor, and one in cooperatives.

[20] 22 U.S.C.A. § 2191(3)(d) and (3)(h).
[21] 22 U.S.C.A. § 2191(3)(m).
[22] Available at <http://www.wto.org/english/docs_e/legal_e/18-trims_e.htm>. See also Article 1146, the North American Free Trade Agreement. Available at <http://www.nafta-sec-alena.org/en/view.aspx?x=343&mtpiID=ALL#mtpi120>.
[23] 22 USCA § 2191(3)(n).
[24] 22 USCA § 2191A.
[25] Pub L 102–549, Title I, § 102, October 28, 1992, 106 Stat 3651, codified at 22 USCA § 2191A (a)(1).
[26] 22 USCA § 2193(b).

The other directors, including the President of OPIC, who is a director *ex officio*, are officials of the United States government, including an official of the Department of Labor. They are appointed by and serve at the pleasure of the President of the United States.[27]

The President of OPIC is appointed by the President of the United States, with the advice and consent of the US Senate, and serves at the pleasure of the President. In appointing OPIC's President, the President of the United States is to take into account the private business experience of the appointee. OPIC's President is its Chief Executive Officer and is responsible for the operations and management of the corporation, subject to the by-laws and policies of the Board.[28]

With its headquarters in Washington, D.C.[29] OPIC is an independent legal entity, with the power to sue and to be sued in its corporate name, to hold real and personal property, and to represent itself or to contract for its representation in arbitral proceedings.[30] All insurance, reinsurance, and guarantees issued by OPIC constitute obligations backed by the full faith and credit of the United States of America.[31]

(d) OPIC Investment Insurance in General

United States law specifically authorizes OPIC to issue insurance "upon such terms and conditions as it may determine" to eligible investors in order to provide protection, in whole or in part, against specified risks.[32] The law's definition of "eligible investor" is considered in section (h). In carrying out its insurance operations, OPIC uses standardized contracts which, while respecting the policies and provisions of the enabling legislation, define in detail the nature and conditions of coverage that is provided; consequently, any consideration of OPIC investment insurance must focus not only on the law but also on the provisions of the insurance contract itself. Although these standard forms normally form the basis for OPIC insurance contracts, OPIC and the insured may agree through negotiation to adapt or modify these provisions to meet the peculiar needs of a specific project or the conditions in particular countries.[33] Moreover OPIC uses other standard form contracts for special types of investments such as oil and gas exploration and leases.

OPIC Investment Insurance is not designed to cover ordinary commercial risks of foreign investment. It is only available for specified political risks: inconvertibility of currency, loss due to expropriation, and loss due to war, revolution, insurrection, or civil strife, as well as "business interruption" caused by the occurrence of any of these three. Thus the law governing OPIC states that OPIC is authorized to issue insurance against any or all of the following risks: (A) inability to convert into United States dollars other currencies, or credits in such currencies, received as earnings or profits from the approved project, as repayment or return of the investment therein, in whole or in part, or as compensation for the sale or disposition of all or any part thereof; (B) loss of investment,

---

[27] 22 USCA § 2193(b) and (c).
[28] 22 USCA § 2193(c).
[29] For additional information, see OPIC's official website, <http://www.opic.gov>.
[30] 22 USCA § 2199(d).
[31] 22 USCA § 2197(c).
[32] 22 USCA § 2199(d).
[33] For a description of such a negotiated modification in the case of an OPIC insurance contract covering an investment in the Dabhol Power Company, a major electrical power generating project in India, discussed in Chapter 10, see the arbitration award in *Bechtel Enterprises International (Bermuda) Ltd; BEn Dabhol Holdings, Ltd; and Capital India Power Mauritius I, (Claimants) against Overseas Private Investment Corporation, (Respondent)*, September 3, 2003, available at <http://www.opic.gov/sites/default/files/docs/2294171_1.pdf>. Further information on the OPIC contracting process may be found on its website at <http://www.opic.gov/publications/forms>.

in whole or in part, in the approved project due to expropriation or confiscation by action of a foreign government or any political subdivision thereof; (C) loss due to war, revolution, insurrection, or civil strife; and (D) loss due to business interruption caused by any of the risks set forth in subparagraphs (A), (B), and (C).[34] The addition of business interruption resulted from a 1985 amendment to the law.[35] The precise nature of the difference between business interruption insurance and insurance against the other three risks would appear to lie in the causal relationship between the occurrence of the covered event and the injury to the investment. For example, a project insured against the risk of war could probably not recover under its policy if war damaged one of the project's principal suppliers, thereby interrupting the project's supply of needed raw materials. Business interruption insurance, on the other hand, would compensate the project for a limited time for the increased costs of obtaining its raw materials from other sources.[36]

The following three sections will consider in detail OPIC coverage against the three basic political risks of inconvertibility, expropriation, and war, revolution, insurrection and civil strife (which OPIC refers to under the general term of "political violence").

(e) OPIC Protection against Inconvertibility

A host country government may at any time through its exchange control regulations or simply through inaction prevent an investor from transferring abroad funds which the investor holds in the host country. Such a situation is known as inconvertibility. OPIC is specifically authorized to issue insurance against the risk of inconvertibility, which is defined in the statute as " ... inability to convert into United States dollars other currencies, or credits in such currencies, received as earnings or profits from the approved project, as repayment or return of the investment therein, in whole or in part, or as compensation for the sale or disposition of all or any part thereof ... "[37]

Inconvertibility coverage does not protect the investor against devaluation of the local currency or losses due to exchange fluctuations.[38] Nor does it protect the investor from the effects of exchange control regulations in force when OPIC issued the insurance contract. Its primary purpose is to assure that earnings, capital, principal, interest, and other eligible remittances may continue to be converted into US dollars to the same extent as they were at the time the OPIC insurance contract was issued. Thus, to obtain compensation under this coverage, the investor must show that at the time the insurance contract was concluded the prevailing host country laws, rules, and practices permitted the conversion of local currency earnings and capital into US dollars. The total amount of such coverage is limited to the insured amount as specified in the contract of insurance.[39]

OPIC contractual provisions on inconvertibility have provided that local currency is deemed inconvertible and OPIC compensation is to be paid ... "if the Investor is unable legally to convert earnings from or returns of the Insured Investment into United States Currency through any channel ... " during a specified number of days immediately prior to

---

[34] 22 USCA § 2194(1).

[35] HR Rep No 285, 99th Cong, 1st Sess 7, reprinted in 1986 US Code Cong & Ad News 2572, 2578.

[36] HR Rep No 285, 99th Cong, 1st Sess 7, reprinted in 1986 US Code Cong & Ad News 2572, 2578.

[37] 22 USCA § 2194(a)(1)(A).

[38] See the arbitral award in the case of *Phillip Morris International Finance Corporation v. OPIC*, (1988) 27 *Int'l Legal Mat* 487 in which the arbitral tribunal found that the action of the El Salvador Central Bank in changing the applicable rate of exchange for repatriation of the dividends from the official rate to the lower "free market" or "parallel" rate constituted a devaluation, not a bar to convertibility, and was therefore not covered by OPIC insurance against inconvertibility.

[39] 22 USCA § 2194.

making a claim to OPIC at a rate that is less favorable than the rate described in the contract.

In order to obtain compensation from OPIC under inconvertibility coverage, the insured investor must establish that any one of the following three situations has arisen: (a) a law, regulation, or administrative decision has prevented the investor from transferring local currency into US dollars for a specified period, a situation often referred to as "active inconvertibility;" (b) the investor is prevented from transferring local currency into US dollars by the failure of the responsible host country agency to grant permission to make such transfer when the investor's application for transfer has been pending for a specified period, a situation often called "passive inconvertibility;" (c) the investor is unable to transfer local currency into US dollars except at a rate of exchange which is less favorable to the investor than the rate generally being used on that date for the type of remittance the investor is seeking to make.[40]

The contract also specifies four conditions which will exclude the payment of compensation for inconvertibility. They are:

(a) *Pre-existing Restriction.* OPIC will not pay an inconvertibility claim if the investor's inability to convert currency is due to the existence of pre-existing restrictions that the investor knew or should have known of, at the time of securing insurance, which renders the investor unable to convert local currency into United States dollars in circumstances similar those for which it is making a claim.

(b) *Investor Diligence.* OPIC will deny recovery if the investor failed to take reasonable efforts to convert local currency into United States currency through all direct and indirect legal mechanisms reasonably open to the investor. Thus, for example, if the investor is prohibited by law from using the facilities of the Central Bank to convert currency but other, private facilities are available legally, the investor would be required to use those facilities.

(c) *Reconversions.* In order to prevent its insurance from being used for currency speculation, the OPIC standard form contract excludes claims for inconvertibility if the local currency the investor seeks to convert was previously converted into another currency.

(d) *Provocation.* An inconvertibility claim will be excluded if the preponderant cause of the inconvertibility is the unreasonable actions, including corruption, of the investor. For example, if because of bribes paid by the investor or unpaid debts, the government blocks currency held by the investor, OPIC would not be bound to pay a claim of inconvertibility.

If the requirements of inconvertibility are met under an insurance contract, OPIC will then proceed to determine the amount of compensation due the investor. The basic principle in this regard is that compensation is to be "United States dollar equivalent of the local currency at the exchange rate in effect sixty days before OPIC receives the completed application for compensation." Such exchange rate is to be the official exchange rate applicable to the type of remittance the investor sought to make; however, if United States dollars are not generally available at the applicable exchange rate and exchanges of local currency for US dollars are normally and legally done through other channels, then OPIC will use the exchange rate obtained through that other channel. For example, if the Central

---

[40] For an analysis of OPIC practice with respect to inconvertibility claims, see PM Zylberglait, "OPIC's Investment Insurance: The Platypus of Governmental Programs and Its Jurisprudence," 25 *Law & Pol'y Int'l Bus* (1993) 359, 394–408.

Bank of a country had an official exchange rate for trade transactions, but required all investors to use the parallel market, where a lower rate prevailed, for all investment transactions, then OPIC would use the parallel market rate, rather than the higher official rate.[41]

To obtain payment, the investor must first present to OPIC the requisite amount of local currency in draft form, or at OPIC's option, in cash. Upon approval of the claim, the local currency becomes the property of OPIC, which may then transfer it to the US Treasury for use in paying the local expenses of the US Embassy and its programs in the host country.

(f) OPIC Protection against Expropriation

By law, OPIC is also authorized to issue insurance against the "...loss of investment, in whole or in part, in the approved project due to expropriation or confiscation by action of a foreign government..."[42] The OPIC legislation states that:

> the term 'expropriation' includes, but is not limited to, any abrogation, repudiation, or impairment by a foreign government, a political subdivision of a foreign government, or a corporation owned or controlled by a foreign government, of its own contract with an investor with respect to a project, where such abrogation, repudiation, or impairment is not caused by the investor's own fault or misconduct, and materially adversely affects the continued operation of the project;..."[43]

Thus, expropriation under OPIC coverage is not limited to the taking of physical assets but also protects against governmental actions that impair the investor's contractual rights with the government of the host country.

Despite this definitional effort, protection against expropriation may raise difficult problems in determining when a compensable expropriation has taken place and, if it has, the amount of compensation due the investor. Both the law and the OPIC insurance contract itself have defined expropriation in such a way that it includes not only the classic nationalization of a company or the immediate seizures of its assets, but also various types of "creeping expropriation" by which the host country government limits or reduces the investor's control and authority over the investment property without actually taking title to it. Under the law, the term "expropriation" also includes, but is not limited to, "any abrogation, repudiation, or impairment by a foreign government of its own contract with an investor with respect to a project, where such abrogation, repudiation or impairment is not caused by the investor's own fault or misconduct, and materially adversely affects the continued operation of the project."[44]

The OPIC contracts deal with expropriation in their article on "Scope of Coverage" and "Amount of Compensation." For a Total Expropriation to take place, the actions taken against the investment must satisfy all of the following four conditions: (1) The acts must be attributable to a foreign governing authority that is in de facto control of the part of the country where the insured investment is located; (2) The acts must be violations of international law or material breaches of local law; (3) The acts must directly deprive the investor of fundamental rights in the insured investment. Rights are fundamental if without them the investor is substantially deprived of the benefits of the investment; and (4) the

---

[41] OPIC, Contract of Insurance, Form 234 KGT 12–85, Article III.
[42] 22 USCA § 2194(a)(1)(B).
[43] 22 USCA § 2198(b).
[44] 22 USCA § 2198(b).

violations of law are not remedied, and the expropriatory effect of the actions continues for one year.[45]

"Expropriation of Funds," as defined under OPIC contracts, exists if an act satisfies the conditions listed in (1), (2), and (4) above (although it does not deprive the investor of fundamental rights in the investment), *and* directly results in preventing the investor from repatriating funds and effectively controlling the funds in the country in which the investment is located.[46]

As can be seen, not all governmental action which restricts an investor's rights in an insured investment will be considered to constitute expropriation. Any host country law or regulation which is *not* by its express terms for the purpose of nationalization, confiscation, or expropriation, is reasonably related to constitutionally sanctioned government objectives, is not arbitrary, is based upon reasonable classification of entities to which it applies, and does not violate generally accepted principles of international law, is not to be considered expropriation. For example, legitimate environmental regulation issued by a government after the investment is made will not be held to be an expropriation because the investor's use of its property has been restricted.

As is the case with inconvertibility coverage, OPIC will not compensate an investor whose own unreasonable actions (including corruption) provoked or instigated the loss through governmental action.

The application of these principles to the diverse situations involving alleged expropriations is difficult and may result in controversy. And indeed, several cases have arisen in which OPIC has opposed investor claims for compensation on the grounds that the loss in question was not the result of an expropriation action.

Individual OPIC contracts may provide that no compensation will be payable under expropriation coverage unless the insured investor has exhausted its available remedies under local law or project agreements. In a case involving the Dabhol Power Company (discussed in Chapter 10), where the project agreement covering this major power project in India provided for international arbitration between the project sponsors and the governmental authorities, as well as for the purchase of the project by the government upon the completion of certain formalities by the sponsors, an Indian court, at the instigation of the governmental authorities, issued injunctions forbidding the sponsors from invoking arbitration and from taking any termination measures pursuant to the project agreement. OPIC refused to pay compensation under the policy, claiming that it had agreed to cover only the risk of an unpaid arbitral decision and that in any event the investors had not taken all the necessary measures to terminate the project and claim compensation from the government. The covered investors therefore brought an arbitration claim against OPIC for compensation pursuant to the OPIC insurance contract. A three-person arbitral panel ruled in favor of the investors and directed OPIC to pay the claimants more than US$57,000,000 as required by the contract, stating "the Panel is cognizant that to enforce compliance with the [OPIC insurance] provisions... [mentioned above]... by Claimants, when the reason for noncompliance was the unforeseen action of a party beyond the control of either Claimants or OPIC, namely MERC [the relevant Indian

---

[45] For a discussion of OPIC practice with regard to expropriation coverage, see PM Zylberglait, "OPIC's Investment Insurance: The Platypus of Governmental Programs and Its Jurisprudence," 25 *Law & Pol'y Int'l Bus* (1993) 359, 369–91.

[46] For information on current OPIC insurance practice, coverage and contracts, see the OPIC website at <http://www.opic.gov/what-we-offer/political-risk-insurance>.

government regulatory agency] and the Indian Courts, would result in forfeiture of Claimants' rights under the insurance agreements."[47]

If a "total expropriation" or "expropriation of funds" has taken place, the insured investor will be entitled to compensation under the OPIC insurance contract. The standard of compensation for total expropriations applicable under the contract is *not* the market value of the investment at the time of the loss, but rather the "book value" as defined in the contract, ie the original amount of the insured investment, adjusted for retained earnings (or losses) or accrued interest as of the date of expropriation; however, OPIC is authorized to make appropriate adjustments to take account of the replacement cost of project assets and to compute a claim of loss in appropriate cases on the basis of net book value attributable to the investment on the date of the loss.[48] In the case of expropriation of funds, the standard of compensation is the US dollar equivalent of the expropriated funds computed as in cases of inconvertibility (see section (e)) on the date the expropriation begins.

If the investor has received compensation from other sources—for example, through payment by the expropriating government—such amount will also be taken into account in determining the amount of OPIC liability to the injured investor. If OPIC agrees to pay a claim for compensation under the contract, the investor must assign to OPIC its rights and securities in the insured investment, as well as any claims and rights related thereto.

(g) OPIC Protection against Political Violence

The third form of OPIC coverage is for "loss due to war, revolution, insurrection or civil strife."[49] Until 1981, the law prevented OPIC from offering insurance for injuries resulting from strife of a lesser degree than revolution or insurrection;[50] however, its governing legislation was specifically amended in 1981 to include civil strife as an insurable risk. Thereafter, OPIC modified its standard contracts to take account of the amendment.[51]

Under the terms of that amendment, an investor protected by Coverage C was entitled to compensation for damage, which "means (a) injury to, (b) disappearance of, or (c) seizure and retention of Covered Property...directly caused by an act of (1) war (whether or not formally declared), (2) revolution or insurrection, or (3) civil strife, terrorism or sabotage."[52]

An application of these definitions to a concrete situation may be seen in the 1988 arbitral award concerning a disputed claim between *Beckman Instruments, Inc and OPIC*.[53] In that case, Beckman ceased operating its wholly owned subsidiary in El Salvador after two of its executives were kidnapped by a radical political organization. The event led it to decide not to send any Americans to El Salvador, thus preventing it from providing its subsidiary with the necessary managerial and technical expertise. The arbitral tribunal

---

[47] Bechtel Enterprises International (Bermuda) Ltd; BEn Dabhol Holdings, Ltd; and Capital India Power Mauritius I, (Claimants) against Overseas Private Investment Corporation, (Respondent), September 3, 2003, at 29, available at <http://www.opic.gov/sites/default/files/docs/2294171_1.pdf>.

[48] 22 USCA § 2197(f).

[49] 22 USCA § 2194(a)(1)(C).

[50] OPIC, Investment Insurance H and book 8 (June 1979).

[51] See OPIC website at <http://www.opic.gov/what-we-offer/political-risk-insurance>.

[52] Article 1.07, Form 12–70 (Rev), 12/2/82. An act of revolution or insurrection was an act committed by an organized group whose principal objective is either the violent overthrow of the established political authorities or the ouster of such authorities from a specific geographic area. An act of civil strife, terrorism, or sabotage was defined as a violent act undertaken by an individual or group with the primary intent of achieving a political objective.

[53] (1988) 27 *Int'l Legal Mat* 1260.

found that the kidnapping was an act of insurrection and directly caused the loss, within the meaning of the OPIC policy covering Beckman's investment in El Salvador.

Since 1985, as a result of the adoption of a new standard form contract, OPIC has employed the term "Political Violence" to designate this type of coverage. It defines Political Violence, a term not found in OPIC legislation, as "a violent act undertaken with the primary intent of achieving a political objective..."[54] The new form contract thus incorporated the notions of war, revolution, insurrection, and civil strife into a single concept, "political violence."

Declared or undeclared wars, hostile actions by armed forces, civil war, revolution, insurrection, civil strife, terrorism, and sabotage all fall within the definition of political violence. While the definition is broad and looks primarily to the political objective of the violent act, it specifically excludes labor and student violence, as did the definition of civil strife in the General Terms and Conditions of the earlier form contract. To obtain compensation under this form of coverage the investor must establish that political violence is "the direct and immediate cause of a permanent loss (including loss of value by damage or destruction) of tangible property of the foreign enterprise used for the project."[55] In a response to the terrorist attacks of September 11, 2001 on the United States, OPIC also offers "stand-alone" terrorism coverage. Terrorism coverage protects against violent acts undertaken by individuals or groups that do not constitute national or international armed forces with the primary intent of achieving a political objective. Coverage includes protection against the use of chemical, biological, radiological, or other weapons of mass destruction. OPIC can provide terrorism insurance for up to ten years on both assets and business income.[56]

Contractual provisions on political violence provide alternative measures of compensation for losses due to political violence: historical cost or replacement cost. If the investor does not repair or replace the property permanently lost due to political violence within three years, the investor may obtain compensation on an historical cost basis only. Historical cost is the investor's share of the least of the following: the original cost of the item, the fair market value of the item at the time it was lost, or the reasonable cost to repair the item. If the investor does repair or replace the property within three years with new or used property equivalent to or better than what was lost, the investor may elect to have OPIC pay compensation based on the actual cost to repair or replace the property, less any other compensation received, up to a maximum of 200 percent of the original cost of the property that was lost.

(h) Eligible Investors

OPIC insurance coverage is available only to "eligible investors" in projects approved by OPIC in "eligible host countries."[57] While OPIC seeks to advance the development of less developed countries, another of its purposes is to assist US investment abroad; consequently, OPIC insurance is available only to US investors. The definition of "eligible investor" under the law is based on the principle of US nationality and includes the following:

---

[54] OPIC, Form 234 KGT 12–85, sec 6.01.
[55] OPIC, Form 234 KGT 12–85, sec 6.01.
[56] See OPIC website at <http://www.opic.gov/what-we-offer/political-risk-insurance>.
[57] 22 USCA § 2194(1).

1. United States citizens;

2. Corporations, partnerships or other associations, including non-profit associations, created under the laws of the United States or any state or territory thereof and substantially beneficially owned by United States citizens; (OPIC considers a US corporation "substantially beneficially owned by United States citizens" if more than 50 percent of each class of its issued and outstanding stock is owned by United States citizens either directly or beneficially); and

3. Foreign corporations, partnerships, or other associations at least 95 percent of which are owned by investors who are eligible as United States citizens or United States corporations substantially beneficially owned by the United States citizens. (Consequently, if a foreign wholly owned subsidiary of an American corporation makes an investment in a country covered by the OPIC program, the foreign corporation is an "eligible investor" and may obtain insurance coverage directly from OPIC.)[58]

The rules on eligibility require that the investor be eligible both at the time the claim arises and at the time the insurance or guarantee is issued; therefore, a foreign corporation whose US ownership falls below 95 percent after the issuance of the insurance contract would be ineligible to receive compensation for any claim which arose thereafter. In cases of loan investments, the final determination of eligibility is made at the time the insurance or guarantee is issued.[59]

In applying the rules on investor eligibility, OPIC does not require that the project in which the insured investment is made be owned or controlled by US investors; consequently, an eligible investor may insure a minority investment interest in a project controlled by non-Americans if the project meets all of the other conditions of eligibility.

(i) Eligible Investments

To obtain insurance, not only must the investor be eligible, but the investment itself must meet various specified criteria relating to the nature of the investment interest to be insured, the type of project in which it is made, and the country in which it is located.

Insurable investments cover a broad range of economic and financial relationships. Under the law, the term "investment" includes any contribution or commitment of funds, commodities, services, patents, processes, or techniques in the form of:

(1) a loan or loans to an approved project,
(2) the purchase of a share of ownership in any such project,
(3) participation in royalties, earnings, or profits of any such project, and
(4) the furnishing of commodities or services pursuant to a lease or other contract.[60]

Thus, not only may eligible investors insure debt or equity investments, but eligible contractors with construction contracts and eligible suppliers of technology may also obtain insurance coverage.

It is OPIC's policy to insure new investments *only* (including expansions of established enterprises); consequently, an existing investment in a foreign country is not itself eligible for OPIC coverage. The apparent reason for this policy is that OPIC's primary objective is to mobilize new capital for investment in developing countries. Insuring existing investments would not, of course, serve to mobilize such new capital infusions.

---

[58] 22 USCA § 2198(c). [59] 22 USCA § 2198(c)(3).
[60] 22 USCA § 2198(a).

In addition to providing coverage for investments in manufacturing, services, and natural resource development, OPIC has certain special programs, including one which provides insurance for investments in oil and gas exploration, development, and production. Coverage is available for virtually all forms of such investments, including production sharing agreements, service contracts, risk contracts, and traditional concessions.[61] Another special program provides coverage for contractors' and exporters' guarantees. Normally, US exporters and construction and service contractors must post bid, performance, or advance payment guarantees in competing for contracts, particularly with host governments, in many parts of the world. Often, such guarantees take the form of on-demand or standby letters of credit or other types of performance bonds which permit the host country contracting party to draw on them virtually at will, by simply alleging non-performance by the contractor or exporter. Since this type of arrangement presents obvious dangers to the US exporter or contractor, OPIC offers insurance against the risk of an unjustified drawing by the host country government on the letter of credit or other guarantee. Under this type of coverage, OPIC will compensate the insured party up to 90 percent of the amount drawn, if subsequent litigation, arbitration, or other dispute settlement procedure concerning the legality of the drawing: a) results in an award to the insured which is not fully paid; b) is frustrated by the host government; or c) results in an award in favor of the host government which is demonstrably caused by fraud, coercion, or corruption or is unsupported by substantial evidence of the record.[62] OPIC insurance of this type does not protect the contractor against commercial risks of the drawing which occur if the contractor fails to perform its obligation or provokes or agrees to the drawing.

(j) Eligible Host Countries

OPIC investment insurance is not available for investments in all countries, or even in all developing countries. US law provides that the purpose of OPIC is to facilitate the economic and social development of "less developed countries and areas and countries in transition from nonmarket to market economies";[63] however, for coverage to be available in a particular country, certain specified factors must be present. First of all, an agreement must exist between the host country and the United States to institute a program of insurance, guarantees, or reinsurance.[64] Secondly, OPIC must determine that suitable arrangements exist for protecting its interest in connection with such insurance, including arrangements on the ownership, use and disposition of currency credits, assets or investments covered by the insurance program.[65] These two requirements have been translated into a specific OPIC policy which provides that no insurance will be issued with respect to projects in a country unless:

(1) a written bilateral agreement between the United States and the host country government is in effect, and

(2) such bilateral agreement provides that OPIC shall be subrogated to the rights of any insured injured investor and that disputes between the United States and the host

---

[61] OPIC, *Handbook* 20–7 available online at <http://www.opic.gov/sites/default/files/docs/OPIC_Handbook.pdf>.

[62] See generally, OPIC, *Handbook* 25 available online at <http://www.opic.gov/sites/default/files/docs/OPIC_Handbook.pdf>.

[63] 22 USCA § 2191.

[64] 22 USCA § 2197(a).

[65] 22 USCA § 2197(b).

country arising out of the payment of any claim are to be settled by international interstate arbitration.[66]

Such bilateral agreements are often formally entitled "Investment Incentive Agreements" and their provisions govern the institution and functioning of the OPIC program in the country concerned.[67] Such Investment Incentive Agreements are to be distinguished from and not to be confused with bilateral investment treaties or treaties of friendship, commerce and navigation, which guarantee specific rights to foreign investors, regardless of whether or not their investments are covered by political risk insurance.[68]

The issues of subrogation and arbitration have in the past been a particular obstacle to the conclusion of OPIC bilateral agreements with certain countries. As with the usual contract of insurance, subrogation means that by compensating the insured investor for the occurrence of an insured injury, OPIC succeeds to the rights of the investor and has the power to advance those rights against the host country government or other party who caused the injury. Thus the agreement with the country concerned specifically states that the government of the country in which the investment is made "shall recognize . . . the transfer to [OPIC] in connection with such payment [to the insured] of the right to exercise the rights and assert the claims . . ." of the insured. It also provides that nothing in the agreement shall limit the right of the government of the United States to assert a claim under international law in its sovereign capacity as a result of such transfer.[69] Subrogation therefore transforms what was essentially a dispute between a private foreign party and a host country government into a diplomatic dispute between the United States government and the host state. In the event of dispute between the United States Government and the host government concerned with respect to the application and interpretation of the Investment Incentive Agreement, the Agreement provides for interstate international arbitration to settle the matter if it cannot be resolved by negotiation and diplomatic means. The only time the United States has formally invoked this provision was in 2004 when it instituted arbitration against India after OPIC had paid approximately $100 million to US insured investors whose rights in the Dabhol Project had been expropriated by Indian governmental action.[70] The dispute between the two governments was ultimately settled through the payment of agreed compensation by India to the US government.[71]

The existence of a valid bilateral agreement is a necessary condition for the eligibility of a country, but that alone is not sufficient. As indicated earlier, the OPIC statute sets down various additional criteria of country eligibility, including maximum per capita gross national product. Other statutory and policy constraints, such as limitations on the extent of exposure in one country, may prevent the issuance of insurance in a country that is otherwise eligible. And finally, the relevant bilateral agreement may prohibit OPIC from issuing insurance on any project unless the host country specifically approves such issuance. As of January 2010, approximately 150 countries were eligible to participate in

---

[66] See OPIC, *Handbook*, available online at <http://www.opic.gov/sites/default/files/docs/OPIC_Handbook .pdf>.

[67] The texts of such agreements may be found on the OPIC website at <http://www.opic.gov/doing-business/ where-we-work>.

[68] With respect to the protection accorded by bilateral investment treaties, see Chapter 15.

[69] See, eg, Investment Incentive Agreement between the Government of the United States of America and the Government of the Republic of Korea, July 30, 1998, Articles 2 and 3, available at <http://www.opic.gov/sites/ default/files/docs/asia/bl_korea07301998.pdf>.

[70] Request for Arbitration between the Government of the United States of America and the Government of India, November 4, 2004, available at <http://www.opic.gov/sites/default/files/docs/GOI110804.pdf>.

[71] See K Hanson, RC O'Sullivan and WG Anderrson, "The Dabhol Power Settlement: How it Happened. Why?" in <http://www.infrastructurejournal.com>.

OPIC programs. They not only included small developing countries, such as Uganda, Laos, and Peru, but also large countries with considerable resources such as Russia, Indonesia, and South Africa.[72]

(k) Obtaining OPIC Political Risk Insurance

In order to obtain investment insurance against any or all of the three above-described risks, the investor must first register its project with OPIC before the investment has been made or irrevocably committed. Registration does not constitute a commitment by OPIC; rather its purpose is to establish the timeliness of the application.

OPIC does not automatically issue investment insurance upon receiving an application. Rather, it evaluates every application carefully, and each year it rejects numerous applications on a variety of grounds. As indicated above, the US Congress has established certain guidelines that OPIC must take into account in evaluating a particular project. For example, it may not issue insurance on investment projects that will have an adverse effect on employment in the United States, or that will not have a sufficient developmental impact on the host country. Moreover, it will also reject applications if existing OPIC exposure in the host country is already above maximum limits.

The maximum amount of coverage that an investor may obtain on a given investment project generally may not exceed 270 percent of the initial investment in the project. One third of this amount (ie, 90 percent of the initial investment) represents coverage on the initial investment itself, and the remaining two-thirds (ie, equivalent to 180 percent of the initial investment) represents a standby commitment to cover future earnings or interest accrued up to the time of the injury.[73] By law, the insurance contract is to be structured so that the investor bears a risk of loss as to at least 10 percent of the investment.[74] While OPIC therefore may not insure more than 90 percent of the value of the initial investment, in certain situations, depending on risk considerations in the host country, the amount of the insurance commitment may be less than 90 percent. According to OPIC, it can cover up to US$250 million per project for up to 20 years and up to US$300 million for projects in the oil and gas sector, with offshore hard currency revenues.[75]

To maintain valid coverage, the investor must pay an annual premium in advance for each year the policy is in force. The maximum duration for OPIC investment insurance is 20 years. Virtually all investors insure their investments for the maximum permissible period. The required premium is computed for each type of coverage on the basis of a contractually stipulated maximum insurance amount, and a current insured amount which may, within the limits of the contract, be elected by the investor on a yearly basis. The current insured amount represents the insurance actually in force during any given year. The difference between the current insured amount and the maximum insured amount for each coverage is called the *standby* amount. Most of the premium is based on the current insured amount; however, a reduced premium rate is also required for any standby amount. For expropriation and war risk coverage, OPIC requires that the insured maintain coverage at a level equal to the amount of the investment at risk; consequently, the current

---

[72] OPIC maintains and publishes the OPIC *Country and Area List*, which is a periodically updated list of countries that are eligible for OPIC programs and is available at <http://www.opic.gov/doing-business/investor-screener#2>.

[73] OPIC, *Handbook* 28, available at <http://www.opic.gov/sites/default/files/docs/OPIC_Handbook.pdf>.

[74] 22 USCA § 2197(f).

[75] OPIC, *Handbook* 16, available at <http://www.opic.gov/sites/default/files/docs/OPIC_Handbook.pdf>.

insured amount may change from year to year to take into account changes in accrued earnings.

The premium rate for insurance on a particular investment depends on the nature of the coverage and the nature of the industry. Thus, for example, in 2010 the annual premium for expropriation coverage in manufacturing and services industries was US$0.50–0.70 for each US$100 of coverage (with the standby rate at US$0.20) and that for inconvertibility was US$0.25–0.45 (with a standby rate of US$0.20 percent for standby). On the other hand, in view of the heightened political risk faced by natural resource projects, the premium rate for expropriation coverage of development and production investment (as opposed to exploration) was US$1.35–1.60 for each US$100 of coverage.[76] Once issued, OPIC insurance is by law an obligation of the United States of America and is backed by the full faith and credit of the United States, in addition to OPIC's own reserves.[77]

(l) Investor Claims Against OPIC

If the insured investor makes a claim for compensation against OPIC for the occurrence of an insured injury, OPIC, like any other insurer, has basically three options: (1) to pay the full amount of the claim; (2) to enter into negotiations with the investor with a view to a settlement for less than the full amount of the claim; and (3) to reject the claim.

In view of the risks of investment in developing countries and the magnitude of OPIC activities, it is not surprising that the agency has to make payments each year in settlement of investor claims. As of September 2009, it had made 290 claim settlements totaling US$969.8 million. These settlements have been structured either as cash payments to insured investors (US$613.7 million) or as OPIC guarantees of host country obligations or similar arrangements (US$356 million). At the same time, during that period, OPIC has made total recoveries from governments of US$892.1 million or a 92 percent recovery rate of the settlements it has paid.[78]

On the other hand, given the nature of this insurance, disputes can arise between OPIC and the investor over a variety of questions including, for example, whether or not an expropriation has taken place and if so, the precise amount of the injury sustained by the investor. In addition to outright rejection, OPIC has settled numerous other claims for less than the investor was seeking.

In the event the investor and OPIC are not able to arrive at a satisfactory settlement of the disputed claim, the OPIC insurance contract provides that "any controversy relating to this contract shall be settled by arbitration in Washington, D.C. according to the then prevailing Commercial Arbitration Rules of the American Arbitration Association." The Contract further provides that the award of the arbitrators is to be final and binding upon the parties and that judgment on such award may be entered in any court having jurisdiction.[79]

As of the end of 2010, eight disputed claims had been submitted to arbitration and resulted in arbitral awards that were made public.[80] One notable example of arbitration

---

[76] OPIC, *Handbook* 29–30.

[77] 22 USCA § 2197(c).

[78] See *Insurance Claims Experience: OPIC and Its Predecessors*, September 30, 2009, available at <http://www.opic.gov/sites/default/files/docs/2009_claims_history_report.PDF>.

[79] See OPIC, *Handbook*.

[80] The eight awards were as follows: (1) *Valentine Petroleum and Chemical Corp v. AID*, (1970) 9 *Int'l Legal Mat* 889; (2) *International Bank v. OPIC*, (1972) 11 *Int'l Legal Mat* 1216; (3) *International Tel & Tel Corp, Sud America v. OPIC*, (1974) 13 *Int'l Legal Mat* 1307; (4) *Anaconda Co and Chile Copper v. OPIC*, (1975) 14 *Int'l Legal Mat* 1210; (5) *Revere Copper & Brass, Inc v. OPIC*, (1978) 17 *Int'l Legal Mat*. 1321; *Philip Morris International Finance*

under the OPIC contract involved the claims of the Revere Copper & Brass Company for alleged losses to their investment in a bauxite-alumina project in Jamaica. Revere asserted that certain acts by the Jamaican government, particularly the imposition of a new tax on the production of bauxite, had the effect of an expropriation, and it therefore claimed compensation of $90 million under its insurance contract, a claim which OPIC denied. The three-person arbitration panel, by a vote of two-to-one, found that the Jamaican government had prevented Revere's subsidiary from exercising "effective control over its operations," within the meaning of its OPIC insurance contract, and that therefore compensation had to be paid. The panel, however, awarded Revere compensation of US$1,131,144, instead of the US$90 million it originally claimed.[81] Another important case, discussed earlier in this chapter, was Bechtel Enterprises International (Bermuda) Ltd; BEn Dabhol Holdings, Ltd; and Capital India Power Mauritius I, (Claimants) against Overseas Private Investment Corporation, (Respondent), which involved coverage on the investments by US investors in the Dabhol Power Project in India, which failed due to actions of Indian governmental authorities and which resulted in numerous conflicts.[82]

As indicated above, once OPIC has paid a claim, it then becomes formally subrogated to that claim and begins discussions with the host country in question in order to seek indemnification for the amount which it has paid. In many instances, such negotiations have resulted in a successful settlement whereby the government in question has agreed to pay OPIC—normally over a period of time—for all or a portion of the loss.

(m) Other OPIC Activities

In addition to the issuance of political risk insurance, OPIC engages in a variety of other activities aimed at fostering the investment of US capital in developing countries and transitional economies. One of the most important of these programs is the provision of loans and loan guaranties to specific projects. OPIC undertakes the financing of projects in two ways: (1) through direct loans from its Direct Investment Fund and (2) through loan guarantees issued to private US financial institutions making eligible loans to the projects in question.[83]

It should be stressed, however, that OPIC will only provide financing to projects which are commercially sound and whose cash flow will be sufficient to pay all operating costs, service all debt, and to provide the owners with an adequate return on their investment. Unlike many government agencies and regional development banks, OPIC does not offer concessionary terms on its loans.[84]

Generally, OPIC can normally guarantee or lend from US$100,000 up to US$250 million per project although projects in the oil and gas sector with offshore, hard currency revenues may be approved for up to US$400 million under certain conditions. However, OPIC also expects a US investor to assume a meaningful share of the risk, generally through ownership of at least 25 percent of the equity in the project. Exceptions to the amount of equity

---

Corp v. OPIC, (1988) 27 *Int'l Legal Mat* 487; *Beckman Instruments, Inc v. OPIC*, (1988) 27 *Int'l Legal Mat* 1260; and *Bechtel Enterprises International (Bermuda) Ltd; BEn Dabhol Holdings, Ltd; and Capital India Power Mauritius I, (Claimants) against Overseas Private Investment Corporation, (Respondent)*, September 3, 2003, at 29, available at <http://www.opic.gov/sites/default/files/docs/2294171_1.pdf>.

[81] <http://www.opic.gov/sites/default/files/docs/2294171_1.pdf>.
[82] See Note, "Looking Beyond the Dabhol Debacle: Examining its Causes and Understanding its Lessons," 41 *Vanderbilt Journal of International Law* (2008) 907.
[83] 22 USCA § 2194(c).
[84] 22 USCA § 2194(c).

requirement may be made in cases where US brand name franchisors, operators, or contractors are significantly involved in the project. OPIC-guaranteed lenders are protected by the full faith and credit of the United States government.[85]

11.5 Multilateral Political Risk Insurance Programs

The desire to encourage the flow of capital from developed to developing countries prompted suggestions in the 1960s for the creation by states of international organizations that would issue political risk insurance. Such organizations would supplement the various national agencies, such as OPIC, and their guarantees would presumably secure the support of both investors and host country governments since both capital-exporting countries and capital-importing countries would be members of such organizations. Moreover, because the guarantee would be issued by an international organization whose members included most important capital exporting states, host countries might be more hesitant to interfere with investment projects insured by such an entity than they would a project insured by a single national program or a private insurer.

The first such proposal to become a reality was the Inter-Arab Investment Guarantee Corporation, established by Arab states by a convention,[86] which was opened for signature in 1971 and entered into force in 1974, as a regional organization for the purpose of encouraging and facilitating the flow of capital from the wealthy Arab countries with a capital surplus to developing Arab countries in need of capital for their development. Its creation was part of the efforts begun in the late 1960s to create institutions to encourage inter-Arab investment for development purposes.[87] The idea of creating such an international organization was first considered at a Conference on Arab Industrial Development in 1966, which asked the Kuwait government to convene financial experts to develop a proposal in detail. The Kuwait government asked the Kuwait Fund for Arab Economic Development, the country's primary agency for providing aid to other Arab countries, to carry out this task and which managed the process leading to the adoption of the Convention.[88] With headquarters in Kuwait and 21 Arab state members as its shareholders, the Inter-Arab Investment Guarantee Corporation insures the investments of Arab investors against political risk in other Arab countries.

Another international organization that would later emerge is the Islamic Corporation for Insurance of Investments and Export Credit[89] established in 1994, and consisting of 35 Islamic countries as of 2011. Sponsored by the Organization of Islamic Conference and the Islamic Development Bank, membership in the Corporation is open only to member states

---

[85] See OPIC, *Handbook* 9–15, available online at <http://www.opic.gov/sites/default/files/docs/OPIC_Handbook.pdf>.

[86] Convention Establishing the Inter-Arab-Investment Guarantee Corporation. The Convention was drafted and adopted in the Arabic language. The Inter-Arab Investment Corporation has published English translations of the Convention. For background on the Corporation, see IIF Shihata, "Arab Investment Guarantee Corporation—A Regional Investment Insurance Project," 6 *Journal of World Trade Law* (1972) 185. For the reflections of a person involved in the development of the Corporation as well as in the creation of the Multilateral Investment Guarantee Agency, see also IIF Shihata, *Multilateral Investment Guarantee Agency and Foreign Investment* (1988) 61–2.

[87] See JW Salacuse, "Arab Capital and Middle Eastern Development Finance," 14 *Journal of World Trade Law* (1980) 283.

[88] See generally, ZA Nasr, *The Kuwait Fund Scheme for the Guarantee of Inter-Arab Investments* (Kuwait: Kuwait Fund for Arab Economic Development, 1971).

[89] Articles of Agreement of the Islamic Corporation for the Insurance of Investment and Export Credit, opened for signature February 19, 1992, available at <http://www.isdb.org/irj/go/km/docs/documents/IDBDevelopments/Internet/English/IDB/CM/About%20IDB/Articles%20of%20Agreement/ICIEC_Articles-of-Agreement.pdf>.

of the Islamic Conference. It operates according to the principles of Islamic law[90] and offers political risk insurance to protect the investments in member states of investors from other member states against four specified risks: restrictions on currency transfers, expropriation and similar measures, breach or repudiation of government contracts with an insured investor, and losses from war and civil disturbance.[91]

The most recent multilateral initiative is the African Trade and Insurance Agency[92] created in 2000 and consisting of African states as members. Its stated purpose is " ... to facilitate, encourage and develop the provision of, or the support for, insurance, including coinsurance and reinsurance, guarantees, and other financial instruments and services, for purposes of trade, investments and other productive activities in Africa in supplement to those which may be offered by the private sector, or in cooperation with the private sector."[93] To achieve this objective, it is specifically authorized by treaty to undertake the " ... provision of, or support for, insurance, coinsurance, reinsurance or guarantees against political, non-commercial and commercial risks"[94]

The most significant of all these multilateral approaches to providing political risk insurance has been global rather than regional in scope. It is the Multilateral Investment Guarantee Agency (MIGA), a member of the World Bank Group. The next section examines MIGA in detail.

11.6 The Multilateral Investment Guarantee Agency (MIGA)

(a) Background

In keeping with its stated goal of encouraging international investment to advance economic development, the World Bank studied the idea of creating a multilateral institution to provide political risk insurance for several years.[95] Ultimately, its staff drafted a Convention establishing an organization, to be known as the Multilateral Investment Guarantee Agency (MIGA). In 1985, the Annual Meeting of the World Bank's Board of Governors approved the Convention establishing the Multilateral Investment Guarantee Agency[96] and transmitted it to Bank member states and to Switzerland for approval.[97]

---

[90] Article 5(3) of its Articles of Agreement states:

'At a suitable time after its establishment the Corporation shall, in accordance with the principles of Shariah, provide Investment Insurance, as well as reinsurance, in respect of investments by Members in a Member State against the risks specified in Article 19(2) hereof, or the risks specified by the Board of Directors in accordance with Article 19(3) hereof.'

[91] Article 19(2), Articles of Agreement.

[92] Agreement Establishing the African Trade and Insurance Agency, opened for signature May 18, 2000, 2200 UNTS 3 (2004). For additional information on the Agency, see its website at <http://www.ati-aca.org/>.

[93] Article 1, Agreement Establishing the African Trade and Insurance Agency.

[94] Article 2(a), Agreement Establishing the African Trade and Insurance Agency.

[95] See generally, IIF Shihata, "Increasing Private Capital Flows to LDCs," *Fin & Dev* (December 1984) 6.

[96] Convention Establishing the Multilateral Investment Guarantee Agency, October 11, 1985, reprinted in (1985) 24 *Int'l Legal Mat* 1598, 1605 [hereinafter MIGA Convention]. The text of the Convention, as well as other pertinent related documents, is available on the MIGA website at <http://www.miga.org/>. For a thorough analysis of the origins, structure, and operations of MIGA, see IIF Shihata, *MIGA and Foreign Investment—Origins, Operations, Policies and Basic Documents of the Multilateral Investment Guarantee Agency (MIGA)* (1988). For an evaluation of the developmental consequences of MIGA for countries in which it insures investments, see generally GT West and EI Tarazona, *Investment Insurance and Developmental Impact* (Washington, D. C.: MIGA, 2003), which concludes at 105: "After evaluating 52 MIGA supported projects, it is clear that the Agency has broadly fulfilled its mission of facilitating productive investments in developing countries.")

[97] For background on MIGA, see its website at <http://www.miga.org/whoweare/index.cfm?stid=1788>. See generally, IIF Shihata, *MIGA and Foreign Investment—Origins, Operations, Policies and Basic Documents of the Multilateral Investment Guarantee Agency (MIGA)* (1988).

To enter into force, the Convention required ratification by at least five developed countries (ie, those listed in Category One of Schedule A to the Convention) and by at least fifteen developing countries (ie, those listed in Category Two of the Schedule), provided the total subscription was not less than one-third the authorized capital (approximately US$360 million).[98]

MIGA was officially created on April 12, 1988, when the required minimum membership and capital were reached, and it held the inaugural meeting of its Council, its governing body, on June 22, 1988, at which time it also adopted its Operational Regulations.[99] The Operational Regulations are particularly important because they set down the basic rules as to the nature and type of political risk guarantees that MIGA may issue, the eligible investors and investments that may obtain such guarantees, and the basic terms and conditions that must be included in MIGA guarantee contracts.

As of December 2010, 175 countries had become members of MIGA. They consisted of 25 industrialized countries and 150 developing countries. Its capital at the end of June 2009 amounted to over $2.5 billion and its underwriting capacity was over $12 billion. MIGA issued its first investment guarantee in January 1990. By June 30, 2010, it had issued a total of 980 "guarantees" (MIGA's term for insurance) against political risk with total assumed contingent liabilities exceeding US$22.4 billion.[100]

MIGA is a member of the World Bank Group and is housed at the World Bank headquarters, although it is an independent international organization having full international juridical personality.

(b) Organizational Structure

MIGA, the newest member of the World Bank Group, is an international corporation whose authorized capital is in excess of $1.9 billion and whose shareholders include both developed and developing countries. Membership in MIGA is open to all members of the World Bank and Switzerland. Ten percent of a member's subscription is paid in cash, another 10 percent is paid in noninterest-bearing promissory notes, and the remainder is subject to call by MIGA when required to meet its obligations.[101]

Despite its close association with the World Bank Group, MIGA is an independent international organization with "full juridical personality" under international law and the domestic laws of its members.[102] Following the organizational pattern of the World Bank, the governing structure of MIGA consists of three levels: a Council of Governors, a Board of Directors, and a President and staff. The Council, which is composed of one governor and one alternate designated by each member state, is vested with all the powers of the Agency[103] and meets at least once a year. It is essentially an oversight and general policy-making body. With certain exceptions, the Council may delegate its powers to the Board of Directors.

---

[98] Article 61, MIGA Convention.
[99] Operational Regulations of the Multilateral Investment Guarantee Agency, June 22, 1988, reprinted in 27 *Int'l Legal Mat* (1988) 1227. The Operational Regulations have been subject to amendment since that time. The current version of the Operational Regulations may be found on the MIGA website at <http://www.miga.org/documents/Operations-Regulations.pdf>.
[100] Multilateral Investment Guarantee Agency, *MIGA Annual Report 2010* (2010) 6, available at <http://www.miga.org/documents/10ar_english.pdf>.
[101] Articles 6, 7, and 8, MIGA Convention.
[102] Article 1, MIGA Convention.
[103] Article 31, MIGA Convention.

The Board of Directors is responsible for the general operations of the Agency, a responsibility covering all matters relating to MIGA's policies and regulations, but not its day-to-day management, which is the responsibility of the President and the staff. The Council elects the Board of Directors, which is to consist of at least 12 directors. The exact number of directors is set by the Council, after taking into account changes in MIGA membership. One-fourth of the directors are elected separately, one each by the member states holding the largest number of shares in the organization. The remaining three-quarters of the Board of Directors are elected by the other MIGA members. As of June 2010, the Board consisted of 25 directors—5 representing the largest shareholders (the United States, Japan, Germany, France, and the United Kingdom) which together hold approximately 35 percent of the voting power—and 18 representing the other states.[104]

The Boards elects the MIGA President and Chairman of its Board, and on June 22, 1988, it selected the President of the World Bank as the first president of MIGA, a position held by subsequent World Bank Presidents. The organization's chief operations officer is its Executive Vice President.

(c) MIGA Investment Guarantee Operations

MIGA's principal function is to guarantee specified risks associated with foreign investment projects, but it is also authorized to engage in consultative and advisory functions whose purpose is to help developing country members increase the flow of foreign investment for productive purposes. The MIGA Convention and its Operational Regulations specify in detail how MIGA is to carry out its functions.[105]

The scope of MIGA guarantee activities is determined by certain eligibility requirements, defined in the Convention and the Operational Regulations. Generally speaking, to qualify for a MIGA guarantee an investment project must meet specified requirements as to: (1) the investor; (2) the time and type of investment; and (3) the type of risk against which coverage is sought.

(i) Eligible Investors

To benefit from MIGA insurance, an investor must be a national of a member country other than the country in which the investment is made. If the investor is a corporation, it will be considered a national of a member country if its meets *either* of two alternative tests: (a) it is incorporated *and* has its principal place of business in a member country; or (b) the majority of its capital stock is owned by nationals of member countries. A juridical person need not be wholly or partially privately owned so long as it is operated on a commercial basis. In addition, the MIGA board, upon the joint application of the investor and the host country, may extend eligibility to a natural person who is a national of the host country or to a juridical person not eligible under the tests described above, provided that the assets to be invested are transferred from abroad.[106] The purpose of this special provision is to encourage the repatriation of flight capital.

---

[104] See Multilateral Investment Guarantee Agency, *MIGA Annual Report 2010* (2010) 10–11, available at <http://www.miga.org/documents/10ar_english.pdf>.

[105] The texts of the MIGA Convention and Operational Regulations may be found on the MIGA website at <http://www.miga.org/whoweare/index.cfm?stid=1788>.

[106] Article 13, MIGA Convention.

(ii) Eligible Investments

To qualify for coverage, an investment must be made in the territory of a member state which is listed as a developing member country in Schedule A to the Convention.[107] The Convention and the Operational Regulations give a broad definition to the term "eligible investment." Under these provisions, two general types of investments qualify for MIGA protection: a) "equity interests," including direct and portfolio investments, preferred stock and shares resulting from the conversion of debt instruments, as well as project loans and guarantees of loans made by holders of equity if such loans have mean repayment periods of not less than three years; and b) "non-equity direct investments," including service contracts, management contracts, franchising agreements, operating/leasing agreements, and turnkey contracts, provided that they have terms of at least three years and the contractor's returns substantially depend on performance; medium- and long-term subordinated debentures of the project enterprise and securities for loans to the project enterprise on condition that the debentures are held and the securities are provided by an equity investor or nonequity direct investor in the project enterprise.[108]

Investments may be made in kind or in any freely convertible currency.[109] MIGA will only guarantee "new" investments, since its purpose is to encourage the flow of new capital to developing countries; however, it takes an expansive view of the meaning of a "new investment." Generally a new investment is one which was neither made nor irrevocably committed before the registration by MIGA of a preliminary application for guarantee. But, reinvested earnings which could otherwise be transferred abroad are considered as new investments, as are contributions to an existing enterprise for the purpose of modernizing, expanding, or restructuring that enterprise. The Operational Regulations also authorize MIGA to consider as new an investment for the purpose of acquiring an existing project in whole or in part if the acquisition accompanies an expansion, modernization, or other enhancement of the enterprise, serves the financial restructuring of the enterprise, or assists the host country in restructuring its public sector.[110]

Equity resulting from the conversion of a debt is in principle eligible for MIGA coverage. Eligibility also extends to portfolio equity investment undertaken by offshore investment funds.

And finally, MIGA will not guarantee an investment without the approval of the host country government.

(d) Risks Covered by MIGA

MIGA affords eligible investments protection against *four* separate non-commercial risks, instead of the usual three normally offered by most national investment insurance programs. The four risks are: (i) host country restrictions on currency conversion and transfer; (ii) expropriation and similar measures that have the effect of depriving the holder of the guarantee of his ownership or control of, or substantial benefit from, his investment; (iii) any repudiation or breach by the host government of a contract when the investor has no access to a competent forum, faces unreasonable procedural delays, or is unable to enforce decisions made in its favor; and (iv) military action or civil disturbance.[111] With the approval of the MIGA Board, other non-commercial risks may be covered upon the joint

---

[107] Article 14, MIGA Convention.
[109] §§ 1.09–1.10, Operational Regulations.
[111] Article 11(a), MIGA Convention.

[108] §§ 1.02–1.13, Operational Regulations.
[110] §§ 1.11–1.13, Operational Regulations.

request of the investor and the host country.[112] The exact scope of the MIGA guarantee depends, of course, on the language of the regulations and the guarantee contract issued to the particular investment covered.

(i) Transfer and Convertibility Risks

This coverage may be provided against active as well as passive restrictions on conversion or transfer of funds of the investment project. An active restriction is a decision by the host government denying conversion and/or transfer of local currency or authorizing such conversion or transfer at an exchange rate less favorable than the lowest exchange rate prevailing in the country at the time of the host country's decision or such other rate specified in the guarantee contract. A passive restriction is a failure by the host country's exchange authority to act on a requested conversion and/or transfer within 90 days from the date of application by the investor or such other period as the MIGA contract may provide.[113]

(ii) Expropriation and Similar Measures

Under the Convention and the Operational Regulations, MIGA may afford broad coverage with respect to the risk of expropriation, including protection against direct, indirect, and creeping expropriation. However, the investor cannot invoke these provisions to claim protection against nondiscriminatory measures of general application which governments normally take in the public interest for the purpose of the regulating economic activity in their territory, such as the bona fide imposition of general taxes, tariffs and price controls and other economic regulations, as well as environmental and labor legislation and measures for the maintenance of public safety.[114]

(iii) Breach of Contract

This form of coverage encompasses losses resulting from any breach or repudiation by an entity of the host government of a contract with the guarantee holder. To avoid embroiling MIGA in the substance of a dispute over a contract, coverage is limited to cases where (i) the aggrieved holder is unable to present its claim to a competent court or arbitral tribunal that is independent of the executive branch, adheres to minimum standards of due process and is empowered to make binding decisions on the complaint; or (ii) such a decision is not rendered within a reasonable time as is specified in the MIGA guarantee (not less than two years); or (iii) the guarantee holder cannot enforce an award in his favor within 90 days from the commencement of the enforcement action or such other period as may be specified in the guarantee contract.[115]

(iv) War and Civil Disturbance

This coverage affords protection for injury to the investment caused by "military action" or "civil disturbance" in the territory of the host country. Military action includes war, both declared and undeclared, hostilities between armed forces of governments of different countries, and, in cases of civil war, between armed forces of rival governments of the

---

[112] Article 11(b), MIGA Convention.   [113] §§ 1.23–1.28, Operational Regulations.
[114] § 1.36, Operational Regulations.   [115] §§ 1.42–1.45, Operational Regulations.

same country. Civil disturbance includes organized violence directed against the government which has as its objective the overthrow of the government or its ouster from a specific region, including revolutions, rebellions, and *coups d'état*. Such coverage is restricted to: (i) the removal, destruction or physical damage of the tangible assets of the investment project; and (ii) the substantial interference with the operation of the project. A mere reduction in business opportunities or a deterioration of operating conditions as a result of military action or civil disturbance is not covered by the MIGA guarantee.[116] In all cases, the civil disturbance must have been caused or carried out by groups primarily pursuing broad political or ideological objectives.[117]

(e) Other Conditions of a MIGA Guarantee

The period of a MIGA guarantee, as a general rule, is for not less than three years or more than fifteen years; however, it may be extended for up to twenty years in special circumstances.[118] The guarantee contract will also specify the "amount of the guarantee," which is the maximum compensation that MIGA will pay in the event of the occurrence of a covered risk. The amount of the guarantee, which is determined by agreement between MIGA and the investor, may be any percentage of the value of the investor's contribution to the project, up to a maximum of 90 percent. For example, an investor who proposes to invest US$5 million in a project may choose any amount for an initial guarantee on his investment up to a maximum of US$4.5 million. Thereafter, the investor may increase the amount of its guarantee to take account of reinvested earnings or additional contributions to the project. The guarantee may also be reduced to take account of write-downs on the investment. Consequently, over the life of the guarantee, the amount of the guarantee may increase and decrease.[119]

The amount of the guarantee is also the basis for calculating the investor's annual premium payable to MIGA for issuing the guarantee.[120] The premium is determined after a risk assessment of the specific investment guarantee, but the Operational Regulations provide that the rates for each type of risk discussed in section (d) shall not be less than 0.3 percent nor more than 1.5 percent of the amount of the guarantee for each individually covered type of risk.[121]

In carrying out its guarantee operations, MIGA, as directed by its Operational Regulations, uses standardized contracts which, while respecting the policies and provisions of the Treaty and the Operational Regulations, also define in detail the nature and conditions of the coverage that is extended to specific investment projects. It has prepared five such documents: (1) Contract of Guarantee for Equity Investments; (2) Contract of Guarantee for Loan Guarantees; (3) Contract of Guarantee for Non-Shareholder Loans; (4) Contract of Guarantee for Shareholder Loans; and (5) the Contract of Guarantee for Non-Shareholder Loans—Non-Honoring of a Sovereign Financial Obligation.[122]

Upon the issuance of a MIGA guarantee, the holder becomes obligated to exercise due diligence to avoid and minimize covered losses and to cooperate with MIGA in the event of a claim or in efforts by the Agency to recover payment from the host country.[123]

---

[116] §§ 1.46–1.52 2, Operational Regulations.
[117] § 1.49, Operational Regulations.
[118] § 2.04, Operational Regulations.
[119] §§ 2.07–2.10, Operational Regulations.
[120] § 3.38, Operational Regulations.
[121] § 3.43, Operational Regulations.
[122] The texts of MIGA's standard contracts of guarantee may be found on its website at <http://www.miga.org/policies/index_sv.cfm?stid=1686>.
[123] § 2.14, Operational Regulations.

Specifically, the holder must comply with the laws of the host country, notify MIGA promptly of any event that might give rise to a covered loss, and seek available administrative, judicial, or other remedies to avoid or minimize the loss.

If a covered loss should occur and the investor presents a claim, MIGA is required to respond with a prompt decision, which may include (i) paying the claim as filed; (ii) denying the claim; (iii) authorizing the negotiation of a settlement with the guarantee holder; or (iv) proceeding otherwise.[124] If MIGA pays a claim under the guarantee, it is subrogated to the rights of the indemnified investor and may proceed to seek a recovery from the host country.[125] In pursuing this course, MIGA is first required to make every effort to reach a negotiated settlement on a sound financial and business basis with the host country concerned. These attempts at negotiation must be pursued for a period of at least 120 days.[126] If negotiations fail, the Agency may then proceed to invoke the dispute resolution proceedings provided by the Convention,[127] particularly Annex II, which affords a flexible approach to dispute resolution.

If the dispute cannot be resolved by negotiations, MIGA and the host country may agree to submit the matter to conciliation. In essence, this procedure entails the selection of a conciliator by mutual consent or by a third person mutually agreed upon. The purpose of the conciliator is to study the conflict and present recommendations, which the parties are free to accept or reject. If the conciliation fails, MIGA may then submit the conflict to binding arbitration as outlined in Annex II of the Convention. Each member of MIGA is required to recognize as binding and enforceable an arbitral award rendered under these procedures.[128]

11.7 Private Sources of Political Risk Insurance

Numerous private companies also provide political risk insurance to foreign investors.[129] Nearly of all these companies are active in offering other types of insurance outside the foreign investment area. Generally, they provide protection against the four basic investment risks covered by governmental and multilateral investment programs: (1) currency inconvertibility and transfer risks; (2) confiscation, expropriation, and nationalization; (3) political violence; and (4) default on governmental obligations.[130] Rather than operate on the basis of standard contracts, as is the case with the governmental programs, private companies tailor their coverage to the nature of the risks presented by specific projects in individual countries. Moreover, because of the magnitude of risk present in certain countries or in particular sections, private companies may be unwilling to offer insurance or to do so at a premium that investors would consider reasonable. Thus, private political risk insurance is unavailable in some countries, a factor causing a coverage gap that justifies the continued need for governmental and multilateral efforts. A further important difference is that whereas governmental and multilateral organizations are willing to enter into insurance contracts for as long as 20 years, most private insurance firms will not make

---

[124] § 4.08, Operational Regulations.
[125] Article 18, MIGA Convention.
[126] §§ 4.20–4.22, Operational Regulations.
[127] Article 57, MIGA Convention.
[128] Article 81, MIGA Convention.
[129] For a listing of 81 governmental, multilateral, and private organizations providing political risk insurance, see the website maintained by MIGA's Political Risk Insurance Center at <http://www.pri-center.com/directories/sub_index.cfm?typenum=661,681>.
[130] K Gordon, *Investment Guarantees and Political Risk Insurance: Institutions, Incentives and Development* (2009) 12.

contractual commitments for such a long period of time.[131] Moreover, because private insurance, unlike governmental and multilateral activities, is not supported by international agreements providing for subrogation and other recovery rights in the event that an insurer is required to compensate an insured investor because of loss, private insurance companies generally have little opportunity to recover loss payments from governments, certainly a factor that affects their willingness to insure certain investments and the level of premiums that they charge to provide political risk insurance generally.[132]

---

[131] R Dolzer and C Schreuer, *Principles of International Investment Law* (2008) 208.
[132] R Dolzer and C Schreuer, *Principles of International Investment Law* (2008) 13–14.

12

Contractual Stability, Instability, and Renegotiation

12.1 The Challenge of Contractual Stability

Experienced lawyers and executives know that the challenge of international investment negotiation is not just "getting to yes,"[1] but also staying there. Despite lengthy negotiations, skilled drafting, and strict enforcement mechanisms, parties to solemnly signed and sealed international investment contracts often find themselves returning to the bargaining table later on to "renegotiate" their agreements. The last half of the twentieth century witnessed numerous examples of renegotiation in international investment: the renegotiation of mineral and petroleum agreements in the 1960s and 1970s, often in the face of threatened host country nationalizations and expropriations,[2] the loan "reschedulings" of the 1980s following the debt crisis in many developing countries,[3] and the "restructuring" of project agreements and financings required by the Asian financial crisis of the late 1990s.[4] The pattern will certainly continue in the twenty-first century.

The renegotiation of investment transaction is a constant and common phenomenon of the international business environment. In today's business world, executives, lawyers, and government officials through renegotiation seem to be seeking continually either to alleviate a bargain that has become onerous or to hold on to a good deal that the other side wants to change. The examples are so numerous that *re*negotiation of investment contracts seems to be as basic to modern business life as is negotiating a new investment transaction for the first time. In an international economy characterized by rapid change, renegotiation may become even more pronounced as companies try to find ways to negotiate contracts that provide stability on the one hand yet give the parties the flexibility to face the unknown on the other.

Although the causes of conflict in individual cases are numerous, two factors in particular contribute to contractual instability and the drive to renegotiate existing investment contracts: (a) the parties' imperfect contract with respect to their underlying transaction, and (b) changing circumstances after they have signed their agreement.

(a) The Parties' Imperfect Contract

The goal of any written contract is to express the full meaning and extent of the parties' understanding and agreement concerning the transaction in which they are about to enter. Despite lawyers' belief in their abilities to capture that understanding in lengthy and detailed contracts, in practice a written contract, particularly in long-term arrangements,

---

[1] R Fisher et al, *Getting To YES: Negotiating Agreement Without Giving In* (2nd edn 1991).

[2] See generally, A Kolo and TW Walde, "Renegotiation and Contract Adaptation in International Investment Projects," 1 *J World Inv* (2000) 5 (offering an excellent summary of major renegotiation cases in petroleum and minerals industry); DF Vagts, "Coercion and Foreign Investment Rearrangements," 72 *Am J Int'l L* (1978) 17, 36.

[3] See, eg, VK Aggarwal, *Debt Games: Strategic Interaction in International Debt Rescheduling* (1996).

[4] See, eg, RM Lastra, "Central Banks as Lenders of Last Resort: Lessons from the Asian Contagion," 7 *J Fin Reg & Comp* (1999) 234, 242.

can only achieve that goal imperfectly, largely for three reasons. First, the parties to long-term agreements are incapable of predicting all of the events and conditions that may affect their transactions in the future. Second, the transaction costs of making contracts limit the resources that the parties are willing to devote to the contracting process and restrict the ability of the parties to arrive at a contract that perfectly reflects their common understanding of the underlying transaction. Thus, an ideal contract for a long-term transaction is impossible to achieve because it would require perfect foresight and limitless resources for negotiating and drafting the contract.[5] Moreover, even if the parties had the requisite foresight and resources to draft a perfect contract reflecting their understanding in all its present and future dimensions, a court, arbitral panel, or other enforcement body might not be unable to apply that contract accurately and inexpensively.

Third, in international transactions, the problem of accurately negotiating and articulating the parties' intent with respect to a long-term arrangement is particularly difficult because of the parties' differing cultures, business practices, ideologies, political systems, and laws—factors that often impede a true common understanding between them and inhibit the development of a working relationship. The world's diverse cultures and legal systems attach differing meanings and degrees of binding force to a signed contract and recognize varying causes to justify avoidance of onerous contractual burdens.[6] For example, a Spanish company in a long-term transaction with an Indian firm may view their signed contract as the essence of the deal and the source of the rules governing their relationship in its entirety. The Indian partner, however, may see the deal as a partnership that is subject to reasonable changes over time; a partnership in which one party ought not to take advantage of purely fortuitous circumstances like radical and unexpected movement in exchange rates or the price of raw materials.[7]

One encounters the problem of cultural misunderstandings particularly in long-term business and financial arrangements. For example, in connection with a contract between the government of the Sudan and an English company for the construction of housing for Nubians forced from their villages by the rising Nile waters resulting from the construction of the Aswan Dam, an executive of the English company stated that it 'expected' to complete the houses by the date specified in the government's public call for tenders. The Sudanese interpreted this as a firm commitment while the English executive later claimed that he was just stating an intent to make a good faith effort. When the construction company failed to complete the houses on time, the Sudanese government demanded compensation. The resulting conflict caused by their imperfect contract was only settled years later in the company's favor through international arbitration.[8]

Although the parties to alliances, joint ventures, and mergers usually announce them with great fanfare at the start, they often become disappointed within a short time and in many cases terminate them earlier than expected. Various studies have found that between 33 percent and 70 percent of international alliances surveyed eventually broke up and that business executives generally consider joint ventures to be notoriously unstable.[9]

[5] See EL Talley, "Contract Renegotiation, Mechanism Design, and the Liquidated Damages Rule," 46 *Stan L Rev* (1994) 1195, 1206; ME Tracht, "Renegotiation and Secured Credit: Explaining The Equity of Redemption," 52 *Vand L Rev* (1999) 599, 623–4.

[6] See JW Salacuse, "Renegotiations in International Business," 4 *Neg J* (1988) 347, 347–54 (1988).

[7] See JW Salacuse, "Ten Ways That Culture Affects Negotiation: Some Survey Results," 14 *Neg J* (1998) 221, 225–7.

[8] *Turriff Construction Co v. The Government of the Sudan*, unpublished file no 862, Attorney General's Chambers, Khartoum, Sudan.

[9] See B Gomes-Casseres, *The Alliance Revolution* (1996) 52.

The obstacles to the creation of effective working relationships are often too great for the parties to overcome.

(b) Changing Circumstances

Investment contracts, which are often intended to govern long-term, if not indefinite, economic and financial relationships, are by their nature also subject to changing circumstances. A sudden fall in commodity prices, the outbreak of civil war, the development of a new technology, or the imposition of currency controls are examples of changes in circumstance that often force the parties back to the negotiating table. Changes in circumstances can either increase or decrease the costs and benefits of the agreement to the parties. When a change in circumstances means that the cost of respecting a contract for one of the parties is greater than the cost of abandoning it, the result is usually rejection of the contract or a demand for its renegotiation.

A traditional theme in international business circles is the lament over the "unstable contract," the profitable agreement for one side that the other side refuses to respect. Although hard data on the subject are lacking, anecdotal evidence suggests that contractual instability is more prevalent in international business than in the domestic setting. Certainly one can say that international business transactions involve special factors not present in domestic deals and that these factors heighten the risk of contractual instability. First, because the international environment itself is so unstable, international business dealings seem particularly susceptible to sudden changes such as currency devaluation, coups, wars, and radical shifts in governments and governmental policies. Second, mechanisms for enforcing agreements are often less sure or more costly in the international arena than in the domestic setting. If one side in an international transaction does not have effective access to the courts or arbitral tribunals to enforce a contract or to seize assets, the other party may have little to lose in rejecting the contract that it judges burdensome or in demanding its renegotiation. Thus, this factor has the effect of reducing the costs to be incurred by not fulfilling its contractual obligations. Third, foreign governments are often important participants in international transactions. They often reserve to themselves, either explicitly or implicitly, the power to repudiate agreement on grounds of protecting national sovereignty and public welfare.[10] Finally, the world's diverse cultures and legal systems attach differing meanings and degrees of binding force to a signed contract and recognize varying causes to justify avoidance of onerous contractual burdens.[11]

12.2 Defining Renegotiation

Discussions of "renegotiation" apply the term to three fundamentally different situations, and it is therefore important to distinguish them at the outset. Each raises different problems, and each demands different solutions. The three situations are: (1) post-contract renegotiations, (2) intra-contract renegotiations, and (3) extra-contract renegotiations.

(a) Post-Contract Renegotiations

Post-contract renegotiation refers to the situation in which negotiations take place at the expiration of a contract when the two sides, though legally free to go their own ways,

---

[10] See generally, JW Salacuse, *Seven Secrets for Negotiating with Government* (2010).
[11] See JW Salacuse, "Renegotiations in International Business," 4 *Neg J* (1988) 347, 347–54.

nonetheless try to renew their relationship.[12] For example, a project company has built an electrical generating station in an emerging market country and has made a 20-year electricity supply contract with that country's state public utility corporation. At the end of 20 years, when local law considers their legal relationship at an end, the project company and the public utility corporation begin discussions on a second long-term electricity supply contract, thereby "renegotiating" their original relationship. While this second negotiation process—a post-contract renegotiation—may seem at first glance to resemble the negotiation of their original contract, it also has some notable differences, as will be seen, that influence renegotiation strategies, tactics, and outcomes.

(b) Intra-Contract Renegotiations

A second type of renegotiation occurs when the agreement itself, explicitly or implicitly, provides that, during its life at specified times or on the happening of specified events, the parties may renegotiate or review certain of its provisions. For example, the 20-year electricity supply contract mentioned above might include a provision calling for the renegotiation of the agreement's pricing terms in the event of dramatic changes in fuel costs. Or in an agreement between a manufacturer and a sales company for the marketing of specific products, the contract may stipulate that if the manufacturer develops new products it will agree to renegotiate its original deal with respect to the marketing of the new products.[13] Here renegotiation is anticipated as a legitimate activity in which both parties, while still bound to each other in a valid contract, are to engage in good faith negotiations. It is an intra-contract renegotiation because it takes places within the legal framework established for the original transaction.

(c) Extra-Contract Renegotiation

The most difficult, stressful, and emotional renegotiations are those undertaken in apparent violation of the contract or at least in the absence of a specific clause authorizing a renegotiation. These negotiations take place "extra-contract," for they occur outside the framework of the existing agreement. Forced renegotiation of mineral concession contracts of the 1960s and 1970s, negotiations to reschedule loans following the Third World debt crisis of the early 1980s, and the restructuring of infrastructure and financial agreements in the wake of the Asian financial crisis of the late 1990s all fit within the category of extra-contract renegotiations. In each case, one of the participants was seeking relief from a legally binding obligation without any basis for renegotiation in the agreement itself. For example, in the illustration given above, if the state public utility company, without justification in the contract, had insisted on negotiations to reduce the price it was committed to pay for electricity under the contract, such discussions would be categorized as "extra-contract renegotiations," because they would be taking place outside the legal framework of the original contract.

(d) Summary

All three types of renegotiation are a constant and ever-present fact of international investment life. All three differ significantly from the situation in which two parties come

---

[12] This process is also sometimes referred to as "contract renewal."
[13] See, eg, *Howtek, Inc v. Relisys, et al*, 958 F Supp 46 (DNH 1997).

together to negotiate an investment contract in first instance. At the same time, all these three types of renegotiation differ among themselves with respect to the dynamics between the parties, as well as the strategies and tactics they may employ. The remainder of this chapter will explore these three renegotiation processes in detail. It will devote particular attention to extra-contract renegotiations because they are a constant risk for an international investment and can have serious implications for investors, financing institutions, and governments. To illustrate the problems and dynamics of this kind of renegotiation, this chapter will examine in some detail a specific case of extra-contract project renegotiation—the renegotiation of the Dabhol Power Project in India, previously discussed in Chapter 10.

12.3 Post-Contract Renegotiations

(a) Distinguishing Characteristics

Although post-contract renegotiations take place when the original transaction has reached or is approaching its end, several factors distinguish it from a negotiation in first instance, factors that may significantly affect the renegotiation process. First, by virtue of local law, customs of the particular business concerned, or the parties' express or implied contractual commitments to one another, the parties may have a legal obligation to negotiate in good faith with one another despite the fact that their original contract has terminated; consequently, their ability to refuse to engage in post-contract renegotiations may be limited. The existence and precise nature of such a duty will depend on the law governing the contract.

English common law has traditionally recognized a broad, unrestrained freedom of negotiation, which permits a party to begin or end negotiation at any time for any reason.[14] The rationale for this rule is that to limit the freedom to negotiate might discourage persons from undertaking to make transactions in the first place. Although the common law has traditionally upheld the freedom to negotiate in commercial matters,[15] the law in certain other countries has taken a less liberal approach to permissible behavior in business negotiations.[16] In such jurisdictions, once the parties have commenced negotiations, they may have an obligation to negotiate in good faith.

In the case of post-contract renegotiations, by reason of an express provision in the original contract itself, the prevailing practices and customs of the business concerned, or the conduct of the parties toward one another, the parties at the termination of their first contract may have an obligation to negotiate in good faith a renewal of their relationship. In contrast, parties seeking to negotiate a transaction in first instance would have no such obligation and could abandon negotiations at any time.

The precise content of the obligation to renegotiate in good faith will vary from country to country. It may include a duty not to negotiate with a third person until post-contract negotiations with a party in the original transaction have failed. It may also impose an obligation not to terminate renegotiations without reasonable cause and without having persevered for a reasonable length of time.[17] Failure by a party to fulfil its obligations to renegotiate in good faith may result in liability in damages.

---

[14] See EA Farnsworth, "Precontractual Liability and Preliminary Agreements: Fair Dealing and Failed Negotiations," 87 *Colum L Rev* (1987) 217, 221–2.

[15] See Farnsworth, n 14, at 217, 221–2.

[16] See generally, S Litvinoff, "Good Faith," 71 *Tulane L Rev* (1997) 1645, 1659–62.

[17] See Farnsworth, n 14, at 269–85 (discussing the meaning of fair dealing in negotiations and offering instances of unfair dealing).

Even if the applicable law imposes no legal obligation to renegotiate in good faith, the original contract, as well as economic factors, may constrain the renegotiation process in ways not present in the original negotiations. For example, the 20-year electricity supply contract mentioned earlier might provide that if the project company and the public utility company fail to successfully negotiate a second 20-year supply contract at the end of the first agreement, the public utility company will be obligated to purchase the project company's electrical generating facility in accordance with a pricing formula specified in the original agreement.

In addition to the factors arising out of law and contract, numerous other elements may influence post-contract renegotiations. First, the parties in a post-contract renegotiation have a shared experience of working together and a knowledge of each other's goals, methods, intentions, capabilities, and reliability. Obviously, the nature of their earlier experience together will significantly affect their renegotiation. For example, the problems of cross-cultural communication that may have complicated their first negotiation will probably be far less important in the second, since the parties, through working together, have learned much about each other's cultures. Second, many of the original questions about their venture—its risks and opportunities—have been answered and that information will shape bargaining positions in the renegotiation.

Finally, the willingness of the participants to reach an agreement will be influenced by their tangible and intangible investments in their first relationship and the extent to which they can use those investments advantageously in their second contract. For example, the project company in the illustration above will have built the generating facility, organized itself, and trained its employees to provide electricity over the long term to a single specific purchaser, the state public utility. All other things being equal, the project company may prefer to enter into a new contract with the utility, rather than to make an agreement with another purchaser, since the latter course of action would entail significant new risks and costs. Similarly, the public utility having come to rely on the project for a major portion of its supply may wish to avoid the costs of finding another supplier or creating its own electrical generating capacity.

In any negotiation, a party's behavior at the negotiating table is influenced by its evaluation of available alternatives to the deal it is trying to negotiate. Rational negotiators will not ordinarily agree to a transaction that is inferior to its best alternative to an agreement at the negotiating table.[18] In a post-contract renegotiation, each party's evaluation of its alternatives to a renegotiated contract will be heavily influenced by the history of its relationship with the other party during their first contract.

In general, the success of post-contract renegotiations will depend on the nature of the relationship that has developed between the parties during the original contract. If that relationship is strong and productive, the atmosphere at the bargaining table will be that of two partners trying to solve a common problem. If the relationship is weak and problematic, the prevailing mood will be that of two cautious adversaries who know each other only too well.[19]

---

[18] See Fisher et al, n 1, at 99–102 (discussing the concept of BATNA, Best Alternative to a Negotiated Agreement).

[19] See generally, JW Salacuse, "After the Contract, What? Negotiating to Work Successfully with a Foreign Partner," 2 *Can Int'l Law* (1997) 195–200.

(b) Principles to Guide Post-Contract Renegotiations

The factors discussed above give rise to the following principles that lawyers, executives, and government officials should consider in structuring and conducting the process of post-contract renegotiations.

(i) Provide for Post-Contract Renegotiations in the Original Contract

In situations in which the desirability or likelihood of post-contract renegotiations is high, the parties should specify in their original contract the process and rules that they will follow in conducting a post-contract renegotiation. For example, the contract should state how soon before the end of the contract that renegotiations are to begin, how long the renegotiations are to continue before either party may legally abandon them, where the renegotiations are to take place, and the nature of the information that each side is to provide the other, among other matters. Recognizing that post-contract renegotiations may become problematic, the contract might also authorize the use of mediators or other third-party helpers in the process.[20]

(ii) Individually and Jointly Review the History of the Original Contract

As part of its preparation, each party to a post-contract renegotiation should review carefully and thoroughly the history of the experience of working together during the first contract. An understanding of the problems encountered during that period will enable each side to shape proposals to remedy the situation during a contemplated second agreement. To make that review an opportunity for creative problem-solving, rather than mutual acrimony over past mistakes, the parties should structure a joint review of past experience, perhaps with the help of a neutral facilitator, at the beginning of the post-contract renegotiation process. For example, as a first step in the renegotiation process, the parties might agree to give a review team consisting of executives from each participating company the task of preparing a mutually acceptable history of the project to be considered by the negotiators as they begin their work on a new agreement. Inevitably, during the course of post-contract renegotiations, each side will refer to past events. The renegotiation process may proceed more smoothly and efficiently if, at the beginning of the process, the parties have a common understanding of their history together, rather than engage in a continuing debate about the existence and significance of past events throughout the renegotiation.

(iii) Understand Thoroughly the Alternatives to a Renegotiated Contract

Negotiation scholars stress the importance of negotiators knowing their alternatives to the deal that they are trying to negotiate and estimating their counterparts' alternatives.[21] Generally, the better a negotiator's alternatives away from the negotiating table, the stronger the negotiator's position at the bargaining table.[22] In a post-contract renegotiation,

---

[20] See JW Salacuse, "Direct Negotiation and Mediation in International Financial and Business Conflicts" in N Horn and J Norton (eds), *Non-Judicial Dispute Settlement in International Financial Transactions* (2003) 53–72 [hereinafter "Direct Negotiation and Mediation"]. See generally C Buhring-Uhle, *Arbitration and Mediation in International Business* (1996).

[21] See Fisher et al, n 1, at 99–102.

[22] See, eg, D Lax and J Sebenius, "The Power of Alternatives or the Limits to Negotiation," in J Breslin and J Rubin (eds), *Negotiation Theory and Practice* (1991) 97–113.

these two tasks are often complicated by the fact that the parties may have conducted their business in such a way during the first contract that few realistic alternatives to a second contract seem possible. For example, the project company that owns a generating facility may feel that it has few other options than to enter into a second contract with the state public utility. Or the government company in a country that has a severe energy shortage may see no realistic alternatives to making a second electricity power purchase agreement with the project company. Rather than accepting the inevitability of a second contract, each side, long before the termination of the first contract, should carefully examine all options and seek to develop possible alternatives before entering into post-contract renegotiations. For example, the state public utility corporation, several years in advance of the end of the first contract, should contact other potential project companies to determine their interest in developing electrical generation plants in the country.

12.4 Intra-Contract Renegotiations

(a) Balancing Contractual Stability and Flexibility

Due to the nature of many international investments, investment contracts cover long time periods, usually many years, include several parties, deal with highly complex technical and financial matters, and involve large sums of money. As a result, all sides in the negotiation process seek contractual stability. At the same time, the parties know that during the long time period covered by their agreement, many unforeseen political, economic, regulatory, and technical circumstances may arise to drastically change the balance of benefits from the project that the parties contemplated at the time that they made their contract. Consequently, one can argue that a certain degree of flexibility is a second imperative that the investment contracting process should seek.

To provide for that flexibility, mechanisms might be included in the contract to allow the parties to adjust their relationship to such changes in circumstances. One approach to balancing the imperatives of stability and flexibility in investment agreements is for the contract itself to authorize the parties to renegotiate key elements of their relationship upon the happening of specified events or circumstances. In appropriate cases, the inclusion in the contract of some type of intra-contract renegotiation clause would appear to be a useful basis for establishing a long-term business relationship. Although commentators have advocated specific renegotiation or revision clauses in long-term international business agreements,[23] these provisions have traditionally not been used extensively.[24] Indeed, prevailing contracting practice among western firms and lawyers is just the opposite. Their preferred approach is to try to anticipate all possible future contingencies and to provide for them in the contract document, while seeking to foreclose any possibility of renegotiating its terms at a later date. Indeed, in order to prevent the possibility of change, many investment contracts include a "stabilization clause" in which the government expressly agrees that any changes in the law that place an additional cost or burden on the project will not be applicable to the project. As discussed in Chapter 7,[25] the specific legal consequences of such stabilization clauses have been the subject of significant debate.[26]

---

[23] KP Berger, "Renegotiation and Adaptation of International Investment Contracts," 36 *Vanderbilt Journal of Transnational Law* (2003) 1347; JY Gotanda, "Renegotiation and Adaptation Clauses in Investment Contracts, Revisited," 36 *Vanderbilt Journal of Transnational Law* (2003) 1461.

[24] M Bartels, *Contractual Adaptation and Conflict Resolution* 65 (trans James E Silva 1985); see also Kolo and Walde, n 2, at 43.

[25] See Chapter 7, section 7.3.

[26] See, eg, R Dolzer and C Schreuer, *Principles of International Investment Law* (2008) 75–7.

The traditional reluctance to use renegotiation clauses stems from a variety of factors, both legal and practical. First is the concern among lawyers that contracts with renegotiation clauses are merely "agreements to agree" and, therefore, may be invalid and unenforceable under the law of many countries.[27] Judicial precedent on the validity of renegotiation clauses is sparse, so guidance in this area comes almost exclusively from judicial doctrine with respect to contract renewal and preliminary agreements.[28] Unlike the English common law, which has tended to dismiss agreements to negotiate as unenforceable, the contemporary approach in many American jurisdictions is to hold that agreements to negotiate in good faith are not unenforceable as a matter of law.[29] According to one case from a US Federal District Court, "the critical inquiry in evaluating the enforceability of an express or implied agreement to negotiate in good faith is whether the standard against which the parties' good-faith negotiations are to be measured is sufficiently certain to comport with the applicable body of contract law."[30] A specific renegotiation clause in an existing contract with definite terms as to how the parties are to conduct the renegotiation process would easily meet this standard of enforceability. The required certainty would be further satisfied by specifying the precise events that give rise to the obligation to renegotiate and by specifically providing for the timing, locale, and conditions of the renegotiation process, among others.

Practical considerations have led western lawyers and executives to view renegotiation clauses with suspicion on the grounds that they increase uncertainty and risk in business transactions and offend western concepts of the sanctity of the contract.[31] Their presence in a contract also creates a risk that one of the parties will use a renegotiation clause as a lever to force changes in provisions that, strictly speaking, are not open to revision. Moreover, the challenges of drafting these provisions and the heightened risks to contractual stability by renegotiation provisions that have yet to be tested in the courts are additional factors that have deterred lawyers from using them in long-term business contracts.[32]

Despite these potential pitfalls, the inclusion of a renegotiation clause may actually contribute to transactional stability in certain situations. First, in cases in which significant changes in circumstances may result in severe unexpected financial hardship, a renegotiation clause may permit the parties to avoid default, with the attendant risk of litigation and extra-contractual renegotiations. At the outset, the parties should recognize the risk of changed circumstances and create within the contract a process to deal with them, rather than to try to predict all eventualities and leave the matter up to the courts or arbitrators when those predictions prove to be flawed.

A second situation in which a renegotiation clause may be helpful occurs in cases in which the parties, by virtue of their differing cultures, understand and perceive the basis of a business transaction in fundamentally different ways. For example, western notions of business transactions as being founded upon law and contract often clash with conceptions in other cultures that hold that business dealings are fundamentally based on the

---

[27] See, eg, JW Carter, "The Renegotiation of Contracts," 13 *J Contract L* (1999) 185, 188.

[28] See generally Farnsworth, n 14.

[29] See *Howtek, Inc v. Relisys, et al.* 958 F Supp 46 (DNH 1996); *Channel Home Ct. v. Grossman*, 795 F 2d 291, 299 (3d Cir 1986).

[30] See *Howtek*, 958 F Supp at 48.

[31] See WA Stoever, *Renegotiations in International Business Transactions* (1981) 27.

[32] See, eg, N Nassar, *Sanctity of Contracts Revisited* 205–30 (1995); Carter, n 27, at 189; and KM Sharma, "From 'Sanctity' to 'Fairness': An Uneasy Transition in the Law of Contracts," 18 *NYL Sch J Int'l & Comp L* (1999) 95, 132–42.

relationship between the parties involved.[33] In many Asian countries, in particular, business executives consider the essence of a business deal to be the relationship between the parties, rather than the written contract which can only describe that relationship imperfectly and incompletely.[34] Often persons from those cultures assume that any long-term business relationship includes an implicit, fundamental principle: in times of change, parties in a business relationship should meet to decide together how to cope with that change and adjust their relationship accordingly.

In long-term business transactions between a western and an Asian firm, the western party may view the transaction as set in the concrete of a lengthy and detailed contract, without the possibility of modification, while the eastern party may see the transaction as floating on fluid personal and social relationships between the parties that contain an implicit commitment to renegotiate the terms of the transaction in the event of unforeseen happenings. In a long-term transaction, such as a joint venture project between eastern and western companies whose success depends on close and continuing cooperation, it may be wise to recognize this difference of view at the time of negotiation and attempt to find some middle ground.

A renegotiation clause may represent such middle ground between total contractual rigidity on the one hand and complete relational flexibility on the other. Thus, rather than dismiss the possibility of renegotiation and then be forced at a later time to review the entire contract, project partners who want to enable their business relationship to weather difficult seas should recognize the possibility of renegotiation at the outset of their dealings with one another and should set down a clear framework within which to conduct that process. Through a renegotiation clause, the parties recognize the possibility of redoing their deal, but control the renegotiation process. An intra-contract renegotiation clause, then, may give stability to an arrangement whose long-term nature creates a high risk of instability.

(b) Approaches to Intra-Contract Renegotiation

In recent times, the use of renegotiation clauses seems to have become somewhat more frequent as a means of dealing with the problem of unpredictable future changes in circumstances in long-term agreements.[35] A review of possible approaches to intra-contract renegotiation clauses may be useful to executives, lawyers, and government officials involved in international investment project contracting.

---

[33] See generally, PJ McConnaughay, "Rethinking the Role of Law and Contracts in East-West Commercial Relations," 41 *Va J Int'l L* (2001) 427; see also JW Salacuse, "Ten Ways That Culture Affects Negotiation: Some Survey Results," 14 *Neg J* (1998) 221, 225–7 (1998) [hereinafter Ten Ways]; L Pye, *Chinese Negotiating Style* (1982).

[34] See Ten Ways, n 33, at 222 (surveying over 300 executives and lawyers from twelve nationalities and finding significant differences among nationalities on whether they viewed the goal of negotiation as creating contract or creating relationship). Whereas 74 percent of the Spanish respondents viewed the goal of a negotiation as concluding a contract (instead of creating a relationship), 67 percent of the Indians claimed that a relationship, rather than a contract, was their negotiating goal.

[35] See Carter, n 27, at 189. See also RJ Weintraub, "A Survey of Contract Practice and Policy" *Wisconsin Law Review* (1992) 1, 16–17 (stating that in a survey asking companies whether they included a renegotiation clause in long-term contracts to protect against substantial changes in market prices, 41.9 percent of the US businesses responded affirmatively).

(i) The Implicit Renegotiation Clause

Persons experienced in investment project implementation know that despite some lawyers' claims to the contrary, project contracts, no matter how detailed, are not a kind of automatic, comprehensive instruction booklet that the parties follow blindly. Time and again, executives involved in the actual implementation of international projects have given the author the same message: "Once the contract is signed, we put it in the drawer. After that, what matters most is the relationship between us and our partner, and we are negotiating that relationship all the time." At best, such contracts are frameworks within which the parties constantly negotiate their relationship.[36] What this view means in practice is that certain matters in the transaction, usually but not always of a minor nature, are subject to renegotiation by the parties as part of the ongoing relationship, despite the fact that their contract contains no specific renegotiation clause.[37] One can therefore argue that an "implicit minor renegotiation clause" is part of the investment project agreement. For example, if the electrical supply agreement in the earlier example provides that the project is to commence delivery of electricity on June 1, 2002, but it later becomes apparent that a four-day national religious holiday falls on that date, making it difficult for the public utility to accept delivery, the parties would renegotiate a more appropriate time for delivery.

(ii) Review Clauses

Long-term contracts, particularly in the oil and mineral industries, sometimes commit the parties to meet to review the operation of their agreement from time to time.[38] Thus, one mining agreement provided that the parties were to meet together every seven years "with a view to considering in good faith whether this Agreement is continuing to operate fairly to each of them and with a view further to discussing in good faith any problems arising from the practical operation of this agreement."[39] Although the words "negotiation" or "renegotiation" are not used in the clause, one reasonable interpretation is that it carries an implicit obligation for the parties to negotiate solutions to problems in good faith.

(iii) Automatic Adjustment Clauses

Project agreements often contain certain terms, such as those concerning prices or interests rates, subject to automatic change by reference to specified indices, such as a cost–of–living index or the London Interbank Offered Rate ("LIBOR").[40] For example, in the electricity supply contract discussed earlier, the price to be paid for the electricity by the public utility might be tied to variations in fuel costs or to the local cost-of-living index. While the aim of such a provision is to provide for flexibility without the risks inherent in renegotiation,

---

[36] See KN Llewellyn, "What Price Contract? An Essay in Perspective,' 40 *Yale L J* (1931) 704, 736–37. The noted American legal scholar underscored a point when he wrote:

'To sum up, the major importance of a legal contract is to provide a frame-work for well-nigh every type of group organization and for well-nigh every type of passing or permanent relation between individuals and groups, up to and including states–a frame-work highly adjustable, a frame-work which almost never accurately indicates real working relations, but which affords a rough indication around which such relations vary, an occasional guide in cases of doubt, and a norm of final appeal when the relations cease in fact to work.'

[37] See Kolo and Walde, n 2, at 45.
[38] See Kolo and Walde, n 2, at 43.
[39] W Peter, *Arbitration and Renegotiation in International Investment Agreements* (1995) 79.
[40] See Kolo and Walde, n 2, at 44.

negotiations may still be necessary during the life of the contract in order to apply the index in unanticipated situations or in the event that the index itself disappears or becomes inappropriate.[41]

(iv) Open-Term Provisions

Because of the difficulties and risks inherent in trying to negotiate arrangements to take place far in the future, some project agreements specifically provide that certain matters will be negotiated at a later time, perhaps years after the contract has been signed and the project established. For example, the electricity project company mentioned earlier might agree to negotiate appropriate senior management training schemes after it has constructed the facility and begun to hire local managers. This type of provision might be called an "open-term" clause because the matter in question has been left open for negotiation at a later time.[42]

In a strict sense, of course, the subsequent negotiation of the open term is not really a *renegotiation* of anything, since the parties have not yet agreed to anything with respect to the open term. In a broader sense, however, the negotiation of the open term at a later time will have the effect of modifying the overall relationship between the parties. Moreover, it is not inconceivable that one or both of the parties could use the opportunity of negotiating the open term as an occasion to seek concessions or changes in other terms through the common negotiating device of linking issues. For example, the project company might offer a particularly attractive management training program if the government would agree to certain desired regulatory changes.

(v) Renegotiation Clauses

In an effort to balance the imperatives of contractual stability with the need for flexibility in long-term arrangements, some investment project agreements may contain a definite clause that obligates the parties to renegotiate specified terms affected by changes in circumstances or unforeseen developments, such as those concerning construction costs, governmental regulations, commodity prices, or product specifications. For example, in a contract for the exploration of petroleum, the government of Qatar and an oil company agreed that they would negotiate future arrangements for the use of natural gas not associated with oil discoveries if commercial quantities of such "non-associated" gas were later found in the contract area.[43] In addition, as Kolo and Walde point out, renegotiation clauses in investment contracts often accompany stabilization clauses, by which a host country promises that any changes in laws or regulations will not adversely affect the foreign investment project. The effect of the two clauses is to obligate the host government and the project company to enter into negotiations to restore the financial equilibrium that such new laws and regulations may have destroyed.[44]

An intra-contract renegotiation clause obligates the parties only to negotiate, not to agree. If the parties have negotiated in good faith pursuant to the clause but fail to reach agreement, that failure cannot justify liability on the part of one of the parties. In the Qatar

---

[41] Kolo and Walde, n 2, at 44.
[42] See Farnsworth, n 14, at 250 (discussing what he calls "agreements with open terms").
[43] *Wintershall, A G, et al v. Government of Qatar,* (1989) 28 *ILM*.795, 814 (Ad Hoc Arbitral Tribunal 1989); J Carver and H Hossain, "An Arbitration Case Study: The Dispute That Never Was," 5 *ICSID Rev* (1990) 311.
[44] Kolo and Walde, n 2, at 44–5.

case mentioned above, the oil company ultimately found commercial quantities of non-associated natural gas and entered into negotiations with the government of Qatar concerning its use. When the two sides failed to reach agreement, the oil company brought an arbitral proceeding against the government. The oil company claimed that, by failing to agree to a renegotiation of their agreement with respect to natural gas, the Qatar government had breached its contract with the oil company. The arbitral tribunal rejected this argument on the grounds that the duty to negotiate in good faith does not include an obligation to accept proposals made by the other side and that the Qatar government's refusal to accept those proposals was based on reasonable commercial judgments.[45]

In order to bring finality to the process of intra-contract renegotiation, parties sometimes include a "contract adaptation clause" in long-term project agreements. A contract adaptation clause stipulates that on the happening of certain specified events the parties will first seek to negotiate a solution and, failing that, refer their problem to a third party for either a recommendation or a binding decision, depending on the desire of the parties to the contract.[46] In 1978, the International Chamber of Commerce issued rules on the adaptation of contracts[47] that parties to a contract might adopt; however, in 1993 ICC withdrew them because it concluded that they had never been used.[48]

12.5 Extra-Contract Renegotiation

(a) The Context of Extra-Contract Renegotiations

In an extra-contract renegotiation, one party insists on renegotiating the terms of a valid contract that contains no express provision authorizing renegotiation. Unlike negotiations for the original transaction, which are generally fueled by both sides' hopes for future benefits, extra-contract negotiations begin with both parties' shattered expectations. One side has failed to achieve the benefits expected from the transaction, while the other is being asked to give up something for which it bargained hard and which it hoped to enjoy for a long time. And whereas both parties to the negotiation of a proposed new venture participate willingly, if not eagerly, one party always participates reluctantly, if not downright unwillingly, in an extra-contract renegotiation.

Beyond mere disappointed expectations, extra-contract renegotiations, by their very nature, can create bad feelings and mistrust. One side believes it is being asked to give up something to which it has a legal and moral right. It views the other side as having gone back on its word, as having acted in bad faith by reneging on the deal. Indeed, the reluctant party may even feel that it is being coerced into participating in extra-contract renegotiations since a refusal to do so would result in losing the investment it has already made in the transaction. Thus, it is very difficult for the parties to see extra-contract renegotiations as anything more than a process in which one side wins and the other side loses. Whereas the negotiation of any transaction in first instance is usually about the degree to which each side will share in expected benefits, an extra-contract renegotiation is often about allocating a loss. At the same time, because the parties are bound together in a legal and economic

---

[45] *Wintershall v. Government of Qatar*, 28 *ILM* at 814.

[46] See generally, JY Gotanda, "Renegotiation and Adaptation Clauses in Investment Contracts, Revisited," 36 *Vanderbilt Journal of Transnational Law* (2003) 1461–73; M Bartels, *Contractual Adaptation and Conflict Resolution* (trans James E Silva, 1985) 65; Norbert Horn (ed), *Adaptation and Renegotiation of Contracts in International Trade* (1985).

[47] Int'l Chamber of Commerce, *Adaptation of Contracts* (ICC Publication no 326, 1978).

[48] JY Gotanda, n 46, at 1461, 1464.

relationship, it is usually much harder for one or both of them to walk away from a troubled transaction than it is for two unconnected parties to walk away from negotiating a prospective business transaction in first instance.   ·

In most countries, the law does not oblige a party to enter into renegotiations, no matter how conditions have changed or how heavy the costs incurred by the other side are since the contract was originally concluded.[49] Indeed, the common law of England at one time viewed some renegotiated contracts as invalid since they lacked consideration in those cases in which as a result of the negotiation a party was promising to do no more than it was already obligated to do.[50] In general, unless some legal doctrine, such as frustration, is applicable to excuse performance, the party being asked to renegotiate an existing agreement has a legal right to refuse to renegotiate and to insist on performance in accordance with the letter of the contract. On the other hand, requests or, in some cases, demands for renegotiation of an existing agreement are often accompanied by express or implied threats, including governmental intervention, expropriation, slow down in performance, or the complete repudiation or cancellation of the contract itself.

In response, of course, the other party usually has a legal remedy in the courts or in arbitration of enforcing its contract and will often threaten to assert it. However, its willingness to pursue a legal remedy to its conclusion, rather than renegotiate, will usually depend on its evaluation of that remedy in relation to the results it expects from renegotiation. To the extent that the net benefits (ie, benefits minus costs) from renegotiation exceed the expected net benefits from litigation, arbitration, or other legal remedy, the rational party will ordinarily engage in the requested renegotiation. But if either before or during the renegotiation, a party judges that the net benefits to be derived from litigation will exceed the net benefits to be gained in any renegotiation, that party will normally pursue its legal remedies. On its side, the party requesting the renegotiation will be making its own cost–benefit analysis of the relative merits of contract repudiation and its probable fate in arbitration or litigation. As long as it judges that the net benefits of repudiating the contract are less than the net benefits of respecting it, the contractual relationship will continue. But when, for whatever reason, it judges the respective net benefits to be the opposite, the result will be a demand for renegotiation with the threat of eventual repudiation in the background.

A party's reluctance to agree to an extra-contract renegotiation may be due not only to the impact of renegotiation on the contract in question, but on other contracts and business relationships as well. The side being asked to relinquish a contractual right may feel the need to show other parties with which it has relationships that it cannot be taken advantage of. Yielding to a demand for the extra-contract renegotiation of one contract may encourage other parties to ask for renegotiation of their agreements as well. Renegotiation of one transaction with one particular party may set a precedent for other renegotiations with other parties. This concern for the potential ripple effect from extra-contract renegotiations clearly contributed to the reluctance of international commercial banks to yield to demands by individual developing countries for a revision of loan terms. Concessions to Mexico

---

[49] Carter, n 27, at 185 (stating "the so-called classical law of contract does not include a doctrine of renegotiation."). "This can be expressed by saying that there are no legal principles which can be invoked by one party to require the other to renegotiate a contract."

[50] *Stilk v. Myrick*, 2 Camp 317, 6 Esp 129 (1809). Recent cases have held that the concern in enforcing renegotiated contracts should not be lack of consideration but presence of duress. *Williams v. Roffey Bros & Nicholls (Contractors) Ltd*, 1 QB 1 (Eng CA 1991). See SM Waddams, "Commentary on 'The Renegotiation of Contracts'," 13 *J Contract L* (1994) 204.

would inevitably lead Argentina to demand equal treatment in its own extra-contract renegotiations.[51]

The causes of extra-contract renegotiations in international project transactions are numerous, perhaps too numerous to be catalogued here. Nonetheless, as indicated at the beginning of this chapter, most factors contributing to the need for extra-contract renegotiations seem to fall into two basic categories: (1) the parties' imperfect contract with respect to their underlying transaction and (2) changed circumstances after they have signed their agreement. Both of these factors contributed to the problems investors encountered in the Dabhol Power Project in India.

12.6 A Case of Extra-Contract Renegotiation: The Dabhol Power Project in India

(a) Background

One may gain an understanding of the dynamics at work in extra-contract renegotiation by examining a specific case, the renegotiations involved in Enron's Dabhol Electricity Power Project in India,[52] an incident that received significant media attention in 1995–1996.[53] The events leading up to the conclusion of the original project agreements were discussed in Chapter 10.[54]

(b) The Forces for Changing the Investment Agreement

Public opposition to the Dabhol Power Project grew as construction activity proceeded. Activists and organizations filed lawsuits in the Bombay High Court, challenging the legality of the project and the processes by which it was negotiated.[55] Although the courts dismissed the complaints, political opposition continued to mount. Specifically, the opposition alliance of the Bharatiya Janata Party ("BJP") and the Shiv Sena took up the issue on the floor of the Maharashtra State Assembly. As they prepared for state elections scheduled for March 1995, they made opposition to the Dabhol Project a centerpiece in their campaign. Emphasizing Hindu nationalism and warning against the dangers of American economic and cultural imperialism, BJP–Shiv Shena politicians encouraged public opposition to the project in their campaign rhetoric. They charged that Enron was offering India nothing that India could not do for itself, that the power tariff was exorbitant and would hurt the poor, that Enron's rate of return was exploitative, and that the whole

[51] See A Mudge, "Sovereign Debt Restructure: A Perspective of Counsel to Agent Banks, Bank Advisory Groups, and Servicing Banks," in WN Eskridge, Jr (ed), *A Dance Along the Precipice: The Political and Economic Dimensions of the International Debt Problem* (1985) 105, 106.

[52] For background, see RP Teisch and WA Stoever, "Enron in India: Lessons From a Renegotiation," 35 *Mid-Atlantic J Bus* (1999) 51–62; Harvard Business School, *Enron Development Corporation: The Dabhol Power Project in Maharashtra, India (A)* (HBS Case no 9-596-099, March 25, 1997) [hereinafter *Harvard Study (A)*]; Harvard Business School, *Enron Development Corporation: The Dabhol Power Project in Maharashtra, India (B)* (HBS Case no 9-596-100, December 16, 1996) [hereinafter *Harvard Study (B)*]; Harvard Business School, *Enron Development Corporation: The Dabhol Power project in Maharashtra, India (C)* (HBS Case no 9-596-101, December 16, 1996) [hereinafter *Harvard Study (C)*].

[53] See, eg, JF Burns, "Indian Politics Derail a Big Power Project," *NY Times*, July 5, 1995, at D1; M Nicholson, "Survey—Maharashtra 1996: U-Turn that Saved the Project," *Fin Times*, July 11, 1996, at 3; "The Mugging of Enron," *Euromoney*, October 1995, at 33; G McWilliams and S Moshavi, "Enron: Maybe Megadeals Mean Megarisk," *Bus Week*, January 22, 1996, at 62; R Rao, "Enron's Power Outage in India," *Fortune*, October 2, 1995, at 35–6.

[54] See section 10.7.

[55] See, eg, *Ramdas Nayak v. Union of India*, 1995 AIR 225.

negotiation process had been tainted by corruption.[56] According to one observer of the campaign, the Dabhol Project became "a national icon...rallying economic nationalists suspicious of the post-liberalization arrival of foreign investment."[57]

In the State Assembly elections of March 1995, the BJP–Shiv Sena alliance won a majority of seats and thereby ousted from government the incumbent Congress Party, which most observers had expected would continue to hold power. In May, the new government appointed a cabinet sub-committee, chaired by the deputy Chief Minister, Shri Gopinath Munde, to investigate the Dabhol Project. The committee submitted a report in July recommending that the State repudiate Phase I of the project and cancel Phase II. The Report based its recommendation on several grounds, including the absence of transparency in the negotiation process, the lack of competitive bidding procedure, the relaxation by the previous government of certain regulations relating to the project, the great expense of the project, the high electricity tariff rate and its continuing escalation, the obligation of the Maharashtra State Electricity Board to pay for electricity whether or not it was actually used, the World Bank Report's objections to the project, and the failure of the project negotiations to address environmental concerns.[58]

On the basis of this report, the State government, under its new Chief Minister, Manohar Joshi, and the Maharashtra State Electricity Board formally canceled the Power Purchase Agreement with the Dabhol Power Company.[59] Chief Minister Joshi stated: "This decision is not against the United States; but against the Dabhol project....The deal is against the interests of Maharashtra. Accepting this deal would indicate an absolute lack of self-respect and would amount to betraying the trust of the people."[60]

At this point in its development, the Dabhol Project had incurred sunk costs of approximately US$300 million and each day of delay on construction was estimated to cost an additional US$250,000.

In response, the Dabhol Power Company and the project sponsors invoked their legal rights under the Power Purchase Agreement by instituting arbitration in London against the Maharashtra Electricity Board and the Maharashtra State government, claiming damages in excess of US$300 million. The State of Maharashtra reacted by bringing suit in the Bombay High Court to invalidate the arbitration clause and the guarantee of MSEB payments on the grounds that both had been secured through illegal means. The US government issued a statement critical of the contract repudiation and asserted that it would have negative consequences for foreign investment in India. Foreign investors considering India became demonstrably more cautious and expressed their concern over the incident. The Indian press appeared to be divided over the wisdom of Maharashtra State's action. In the face of this growing controversy, the Deputy Chief Minister Munde, who had chaired the Dabhol Project review committee, stated, "Our decision is firm. We do not wish to renegotiate."[61]

---

[56] See Burns, n 53, at D1.
[57] See Nicholson, n 53, at 3.
[58] See *Report of the Cabinet Sub-Committee to Review the Dabhol Power Project*, reprinted in *Human Rights Watch Report, The Enron Corporation: Corporate Complicity in Human Rights Violations, Appendix B* (January 1999) available at <http://www.hrw.org/reports/1999/enron/>; see also *Harvard Study (B)*, n 52, at 2–3.
[59] MW Brauchli, "Enron Project Is Scrapped by Indian State," *Wall St J*, August 4, 1995, at A3; Rao, n 53, at 35–6.
[60] See Rao, n 53.
[61] *Harvard Study (B)*, n 52, at 5.

(c) Renegotiating the Dabhol Project

While pursuing its legal remedies in arbitration, Enron made it clear to the Maharashtra State authorities that it would be willing to renegotiate the Dabhol Project. In the fall of 1995, discussions took place between Enron executives and Maharashtra officials and political leaders, which culminated in a meeting between Chief Minister Joshi and the chief executive officers of the Enron Corporation and its subsidiary, the Enron Development Corporation, intended to find a way of reviving the Dabhol Project. Shortly thereafter, Chief Minister Joshi announced that Maharashtra State would undertake a review of the project and promised to reopen negotiations in November. To carry out the review and renegotiation, he appointed a panel consisting of the President of the MSEB, the Power Secretary of Maharashtra State, and four other academic and industry experts, in contrast to the first review panel, which had consisted of government ministers.[62]

During a period of two weeks, the Review Panel not only met with Enron to discuss proposals for restructuring the Dabhol Project, but it also listened to principal critics of the project. The key issues in the discussions with Enron concerned the electricity tariff, capital costs, payment terms, and the environment.[63] Finally, on November 19, 1995, the Panel submitted a proposal to the Maharashtra State government embodying the renegotiated terms of the Dabhol project to which the Panel and Enron had agreed. Enron agreed to suspend its arbitration proceedings in London until December 10. Ultimately, on January 8, 1996, after some delay, the Maharashtra government agreed to accept the Panel proposal for renegotiated terms,[64] which eventually became the basis for amending the Power Purchase Agreement between the Dabhol Power Company, the State of Maharashtra, and the MSEB, an event that took place on February 23, 1996. Ultimately, in July after much debate, the Indian central government, which had also undergone a recent election that led to a new governing coalition, approved the amended Power Purchase Agreement and extended the central government's counter-guarantee of Maharashtra's obligations, thereby removing the final barrier to the revived project. In August 1996, Enron agreed to abandon its arbitration proceeding in London, and Maharashtra State agreed to drop its case in the Mumbai high court.

Despite the renegotiation and government approvals, Enron was not able to resume construction immediately. While the conflict and renegotiation between Enron and the government was evolving, various labor unions, public interest groups, and activists brought some 24 suits in the Indian courts to stop the project. Even though the Maharashtra government had approved the terms of the renegotiated agreement, the courts ruled that until these suits were resolved, construction on the project would have to remain suspended. Eventually, the Indian courts held against the plaintiffs in all of these cases, but it was not until December 1996 that the last suit was dismissed and construction resumed on the Dabhol Project.[65]

---

[62] *Harvard Study (C)*, n 52, at 1.

[63] S Hattangadi, "Enron, Indian State Revive Power Project," *Wall St J*, November 22, 1995, at A4.

[64] See McWilliams and Moshavi, n 53, at 62.

[65] Enron, Press Release: "Court Rules in Favor of Dabhol Power, Dabhol Construction to Resume," available at <http://www.enron.com/india/Newsroom/Press-Releases03.htm> (December 2, 1996); Enron, *Press Release: Dabhol Project Achieves Financial Close: Resumes Construction,* available at <http://www.enron.com/india/Newsroom/Press_Release02.htm> (December 10, 1996).

(d) The Terms of the Renegotiated Investment Agreement

The renegotiation resulted in a modification of all of the principal terms of the Power Purchase Agreement. A summary of the changes is as follows:

a. *Equity Participation.* Although the project company originally had only three US shareholders (Enron 80 percent; Bechtel, 10 percent; and General Electric, 10 percent), the renegotiated deal provided for the introduction of the Maharashtra State Electricity Board as a 30 percent shareholder with a proportionate reduction in Enron's interest. Thus the new equity structure was Enron, 50 percent; MSEB, 30 percent; Bechtel, 10 percent; and General Electric, 10 percent. The introduction of an Indian partner seemed a way of meeting public suspicion over foreign investment.

b. *Output Capacity.* Although the World Bank's report had criticized the original proposed power plant as being too large, the renegotiated terms provided for a plant of even greater output capacity. The capacity of Phase I was increased from 695MW to 826MW and total capacity after the completion of Phase II under the renegotiated agreement was increased to 2,450MW, as compared with 2,105MW in the original proposal.

c. *Capital Costs.* To respond to the criticism that the project was too expensive, the renegotiation reduced the capital costs from US$2.85 billion to US$2.5 billion. The panel achieved this result by removing the regasification plant from the Dabhol project and treating it as a separate project, for which the power plant would pay a fixed charge. This change transformed a portion of capital costs to an ongoing variable cost that would be included in the new power tariff.[66] A portion of the reduction in capital costs can also be attributed to the worldwide fall in the price of generation equipment.

d. *Power Tariff.* The politics of Maharashtra demanded a reduction in the power tariff to be paid by the MSEB. Accordingly, the panel with the agreement of Enron recommended a reduction in the power tariff from approximately 7.03 US cents per kWh, subject to a 4 percent annual escalation on fixed charges, to 6.03, subject to fuel price and exchange rate fluctuations, until Phase II became operational, at which time the tariff would become 5.08 US cents per kWh, subject to fuel price and exchange rate fluctuations for 20 years, but with no escalation.

e. *Fuel.* The original proposal had called for distillate oil to be used in Phase I and liquefied natural gas in Phase II. The renegotiated terms provided in Phase I for the use of naphtha, a fuel that was produced locally, thus sparing India foreign exchange costs of importing oil for the project.

f. *Environment.* The original power purchase agreement contained no provisions with respect to environmental protection. The renegotiated terms stated that Enron and the Dabhol Power Company would pay for monthly air and water surveys, would plant trees, manage effluent discharged into the sea so as to protect marine life, and would employ one person from any family displaced due to the construction of the plant.[67]

---

[66] See "BJP Collapse Muddies Enron/Dabhol Waters," *Power Asia*, June 10, 1996. Later, the Central Electricity Authority and the Ministry of Power, both agencies of the Indian central government, persuaded the state to put the regasification facility back into the project without any changes in the renegotiated power purchase agreement. This further development resulted in a real capital cost increase but a small tariff reduction since the lower rate no longer included amortization of the LNG facility.

[67] *Harvard Study (C)*, n 52, at 4.

g. *Other Terms.* Various other terms were introduced into the renegotiated agreement. For example, Enron and the Dabhol Power Company agreed to use local suppliers and supplies to the extent possible and to employ a bidding procedure in purchasing power equipment. Moreover, Enron agreed to bear costs of approximately US$175 million caused by the State's cancelation of the contract, provided that the construction was renewed by February 1, 1996. Although Maharashtra State failed to meet this deadline, Enron later also agreed to waive the daily interest charges of US $250,000 that had been accruing as a result of work stoppage, thereby saving Maharashtra State an additional approximately US$10 million.[68]

(e) The Aftermath

Both Enron and the State of Maharashtra claimed the renegotiation as a victory. The Maharashtra government pointed to the reduction in the power tariff and capital costs as major concessions favoring the State.[69] On the other hand, the enlarged project capacity was clearly a renegotiated term favorable to Enron since the Power Purchase Agreement was a "take-or-pay contract." Moreover, a significant portion of the capital cost reduction resulted from favorable market developments with respect to generating equipment, not a transfer of value from Enron to the State of Maharashtra.

Despite government statements of satisfaction with the renegotiation, significant public opposition to the project continued. Although the Indian courts eventually dismissed all the numerous lawsuits against the project, public protests and demonstrations at the project site persisted. The measures taken by the Maharashtra State government and the police to deal with these protests prompted concerns with respect to human rights violations.[70] Nonetheless, in May 1999, the Dabhol Power Project was completed and began commercial operation. In that same month, on the strength of projected cash flows promised by the Power Purchase Agreement and guaranteed by the government of India, Enron secured financing of US$1.87 billion for Phase II of the Project,[71] which was scheduled for completion at the end of 2001.[72]

(f) The Aftermath of the Aftermath

By 2001, the Maharashtra State Electricity Board found itself unable to meet it payments to the Dabhol Power Company for the electricity it was required to take under the Power Purchase Agreement. The projected demand for electricity had not materialized, primarily because of a downturn in the economy due to the Asian financial crisis of 1997–1998 and because of the failure of the MSEB to rationalize its internal operations to secure the needed revenue from its consumers. Faced with this failure of payment, the Dabhol Power Company sent a notice of arbitration to the MSEB, invoking its remedy under the Power Purchase Agreement. In response, the Maharashtra State government took three actions. It repudiated the Power Purchase Agreement, refused to permit the testing of the turbines

---

[68] "Legal Hurdles Dropped as Dabhol Project Gets Set," *Power Asia*, August 4, 1996.

[69] "India: Power Struggle," *Economist*, January 13, 1996, at 37; G McWilliams and S Moshavi, "More Power To India," *Bus Week*, January 22, 1996, at 62.

[70] See n 59.

[71] "Enron, Financing Complete, Construction Commences on Second Phase of Dabhol Power Project," Press Release (May 6, 1999) available at <http://www.enron.com>.

[72] Enron International, Our Presence in India, available at <http://www.ei.enron.com/presence/projects/ India>.

in Phase II, thereby effectively bringing that aspect of the project to a stop, and obtained an injunction from the Indian courts against the arbitration and Dabhol's participation in it. Ultimately, with all income ceased, the Dabhol Power company closed down operations and stopped construction on Phase II of the project, which was then about 95 percent complete.[73]

In the summer of 2001, Enron sought to sell the project to the Indian government, but this initiative failed. By December of the same year, Enron's entire operations were in serious financial difficulty and the company entered bankruptcy in the United States. While pursuing various litigations against the government of India, the state of Maharashtra and the MSEB, the equity investors also filed claims for payment under their political risk insurance policies with the United States Overseas Private Investment Corporation. During that process as a result of negotiations, the bankrupt Enron agreed to drop its US$142 million claim against OPIC and to transfer its full interest in the project to OPIC or its designee in return for a payment of about US$16 million, which represented the equivalent of what Enron had paid OPIC in insurance premiums. Thus, Enron formally left the project in 2002.

Bechtel and General Electric continued to press their claims against OPIC. When OPIC refused payment, they began arbitration against OPIC as provided by their insurance policies. In September 2003, a three-person arbitral panel ruled in favor of the insured investors, awarding them each approximately US$27.5 million.[74] The interests of the private equity investors, as a result of subrogation, now passed into the hands of the United States government. Having made insurance payments of over US$110 million to insured investors in the Dabhol Project, the US government then began negotiation with the government of India for reimbursement as provided by the Investment Incentive Agreement[75] between the government of the United States of America and the government of India governing the operation of the OPIC program of political risk insurance in India. When those talks failed to yield tangible results, the United States, invoking its rights under its agreement with India, filed a request for international interstate arbitration against the Indian government in November 2004,[76] the first and only time that the United States had invoked arbitration against a foreign state to recoup payments made under an OPIC insurance policy. Ultimately, the two countries negotiated a settlement in March 2005. By summer of 2005, the Indian government had settled the remaining claims of Bechtel and GE. Their positions in Dabhol and those of the foreign lenders were transferred to a special purpose vehicle controlled by state-owned Indian banks. As a result, the assets of the Dabhol Power Company, which at one time was the largest foreign investment in India, became completely owned and controlled by the government of India.[77] In July 2005, to revive the project, a special purpose vehicle, Ratnagiri Gas and Power Pvt Limited

---

[73] K Hanson, R O'Sullivan and WG Anderson, "The Dabhol Power Project Settlement—What Happened? Why?" <http://www.infrastructurejournal.com>.

[74] Bechtel Enterprises International (Bermuda) Ltd; BEn Dabhol Holdings, Ltd; and Capital India Power Mauritius I, (Claimants) against Overseas Private Investment Corporation, (Respondent), September 3, 2003, at 29, available at <http://www.opic.gov/sites/default/files/docs/2294171_1.pdf>.

[75] Investment Incentive Agreement, signed on November 19, 1997 and entered into force on April 16, 1998.

[76] *Request for Arbitration Under the Investment Incentive Agreement between the Government of the United States of America and the Government of India 19 November 1997*, November 4, 2004 available <http://www.opic .gov/sites/default/files/docs/GOI110804.pdf>. See also "U.S. Initiates Arbitration Against India Over OPIC Claims for the Dabhol Power Project," 99 *Am J Int'l L* (2005) 271.

[77] K Hanson, R O'Sullivan and WG Anderson, "The Dabhol Power Project Settlement—What Happened? Why?" at 4, available at <http://www.infrastructurejournal.com>. See also, "Looking Beyond the Dabhol Debacle: Examining its Causes and Understanding its Lessons," 41 *Vanderbilt Journal of International Law* (2009) 907.

(RGPPL), was created to take ownership of the former Dabhol power plant. By October of that year, the principal shareholders in the new company were NTPC National Thermal Power Corporation of India (NTPC) and Gas Authority of India Limited (GAIL), each of which held approximately 30 percent of the equity, and the Maharashtra State Electricity Board (MSEB), which owned close to 17 percent of the equity while the remaining 20 percent was owned by various financial institutions. In April 2009, RGPPL was operating the plant at one half its capacity, producing 900 MW of electricity, but by March 2010 it had achieved full operational capacity of 1,940 MW.[78]

(g) The Lessons of Dabhol: Principles to Guide Extra-Contract Project Renegotiations

Since the risk of extra-contract investment renegotiations is always present in any project, international investors planning projects need to ask two basic questions:

1. How can the likelihood of extra-contract renegotiations be reduced?
2. When renegotiations actually occur, how should the parties conduct them to make the process as productive and fair as possible?

In answering these questions, project participants should distinguish actions they may take before and after the transaction has broken down and one party is demanding renegotiation or threatening to reject the deal entirely. Thus, in the case of the Dabhol Project, one needs to consider the actions that Enron might have taken to have avoided the conflict and the renegotiation that actually took place, as well as those it should have taken when faced with the cancellation of the Power Purchase Agreement.

(i) Principles to Follow before Contractual Breakdown

1. Work to Create a Business Relationship between the Parties and Recognize that a Signed Contract Does Not Necessarily Create an International Business Relationship

For a long-term transaction to be stable and productive for both sides, it must be founded on a business relationship, a complex set of interactions characterized by cooperation and a minimal degree of trust. A relationship also implies a connection between the parties. It is the existence of a solid business relationship between the parties to a transaction that allows them to face unforeseen circumstances and hardships in a productive and creative manner. A contract, no matter how detailed and lengthy, does not create a business relationship. Just as a map is not a country, but only an imperfect description thereof, a contract is not a business relationship, but only an imperfect sketch of what the relationship should be. A contract may be a necessary condition for a business relationship in some, but not all, countries; however, it is never a sufficient condition for a business relationship in any country. A business negotiator, while necessarily concerned about contractual provisions, should also be concerned that a solid foundation for a business relationship is in place. Accordingly, a project negotiator should also ask a variety of nonlegal and noncontractual questions during the contracting process: How well do the parties know one another? What mechanisms are in place to foster communications between the two sides after the contract is signed? To what extent

---

[78] "Dabhol Power Project," *Indian Power Sector*, March 25, 2012, available at <http://indianpowersector.com/about/case-study/>.

are there genuine business links and connections between the parties to the project? Is the deal balanced and advantageous for both sides?

One may argue that these issues are management problems or personnel questions, matters that have nothing to do with law or the lawyer's work in negotiating and structuring international transactions. On the other hand, if the lawyer's fundamental task is to help the client establish the best possible basis for an international transaction, not just to draft a contract, then these issues should be of concern from the very start of negotiations. Rather than see his or her basic objective in an international business negotiation as merely securing an advantageous contract for the client, an international lawyer ought also to strive for the goal of negotiating a basis for the client to work productively with a foreign partner and to help the parties find an overriding mutuality of purpose. Throughout project negotiations, international business lawyers must keep asking themselves a basic first question: "After the contract, what?"

In reviewing the Dabhol Project case, one concludes that although a detailed contract governed the project, no real business relationship appears to have existed at all between Enron, on the one hand, and the Maharashtra State Electricity Board and the various concerned Indian government departments, on the other. Specifically, at the time the Power Purchase Agreement was signed, there was no real connection between Enron and India itself. No Indian party was to participate in any meaningful way in the development and management of the Dabhol Power Company. The Indian public had little knowledge of Enron or of the proposed Dabhol Project, which was negotiated largely in secrecy. The only role for any Indian entity was to buy electricity according to the Power Purchase Agreement. The negotiation of the contract had been contentious, and Enron appeared to have little appreciation for the concerns of the Indian public about foreign investment in general and the manner in which the Dabhol Power Project was being negotiated and developed in particular. Finally, given the size and importance of the Dabhol Project, Enron and India seemed to know relatively little about one another. Thus, after nearly eighteen months of negotiation, Enron emerged with a contract but no real business relationship. It had no real connection to any Indian party, and had established no basis for cooperation and trust with Maharashtra State Electricity Board, the Maharashtra State government, or the Indian public. Indeed, the situation was quite the contrary. Before ground had been broken for the project, important segments of the Indian public were either suspicious of, or downright hostile toward, Enron.

Had Enron thought in terms of relationship building, in addition to contract negotiation, and taken actions accordingly, it might have avoided the cancelation of the contract. For example, the involvement of the Maharashtra State Electricity Board as a partner in the project from the very start might have been a crucial first step in building an effective business relationship between Enron and India. Moreover, given India's historical ambivalence toward foreign investment, it was essential that a transaction of the magnitude of the Dabhol Project be, and *appear* to be, balanced and fair to both sides. The Project's high rate of return and high power tariff raised important questions in the minds of the Indian public that Enron should have sought to address.

2. Building a Relationship Takes Time, so Don't Rush Negotiations and Use Negotiation Preliminaries Fully

Project negotiators who wish to lay the foundation for a business relationship as well as to conclude a contract know that sufficient time is required to achieve these goals. In the case of the Dabhol Project, the speed with which Enron and the Maharashtra State

Electricity Board achieved a contract not only did not permit the parties to develop a relationship, but also the project's opponents viewed that speed as a defect in the negotiation process. Opponents and the Indian press criticized the original Enron transaction as having been done in "unseemly haste," and the Maharashtra State government based one of its grounds for canceling the Power Purchase Agreement on flawed "fast track procedures," which had circumvented established practice for developing power projects in the past. In particular, the Cabinet subcommittee pointed to the fact that the Memorandum of Understanding had been signed less than three days after the Enron team's arrival in Bombay.[79]

While speed of negotiation may appeal to American negotiators as "efficient" and a recognition of the fact that "time is money,"[80] for other cultures a quick negotiation of a complicated project transaction may imply overreaching by one of the parties, insufficient consideration of the public interest, or even corruption. Thus negotiations done in haste may be subject to challenge later on.

The difference in view between American and other negotiators concerning desirability of fast negotiations may explain why Asians tend to give more time to negotiation preliminaries, while Americans want to rush through this first phase in deal making. Asians consider negotiation preliminaries, whereby the parties seek to get to know one another thoroughly, a crucial foundation for a good business relationship. For negotiators who are concerned primarily with achieving a contract and are less cognizant of the need to lay a foundation for a relationship, negotiation preliminaries may seem less important when the goal is merely a contract.[81]

As a general rule, North American executives and lawyers want to "dispense with the preliminaries" and "to get down to cases." Consequently, they have a tendency to rush through prenegotiation and to view it as not really important to building a strong deal. Enron clearly followed the typical North American pattern, for it secured a memorandum of understanding on establishing the largest foreign investment project ever undertaken in India just five days after the Enron team had entered the country for the first time.

Asians tend to devote more time and attention to the preliminary phase of deal making than do Americans. Most Asians view the preliminaries as an essential foundation to any business relationship; consequently they recognize the need to conduct them with care before actually making a decision to undertake substantive negotiations of a deal. No Japanese power development firm would have pushed to conclude a memorandum of understanding on a Power Purchase Agreement within five days of arriving in India.

While Enron seems to have taken pride in the speed with which it concluded the memorandum of understanding and the Power Purchase Agreement, one may ask whether a greater investment of time in the negotiation process would have in the end proved cost-effective by avoiding the costs and delays of renegotiation later on.

---

[79] See *Report of the Cabinet Sub-committee to Review the Dabhol Power Project*, n 58.

[80] "Enron's Rebecca Mark: 'You Have To Be Pushy and Aggressive,'" *Bus Week* (February 24, 1997) available at <http://www.businessweek.com/1997/08/b351586.htm>. In a 1997 interview in *Businessweek*, Rebecca Mark, chairman and CEO of Enron International, reflected this attitude with regard to the process leading up to the Dabhol Project:

> We were extremely concerned with time, because time is money for us. People thought we were pushy and aggressive. But think of the massive bureaucracy we had to move. How do you move a bureaucracy that has done things one way its entire collective life? You have to be pushy and aggressive.

[81] See JW Salacuse, "Making Deals in Asia," in *Private Investments Abroad—Problems and Solutions in International Business in 1995*, (1995) at 23–31.

3. Consider Providing for Renegotiation in Appropriate Transactions

If the risk of change and uncertainty is constant in international business, how should deal-makers cope with it? The traditional method is to write detailed contracts that seek to foresee all possible eventualities. Most modern contracts deny the possibility of change. They therefore rarely provide for adjustments to meet changing circumstances. This assumption of contractual stability has proven false time and time again.

As suggested above, rather than to view a long-term transaction as frozen in the detailed provisions of a lengthy contract, it may be more realistic and wiser to think of an international deal as a *continuing negotiation* between the parties to the transactions as they seek to adjust their relationship to the rapidly changing international environment in which they must work together. Accordingly, another approach to the problem of contractual instability is to provide in the contract that at specified times or on the happening of specified events, the parties may renegotiate or at least review certain of the contract's provisions. In this approach, the parties deal with the problem of renegotiation before, rather than after, they sign their contract. Both sides recognize at the outset that the risk of changed circumstances is high in any long-term relationship and that at some time in the future either side may seek to renegotiate or adjust the contract accordingly. Rather than dismiss the possibility of renegotiation and then be forced to review the entire contract at a later time in an atmosphere of hostility between the partners, it may be better to recognize the possibility of renegotiation at the outset and set down a clear framework within which to conduct the process. Although commentators[82] have urged this approach in long-term business relationships, it is rarely used. Perhaps the new era of global finance and business requires a re-examination of renegotiation provisions.

Other than through the use of force majeure clauses, most contracts implicitly deny the possibility of change and therefore make no provision whatsoever to meet changing circumstance. This assumption of contractual stability has proven false time and again. For example, most mineral development agreements assume they will continue unchanged for a period of up to 99 years, yet they rarely remain unmodified for more than a few years.[83] The traditional approach in international business has been to assume and insist on the stability of international agreements and only grudgingly and bitterly agree to renegotiations in the face of changing circumstances.

4. Consider a Role for Mediation or Conciliation in the Deal

A third party can often help the two sides with their negotiations and renegotiations. Third parties, whether called mediators, conciliators, advisers, or something else, can assist in building and preserving business relations and in resolving disputes without resorting to arbitration or adjudication. Consequently, persons planning and negotiating international business and financial transactions should consider the possibility of building into their deals a role for some form of mediation. For example, the contract might provide that before either party can invoke arbitration to settle their dispute, they must use the services of a mediator or conciliator in trying to negotiate a settlement of their conflict.

---

[82] See, eg, Stoever, n 31, at 27.
[83] See DN Smith and LT Wells, *Negotiating Third-World Mineral Agreements* (1975) 18.

(ii) Renegotiation Principles after Contractual Breakdown

When one side has demanded renegotiation of the basic contract governing their relationship, how should one or both of the parties proceed? The following are a few principles to
consider.

1. Hostile, Belligerent, or Moralistic Responses to Demands for Renegotiation are Generally Ineffective

Demands for renegotiation of the contract by one party to a project contract are often met
with hostility, belligerency, or moralistic objections by the other side. Such arguments are
hardly ever effective in persuading the other side to end its insistence on renegotiation. The
party asking for renegotiation almost always is able to assert equally moralistic arguments
justifying the need to renegotiate the contract. Like the Maharashtra State government, a
party resisting a contract will usually offer a variety of legal and moral arguments for its
action: the contract is exploitative, the negotiators were corrupt, one side used duress, the
other side was ignorant of all the underlying factors, and the basic circumstances of the deal
have changed in a fundamental way.

While respect for agreements is indeed a norm in virtually all societies and may even
rise to the level of a universal principle of law, most cultures also provide relief, in varying
degrees, from the binding force of a contract in a variety of circumstances. "A deal is a
deal" (*pacta sunt servanda*) is certainly an expression of a fundamental rule of human
relations, but so is the statement "things have changed" (*rebus sic stantibus*). While a
request for extra-contract renegotiations may provoke bad feelings in one party, an
outright refusal to renegotiate may also create ill will on the other side since it will be
seen as an attempt to force adherence to a bargain that has become unreasonable. Thus,
throughout the crisis provoked by the Maharashtra State government's cancelation of the
Power Purchase Agreement, Enron consistently and quite wisely made known its willingness to renegotiate the Power Purchase Agreement, a posture that ultimately led to a
satisfactory resolution of the conflict. While it did begin to pursue its legal remedy in
arbitration immediately, it did not become belligerent or hostile toward the Maharashtra
government.[84]

2. It is Important to Understand the Basis of the Other Side's Demand for Renegotiation.

How can renegotiation be justified in the face of a detailed contract that contains no specific
provision authorizing it? One may argue that in many transactions, particularly between
parties from different cultures, there are in effect two agreements, the legal contract that
sets out enforceable rights and duties and their "foundation relationship" that reflects their
fundamental understanding in all its dimensions, legal and non-legal. An important,
implied aspect of this relationship is an understanding, given the impossibility of predicting
all future contingencies, that if problems develop in the future the two sides will engage in
negotiations to maximize the joint gains in their relationship. At the same time, the legal
contract grants the parties the right to invoke certain enforcement mechanisms, such as
litigation or arbitration, if specified legal obligations have not been performed by the other
side. The aggrieved party will only pursue them fully, however, if it judges the benefits of a
legal remedy to be greater than its costs, one of which is the loss of any relationship with the
other side. But a party usually cannot accurately make that calculation unless it has engaged

---

[84] See Teisch and Stoever, n 52, at 62.

in some form of renegotiation first. One can argue that one of the purposes of the delays inherent in pursuing legal remedies, such as a lawsuit or arbitration, is to give the parties an opportunity to negotiate an efficient solution to their conflict.[85] Thus, although Enron began arbitration in London immediately after the Maharashtra government's cancelation of the power purchase agreement, it also immediately communicated to the government its willingness to renegotiate. The delay inherent in the arbitration process allowed the renegotiation to take place, and Enron eventually abandoned its arbitration because it judged the value of the renegotiated agreement to be worth much more than any damages it might receive in arbitration.

3. Evaluate the Worth of the Claim for Breach of Contract against the Value of a Continuing Relationship with the Other Side

The extent of a party's willingness to renegotiate a project agreement will usually be in direct proportion to the value it attaches to its potential future relationship with the other side, particularly if it judges the potential relationship with the other side to be worth more than the claim for breach of contract. For example, one of the factors that encouraged Enron to renegotiate with the Maharashtra government after it had canceled the contract was the prospect of long-term relationships in India involving many energy projects in the future. Enron clearly evaluated that relationship to be worth much more than winning an arbitral award in a case that would certainly be a long protracted struggle. Even if it won an award for US$300 million, that victory would not only drastically reduce its business prospects in the economically important state of Maharashtra but probably in all of India as well.

4. Look for Ways to Create Value in the Renegotiation

Because of differences in culture or personality, or both, persons appear to approach deal making with one of two basic attitudes: that a negotiation is either a process in which both can gain (win/win) or a struggle in which, of necessity, one side wins and the other side loses (win/lose). Win/win negotiators see deal making as a collaborative and problem-solving process; win/lose negotiators see it as confrontational. In a reflection of this dichotomy, negotiation scholars have concluded that these approaches represented two basic paradigms of the negotiation process: (1) distributive bargaining (ie, win/lose) and (2) integrative bargaining or problem solving (ie, win-win).[86] In the former situation, the parties see their goals as incompatible, while in the latter they consider themselves to have compatible goals.

In an extra-contract renegotiation, the general tendency of the party who feels it has been forced into renegotiation is to fight a rear guard action, to raise recriminations, to see the process as the worst kind of win/lose activity in which anything gained by the one side is an automatic loss to the other party. The challenge for both sides in a renegotiation is to create a win/win process, an atmosphere of problem solving, joint gains negotiation. Even if a party feels forced into an extra-contract renegotiation, it should approach the process as an opportunity to create value, to make the pie bigger. Thus in the renegotiations between Enron and the Maharashtra State government over the Dabhol Project, while Maharashtra

---

[85] See Tracht, n 5, at 622 (arguing that a well-crafted security arrangement should encourage lender and borrower to renegotiate their loan if renegotiation is efficient).

[86] See, eg, R Lewicki et al, *Negotiation—Readings, Exercises and Cases* (1993); T Hoppman, "Two Paradigms of Negotiation: Bargaining and Problem Solving," 542 *Annals Am Acad Pol & Soc Sci* (1995) 24–47; JW Salacuse, *The Global Negotiator: Making, Managing and Mending Deals Around the World in the Twenty-first Century* (2003) 7–16.

State gained a reduced power tariff and project that was no longer exclusively foreign, Enron secured certain additional benefits including a large power plant, increased capital from a new joint venture partnership, and an influential local partner who now had an interest in the success of the project.

5. The Parties should Fully Understand the Alternatives to Succeeding in the Renegotiation—Especially their Costs

Negotiation scholars[87] have identified the importance of each side understanding its Best Alternative to a Negotiated Agreement ("BATNA") and of estimating the other side's BATNA. Recognizing the costs and benefits of a BATNA, for example, pursuing a claim in arbitration or being sued in a court, may encourage both sides to work harder at resolving their problems at the negotiating table. In the case of the Dabhol Project, at the time the Maharashtra government canceled the Power Purchase Agreement, it probably assumed that its action would entail relatively little cost. Moreover, it seemed to have assumed that other investors would be willing to step into the shoes vacated by Enron or that it would be able to find indigenous means of solving India's power shortage. When it fully understood that its alternatives to dealing with Enron were potentially very costly, it looked more favorably on renegotiation than it had at the time it canceled the contract as a result of the Cabinet subcommittee's report. Once it fully understood the costs that it might entail in an international commercial arbitration and the difficulty it would encounter in attracting other investors, it became considerably more open to agreeing to renegotiation and to arriving at a satisfactory conclusion to the conflict.

6. Make Sure All Necessary Parties in the Renegotiation are Involved Either Directly or Indirectly

In any renegotiation, a variety of parties may need to be involved, either directly or indirectly, even though they are not themselves insisting on a renegotiation. It is therefore important to determine who those parties are and how they should be connected to the renegotiation process. For example in the Enron–Maharashtra renegotiation, the Indian central government was such a party since it had counter-guaranteed the Maharashtra government's payments under a Power Purchase Agreement and would have to approve the terms of any renegotiated contract. Whether such parties should be at the negotiating table is another question. It may be preferable to conduct discussions with them separately.

7. The Right Process for the Renegotiation is Important

It is important for both sides to think hard about the appropriate process for launching and conducting extra-contract renegotiations. Renegotiations often emerge out of crisis characterized by severe conflict among the parties, threats, and high emotion. An appropriate process for the renegotiation may help to mollify the parties and reduce the negative consequences of the crisis on their subsequent discussions. An inappropriate process, on the other hand, may serve to heighten those negative consequences and impede the renegotiations. Thus in the case of the Dabhol Project, the government of the State of Maharashtra, having repudiated the original contract while declaring that renegotiations were out of the question, needed to find a process later on that would allow renegotiations to take place while preserving its dignity and prestige. The use of a committee of experts, rather than face-to-face renegotiations between the government and Enron to start the

---

[87] See Fisher et al, n 1.

process, served this purpose. The committee, in effect, conducted the renegotiations, which the government had the discretion to approve or disapprove. Moreover, its status as a committee of independent experts, rather than of politicians, tended to give its recommendations the legitimacy needed to persuade the public that Indian interests had been protected.

In some cases, the way in which a renegotiation is framed may influence its success. For example, rather than use the label "renegotiation," a term that conjures up negative implications of fundamental changes in the sanctity of contract, the parties in some cases can cast the renegotiation as an effort to clarify ambiguities in the existing agreement, rather than to change basic principles. This approach, at least formally, respects the sanctity of contract and thereby may avoid some of the friction and hostility engendered by demanding outright extra-contract renegotiations. For example, a host country government finding that a foreign investment project exempted from "all taxes and duties" is placing increasing demands on public services may seek to require the project to pay "user fees" for certain governmental services on the grounds that they are not taxes or duties. Another approach is to request "review" or "reinterpretation" of key terms in the contract in light of changes in circumstances, while still preserving the principles in the original agreement. For example, even if the host government had specifically agreed that the investment project would be exempt from user fees, requiring it to pay additional costs incurred by the government to supply power to the project during an energy crisis might be a principled way for redefining the scope of the exemption without altering the fundamental principles agreed by the parties. Waiver is yet another way of framing a renegotiation, an approach that respects the sanctity of the agreement yet enables the burdened party to obtain the relief it seeks. For example, during the energy crisis mentioned above, the government might seek a temporary waiver of certain of its obligations until the crisis ends.

8. Consider a Role for a Mediator in the Renegotiation Process

Mediation is basically a "voluntary, non-binding process in which a third person tries to help the parties reach a negotiated settlement."[88] Although mediators are not used frequently in resolving international investment disputes, they may play a useful role in assisting the parties to achieve agreement during a renegotiation. A mediator can help in any or all of the following three functions: (1) helping design and manage the renegotiation process so that the parties will have the maximum opportunities to create value through their interaction, (2) assisting with the communications between the two sides in a way that will facilitate positive results from their renegotiation, and (3) suggesting substantive solutions to the problems that the parties are encountering during the course of their extra-contract renegotiation.

12.7 Conclusion

Renegotiation, whether post-contract, intra-contract, or extra-contract, is a constant fact of life in international investment. As a result, investors, project developers, financing institutions, and their lawyers need to understand this phenomenon and devise strategies and mechanisms to deal with it productively. For many persons, renegotiation is an aberration and a somewhat disreputable practice. It provokes images of disappointed expectations, of

---

[88] See J Bercovitch and JZ Rubin, *Mediation in International Relations: Multiple Approaches to Conflict Management* (1992) 7 (offering similar, but more elaborate, definition of mediation); JW Salacuse, *The Global Negotiator: Making, Managing and Mending Deals around the World in the Twenty-first Century* (2003) 257–66.

broken promises, of bargains made but not kept. For others, particularly governments, it is a necessity and a means of fostering the public interest. But from the vantage of international investment life in general, renegotiation can be seen as playing a constructive and facilitating role. In 1931, the American legal scholar Karl Llewellyn made a thoughtful inquiry into the role of contract in the social order and concluded: "One turns from the contemplation of the work of contract as from the experience of a Greek tragedy. Life struggling against form."[89] In the realm of modern international investment, the struggle of life against form continues. The case of the Dabhol Power Project was essentially a struggle between the political life of India and the form of the Power Purchase Agreement. As that case demonstrates, the role of renegotiation in the social order of international investment is to mediate the struggle between life and form, to allow life and form to adjust to one another over the long term at the least cost.

---

[89] KN Llewellyn, "What Price Contract? An Essay in Perspective," 40 *Yale L J* (1931) 704, 751.

PART IV

THE INTERNATIONAL
LEGAL FRAMEWORK

13

The Foundations of the International Legal Framework for Investment

13.1 In General

The international legal framework for investment is built on international law. Whereas the national legal framework for investment is the product of legislative and regulatory action by individual states and whereas the contractual framework results from negotiations between states and investors, as well as among investors, the international legal framework has grown through agreements and other practices that states have made with one another.

International law has traditionally been conceived as the law governing relations among states.[1] Strictly speaking, in former times, international law did not apply to individuals and private organizations. In the contemporary era, however, international law has given a growing role to non-state actors. One authoritative definition provides: "International law ... consists of the rules and principles of general application dealing with the conduct of states and of international organizations and with their relations *inter se*, as well as with some of their relations with persons, whether natural or juridical."[2] As will be seen, international investment law in particular is an area of international law that has given an increasing role to legal and physical persons. Since states are obligated to follow international law, its importance in the domain of international investment resides in the fact that it is potentially a mechanism to limit the exercise of state sovereignty and governmental actions affecting investors and their assets.

The world is organized on the basis of sovereign and equal states. It has no supranational legislature or court with authority to make rules to govern states. As a result, the rules of international law are those that have been accepted as such by states themselves. Where is one to find those rules? What are the sources of international law?

The most generally accepted statement of the sources of international law is found in Article 38(1) of the Statute of the International Court of Justice, which provides:

1. The Court, whose function is to decide in accordance with international law such disputes as are submitted to it, shall apply:
    a. international conventions, whether general or particular, establishing rules expressly recognized by the contesting states;
    b. international custom, as evidence of a general practice accepted as law;
    c. the general principles of law recognized by civilized nations;
    d. subject to the provisions of Article 59, judicial decisions and the teachings of the most highly qualified publicists of the various nations, as subsidiary means for the determination of rules of law.[3]

---

[1] "International law governs relations between independent States. The rules of law binding upon States therefore emanate from their own free will as expressed in conventions or by usages generally accepted as expressing principles of law and established in order to regulate relations between these co-existing independent communities or with a view to the achievement of common aims." *The Case of the S.S. Lotus (France v. Turkey)* (1927) PCIJ Series A No 10; 2 Hudson, World Ct Rep 20.

[2] The American Law Institute, *Restatement of the Law, The Foreign Relations Law of the United States* (3rd edn 1987) vol 1, § 101 at 22.

[3] Statute of the International Court of Justice (June 26, 1945) 33 UNTS 993; 59 Stat 1055 Article 38(1).

According to this provision, there are three fundamental sources of international law: (1) international conventions; (2) international custom; and (3) general principles of law recognized by states. Judicial decisions and the writing of legal scholars are not in themselves autonomous sources of international law. They are supplemental or secondary sources which are used by courts, tribunals, governments, and others to establish what a specific rule of international law is.[4] Since these three sources constitute the foundations of international investment law, let us examine each briefly.

13.2 International Conventions

International conventions are binding agreements between or among states. International conventions have a variety of designations: treaty, agreement, protocol, pact, convention, and covenant, among others. Thus, in the field of investment law, important international sources of law include the North American Free Trade *Agreement*,[5] the Energy Charter *Treaty*,[6] and the *Convention* on the Settlement of Investment Disputes between States and Nationals of Other States.[7] Despite their differences in name, each of these three documents has the same binding effect on the states that have consented to them. The particular name given to an international agreement has no consequence as to its legal force or the binding effect it has on its parties.[8]

The basic international law governing treaties and their interpretation and application is the Vienna Convention on the Law of Treaties.[9] Like contracts, treaties bind only the state parties who have consented to them. If a state's internal law is inconsistent with its obligations under the treaty, that state may not invoke that internal law as a justification for not performing its obligations under the treaty.[10] Thus, for example, if a state has entered into a treaty in which it promises not to expropriate property without payment of full compensation, the existence of a domestic law that authorizes the taking of property without compensation does not excuse failure to live up to its treaty obligations. On the other hand, states that are not signatories to an international agreement or treaty are usually not bound by its terms. But, if a treaty gains wide enough acceptance among states, it will be deemed to constitute international customary law and will have binding effect even on nonsignatories.[11]

Article 38 of the Statute of the International Court of Justice places international conventions first in its listing of the sources of international law, but it does not specifically state that they will have precedence over the other two sources, that is, customary international law and general principles of law.[12] It is generally agreed that should a custom

---

[4] I Brownlie, *The Principles of Public International Law* (6th edn 2003) 19, 23.

[5] North American Free Trade Agreement (signed December 17, 1992) (1993) 32 *ILM* 289, 605 (NAFTA).

[6] Energy Charter Treaty (December 17, 1994) (1995) 34 *ILM* 360 (ECT).

[7] ICSID Convention (March 18, 1965) 17 UST 1270, TIAS 6090, 575 UNTS 159.

[8] Brownlie (n 4) 23; A Aust, *Modern Treaty Law and Practice* (2000) 15.

[9] Vienna Convention on the Law of Treaties (opened for signature May 23, 1969) 1155 UNTS 331; UN Doc A/ Conf.39/27; 8 ILM 679 (1969); 63 *AJIL* 875 (1969) (Vienna Convention).

[10] Vienna Convention, Article 27; Aust (n 8) 144.

[11] AD McNair, *Law of Treaties* (1961) 5, 124, 749–52; RR Baxter, "Treaties and Custom" 129 *Recueil des Cours* (1970-I) 25, 101; RR Baxter, "Multilateral Treaties as Evidence of Customary International Law" (1965–6) 41 *BYIL* 275.

[12] Brownlie notes that: "[Article 38] itself does not refer to 'sources' and, if looked at closely, cannot be regarded as a straightforward enumeration of the sources. They are not stated to represent a hierarchy, but the draftsmen intended to give an order and in one draft the word 'successively' appeared. In practice the Court may be expected to observe the order in which they appear: (a) and (b) are obviously the important sources, and the priority of (a) is explicable by the fact that this refers to a source of mutual obligation of the parties." Brownlie (n 4) 5. Lauterpacht has a similar view: "The rights and duties of States are determined in the first instance, by their agreement as

of international law conflict with a treaty provision, the treaty provision will prevail unless the custom is determined to fall under Article 53 of the Vienna Convention on the Law of Treaties, which describes "peremptory norm[s] of general international law," sometimes referred to as *jus cogens*. A peremptory norm of international law is one that is "accepted and recognized by the international community of States as a whole as a norm from which no derogation is permitted and which can be modified only by a subsequent norm of general international law having the same character."[13]

Just as national legislation and regulation have increasingly supplanted custom and common law to become the legal foundation of domestic economies, international treaties have increasingly become the foundation for international economic relations. As will be seen, this shift has been particularly clear in the area of international investment, and the reasons for it will be explained in more detail in the following chapter. At the same time, the existence of a treaty does not mean that the other sources of international law, namely custom and general principles of law, are not relevant or applicable. Often treaties incorporate concepts whose full meaning cannot be understood without reference to customary international law. Moreover, treaties may specifically declare that the other sources of international law are to supplement the treaty if its provisions are silent about a particular issue or problem. Thus, for example, if an investment treaty declares that an investor is to be given "full protection in accordance with international law," an arbitration tribunal would have to refer to customary international law to determine the extent of protection provided.[14]

13.3 International Custom

International custom is a second source of international law under Article 38 of the Statute of the International Court of Justice. International custom is defined simply as "a general practice accepted as law." Thus, a customary rule of international law must meet two criteria: (1) it must be a general practice of states, and (2) states must engage in that practice out of a sense of a legal obligation.[15] With respect to the first criteria, the practice of states is the actions states undertake to carry out government business. Such actions can include policy pronouncements, statements at international conferences, diplomatic communications and correspondence with other states, national legislation, decisions of domestic courts, and other actions taken by governments in respect of international matters.[16] To satisfy this first criterion, the practice, according to the International Court of Justice, must be "both extensive and virtually uniform."[17] The practice need not be particularly long-

---

expressed in treaties—just as the case of individuals their rights are specifically determined by any contract which is binding upon them. When a controversy arises between two or more States with regard to a matter regulated by a treaty, it is natural that the parties should invoke and the adjudicating agency should apply, in the first instance, the provisions of the treaty in question." H Lauterpacht, *International Law: Collected Papers* (1970) 86–7.

[13] Vienna Convention (n 9) Article 53.

[14] For example, Article 1131 of the North American Free Trade Agreement (NAFTA) empowers the NAFTA Free Trade Commission to make authoritative interpretations of NAFTA provisions that are binding on investment arbitration tribunals. In the exercise of that power, the Commission issued an interpretation holding that Article 1105(1) of NAFTA "prescribes the customary international law minimum standard of treatment of aliens as the minimum standard of treatment to be afforded investments of investors of another Party" and that "the concepts of 'fair and equitable treatment' and 'full protection and security' do not require treatment in addition to or beyond that which is required by the customary international law minimum standard of treatment of aliens." NAFTA Free Trade Commission, "NAFTA Commission Notes of Interpretation of Certain Chapter 11 Provisions" (2001) available at <http://www.dfait-maeci.gc.ca/tna-nac/NAFTA-Interpr-en.asp>.

[15] The American Law Institute (n 2) vol 1, § 102(2) at 24.

[16] The American Law Institute, § 102, comment b, at 25. See also Brownlie (n 4) 6.

[17] *North Sea Continental Shelf (FRG v. Den; FRG v. Neth)* [1969] ICJ Rep 3, 43.

standing to be a custom, for as the Court has also stated, "the passage of only a short period of time is not necessarily, or of itself, a bar to the formation of a new rule of customary international law."[18]

Just because states act in a particular way does not mean that such actions automatically constitute customary international law. States must act in a particular way out of a sense of legal obligation. This is the second requirement under Article 38, the requirement of *opinio juris sive necessitatis*, that state practice should "occur... in such a way as to show a general recognition that a rule of legal obligation is involved."[19]

These two requirements for international customary law can make it difficult to establish a particular rule of customary law even under the best of conditions. Where there is significant disagreement among states or significant differences in practice, the determination of a rule of customary international law may be next to impossible. As will be seen, the field of international investment law has generated significant disagreement among nations as to the nature and content of applicable customary international rules. As a result, in many forums the very existence of customary international investment law has been questioned, if not challenged outright, over the years.

13.4 General Principles of Law

The third and final source of international law is the "general principles of law recognized by civilized nations."[20] This source of law refers to the legal principles that are common to the world's major legal systems.[21] These "general principles" are often seen as a source to help fill in gaps where no applicable treaty provision or international custom exists. While certain general principles, such as *pacta sunt servanda*, have emerged to become custom, tribunals will generally be hesitant to find such a general principle, unless it is clear there is broad acceptance in the world's legal systems.[22]

13.5 Customary International Law and General Principles of Law Governing Investment

(a) Introduction

Two fundamental questions arise with respect to the customary international obligations of states toward foreign investors: (1) What standard of treatment do host states owe to foreign persons with respect to making investments in host state territory? and (2) What standard of treatment do host states owe to foreign persons and their assets once such foreign persons have made investments in host state territory?

The answer to the first question is clear. As was discussed in Chapter 5, it is well settled in international law that a state has the right to control the movement of capital into its territory, to regulate all matters pertaining to the acquisition and transfer of property

---

[18] *North Sea Continental Shelf.*
[19] *North Sea Continental Shelf.*
[20] On their status as a source of law, Brownlie observes that they are "a source which comes after those depending more immediately on the consent of states and yet escapes classification as a 'subsidiary means'." Brownlie (n 4) 15.
[21] O Schachter distinguishes five categories of general principles that have been invoked and applied in international law discourse and cases. O Schachter, *International Law in Theory and Practice* (1991) 50. Brownlie notes: "the view expressed in Oppenheim is to be preferred: 'The intention is to authorize the Court to apply the general principles of municipal jurisprudence, in particular of private law, in so far as they are applicable to relations of States.'" Brownlie (n 4) 16.
[22] Schachter (n 21) 50–5.

within its national boundaries, to determine the conditions for the exercise of economic activity by natural or legal persons, and to control the entry and activities of aliens.[23] Thus, unless there is a specific treaty to the contrary, a home state may prevent or impose conditions on the exit of capital from its territory for purposes of foreign investment, and a host state may prohibit or impose conditions on the movement of that capital into its territory. Customary international law does not grant investors rights to move their capital from one country to another. In short, an investor does not have a right under customary international law to make an international investment or even to engage in the international movement of capital.

The answer to the second question—the treatment owed by states toward foreign investment made in their territory—has been far less clear. Indeed, this area of international law has for many years been fraught with disagreement among states, particularly between developed, capital-exporting states, on the one hand, and developing, capital-importing states, on the other. Doctrines and rules that seemed settled in earlier times, particularly during the era of colonialism, have been challenged as the territories formerly under colonial rule emerged as fully independent and sovereign states after the end of World War II. In that earlier era, the effort to develop principles of customary international law respecting the rights of investors abroad evolved out of the law of state responsibility for injury to aliens and alien property.[24] The basic questions asked by this area of international law are: (1) What is the legal standard that states must respect in their treatment of aliens living and working in their territories? (2) What means are available for aliens and their home governments to ensure that host countries live up to those standards? (3) How specifically do those standards and means of enforcement apply to investment activities of aliens in host countries? We consider each of these questions in turn.

(b) Standard of Treatment Owed to Aliens by Host States

A fundamental, recurring issue in international law and international relations is: What is the standard of treatment that a host country government owes to aliens residing and working in its territory? One possible answer is that a host government need not treat aliens any better than its own nationals. This view incorporates the *principle of equality*. It draws its justification from the fact that as a sovereign state in the international system a host country is not subject to any legislative authority other than its own. Moreover, a foreigner who voluntarily takes up residence in a host country must accept that he or she is subject to host country law and is assumed to understand the risks that such a situation entails. In a famous exchange of correspondence between US Secretary of State Cordell Hull and Mexican Foreign Minister Eduardo Hay in 1938 concerning the expropriation of agricultural land in Mexico that was owned by US citizens but that equally affected Mexican owners, the Mexican Foreign Minister argued the principle of equality quite forcefully: "the foreigner who voluntarily moves to a country which is not his own, in search of a personal benefit, accepts in advance, together with the advantages he is going to enjoy, the risks to which he may find himself exposed. It would be unjust that he should aspire to a privileged position."[25]

---

[23] See section 5.2 of Chapter 5. See also A Fatouros, *Government Guarantees to Foreign Investors* (1962) 40–1.
[24] See generally R Lillich, *The International Law of State Responsibility for Injuries to Aliens* (1983).
[25] "Official Documents" (1938) 32 *AJIL Supp* 181, 188.

An opposing view, which evolved in the nineteenth century among European countries and the United States, was that a host state has an obligation under international law to observe *an international minimum standard* of treatment toward foreign persons and their property regardless of the host state's domestic legislation and practices. This doctrine takes into account the possibility that the standards prevailing in a given state may be so low that, even if nationals and aliens are treated alike, the norms of international law may be violated. Thus, in the exchange of correspondence noted above, US Secretary of State Hull opposed the position of the Mexican Foreign Minister, asserting that "when aliens are admitted into a country the country is obligated to accord them that degree of protection of life and property consistent with the standards of justice recognized by the law of nations"[26] and that the confiscation of American property could not be excused by the "inapplicable doctrine of equality."[27] The American Law Institute, a leading body of US legal scholars, made the following authoritative statement of the minimum international standard:

> The prevailing rule [is] that such national treatment is not always sufficient, and that there is an international standard of justice that a state must observe in the treatment of aliens, even if the state does not observe it in the treatment of its own nationals, and even if the standard is inconsistent with its own law.[28]

With respect to the treatment of aliens, including foreign investors, by host states, there is thus a fundamental tension between the equality principle and the minimum international standard principle. This tension has in varying degrees pervaded the evolution and content of international investment law over the years. While the partisans of each view often justify their positions by reference to abstract notions of justice, the fundamental interests of nations have also shaped the debate and influenced positions on the question. Countries that had expanding foreign economic interests have quite naturally sought to protect those interests by advancing the principle of a minimum international standard of protection. Countries that had few foreign interests and saw themselves as the target of other countries' expansionist activities quite naturally asserted the equality principle as a means to protect themselves and to assure their full sovereignty over foreign economic actors in their territory.

During the nineteenth and first half of the twentieth century, with the expansion of western economic powers, the spread of European colonialism and American influence in Latin America and Asia, the principle of a minimum international standard became dominant, at least among western states. Despite this affirmation of a minimum standard of international law, legal scholars and government officials in the countries subject to the intervention of European and American influence continued to assert that customary international law did not recognize such a standard. Probably the most important formulation of this position was that of the Argentine jurist and foreign minister Carlos Calvo (1824–1906), whose "Calvo doctrine" was adopted throughout Latin America at a time when many countries felt threatened by US domination. Calvo argued that a sovereign independent state was entitled by reason of the principle of sovereign equality to complete freedom from interference in any form, whether by diplomacy or by force, by other states. Therefore, according to the Calvo doctrine, when an alien suffers an alleged injury his only remedies are local ones. Absent a denial of justice, which Calvo defined narrowly, diplomatic protection is unavailable to an injured alien. Calvo argued that aliens and nationals

---

[26] "Official Documents" (1938) 32 *AJIL Supp* 198.   [27] "Official Documents" 198.
[28] The American Law Institute, *Restatement (Second) of Foreign Relations Law* (1965) § 165, comment (a), at 502.

are entitled in principle to equal treatment, but once equality of treatment is granted, the host State has fulfilled its obligations regardless of whether the alien or his State is dissatisfied with the treatment received. Thus, Latin America's response to the international minimum standard was the doctrine of national treatment.[29] European governments, the United States, and many international forums and tribunals tended to dismiss this approach as not representing customary international law. Nevertheless, as will be seen later in this chapter, individual Latin American countries took significant measures to implement the Calvo doctrine through the inclusion of "Calvo clauses" in their constitutions, legislation, and contracts with foreign companies.

(c) The Application and Enforcement of a Minimum Standard

The debate between the minimum international standard and national treatment principles was by no means a purely theoretical one. It had its application in diplomatic relations between nations and in various forums of international adjudication in the nineteenth and twentieth centuries.

Investors, for example, had little effective means to press claims directly against offending host governments based on the international minimum standard of treatment. Customary international law did not give individuals or companies the right to press such claims directly against an offending host government, nor did it provide them with any other enforcement mechanism. Rather, investors had to rely on their home governments to give them "diplomatic protection."

The interest of investor home governments in protecting their nationals abroad was not just to satisfy powerful domestic constituencies but also to advance important economic and political interests abroad. Their investors were one means of achieving that goal. Aliens have always been subject to discrimination and abuse in foreign countries. What right under international law did their home governments have to protect them? Drawing on the work of the eighteenth century Swiss philosopher, diplomat, and jurist Emerich de Vattell (1714–1767), who declared "[w]hoever ill-treats a citizen injures the state, which must protect that citizen,"[30] countries developed the concept of diplomatic protection of aliens. Thus, under international law a host country that injured an alien was simultaneously injuring the state of that national and that state therefore had the right to protect itself from such injurious acts.[31]

Home country governments therefore took the position that international law gave them a right to pursue claims against foreign countries that illegally injured their nationals. The violation of the minimum standard of treatment was considered to be such an injury under international law and, provided that the alien had exhausted local remedies, could give rise to international action on behalf of the injured alien by his home state. The doctrine of diplomatic protection, in turn, provided a procedural vehicle for a home state to seek redress in cases where a foreign state allegedly violated the international minimum

---

[29] R Lillich, *The Human Rights of Aliens in Contemporary International Law* (1984) 16–17; SKB Asante, "International Law and Investments," in M Bedjaoui (ed), *International Law: Achievements and Prospects* (1991) 670. I Brownlie observes that "legal doctrine has opposed an 'international minimum standard', a 'moral standard for civilized States', to the principle of national treatment." Brownlie (n 4) 502. The most complete exposition of the Calvo doctrine by the jurist himself is C Calvo, *Le Droit international théorique et pratique* (5th edn 1896) vols 1–6. See also A Freeman, "Recent Aspects of the Calvo Doctrine and the Challenge to International Law," 40 *AJIL* (1946) 121.

[30] E de Vattel, *The Law of Nations*, trans C Fenwick (1919) Book II, Ch 6 at 136.

[31] RB Lillich, "The Current Status of the Law of State Responsibility for Injuries to Aliens," in Lillich (n 24) 1.

standard in its treatment of home country nationals.[32] During the nineteenth and early twentieth centuries, in the era of "gunboat diplomacy," states sometimes also sought redress through military interventions when nationals suffered injuries in foreign countries.[33] In most cases, however, they used diplomatic or international judicial means to press their claims. The legal basis for such actions was explained by the Permanent Court of International Justice in the *Mavromatis* case:

> It is an elementary principle of international law that a State is entitled to protect its subjects, when injured by acts contrary to international law committed by another State, from whom they have been unable to obtain satisfaction through the ordinary channels. By taking up the case of one of its subjects and by resorting to diplomatic action or international judicial proceedings on his behalf, a State is in reality asserting its own rights—its right to ensure, in the person of its subjects, respect for the rules of international law.... Once a State has taken up the case on behalf of one of its subjects before an international tribunal, in the eyes of the latter the State is sole claimant.[34]

The concept of "diplomatic protection of aliens" by their home states did not receive universal acclaim. As one might imagine, certain states, notably those in Latin America, viewed the concept as another tool by which the United States and European powers could undermine their national sovereignty. As noted earlier in this chapter, the Calvo doctrine represented an opposing view, holding that in pressing a claim against a host government a foreigner had no right to seek the diplomatic protection of its government and that customary international law did not allow a home country to extend diplomatic protection to its nationals living and working in another sovereign state.[35] Governments of injured aliens nonetheless sought redress through diplomatic representations for injuries suffered by their nationals in host countries. A famous example of such a representation was the exchange of diplomatic correspondence, referred to earlier in this chapter, between Mexico and the United States concerning the expropriation of agricultural land owned by Americans in Mexico.

During the nineteenth and twentieth centuries, various international tribunals applied the minimum international standard to protect aliens in foreign countries and to recognize the right of home countries to extend diplomatic protection to their nationals injured abroad. For example, in 1926 the Permanent Court of International Justice in the *Chorzów* case recognized "the limits set by generally accepted principles of international law" regarding the treatment of aliens and stated that "the only measures prohibited are those which generally accepted international law does not sanction in respect of foreigners."[36]

A number of arbitral awards also recognized the duty of a state to conform to international standards of justice even when there may be a conflict with domestic law, and imposed obligations on the offending state to pay damages. It should be noted, however, that for a tribunal to have jurisdiction in any case the offending state had to agree to submit

---

[32] "In precise language, diplomatic protection can be defined as a procedure for giving effect to State responsibility involving breaches of international law arising out of legal injuries to the person or property of the citizen of a State. With the expansion of economic and commercial intercourse between nations, diplomatic protection evolved into a rule of customary international law." J Cuthbert, *Nationality and Diplomatic Protection* (1969) 1.

[33] Lillich (n 31) 14–15, 24.

[34] *Case Concerning Mavromatis Palestine Concessions* (1924) PCIJ Series A No 2 p 2. See also A Bagge, "Intervention on the Ground of Damage Caused to Nationals, with Particular Reference to Exhaustion of Local Remedies and the Rights of Shareholders" *BYIL* (1958) 162.

[35] Lillich (n 31) 2–6; R Lillich, *The Human Rights of Aliens* (1984) 16–17.

[36] The American Law Institute, *Restatement of the Law, The Foreign Relations Law of the United States* (1965) § 165, reporters' note 1, at 505, citing the *Case Concerning Certain German Interests in Polish Upper Silesia* (1926) PCIJ Rep Series A No 7 at 22.

to its jurisdiction. For example, in the *Hopkins* case before the United States–Mexico General Claims Commission of 1923 the tribunal concluded that under the minimum international standard " ... a nation is required to accord aliens broader and more liberal treatment than it accords to its own citizens under municipal laws."[37] Other claim cases reached similar conclusions, finding that the test, broadly speaking, is whether aliens are treated in accordance with "the ordinary standards of civilization"[38] and whether "[t]he international minimum standard has been extended to cover the instances of discrimination against aliens, denial of justice and injuries to aliens' economic interests (eg, expropriation)'.[39]

Despite the pronouncements of diplomats and international tribunals, foreign investors considered diplomatic protection to be far from a complete protection for their property and activities in host countries. For one thing, the existence of diplomatic protection depended entirely on the willingness of the investor's home country to extend it in any given situation. Home country governments were not then, and are not now, required to take up or "espouse" a claim against an offending host state, no matter how egregious its conduct might have been. The decision to take up a claim or not, and to pursue it with vigour or not, is completely within the discretion of the home government.

Second, once the home country government has espoused the claim, it effectively "owns" it. It controls how the claim will be made, what settlement if any to accept, and whether any portion of that settlement should be paid to its aggrieved national. Thus, for example, the home country might settle or abandon a claim for injury to its nationals if it judged that it is justified by other factors in its relations with the host country, such as security or broader economic concerns. In such a situation, the injured investor is left with no redress either against the offending host country or its unsympathetic home country.

A further complication involved a home country's ability to extend diplomatic protection to nationals who are shareholders in foreign corporations. In the *Barcelona Traction* case,[40] Belgium sued Spain in the International Court of Justice on behalf of injured Belgian shareholders of a Canadian corporation, Barcelona Traction. Barcelona Traction was supplying electricity to that Spanish city when it was expropriated by the government of Spain. The Court ruled that Belgium had no right to make a claim on behalf of the Belgian shareholders, since the primary party injured by the expropriation was the Canadian corporation, not the Belgian shareholders. Although this decision has been strongly criticized over the years,[41] it remains difficult for shareholders of one nationality to press claims for injuries to a corporation that was incorporated in a country other than that of their nationality—an obstacle that is particularly problematic, since investors commonly purchase shares in companies and corporations organized or with headquarters in other countries.

And finally, once the era of gunboat diplomacy ended, the process of diplomatic protection of aliens and foreign investors in many cases did not necessarily result in a meaningful remedy. Often, nothing more than an exchange of oral or written statements took place between the two states, and the injured investor received no compensation. The

---

[37] *Hopkins (US) v. Mexico*, (March 21, 1926), I Opinions of Commissioners, General Claims Commission (US and Mexico, 1923), 42, 50–1 (1927).

[38] *Roberts (US) v. Mexico*, (November 2, 1926), I Opinions of Commissioners, General Claims Commission (US and Mexico, 1923), 100, 105 (1927).

[39] The American Law Institute, *Restatement of the Law, The Foreign Relations Law of the United States* (1965) citing "France v Great Britain (1931)" (1933) 27 *AJIL* 153, 160. See also A Freeman, *The International Responsibility of States for Denial of Justice* (1938) 502 et seq.

[40] *Barcelona Traction, Light and Power Company, Limited (Belgium v. Spain)* (1970) ICJ Rep 3; (1970) 64 *AJIL* 653.

[41] eg, RB Lillich, "Two Perspectives on the Barcelona Traction Case" (1971) 65 *AJIL* 3, 522–32.

investor's home state could bring the matter to an international tribunal only if the offending state agreed to submit the case to that tribunal, whose jurisdiction always depended on the consent of the states concerned. Thus, diplomatic protection proved to be a very uncertain and often ephemeral remedy for injured international investors.

13.6 Customary International Law Concerning Expropriation and Breach of State Contracts

(a) In general

Traditionally, foreign investors in host countries have had two primary concerns: (1) the protection of their investments from expropriation or other unjustified interference by host governments with their property rights, and (2) the assurance that host country governments will respect the contracts they have made with investors. During the nineteenth and twentieth centuries, when western states dominated the international system, their governments sought to develop customary international law to deal with both problems.

With respect to expropriation, international law has always recognized the state's power of eminent domain to take property—at least for public purposes and on payment of compensation. Indeed, this power, which is derived from the sovereignty of the state over all things within its boundaries, is an essential attribute of state sovereignty. In fact, it has been asserted that a state may not validly bind itself not to exercise it. The justification for this principle is that a state's fundamental purpose is to safeguard the public interest of its citizens and, if such interest will be properly safeguarded by nationalization, the state must be free to pursue that course of action.[42]

At the same time, western governments and jurists appeared to agree that even though a government taking of foreign property may be legal under host country law such a taking was also subject to certain minimum standards of international customary law. One example of such a standard was that customary international law permitted expropriation of an alien's assets provided it was for a public purpose, was nondiscriminatory, and was accompanied by compensation to the injured alien.[43] In 1903, in the *Upton* case (1903), the Mixed Claims Commission held that "the right of the State . . . to appropriate private property for public use is unquestioned, but always with the corresponding obligation to make just compensation to the owner thereof."[44] In the *De Sabla* case, the United States–Panama General Claims Commission held that "[i]t is axiomatic that acts of a government in depriving an alien of his property without compensation impose international responsibility."[45] And in one of the leading pre-World War II cases on the subject, the Permanent Court of International Justice in the *Chorzów Factory* case,[46] which involved the expropriation by Poland of German-owned industrial property in Upper Silesia, declared that in the event of expropriation the expropriating state had the obligation to pay the "just price of what was expropriated." This meant "the value of the undertaking at the moment of dispossession, plus interest to the day of payment." In an often cited passage in this case, the Court set down the basic standard of compensation to be applied to repair injuries to aliens caused by a state's illegal acts under international law:

---

[42] I Delupis, *Finance and Protection of Investments in Developing Countries* (1973) 31.
[43] CF Amerasinghe, *State Responsibility for Injuries to Aliens* (1967) 124–5.
[44] *United States–Venezuela Mixed Claims Commission* (1903) 174.
[45] (1934) 28 *AJIL* 602, 611–12.
[46] *Factory at Chorzów (Germany v. Poland)* (Indemnity), (Judgment of September 13, 1928) PCIJ Series A No 17 at 47.

The essential principle contained in the actual notion of an illegal act—a principle which seems to be established by international practice and in particular by the decisions of arbitral tribunals—is that reparation must, as far as possible, wipe out all consequences of the illegal act and reestablish the situation which would, in all probability, have existed if that act had not been committed. Restitution in kind, or, if that is not possible, payment of a sum corresponding to the value which a restitution in kind would bear [must be made].

The traditional western position with respect to expropriation is perhaps best summed up in § 712 of the *Restatement (Third) of the Foreign Relations Law of the United States*, which provides:

A state is responsible under international law for injury resulting from:
(1) a taking by the state of the property of a national of another state that
    (a) is not for a public purpose; or
    (b) is discriminatory; or
    (c) is not accompanied by provision for just compensation.

A consideration of this principle requires a discussion of the meaning of its constituent elements.

(b) Taking under International Law

In any case of an alleged interference by the host country with a foreign investment, one must first of all determine whether such interference constitutes a "taking" under international law that would thereby give rise to the application of international legal principles of expropriation. In years past, such a determination was not difficult to make, since the host country government, in effecting an expropriation or nationalization, would specifically transfer title of the foreign investor's assets to the government or a public agency. Such instances were clearly an exercise of the power of eminent domain. In recent years, however, governments have engaged in more subtle means of interference—often through the arbitrary or discriminatory exercise of their police power—by imposing onerous regulations and taxation upon the investor or the investment project. This approach, sometimes referred to as "creeping expropriation," "indirect expropriation" or "regulatory taking," is designed to increase the amount of benefits flowing to the government from the investment. In some cases, it may gradually achieve the same result as a formal act of expropriation, for example inducing the investor either to abandon the investment entirely or to transfer it to the host country government at a bargain price.[47]

While western views of international law hold such use of state regulatory power to be a taking in certain situations,[48] they also recognize that a state is not responsible for losses resulting from the bone fide exercise of its regulatory or taxation authority. If not exercised discriminatorily, such authority is commonly accepted as part of a state's police powers.[49]

---

[47] See generally, SR Ratner, "Regulatory Takings In Institutional Context: Beyond the Fear of Fragmented International Law," 102 *AJIL4* (2008) 75; D Vagts, "Coercion and Foreign Investment Rearrangements," 72 *AJIL* (1978) 17; B Weston, ""Constructive Takings" under International Law: A Modest Foray into the Problem of "Creeping Expropriation,"" (1975) 16 *Va J Int'l L* (1975) 103.

[48] eg, *Restatement (Third)*, § 712, comment g, at 200 states:"A state is responsible for an expropriation of property when it subjects alien property to taxation, regulation, or other action that is confiscatory or that prevents, unreasonably interferes with, or unduly delays, effective enjoyment of an alien's property or its removal from the state's territory." The American Law Institute, *Restatement of the Law, The Foreign Relations Law of the United States* (3rd edn 1987) vol 2.

[49] The American Law Institute (n 48).

Determining whether a specific governmental regulation is an ordinary exercise of police power or is instead a disguised form of expropriation is not an easy matter, since the precise boundary between the two situations is not always clear. For example, the commentary to the *Restatement (Third)* asserts that regulatory action that is "confiscatory" or "unreasonably interferes with" a foreign national's use of his property is to be considered a taking. These concepts, of course, are subject to a variety of interpretations. In the Reporters' Notes, the *Restatement (Third)* further contends that the distinction between a taking requiring compensation and a lawful exercise of police power not requiring compensation "is similar to that drawn in United States jurisprudence for purposes of the Fifth and Fourteenth Amendments to the Constitution in determining whether there has been a taking requiring compensation."[50]

In determining the nature of a regulatory action, one might also consider the government's intent. A determination of such intent could be established, for example, if the government issued a series of discriminatory regulations making continued profitable operation impossible, purchased the property from the investor at a low price, and then later rescinded the regulations.

A government can also effect a taking under international law if it nullifies important contractual relationships with the investor. Canceling a concession agreement or investment contract with an investor could constitute a taking, since the contractual right to operate a concession or carry out an investment project is a valuable property right. Moreover, if a host country, in order to raise revenues, imposes a levy upon a mining concession in violation of an agreement, that levy might constitute a taking even if the investor continues to control the mining investment.[51]

A taking can also occur when a government, instead of asserting property rights in foreign-owned property, merely seizes control of an investment. For example, a government might appoint a new manager to administer a property or operate the investor's business. Provided the deprivation of the investor's right of control is not merely ephemeral, this might also qualify as a taking.[52]

(c) Public Purpose

The traditional rules of international law require that the taking be for a public purpose; however, this requirement has not figured prominently in international claims in recent years. For one thing, the concept is extremely broad and is not subject to precise definition. Indeed, it can be argued that virtually any expropriation by a government is done for a public purpose such as developing the national economy, executing development plans, or protecting foreign currency reserves. Moreover, there appears to be no effective means under customary international law for reviewing whether or not a particular expropriation is for a public purpose.[53]

---

[50] The American Law Institute (n 48), vol 2, § 712 at 211.

[51] See *Revere Copper and Brass, Inc v. Overseas Private Investment Corporation (OPIC)* (1978) 17 *ILM* 1321, particularly the majority and minority opinions as to whether the Jamaican government's repudiation of its agreement with the investor on taxation prevented the investor from exercising effective control of its investment.

[52] GH Aldrich, "What Constitutes a Compensable Taking of Property? The Decisions of the Iran–United States Claims Tribunal," 88 *AJIL* (1994) 585–610.

[53] See generally, M Sornarajah, *The International Law on Foreign Investment* (2nd edn 2004) 395–8.

(d) Discrimination

Although traditionally international law has prohibited discriminatory taking, the application of this principle also poses considerable difficulties. Often, the investor stands in a class by itself within the host country because nationals or other foreigners do not own comparable investments. Consequently, it is difficult to establish whether or not an act of expropriation directed against a foreign investor is discriminatory in nature. For example, if a foreign consortium owns the only mine in a small developing country, it is difficult to show that the nationalization of that mine was discriminatory. Unlawful discrimination requires the government of the host country to make arbitrary or unreasonable distinctions among investors. It may well be that the reasons for the expropriation bear a reasonable relationship to the security interests or economic policy of the host government. As a practical matter, injured investors will only claim discrimination or lack of public purpose if the host country government does not provide adequate compensation.

(e) Compensation

In contemporary international economic life, the essential objective of an injured investor is to secure adequate compensation for its expropriated investment. Even though the taking may not have been for a public purpose, and even though it may have been grossly discriminatory, no investor has a realistic hope—through legal, diplomatic, or other means—of obtaining restitution of the nationalized property, unless, of course, a radical change of regime takes place in the country of expropriation. Indeed, even if the expropriation has been discriminatory and not for a public purpose, most investors would not raise a claim if they received adequate compensation.

Generally speaking, almost all of the nations in the world today would claim to recognize the principle that a state which has expropriated the property of a foreign investor has an obligation to pay compensation to that investor. However, all nations do not agree on the appropriate standard of compensation for expropriation or on its application in specific cases. One traditional formulation of the appropriate standard is the "Hull formula," which was derived from the correspondence, previously referred to, between US Secretary of State Cordell Hull and Mexican Minister of Foreign Affairs Eduardo Hay. In that correspondence, Hull declared that the property of aliens was protected by an international standard under which expropriation was subject to limitations, which required that there be "prompt, adequate and effective compensation."[54] In its international relations, the US government has consistently maintained that the standard to be applied in cases of expropriation is the "prompt, adequate, and effective standard of compensation."[55] As will be seen, the United States and various European countries have at times incorporated the Hull formula into their investment treaties.

Many western countries and several international tribunals, while recognizing a host state's international obligation to pay compensation when alien property is taken or injured by a state, have not employed the Hull formula, but instead have used different terms that seem to be its functional equivalent.[56] On the other hand, it appears that the Hull formula

---

[54] "Official Documents," 32 *AJIL Supp* (1938) 181, 193.

[55] E Mcdowall, *Digest of U.S. Practice in International Law* (1975) 488; *Digest of U.S. Practice in International Law* (1978) 1226–7.

[56] O Schachter, "Compensation for Expropriation" (1984) 78 *AJIL* 121.

has not won widespread acceptance in state practice as reflected in the negotiated settlements paid by host states.[57]

Arbitral tribunals in their determination of damages for expropriation have tended to apply standards calling for full reparation of the injury sustained by the investor, similar to that enunciated by the Permanent Court of International Justice in the *Chorzów* case quoted above. For example, in the *De Sabla* case the tribunal found that the claimant was entitled to the "full value" of property that had been adjudicated to third parties.[58] In *Delagoa Bay*, the tribunal stated, "... the State, which is the author of such dispossession, is bound to make full reparation for the injuries done by it."[59] In the *Norwegian Claims* case, the Permanent Court of Arbitration held that the claimants were entitled to "just compensation ... under the municipal law of the United States, as well as under the international law."[60] After reviewing the arbitral jurisprudence on the question, one commentator noted: "Some sixty international claims tribunals sat between the early nineteenth century and the Second World War, many dealing with claims arising out of takings of alien property. Although their reasoning is sometimes obscure, none held that the appropriate measure of compensation was less than the full value of the property taken, and many specifically affirmed the need for full compensation."[61]

As far as specific rules regarding determination of the precise amount of compensation to be paid in specific cases are concerned, other commentators observed that "it is extremely difficult, if not entirely impossible, to set out systematically the criteria which seem to have been observed in practice."[62] Although the Permanent Court of International Justice in the *Chorzów Factory* case set down, albeit indirectly, the criterion of the "value of the undertaking at the moment of dispossession, plus interest to the day of payment,"[63] this formula has not been followed in the same way in all cases.[64]

Following more general usage, the *Restatement (Third) of the Foreign Relations Law of the United States*, unlike its predecessor, does not use the formulation "prompt, adequate, and effective compensation." Rather, it simply provides for the payment of "just compensation." For compensation to be just, "it must, in the absence of exceptional circumstances, be in an amount equivalent to the value of the property taken and be paid at the time of taking, or within a reasonable time thereafter with interest from the date of taking, and in a form economically usable by the foreign national."[65] The *Restatement*'s view, which repeats the Hull formula's three elements in different words, would seem to represent the current position of most western states on the standard of compensation due to investors for the illegal acts of host states under international law.

---

[57] O Schachter, "Compensation for Expropriation" (1984) 78 *AJIL* at 124.

[58] (1934) 28 *AJIL* 602, 611–12. This passage is also cited in Report of BL Hunt, "American and Panamanian General Claims Arbitration" (1934) 447.

[59] *Delagoa Bay and East African Railway Co (US and Great Britain v. Portugal)* (1900) in A Moore, *Digest and History of the International Arbitrations* (1908) vol 2, at 1875.

[60] *Norwegian Claims* case (1922) in *The Hague Reports* (1932) vol 2, at 69.

[61] PM Norton, "A Law of the Future or a Law of the Past? Modern Tribunals and the International Law of Expropriation," 85 *AJIL* (1991) 474, 477.

[62] FV Garcia-Amador, LB Sohn, and RR Baxter, *Recent Codification of the Law of State Responsibility for Injuries to Aliens* (1974) 55.

[63] *Factory at Chórzow* (n 46) 47.

[64] Garcia-Amador et al (n 62) 55.

[65] The American Law Institute, *Restatement of the Law, The Foreign Relations Law of the United States* (3rd edn 1987) vol 2, § 712 at 198–9.

(f) Breaches of State Contracts

Under traditional principles of customary international law, a state that is a party to a contract with a foreign national may be liable for its repudiation or breach in certain instances. According to the *Restatement (Third) of the Foreign Relations Law of the United States*, a state is liable: (a) if the repudiation or breach is discriminatory or motivated by noncommercial considerations and compensation is not paid or (b) if the foreign national is not given an adequate forum to hear his claim or is not compensated. On the other hand, if a state repudiates or breaches a commercial contract with a foreign national for commercial reasons, for example, where performance becomes uneconomical, international law will not be applicable. In such cases, where the state is acting as any private contractor might, the state is only liable under the law applicable to the contract.[66] Nonetheless, breaches of concession agreements, development contracts, and investment contracts may be akin to an expropriation, since through such a breach the investor is effectively deprived of its investment.[67]

As a general rule, contracts between a state and a foreign private investor are governed by the law of that state.[68] At the same time, the parties to that contract may agree to a choice-of-law clause expressly stipulating that the contractual relationship shall be governed, either wholly or in certain particulars, by a legal system or specified legal rules other than the municipal law of the contracting state, including the principles of international law. Sometimes, as discussed in Chapter 7,[69] major contracts involving large projects or long-term concessions, in order to gain added protection against unjustified cancelation by the host country government, may include a clause stating that the contract is to be governed by general principles of international law or general principles of law common to the world's legal systems. The purpose of this type of clause is to "internationalize" the contract and thus protect it from attempts by the state party to cancel or modify it without the consent of the investor. In order to give additional assurance of the enforceability of their contract, the parties might also agree to settle any dispute arising under the agreement by international arbitration rather than in the courts of the host country.

By analogizing treaties between states to contracts between a state and an alien, various jurists and tribunals have argued that the principle of *pacta sunt servanda* is applicable to state contracts as a matter of international law. The basis of this view lies in the contracts' international character and also the fact that failure to apply the principle would place the validity and effectiveness of obligations made to aliens at the mercy of the unilateral decisions of the host country government. Moreover, it has also been argued that the principle of *pacta sunt servanda* is applicable as one of "the general principles of law recognized by civilized nations." Thus, once a state has entered into an international agreement with an investor, such state must abide by that agreement. Various tribunals have confirmed that the principle of *pacta sunt servanda* underlies contracts entered into by states and foreign investors.[70] The Permanent Court of International Justice in the *Chorzów*

---

[66] The American Law Institute (n 65), vol 2, § 712, reporters' n 8, at 212.

[67] It is for this reason that the Multilateral Investment Guarantee Agency (MIGA) includes as one of its covered, non-commercial risks "any repudiation or breach by the host government of a contract when the investor has no access to a competent forum, faces unreasonable procedural delays, or is unable to enforce decisions made in its favor." Convention Establishing the Multilateral Investment Guarantee Agency (October 11, 1985) 24 ILM 1598, 1605 (The MIGA Convention) Article 11(a). See Chapter 11, section 11.6.

[68] G Schwarzenberger, *Foreign Investments and International Law* (1969) 5–7.

[69] See particularly section 7.3 of Chapter 7.

[70] For example, in the *Sapphire* case the tribunal stated: "It is a fundamental principle of law, which is constantly being proclaimed by international courts, that contractual undertakings must be respected. The rule

case also confirmed that a lawfully concluded public contract is a property or "vested" right in the technical sense.[71] Contractual rights, like any other property rights, are protected by international law against confiscation by the state party to the contract. According to the traditional view of international law prevailing in western countries, a state that breaks its obligations of non-interference with a public contract violates both the minimum standards of international law and the general principles of law recognized by civilized nations.

13.7 Challenges to the Capital-Exporting States' Position on International Investment Law

(a) Introduction

Not all countries meekly accepted the western position on the customary international law governing foreign investments. Indeed, there were numerous challenges to western views, and those challenges had an impact on the investment treaty movement that emerged after World War II. The three most notable challenges were (1) the Soviet challenge, (2) the Latin American challenge, and (3) the postcolonial challenge. Each of these challenges is considered briefly.

(b) The Soviet Challenge

The October Revolution of 1917 in Russia and the subsequent establishment of the Dictatorship of the Proletariat resulted in the confiscation of foreign private property on a vast scale.[72] The new Soviet Government refused to make restitution or pay compensation for the seized foreign property. In response, western governments of nationals affected by the seizures lodged vigorous protests with the Soviet government. For example, on February 13, 1918, the US Ambassador protested in the name of fourteen Allied powers and sixteen neutrals, stating that: "In order to avoid any misunderstandings in the future, the representatives at Petrograd of all the foreign powers declare that they view the decrees relating to the repudiation of the Russian state loans, the confiscation of property and other similar measures as null and void insofar as their nationals are concerned."[73]

At the Brussels Conference on Russia of October 1921, the delegates passed a resolution stating what they perceived as a well-established principle of international law on the question of expropriation: "The forcible expropriations and nationalizations without any compensation or remuneration of property in which foreigners are interested is totally at

---

of *pacta sunt servanda* is the basis of every contractual relationship." *Sapphire International Petroleum Limited (Sapphire) v. National Iranian Oil Co* (1953) 35 *ILR* 136, 181. In *TOPCO*, sole arbitrator Dupuy reiterated that "the maxim *pacta sunt servanda* should be viewed as a fundamental principle of international law." *Texaco Overseas Petroleum Company and California Asiatic Oil Company (TOPCO) v. Government of the Libyan Arab Republic* (1978) 17 *ILM* 1.

[71] *Case Concerning Certain German Interests in Polish Upper Silesia* (1926) PCIJ Rep Series A No 7 at 21–2, 42.

[72] The Decree of October 26, 1917, adopted by the Second All-Russian Congress of Soviets, abolished private property in land without compensation. The Decrees of December 14, 1917 and January 26, 1918, socialized the banks "in order to liberate the workers and peasants and the whole population from the exploitation of the capitalist banks" and provided that the assets of the former private banks were to be confiscated. By June 1920 most industry had been socialized in the USSR. S Friedman, *Expropriation in International Law* (1953) 17–23; BA Wortley, *Expropriation in Public International Law* (1959) 61–2; Legislative Reference Service, Library of Congress for the Comm on Foreign Affairs, 88th Cong, 1st Sess, Report on Expropriation of American-Owned Property by Foreign Governments in the Twentieth Century (July 19, 1963) 8–10.

[73] S Friedman (n 72) 18, quoting *Correspondence between His Majesty's Government and the French Government respecting the Anglo-Russian Trade Agreement, 1921*.

variance with the practice of civilised states. Where such expropriation has taken place, a claim arises for compensation against the Government of the country."[74]

In the 1920s, the Soviet Union, still unrecognized by the major powers and with an economy in ruin, launched its New Economic Policy and actively sought to obtain international recognition and economic assistance. As part of this effort, it expressed a readiness to consider foreign claims arising out of the expropriations that followed the Russian Revolution.[75] However, the offer was conditioned on a satisfactory settlement of the Soviet Union's own claims against the western countries that had militarily intervened in Soviet territory after the October Revolution. Throughout this period, the Soviet Union refused to recognize the duty of a state, as a principle of customary international law, to make restitution or pay compensation for foreign property it had seized.[76]

After the failure of the 1922 Cannes and Hague conferences seeking a possible multilateral settlement of the various claims and counter-claims between Soviet Russia and Western countries, individual western governments, desiring access to the large Russian market, began to conclude bilateral agreements with the Soviet government. The result of these efforts was generally little compensation compared to investors' actual losses. In 1924, for example, the British concluded a treaty in which they agreed in principle to Russian counter-claims based on the British intervention that occurred after the Russian Revolution and recognized the possibility of setting them off against claims by British nationals arising out of Soviet confiscations. The British also promised a financial loan, while the Soviet Union, in its turn, undertook to open negotiations for these purposes with interested parties in the United Kingdom. A separate agreement was reached between the Soviet Government and one of the nationalized British enterprises, *Lena Goldfields Limited*, whereby the enterprise renounced its claims in return for the concession of its former properties.[77] A subsequent change in Soviet policy led to a revocation of the concession and, ultimately, to one of the first investor–state arbitrations, the *Lena Goldfields* case.[78]

A similar development took place between the United States and the USSR. In an exchange of communications by which the United States recognized the Soviet government on November 16, 1933, the government of the Soviet Union released and assigned to the US government all amounts due to the Soviet government from American nationals.[79] This agreement, known as the Litvinov Assignment, formed the basis of a fund out of which some of the claims against Russia made by American nationals for confiscation of their property could be paid. Although the Litvinov Assignment was only intended as a

---

[74] BA Wortley, *Expropriation in Public International Law* (1959) 61, citing McNair, *International Law Opinions* (1956) vol 1, at 9.

[75] Friedman (n 72) 19, citing Correspondence between the British and Russian Governments concerning Russia's Foreign Indebtedness, 114 *BFSP* (1921) 380.

[76] Friedman (n 72) 19; Legislative Reference Service, Library of Congress for the Comm on Foreign Affairs, 88th Cong, 1st Sess, Report on Expropriation of American-Owned Property by Foreign Governments in the Twentieth Century (July 19, 1963) 9.

[77] Friedman (n 72) 21.

[78] In accordance with the concession agreement, the company holding the concession instituted arbitration proceedings against the USSR. The *Lena Goldfields* arbitral award of 1930 decided in favor of the company after the abrupt withdrawal of the Soviet government from the arbitral proceedings. It was not until 1934, when the Anglo-Soviet Trade agreement was signed, that the Soviet Union, after protracted diplomatic negotiations, gave the company transferable but noninterest-bearing notes payable over 20 years. This sum (£3 million) was considerably less than the arbitration award (£13 million); however, even this compensation arrangement was repudiated by the USSR in 1940. BA Wortley, *Expropriation in Public International Law* (1959) 62. The circumstances surrounding the *Lena Goldfields* case have prompted one commentator to note that "[h]istorically, the *Lena* case remains a baleful monument to the absolute power of a State." VV Veeder, "The Lena Goldfields Arbitration: The Historical Roots of the Three Ideas," 74 *ICLQ* (1988) 747–92.

[79] "Exchange of Communications between the President of the United States and the President of the All Union General Executive Committee," 28 *AJIL Supp* (1934) 1–20.

temporary measure preceding a final settlement of the claims and counterclaims, subsequent negotiations between the two governments on an overall settlement proved unsuccessful. As of the early 1960s, only a portion of the claims of American nationals had been paid from the Litvinov Assignment funds. Those that were paid were distributed by the Foreign Claims Settlement Commission under title III of the International Claims Settlement Act of 1949.[80]

Reviewing the history of efforts to secure compensation from the Soviet Union for foreign property seized by the Soviet government, one commentator concluded: "[o]ne after another, States ceased to press their claims arising out of the Soviet socialization measures. They even went so far as actually renouncing these claims, either expressly as in the case of Germany, or tacitly as in the case of the United States."[81]

Thus, by its actions and inactions, the Soviet Union, one of the world's great powers, expressed its clear opposition to the traditional western position on expropriation and the enforcement of state contracts under international law.

(c) The Latin American Challenge

Latin American countries also challenged the western view of the customary international law of investment, primarily through their efforts to implement the Calvo doctrine. One common method was to include "Calvo clauses" in their constitutions. These clauses purported to make all property within their territories subject only to domestic law. For example, the 1933 Constitution of Peru provided: "Property, whoever may be the owner, is governed exclusively by the laws of the Republic and is subject to the taxes, charges and limitations established in the laws themselves. The same provision regarding property applies to aliens as well as [nationals], except that in no case may said aliens make use of their exceptional position or resort to diplomatic appeals."[82]

A similar provision was incorporated into the Bolivian Constitution: "Foreign subjects and enterprises are, in respect to property, in the same position as Bolivians, and can in no case plead an exceptional situation or appeal through diplomatic channels unless in case of denial of justice."[83]

Another approach was to implement the Calvo doctrine through legislation. Thus, for example, in 1938, Article 26 of a 1938 law of Ecuador provided that "the foreigners, by the act of coming to the country, subjected themselves to the local laws without any exception and may in no case, nor for any reason, avail themselves of their status as foreigners against laws, jurisdiction and police." Furthermore, Article 30 of the law subjected contractual rights of foreigners "to exclusive jurisdiction of the national judges and courts," while Article 31 flatly stated that "the renunciation of diplomatic claims will be an implicit and essential condition of all contracts concluded by foreigners with the state" and "foreigners who have been employed or carried out a commission subjecting them to the Ecuadorian laws and authorities may not claim indemnification through diplomatic channels."[84]

A third approach to implementing the Calvo doctrine was to include "Calvo clauses" in contracts with foreign companies by which the companies agreed to pursue claims only in

---

[80] Legislative Reference Service, Library of Congress for the Comm on Foreign Affairs, 88th Cong, 1st Sess, *Report on Expropriation of American-Owned Property by Foreign Governments in the Twentieth Century* (July 19, 1963) 9.

[81] Friedman (n 72) 23.

[82] R Fitzgibbon, *Constitutions of the Americas* (1948) 670, citing Article 31 of the 1933 Constitution of Peru.

[83] Fitzgibbon (n 82) 35.

[84] DR Shea, *The Calvo Clause* (1955) 26, quoting (1938) 32 *AJIL Supp*.

local courts and to relinquish the right to diplomatic protection in any dispute arising out of the contractual relationship.[85] In such cases, the enforceability of the Calvo clause gained additional force because the foreign company had specifically agreed to it.[86]

The widespread use of the Calvo clause in Latin America raised the question of whether such use was compatible with international law. Some opponents argued that the right to protect investors under international law belonged to the investors' states of nationality and so only those states, not the investors, could waive the right to diplomatic protection.

The issue of the Calvo clause's compatibility with international law was considered in the decision of the United States–Mexican Claims Commission in the *North American Dredging Company* case,[87] which is regarded as the leading case on the subject.[88] The Commission stated that, for the clause to be declared void, one would have to prove that a generally accepted rule of international law exists that condemns the Calvo clause and that denies "an individual the right to relinquish to any extent, large or small, and under any circumstances or conditions, the protection of the government to which he owes allegiance." After declaring that no such rule exists, the Commission held that because of its Calvo clause contractual commitment "the present claimant is precluded from presenting to its Government any claim relative to the interpretation or fulfilment of this contract." The claimant, because it violated its contractual renunciation, "has not put itself in a position where it may rightfully present this claim to the Government of the United States for its interposition."[89]

Summarizing the international jurisprudence dealing with the Calvo clause from the *Dredging* decision of 1926 through the 1950s (a period when the clause gained significant use), one commentator observed that in five out of seven cases international tribunals applied the rule to bar claims that would have been otherwise admissible in the absence of the renunciatory provision (among them are *International Fisheries, Mexican Union Railway, Interoceanic Railway, Veracruz Railway,* and *Pilot* cases). There were two cases where the Calvo clause did not bar the claims: in the *McNeil* case the clause's wording was found so vague that the intent of the parties was not clear to the Commission, and in the *El Oro Mining and Railway Co* the case was based on claims of a flagrant denial of justice.[90]

[85] An example of a Calvo clause is found in the contract between Mexico and the North American Dredging Company of Texas, later subject to an international law claim, which reads as follows:

> The Contractor and all persons, who as employees or in any other capacity may be engaged in the execution of the work under this contract either directly or indirectly, shall be considered as Mexicans in all matters, within the Republic of Mexico, concerning the execution of such work and the fulfillment of this contract. They shall not claim, nor shall they have, with regard to the interests and the business connected with this contract, any other rights or means to enforce the same than those granted by the laws of the Republic to Mexicans, nor shall they enjoy any other rights than those established in favor of Mexicans. They are consequently deprived of any rights as aliens, and under no conditions shall the intervention of foreign diplomatic agents be permitted, in any matter related to this contract.

Shea (n 84) 29, quoting *United States (North American Dredging Co) v. United Mexican States*, Opinions of Commissioners, I at 21–2.

[86] Shea (n 84) 28. Shea argues that the Calvo clause differs from the Calvo doctrine in one very important respect: the enforcement of the latter was a unilateral act, whereas in the case of the former the individual has consented of his own free will to surrender of the right of recourse to his government in case of contractual controversies or disputes.

[87] *North American Dredging Company of Texas (United States v. United Mexican States)* (March 31, 1926), reproduced in 20 *AJIL* (1926) 800.

[88] UNGA, "Diplomatic Protection," Report of the International Law Commission Fifty-fourth Session (29 April to 7 June and 22 July to August 16, 2002) GAOR 57th Sess Supp No 10 (A/57/10) c V 253. The Special Rapporteur noted, in particular: "[in the case] it had been shown that the Calvo clause was compatible with international law in general and with the right to diplomatic protection in particular, although the decision in that case had been subjected to serious criticism by jurists."

[89] Shea (n 84) at 263, citing *Opinions of Commissioners*, vol 1, at 30–3.

[90] Shea (n 84) 255–6.

In 2002, the International Law Commission issued its *Third Report on Diplomatic Protection* to the United Nations General Assembly. The Special Rapporteur on Diplomatic Protection referred to several considerations concerning the Calvo clause's purpose and scope. First, the Calvo clause was of limited validity in that it did not constitute a complete bar to diplomatic intervention. It applied only to disputes relating to the contract between the alien and host state containing the clause, but it did not apply to breaches of international law. Second, the Calvo clause confirmed the importance of the rule requiring the exhaustion of local remedies. Some writers had suggested that the clause was nothing more than a reaffirmation of that rule, but most saw it as extending beyond that principle. Third, international law placed no bar on the right of an alien to waive by contract his right to request his state of nationality to exercise diplomatic protection. Fourth, an alien could not waive rights that under international law belonged to his government through a Calvo clause. Fifth, the waiver in a Calvo clause extended only to disputes arising out of the contract or out of a breach of the contract. The waivers did not cover disputes that constitute a breach of international law and, in particular, did not extend to breaches that represented a denial of justice.[91]

(d) The Postcolonial Challenge

In the aftermath of decolonization in the post-World War II era, the legitimacy and content of traditional principles of the law regarding states' international responsibility for injuries to investors came under increased attack from the newly emerging states. Developing countries challenged its legitimacy by arguing that customary international law had been shaped exclusively by western countries and that they, being under colonial or imperialist domination at that time, played no part in its formation and evolution. One commentator aptly summarized their position with respect to the international law on this point:

> The law of responsibility ... is not founded on any universal principles of law or morality. Its sole foundation is custom, which is binding only among states where it either grew up or came to be adopted. It is thus hardly possible to maintain that it is still part of universal international law. Whatever the basis of obligation of international law in the past, when the international community was restricted to only a few states ... the birth of a new world community has brought about a radical change which makes the traditional basis of obligation outmoded.[92]

Developing countries also viewed the content of traditional international law—with its emphasis on the protection of foreign investment—as playing an important role in their economic underdevelopment and continued dependence on western countries. In short, they saw international law as an obstacle to their economic advancement. International law, as shaped by their former colonial masters, elevated the protection of foreign-owned property and contracts over the right to nationalize ownership of property on their territories and prioritized the commercial and economic freedom of foreigners over the right of the state to regulate economic activities in its own territory.[93]

To deal with this problem, developing countries sought to use their numerical superiority in the United Nations to shape the international law of state responsibility to foreign investors in a way that was more in keeping with their interests. An early effort in this

---

[91] UNGA (n 88) 256 at 162.

[92] SN Guha Roy, "Is the Law of Responsibility of States for Injuries to Aliens a Part of Universal International Law?" 55 *AJIL* (1961) 863.

[93] T Wälde, "Requiem for the 'New International Economic Order,'" in G Hafner et al (eds), *Festschrift für Ignaz Seidl-Hohenveldern* (1998) 761.

respect was the 1962 General Assembly Resolution 1803 on Permanent Sovereignty over Natural Resources. Establishing sovereignty over the natural resources in their territories was a prime concern for developing countries. They therefore sought to secure international recognition of their right to nationalize and reestablish sovereignty over the natural resources contained in their territories, without regard to the necessity or adequacy of compensation. Developed nations, for their part, were willing to recognize such a right only if the developing nations abided by established rules of international law providing for the payment of adequate compensation.[94]

In fact, investors' home countries had good reason to emphasize the importance of adequate compensation. From 1960 through mid-1974, some 62 different developing countries engaged in 875 nationalizations or takeovers of foreign enterprises. The majority of the cases (591) took place in 10 states.[95] As a result, disputes about the existence and nature of obligations to pay compensation for expropriation of alien property under international law increased dramatically

Beginning in the 1960s and continuing through the 1970s, developing countries attempted to revise the established principles regarding compensation and to bring about what they termed the "New International Economic Order" (NIEO). They did this through a series of UN General Assembly resolutions dealing with the issue of permanent sovereignty over natural resources and the economic rights and duties of states.

In 1962, the UN General Assembly adopted Resolution 1803 (XVII), which contained the Declaration on Permanent Sovereignty over Natural Resources. It provided in part:

3. In cases where authorization is granted, the capital imported and the earnings on that capital shall be governed by the terms thereof, by the national legislation in force, and by international law. The profits derived must be shared in the proportions freely agreed upon, in each case, between the investors and the recipient State, due care being taken to ensure that there is no impairment, for any reason, of that State's sovereignty over its natural wealth and resources.

4. Nationalization, expropriation or requisitioning shall be based on grounds or reasons of public utility, security or the national interest which are recognized as overriding purely individual or private interests, both domestic and foreign. In such cases the owner shall be paid appropriate compensation, in accordance with the rules in force in the State taking such measures in the exercise of its sovereignty and in accordance with international law. In any case where the question of compensation gives rise to a controversy, the national jurisdiction of the State taking such measures shall be exhausted. However, upon agreement by sovereign States and other parties concerned, settlement of the dispute should be made through arbitration or international adjudication.

. . .

8. Foreign investment agreements freely entered into by or between sovereign States shall be observed in good faith.[96]

Some observers interpreted the Declaration as not being too radical a departure from the traditional international customary law understood by western nations.[97] The Declaration incorporated by reference the international law requirement that foreign capital not be subject to discriminatory treatment and it affirmed the binding character of foreign

---

[94] M Mugharby, *Permanent Sovereignty over Oil Resources* (1966) 15.

[95] UNGA, "Permanent Sovereignty over Natural Resources," UN Doc A/9716 (September 20, 1974) annex at 2, table 1.

[96] UNGA Res 1803 (XVII) (December 14, 1962) UN Doc A/RES/1803 (XVII) (1962). <http://www.un.org/documents/ga/res/17/ares17.htm> last accessed March 22, 2009.

[97] SM Schwebel, "The Story of the United Nations Declaration on Permanent Sovereignty over Natural Resources," 49 *ABAJ* (1963) 463, 469.

investment agreements. Although the stipulation that compensation need only be "appropriate" was ambiguous, the legislative history was said to support the US interpretation that "appropriate compensation" meant "prompt, adequate, and effective compensation."[98] Adopted by a vote of 87 to 2 with 12 abstentions, the Declaration has been viewed as the last consensus on the issue of expropriation under international law.[99]

In the 1970s, developing countries became more assertive in their efforts to reshape the customary international law affecting foreign investments. Under their impetus, the UN General Assembly in 1973 adopted Resolution 3171, which affirmed that:

> 3 ... the application of the principle of nationalization carried out by States, as an expression of their sovereignty in order to safeguard their natural resources, implies that each State is entitled to determine the amount of possible compensation and the mode of payment, and that any disputes which might arise should be settled in accordance with the national legislation of each State carrying out such measures.[100]

The Resolution omitted language concerning the guarantee of compensation for foreign investors and also references to international law and thus left host states wide discretion in determining what if any compensation was due under its municipal law and without regard to the objective standards under international law.

The following year, developing countries pushed the UN General Assembly to adopt resolutions departing even further from the traditional western positions on the international law governing foreign investments. In May 1974, the General Assembly adopted Resolution 3201 containing the Declaration on the Establishment of a New International Economic Order.[101] Resolution 3201 declared the right of each state to exercise control over and exploit its natural resources, "including the right to nationalization or transfer of ownership to its nationals."[102] It was followed on December 12, 1974 by Resolution 3281 containing the Charter of Economic Rights and Duties of States.[103] Resolution 3281 was adopted by a vote of 120 to 6, with 10 abstentions (the states voting "against" included Belgium, Denmark, German Federal Republic, Luxembourg, the United Kingdom, and the United States).[104] This Resolution reiterated the urgent need "to establish generally accepted norms to govern international economic relations systematically." It also recognized that "it is not feasible to establish generally accepted norms to govern international economic relations systematically" and "to establish a just order and a stable world as long as a charter to protect the rights of all countries and in particular the developing states is not formulated." It further noted that the Charter was designed as "the first step in the codification and development" of the norms for "the development of international economic relations on a just and equitable basis."

The most contentious provisions in the Charter were contained in Article 2 on private foreign investment. Article 2(2) of the Charter provided that each state has the right:

---

[98] Schwebel, "The Story of the United Nations Declaration on Permanent Sovereignty over Natural Resources," 49 *ABAJ* (1963) 469.

[99] P Norton, "A Law of the Future or a Law of the Past? Modern Tribunals and the International Law of Expropriation," 85 *AJIL* (1991) 474, 479.

[100] UNGA Res 3171 (XXVIII) (December 17, 1973) UN Doc A/RES/9030 (XVIII) (1973) <http://www.un.org/documents/ga/res/28/ares28.htm> last accessed March 22, 2009.

[101] UNGA Res 3201 (S-VI) (May 1, 1974) UN Doc A/RES/3201 (S-VI) (1974), reprinted in 13 *ILM* 715 (1974).

[102] UNGA, (n 101) 6.

[103] UNGA Res 3281 (XXIX) (December 12, 1974) UN Doc A/RES/3281 (XXIX) (1974) reprinted in 14 *ILM* 251 (1975).

[104] GAOR, 29th Sess, annexes, agenda item 48 at 31.

(a) To regulate and exercise authority over foreign investment within its national jurisdiction in accordance with its laws and regulations and in conformity with its national objectives and priorities. No State shall be compelled to grant preferential treatment to foreign investment; . . .

(c) To nationalize, expropriate or transfer ownership of foreign property, in which case appropriate compensation should be paid by the State adopting such measures, taking into account its relevant laws and regulations and all circumstances that the State considers pertinent. In any case where the question of compensation gives rise to a controversy, it shall be settled under the domestic law of the nationalizing State and by its tribunals, unless it is freely and mutually agreed by all States concerned that other peaceful means be sought on the basis of the sovereign equality of States and in accordance with the principle of free choice of means.

Most developed countries opposed the Resolution. They argued it did not take into account traditional principles of international law on the treatment of foreign investment and the respect for international obligations.[105] Two basic reasons prevented developed countries from accepting the Charter. First, the document was an attempt to assert principles of international law, or at least *opinio juris*, without specific reference to established international legal doctrine and practice. Second, the Charter failed to formulate and articulate propositions that would give predictability to international economic transactions. The developed states, therefore, had no assurance that their economic relations with the developing states would be subject to a predictable or stable legal regime,[106] which was a fundamental requirement for their nationals to undertake international investments.

Commentators argued that Article 2 of the Charter departed dramatically from the existing international law in several important respects. Critics claimed that its most fundamental weakness was its general failure to clearly state that the economic rights and duties of states are subject to international law, or, at a bare minimum, that international law is a relevant consideration. In dealing with the compensation of an alien whose property has been dispossessed, Article 2(2)(c) provided only that "appropriate compensation should be paid by the State adopting such measures, taking into account its relevant laws and regulations and all circumstances that the State considers pertinent."

In analyzing its text, critics also noted that Article 2 is prefaced with the precatory "should" rather than the mandatory "shall." Thus, they argued that if there is an obligation, it is solely to grant whatever compensation a host state subjectively thinks to be "appropriate," with consideration given only to local law and circumstances and not necessarily to international law, which may not be "pertinent." They also pointed to the fact that the text contains no requirement that a taking must be for a public purpose and that Article 2 is also silent on the traditional principle that any taking of alien property by a state must not be discriminatory. They found this particularly strange because the Charter stipulates that "no state shall be compelled to grant preferential treatment to foreign investment," which is the natural corollary of nondiscrimination. The Charter also denied the inviolability of contracts by boldly proclaiming without limitation that "every state has and shall freely exercise full permanent sovereignty, including possession, use and disposal, over all its wealth, natural resources and economic activities."[107]

---

[105] G White, "A New International Economic Order?" 16 *Va J Int'l L* (1975–76) 323, 334.
[106] White (n 105), 335.
[107] CN Brower and JB Tepe, "The Charter of Economic Rights and Duties of States: A Reflection or Rejection of International Law?" 9 *Int'l L* (1975) 295, 304–7. But cf EJ de Arechaga, "Application of the Rules of State Responsibility to the Nationalization of Foreign-Owned Property," in K Hossain (ed), *Legal Aspects of the New International Economic Order* (1980) 225–7.

The Charter also departed significantly from traditional international law with respect to the settlement of disputes between aggrieved investors and host countries. First, instead of exhausting local remedies and then proceeding to arbitration and international adjudication, cases were to be decided nationally (in the host country) or possibly by other peaceful means. Second, any agreement to utilize other peaceful means was required to be between "states concerned" rather than "upon agreement by sovereign states and other parties," which effectively excluded private companies as parties.[108]

The adoption of the Charter provoked a vehement debate not only regarding its content but also its legal nature and effect on existing international law. The original intent of the Charter's sponsors was for it to be a legally binding document. However, as the divergence of opinion between the developing and developed nations became apparent, the latter grew increasingly opposed to creating legally binding obligations in the Charter.[109] The question of the legal nature of the Charter was left to the General Assembly, but it never reached any determination on the matter, leaving developing countries free to try to bring the document into line with their preferences.[110]

Commentators' views on the legal effect of the Charter varied greatly. Some emphasized the norm-making power of the Charter, equating the instrument to "a constitution" that served the dual purpose of codifying existing customary law and progressively developing new rules to address the current and future needs of international society.[111] Others asserted that the Charter expressed both traditional principles of international law that were binding on all states and also new principles that were a stage in the progressive development of international law, but possessed no more weight than an unratified treaty.[112] Still others, primarily from developed countries, emphasized the General Assembly's lack of law-making authority[113] and concluded that the Charter "is not a legally binding instrument."[114]

The *TOPCO* arbitration[115] considered the legal validity of the various UN resolutions on the New International Economic Order and the possible existence of a custom resulting from them. Sole Arbitrator Dupuy, by looking at the circumstances under which the resolutions were adopted and analyzing the principles that they stated, concluded that only Resolution 1803 (XVII) of 1962 reflected the state of existing customary international law.[116] He further stated that "Article 2 of this Charter must be analyzed as a political rather than as a legal declaration concerned with the ideological strategy of development and, as

---

[108] RF Meagher, *An International Redistribution of Wealth and Power: A Study of the Charter of Economic Rights and Duties of States* (1975) 53–4. Meagher summarized the thrust of the Charter as follows:
[T]here has been an expansion of the concept of permanent sovereignty; nationalization is now an unqualified right; transnational corporations have become a special category of institutions subject to particular rules; the standards for compensation are determined by national laws based upon what nationalizing state considers pertinent; and disputes over compensation are to be decided by national tribunals utilizing national laws, unless states agree on other peaceful means. (1975) 54.

[109] UN Doc, TD/B/AC.12/4 at 2. See also Brower and Tepe (n 107) 295, 300.

[110] Meagher (n 108) 89.

[111] Meagher (n 108), 90, citing J Castaneda, "La Charte des Droits et Devoirs Economique des Etats," *Annuaire Français de Droit International* (1974) XX at 39.

[112] Meagher (n 108) 90, citing G Feuer, "Reflexions sur La Charte des Droits et Devoirs Economique des Etats," *Revue Generale de Droit International Public* (1975) 274.

[113] "[A]part from its control over the budget, all the General Assembly can do is to discuss and recommend and initiate studies and consider reports from other bodies. It cannot act on behalf of all members, as the Security Council does, and its decisions are not directions telling the member states what they are or are not to do." JL Brierly, *The Law of Nations* (1963) 110.

[114] Brower and Tepe (n 107) 295, 301.

[115] *Texaco Overseas Petroleum Company and California Asiatic Oil Company (TOPCO) v. Government of the Libyan Arab Republic* (Award on the Merits) (1977) 17 *ILM* 1 (1978); 53 *ILR* 389 (1977).

[116] *TOPCO* arbitration (n 115) 87.

such, supported only by non-industrialized States."[117] Moreover, as will be seen, state practice among developing countries, particularly their subsequent willingness to consent to investment treaties giving strong protection to investor interests, demonstrated that customary international law had not evolved in the direction developing countries had hoped in the 1970s.[118]

Regardless of its legal effect, the Charter of Economic Rights and Duties of States, even though it did not create international law, was a clear challenge to the traditional western view of international law.[119] That challenge, added to the earlier challenges of the Soviet Union and Latin America, served to undermine the solidity of the traditional international legal framework for foreign investment as conceived by western capital-exporting states and led both investors and their home countries to search for other means to strengthen it in order to protect their economic interests in a new era.

13.8 Perceived Deficiencies of International Investment Law

International investment gained momentum as an increasingly important international economic activity in the period after World War II when new states joined the international community. Foreign investors and their home governments seeking the protection of international investment law in this period encountered an ephemeral structure consisting of scattered treaty provisions, a few questionable customs, and contested general principles of law. From their point of view, the resulting international legal framework was a weak structure on which to rely for it was seriously deficient in several respects.

First, the applicable international law failed to take account of contemporary investment practices and to address important issues of concern to foreign investors.[120] For example, customary international law had virtually nothing to say about the right of foreign investors to make monetary transfers from a host country or to bring foreign managers into the host country to manage their investments. Second, the principles that did exist were often vague and subject to varying interpretations. Thus, although there was strong evidence that customary international law required the payment of compensation upon nationalization of an investor's property, no specific principles had crystallized as to how that compensation was to be calculated.

---

[117] *TOPCO* arbitration (n 115) 87.

[118] See, eg, BH Weston, "The New International Economic Order and the Deprivation of Foreign Proprietary Wealth: Some Reflections upon the Contemporary International Law Debate" in RB Lillich (ed), *International Law of State Responsibility for Injuries to Aliens* (1983) 106, stating:

> Because the UN majority did not actually assume they were creating law in the binding or codificatory sense when they adopted the NIEO Charter, because a substantial and critical segment of the international economic community refused to endorse the Charter as written, and, most importantly, because State practice since the Charter's creation and adoption demonstrates a continued adherence to the customary international law principle of compensation (at least as interpreted since World War II), it is appropriate—necessary—to conclude that Article 2(2)(c) is not presently an authoritative statement of existing international law, ie, not *lex lata*.

See also Brownlie (n 4) 518.

[119] O Schachter, "The Evolving International Law of Development," 15 *Col J Transnat'l L* (1976) 1, 4.

[120] In 1970, the International Court of Justice in the *Barcelona Traction* case found it "surprising" that the evolution of international investment law had not gone further and that no generally accepted rules had yet crystallized in the light of the growth of foreign investments and the expansion of international activities by corporations in the previous half-century. *Barcelona Traction, Light and Power Co, Ltd (Belg v. Spain)* 1970 ICJ 3, 46–7 (5 February). As recently as 2004, a noted commentator on international investment law stated: "There are few customs in this sense in the field of foreign investment." M Sonorajah, *The International Law on Foreign Investment* (2nd edn 2004) 89.

Third, the content of the existing international legal framework was subject to sharp disagreement between industrialized countries and newly decolonized developing nations. For example, as we have seen, capital-exporting states claimed that international law imposed an obligation on host countries to accord foreign investors a minimum standard of protection and required that states expropriating the property of foreign investors needed to provide compensation. Many developing countries, believing that the existing international rules served only to maintain their poverty, rejected this view and, beginning in the 1970s, demanded that their particular needs and circumstances be taken into account.[121] As was discussed above, their position on foreign investment was incorporated into Article 2 of the 1974 UN Charter of Economic Rights and Duties of States, which was adopted by the UN General Assembly and which seemed a strong rejection of the traditional western views of international investment law.

Finally, existing international law offered foreign investors no effective enforcement mechanism to pursue claims against host countries that seized their investments or refused to respect their contractual obligations. As a result, investors had no assurance that investment contracts and arrangements made with host country governments would not be subject to unilateral change at some later time. Although an affiliate of the World Bank, the International Centre for Settlement of Investment Disputes (ICSID), formally established in 1966 to resolve disputes between host countries and foreign private investors,[122] it required the specific consent of the parties to exercise jurisdiction over an investor–state dispute. As a result, the Centre did not hear its first case until 1972.[123] Injured foreign investors who were unable to negotiate a satisfactory settlement, secure an arbitration agreement with a host government, or find satisfaction in the local courts had few options other than to seek espousal of their claims by their home country governments. By its very nature, this process was more political than legal and, in any event, yielded results that were always uncertain and invariably slow.

In sum then, as global economic expansion began to accelerate in the years following World War II, the existing international legal framework for foreign investment was for most investors incomplete, vague, contested, and without an effective enforcement mechanism. Because of these defects, investors and their home governments needed to find another means to protect their investments abroad from the injurious actions of host country governments. That means would lie in negotiating investment treaties.

---

[121] Inspired by the success of the oil-producing countries in raising petroleum prices in 1973–4, developing countries had hoped that by building a numerically strong coalition amongst themselves, they would be able to bring about desired change in various international fora. As a result of the debt crisis in the early 1980s, the internal economic restructuring demanded by international financial institutions, such as the International Monetary Fund (IMF) and the World Bank, and the abandonment of command economy models by developing countries, the movement for a "New International Economic Order" lost steam and was virtually dead by 1990. Wälde (n 93) 771. See generally J Hart, *The New International Economic Order* (1983); JN Bhagwati (ed), *The New International Economic Order: The North–South Debate* (1977).

[122] The ICSID Convention (n 7).

[123] ICSID, "List of Concluded Cases" <http://www.worldbank.org/icsid/cases/conclude.htm> (listing concluded cases in chronological order).

14

The Treatification of International Investment Law

14.1 Introduction

As a result of the perceived deficiencies of the customary international law applicable to foreign investments, discussed in the preceding chapter, international investors in the mid-twentieth century had no assurance that investment arrangements and contracts made with host country governments would not be subject to unilateral change by those governments at some later time. In fact, they did experience expropriations, nationalizations, and forced renegotiation of contracts on many occasions.[1] As a result, foreign investments at that time, particularly in developing countries, seemed to be, in the oft-quoted words of Professor Raymond Vernon, "obsolescing bargains" between the investor and the host country.[2] In the continuing tension between negotiated agreements and subsequent reality which Karl Llewellyn had earlier characterized as a Greek tragedy of "Life struggling against form,"[3] the postcolonial era of nationalizations and contract renegotiations seemed to indicate that life was indeed triumphing over form.

To change the dynamics of this struggle so as to protect the interests of their companies and investors, capital-exporting countries began a process of negotiating international investment treaties that, to the extent possible, would be: (1) complete, (2) clear and specific, (3) uncontestable, and (4) enforceable. A secondary purpose was to facilitate the entry of investment into the territories of their treaty partners. These treaty efforts took place at both the bilateral and multilateral levels, which, though separate, tended to inform and reinforce each other. As a result of this process, a wide spread *treatification*[4] of international investment law took place in a relatively short time. By the beginning of the twenty-first century, foreign investors in many parts of the world were protected primarily by international treaties, rather than by customary international law alone. Investment treaties, often referred to as "international investment agreements" (IIAs), are essentially instruments of international law by which states (1) make commitments to other states with respect to the treatment they will accord to investors and investments from those other states and (2) agree on some mechanism for the enforcement of those commitments.

---

[1] From 1960 through mid-1974, some 62 different developing countries engaged in 875 nationalizations or takeovers of foreign enterprises. The majority of the cases (591) took place in 10 states. UNGA, "Permanent Sovereignty over Natural Resources", UN Doc A/9716 (September 20, 1974) annex at 2, table 1.

[2] Raymond Vernon, *Sovereignty at Bay: The Multinational Spread of U.S. Enterprises* (1971) 46.

[3] "One turns from the contemplation of the work of contract as from the experience of Greek tragedy. Life struggling against form...." KN Llewellyn, "What Price Contract? An Essay in Perspective," 40 *Yale LJ* (1931) 704, 704–51

[4] The word "treatification," while not recognized by any standard English dictionaries, has been used on rare occasions previously. See, eg, the executive summary on missile proliferation on the website of the Canadian Department of Foreign External Affairs, available at <http://www.dfait-maeci.gc.ca/arms/MTCR/page2-en.asp>. The origin of this derivation of the word "treaty" may perhaps be found in the 1908 Nobel lecture of the Peace Prize Laureate Frederik Bajer, who urged that a treaty be established to govern the canals between the North and Baltic seas, stating "there is a need to "treatify," if I may coin this expression, the waterways—the French call them "canaux interocéaniques"—which connect the two seas." Available at <http://nobelprize.org/peace/laureates/1908/bajer-lecture.html>. See also JW Salacuse, "The Treatification of International Investment Law," 13 *Law & Bus Rev Am* (2007) 155.

Three basic types of investment agreements have evolved during that period: (1) bilateral investment treaties, commonly known as "BITs," (2) bilateral economic agreements with investment provisions, and (3) other investment-related agreements involving more than two states.

For all practical purposes, treaties have now become the fundamental source of international law in the area of foreign investment.[5] They form the principal pillar of a new international legal framework for investment. Indeed, one can say that because of the similarities in concepts, language, rules, processes, and structure among investment treaties they form together a "regime" for global investment.[6]

This change has been anything but theoretical. For one thing, it has imposed a discipline on host country treatment of foreign investors by obligating them to grant covered investors full protection and security, fair and equitable treatment, national treatment, most-favored nation treatment, full rights to make international monetary transfers, and protection against arbitrary treatment and expropriation without adequate compensation. In those cases where host governments failed to abide by their treaty commitments aggrieved investors have invoked their rights to sue those governments in arbitration, a phenomenon that has become increasingly common in the new century. As beneficiaries of resulting arbitral awards, many of which were substantial, investors had the power to seek enforcement in national courts throughout the world under treaties such as the ICSID Convention[7] and the New York Convention.[8] Today, as a result, it increasingly seems that in the international investment domain legal form is winning out in its struggle with life, or at least holding its own.

The purpose of this chapter is to examine the history, purposes, and consequences of the investment treatification process. The following chapter will analyze the structure and content of investment treaties and examine how their provisions have been applied to protect, advance, and accommodate the diverse interests of international investors, capital-exporting countries, and host states.

14.2 Historical Background of the Treatification Process

The modern investment treaty is the product of a historical process that has passed through several phases.[9] Let us briefly examine each phase.

(a) The Early Beginnings

Since the very inception of international investment, foreign investors have sought assurances from the sovereigns in whose territory they invest that their interests would be protected from negative actions by the sovereign and local individuals. Investors have even requested that sovereigns grant them privileges and benefits that nationals themselves did not enjoy. Often these assurances and grants of privilege would be embodied in a document that the sovereign issued or agreed to. In the era before the formation of states that

[5] P Juillard, "L'Evolution des Sources du Droit des Investissements," 250 *Recueil Des Cours de L'Academie de Droit International* (1994) 74.

[6] JW Salacuse, "The Emerging Global Regime for Investment," 51 *Harv Int'l LJ* (2010) 427.

[7] Convention on the Settlement of Investment Disputes Between States and Nationals of Other States (March 18, 1965) 17 UST 1270, TIAS 6090, 575 UNTS 159 (ICSID Convention).

[8] Convention on the Recognition and Enforcement of Foreign Arbitral Awards (done June 10, 1958) 330 UNTS 3, 21 UST 2517.

[9] For a more detailed historical treatment, see JW Salacuse, *The Law of Investment Treaties* (2010) 78–108, 370.

conducted foreign relations, traders and investors often formed themselves into associations and negotiated directly with foreign sovereigns to obtain such assurances and grants. For example, as noted earlier in this volume, in 991 AD the Byzantine Emperors Basil II and Constantine VIII, in a document known in Latin as a *chrysobul*, granted to the merchants of Venice the rights to trade in the ports and other places of the Byzantine Empire without paying customs duties, as well as the right to a quarter in Constantinople, known as an *embolum*, for dwelling and trading.[10] Various other sovereigns also granted concessions and franchises to individuals or groups of traders and investors. Similar developments were taken at the same time across Western, Northern, and Eastern Europe. For example, King Henry II of England issued a grant, dated 1157 AD, guaranteeing protection to German merchants from Cologne and to their establishment in London.[11]

Although these documents were called "grants" or "concessions" and not agreements and usually took the form of a unilateral act by the sovereign, they were usually the product of some degree of negotiation between the sovereign or his representatives and the foreign traders who were their beneficiaries. Sovereigns were motivated to grant protection and privileges to foreign traders out of a desire to secure certain advantages for themselves, such as the promotion of foreign trade or the improvement of relations with groups in foreign territories. Thus the basis of these early grants and concessions was reciprocity of benefits. This rationalization was articulated, for example, by King Erik of Norway in 1296 AD when he granted the Hamburg merchants extensive privileges for the purpose of '*ad meliorandum terram nostram cum mercaturis*–"for the amelioration of our territories through trade."[12]

While the instruments issued by sovereigns during this period are most directly analogous to modern international concession contracts granted to foreign companies, one can also view them, in their enunciation of certain standards of investor treatment, as the distant ancestors of modern investment treaties.

(b) The Emergence of a Treaty Framework for Investment Protection in the Seventeenth and Eighteenth Centuries

As Europe emerged from the Middle Ages and began to form nation-states, the sovereigns of those states acted in various ways to protect and advance the interests of their nationals in other countries.[13] Toward this end, they would often negotiate with foreign countries to obtain commercial and trading rights for their nationals. The product of such negotiations was usually a written agreement between the two sovereigns. This historical period witnessed an increase in the reliance on treaties between two sovereigns as an important means of regulating transborder economic activity. The result was a welter of bilateral agreements among the states and principalities of Europe, which, over time, began to demarcate principles of protection for aliens and their property that would later be echoed in modern-day investment treaties. Specifically, in varying degrees one can find

---

[10] P Fischer, "Some Recent Trends and Developments in the Law of Foreign Investment," in K-H Boeckstiegel et al (eds), *Völkerrecht, Recht der internationalen Organisationen, Weltwirtschafatsrecht: Festschrift für Ignaz Seidl-Hohenveldern* (1988) 97. See also "Concessions granted to the Merchants of Venice, by the Byzantine Emperors Basilius and Constantinus, executed in March 991," in P Fischer, *A Collection of International Concessions and Related Instruments* vol I, at 15–18.

[11] Fischer (n 10) 97. Hansa societies worked to acquire special trade privileges for their members. For example, in 1157 the merchants of the Cologne (Köln) Hansa persuaded Henry II of England to grant them special trading privileges and market rights which freed them from all London tolls and allowed them to trade at fairs throughout England.

[12] P Fischer, *A Collection of International Concessions and Related Instruments* (1976) xix.

[13] R Lillich, *Human Rights of Aliens in Contemporary International Law* (1981) 8–11.

the following principles of treatment in these early international agreements: (1) protection and security of aliens and their property;[14] (2) special means of protection for asset recovery and monetary transfers; (3) most-favored-nation treatment[15] (which requires equality of treatment with other foreigners); (4) national treatment (which prohibits unfavorable discrimination in favor of nationals); and (5) guarantees of access to justice and safeguards against its denial.[16] Thus, during this period one can say that the sovereigns of Europe laid the foundation for what would later become the framework for the international investment treaty. And, like modern investment treaties between states, the subjects of the sovereigns concerned were not themselves parties to these agreements—they were mere beneficiaries.[17]

During this period, treaties were not only used to establish mutual economic relationships among nations, but were also employed as instruments of economic domination. An important example was the treaty between the King of France and the Ottoman Sultan in 1536.[18] However, although this agreement and others like it purported to be based on principles of equality and mutuality, they in fact favored European nationals, not Ottoman subjects, because of their superior economic and technological power. These treaties were the basis of what became known as the capitulary system. Individual treaty chapters (*capitula* in Latin) granted foreign traders a variety of privileges, including exemptions from customs duties, the right to be governed by their home country law, freedom from the jurisdiction of local courts, and the right to sue and be sued exclusively in special consular courts. In many places, these treaties became the basis of a full-fledged extra-territorial system of privilege and immunity that applied not only to all European nationals but also to a select group of Ottoman subjects.[19]

These capitulations were an institutionalized symbol of the inferiority and subservience of local institutions and individuals to European power, and they facilitated the domination of much of the non-western world by Western states. Treaties having a similar effect were negotiated in many areas, including the Middle East and Asia.[20] Thus the international

---

[14] For example, the Peace Treaty between Spain and the Netherlands of 1648 provided that the assets of the merchants were not to be seized, not even on account of war, except by judicial process to satisfy debts, other obligations, and contracts. Several treaties between European nations accepted the principles of freedom and security of an alien's person and property, with the exception of those made by Russia, which granted that treatment to merchants only. Because of such provisions, these treaties were called "an international bill of rights". H Neufeld, *The International Protection of Private Creditors from the Treaties of Westphalia to the Congress of Vienna* (1971) 98.

[15] One of the earliest bilateral treaties to have employed the term "the most-favored-nation" was the Trade Treaty of Nijmwegen of 1679 between Sweden and Holland. Since the Treaties of Utrecht of 1713, the term has had regular usage in the treaties of European nations. Neufeld, *The International Protection of Private Creditors from the Treaties of Westphalia to the Congress of Vienna* (1971) 29, 110.

[16] Neufeld, *The International Protection of Private Creditors from the Treaties of Westphalia to the Congress of Vienna* (1971) 10

[17] R Lillich, *Human Rights of Aliens in Contemporary International Law* (1981) 2–3.

[18] See generally, H Maurits van den Boogert and K Fleet (eds), *The Ottoman Capitulations: Text and Context* (2003). In 1536, Francis I of France and Süleyman I of Turkey signed a *capitulation treaty* that became the model for later treaties with other powers. It allowed the establishment of French merchants in Turkey, granted them individual and religious liberty, and provided that consuls appointed by the French king should judge the civil and criminal affairs of French subjects in Turkey according to French law, with the right of appeal to officers of the sultan for assistance in carrying out their decisions. During the eighteenth century nearly every European power obtained capitulations in Turkey, and in the nineteenth century such newly established countries as the United States, Belgium, and Greece followed suit. *The New Encyclopaedia Britannica* (15th edn 2002) vol II, at 832.

[19] B Lewis, *The Emergence of Modern Turkey* (1968) 455.

[20] The capitulation system spread widely in the seventeenth, eighteenth, and early nineteenth centuries, when traders from the West extended Western influence by a process of infiltration rather than by annexation. "Unequal treaties" soon developed, and such treaties as the Sino-British supplementary treaty (1843) and its later amendments established a system of provincial courts and a British supreme court in China to try all cases

economic treaty became an important instrument for spreading European economic power and influence. For people in the non-western world, however, these treaties were an instrument of economic exploitation. In time, with the end of colonialism and the emergence of newly sovereign states in many parts of the non-western world, the capitulary system would end. However, the memory of these experiences would die much less quickly and would influence some groups in these countries to resist investment treaties in the modern era.[21] Nonetheless, the historical foundations of the investment treaties that proliferated in the twentieth and twenty-first centuries can be found in these early trading agreements.

(c) Further Developments in the Eighteenth, Nineteenth, and Early Twentieth Centuries

Most foreign investment in the eighteenth, nineteenth, and early twentieth centuries was made in the context of colonial expansion. Because imperial powers imposed their political and military power on colonized territories and controled the actions of colonial governments and their legal systems, the European countries felt no need for commercial and investment treaties.[22] A blend of diplomacy and force[23] was relied on to prevent adverse interference with the investments and commercial activities of European nationals in the colonies and protectorates.

Beginning in the eighteenth century, western countries began to conclude commercial treaties among themselves on a basis of greater equality than what they had negotiated with non-western nations.[24] The purpose of these agreements was to facilitate trade, rather than investment. For example, from its foundation at the end of the eighteenth century the United States made large numbers of agreements known as treaties of friendship, commerce and navigation (often called FCN treaties),[25] and their geographic spread reflected the expansion of US foreign trade.[26] Although these treaties were intended to facilitate trade and shipping, they occasionally contained provisions affecting the ability of one country's nationals to own property or do business in the territory of the other country. European countries made similar treaties, although they did not use the same

---

involving British subjects while granting no corresponding rights to Chinese residents in Britain. The evils to which the system gave rise were experienced particularly in Turkey and China. *The New Encyclopaedia Britannica* (15th edn 2002) vol II, at 832–3.

[21] eg, JW Salacuse, "Foreign Investment and Legislative Exemptions in Egypt: Needed Stimulus or New Capitulations," in LD Michalak and JW Salacuse, *Social Legislation in the Contemporary Middle East* (1986) 241–61.

[22] On the general history of international law on foreign investments see M Sornarajah, *The International Law on Foreign Investment* (2004) 18–30.

[23] See generally, G Schwarzenberger, *Foreign Investments and International Law* (1969) 22–4; A Bagge, "Intervention on the Ground of Damage Caused to Nationals, with Particular Reference to Exhaustion of Local Remedies and the Rights of Shareholders," in *Selected Readings on Protection by Law of Private Foreign Investments by International and Comparative Law Center* (1964).

[24] R Lillich, *Human Rights of Aliens in Contemporary International Law* (1981) 18–21.

[25] R Wilson, *United States Commercial Treaties and International Law* (1960); K Vandevelde, *United States Investment Treaties* (1992); R Wilson, "Property-Protection Provisions in United States Commercial Treaties," 45 *AJIL* (1951) 83; H Walker, "Modern Treaties of Friendship, Commerce and Navigation," 42 *Minnesota L Rev* (1957–1958) 805.

[26] Thus, the United States first made bilateral commercial treaties with Western Europe, then with Latin America, later with Asia, and still later with Africa. K Vandervelde, "The Bilateral Investment Treaty Program of the United States," 2 *Cornell Int'l LJ* (1988) 201, 203–6.

designation.[27] Many of the concepts and terms used in these agreements would find their way into the investment treaties concluded in the twentieth and twenty-first centuries.

Emerging countries at that time, such as the United States, felt the need to develop a new international legal instrument that would serve two important purposes: (1) establish a comprehensive legal framework for developing good relations with stronger powers to assure national security and further commerce, and (2) create new commercial relations with other emerging nations. The solution to this problem was to create a broad treaty covering amity/friendship, establishment, commerce and navigation. This was the origin of the "friendship, commerce and navigation treaty," of which the United States became a leading exponent.[28] The FCN treaties evolved to play an important role in the articulation and implementation of US policy concerning standards of treatment and protection of foreign investment.[29] Their provisions developed over time to respond to business practices, US commercial interests, and the political and legal environment affecting investment activities.[30]

The first Treaty of Amity and Commerce, concluded by the US with France in 1778, established bilateral trade on a most-favored-nation basis and provided for protection of vessels, crews, passengers, and cargoes;[31] however, it did not include any general property protection provisions.[32] The early FCN treaties were principally trade-oriented agreements and investment protection did not play an important role in their provisions, though they did include the obligation to protect the property of nationals of the other party in its territory. The standard was an "absolute" one, because it did not depend upon the level of protection afforded to the property of nationals of other countries, typically guaranteeing "special protection" or "full and perfect protection" to the covered property.[33]

In addition to broad terms of property protection clauses, these early treaties developed specific provisions covering only commercial property and persons engaged in commerce. For example, an 1815 treaty between the United States and Great Britain restricted protection to "merchants and traders" and promised "the most complete protection and security for their commerce." The 1903 US-Ethiopia FCN treaty assures "security of those engaged in business and of their property" in order to facilitate bilateral commercial relations.[34] Implicit in all of the provisions is the idea that the persons and property of foreigners are entitled to a minimum of respect and protection. Similarly, and regardless of

---

[27] Before the adoption of their bilateral investment treaty programs, European nations relied predominantly on agreements regarding establishment, trade/commerce, and double-taxation avoidance. For the references to such agreements, see KW Hancock, *Survey of British Commonwealth Affairs, Vol. II: Problems of Economic Policy* (1940) 278; J Alenfeld, *Die Investionsförderungsverträge der Bundes Republic Deutschland* (1971) 2–21; M Banz, *Völkerrechtlicher Eigentumschutz durch Investitionsschutzabkommen* (1987) 3–17; M Kamyar, "Ownership of Oil and Gas Resources in the Caspian Sea," 94 *AJIL* (2000) 1, 179–89.

[28] K Vandevelde observes that the earliest FCNs were thus concluded with important European powers that became major US trading partners, and then were utilized as the principal legal basis for establishing commercial relations with newly emerged Latin American republics, and other nations in Asia and Africa. K Vandevelde, *United States Investment Treaties* (1992) 15.

[29] In 1776 the US Congress approved the Plan for Treaties that provided guidance for American negotiators to conclude first treaties of amity and commerce. See generally R Wilson, *United States Commercial Treaties and International Law* (1960) 1–26.

[30] See generally, K Vandevelde, *United States Investment Treaties* (1992).

[31] Vandevelde, *United States Investment Treaties* (1992) 14.

[32] A Benton, "The Protection of Property Rights in Commercial Treaties of the US," in 25 *Zeitschrift für ausländisches öffentliches Recht und Völkerrecht* (1965) 50, 52.

[33] K Vandevelde, *United States Investment Treaties* (1992) 15.

[34] A Benton, "The Protection of Property Rights in Commercial Treaties of the US," in 25 *Zeitschrift für ausländisches öffentliches Recht und Völkerrecht* (1965) 50, 55.

the fact that domestic law might offer a lower level of protection, host governments may not take such property by mere arbitrary executive decree and are subject to FCN provisions that must be applied according to a broad rule of reason.[35] Thus, a fundamental objective of the treaty-making process was to secure minimum international standards of treatment for investors and investments abroad.

The early FCN treaties also granted foreign nationals the right of equal access to domestic courts and later began to include most-favored-nation[36] and national treatment provisions covering other activities potentially related to investment. FCN treaties of this era also began to include provisions dealing explicitly with the problem of expropriation. Typical provisions prohibited the seizures of "vessels, cargoes, merchandise and effects" of the other party's nationals without payment of "equitable and sufficient compensation" or "sufficient indemnification". Later, this protection was extended to cover "property" generally. These FCN treaties also prohibited the confiscation of debts or other property during hostilities.[37] Toward the end of the nineteenth century, FCN treaties extended the scope of protection in an important new domain when they began to address restrictions on earnings repatriation. After World War I, these principles became the foundation for more explicit and effective investment provisions.

(d) From World War I until World War II

After World War I, US FCN treaties increasingly dealt with investment abroad by focusing on the treatment given to US nationals and companies regarding establishment of businesses, the protection of American property from arbitrary and discriminatory governmental actions, expropriation, the processes for settling disputes, and the protection of intellectual property. Nonetheless, during this time US direct foreign investment was not significant and European investment, with certain exceptions, still favored their colonial and dependent territories. In such dependencies, Europeans judged that special agreements to protect investment were not needed.

Immediately after World War I, under the leadership of the Secretary of State Charles Evans Hughes the United States broadened and revitalized its commercial treaty program and focused particularly on the expansion of US foreign trade. One of the results of the effort was the development of a new FCN treaty model containing a uniform clause for investment protection whose provisions, though clothed in new language, were analogous to those initiated in the nineteenth century. Inter-war FCN treaties distinguished between absolute and relative standards of treatment. The absolute treatment standard required each party to provide "the most constant protection and security" as well as "protection required by international law." The relative standard guaranteed national and MFN treatment with respect to the right to "engage in scientific, religious, philanthropic, manufacturing and commercial work" by a national of one party in the territory of the other party, thus broadening the list of protected activities to include noncommercial enterprises. To address the problem of expropriation, a refinement was introduced providing that the property of the other party's national "shall not be taken without due process of

---

[35] For a detailed discussion of property protection provisions, see R Wilson, *United States Commercial Treaties and International Law* (1960) 105–12.

[36] One of the earliest MFN provisions appeared in a US–France FCN that dealt with the "enjoyment of all rights, liberties, privileges, immunities, and exemptions in trade, navigation, and commerce". A Benton "The Protection of Property Rights in Commercial Treaties of the US" in 25 *Zeitschrift für ausländisches öffentliches Recht und Völkerrecht* (1965) 50, 55.

[37] K Vandevelde, *United States Investment Treaties* (1992) 16.

law and without payment of just compensation."[38] Although these inter-war treaties in many respects provided for a heightened standard of protection compared to the pre-WWI treaties, they nevertheless failed to provide protection to property owned by corporations, a matter to be addressed only in the post-WWII period.

(e) The Immediate Aftermath of World War II

In the immediate aftermath of the war, the nations of the world laid the foundations for a set of new institutions that they hoped would lead to global economic expansion and prosperity. One of the envisaged goals was the facilitation of the international flow of capital and investment. The new institutions, all of which were based on international treaties, included the International Bank for Reconstruction and Development, one of whose stated purposes was "... to promote private foreign investment,"[39] the International Monetary Fund,[40] and the General Agreement on Tariffs and Trade,[41] which set the foundation for a multilateral trading system that nearly fifty years later would evolve into the World Trade Organization.[42]

Just as the nations of the world in the immediate postwar era attempted to create a multilateral framework for trade and currency, so too did they attempt to establish a framework for investment. This effort took the form of the Havana Charter of 1948,[43] which would have created the International Trade Organization (ITO) with the power to promulgate rules on international investment as well as trade.[44] Notwithstanding its focus on international trade, however, an important objective of the Charter was to encourage economic development, especially in developing countries, and to foster "the international flow of capital for productive investment." Consequently, the Havana Charter contained a number of provisions concerning foreign investment and the relationship between host states and foreign investors.[45] For example, Article 11(2) (a) of the Charter would have authorized the ITO, inter alia, to make recommendations for and promote bilateral or multilateral agreements on measures designed *to assure just and equitable treatment* for the skills, capital, enterprise, arts, and technology brought from one Member country to another. This was done in order to avoid international double taxation and stimulate foreign private investments. Article 11(2) (c) of the Charter also envisaged that the ITO would formulate and promote the adoption of a general agreement or statement of principles regarding the conduct, practices, and treatment of foreign investment.

---

[38] K Vandevelde, *United States Investment Treaties* (1992) 17; A Benton, "The Protection of Property Rights in Commercial Treaties of the US," in 25 *Zeitschrift für ausländisches öffentliches Recht und Völkerrecht* (1965) 50, 57–9.

[39] Articles of Agreement of the International Bank for Reconstruction and Development (formulated at the Bretton Woods Conference July 1–22, 1944) (opened for signature at Washington December 27, 1945, entered into force December 27, 1945) 2 UNTS 134; 60 Stat 1440; TIAS 1502; 3 Bevans 1390.

[40] Articles of Agreement of the International Monetary Fund (formulated at the Bretton Woods Conference July 1–22, 1944) (opened for signature at Washington December 27, 1945, entered into force December 27, 1945) (1944) 2 UNTS 39; 60 Stat 1401; TIAS 1501; 3 Bevans 1351.

[41] General Agreement on Tariffs and Trade (October 30, 1947) 55 UNTS 194; 61 Stat A-11, TIAS 1700 (GATT).

[42] *General Agreement on Tariffs and Trade 1994 (April 15, 1994), Marrakesh Agreement Establishing the World Trade Organization, Annex 1A, The Legal Texts: The Results of the Uruguay Round of Multilateral Trade Negotiations* 17 (1999) 1867 UNTS 187; 33 ILM 1153 (1994).

[43] Havana Charter for an International Trade Organization (March 24, 1948) UN Doc E/Conf. 2/78.

[44] W Diebold, Jr, "The End of ITO" 9 *Princeton Essays in International Finance No. 16* (1952), cited in TS Shenkin, "Trade-Related Investment Measures in Bilateral Investment Treaties and the GATT: Moving toward a Multilateral Investment Treaty," 55 *U Pittsburgh LR* (1994) 541, 555.

[45] United Nations Conference on Trade and Development: Fair and Equitable Treatment (1999) UNCTAD/ITE/IIT/11 (vol III) 24 (UNCTAD).

In Article 12(2) of the Charter, participating states were to *provide reasonable opportunities* for investments acceptable to them and *adequate security* for existing and future investments and to give *due regard to the desirability of avoiding discrimination* as between foreign investments.[46]

Capital-exporting countries and investors perceived the Charter's investment-related provisions as falling short of establishing an effective investment protection regime. For instance, the reference in Article 11(2) to "just and equitable" treatment did not place a legal obligation on host countries but merely authorized the ITO to recommend that this standard be included in future agreements. This rendered the provision simply an exhortation with respect to future activities.[47] The vague language of Article 12(2) provided only a qualified protection against discriminatory treatment and expropriation, which was deemed insufficient to meet the challenges that began to arise during the decolonization period. Because of these concerns, coupled with other broader trade issues, the capital-exporting nations opted not to ratify the Havana Charter.[48] Due partly to opposition from the western business community, the Havana Charter failed to be ratified by participating countries and, as a result, never became a reality.

Despite this early failure to create a global treaty on investment, capital-exporting nations in the following years continued to make international rules in other forums through treaties that facilitated and protected the investments of their nationals and companies abroad. These efforts took place at both the bilateral and multi-lateral levels, which, though separate, tended to inform and reinforce one another through the next 50 years.

(f) The Later Post-World War II Years

(i) Bilateral Efforts

The post-World War II years witnessed a great expansion in foreign investment, led initially by the United States, then joined by Europe, later by Japan, and still later by other parts of the world. Responding to the great expansion in US foreign investment after World War II, the US government undertook a program to conclude a network of bilateral treaties of friendship, commerce, and navigation that, in addition to other commercial matters, specifically sought to facilitate and protect US direct foreign investments abroad.[49] Indeed, because of the diminished importance of bilateral commercial treaties as means to promote trade in the postwar era of multilateral trade rules, the US increasingly viewed FCN treaties as the preferred method for investment protection.[50] Starting with the existing FCN framework, the United States added various new provisions that were basically of two types: (1) those dealing with protection of the investment property itself, and (2) those dealing with subjects other than property, but which nevertheless were vital in determining

---

[46] Havana Charter for an International Trade Organization (March 24, 1948), UN Doc E/Conf.2/78). <http://www.wto.org/English/docs_e/legal_e/havana_e.pdf> accessed March 27, 2009.

[47] See generally, United Nations Conference on Trade and Development, *Fair and Equitable Treatment* (1999) UNCTAD/ITE/IIT/11 (vol III) 24–5.

[48] See generally, United Nations Conference on Trade and Development, *International Investment Instruments: A Compendium* (1996) vol I, at xx.

[49] For a concise overview of the history of US bilateral investment treaties, see the United States Supreme Court decision in *Sumitomo Shoji America v. Avagliano*, 457 US 176 (1982). See also JW Salacuse, "BIT By BIT: The Growth of Bilateral Investment Treaties and Their Impact on Foreign Investment in Developing Countries," 24 *Intl Lawyer* (1990) 655, 656–61.

[50] K Vandevelde, *United States Investment Treaties* (1992) 17; A Benton "The Protection of Property Rights in Commercial Treaties of the US," in 25 *Zeitschrift für ausländisches öffentliches Recht und Völkerrecht* (1965) 50, 60.

the legal and economic status of foreign-owned property. The provisions under the first category dealt with (a) taking of property, (b) protection and security of property, (c) equitable treatment, (d) unreasonable and discriminatory measures, and (e) public ownership.[51] The provisions under the second category concerned most-favored nation and national treatment and expanded those standards to cover new investment activities and intellectual property. This second category also included dispute settlement clauses.[52]

The post-World War II US FCN treaties contained a number of innovations that would later shape the investment treaty practice of other nations. One important innovation of the revised FCN treaties lies in the application of traditional FCN treaty benefits to corporate activities, including those of local subsidiaries.[53] The FCN treaties also sought to strengthen enforcement of its provisions in several ways. First, where parties have agreed to arbitrate their disputes, the treaties encouraged settlement of private controversies through commercial arbitration by including a clause providing for judicial enforcement of arbitration awards. Further, the entire treaty was strengthened by a provision requiring state parties to submit to the jurisdiction of the International Court of Justice (ICJ) to settle all disputes over the interpretation or application of its provisions.[54]

The FCN treaties of this period specifically incorporated the "Hull formula" by requiring "prompt, adequate, and effective compensation" for the expropriation of property of nationals and companies of the other party, a provision intended to significantly expand the previous requirement of "just compensation."[55] Seeking for the first time to protect US investors from host country exchange controls, the new treaties also constrained the rights of state parties to impose restrictions on currency transfers.[56] The clear intent of the FCN of this era was to establish binding principles for the treatment of foreign nationals and their property.[57]

Although the United States signed approximately 23 such treaties between 1946 and 1966,[58] the effort soon lost momentum as developing countries, increasingly skeptical of the benefits of foreign investment, demonstrated growing reluctance to make the types of guarantees requested by the United States government to protect US investments abroad.

(ii) Multilateral Efforts

At the same time, despite the defeat of the Havana Charter, official and non-governmental efforts were made to prepare multilateral conventions governing foreign investment exclusively. These included the International Chamber of Commerce's International Code of Fair

[51] Benton, "The Protection of Property Rights in Commercial Treaties of the US," in 25 *Zeitschrift für ausländisches öffentliches Recht und Völkerrecht* (1965) 50, 60–7.
[52] Benton, "The Protection of Property Rights in Commercial Treaties of the US," in 25 *Zeitschrift für ausländisches öffentliches Recht und Völkerrecht* (1965) 67–72.
[53] KS Gudgeon, "United States Bilateral Investment Treaties: Comments on their Origin, Purposes, and General Treatment Standards," 4 *Intl Tax & Business L* (1986) 105, 108.
[54] A Benton, "The Protection of Property Rights in Commercial Treaties of the US," in 25 *Zeitschrift für ausländisches öffentliches Recht und Völkerrecht* (1965) 50, 72; K Vandevelde, *United States Investment Treaties* (1992) 19; R Wilson, "Postwar Commercial Treaties of the US," 43 *AJIL* (1949) 262, 275. A dispute between the United States and Italy over Italy's treatment of an American subsidiary in Sicily under the 1948 United States–Italy FCN Treaty did in fact result in a decision by the International Court of Justice. *Elettronica Sicula SpA. (ELSI), (US v. Italy),* (Judgment) (July 20, 1989) ICJ Rep 15.
[55] K Vandevelde, *United States Investment Treaties* (1992) 19.
[56] Vandevelde, *United States Investment Treaties* (1992) 19.
[57] R Wilson, "Postwar Commercial Treaties of the US," 43 *AJIL* (1949) 262, 277.
[58] TS Shenkin, "Trade-Related Investment Measures in Bilateral Investment Treaties and the GATT: Moving toward a Multilateral Investment Treaty," 55 *U Pittsburgh L Rev* (1994) 541, 555. See also K Kunzer, "Developing a Model Bilateral Investment Treaty," 14 *L Policy Intl Business* (1983) 273, 276.

Treatment of Foreign Investment (1949),[59] the International Convention for the Mutual Protection of Private Property Rights in Foreign Countries (1957),[60] a private effort known as the Abs-Shawcross Convention, and the OECD Draft Convention on the Protection of Foreign Property (1967), among others.[61] Although none of these efforts was ever adopted, they did inform and influence the development of the investment treaty movement that was to come.[62]

One multilateral effort in the mid-twentieth century that did have great significant lasting impact was the creation of the European Economic Community in 1957,[63] which would evolve later into the European Union. Like its predecessors, the European Union is founded on a treaty[64] (the EU Treaty) among its members, and that treaty contains important provisions relating to inter-European investment. Thus, in part, the European Union treaty is an investment treaty designed to promote and protect the flow of capital among its members. For example, Article 43 of the EEC grants all member state firms the right of establishment in all EU countries, while Article 47 guarantees that such firms will receive national treatment.

Moreover, the treaty grants investors from EU member states the right to transfer capital and earnings freely, and to receive national treatment on expropriation. Indeed, Article 56 of the EU Treaty specifically prohibits restrictions on the movement of capital and payments between member states and between member states and third countries. Finally, the European Court of Justice has jurisdiction both to hear cases related to violations of treaty rights directly and to overturn national court decisions inconsistent with the treaty. The EU Treaty also authorizes the European Commission to reduce barriers to investment both among EU members and from third countries, a task that the Commission has pursued quite energetically.[65]

---

[59] For text, see United Nations Conference on Trade and Development, *International Investment Instruments: A Compendium* (1996) vol III, at 273–8.

[60] Abs and Shawcross, "The Proposed Convention to Protect Private Foreign Investment: A Round Table: Comment on the Draft Convention by its Authors," 9 *J of Public L* (1960) 119.

[61] For the text of the OECD Draft Convention on the Protection of Foreign Property, see 7 *Intl Legal Mat* (1968) 241. For a survey of the various multilateral efforts to prepare treaties on foreign investment, see F Tschofen, "Multilateral Approaches to the Treatment of Foreign Investment," 7 *ICSID REVIEW—Foreign Investment Law Journal* (1992) 384, 385–6.

[62] TW Walde, "Introductory Note, European Energy Conference: Final Act, Energy Charter Treaty, Decisions, and Energy Charter Protocol on Energy Efficiency and Related Environmental Aspects," 34 *ILM* (1995) 360 (noting the strong influence of BITs on the trade provisions of a multilateral energy treaty); P Juillard, "Le Réseau Français des Conventions Bilatérales d'Investissement: á la Recherche d'un Droit Perdu?" 13 *Droit et Pratique du Commerce Internationale* (1987) 9, 16 (noting that France based its model BIT on the 1967 Organization for Economic Cooperation and Development ("OECD") Draft Convention on the Protection of Foreign Property).

[63] Treaty Establishing the European Economic Community, (EEC Treaty) in Treaties Establishing the European Communities (EC Off l Pub Off).

[64] Treaty on European Union (TEU) (amending EEC Treaty), as amended by Single European Act, OJL 169/1 (1987), [1987] 2 *CMLR* 741 (SEA) in Treaties Establishing the European Communities (EC Off l PubOff 1987).

[65] For example, in June 1997, the European Commission issued an interpretative Communication clarifying the scope of EU Treaty provisions on capital movements and the right of establishment. It took this initiative because certain Member States had imposed limits on the number of voting shares that investors from other Member States could acquire in privatization operations. The Communication stresses that free movement of capital and freedom of establishment constitute fundamental and directly applicable freedoms established by the EU Treaty. Nationals of other Member States should, therefore, be free to acquire controlling stakes, exercise the voting rights attached to these stakes and manage domestic companies under the same conditions laid down in a Member State for its own nationals. Communication of the European Commission on Certain Legal Aspects Concerning Intra-EU Investment (EC) (July 19, 1997) OJ C 220 15–18. In April 2001, the Commission reaffirmed the validity of its interpretative Communication on investment.

(g) The Development of the Bilateral Investment Treaty (BIT) and the Creation of the International Centre for Settlement of Investment Disputes (ICSID)

A new and important phase in the historical development of investment treaties began on the eve of the 1960s when individual European countries began to negotiate bilateral treaties that were unlike previous bilateral commercial agreements but that were similar to the multilateral efforts mentioned above. These new treaties dealt exclusively with foreign investment and sought to create an international legal framework governing investments by the nationals of one country in the territory of another. The stated purpose of nearly all of these treaties was to protect and promote foreign investment. The modern bilateral investment treaty (BIT) was thus born.

Germany, which had lost all of its foreign investments as a result of its defeat in World War II, took the lead in this new phase of investment treaty-making. Beginning with the first such agreement with Pakistan in 1959, Germany proceeded to negotiate similar investment treaties with countries throughout the developing world. Eventually, Germany would become one of the nations with the greatest number of BITs, having concluded 138 by 2009.[66] At the same time, various European countries were in the process of liquidating their colonial empires. As part of that process, their governments felt a need to safeguard the existing investments of their nationals in the newly independent territories, and also to facilitate future investments. Therefore, the former colonial powers also began to develop bilateral treaty programs,[67] concluding BITs not only with their former colonies but also with other developing countries. Moreover, not only did former colonial powers like the United Kingdom, Belgium, France, and the Netherlands actively negotiate BITs, but European countries that had no colonies, such as Switzerland, Austria, and Italy, joined the BIT movement in relatively short order.[68] By 1980, European countries had concluded approximately 150 BITs with a broad array of developing countries.[69]

The European BITs incorporated many of the principles that had been elaborated in earlier bilateral commercial agreements, as well as in the various unsuccessful multilateral efforts. To implement their bilateral treaty programs, each capital-exporting state developed a model or prototype treaty which it used in negotiations with other countries. The models prepared by the European states bore significant similarities.[70] Generally, the BITs guaranteed investors of one treaty partner in the territory of another treaty partner various standards of protection, including protection from expropriation without just compensation, and the right to make monetary transfers.

---

[66] UNCTAD, *World Investment Report 2008* (2008) 15.

[67] F A Mann, "British Treaties for the Promotion and Protection of Investments," 52 *Brit YB Intl L* (1981) 241; P Juillard, "Les conventions bilatérales d'investissements conclues par la France," 106 *Journal du Droit International* (1979) 274; J Karl, "The Promotion and Protection of German Foreign Investment Abroad," 11 *ICSID Rev- FILJ* (1996) 1; M Bos, "The Protection of Foreign Investments in Dutch Court and Treaty Practice," 3 *Intl in the Netherlands* (1980) 221; W Van de Voorde, "Belgian Bilateral Investment Treaties as a Means for Promoting and Protecting Foreign Investment," 44 *Studia Diplomatica* (1991) 87; Y Matsui, "Japan's International Legal Policy for the Protection of Foreign Investment," 32 *Japanese Annual Intl L* (1989) 1.

[68] M-Ch Kraft, "Les accords bilatéraux sur la protection des investissements conclus par la Suisse," in D Dicke (ed), *Foreign Investment in the Present and a New International Economic Order* 72–95 (1987); N Huu-tru, "Le réseau suisse d'accords bilatéraux d'encouragement et de protection des investissements," 92 *Revue Générale de Droit International Public* (1988) 577; O M Maschke, "Investitionsschutzabkommen: Neue vertragliche Wege im Dienste der Österreichischen Wirtschaft," 37 *Österreichische Zeitschrift für Öffentliches Recht und Völkerrecht* (1986) 201.

[69] International Chamber of Commerce, *Bilateral Investment Treaties for International Investment* (1980).

[70] The similarity is attributed to the fact that some European countries seemed to have emulated the German BIT model. "Reforming the International Legal Order: German Legal Comments," in Th Oppermann and E-U Petersman (eds), *Tübinger Schriften zum internationalen und europäischen Recht*, Band I (1987) 37.

One important innovation of the BIT movement in its initial phase was the provision in the treaties for investors to bring claims against host states for violation of their treaty rights directly to an international arbitration tribunal. This process, known as investor–state arbitration, would become a powerful enforcement tool to protect treaty standards. Prior to this time, unless an investor had concluded a separate agreement with a host government calling for arbitration, an aggrieved investor could only rely on its home country to press claims against the host government. As indicated in Chapter 13, a home government was not obligated to press such claims, and if it chose to do so, it became the owner of that claim with the full and exclusive power to decide how to press it, whether and how to settle it, and what should be done with any settlement payments.

An important institutional support for the enforcement of BIT provisions was the creation of the International Centre for Settlement of Investment Disputes (ICSID) in 1965. In the early 1960s, the World Bank directed its attention to the problem of resolving disputes between foreign investors and host governments because it believed that problem was impeding the flow of capital necessary for the development of less developed countries.[71] The concern of investors that host countries would not respect their commitments was an important element of political risk and created an unfavorable investment climate. The Bank came to believe the problem of unfavorable investment climates in many poor countries might be attacked *procedurally* by creating international machinery that would be voluntarily available for the conciliation and arbitration of investment disputes.[72] In other words, the Bank saw the establishment of an adequate method for investment dispute settlement as a way to improve a country's investment climate and thus promote foreign private investments.

The World Bank therefore proposed the adoption of an international convention that would create a new international institution: the International Centre for Settlement of Investment Disputes (ICSID). The ICSID was meant to provide conciliation and arbitration facilities for investment disputes between foreign investors and host country governments. In 1965, the Convention on the Settlement of Disputes between States and the Nationals of Other States[73] was concluded and was initially adopted by 30 states.[74] It sought to foster a climate of mutual confidence between capital-importing and capital-exporting states by providing basic rules to protect the legitimate interests of governments and foreign investors alike. This enabled both capital-exporting and capital-importing states to be members of the Centre and participate in its governance.[75] After the adoption of the Convention, investment treaties began to refer to it as a forum for resolution of treaty disputes and signatory countries consented to ICSID jurisdiction in treaties themselves. The first investment treaty to include an ICSID clause was the Netherlands–Indonesia treaty signed in 1968.[76] Since then, it has become standard practice for treaties to make

[71] Paper Prepared by the General Counsel of the World Bank and transmitted to the members of the Committee of the Whole, SID/63–2 (February 18, 1963) 3 in ICSID, *History of the ICSID Convention* (1968) vol II, part I at 73.

[72] Note by the President of the Executive Directors, R 61–128 (December 28, 1961) in ICSID, *History of the ICSID Convention* (1968) vol II, part I at 4–6.

[73] Convention on the Settlement of Investment Disputes Between States and Nationals of Other States (March 18, 1965) 575 UNTS 159; 17 UST 1270; TIAS 6090 (ICSID Convention).

[74] Chronological List of Contracting States and other Signatories of the Convention, available at <http://www.worldbank.org/icsid/constate/c-states-en.htm>.

[75] Report of the World Bank Executive Directors on the ICSID Convention, Doc ICSID/2 in ICSID, *History of the ICSID Convention* (1968) vol II, part II at 1072–4.

[76] ICSID clauses were added to several other early treaties, by reference to the Convention in subsequent protocols. See eg, Netherlands-Cote d'Ivoire BIT of 1965 and the Protocol thereto of 1971. R Dolzer and M Stevens, *Bilateral Investment Treaties* (1995) 130.

reference to the ICSID for the settlement of disputes arising under their provisions and for treaty signatories to give their consent to ICSID jurisdiction. In addition, the membership of ICSID grew steadily over the years and by 2012 included 148 states.[77] Owing to the great number of BITs and the incorporated references to ICSID arbitration within them, some commentators claim ICSID is the natural forum for resolution of investor–state disputes.[78] At the same time, many, if not most BITs also offer ad hoc arbitration under UNCITRAL Rules as an alternative method of resolving investor–state disputes.

Although ICSID was formally established in 1965,[79] it did not hear its first case until 1972.[80] Despite this somewhat delayed start, ICSID was destined to become an important institution for international investment dispute resolution.[81] By the end of 2011, for example, out of an estimated total of 450 investor–state arbitrations initiated since 1987, nearly 350 cases were brought before ICSID.[82] From the point of view of the investor, a mechanism in international law finally existed to deal with investors' historical inability to enforce international legal provisions against host states.[83] The growing number of cases and the sometimes large resulting monetary awards were also causing considerable consternation among certain host states.[84]

(h) The Gathering Momentum of the BIT Movement

The reason for the greater success of the European BIT programs as compared with earlier US efforts is not completely clear, but the answer may lie in the fact that the European countries were less demanding with respect to guarantees on such matters as free conversion of local currency, abolition of performance requirements, and protection against expropriation. Moreover, specific foreign aid relationships between some European countries and the European Community, on the one hand, and individual developing countries, on the other, may have predisposed the developing countries to look more favorably on concluding BITs with European states.

Nonetheless, spurred in part by the experience of the Europeans, the United States launched its own BIT program in 1981.[85] By July 2012, the US had signed 48 BITs with developing countries and emerging markets, of which 41 had entered into force.[86] As non-

---

[77] Of 158 states that signed the Convention on the Settlement of Investment Disputes between States and Nationals of Other States as of July 2012, 148 States had deposited their instruments of ratification and attained the status of Contracting State. See the ICSID website at <http://icsid.worldbank.org/ICSID/FrontServlet?requestType = CasesRH&actionVal = ShowHome&pageName = MemberStates_Home>.

[78] BM Cremades, "Arbitration in Investment Treaties: Public Offer of Arbitration in Investment-Protection Treaties," in R Briner and K-H Böckstiegel (eds), *Law of International Business and Dispute Settlement in the 21st Century: liber amicorum Karl-Heinz Böckstiegel* (2001) 158.

[79] Convention on the Settlement of Investment Disputes Between States and Nationals of Other States (March 18, 1965), 575 UNTS 159; 17 UST 1270; TIAS 6090 (ICSID Convention).

[80] ICSID, *List of Concluded Cases*, <http://www.worldbank.org/icsid/cases/conclude.htm> accessed November 30, 2004 (listing concluded cases in chronological order).

[81] ICSID, *List of Concluded Cases.*

[82] UNCTAD, *World Investment Report 2012* (2012) 86–7.

[83] For a thorough analysis of the ICSID Convention and ICSID arbitration rules, see C Schreuer, *The ICSID Convention: A Commentary* (2001).

[84] Schreuer, *The ICSID Convention: A Commentary* (2001).

[85] K Vandevelde, *United States Investment Treaties* (1992) 29–45; P B Gann, "The U.S. Bilateral Investment Treaty Program," 21 *Stanford J Int'l L* (1985) 73; KS Gudgeon, "United States Bilateral Investment Treaties: Comments on their Origin, Purposes, and General Treatment Standards," 4 *Int'l Tax & Bus Law* (1986) 105, 107–11; JW Salacuse, "BIT by BIT: The Growth of Bilateral Investment Treaties and Their Impact on Investment in Developing Countries," 24 *The Intl Lawyer* (1990) 655–75.

[86] US Dept of State website at <http://www.state.gov/e/eb/ifd/bit/117402.htm>.

western countries began to export capital, like Japan and Kuwait, they too negotiated BITs to create a legal framework for their nationals' investments in specific countries.[87]

With the end of the communist era and the abandonment of command economies in many parts of the world, the late 1980s witnessed a new phase in the history of the BIT movement. The emerging economies of Eastern and Central Europe, as well as some Latin American, African, and Asian countries that had previously been hostile to foreign investment, now actively sought foreign capital to finance their development. This dramatic transformation entailed sweeping changes in law and policy.[88] Reflecting this policy shift, countries with emerging markets entered into BITs with industrialized states in order to attract capital and technology to advance their development, and did so at an accelerating pace. Whereas some 309 BITs had been concluded by the end of 1988,[89] more than 2,833 BITs were concluded by the end of 2001.[90] This dramatic change in so short a time period represents a substantial feat of international law-making. In 2001 alone, a total of 97 countries concluded some 158 BITs, a numerical record for any single year since the BIT movement began in 1959.[91] The cumulative result of this effort has been the creation of an increasingly dense BIT network linking over 179 different countries by the end of 2011.[92]

Meanwhile, the number of BITs involving two developing countries, what one may call "South-South" BITS, has also been increasing steadily. By the end of 2005, the number of "South-South" BITs had grown to 644, representing 26 percent of BITs overall. Countries with large FDI outflows, such as China, Malaysia, and the Republic of Korea, are among those with the highest number of BITs. As of 2008, the leading developing countries among BIT signatories were China with 120 BITs and Egypt with 100, many of which were signed with other developing economies.[93]

While BITs are usually made between capital-exporting states and developing countries, on occasion two developing countries or two industrialized countries have formed such agreements. Examples of the former include BITs between Thailand and China and between Egypt and Morocco.[94] The most notable example of the latter is the 1988 agreement between the United States and Canada that created a free trade area.[95] This agreement included a special chapter that in effect functioned as a BIT and closely paralleled BITs that the United States has negotiated with other countries.[96] By 1994, this treaty evolved into the North American Free Trade Agreement ("NAFTA") among Canada, Mexico, and the United States.[97] For all intents and purposes, NAFTA's section on investment, Chapter Eleven, constitutes a BIT among the three countries.

---

[87] United Nations Conference on Trade and Development, *Bilateral Investment Treaties in the Mid-1990s* (1998) 185–6.

[88] JW Salacuse, "From Developing Countries to Emerging Markets: A Changing Role for Law in the Third World," 33 *The Intl Lawyer* (1999) 875, 875–7.

[89] A J Pappas, "References on Bilateral Investment Treaties," 4 *ICSID Rev-Foreign Inv LJ* (1989) 189, 194–203.

[90] UNCTAD, *World Investment Report 2008* (2008) 14.

[91] UNCTAD, *World Investment Report 2002: Transnational Corporations & Export Competitiveness* (2002) 8.

[92] UNCTAD, *World Investment Report 2012* (2012) 89.

[93] UNCTAD, *World Investment Report 2008* (2008).

[94] Agreement for the Promotion and Protection of Investments (PRC–Thailand) (March 12, 1985) <http://www.unctad.org/sections/dite/iia/docs/bits/china_thailand.pdf> accessed April 1, 2009; Agreement regarding the Encouragement and Protection of Investment (Egypt–Morocco) (June 6, 1976) <http://www.unctad.org/sections/dite/iia/docs/bits/egypt_morocco_arb.pdf> accessed April 1, 2009.

[95] Free Trade Agreement (US–Canada) (January 2, 1988) 27 *ILM* 281 (1988).

[96] Free Trade Agreement (US–Canada) (January 2, 1988) 27 *ILM* 281 (1988) 373–80.

[97] North American Free Trade Agreement (US–Canada–Mexico), (December 17, 1992) 32 *ILM* 289 (1993) (NAFTA).

(i) The Development of Multilateral Regional and Sector Investment Agreements

The 1980s and 1990s also witnessed a new phase in the evolution of investment treaties: the development of regional investment agreements whose purpose was to promote and protect investments among countries within a geographic region. Up to that point, the most famous and most successful of such endeavors was the European Union, discussed earlier, which had been launched in the late 1950s and had become increasingly integrated in the following years. With varying degree of success, other regions also sought to develop regional international investment arrangements. The principal regional arrangements are examined briefly.

(1) Arab States Investment Agreement

One of the earliest of these was the *Unified Agreement for the Investment of Arab Capital in the Arab States*,[98] which was signed on November 26, 1980 in Amman, Jordan, during the Eleventh Arab Summit Conference. It entered into force on September 7, 1981.[99] The Middle East includes countries, such as Kuwait, Saudi Arabia, and the United Arab Emirates, that have accumulated significant capital reserves as a result of their oil revenues, and other poorer countries like Egypt, Sudan, and Syria, that have a significant need for investment funds.[100] One of the purposes of the Unified Agreement for the Investment of Arab Capital in the Arab States was to encourage nationals of the wealthy Arab states to invest in the region's poorer countries. As a general matter, this treaty does not provide high standards of protection to foreign Arab investors. For example, it contains no specific guarantees of full protection and security or of fair and equitable treatment. Nor does it provide strong enforcement by guaranteeing the right to dispute settlement under ICSID's auspices. Instead, it states that until the Arab Court of Justice is established and its jurisdiction is determined, investment disputes under the Agreement will be settled by an Arab Investment Court, which was not created until 2003. Since that time, the Arab Investment Court has heard a few cases.[101]

(2) ASEAN Investment Agreement

The second regional investment treaty is the Agreement Among The Government of Brunei Darussalam, The Republic of Indonesia, Malaysia, The Republic of The Philippines, The Republic of Singapore, and The Kingdom of Thailand for the Promotion and Protection of Investments (December 15, 1987),[102] referred to as the ASEAN Agreement for the Promotion and Protection of Investments. Similar to many BITs, this treaty provides a higher level of protection for other ASEAN investors than that found in the Unified Agreement for the Investment of Arab Capital in Arab States. For example, each country

---

[98] League of Arab States (1982). "Unified Agreement for the Investment of Arab Capital in the Arab States", *Economic Documents*, No 3 (Tunis: League of Arab States) <http://www.unctad.org/sections/dite/iia/docs/Compendium//en/36%20volume%202.pdf> accessed September 29, 2007.

[99] The agreement has been ratified by all member States of the League except Algeria and the Comoros. The text of the "Unified Agreement for the Investment of Arab Capital in the Arab States" is available in *Transnational Dispute Management* vol I, issue 4 (October 2004).

[100] JW Salacuse, "Arab Capital and Trilateral Ventures in the Middle East: Is Three a Crowd?" in Kerr and Yassine (eds), *Rich and Poor States in the Middle East* (1982) 129–63.

[101] W B Hamida, "The First Arab Investment Court Decision," 7 *JWIT* (2006) 699, 702.

[102] The ASEAN Agreement for the Promotion and Protection of Investments of 1987, (1988) 27 *ILM* 612.

undertakes an obligation to ensure full protection to investments made by investors of other member nations and not to impair by unjustified or discriminatory measures the management, maintenance, use, enjoyment, extension, disposition or liquidation of such investments. All investments made by investors of a member country are to be accorded fair and equitable treatment in the territory of other treaty members. Moreover, the treatment accorded to investors can be no less favorable than that granted to investors from other countries.

Investments made by nationals or companies of a member country are not to be subject to expropriation or nationalization or any equivalent measure, except for public use or in the public interest, under due process of law, on a nondiscriminatory basis and upon payment of adequate compensation. The compensation should amount to the market value of the investment that prevailed immediately before the measure of dispossession became public knowledge, and it should be freely transferable in usable currencies from the host country. The compensation is to be determined and paid without undue delay. The national or company affected has the right to a prompt review of the amount by a judicial body or some other independent authority.

The treaty provides for various dispute settlement options to be decided upon by mutual agreement of the parties, including: (a) the International Centre for Settlement of Investment Disputes (ICSID); (b) arbitration under the rules of the United Nations Commission on International Trade Law (UNCITRAL); (c) the Regional Arbitration Centre at Kuala Lumpur; or (d) any other regional centre for arbitration in ASEAN. The first arbitral decision under the treaty was rendered in 2003.[103] In an effort to increase economic cooperation, ASEAN ministers signed a new Comprehensive Investment Treaty, which upon ratification by ASEAN states will supersede the 1987 Agreement.[104]

(3) Mercosur Investment Treaties

Yet a third regional treaty effort took place within Latin America among the countries of the Common Market of the Southern Cone ("Mercosur"), a customs union and trade bloc comprising Argentina, Brazil, Paraguay, and Uruguay, established in 1991 by the Treaty of Asunción.[105] The Mercosur members concluded two regional investment treaties in 1994 as protocols to the Treaty of Asunción. The first, the Protocol of Colonia for the Promotion and Reciprocal Protection of Investments in Mercosur, is intended to serve as the region's main investment legal regime.[106] As such, it defines the rights enjoyed by persons from a member state who make investments in other member states.

Mercosur's second regional investment treaty—the Protocol of Buenos Aires for the Promotion and Reciprocal Protection of Investments Coming from Non-Mercosur State Parties—serves as a baseline agreement, outlining the "general legal principles to be applied by each of the State Parties to investments coming from non-Mercosur states...so as not to create differentiated conditions that would distort the flow of investments."[107] Despite their relatively broad investor protection provisions, the Colonia and Buenos Aires Protocols

---

[103] *Chi Oo Trading Pte Ltd v. Government of the Union of Myanmar* (Award), ASEAN Case No ARB/01/1 (March 31, 2003) (2003) 42 *ILM* 3 at 540.

[104] Available at <http://www.asean.org/documents/FINAL-SIGNED-ACIA.pdf>.

[105] Treaty Establishing a Common Market.

[106] Protocol of Colonia for the Promotion and Reciprocal Protection of Investments in Mercosur (January 17, 1994) MERCOSUR/CMC/DEC No 11/93 (Colonia Protocol).

[107] Protocol of Buenos Aires for the Promotion and Reciprocal Protection of Investments Coming from Non-Mercosur State Parties (August 5, 1994) MERCOSUR/CMC/DEC No 11/94 at pmbl (Buenos Aires Protocol) <http://www.sice.oas.org/trade/mrcsrs/decisions/dec1194e.asp> accessed April 2, 2009.

were not in force as of 2008. Both treaties require ratification by the four Mercosur member countries.[108] However, the first had been ratified only by Argentina and Uruguay and the second only by Argentina, Paraguay, and Uruguay.

(4) Comesa Treaty

A fourth regional treaty occurred within Africa: The Common Market for Eastern and Southern Africa (COMESA).[109] COMESA is one of the largest trading organizations in Africa, and includes 374 million people.[110] It is a preferential trading area with 19 members that stretches from Libya to Zimbabwe.[111] COMESA replaced a Preferential Trade Area that had existed since 1981.[112] By 2000, COMESA aimed for the removal of all internal tariffs through a free trade area, and by 2004, a common external tariff was meant to be created. Unfortunately, by 2005 the 2000 goals had only been partially achieved.[113]

In 2007, member states agreed to impose a common external tariff, which is a vital step to imposing a custom union. Having reservations about liberalized trade, Angola, Ethiopia, and Uganda declined to adopt the measure.[114] COMESA representatives have met with their European counterparts to discuss a new economic partnership agreement.[115] In 2008, COMESA agreed to expand the free trade zone to include the East African Community and the Southern Africa Development Community.

(5) North American Free Trade Agreement

Certainly the most famous and successful of the regional arrangements concluded at the end of the twentieth century was the North American Free Trade Agreement (NAFTA), signed by the United States, Canada, and Mexico on December 17, 1992.[116] NAFTA put in place the legal structure for one of the largest free trade areas in the world with over 360 million consumers and $6 trillion in annual output. Despite the omission of the word "investment" from its title, NAFTA governs both trade and investment among its three member states. In effect, Chapter Eleven of NAFTA, entitled "Investment," constitutes an investment treaty among the three countries and its text has clearly been influenced by the provisions of earlier bilateral investment treaties.

In order to facilitate the flow of capital within the NAFTA area, Chapter Eleven seeks: (1) to reduce or remove barriers to investment in one country by investors of another member country, (2) to create a secure investment climate by specifying clear rules

---

[108] Colonia Protocol (n 106 above) Article 11 at 1; Buenos Aires Protocol (n 107) Article 4.

[109] Treaty Establishing the Common Market for Eastern and Southern Africa (November 5, 1993) 33 *ILM* 1067.

[110] S Flatto, Note, "Too Much of a Good Thing?: Reassessing the Proliferation of African Regional Agreements," 30 *Sufflk Transnat'l L Rev* (2007) 407, 415 (2007).

[111] Current members include: Burundi, Comoros, Democratic Republic of Congo, Djibouti, Egypt, Eritrea, Ethiopia, Kenya, Libya, Madagascar, Malawi, Mauritius, Rwanda, Seychelles, Sudan, Swaziland, Uganda, Zambia, and Zimbabwe. Former members include: Angola, Lesotho, Mozambique, Tanzania, and Namibia.

[112] M Oduor, "Resolving Trade Disputes in Africa: Choosing Between Multilateralism and Regionalism: The Case of COMESA and the WTO," 12 *Tulane J Intl Comparative* (2005) 177, 189.

[113] Oduor, "Resolving Trade Disputes in Africa: Choosing Between Multilateralism and Regionalism: The Case of COMESA and the WTO," 12 *Tulane J Intl Comparative* (2005) at 189–90.

[114] "International Legal Developments in Review: 2007 Regional and Comparative Law," 42 *Intl Law* (2008) 863, 875.

[115] "International Legal Developments in Review: 2007 Regional and Comparative Law," 42 *Intl Law* (2008) 863, 875.

[116] North American Free Trade Agreement Between the Government of the United States of America, the Government of Canada and the Government of the United Mexican States (US Government Printing Office, 1993).

concerning the treatment to which NAFTA investors and their investments are entitled, and (3) to provide a fair means for the settlement of disputes between a NAFTA investor and the host country. Section A of the chapter contains provisions on the establishment and treatment of investment and Section B governs dispute settlement.

Key NAFTA investment provisions in facilitating the flow of capital and the making of investments are found in Articles 1102 and 1103, which guarantee that investors and investments will receive national treatment or most favored nation treatment with respect to the "establishment, acquisition, expansion, management, conduct, operation and sale or other disposition of investments." Article 1106 of NAFTA prohibits a host country from imposing any specified performance requirements on an investment undertaken not only by an investor of a NAFTA country (including investors of the host country) but of other foreign investors in connection with the establishment, acquisition, expansion, management, conduct, or operation of any investment.

Other important provisions in NAFTA require each member country to permit all monetary transfers by an investor relating to an investment of another NAFTA country to be made freely, without delay, and in freely usable currency at the market exchange rate prevailing on the date of transfer. NAFTA also prohibits member states from directly or indirectly nationalizing or expropriating an investment of an investor from another NAFTA state or taking a measure tantamount to nationalization or expropriation except for a public purpose, on a nondiscriminatory basis, and upon payment of just compensation.[117] In addition, the NAFTA chapter on investment requires each country to accord investments from other member countries the minimum treatment required by international law, including fair and equitable treatment and full protection and security. NAFTA also gives aggrieved investors the right to bring a claim in arbitration against a state that has violated NAFTA treatment standards. In the years since NAFTA was launched, it has been the subject of significant investor–state arbitration, and each of the three member states have been respondents.

(6) The Energy Charter Treaty

Another potentially important multilateral treaty affecting international investment is the Energy Charter Treaty,[118] which was opened for signature in Lisbon on December 17, 1994 and had gained 53 members by 2007. The Charter Treaty has a sector, rather than a regional, focus. It aims to create a legal framework that will encourage the development of a secure international energy supply through liberalized trade and investment among member states. The Treaty arose out of the idea, emerging with the end of communism, that western countries were in need of stable, efficient sources of energy while the states of the former Soviet Union, because of their natural resource endowment, had great energy potential whose development required the capital and technology held by the West. Consequently, cooperation in the international energy sector could bring benefits to all sides. The Treaty became effective in 1998.

Part III of the Energy Charter Treaty, entitled "Investment Promotion and Protection," is in effect a bilateral investment treaty, and it clearly has been profoundly influenced by the

---

[117] T Levy, "NAFTA's Provision for Compensation in the Event of Expropriation: A Reassessment of the Prompt, Adequate and Effective Standard," 31 *Stanford J Intl L* (1995) 423–53.

[118] The text of the Energy Charter Treaty may be found in The Final Act of the European Energy Charter Conference (December 12, 1994) AF/EECH en 1, reprinted at 34 *International Legal Materials* 373 (1995). For an extensive discussion of the provisions of the Energy Charter Treaty, see TW Walde (ed), *The Energy Charter Treaty: An East-West Gateway for Investment and Trade* (1996).

language of the various European and American BITs in its structure, content, and drafting.[119] One of the unique features of the Treaty, which distinguishes it from other international investment agreements, is that it is a sector agreement, meaning that it only applies to investments in a particular economic sector. According to Article 1, the Energy Charter Treaty's scope is limited to investments associated with economic activities concerning the exploration, extraction, refining, production, storage, land transport, transmission, distribution, trade, marketing, or sale of energy materials and products. On the other hand, its substantive provisions on the protection and treatment of investments and investors, as well as their enforcement through investor–state arbitration, are very similar to what one might find in a western BIT with a developing country. The resemblance is not accidental. Virtually all of the states participating in the Conference that wrote the Treaty had previously signed at least one bilateral investment treaty, and many had concluded several. By 2008, aggrieved investors had brought several claims in arbitration against member states under Energy Charter Treaty provisions, and several awards had been rendered by international tribunals.[120]

(7) Dominican Republic–Central America–United States Free Trade Agreement

(CAFTA-DR)

In an effort to build an eventual free trade area for North and South America and the Caribbean and thereby expand on the work of NAFTA, the United States concluded an agreement with the Dominican Republic and five Central American states, Costa Rica, El Salvador, Honduras, Nicaragua, and Guatemala, in 2004. Signed on August 5, 2004, it is known as the Dominican Republic–Central America–United States Free Trade Agreement (CAFTA-DR), sometimes simply referred to as "CAFTA." After contentious debate, the US Congress approved the CAFTA-DR Agreement in July 2005, and the US President signed the implementing legislation on August 2, 2005.[121] The agreement was implemented on a rolling basis: El Salvador was the first to ratify on March 1, 2006, and Costa Rica the last, on January 1, 2009. The Agreement went into effect fully among all seven signatories on January 1, 2009. According to its preamble, one of the objectives of CAFTA-DR is "to contribute to hemispheric integration and to provide impetus toward establishing the *Free Trade Area of the Americas*."[122] Although CAFTA-DR, like the North American Free

---

[119] The Legal Counsel of the International Energy Agency, a principal adviser to the European Energy Charter Conference, has stated that the investment provisions of the Energy Charter Treaty "...resemble provisions in bilateral investment treaties although their drafting has not been based on any single negotiating party's treaty practice." Legal Counsel of the IEA, *The Energy Charter Treaty—A Description of Its Provisions* 15 (1994). For a comparison of the Energy Charter's investment provisions with the BITs, see JW Salacuse, "The Energy Charter Treaty and Bilateral Investment Treaty Regimes," in TW Walde (ed), *The Energy Charter Treaty: An East-West Gateway for Investment and Trade* (1996) 321–48.

[120] Texts of the awards in *Nykomb Synergetics Technology Holding v. Latvia* (Award) (December 16, 2003) and *Petrobart Limited v. Kyrgyz Republic* (Award) (March 29, 2005) may be found at <http://ita.law.uvic.ca/alphabetical_list.htm> accessed April 2, 2009.

The *Plama Consortium Limited v. Bulgaria* is the first Energy Charter Treaty investment dispute to be brought before the ICSID (Case No. ARB/03/24; Decision on Jurisdiction, February 8, 2005) <http://ita.law.uvic.ca/alphabetical_list.htm> accessed April 2, 2009.

[121] Dominican Republic–Central America–United States Free Trade Agreement Implementation Act 2005 (PL 109-53, 119 Stat 462). See generally, JR Hornbeck, *The Dominican Republic-Central America-United States Free Trade Agreement (CAFTA-DR)* (Congressional Research Service 2008).

[122] The full text of the Agreement may be found on the website of the United States Trade Representative, <http://www.ustr.gov>. See also Vivian HW Wang, "Investor Protection of Environmental Protection? 'Green' Development Under CAFTA," 32 *Columbia Journal of Environmental Law* (2007) 251; Mark B Baker, "No Country Left Behind: The Exporting of US Legal Norms Under the Guise of Economic Integration," *Emory International Law Journal* no. 19 (2005) 1346.

Trade Agreement (NAFTA), does not refer to investment in its title, it is similar to NAFTA in that it covers both trade and investment. Indeed, CAFTA-DR's investment chapter borrows heavily from Chapter 11 of NAFTA, as well as from the US Model BIT. CAFTA contains 22 chapters and annexes detailing, inter alia, country-specific tariff schedules and rules of origin. Chapter 10, which contains the investment provisions, is highly similar to the investment provisions in prior US agreements, particularly NAFTA. As such, it is safe to assume that US views and interests were critical in shaping Chapter 10 and that the influence of the other six parties seems limited primarily to the reservations and certain limitations in the party-specific annexes, particularly those with respect to sectors in which national treatment is not required for foreign investors. Like NAFTA Chapter 11, CAFTA Chapter 10 on investment is divided into three sections. Section A contains the substantive investment protections. Section B sets down the rules for investor–state dispute settlement. Section C contains definitions of key terms employed in the Chapter. The provisions on investment largely follow the structure and content of NAFTA. As in most other investment treaties, CAFTA's main protections are national treatment (Article 10.3), most-Favored Nation Treatment (Article 10.4), minimum standard of treatment (Article 10.5, encompassing "fair and equitable treatment"[123] and "full protection and security"[124]), and protection against expropriation (Article 10.7). The treaty prohibits certain performance requirements (Article 10.9), and allows states to maintain nonconforming measures that predate CAFTA (Article 10.13). It also allows member states to deny the benefits of the treaty to investors of nonparties with which those CAFTA states do not have diplomatic relations.

CAFTA, like other modern investment treaties, also provides for investor–state arbitration for the settlement of disputes arising under its provisions.[125]

(j) The Evolution of BIT Provisions into Free Trade Agreements

NAFTA and the Energy Charter Treaty also signaled the development of another trend in investment-treaty making: the incorporation of investment treaty provision into free-trade agreements. Following NAFTA, the United States proceeded to make a number of free trade agreements (FTAs) all of which included a separate chapter that was virtually indistinguishable from a BIT.[126] Such agreements were concluded, for example, with Israel,[127] Jordan,[128]

---

[123] CAFTA-DR, ch 10, Article 10.5(a).

[124] CAFTA-DR, ch 10, Article 10.5(b).

[125] See *Investor-State Dispute Resolution Under DR-CAFTA* (accessed July 13, 2012); available from <http://www.whitecase.com/idq/fall_2007/ia2/>. For one of the first investor–state cases to arise under its provisions, see *Railroad Development Corporation v. Guatemala* (ICSID Case No Arb/07/23) Award of June 29, 2012.

[126] For the text of the various free trade agreements concluded by the United States, see the website of the United States Trade Representative at <http://www.ustr.gov/Trade_Agreements/Section_Index.html> accessed April 2, 2009.

[127] Agreement on the Establishment of a Free Trade Area (signed April 22, 1985, entered into force August 19, 1985). US Dept of State, *Treaties in Force: A List of Treaties and Other International Agreements of the United States in Force on January 1, 2007* <http://www.state.gov/s/l/treaty/treaties/2007/section1/index.htm> accessed April 2, 2009.

[128] Agreement on the Establishment of a Free Trade Area (signed October 24, 2000, entered into force December 17, 2001) US Dept of State, *Treaties in Force: A List of Treaties and Other International Agreements of the United States in Force on January 1, 2007* <http://www.state.gov/s/l/treaty/treaties/2007/section1/index.htm> accessed April 2, 2009.

Bahrain,[129] Chile,[130] and Singapore,[131] as well as the Dominican Republic-Central America-United States Free Trade Agreement (CAFTA-DR), already discussed.[132]

Japan would follow a similar approach in the promotion of its Economic Partnership Agreements (EPAs),[133] which also contain chapters on investment and provide for investor–state arbitration as a means of enforcement. Other Asian countries have also followed this approach, so that by the year 2012 there were over 300 such agreements and many others were in the process of negotiation.[134] Thus, it appears that the investment treaty, which arose out of trade agreements, is returning to its origins.

The connection between trade and investment was also formally recognized by the General Agreement on Tariffs and Trade, which would later become the World Trade Organization, during its Uruguay Round of negotiations between 1986 and 1994.[135] One of the products of that negotiation, to which all WTO members must now adhere, is the Agreement on Trade Related Investment Measures.[136] This Agreement forbids the imposition of measures that are inconsistent with GATT's Article III on national treatment[137] and it's Article XI on the elimination of quantitative restrictions.[138] Its purpose is to prevent WTO members from imposing local content and trade balancing requirements as a condition for the creation or operation of foreign investment projects. One WTO dispute settlement case has applied the Agreement to invalidate an Indonesian measure used to favor the development of a "national car" enterprise.[139] In addition, the WTO's General Agreement on Trade in Services[140] also includes provisions affecting investment related to the provisions of services.

(k) Toward a Global Treaty on Investment

While negotiations over the years have led to a substantial number of investment treaties, the results of these efforts have been limited in geographic scope, being either bilateral or regional, or in the case of the Energy Charter Treaty, restricted to a particular sector. Given the success of their efforts at international rule making, it was natural for capital-exporting countries to contemplate the negotiation of a global treaty on investment; however, thus

---

[129] Agreement on the Establishment of a Free Trade Area (signed September 14, 2004, entered into force August 1, 2006) US Dept of State, *Treaties in Force: A List of Treaties and Other International Agreements of the United States in Force on January 1, 2007* <http://www.state.gov/s/l/treaty/treaties/2007/section1/index.htm> accessed April 2, 2009.

[130] United States–Chile Free Trade Agreement (signed June 6, 2003, entered into force January 1, 2004) US Dept of State, *Treaties in Force: A List of Treaties and Other International Agreements of the United States in Force on January 1, 2007* <http://www.state.gov/s/l/treaty/treaties/2007/section1/index.htm> accessed April 2, 2009.

[131] United States–Singapore Free Trade Agreement (signed May 6, 2003, entered into force January 1, 2004) US Dept of State, *Treaties in Force: A List of Treaties and Other International Agreements of the United States in Force on January 1, 2007* <http://www.state.gov/s/l/treaty/treaties/2007/section1/index.htm> accessed April 2, 2009.

[132] For text of CAFTA-DR, see the website of the US Trade Representative at <http://www.ustr.gov/trade-agreements/free-trade-agreements/cafta-dr-dominican-republic-central-america-fta/final-text>.

[133] M Yasushi, "Economic Partnership Agreements and Japanese Strategy" (Fall 2006) 6 *Gaiko Forum*, No 3 at 53.

[134] UNCTAD, *World Investment Report 2012* (2012) 84.

[135] Final Act Embodying the Results of the Uruguay Round of Multilateral Trade Negotiations (April 15, 1994) Legal Instruments—Results of the Uruguay Round, 33 *ILM* 1125 (1994).

[136] Agreement on Trade-Related Investment Measures (April 15, 1994) 1868 UNTS 186 (TRIMs).

[137] General Agreement on Tariffs and Trade (October 30, 1947) 55 UNTS 194; 61 Stat A-11; TIAS 1700, (GATT).

[138] General Agreement on Tariffs and Trade (October 30, 1947) 55 UNTS 194; 61 Stat A-11; TIAS 1700, (GATT) Article XI.

[139] *Indonesia—Certain Measures Affecting the Automobile Industry* (WT/DS54/15 of December 7, 1998) <http://www.tripsagreement.net/PanelDecisions.php#Panel6> accessed April 2, 2009.

[140] General Agreement on Trade in Services (April 15, 1994) UNTS 183; 33 *ILM* 1167 (1994) (GATS).

far, the results in this domain have been virtually nonexistent. Two initiatives at the end of the twentieth century are worthy of note, in addition to those that took place immediately after World War II.

The first of these began in April 1991 when the Development Committee, which is a Joint Ministerial Committee of the Boards of Governors of the International Monetary Fund and the World Bank, requested that the Multilateral Investment Guarantee Agency (MIGA) prepare a "legal framework" to promote foreign direct investment. The resulting *Guidelines on the Treatment of Foreign Investment*,[141] which had a long gestation period in the World Bank Group (mainly at the IBRD, MIGA, and IFC) and was based upon extensive consideration of important legal instruments in the field, such as bilateral investment treaties, was then submitted to an international conference held under the auspices of the Bank Group and the French Ministry of Finance in July 1992. It was later resubmitted to the Development Committee, which gave its approval in September 1992. Because of its source and the careful process by which it was developed, the *Guidelines*, although not law, have enjoyed considerable influence and credibility.[142] The *Guidelines* set out a general framework for the treatment of foreign investors by host states and cover areas of concern to investors, such as the admission of foreign investment, standards of treatment and transfer of capital and net revenues, expropriation and its compensation, and the settlement of disputes.[143] The basic goal of the *Guidelines* is to set down a global framework.

The second notable initiative to establish global rules on investment took place within the Organization for Economic Cooperation and Development (OECD). In September 1995, negotiations to establish a Multilateral Agreement on Investment (MAI) began at the OECD with the goal of completing a draft treaty in time for the 1997 ministerial meeting. The OECD mandate called for "a broad multilateral framework for international investment with high standards of liberalization of investment and investment protection and with effective dispute settlement procedures."[144] Thus, the dual objectives of investment liberalization and investment protection which had directed developed countries' BIT efforts also appeared in the search for a workable MAI.

In developing a treaty framework, the MAI negotiators drew heavily on NAFTA and the BITs; for example, the draft MAI structure addressed the same issues as the earlier documents. While a structure for the MAI was agreed upon relatively quickly, the precise content of the rules to govern that structure were not. The negotiating states achieved consensus fairly quickly on the issues of investment protection and dispute resolution. Following the BITS, the states seem to have agreed on strong dispute settlement procedures and on postinvestment national or most-favored-nation treatment, whichever was the most favorable. They also agreed on extensive rights to monetary transfers and to require prompt, adequate, and effective compensation in cases of expropriation.

It was on the question of investment liberalization that significant disagreements surfaced—disagreements that often brought the United States into conflict with European countries. All the principal negotiating states had substantial investments abroad and so had a common interest in seeing that those investments received maximum protection.

---

[141] World Bank, "Report to the Development Committee and Guidelines on the Treatment of Foreign Direct Investment" (1992) 31 *ILM* 1363.

[142] SJ Rubin, "Introductory Note for International Legal Materials" 31 *ILM* (1992) 1363.

[143] IFI Shihata, "Introductory Note of September 25, 1992," in *Legal Framework for the Treatment of Foreign Investment: Volume II* (1992) 31 *ILM* 1367.

[144] OECD, *Multilateral Agreement on Investment: The Original Mandate*, <http://www.oecd.org/daf/investment/fdi/mai/mandate.htm> accessed April 2, 2009. See also G Kelley, "Multilateral Investment Treaties: A Balanced Approach to Multinational Corporations," 39 *Columbia J of Transnational L* 483 (2001).

Moreover, the developed OECD members had already established strong systems of investment protection within their own borders. On the other hand, the OECD states each had different economic interests with respect to investment liberalization, particularly with regard to foreign investments that might be undertaken in their own territories. Each had different procedures governing investments and different local industries they wished to protect from the competition of foreign investors. The negotiators seemed to find no common ground with respect to investment liberalization.

Beyond disagreement among OECD members, other parties raised their voices to contest the MAI negotiations. First, developing countries, led by India, opposed the MAI and any attempt to create new rules of international law to protect and liberalize foreign investment. They saw the prospect of a global treaty on investment as a threat to their national sovereignty and economic independence. They challenged the legitimacy of a forum that did not allow developing countries to fully participate in the negotiating process. Second, a broad coalition of nongovernmental organizations (NGOs), based largely in developed countries, arose to challenge both the process and content of the MAI negotiations. In 1997, the NGOs obtained a draft of the MAI. Discovering that negotiators had consulted business interests but not other elements of civil society, the NGOs mounted an effective worldwide protest through the internet, arguing that the drafting process was flawed, because the OECD chose to conduct secret negotiations with business interests at the expense of labor unions, environmentalists, human rights organizations, and others. Seeing the MAI as yet another instrument that would advance globalization at the expense of local groups and interests, anti-globalization forces soon joined the protest.

As the public within OECD countries became aware of the contested MAI negotiations various American and European politicians and groups took opposing stands on the issue and their governments became more cautious in pressing for conclusion of the treaty. Ultimately, in the face of strong opposition from various quarters, the OECD countries abandoned the effort to create the MAI in December 1998.[145]

(l) Conclusion

Since World War II, the nations of the world have been actively engaged in creating an international law based on treaties, both bilateral and multilateral, in order to remedy the defects perceived by capital-exporting states and their investors in customary international investment law. The process of treatification has proceeded rapidly and will almost certainly continue as countries create an increasingly dense treaty network. Already, that network is having a growing impact on international investments and on the behavior of host states towards investments and investors.

14.3 The Objectives of the Movement to Negotiate Investment Treaties

Having reviewed the history of the development of investment treaties, a history that has largely been driven by capital-exporting countries' nationals and companies, one may well ask: What was the objective of this international law making during the last half of the twentieth century and the beginning of the twenty-first? An understanding of these

---

[145] For a description of the OECD's failed process to negotiate the Multilateral Investment Agreement, see C Devereaux and M Watkins, *A Virtual Defeat: Stalling the Multilateral Agreement on Investment* (Cambridge: JF Kennedy School of Government Case Program).

objectives is an important element in interpreting the treaty texts and successfully applying them to specific situations. It is to be recalled that Article 31 (1) of the Vienna Convention on the Law of Treaties[146] provides:

> A treaty shall be interpreted in good faith in accordance with the ordinary meaning to be given to the terms of the treaty in their context and in light of *its object and purpose*. (emphasis added)

The objects and purposes of investment treaties are often specifically stated in the body of the treaty, its preamble, and in related documents. Although specific objectives may vary from treaty to treaty, as a group, contemporary investment treaties appear to share remarkably similar goals. In reviewing investment treaties and their surrounding circumstances, one can identify three orders of objectives: (1) primary objectives; (2) secondary objectives, and (3) long-term objectives. The following sections will examine each of these three.

14.4 The Primary Objectives of Investment Treaties

Nearly all investment treaties pursue two primary objectives: (a) investment protection and (b) investment promotion. Thus, most BITs bear the title "Treaty Concerning the Promotion and Protection of Investment . . . ," or some variation thereof.[147]

(a) Investment Protection

The primary motives behind the rapid expansion of international investment treaties were the desire of investors from capital-exporting states to invest safely and securely abroad and the need to create a stable international legal framework to facilitate and protect those investments. The risks against which such protection has been aimed are the injurious acts and omissions by host governments themselves and also the injurious acts and omissions by other persons in the host country. Without an applicable investment treaty, international investors would be forced to rely on host country law alone for protection, a reliance that entails a variety of risks to their investments. Host governments can easily change their own domestic law after a foreign investment is made, and host country officials may not always act fairly or impartially toward foreign investors and their enterprises. Moreover, host country officials may fail to take action to protect foreign investors and their investments from injurious actions by other persons. Investor recourse to local courts for protection may prove to be of little value in the face of prejudice against foreigners or governmental interference in the judicial process.[148]

The lack of consensus on the customary international law applicable to foreign investments, discussed in Chapter 13, created further uncertainty in the minds of investors about the degree of protection they could expect under international law. To decrease their uncertainty and counter the threat of adverse national law and regulation, the home countries of these investors attempted to conclude a series of treaties that would provide

---

[146] Vienna Convention on the Law of Treaties (May 22, 1969) 1155 UNTS 331; (1969) 8 *ILM* 679 (1969); (1969) 63 *AJIL* 875; UN Doc A/Conf. 39/27 (1969)) (VCLT).

[147] Treaty Concerning the Reciprocal Encouragement and Protection of Investment (US–Armenia) (September 23, 1992), S Treaty Doc No 103–11 (1993); Treaty Concerning the Promotion and Reciprocal Protection of Investments, (Federal Republic of Germany–Poland) (November 10, 1989 29 *ILM* 333 (1990); Agreement for the Promotion and Protection of Investments (Indonesia–United Kingdom) (April 27, 1976) Treaty Series no 62. Similarly, Part III of the Energy Charter Treaty is entitled "Investment Promotion and Protection."

[148] UNCTAD, *Bilateral Investment Treaties in the Mid-1990s* (1998) 114–18.

clear rules and effective enforcement mechanisms, at least with regard to their treaty partners. Their primary goal was therefore the *protection* of investments made by their nationals and companies in foreign countries.

(b) Investment Promotion

A second primary objective of investment treaties is the promotion or encouragement of investment. This objective is based on the assumption that increased investment will further a country's economic development and prosperity and that foreign sources of capital and technology can usefully contribute to a country's economic advancement.

Concluding and maintaining a treaty requires a bargain from which both parties believe they derive benefits. An investment treaty between two developed states, both of whose nationals expect to invest in the territory of the other, would be based on the notion of reciprocity and mutual protection. That is, a host state is induced to grant protection to investors from another country to be assured that the other state will grant similar protection to investors from the host state. However, this bargain would not seem to apply to a treaty between a developed, capital-exporting state and a developing, capital-importing country whose nationals are unlikely to invest abroad. One might therefore ask: why would developing countries enter into such agreements? Why would they constrain their sovereignty by entering into treaties that specifically limit their ability to take necessary legislative and administrative actions to advance and protect what they perceive as their national interests?[149]

The answer to this question is that many countries sign investment treaties to *promote* foreign investment, thereby increasing the amount of capital and associated technology that flows to their territories. The basic assumption in this respect is that treaties with clear and enforceable rules to protect and facilitate foreign investment reduce risk and that such reduction in risks, all things being equal, encourages investment. In the 1980s and 1990s, as other forms of financial assistance became less available from commercial banks and official aid institutions, developing countries increasingly felt the need to promote private foreign investment in order to foster economic development. Investment treaties were seen as one means of pursuing a broader campaign of investment promotion and so developing nations signed them in increasing numbers.[150] Thus, an investment agreement between a developed and a developing country is founded on a grand bargain: a *promise* of protection of capital in return for the *prospect* of more capital in the future.[151]

Developing countries have sometimes entered into investment treaty negotiations with the expectation that the capital-exporting country would take affirmative measures to encourage its nationals to invest in the developing country—an expectation no doubt fostered by the word "encouragement" appearing in the titles of most draft treaties. Capital-exporting states, however, have generally refused to agree to any provision obligating them to encourage or induce their nationals to invest in the foreign state. On the contrary, many BITS have terms that encourage or obligate the *host* country to create favorable investment conditions in its territory.

---

[149] This question assumes that the developing country is not expecting other benefits from its developed country treaty partner, such as increased foreign aid or enhanced security guarantees, which are extraneous to a bilateral investment treaty relationship.

[150] UNCTAD, *Bilateral Investment Treaties in the Mid-1990s* (1998) 85.

[151] JW Salacuse and NP Sullivan, "Do BITs Really Work? An Evaluation of Bilateral Investment Treaties and Their Grand Bargain," 46 *Harvard Intl L J* (2005) 67.

It should also be noted that some investment treaties have sought to *facilitate* the entry and operation of investments by inducing host countries to remove various impediments in their regulatory systems. This has clearly been the goal of the European Union treaty, and particularly Article 43 of that treaty, which grants investors from any EU Member State a right of establishment, ie the right to set up business, in any other EU Member State. Other measures designed to create a single European market for the movement of capital have also supported this goal. The North American Free Trade Agreement pursued a similar purpose, as is clear from the fact that in Article 102 (1)(b), one of its stated purposes is "to increase substantially investment opportunities in the territories of the Parties." Accordingly, that treaty grants investors from other member states national treatment and most-favored-nation treatment in undertaking investments.[152] Some, but not all, other BITs and FTAs have taken a similar approach with respect to the entry and establishment of investment from treaty partners.

14.5 Secondary Objectives of Investment Treaties

Countries often have various secondary objectives in concluding investment treaties. The specific secondary objective pursued by a particular country may vary according to its economic situation, policy goals, ideology, or the state of its international relations. Sometimes such objectives are not stated in the treaty and sometimes government officials may not even be willing to acknowledge them publicly. Among some of the more common secondary goals are the following.

(a) Market Liberalization

In negotiating investment treaties with developing countries, some capital exporting states have sought to use the investment treaty as a means to encourage or induce investment and market liberalization within their negotiating partners.[153] Moreover, in the view of certain developed countries, investment treaties can have the effect of liberalizing a country's whole economy by facilitating the entry of investment and creating conditions favoring their operation. In the process of reforming their economies to foster private enterprise, some developing countries have concluded that creating favorable conditions for foreign investment can be integral to their success.[154] Although the BITs themselves do not specifically enunciate the goal of investment and market liberalization, it is clear those goals are in the minds of developed country negotiators and are sometimes reflected in background documents.[155]

---

[152] NAFTA Articles 1102 and 1103.
[153] The Deputy United States Trade Representative stated the US goals in negotiating BITs as follows:

> The BIT program's basic aims are to: (1) protect U.S. investment abroad in those countries where U.S. investors' rights are not protected through existing agreements; (2) encourage adoption in foreign countries of market-oriented domestic policies that treat private investment fairly; and (3) support the development of international law standards consistent with these objectives.

J Lang, "Keynote Address," 31 *Cornell Intl L J* (1998) 455, 457. See also US Trade Rep, *USTR Focus on Investment* <http://ustr.gov/Trade_Sectors/Investment/Section_Index.html> accessed September 19, 2007.
[154] See generally, JW Salacuse, "From Developing Countries to Emerging Markets: A Changing Role for Law in the Third World," 33 *Intl Lawyer* (1999) 875, 875–7.
[155] See, eg, Investment Treaty With Albania (US–Albania) (January 11, 1995) S Treaty Doc No 104–19 (1995) (In the message from the President of the United States transmitting the Treaty Between the Government of the United States of America and the Government of the Republic of Albania Concerning the Encouragement and Reciprocal Protection of Investment With Annex and Protocol Signed at Washington on January 11, 1995, President Clinton stated: "The bilateral investment treaty (BIT) with Albania will protect U.S. investment and

It should be noted that investment promotion, a fundamental objective of developing countries, and investment and market liberalization, a subsidiary aim of developed countries, are separate and distinct goals.[156] Within the context of BITs, for example, host country investment promotion means attracting investment projects that the host country determines are in *its* best interests. Investment liberalization, on the other hand, is a favorite term of capital-exporting countries that generally means creating a climate in which investors may undertake investments they judge to be in *their* interests. For example, a host country government might seek to promote investments in its electronics industry if it judged doing so would develop its economy in ways not yet present in the country. At the same time, that country may desire to impede investment in the retail industry if that industry is already served by politically powerful local entrepreneurs who fear foreign competition. In such a situation the developing country, through its treaty relationships and internal legislation, would be following a policy of investment promotion but not of investment liberalization.

(b) Relationship Building

Some developing countries have also been led to sign bilateral investment treaties with developed capital-exporting countries to strengthen their relationship with those countries and obtain the benefits and favors, such as increased trade or foreign aid, that such a relationship may yield. Thus, even though a developing country may not be certain of increased investment flows from its developed country treaty partner after signing an investment treaty, it may well expect that the treaty will result in closer ties that will lead to increased trade, foreign aid, security assistance, technology transfers, or other benefits. For example, when a left-of-center government came to power in Uruguay in 2005 after a previous government had signed but not yet ratified a BIT with the United States, the new government renegotiated but ultimately ratified the BIT. The Uruguayan government justified its action on the grounds that ratifying the BIT would protect and strengthen its important export markets in the United States. To the extent that investment treaty provisions are embedded in free trade agreements, such as those advanced by the United States and Japan, the prospect of improved trade relations as an inducement to agree to investment treaty provisions is quite explicit.

(c) Domestic Investment Encouragement

Related to the objective of economic liberalization is the goal of encouraging domestic entrepreneurs, who may be skeptical of their government's intentions toward private

assist the Republic of Albania in its efforts to develop its economy by creating conditions more favorable for U.S. private investment and thus strengthen the development of its private sector.")

See also United States Trade Representative, *USTR Focus on Investment* <http://ustr.gov/Trade_Sectors/ Investment/Section_Index.html> accessed September 19, 2007.

[156] Investment protection and investment liberalization are also distinct concepts. Investment liberalization refers to facilitating the entry and operation of foreign investments in the host country. Investment protection refers to protecting the investment, once it has entered the country, from actions by governments and others that would interfere with investor property rights and the functioning of the investment in general. For example, in launching negotiations for a Multilateral Agreement on Investment in September 1995, the OECD mandate called for "a broad multilateral framework for international investment with high standards of liberalisation of investment regimes and investment protection...." OECD, Multilateral Agreement on Investment: Launch of the Negotiations:1995 CMIT/CIME Report and Mandate, <http://www.oecd.org/daf/mai/htm/cmitcime95.htm> accessed September 18, 2007.

capital, to undertake productive investments. An investment treaty therefore serves as a "signaling device" to the domestic private sector that the government's intentions toward private capital, both foreign and domestic, are benign. This is clear from the international commitments the home government has made in the treaty to protect the capital of foreigners.

(d) Improved Governance and a Strengthened Rule of Law

Another secondary purpose for some developing countries in signing investment treaties is to remedy the deficiencies in their own governance institutions and enforcement of the rule of law. Investment treaties thus become international substitutes for domestic institutions.[157] The theory underlying this rationale is that developing country authorities and institutions that have prevented themselves from acting in arbitrary and abusive fashion toward foreign investors will also be led to avoid arbitrary and abusive actions toward their own nationals. Over time those authorities and institutions may demonstrate improved governance and a heightened respect for the rule of law. Thus, as the Minister of Finance of Uruguay explained at the time his country ratified its BIT with the United States, "We are not signing this treaty for *them* [ie the United States], we are signing it for *us*."

14.6 Long-Term Goals of Investment Treaties

Lawyers, arbitrators, government officials, and corporate executives sometimes view investment treaties solely as being about foreign investors and foreign investment. That view may lead to distortions in understanding and interpreting investment treaty texts. Investment treaties are basically instruments of international relations, and the parties to them—sovereign states, not investors—undertake them in order to further certain long-term goals that may go well beyond the domain of investment. For investors, investment treaties are quite naturally about investments, but for states that are a party to them they may be about "economic cooperation," "economic development," or "mutual prosperity." A careful reading of investment treaty preambles reveals these long-term objectives. For example, the Preamble of the BIT between France and Argentina[158] asserts the parties' purpose as "...Desiring to intensify economic cooperation for the economic benefit of both countries..." and the Preamble to an investment agreement between the Netherlands and the then Czechoslovakia[159] states the parties' aims as "...Desiring to extend and intensify the economic relations between them..." and to "...stimulate the flow of capital and technology and the economic development of the Contracting Parties..." It is important to place treaty texts within the context of their stated long-term objectives in order to interpret and understand fully their provisions. This is especially so since Article 31(1) of the Vienna Convention on the Law of Treaties requires that such context be taken into account in interpreting a treaty. The arbitral tribunal in the case of *Saluka Investments BV v. The Czech Republic* took precisely this approach in interpreting the term "fair and

---

[157] T Ginsburg, "International Substitutes for Domestic Institutions: Bilateral Investment Treaties and Governance," 25 *Intl R of L Economics* (2005) 107–23.

[158] Accord entre le Gouvernement de la République française et le Gouvernement de la République Argentine sur l'encouragement et la protection réciproques des investissements (Agreement between the Argentine Republic and the Republic of France for the Promotion and Reciprocal Protection of Investments) (signed July 3, 1991, entered into force March 3, 1993) 1728 UNTS 298.

[159] Agreement on Encouragement and Reciprocal Protection of Investments Between the Kingdom of The Netherlands and the Czech and Slovak Federal Republic (signed April 29, 1991).

equitable treatment" to take into account the stated long-term objectives as expressed in the preamble of the above-quoted Netherlands–Czech and Slovak BIT:

> This is a more subtle and balanced statement of the Treaty's aims than is sometimes appreciated. The protection of foreign investments is not the sole aim of the Treaty, but rather a necessary element alongside the overall aim of encouraging foreign investment and extending and intensifying the parties' economic relations. That in turn calls for a balanced approach to the interpretation of the Treaty's substantive provisions for the protection of investments, since an interpretation which exaggerates the protection to be accorded to foreign investments may serve to dissuade host States from admitting foreign investments and so undermine the overall aim of extending and intensifying the parties' mutual economic relations.[160]

14.7 The Treaty Negotiation Process

Investment treaties do not simply spring into being. They are usually the product of long and hard negotiations between the countries concerned. Those negotiations explain why textual differences occur among investment treaties. It is therefore worthwhile to consider briefly the processes by which investment treaties come into existence. In doing so, one must distinguish the negotiation of bilateral investment treaties from those involving more than two countries.

(a) Bilateral Treaty Processes

Having determined the need for treaty protection for their investors abroad, capital-exporting countries did not immediately proceed to negotiate BITs or FTAs with developing nations. First, they devoted considerable time and effort to the preparation of what they called a "model treaty," "prototype treaty," or "draft treaty," to serve as the basis for negotiations with individual developing countries. Preparing the draft treaty usually involved intensive consultation with various organizations, including relevant government agencies and representatives from the country's private sector. For example, preparation of the US model treaty took nearly four years.[161] For capital exporting states, which without exception have been the ones to initiate negotiations, model or prototype treaties have been the basic and essential elements in their attempts to conclude BITs or FTAs.

The prototype treaty serves several purposes. First, its preparation is an occasion for capital-exporting states to study the entire question of investment protection and promotion, to consult with interested governmental and private sector organizations, and to formulate a national position on the question. The government emerges from this process with a firm idea of the kind of treaty that would be acceptable to various domestic constituencies, knowledge that is essential if a negotiated treaty is to secure the approval and ratification of home country authorities. Second, since the capital-exporting countries desire to negotiate BITs and FTAs with many developing countries, the prototype is an efficient means of communicating to those countries concretely what type of treaty the capital-exporting state seeks. Thirdly, to the extent possible, a capital-exporting state usually wants relative uniformity in its BITs and FTAs with developing countries. Starting all negotiations with the same draft treaty is a way to attain that goal. An additional motivation for the preparation of a prototype is that it gives the capital-exporting state a

---

[160] *Saluka Investment BV v. The Czech Republic* (Partial Award) (March 17, 2006) 300 (UNCITRAL).
[161] K Vandevelde, "The Bilateral Investment Treaty Program of the United States," 21 *Cornell Intl L J* (1988) 201, 210.

negotiating advantage, as the party who controls the draft usually controls the negotiation. By preparing a draft BIT or FTA which will become the basis of discussion, the capital-exporting country has, in effect, determined the agenda of the negotiation and has established the conceptual framework within which bargaining will take place. The developing country, at least at the outset, is placed in a position of merely reacting to the draft.[162]

After completing the preparation of the prototype, a capital-exporting state often informally makes contact with a target country to determine its level of interest in concluding a BIT or FTA. When selecting countries to approach for an indication of interest, a capital-exporting country considers a variety of factors including the state of friendly diplomatic relations between the two countries, the extent to which its nationals have already invested in that country, whether their nationals can be expected to invest in the host country in the future, and finally, the extent to which the potential host country's existing economic policies are conducive to foreign private investment.

If a developing country decides to enter into BIT or FTA negotiations with a capital-exporting state, it too must engage in a consultative process among various government agencies and representatives of its private sector to formulate a negotiating position. Often this consultative process is accomplished by creating a team of representatives to carry on the negotiations. Inevitably, the views of individual negotiating team members may differ on many questions with respect to the proposed BIT or FTA. For example, officials of the Central Bank normally oppose treaty obligations that increase demands on the country's foreign exchange reserves. Others with a different viewpoint, such as representatives of the government's investment promotion agency, stress the importance of securing new investment for the country and accordingly often urge quick acceptance of the proposed BIT or FTA with as few changes as possible.

A BIT or FTA purports to create a symmetrical legal relationship between the two states, in that it provides that either party may invest under the same conditions in the territory of the other. In reality, an asymmetry often exists between the parties to many BITs and FTAs, especially in negotiations between industrialized and developing countries, since one state will be the source and the other the recipient of most investment flows. This asymmetry affects the dynamics of the BIT negotiation. Recognizing that the BIT essentially defines the developing country's obligations toward investment from the developed country, the developing country tends to negotiate obligations that are more general than specific, vague rather than precise, and subject to exceptions rather than absolute requirements. On the other hand, capital-exporting countries seek guarantees of protection that are precise and all-encompassing. Thus, for example, a capital-exporting country will want the treaty in all cases to guarantee investors the right to transfer revenues and capital out of an investment. In contrast, a developing country will try to negotiate exceptions in appropriate situations, so that the transfer obligation will not apply, say, if the country is suffering from balance-of-payment difficulties. Generally, negotiations that result in a successful agreement do not depart significantly from the capital-exporting state's model.

(b) Multilateral Negotiation Processes

The process for negotiating a multilateral investment treaty is usually more complex and lengthy than the process for negotiating a bilateral treaty. This complexity arises from the

---

[162] For a discussion of this negotiating problem, see JW Salacuse, *The Global Negotiator* (2003) 39–42.

number of parties at the negotiating table, which usually takes the form of a diplomatic conference. This means that the interests and resulting issues that have to be accommodated are more numerous than in a bilateral setting. Moreover, the existence of more than two parties in the negotiation enables the parties to form blocs and coalitions to increase their influence, a factor that further complicates and lengthens the multilateral process. In addition, a multilateral negotiation usually attracts significant public attention and may invite the intervention of nongovernmental organizations and other elements of civil society, and their presence may also increase the difficulty of arriving at an agreement.[163]

An interesting related question is why the nations of the world have been willing to conclude BITs and FTAs in growing numbers over the last 50 years but have steadfastly refused to join global agreements on investment. One technical explanation is that a bilateral treaty needs to accommodate the interests of only two parties and, therefore, is far less complicated to negotiate than a multilateral global treaty, which must accommodate the interests of many countries.[164] Politically, given the asymmetric nature of BIT negotiations, the bilateral setting allows the developed country to use its power more effectively than in a multilateral setting where that power may be much diluted.

For example, in multilateral settings, developing countries have the opportunity to form blocking coalitions to enhance their power in the negotiations, something that is obviously impossible in bilateral negotiations. On the other hand, the prospect of investment capital from specific developed countries, along with other political and economic benefits arising from a definite bilateral relationship, may make a developing country more willing to enter into a BIT than a multilateral agreement where those benefits may seem more tenuous and theoretical. Moreover, whereas developed countries may be willing to enter into bilateral treaties with developing countries for investment liberalization knowing that few if any enterprises from the developing country will invest in the developed state, developed countries have been unwilling to enter into treaties that would grant such liberalization to investors from other developed states, who could become strong competitors in the host countries' own enterprises.[165]

14.8 Conclusion

The nature and sources of international investment law have undergone a significant transformation in a relatively short time. The creation of an increasingly dense network of international investment treaties therefore represents an important step in the development of the international legal framework for investment and of international economic law in general.

One important consequence of treatification is that it has increased the importance of international investment law in economic relations to a level that it had never enjoyed

---

[163] For discussion of a multilateral treaty process that successfully resulted in the creation of the Energy Charter Treaty, see J Doré, "Negotiating the Energy Charter Treaty," in T Walde (ed), *The Energy Charter Treaty: An East-West Gateway for Investment and Trade* (1996) 137–53. For a description of the OECD's failed process to negotiate the Multilateral Investment Agreement, see C Devereaux and M Watkins, *A Virtual Defeat: Stalling the Multilateral Agreement on Investment* (Cambridge: JF Kennedy School of Government Case Program).

[164] For a discussion of the differences between bilateral and multilateral negotiations, see FO Hampson, *Multilateral Negotiations: Lessons from Arms Control, Trade and the Environment* (1995) 1–51, 345–60; IW Zartman (ed), *International Multilateral Negotiation: Approaches to the Management of Complexity* (1994) 1–10, 213–22.

[165] As indicated earlier in this chapter, such a problem arose during the negotiation of the failed OECD Multilateral Agreement on Investment, conducted between 1995 and 1998. G Kelley, "Multilateral Investment Treaties: A Balanced Approach to Multinational Corporations," 39 *Columbia J Transnational L* (2001) 483, 494–8.

before. Prior to treatification, international investment law was basically an arcane subject that interested only a few academic international lawyers. It had little practical effect. Today, it has become of immense practical concern to a much wider audience, including the practicing bar, environmentalists, nongovernmental organizations, multinational companies, and governments, both industrialized and developing, who sometimes question the consequences of what they have created over the last five decades. As a result, unlike the situation that prevailed in the mid-twentieth century, government officials, international executives, lawyers, and financiers must increasingly take investment treaties into account in planning, negotiating, undertaking, and managing international investment transactions.

15

The Nature and Content of Investment Treaties

15.1 Introduction

The world's more than three thousand investment treaties constitute the basic pillar of the international legal framework for investment. An investment treaty is an agreement by which two or more states agree to accord specified legal treatment to investments undertaken in their territory by nationals of another treaty party and to resolve related disputes in the event that a state is alleged to have denied such legal treatment to a protected investment. Although the specific provisions of individual investment treaties are not identical and some investment treaties restrict host country governmental action more than others, virtually all investment treaties address the same issues, adopt a similar structure, and employ common concepts and terminology. The purpose of this chapter is to discuss the content of this increasingly important source of the international rights and obligations pertaining to investments.

15.2 Treaty Structure

The basic structure of most modern investment treaties encompasses ten topics:

1. Treaty Title and Statement of Purpose
2. Definitions and Scope of Application
3. Investment Promotion, Admission, and Establishment
4. General Standards of Treatment of Foreign Investments
5. Monetary Transfers
6. Expropriation and Dispossession
7. Operational and Other Conditions
8. Losses from Armed Conflict or Internal Disorder
9. Dispute Settlement
10. Treaty Exceptions, Modifications, and Terminations

This chapter briefly examines the content of these topics in order to provide a general understanding of the nature of international investment treaties.[1]

15.3 Treaty Title and Statement of Purpose

All investment treaties have a title and preamble. The title usually states the general aim of the treaty and, if it is a bilateral agreement, identifies the parties to it, for example "Agreement between the Government of the United Kingdom of Great Britain and Northern Ireland and the Government of the Republic of Albania for the Promotion and

---

[1] For a more detailed consideration of investment treaties, see generally, JW Salacuse, *The Law of Investment Treaties* (2010).

Protection of Investments."[2] The title of a multilateral investment treaty usually states its nature but not the names of the party to it; for example, "The Energy Charter Treaty."[3] As noted previously, the precise designation or title given to a treaty does not affect its status as a binding international agreement.

Directly after the title, an investment treaty normally contains a preamble in which the parties state the aims and purposes of the treaty. While neither the title nor the preamble impose legal obligations, they may be relevant to the interpretation of the treaty's substantive provisions. Article 31(1) of the Vienna Convention on the Law of Treaties[4] provides that "[a] treaty shall be interpreted in good faith in accordance with the ordinary meaning to be given to the terms of the treaty in their context and in light of *its object and purpose*" (emphasis added). Accordingly, an important source for determining a treaty's objects and purposes is its title and preamble.[5]

An investment treaty usually consists of a single document. However, the parties may use an exchange of letters or separate protocols to explain, modify, or elaborate on certain treaty provisions. For example, an investment treaty may provide that it applies to "companies controlled by nationals of the other state Party," and a subsequent exchange of letters between the countries' foreign ministers or ambassadors may define in detail the meaning of "control."[6] Such documents are considered an integral part of the treaty and have the same binding effect as the treaty text. They are often published as an annex to the treaty in the contracting states' official publications.

15.4 Definitions and Scope of Application of Investment Treaties

(a) In General

A key element in any investment treaty is its provisions defining the treaty's terms and its scope of application, especially the persons, organizations, and investments that may benefit from the treaty. Persons, organizations, or investments that fall outside a treaty's terms or scope of application are not entitled to the benefit of its provisions. Thus, if a particular asset or enterprise in a host country lies within the definition of "investment" in an investment treaty, that enterprise may take advantage of the treaty's privileges and benefits, as well as its enforcement mechanisms. If not, then it may not take advantage of the treaty.

---

[2] Agreement between the Government of the United Kingdom of Great Britain and Northern Ireland and the Government of the Republic of Albania for the Promotion and Protection of Investments (March 30, 1994) Treaty Series No 17 (1996).

[3] The Energy Charter Treaty (December 17, 1994) 34 *ILM* 360 (1995) (ECT).

[4] Vienna Convention on the Law of Treaties (adopted May 22, 1969, entered into force January 27, 1980) 1155 UNTS 331; 8 *ILM* 679; UN Doc A/Conf 39/27 (VCLT).

[5] In the ICSID case of *LG&E Energy*, for example, the tribunal in considering the context within which Argentina and the United States included the fair and equitable treatment standard, and its object and purpose, observed in para 124 that:

> ...in the Preamble of the Treaty...the two countries agreed that 'fair and equitable treatment of investment is desirable in order to maintain a stable framework for investment and maximum effective use of economic resources.' In entering the Bilateral Treaty as a whole, the parties desired to 'promote greater economic cooperation' and 'stimulate the flow of private capital and the economic development of the parties'. In light of these stated objectives, this Tribunal must conclude that stability of the legal and business framework is an essential element of fair and equitable treatment in this case, provided that they do not pose any danger for the existence of the host State itself.

LG&E Energy Corp v. Argentine, ICSID Case No ARB/02/1 (Decision on Liability) (October 3, 2006).

[6] See, eg, the letters annexed to the Agreement between the Government of the French Republic and the Government of the Republic of Argentina on the Reciprocal Encouragement and Protection of Investment (July 3, 1991; *Journal Officiel* du 5 juin 1993, 8164).

Definitions of treaty terms and rules on scope of application are generally found at the beginning of the treaty in sections defining "investors," "companies," "nationals," "investments," and "territory."[7] As a result of entering into an investment treaty a contracting state owes obligations only to the investors of contracting states who make investments in its territory. Conversely, a contracting state has no obligation to persons or investments that do not come within the definitions of these terms as defined in the treaty document. This section of the chapter will examine the meaning of two key defined treaty concepts: (1) "investments" and (2) "investors."

(b) "Investments" Covered by Investment Treaties

In defining the nature of covered investments, most investment treaties provide a general definition of investments covered by the treaty and then proceed to impose on that definition certain limitations such as the area of the investment's economic activity, the time when the investment is made, and prescribed legal requirements.

Most modern investment treaties adopt a broad asset-based definition of investment.[8] Such a definition recognizes the fact that investment forms are constantly evolving in response to the creativity of investors and the rapidly changing world of international finance, so a broad definition is necessary to cover the wide and potentially growing spectrum of investments. The effect of this approach is to create an expanding umbrella of protection for investors and investments. Treaties achieve this result by employing a formula in which the term "investment" is defined as "every kind of asset" and is then followed by a *nonexhaustive* list of asset categories that usually includes: (1) movable and immovable property and any related property rights; (2) various types of interests in companies or any other form of participation in a company, business enterprise, or joint venture; (3) claims to money and claims under a contract having a financial value; (4) intellectual property rights; and (5) business concessions.[9]

In interpreting a similar provision, one tribunal noted that "[t]he specific categories of investment included in the definition are included as examples rather than with the purpose of excluding those not listed."[10] The tribunal also emphasized that "[t]he drafters were careful to use the words 'not exclusively' before listing the categories of 'particularly' included investments."[11] Since one of the investment categories in that case consisted of "shares, rights of participation in companies and other types of participation in

---

[7] See, eg, Agreement for the Liberalization, Promotion and Protection of Investment, Japan-Vietnam (November 14, 2003) Article 1 (defining "investor," "investments," and "Area"); Treaty Concerning the Reciprocal Encouragement and Protection of Investment (United States–Czech Republic) (October 22, 1991) Articles 1(a)–(b) (defining "investment" and "company of a Party"); Treaty concerning the Reciprocal Encouragement and Protection of Investments (United States–Turkey) (December 3, 1985) Articles 1(a)(c)(e) (defining "company," "Investment," and "national").

[8] UNCTAD, *Bilateral Investment Treaties 1995–2006: Trends in International Rulemaking* (2007) 7–12. See also *Fedax NV v. Venezuela*, ICSID Case No ARB/96/3; (1998) 37 *ILM* 1358 (Decision of the Tribunal on Objections to Jurisdiction) (July 11, 1997), in which the tribunal stated at para 34: "A broad definition of investment . . . is not at all an exceptional situation. On the contrary, most contemporary bilateral treaties of this kind refer to 'every kind of asset' or to 'all assets'." The tribunal also found that "[a] similar trend can be found in the context of major multilateral instruments" (Decision of the Tribunal on Objections to Jurisdiction, 35).

[9] For an example of this approach, see Article 1(1), Treaty between the Federal Republic of Germany and Bosnia and Herzegovina concerning the Encouragement and Reciprocal Protection of Investments, October 18, 2001, available at UNCTAD, Investment Instruments Online <http://www.unctad.org/sections/dite/iia/docs/bits/germany_bosnia.pdf>.

[10] *Siemens v. Argentina*, ICSID Case No ARB/02/8 (Decision on Jurisdiction) (August 3, 2004) 137 Germany–Argentina BIT.

[11] *Siemens v. Argentina*, ICSID Case No ARB/02/8 (Decision on Jurisdiction) (August 3, 2004).

companies," the tribunal found that the plain meaning of the term "investment" in the applicable BIT included shares held by a German shareholder.[12]

On the other hand, even if a treaty uses a broad asset-based approach to defining investment, it may still state definitional limitations by specifying particular assets that are *not* to be covered. For example, the North American Free Trade Agreement (NAFTA) definition of "investment" in Article 1139 is broad, but it also specifies certain limits. It provides that "investment" does not mean, among other things, "(i) claims to money that arise solely from . . . commercial contracts for the sale of goods or services by a national or enterprise in the territory of a Party to an enterprise in the territory of another Party, or . . . (ii) the extension of credit in connection with a commercial transaction, such as trade financing." Thus, NAFTA is clearly seeking to exclude purely commercial transactions from the coverage of Chapter Eleven, which is intended to protect investments.

An approach often used in treaties is to define an investment as "any asset" and then list illustrative assets, such as "shares," patents, rights in land, in a nonexclusive manner. One of the purposes of this broad language is to make clear that both tangible and intangible assets are protected by treaty and to clarify that customary international law's protection of investments does not depend on the particular form an investment takes. Thus, for example, while it has been claimed that customary international law does not protect portfolio investments and patents,[13] virtually all investment treaties affirm that shares and participations are "investments" and so are subject to treaty protection. Most also provide protection to patents and other forms of intellectual property.

(c) Limitations on Definitions of "Investment"

Regardless of whether a treaty defines "investment" broadly or narrowly, assets that fall within a treaty's definition nonetheless may have to meet additional qualifications or requirements in order to come within that treaty's scope of application and protection. Such additional qualifications may require that an investment: (i) comply with certain laws and regulations of the host state, (ii) meet certain temporal requirements as to the time when the investment must have been made, (iii) be made in specific sectors of the economy, (iv) comply with specified territorial requirements, or (v) be made in projects classified as "approved" by appropriate governmental authorities. Let us now examine the nature and application of each of these limiting conditions.

(i) Legal Requirements

The practice of conditioning coverage of an investment on its compliance with local laws is an attempt to achieve a very important public purpose—ensuring that foreign investors observe host state's laws and regulations. This requirement also corresponds to the principle that persons should not benefit from their own wrongdoing. For example, Article 1(1) of the Austria–Saudi Arabia BIT defines "investment" to mean "every kind of asset, owned or controlled by an investor of a Contracting Party in the territory of the other Contracting Party *according to its legislation* and in particular, but not exclusively,

---

[12] *Siemens v. Argentina*, ICSID Case No ARB/02/8 (Decision on Jurisdiction) (August 3, 2004).
[13] M Sornarajah, *The International Law on Foreign Investment* (2nd edn 2004) 8, 12 (without citing supporting authority for the statement).

includes..."[14] (emphasis added). Thus, under this definition an investment will enjoy treaty protection only if a claimant establishes that its investment has been owned and controlled in accordance with the host state's legislation. Conversely, a host government and ultimately a tribunal may deny treaty protection of an investment that is found not to be in compliance with host state national law.

Two arbitration cases illustrate some of the issues involved in applying this type of provision. In *Salini Construtorri SpA and Italstrade SpA v. Morocco*,[15] the claimants relied on the broad definition of investment in the Italy–Morocco BIT, which included "rights to any contractual benefit having an economic value" and "any rights of an economic nature conferred by law or by contract" to argue that the contract in question gave them a right to economic value and that a breach of the treaty entitled them to damages. Morocco, however, responded that those categories of investments, when analysed in conjunction with the language "invested in accordance with the laws and regulations of the party," should lead to the conclusion that "Moroccan law, not the Italy–Morocco BIT, should define the notion of investment."[16] Accordingly, Morocco argued that because the transaction in question was characterized as a contract for services and not as a contract for investment under Moroccan law, the complaint did not allege violations of the BIT but only a contractual breach governed by Moroccan domestic law. The tribunal rejected this argument, concluding that "[i]n focusing on *the categories of investment assets (. . .) in accordance with the laws and regulations of the aforementioned party*," this provision refers to the validity of the investment and not to its definition" (emphasis added).[17] More specifically, the tribunal stressed, "[S]uch language seeks to prevent the BIT from protecting investments that should not be protected, particularly because they would be illegal."[18] The tribunal found that the contract was legally valid in Morocco and that it constituted an investment under the Morocco–Italy BIT.

In *Tokios Tokelés v Ukraine*,[19] the Ukrainian government argued that the claimant's investments were not made in accordance with Ukrainian law as required by Article 1(1) of the Ukraine–Lithuania BIT. The Ukrainian government based its argument on the grounds that "the full name under which the Claimant registered its subsidiary...is improper, because 'subsidiary enterprise' but not 'subsidiary *private* enterprise' is a recognized legal form under Ukrainian law." Ukraine also asserted that "it has identified errors in the documents provided by the Claimant related to asset procurement and transfer, including, in some cases, the absence of a necessary signature or notarization."[20] In responding to these allegations, the tribunal noted that Ukraine did not allege that the claimant's investments were illegal per se. Moreover, it found that Ukrainian authorities registered the claimant's subsidiary as a valid enterprise and had also subsequently had registered each of

---

[14] Agreement between The Kingdom of Saudi Arabia and The Republic of Austria concerning the Encouragement and Reciprocal Protection of Investments of June 30, 2001, UNCTAD, Investment Instruments Online <http://www.unctad.org/sections/dite/iia/docs/bits/saudi_austria.pdf>.

[15] *Salini Construtorri SpA and Italstrade SpA v. Morocco*, ICSID Case No ARB/00/4 (Decision on Jurisdiction) (July 23, 2001).

[16] *Salini Construtorri SpA and Italstrade SpA v. Morocco*, ICSID Case No ARB/00/4 (Decision on Jurisdiction) (July 23, 2001) 38.

[17] *Salini Construtorri SpA and Italstrade SpA v. Morocco*, ICSID Case No ARB/00/4 (Decision on Jurisdiction) (July 23, 2001) 46.

[18] *Salini Construtorri SpA and Italstrade SpA v. Morocco*, ICSID Case No ARB/00/4 (Decision on Jurisdiction) (July 23, 2001).

[19] *Tokios Tokelés v. Ukraine*, ICSID Case No ARB/02/18 (Decision on Jurisdiction) (April 29, 2004) (Lithuania–Ukraine BIT).

[20] *Tokios Tokelés v. Ukraine*, ICSID Case No ARB/02/18 (Decision on Jurisdiction) (April 29, 2004) (Lithuania–Ukraine BIT) 83.

the claimant's investments. Although Ukraine claimed that some of the registered investments' underlying documents contained various defects, some of which related to matters
of Ukrainian law, the tribunal concluded: "Even if we were able to confirm the Respondent's allegations, which would require a searching examination of minute details of
administrative procedures in Ukrainian law, to exclude an investment on the basis of
such minor errors would be inconsistent with the object and purpose of the Treaty
[...which is to protect investments]."[21] The fact that Ukraine registered each of the
claimant's investments was sufficient evidence for the tribunal to conclude that the "investment" in question was made in accordance with Ukrainian laws and regulations.

It is to be noted that the requirement that investments be in accordance with law raises a
possible defence in investor–state arbitration, for example, where an investment has been
made through corruption or illegal payments by the investor to governmental authorities, a
situation that unfortunately occurs with some frequency. In *Inceysa Vallisoletana SL v.
Republic of El Salvador*, El Salvador claimed that the investor made investments through
fraud and misrepresentation. Since the investments had not been established "in accordance with law" as required by the BIT, El Salvador argued that the claimant should be
deprived of the protections of the treaty. In light of these facts, the tribunal dismissed
the claims of the Spanish company Inceysa Vallisoletana SL for lack of jurisdiction, since
the treaty conditioned the tribunal's jurisdiction on investments being made "in accordance with law." It also noted that any contrary finding would run counter to the general
principle, inherent in the notion of the international public order, that parties should not
benefit from their own wrongdoing.[22] Similarly, in *Alasdair Ross Anderson v. The Republic of
Costa Rica*, the tribunal declined jurisdiction over claims by a group of Canadian nationals
that had participated in a Ponzi scheme, which was illegal under the country's Central Bank
Law, since the Canada–Costa Rica BIT only protected investments that had been owned and
controlled, "directly or indirectly...in accordance with Costa Rica's law."[23]

In general, the inclusion of the qualification "in accordance with the laws and regulations
of the host State" in the definition of "investment" refers to the validity of the investment
and is designed to prevent the treaty from protecting investments that were not made in
compliance with the host state's national legislation. It should be noted that such provisions
usually place an absolute obligation on the investor to make its investment in accordance
with the host country law. The fact that an investor made a "reasonable effort" or "exercised
due diligence" to assure the legality of its investment would not be sufficient to meet the
obligation imposed by such treaty language.

(ii) Temporal Requirements

Another issue faced in investment treaty negotiation is whether investments made prior to
the treaty will benefit from its provisions. Developing countries have sometimes sought to
limit a treaty's application to future investment only or at least to those investments made

---

[21] *Tokios Tokelés v. Ukraine*, ICSID Case No ARB/02/18 (Decision on Jurisdiction) (April 29, 2004) (Lithuania–
Ukraine BIT) 86.
[22] Summary of Award by counsel for El Salvador, *Inceysa Vallisoletana SL v Republic of El Salvador*, ICSID Case
No ARB/03/26 (Award) (August 2, 2006) (Spain–El Salvador BIT).
[23] *Alasdair Ross Anderson v. Republic of Costa Rica*, ICSID Case no ARB/AF/07/3 (Award), May 19, 2010.
Article I (g) of the Canada–Costa Rica BIT provided: "'investment' means any kind of asset owned or controlled
either directly, or indirectly through an enterprise or natural person of a third State, by an investor of one
Contracting Party in the territory of the other Contracting Party in accordance with the latter's laws..."

in the relatively recent past.[24] Viewing the treaty primarily as an investment promotion mechanism, they claim to see little purpose in granting additional protections to investments already made in the host country. Moreover, they argue that their governments might not have approved such investments if they had realized an investment treaty would later expand the investor's rights and privileges.[25] Capital-exporting states, on the other hand, have generally sought to protect all investments made by their nationals and companies, regardless of when they were made.

Most investment treaties also seek to provide continued protection to investors even after a host country has terminated or withdrawn from the treaty. These continuing effects provisions protect investors who have made investments based on the expectation of treaty protection. The usual period of continued protection is between 15 and 20 years. Investment treaties generally provide that they shall be in force for a term of 15 years.[26] Upon the expiry of this initial period, the treaty may continue either for a fixed additional period or until it is terminated by one of the parties.[27] As a rule, a treaty may be terminated by the parties only after the end of the initial period or after the submission of advance written notice;[28] however, the termination of a treaty usually does not result in the immediate denial of treaty protection for investments made while it was in effect. Most treaty termination provisions contain a continuing effects clause which provides that investments made, acquired, or approved prior to the date of the termination of the treaty will remain in force for a further period of 10, 15, or 20 years.[29] Thus, for example, on February 1, 2010, a tribunal hearing claims against Russia under the Energy Charter Treaty held that Russia's termination of the Treaty's provisional application did not affect the continuing protection of investment under its provisions, including dispute settlement, of investments made before the withdrawal of provisional application for another 20 years.[30]

(iii) Sector Requirements

Some treaties provide that for an asset to qualify as an investment that asset must be in a specified sector of the economy. For example, Article III(1) of the 1977 Egypt–Belgo-

---

[24] See, eg, Agreement for the Promotion and Protection of Investments (United Kingdom–Indonesia), (April 27, 1976) Article 2(3) ("The rights and obligations of both Contracting Parties with respect to investments made before January 10, 1967 shall be in no way affected by the provisions of this Agreement").

[25] UNCTAD, *Bilateral Investment Treaties in the Mid-1990s* (1998) 42.

[26] See, eg, Agreement Between the Government of the Republic of Botswana and the Government of the People's Republic of China on the Promotion and Protection of Investments, Bots–PRC, Article 14, June 12, 2000 (ten years); Agreement on Encouragement and Reciprocal Protection of Investments between the State of Eritrea and the Kingdom of the Netherlands, Eri–Neth, Article 13, April 14, 2004 (fifteen years).

[27] eg, Agreement Between the Government of the Republic of Indonesia and the Government of the People's Democratic Republic of Algeria Concerning the Promotion and Protection of Investments, Indon–Alg, Article 13, March 21, 2000, provides: "The present Agreement . . . shall remain force for a period of *ten years* and shall continue in force thereafter for *another period of ten years* and *so forth* unless denounced in writing by either Contracting Party one year before its expiration." (emphasis added).

[28] For example, Article 10 of the Jordan–Yemen BIT provides: "Each Contracting Party has the right to terminate this agreement at the end of its duration or at any time after the expiry of the initial ten years period by a written notice served to the other Contracting party one year prior to the intended termination date." Agreement between the Government of the Hashemite Kingdom of Jordan and the Government of the Republic of Yemen on the Mutual Promotion and Protection of Investments, Jordan-Yemen, Article 10, May 8, 1999.

[29] For example, Article 14 of the Japan–Bangladesh BIT provides: "In respect of investments and returns acquired prior to the date of termination of the present Agreement, the provisions of Articles 1 to 13 shall continue to be effective for further period of fifteen years from the date of termination of the present Agreement." Agreement between Japan and the People's Republic of Bangladesh Concerning the Promotion and Protection of Investment, Japan–Bangl, Artile 14, November 10, 1998.

[30] "Tribunal Allows Claims by Yukos Shareholders Against Russia," *Lovells*, February 9, 2010, <http://elovells.com/ve/ZZ9191307269L9680604>.

Luxemburg Economic Union BIT contains the following general definition of investment: "The term "investments" shall comprise every direct or indirect contribution of capital and any other kind of assets, invested or reinvested in enterprises in the field of agriculture, industry, mining forestry, communications, and tourism."[31]

The challenges that may arise in interpreting provisions of this kind are illustrated in *Jan de Nul NV and Dredging International NV v. Arab Republic of Egypt*.[32] In that dispute, the tribunal was faced with the question of whether a contribution of capital was invested in one of the fields specified in the above-quoted Article III (1) of the 1977 Egypt–Belgo–Luxemburg Economic Union BIT. More specifically, the issue was whether the dredging of the Suez Canal was related to "communications" within the meaning of that Article. Egypt argued that the dredging of the Canal did not relate to communications, since the ordinary meaning of "communications" in English is limited to the exchange of information. In response, the claimants relied on authoritative English language dictionaries to support the argument that the word "communications" is not limited to the transmission of information but includes a geographic dimension. For example, it may include: "any connective passage or channel," "a system of routes for moving troops, supplies, and vehicles," or "passage or an opportunity or means of passage between places." The tribunal ultimately decided the issue in favor of the claimants, stating that it failed "to see how the Respondent can argue that including 'road of communication' or 'transport of persons and goods' in the meaning of 'communications' under Article III(1) can be 'at odds with the common and ordinary meaning of the term communications.'" The tribunal also found that just because the claimants' activities related to dredging the canal, and not communicating through the canal, it did not mean that the claimants had not invested in an enterprise in the field of communications within the meaning of the BIT.[33]

Although limiting an investment to certain economic sectors may be justified by economic development or the protection of national economy, most modern bilateral investment treaties have not followed this practice.[34] However, the Energy Charter Treaty, a sector-specific investment treaty, has done so out of necessity. Intended to cover the energy sector alone, the Treaty had to define that sector with some precision. Article 1(6) of the ECT states: "'Investment' refers to any investment Associated with an Economic Activity in the Energy Sector and to investments or classes of investments designated by a Contracting Party as 'Charter efficiency projects' and so notified to the [Energy Charter] Secretariat." Under Article 1(4), "'Economic Activity in the Energy Sector' is defined broadly as 'an economic activity concerning the exploration, extraction, refining, production, storage, land transportation, transmission, distribution, trade, marketing or Sale of Energy Materials and Products'" with certain specified exceptions. The Understandings in the Final Act of the European Energy Charter Conference give examples of permitted "Economic Activity in the Energy Sector" and further underscore the sectorial character of the Treaty by stating that it confers no right to engage in economic activities other than in the Energy Sector.

---

[31] Article III, Agreement between the Arab Republic of Egypt on the one Hand, and the Belgo-Luxemburg Economic Union on the other Hand, on the Encouragement and Reciprocal Protection of Investments of 1977, UNCTAD, Investment Instruments Online <http://www.unctad.org/sections/dite/iia/docs/bits/egypt_belg_lux .pdf> accessed May 22, 2009.

[32] *Jan de Nul NV and Dredging International NV v. Arab Republic of Egypt*, Decision on Jurisdiction, June 16, 2006, ICSID Case No ARB/04/13 (Belgo–Luxembourg–Egypt BIT).

[33] *Jan de Nul NV and Dredging International NV v. Arab Republic of Egypt*, Decision on Jurisdiction, June 16, 2006, ICSID Case No ARB/04/13 (Belgo–Luxembourg–Egypt BIT) 101–2, 104.

[34] See generally, UNCTAD (n 8) 7–12.

Because most other investment treaties are general rather than sectorial in scope, they have usually not employed such elaborate provisions to define the sectors in which investments are permitted. On the other hand, investment treaties rarely allow investments in all economic sectors. Most bilateral investment treaties either specifically identify sectors in which nationals from the other country may not invest, for example, banking or maritime shipping, or they state that investments are permitted only in those sectors permitted by domestic law, a provision that incorporates by reference legislation prohibiting foreign investment in defined economic areas into the treaty.[35]

(iv) Territorial Requirements

Investment treaties often specifically limit their application to investments made within the territory of the respective contracting parties. The rationale behind this provision is to ensure that the host state obtains the benefits from the operation of foreign investments within its territory, whether such benefits consist of obtaining new technologies, developing important economic sectors, creating employment, or collecting additional tax revenues. Such a condition may be included either in the definition of the term "investment" or in the provision on the treaty's scope of application. The former approach is illustrated in Article 1 of the 2006 Canada–Peru BIT, which provides: "'Covered investment' means, with respect to a Party, *an investment in its territory of an investor of the other Party* existing on the date of entry into force of this Agreement, as well as investments made or acquired thereafter" (emphasis added).[36] The latter approach is illustrated in Article II of the 1997 Switzerland–Philippines BIT, which provides: "The present agreement applies to investments in the territory of the one Contracting Party made in accordance with its laws and regulations by investors of the other Contracting Party, whether prior to or after the entry into force of the Agreement."[37] Thus, according to such provisions treaty protection extends to an investment only if it is made in the territory of the host State.

The application of such provisions to certain kinds of investment transactions sometimes poses challenges. In *Fedax NV v. Venezuela*,[38] Venezuela argued that Fedax did not qualify as an investor because, only being the holder of promissory notes, it did not make any "investment" in the territory of the host state. In response to this argument, the tribunal recognized that "it is true that in some kinds of investments, such as the acquisition of interests in immovable property, companies and the like, a transfer of funds or value will be made into the territory of the host country" but it stressed that "this does not necessarily happen in a number of other types of investments, particularly those of financial nature."[39] The test in such circumstances, according to the tribunal, is whether the available

---

[35] UNCTC, *Bilateral Investment Treaties* (1988) 27.

[36] Agreement between Canada and the Republic of Peru for the Promotion and Protection of Investments of 2006. Available at Foreign Affairs and International Trade Canada at <http://www.international.gc.ca/assets/trade-agreements-accords-commerciaux/pdfs/Canada-Peru10nov06-en.pdf>.

[37] Accord entre la Confédération suisse et la République des Philippines concernant la promotion et la protection réciproque des investissements (1997). UNCTAD, Investment Instruments <http://www.unctad.org/sections/dite/iia/docs/bits/switzerland_philippines_fr.pdf>.

[38] *Fedax NV v. Venezuela*, ICSID Case No ARB/96/3 (Award on Jurisdiction) (July 11, 1997) (The Netherlands–Venezuela BIT).

[39] On this point the tribunal observed: "It is a standard feature of many international financial transactions that the funds involved are not physically transferred to the territory of the beneficiary, but put at its disposal elsewhere. In fact, many loans and credits do not leave the country of origin at all, but are available to suppliers or other entities. The same is true of many important offshore financial operations relating to exports and other kinds of business. And, of course promissory notes are frequently employed in such arrangements."

Fedax NV v. Venezuela, ICSID Case No ARB/96/3 (Award on Jurisdiction) (July 11, 1997) (The Netherlands–Venezuela BIT) 41.

funds are used by the beneficiary of the credit to finance its various governmental needs.[40] Since it was not disputed that through its promissory notes Venezuela had received credit that was put to work for its financial needs, those promissory notes were determined to be invested in the territory of Venezuela within the meaning of the treaty.

The issue of whether an investment was made in the territory of a treaty party also arose in two cases by the same claimants involving similar transactions, one against Pakistan and the other against the Philippines. In *SGS Société Générale de Surveillance SA v. Islamic Republic of Pakistan*,[41] and *SGS Société Générale de Surveillance SA v. Republic of the Philippines*,[42] the disputes arose out of the alleged wrongful termination of contracts under which SGS, a Swiss group, was to provide "preshipment inspection services," including comprehensive import supervision of goods before shipment to the Philippines and Pakistan. Because of the nature of the services to be rendered, the SGS activity was carried out in the territories of exporting countries. In both cases the respondent states objected to the tribunal's jurisdiction by arguing that SGS's investments were not made in the territory of the host states and so were not covered by the applicable BITs, which included the territoriality investment requirement. As a result, they argued, the dispute did not arise out of an investment. In determining whether SGS made an "investment" "in the territory of Pakistan," the tribunal noted that the Pre-Shipment Inspection (PSI) Agreement defined SGS's commitments in such a way as to ensure that SGS, if it were to comply with them, had to make certain expenditures within Pakistan. It observed that "[w]hile the expenditures may be relatively small (Pakistan's Reply estimated them as amounting to approximately US$800,000, while SGS estimate put them at US$1.5 million), they involved the injection of funds into the territory of Pakistan for the carrying out of SGS's engagements under the PSI Agreement."[43] The tribunal also found relevant the fact that the claimant adduced evidence of expenditures to establish and operate liaison offices in Pakistan to perform its obligations under the PSI Agreement,[44] and that Pakistan itself recognized that the PSI Agreement involved the delegation of some of the state's customs powers to the private party in order to increase the customs revenue of that state.[45] Therefore, the tribunal held that the expenditures made by SGS pursuant to the PSI Agreement constituted an investment within the meaning of the BIT and, moreover, that the ICSID Convention's requirement that there be a legal dispute arising directly out of an "investment" was satisfied.[46] In the SGS arbitration against the Philippines, a different tribunal arrived at the same conclusion, finding that to accomplish the purposes of the contract the claimants had made certain expenditures in the territory of the Philippines.[47]

(v) Approved Project Requirements

Some treaties may also limit their scope to investments in projects specifically approved by appropriate governmental authorities. The aim of this provision is to confine a treaty's

[40] *Fedax NV v. Venezuela*, ICSID Case No ARB/96/3 (Award on Jurisdiction) (July 11, 1997) (The Netherlands–Venezuela BIT).
[41] *SGS Société Générale de Surveillance SA v. Islamic Republic of Pakistan*, ICSID Case No ARB/01/13 (Decision on Jurisdiction) (August 6, 2003) (Swiss Confederation–Pakistan BIT).
[42] *SGS Société Générale de Surveillance SA v. Republic of the Philippines*, ICSID Case No ARB/02/6 (Decision on Jurisdiction) (January 29, 2004) (Swiss Confederation–Republic of the Philippines BIT).
[43] See *SGS Société Générale de Surveillance SA* (n 41) 136.
[44] *SGS Société Générale de Surveillance SA* (n 41) 137.
[45] *SGS Société Générale de Surveillance SA* (n 41) 139.
[46] *SGS Société Générale de Surveillance SA* (n 41) 140.
[47] See *SGS Société Générale de Surveillance SA* (n 42) 101–2.

encouragement and protection only to investment in projects perceived by its governing authorities to be contributing to the state's economic development or national interest. For example, Article 1 of the 1979 Sweden–Malaysia BIT, like many treaties, defines "investment" as "any kind of asset"; however, the definition also contains an important proviso:

> that such asset when invested:
>
> (i) in Malaysia, is *invested in a project classified by the appropriate Ministry in Malaysia in accordance with its legislation and administrative practice as an "approved project."* The classification as an "approved project" may, on application, be accorded to investments made prior to the date of the entry into force of this Agreement on conditions to be stipulated for each individual case. . . .[48] (emphasis added)

A failure to satisfy the requirement of ministry approval would deprive an asset of the BIT's protection because it would not constitute a covered investment within the meaning of the treaty.

The ICSID case of *Gruslin v. Malaysia*,[49] which involved an alleged investment made in securities listed on the Malaysian Stock Exchange (KLSE), required the tribunal to interpret the proviso quoted above. Relying on that provision, Malaysia argued that the assets in question did not constitute an investment within the meaning of the treaty because they were not made in an approved project and because "mere investment in shares in the stock market, which can be traded by anyone and are not connected to the development of an approved project, are not protected." The sole arbitrator upheld Malaysia's position and rejected the claimant's contention that the approval given to participate in the KLSE listing processes was sufficient to satisfy the "approved project" requirement. The arbitrator noted, "What is required is something constituting regulatory approval of a 'project', as such, and not merely the approval at some time of the general business activities of a corporation."[50] He therefore concluded that the shares in question did not satisfy the treaty's definition of "investment" and consequently were not protected by the BIT. Thus, it would seem that clauses similar to the proviso found in the Sweden–Malaysia BIT require specific governmental authorization for the investment. The fact that an investment was made in accordance with the host country's laws and regulations, as was discussed earlier, is not sufficient to meet this requirement.

(c) Definitions of "Investors" Covered by the Treaty

Even though an asset qualifies as an "investment" under an investment treaty, a person or entity will not be able to claim treaty protection for that asset unless that person or entity is deemed to be an "investor" as that term is defined in the applicable treaty. Defining which investors can benefit from the treaty is an important issue, since the goal of a contracting state is to secure benefits for its own nationals, companies, and investors, rather than those of other countries. The problem is essentially one of determining what links need to exist between an investor and a state party to a treaty for the investor to receive the maximum

---

[48] Agreement between the Government of Sweden and the Government of Malaysia concerning the Mutual Protection of Investments of 1979, Article 1. *Sveriges oeverenskommelser med fraemmande makter*, SO 1979:17, UNCTAD InvestmentInstruments Online <http://www.unctad.org/sections/dite/iia/docs/bits/sweden_malaysia.pdf>.

[49] *Gruslin v. Malaysia*, Final Award, ICSID Case No ARB/99/3 (November 27, 2000) (Belgo–Luxembourg–Malaysia BIT).

[50] *Gruslin v. Malaysia*, Final Award, ICSID Case No ARB/99/3 (November 27, 2000) (Belgo–Luxembourg–Malaysia BIT) 25.5.

benefit from the treaty's provisions. In examining this problem, one must distinguish between two types of investors: (a) natural persons and (b) legal entities. Virtually all treaties make this distinction in setting out their definitions of "investor."

(i) Natural Persons as "Investors"

In the case of physical persons or individuals, investment treaties specify the necessary link between the individual and a contracting state primarily on the basis of nationality or citizenship and to a lesser extent by domicile, permanent residence, or some combination thereof. Thus, for example, Article 1(7)(a)(i) of the Energy Charter Treaty defines "investor" as including a "natural person having the citizenship or nationality of or who is permanently residing in that Contracting Party in accordance with its applicable law."[51] Whether a person has the necessary link is determined by the domestic law of the country with which the link is claimed.

Persons having more than one nationality pose a special problem under investment treaties. Unless the treaty specifically treats this question, a variety of possible solutions present themselves. One possibility is to follow the principle of international law that a person with more than one nationality is a national of the state of that person's dominant and effective nationality.[52] Another approach is to hold that if a person is a national of both contracting states that fact automatically denies that person protection, since the treaty is not meant to provide protection to nationals who invest in their own state. Such individuals receive protection from the legal system of the state of which they are nationals.

(ii) Companies and other Legal Entities as "Investors"

For investors that are companies or other legal entities, the problem of determining an appropriate link with a contracting state becomes more complex. Such legal entities may be created and owned by persons who have no real connection with the countries that are parties to the treaty. In particular, three types of cases raise problems in this respect: (1) companies organized in a treaty country by nationals of a non-treaty country; (2) companies organized in a non-treaty country by nationals of a treaty country; and (3) companies in which nationals of a non-treaty country hold a substantial interest. For a company to be covered by the treaty, most BITs require that a treaty partner at least be one of the following: (1) the country of the company's incorporation,[53] (2) the country of the company's seat, registered office, or principal place of business,[54] or (3) the country whose nationals have control over, or a substantial interest in, the company making the

---

[51] The Energy Charter Treaty, Article 1(7)(a)(i).

[52] UNCTAD (n 8) 14. It is to be noted that Article 1 of the Uruguay–US BIT of 2005 specifically adopts this position in its definition of "investor," which states "provided however, that a natural person who is a dual citizen shall be deemed to be exclusively a citizen of the State of his or her dominant and effective citizenship."

[53] See, eg, Treaty Concerning the Encouragement and Reciprocal Protection of Investment, (United States-Sri Lanka) (September 20, 1991) Article 1(b) ("'[C]ompany' of a Party means any kind of corporation, company, association, partnership or other organization, legally constituted under the laws and regulations of a Party or a political subdivision thereof..."). BITs concluded by Denmark, the Netherlands, the United Kingdom, and the United States are frequently of this type. *See* UNCTAD, *Bilateral Investment Treaties in the Mid-1990s* (1998) 39.

[54] See, eg, Treaty Concerning the Encouragement and Reciprocal Protection of Investments, (Federal Republic of Germany–Swaziland) (April 5, 1990) Article1(4)(a) ("The term 'companies' means...in respect of the Federal Republic of Germany: any juridical person as well as any commercial or other company or association with or without legal personality having its seat in the German area of application of this Treaty, irrespective of whether or not its activities are directed at profit."). BITs concluded by Belgium, Germany, and Sweden are frequently of this type. eg, UNCTAD, *Bilateral Investment Treaties in the Mid-1990s* (1998) 40.

investment.[55] Sometimes these requirements are combined so that an investing company must satisfy two or more conditions to qualify for coverage under a particular investment treaty.

One example of an approach taken to corporate investors in a treaty regime is the Energy Charter Treaty (ECT), which adopts the relatively simple rule that a company is an investor of a contracting party if it has been organized in accordance with the law applicable in the contracting state. Thus, even if nationals of a non-ECT state organize a company in an ECT state, such company would qualify as an investor of a contracting party under the treaty. Moreover, unlike most BITs, the ECT explicitly recognizes the possibility that a natural or legal person from a "third state" (ie non-ECT state) can be considered an investor if it fulfils the treaty conditions, *mutatis mutandis*, specified for contracting states.[56] So, if under the laws of an ECT state a company organized in another state was considered to be organized under the laws of the ECT state, that company would still qualify as an investor under the treaty. In order to prevent these provisions from being abused by nationals and companies of non-ECT states, Article 17 of the Energy Charter Treaty, in terms almost identical to Article 1(2) of the United States BIT Prototype,[57] gives each contracting party the right to deny the advantages of the treaty to a legal entity if it is owned or controlled by third country nationals and has no substantial business activities in the state of the contracting party. A contracting party may also deny the advantages of the treaty to the investments of investors from countries not a member of the treaty and investors with which the host country does not maintain diplomatic relations or prohibits transactions.

To be protected under many investment treaties, an investor must "own" or "control" the investment. While determining ownership is usually easy, control is a more vague and ambiguous concept. In order to give some specificity to the term, some treaties contain an annexed or supplementary agreement defining the term "control" in the treaty. For example, the Understandings of the Final Act, IV 3, of the European Energy Charter Conference that adopted the Energy Charter Treaty provides that

> control of an Investment means control in fact, determined after examining the actual circumstances in each situation, including the Investor's a) financial interest, including equity interest in the Investment; b) ability to exercise substantial influence over the management and operation of the Investment; and c) ability to exercise substantial influence over selection of members of the board of directors or other managing body.

Bilateral treaty negotiations have sometimes dealt with the issue of control in the text of the BIT itself or in separate protocols or an exchange of letters. The concern in most investment treaties has been the same: to prevent persons and companies having no genuine link with treaty partners from obtaining benefits under the treaty.

Two arbitration decisions illustrate some of the challenges in determining whether a corporation qualifies as an "investor" under an investment treaty. In *Tokios Tokelés v.*

---

[55] See, eg, Agreement on Encouragement and Reciprocal Protection of Investments (Lithuania–Netherlands) (January 26, 1994) Article 1(b)(iii):

> The term 'investor' shall comprise with regard to either contracting party:...(iii). legal persons not constituted under the law of that Contracting Party but controlled, directly or indirectly, by natural persons as defined in (i) [of the Contracting Party's nationality] or by legal persons as defined in (ii) [legal persons constituted under the law of the Contracting Party] above, who invest in the territory of either Contracting Party.

"Ownership or control," as these provisions are called, is used in BITs concluded by the Netherlands, Sweden, and Switzerland. UNCTAD, *Bilateral Investment Treaties in the Mid-1990s* (1998) 39.

[56] The Energy Charter Treaty, Article 1(7)(b).

[57] Reprinted in UNCTC, *Bilateral Investment Treaties* (1988) 184.

Ukraine,[58] Tokelés, a Lithuanian corporation, brought an arbitration proceeding against the government of Ukraine under the Ukraine–Lithuania BIT[59] for Ukraine's alleged violation of the BIT's guarantees of investor treatment. Ukraine argued that Tokios Tokelés was not an "investor" under the treaty since 99 percent of its shares were owned by Ukrainian nationals, who also constituted two-thirds of its management. Ukraine argued that, therefore, while Tokios Tokelés was technically a Lithuanian corporation, it was effectively a Ukrainian corporation since it was owned and operated by Ukrainian nationals. Relying on the BIT's definition of investor, which included "any entity established in the territory of the Republic of Lithuania in conformity with its laws and regulations," the tribunal, with a strong dissent by its president, found that Tokios Tokelés satisfied the requirements of the treaty. The majority acknowledged that many investment treaties expressly provide that an entity controlled by nationals of the host country shall not be considered an investor of the other contracting party but found no such limitation in the Ukraine–Lithuania BIT. In a statement that negotiators and drafters of investment treaties should bear in mind, the majority observed: "We regard the absence of such a provision as a deliberate choice of the Contracting Parties. In our view, it is not for tribunals to impose limits on the scope of BITs not found in the text, much less limits nowhere evident from the negotiating history."[60]

In a second ICSID case, *Rompetrol Group NV v. Romania*,[61] the claimant, a Dutch corporation whose principal shareholder was a Romanian national, commenced arbitration against Romania under the Netherlands–Romania BIT. That BIT defined an "investor" of a contracting party as "legal persons constituted under the law of that Contracting Party."[62] Romania sought dismissal of the case on the grounds that Rompetrol was merely a shell company controlled by Romanian nationals and that it therefore did not qualify as an "investor" under the BIT. The tribunal rejected this argument and found that the treaty very clearly stated that an entity merely had to be constituted under the law of a contracting party to establish a legal link with that state and qualify it as an investor. On the basis of these two cases, it would seem that tribunals are reluctant to impose on corporate investors substantive conditions that the applicable investment treaty does not specifically require.

15.5 Investment Promotion, Admission, and Establishment

Virtually all investment treaties deal with the promotion, entry, and establishment in the territory of one treaty partner of investments from other treaty partners. Let us examine each of these three functions separately.

(a) Investment Promotion

Believing that increased foreign investment will foster economic prosperity and global well-being, numerous countries have undertaken to negotiate investment treaties as a means to

---

[58] *Tokios Tokelés v. Ukraine*, ICSID Case No ARB/02/18 (Decision on Jurisdiction) (April 29, 2004) (Lithuania–Ukraine BIT).

[59] Agreement between the Government of Ukraine and the Government of the Republic of Lithuania for the Promotion and Reciprocal Protection of Investments (entered into force on February 27, 1995).

[60] Agreement between the Government of Ukraine and the Government of the Republic of Lithuania for the Promotion and Reciprocal Protection of Investments (entered into force on February 27, 1995) 36.

[61] *Rompetrol Group NV v. Romainia*, ICSID Case No ARB/06/3 (Decision on Respondent's Preliminary Objections on Jurisdiction and Admissibility) (April 18, 2008).

[62] *Rompetrol Group NV v. Romainia*, ICSID Case No ARB/06/3 (Decision on Respondent's Preliminary Objections on Jurisdiction and Admissibility) (April 18, 2008) Article 1(b).

facilitate the entry of capital, technology, and people from their territories into the territories of their treaty partners. In doing so, such states have hoped that treaty commitments would lead potential host countries to reduce or lower their own barriers to foreign investment. This goal has been apparent from the titles given to most investment treaties— "A Treaty for the *Promotion* and Protection of Investment"[63] or "A Treaty for the Reciprocal *Encouragement* and Protection of Investment."[64] This goal is also clear from the objectives given in treaty preambles, which state that the Contracting Parties desire to "...create favorable conditions for greater investment by nationals of one state in the territory of the other state...,"[65] wish "...to develop economic cooperation between the two states and to create favorable conditions for investments..."[66] or seek "...to intensify economic cooperation for the economic benefit of both countries."[67] Thus, it would seem that many investment treaties foresee more than a lack of resistance or even passivity toward investment by the contracting parties; rather, they contemplate treaty partners somehow actively seeking to promote and encourage the entry of investment into their territories.

In pursuit of this goal, all treaties impose an obligation on each contracting party "to promote" or "encourage" investments by nationals and companies of other contracting parties; however, the nature of that obligation is usually very general and vague. For example, the BIT between Egypt and France simply states that "[e]ach of the contracting parties shall encourage investment made in its territory by nationals and companies of the other contracting party."[68] Notably, it does not specifically state what each country must to do to encourage investment from the other. Even in the absence of treaties, as a matter of national policy many countries promote specific kinds of foreign investment to secure needed capital and technology. These countries undertake promotional activities such as placing advertisements in international publications, holding investment conferences in their countries to which potential investors are invited, and sending missions abroad to conduct "road shows" that give presentations about investment opportunities in their countries. No investment treaty, however, obligates a contracting state to undertake such specific promotional activities.

Investment treaties generally impose an obligation to promote or encourage investments in the following terms: "Each contracting state shall encourage and create favourable conditions for investors of the other Contracting party to make investments in its territory..."[69] A variation of this obligation is found in Article 10 of the Energy Charter

[63] eg, Agreement between the Government of the United Kingdom of Great Britain and Northern Ireland and the Government of the Republic of Albania for the Promotion and Protection of Investments (March 30, 1994) Treaty Series No 17 (1996); Treaty Concerning the Promotion and Reciprocal Protection of Investments (Germany–Poland) (November 10, 1989) (1990) 29 *ILM* 333; Agreement for the Promotion and Protection of Investments (Indonesia–United Kingdom)(April 27, 1976) Treaty Series No 62.

[64] Treaty Concerning the Reciprocal Encouragement and Protection of Investment (United States–Armenia) (September 23, 1992) S Treaty Doc No 1993 103-11.

[65] "Draft Agreement between the Government of the United Kingdom of Great Britain and North Ireland and the Government of [...] for the Promotion and Protection of Investments," in R Dolzer and Ch Schreuer, *Principles of International Investment Law* (2007) 376.

[66] Convention entre le Governement de la République Française et le Gouvernement de la République Arabe d'Egypte sur l'Encouragement et la Protection Reciproques des Investissements (December 22, 1974) in J Officiel Française (November 8, 1974) 11486.

[67] Agreement Between the Argentine Republic and the Kingdom of Spain on the Reciprocal Promotion and Protection of Investments (entered into force September 28, 1992).

[68] Convention entre le Gouvernement de la République Française et le Gouvernement de la République Arabe d'Egypte sur l'Encouragement et la Protection Réciproques des Investissements (December 22, 1974) Article 2 in *J Officiel Français* (November 8, 1974) 11486.

[69] eg, Agreement between the Government of the United Kingdom of Great Britain and Northern Ireland and the Government of the Republic of India for the Promotion and Protection of Investments (March 14, 1994) Article 3(1) in (1995) 34 *Int'l Legal Mats* 935.

Treaty, entitled "Promotion, Protection, and Treatment of Investment," which states: "Each Contracting Party shall, in accordance with the provisions of this Treaty, encourage and create stable, equitable, favourable and transparent conditions for Investors of other Contracting Parties to make Investments in its Area."

Thus, investment treaties place an obligation upon host countries to promote investment by the nationals and companies of other treaty partners by creating "favorable conditions" within their territories for making and operating such investments. The notion of "favorable conditions" can conceivably cover a wide range of political, economic, and social situations in areas from exchange rates to security in rural areas. Regardless, investment treaties do not normally specify the precise kinds of conditions that a contracting state must create. Presumably, a country is to create favorable conditions through its laws, policies, and administrative actions; however, investment treaties are rarely even that specific. Often they do not even indicate the kind of laws and administrative actions that must be enacted to meet their investment promotion obligations.

In view of its generality and vagueness, it is difficult to determine if the obligation to promote investment has been effective in influencing the behavior of host country governments. No arbitration cases appear to have arisen against a state purely on the grounds that it failed to create favorable conditions for investment promotion. The generality and vagueness of the language in which treaties express the obligation to promote investments gives contracting states great latitude to argue that the nature of such conditions makes their application a matter fully within a host country's legislative and administrative discretion. On the other hand, it is clear from the language of most treaties that a contracting party has no obligation to encourage and promote investors from *its own* country to invest in a treaty partner's territory, a goal sometimes sought by developing countries when negotiating bilateral investment treaties with wealthy industrialized states. Investment treaties impose the duty to promote investment on the potential host country, not the prospective investor's home country.[70] Moreover, whatever the scope and nature of the obligation to promote, it is also clear that such obligations do not include an obligation to admit investments from other contracting states to their territories. Investment treaties view investment promotion and investment admission as two separate and distinct functions governed by different treaty provisions.

(b) Admission and Establishment of Investments

Although the investment treaty movement has caused 3000 agreements to be concluded in the last half-century, that movement has not created a truly open door to the flow of capital among treaty partners nor led to the total dismantling all the pre-existing laws and policies restricting the entry of foreign investors and investment. While countries have participated in the investment treaty movement in the hope of obtaining increased foreign capital and technology vital for their economic development and prosperity, they have also perceived a need to protect important national interests that might be threatened by the uncontrolled

---

[70] See, however, Article 2(3) of the Convention between the Belgo-Luxembourg Economic Union and the United Republic of Cameroon Concerning the Reciprocal Promotion and Protection of Investments (March 27, 1980) 1284 UNTS 21115, which states: "Aware of the importance of investments for the promotion of its development and cooperation, the Belgo-Luxembourg Economic Union shall adopt measures to encourage its economic agents to participate in the development of the United Republic of Cameroon, in accordance with its priority objectives." While one interpretation of this provision might lead to the conclusion that the Belgo–Luxembourg Economic Union is to encourage its own companies and nationals to invest in Cameroon, an equally plausible interpretation is that the Union is only obligated to encourage governmental agencies to participate in Cameroon development.

entry of foreign investment. Consequently, no country has been willing to sacrifice those interests by creating an unrestricted "open door" to investors from treaty partners. In treaty negotiations, countries have had to balance two imperatives: their need for foreign investment and their need to protect certain domestic interests. That fact does not mean, however, that treaties have no effect on the admission and establishment of investment.

The totality of treaty obligations that a host country owes to foreign investors is generally referred to as the "treatment" to be accorded to the investor or the investment. Most treaties make a distinction between the treatment to be accorded in making an investment and the treatment to be given after that investment is made. The former is referred to as "preentry" or "preestablishment" treatment, while the latter is referred to as "postentry" or "postestablishment" treatment. While most investment treaties establish similar firm obligations with respect to the latter, they express much more diverse and flexible commitments with respect to the former.

Despite a contracting state's obligation to promote investment and create favorable conditions for investment, there is no requirement that a host country admit any investments proposed by investors from another treaty country. Nonetheless, all investment treaties have endeavored to restrain a host country's discretion regarding the admission of investment to a greater or lesser extent. A review of investment treaties to this point reveals three approaches to preentry treatment: (1) the admission of investment according to host country law, which one might call the "controlled entry model";[71] (2) grants of a relative right of admission or establishment, which can be described as the "liberalized entry model"; and, in rare cases, (3) grants of an absolute right of admission or establishment known as the establishment model.

1. *Admission according to National Law.* Most investment treaties admit investments of other contracting parties only if they comply with the host country's legislation.[72] This type of provision is normally referred to as an "admissions clause."[73] An example of such a clause is Article 2(1) of the Germany–Antigua and Barbuda BIT of 1998, which provides: "Each Contracting State shall in its territory promote as far as possible investments by investors of the other Contracting State and *admit such investments in accordance with its legislation*"[74] (emphasis added). Similarly, Article 2(1) of China–Bosnia–Herzegovina BIT of 2002 represents a variation on this approach: "Either Contracting Party shall encourage and create favourable, stable and transparent conditions for investors of the other

[71] I Gomez-Palacio and P Muchlinsky, "Admission and Establishment," in *The Oxford Handbook of International Investment Law* (2008) 240.

[72] UNCTAD, *Bilateral Investment Treaties 1995–2006: Trends in Investment Rulemaking* (2007) 21.

[73] UNCTAD, *Bilateral Investment Treaties 1995–2006: Trends in Investment Rulemaking* (2007). See also *Aguas del Tunari SA v. Republic of Bolivia*, ICSID Case No ARB/02/3 (Decision on Respondent's Objections to Jurisdiction) (October 21, 2005), in which the tribunal interpreted Article 2 of the 1992 Bolivia–Netherlands BIT, which provided: "Each Contracting Party shall, within the framework of its laws and regulations, promote economic cooperation through the protection in its territory of investments of nationals of other Contracting Parties. Subject to its right to exercise powers conferred by its laws or regulations, each Contracting Party shall admit such investments." The tribunal also stated: "This obligation to allow the entry of foreign investment is a common provision in bilateral investment treaties, and is often termed an "admission clause." *Aguas del Tunari SA v. Republic of Bolivia*, ICSID Case No ARB/02/3 (Decision on Respondent's Objections to Jurisdiction) (October 21, 2005) 147.

[74] Treaty between the Federal Republic of Germany and Antigua and Barbuda concerning the encouragement and reciprocal protection of investments (November 5, 1998) Bundesgesetzblatt,Teil II, Nr 23, 859 (2002) <http://www.bundesgesetzblatt.de/> accessed May 25, 2009.

Contracting Party to make investment in its territory and *shall admit such investments, within the framework of its laws and regulations*"[75] (emphasis added).

These admissions clauses have two important implications. The first and most obvious is that under a treaty containing an admissions clause a host country agrees to allow investments from a treaty partner only to the extent that it decides they meet the requirements of its national laws and regulations. Consequently, the admissions clause allows the host state to retain control over the entry of foreign capital, to screen investments to ensure their compatibility with the state's national security, economic development, and public policy goals, and to determine the conditions under which foreign investments will be permitted, if at all. For example, in *Aguas del Tunari SA v. Republic of Bolivia*, a tribunal interpreted a Bolivia–Netherlands BIT in which the contracting parties agreed to admit investments of the other contracting party " ... [s]ubject to its right to exercise powers conferred by its laws or regulations ...." Based on this language, the tribunal found in the case of Bolivia that " ... the obligation to admit investments was subject to the decision of Bolivia to exercise powers conferred by its laws or regulations."[76]

Furthermore, unless the treaty provides otherwise, when considering the admission of investments from a treaty partner the host state is under no obligation to grant investors from treaty partners the same treatment that it grants to its own nationals or to investors of third parties. Similarly, it is not required to amend its laws and regulations subsequent to a treaty's ratification to facilitate their entry. Indeed, each contracting party is free to change its legislation after the treaty has entered into effect in ways that create new barriers to investments. Thus, a host government may subject the admission of investments from a treaty partner to less favorable treatment than is enjoyed by host country nationals or investors from third countries.

Similar to the definition of "investment" discussed earlier in this chapter, the inclusion in an admission clause of the phrase "in accordance with laws and regulations" may serve as a limitation on a treaty's scope of protection and the host state's consent to arbitral jurisdiction over related investment disputes. Thus, if a treaty protects only investments made in accordance with host country law and an investment in an arbitration case is shown not to have been made in accordance with such law, a tribunal may conclude that it has no jurisdiction to hear the dispute.

2. *Grants of a Relative Right of Establishment.* In negotiating investment treaties, some capital-exporting states have sought to protect their nationals and companies from unfavorable discrimination by securing admission treatment no less favorable than that given to investments made by the nationals of the host country, nationals of a third country, or both, whichever is the more favorable. This approach has been labeled a "right of establishment"[77]; however, if it is right to establish an enterprise, it is only a conditional and relative right in that it exists only if other parties have been treated in a more favorable way.

The United States has traditionally sought this type of relative right of establishment in its BIT negotiations. Canada and Japan have subsequently adopted a similar approach. As a

---

[75] The Agreement on Facilitating and Protecting Investment between the People's Republic of China and the Republic of Bosnia–Herzegovina (June 26, 2002) Ministry of Foreign Affairs of the People's Republic of China, <http://www.fmprc.gov.cn/eng/wjb/zzjg/xos/gjlb/3145/t16628.htm> accessed May 28, 2009.

[76] *Aguas del Tunari SA v. Republic of Bolivia*, ICSID Case No ARB/02/3 (Decision on Respondent's Objections to Jurisdiction) (October 21, 2005) 147.

[77] UNCTAD, *Bilateral Investment Treaties 1995–2006: Trends in Investment Rule Making* (2007) 22.

result, with respect to the admission of investment, investment treaties increasingly reflect two models: a "controlled entry model" (found mostly in BITs with European countries), in which investment admission is subject to the application of local law, and a "liberalized entry model" (mainly found in treaties concluded by the United States, Japan, and Canada), in which contracting parties are to treat the admission of investments from other contracting parties no less favorably than investors and investments from nationals or third countries.[78] The purpose of these provisions is to equalize competitive conditions for market entry among potential investors.

   3. *Grants of an Absolute Right of Establishment.* A true right of establishment would allow investors from other treaty partners to invest freely and unconditionally in a host state. The only significant international treaty that grants such an absolute right is the European Union Treaty.[79] The European Union Treaty is constitutional in nature, but it is also partly an investment treaty designed to promote and protect the flow of capital among its members. An important provision in this respect is Article 43, which grants all persons and firms of member states the right of establishment in all EU countries. Article 43 provides that " . . . restrictions on the freedom of establishment of nationals of a Member State in the territory of another Member State shall be prohibited" and that: "Freedom of establishment shall include the right to take up and pursue activities as self-employed persons and to set up and manage undertakings in particular companies or firms within the meaning of the second paragraph of Article 48, under the conditions laid down for its own nationals by the law of the country where such establishment is effected, subject to the provisions of the chapter relating to capital." Article 48 states that "Companies or firms formed in accordance with the law of a Member State and having their registered office, central administration or principal place of business within the Community shall, for the purposes of this Chapter, be treated in the same way as natural persons who are nationals of Member States," thereby guaranteeing such firms national treatment. Furthermore, under the treaty investors from other EU Member States have the right to transfer capital and earnings freely and are guaranteed national treatment on expropriation. Indeed, Article 56 of the EU Treaty specifically prohibits restrictions on the movement of capital and payments between Member States and between Member States and third countries. Finally, any violation of these rights can be adjudicated by the European Court of Justice.

   Although no other investment treaty has gone so far to create an "open door" for investments from treaty partners as the European Union, the EU treaty may stand as a model for countries that desire increased economic integration through the treaty-making process.

(c) Performance Requirements

Related to the issue of the entry or establishment of investment is the ability of the host country to impose conditions on that entry. One type of condition that host countries often impose is a "performance requirement" or "trade-related investment measure" ("TRIM")

---

[78] UNCTAD, *Bilateral Investment Treaties 1995–2006: Trends in Investment Rule Making* (2007) 23.
[79] Treaty on European Union (February 7, 1992) OJ C 224/1 (1992)1 CMLR 719, 31 ILM 247 (hereinafter "TEU") (amending Treaty Establishing the European Economic Community (March 25, 1957) 298 UNTS 11; 1973 Gr Brit TS No 1 (Cmd. 5179-II) (hereinafter "EEC Treaty," as amended by Single European Act, OJ L 169/1 (1987); 2 CMLR 741 (hereinafter "SEA"), in Treaties Establishing the European Communities (EC Off 'l Pub Off 1987)).

which impose on an investment project, as a condition of entry, such requirements as exporting a certain proportion of its production, restricting its imports to a certain level, or purchasing a minimum quantity of local goods and services. Although most investment treaties have not dealt with the question of performance requirements,[80] the United States, with some success, has sought to protect its investors from them through its BIT negotiations.[81] For example, Article 1106 of the North American Free Trade Agreement specifically provides that no NAFTA party may impose any of seven defined performance requirements in connection with the "establishment, acquisition, expansion, management, conduct or operation of an investment . . ."[82]

15.6 General Standards of Treatment of Foreign Investments

In order to protect foreign investors against the political risk resulting from placing their assets under a host country's jurisdiction, investment treaties impose obligations on host countries regarding the "treatment" they must accord to covered investments and investors. Although the treaties do not usually define the meaning of "treatment," the term treatment in its ordinary dictionary sense includes the "actions and behavior that one person takes toward another person." In other words, by entering into an investment treaty, a state makes promises about the actions and behaviors it will take toward investments and investors of treaty partners.[83] The treaty provisions on investor and investment treatment are intended to restrain host country government behavior and impose a discipline on governmental actions. To achieve this goal, treaties define a *standard* that host countries must conform to in their treatment of investors and investments. State actions that fail to meet that defined standard constitute a treaty violation, making the offending state internationally responsible and potentially rendering it liable to pay compensation to the injured investor.

Investment treaties normally contain treatment provisions with respect to numerous matters that investors consider important. One may categorize the various treatment standards included in treaties as "general" or "specific." General standards of treatment apply to all facets of an investment's activities in the host country. These include host government commitments to grant investors and investments "fair and equitable treatment," "full protection and security," and "treatment in accordance with international law." Specific treatment standards concern particular matters relating to an investment, such as monetary transfers, expropriation, and investor rights in times of war, revolution, or civil disturbance.[84] Further, general treatment standards consist of two types: (a) *absolute standards*, that are not contingent upon specified factors, happenings, or government behavior toward other investors or persons; and (b) *relative standards*, that are dependent upon the host government's treatment of other investments or investors.

---

[80] UNCTC, *Bilateral Investment Treaties* (1988) 69.

[81] See, eg, Treaty Concerning the Encouragement and Reciprocal Protection of Investment, (United States–Albania) (January 11, 1995) Article VI (prohibiting four specified types of performance requirements).

[82] Article 1106, North American Free Trade Agreement (December 17, 1992) (1994) 32 *ILM* 612.

[83] In the ICSID case of *Suez, Sociedad General de Aguas de Barcelona SA, and Vivendi Universal SA v. The Argentine Republic*, ICSID case no. ARB/O3/19, the tribunal defined "treatment" as follows: "The word 'treatment' is not defined in the treaty text. However, the ordinary meaning of that term within the context of investment includes the rights and privileges granted and the obligations and burdens imposed by a Contracting State on investments made by investors covered by the treaty." *Suez, Sociedad General de Aguas de Barcelona SA, and Vivendi Universal SA v. The Argentine Republic* ICSID case no ARB/O3/19 (Decision on Jurisdiction) (August 3, 2006) 55.

[84] UNCTAD, *Bilateral Investment Treaties 1995–2006: Trends in Investment Rulemaking* (2007) 28.

Examples of absolute standards include guarantees of full protection and security, fair and equitable treatment, or treatment in accordance with the minimum standard of international law. Examples of relative standards are most-favored-nation treatment and national treatment. Whereas the latter type of standard requires a comparator for its application,[85] the former does not.

It should be noted that while investment treaties specify standards for state behavior toward investors, they generally do not impose standards for the behavior of investors toward the host country or its government. Presumably, the reason for this is the assumption by treaty negotiators that host country laws and legal institutions are sufficient to ensure proper investor behavior.

One may identify six general standards of treatment that appear commonly in investment treaties: (a) fair and equitable treatment; (b) full protection and security; (c) protection from unreasonable or discriminatory measures; (d) treatment no less than that accorded by international law; (e) the requirement to respect obligations made to investors and investments; and (f) national and/or most-favored-nation treatment. An individual investment treaty may provide for some or all of these treatment standards. Each treatment standard is considered briefly below.

(a) Fair and Equitable Treatment

One of the most common standards of treatment found in investment treaties is an obligation that the host country accord foreign investment "fair and equitable treatment,"[86] a phrase that has been the subject of much commentary and state practice.[87] Its precise meaning in specific situations is nonetheless open to varying interpretations. A vague and ambiguous expression on its face, the term is not defined in investment treaties even though virtually all such treaties include it as a mandatory standard of treatment. It has been interpreted in a large number of arbitral awards, and has been extensively analyzed by scholars. Indeed, it is invoked so often in contemporary investor–state arbitration that one observer has labeled it "an almost ubiquitous presence" in investment litigation.[88]

The term's undefined and potentially elastic nature has made it a favorite for aggrieved investors and their lawyers when seeking compensation for the allegedly injurious acts of host country governments. Indeed, it has been claimed that a majority of successful claims in investor–state arbitrations have been based on the fair and equitable clause.[89]

An examination of treaty practice, jurisprudence, and scholarly commentary reveals two different conceptions of the nature of the fair and equitable standard: (1) that fair and equitable treatment merely reflects the *international minimum standard* required by customary international law, or (2) that the standard is *autonomous and additional* to general international law. Let us examine each of these views briefly.

As was discussed in Chapter 13, the traditional position of western governments and commentators has been that states owe aliens and their property a certain minimum level

---

[85] TJ Grierson-Weiller and IA Laird, "Standards of Treatment," in P Muchlinski et al, *The Oxford Handbook of International Investment Law* (2008) 262.

[86] M I Khalil, "Treatment of Foreign Investment in Bilateral Investment Treaties," 7 *ICSID Rev-Foreign Inv LJ* (1992) 339, 351.

[87] UNCTC, *Bilateral Investment Treaties*, UN Doc ST/CTC/65 (1988) 41–5.

[88] R Dolzer, "Fair and Equitable Treatment: A Key Standard in Investment Treaties," 39 *The Intl Lawyer* (2005) 87.

[89] R Dolzer and C Schreuer, *Principles of International Investment Law* (2008) 119.

of treatment regardless of the treatment each state gives to its nationals. Treatment short of this required minimum creates state responsibility for any resulting injuries. One view of the fair and equitable treatment standard is that it merely refers to that minimum international standard and does not give investors any additional rights. This position has often been advanced by developing countries, which have sought to limit the scope of the fair and equitable treatment standard. For example, during the negotiations for the Draft United Nations Code of Conduct on Transnational Corporations, some claimed that the Group of 77, which is constituted exclusively of developing countries, collectively asserted that the fair and equitable treatment language amounted to the international minimum standard advocated by developed countries.[90]

The treaty practice of certain countries also seems to support this view of fair and equitable treatment. Article 5 of the 2004 US Model BIT, entitled "Minimum Standard of Treatment," as well as the investment chapters of recently concluded US Free Trade Agreements go even further and attempt to define a minimum standard of treatment. They provide that:

1. Each Party shall accord to covered investments treatment in accordance with customary international law, including fair and equitable treatment and full protection and security.

   Paragraph 2 of Article 5 makes clear that the fair and equitable treatment standard does not go beyond the minimum standard:

2. For greater certainty, paragraph 1 prescribes the customary international law minimum standard of treatment of aliens as the minimum standard of treatment to be afforded to covered investments. The concepts of "fair and equitable treatment" and "full protection and security" do not require treatment in addition to or beyond that which is required by that standard, and do not create additional substantive rights.... [91]

Canada has taken a similar approach in its model Foreign Investment Protection and Promotion Agreement.[92]

The most significant and explicit adoption of the concept of fair and equitable treatment as a minimum international standard is found in the text of NAFTA and related practice. Article 1105(1) of NAFTA, entitled "Minimum Standard of Treatment" states: "Each Party shall accord to investments of investors of another Party treatment in accordance with international law, including fair and equitable treatment and full protection and security." In 2001, the North American Free Trade Commission, which is empowered to make binding interpretations of the NAFTA text, issued a Note of Interpretation which provided that "...the concepts of "fair and equitable treatment" and "full protection and security" do not require treatment beyond that which is required by the customary international law minimum standard of treatment of aliens."[93] The Dominican Republic–Central America–United States Free Trade Agreement, signed in 2004 and effective as of 2009, adopts a similar position.[94]

---

[90] P Robinson, "The June 1985 Reconvened Special Session on the Code," The CTC Reporter No 20 (1985) 15.
[91] <http://www.ustr.gov/assets/Trade_Sectors/Investment/Model_BIT/asset_upload_file847_6897.pdf> accessed May 28, 2009.
[92] C Yannaca-Small, *Fair and Equitable Treatment Standard in International Investment Law* (OECD, 2005) 87.
[93] Notes of Interpretation of Certain Chapter 11 Provisions (NAFTA Free Trade Commission, July 31, 2001).
[94] Article 10.5, Dominican Republic-Central America-United States Free Trade Agreement, available at <http://www.ustr.gov/trade-agreements/free-trade-agreements/cafta-dr-dominican-republic-central-america-fta/final-text>.

Certain arbitral decisions have also adopted this concept of fair and equitable treatment. In *Genin v. Estonia*,[95] the tribunal considered whether certain actions by Estonia amounted to a violation of its obligation to accord "fair and equitable treatment" and "non-discriminatory and non-arbitrary treatment" under the 1994 US–Estonia BIT. The tribunal ultimately dismissed the claim, viewing the fair and equitable treatment standards as incorporating the minimum standard under international law.[96] In *Occidental v. Ecuador*[97] the tribunal examined " … whether the fair and equitable treatment mandated by the Treaty is a more demanding standard than that prescribed by customary international law" and concluded that in the case in question " … the BIT standard was not different from the minimum standard required under customary international law concerning both the stability and predictability of the legal and business framework of the investment."[98]

Many scholars and non-NAFTA tribunals have held a different view and concluded that the fair and equitable standard, when expressed without qualification or condition, is an autonomous, additional standard whose interpretation is not limited by the minimum standards required by international law. According to this view, the fair and equitable clause imposes a higher standard of treatment on host states than customary international law does. For example, FA Mann states that:

> The terms "fair and equitable treatment" envisage conduct which goes far beyond the minimum standard and afford protection to a greater extent and according to a much more objective standard than any previously employed form of words. A tribunal would not be concerned with a minimum, maximum or average standard. It will have to decide whether in all circumstances the conduct in issue is fair and equitable or unfair and inequitable. No standard defined by other words is likely to be material. The terms are to be understood and applied independently and autonomously.[99]

Various arguments support this view. First, if states and investors believed that the fair and equitable standard was entirely interchangeable with the international minimum standard, they could have stated so clearly in their investment treaty texts; instead, most investment instruments do not make an explicit link between the two. Therefore, one may reasonably infer that to this point most contracting states do not believe that fair and equitable treatment is implicitly the same as the international minimum standard. Second, attempts to equate the two standards fail to take into account the significant historical debate between developed, capital-exporting countries and developing capital-importing countries concerning the very existence of the international minimum standard. While developed countries have strongly supported the existence of a minimum international standard, many developing countries have denied its very existence in customary international law. Against this uncertain background, it is difficult to assume that countries participating in investment treaties intended to incorporate the international minimum standard into their treaties without expressly stating so.[100] One may therefore conclude that the fair and equitable standard is autonomous and is not necessarily equivalent to the international minimum standard. Indeed, in view of the various historical challenges to

---

[95] *Alex Genin, Eastern Credit Limited, Inc and AS Baltoil (US) v. Republic of Estonia*, ICSID Case No ARB/99/2 (Award) (June 25, 2001).

[96] *Alex Genin, Eastern Credit Limited, Inc and AS Baltoil (US) v. Republic of Estonia*, ICSID Case No ARB/99/2 (Award) (June 25, 2001) 67.

[97] *Occidental Exploration and Production Co v. Ecuador*, LCIA Case No UN3467 (Award) (July 1, 2004).

[98] *Occidental Exploration and Production Co v. Ecuador*, LCIA Case No UN3467 (Award) (July 1, 2004) 188, 190.

[99] FA Mann, "British Treaties for the Promotion and Protection of Investments," 52 *BYIL* (1981) 241, 244.

[100] UNCTAD, *Fair and Equitable Treatment* (1999) 13.

the international minimum standard and the fact that capital-exporting countries have been the driving force behind the investment treaty movement, it is likely that the fair and equitable treatment provision is intended to be a higher standard of protection than that provided under the disputed international minimum standard. The inclusion of the fair and equitable standard, unknown to customary international law prior to the advent of investment treaties, seems to be intended to provide investors with a basic level of protection in situations where the other substantive provisions of international and national law are inapplicable.[101] Its function in the treaty can thus be seen as filling gaps not covered by other treaty provisions.[102] It also serves to guide the interpretation of other treaty provisions and assure that the general standard of fair and equitable treatment, a fundamental treaty goal, is attained.

The application of the fair and equitable standards in most cases is difficult for a variety of reasons. First, investment treaties do not define the term. Thus, arbitrators, government officials, investors' legal counsel and others who would apply the term must begin interpretation by confronting two words, "fair" and "equitable," that because of their vagueness and generality allow for great subjectivity. Second, as a result, the standard created will be highly flexible and may result in a subjective decision-making process that disappointed litigants may consider unprincipled. Third, the situations in particular cases to which the term must be applied are highly complex and in many instances involve troubled relationships between investors and host governments stretching over significant periods of time and involving multiple interactions. Thus, determining whether a particular governmental action violates the fair and equitable standards depends greatly on the facts of the individual case.[103]

In actual practice, it is impossible to anticipate the entire range of state actions that may injure an investor's legal position.[104] Some might consider the standard's lack of precision a virtue rather than a shortcoming because it promotes flexibility in the investment process. Like other broad legal principles (such as "due process of law," a term found in many domestic legal systems) the fair and equitable standard has been and will continue to be elaborated and given specific content through judicial and arbitral practice.[105] Thus, its very vagueness and generality endow it with a flexibility that will permit it to evolve in the light of experience by investors, host countries, and international arbitration tribunals. At the same time, interpreters of the standard must guard against the danger of subjectivity, bias, and lack of discipline in the interpretation process.

An examination of the cases applying the fair and equitable standard reveals that arbitral tribunals have developed specific criteria, norms and principles to determine whether host states have given fair and equitable treatment to investors. In general, tribunals have been called upon to determine whether specific governmental actions, such as amending legislation, revising administrative regulations, and modifying contracts in ways that adversely affect an investor's interests, have thereby denied investors fair and equitable treatment. Not all such actions are a violation of the fair and equitable standard. States have a right to regulate persons and activities on their territories and do not cede that right when they sign an investment treaty. Therefore, in interpreting the meaning of fair and equitable treatment

---

[101] K Vandevelde, *United States Investment Treaties* (1992) 76.

[102] R Dolzer and C Schreuer, *Principles of International Investment Law* (2008) 123.

[103] *Noble Ventures, Inc v. Romania*, ICSID Case No ARB/01/11 (Award) (October 12, 2005) 181.

[104] S Vasciannie, "The Fair and Equitable Treatment Standard in International Investment Law and Practice," 70 *BYIL* (1999) 100, 104, 145.

[105] P Weil, "The State, the Foreign Investor, and International Law: The No Longer Stormy Relationship of Menage a Trois," 15 *ICSID Rev-FILJ* (2000) 401, 415.

with respect to investors, tribunals must balance the legitimate and reasonable expectations of investors with the host country's legitimate regulatory interests.

Among the principles most often relied upon by tribunals when applying the fair and equitable standard is whether the host state has: (1) failed to protect the investor's legitimate expectations; (2) failed to act transparently; (3) acted arbitrarily or subjected the investor to discriminatory treatment; (4) denied the investor access to justice or procedural due process; or (5) acted in bad faith. It must be recognized, however, that these five general principles are not separate and distinct, but often overlap and blend into one another. It should also be noted that some of these principles, such as the prohibition on arbitrary or discriminatory actions or on measures that are a denial of access to justice, are stated in particular treaties as explicit, independent standards in addition to being subsumed within the meaning of fair and equitable treatment.

(b) Full Protection and Security

Another general standard of treatment found in most investment treaties is the obligation of the host country to accord "full protection and security" or "constant protection and security" to investments made by nationals and companies of its treaty partners. Here too, the precise meaning of the term may be open to widely varying interpretations in different situations. Consequently, courts, including the International Court of Justice, and arbitration tribunals have struggled to determine the proper scope of its protection. Two cases have held that the standard does not make the host country responsible for all injuries that befall the investment.[106] Thus, although the host country is not a guarantor, it is liable when it fails to show due diligence in protecting the investor from harm. One definition of due diligence that was cited favorably by an ICSID arbitral tribunal is "reasonable measures of prevention which a well-administered government could be expected to exercise under similar circumstances."[107] Consequently, the failure by a host government to take reasonable measures to protect the investment against threats such as brigands or violence by police and security officers renders that government liable to compensate an investor for resulting injuries. Other cases have found host governments liable for not taking steps to protect an investor's factory from looting by government troops, in Zaire,[108] and for not taking measures to prevent the seizure of a hotel by disgruntled employees, in Egypt.[109]

(c) Unreasonable or Discriminatory Measures

Many investment treaties provide that "no Contracting Party shall in any way impair by unreasonable or discriminatory measures the management, maintenance, use, enjoyment or disposal" of an investment.[110] The specific application of this provision to the individual

---

[106] cf *Asian Agricultural Products Ltd v. Sri Lanka*, ICSID Case No ARB/87/3 (Final Award) (June 27, 1990) (1991); 6 *ICSID Rev–Foreign Inv LJ* 526 (interpreting the words "full protection and security" in the UK–Sri Lanka BIT), and Elettronica Sicula SPA (*United States v. Italy*) 1989 ICJ 15 (20 July) (interpreting the words "constant protection and security" in the United States–Italy Treaty of Friendship, Commerce and Navigation).

[107] *Asian Agricultural Products Ltd v. Sri Lanka*, ICSID Case No ARB/87/3 (Final Award) (June 27, 1990) (1991); 6 *ICSID Rev–Foreign Inv LJ* 558 citing A V Freeman, *Responsibility of States for Unlawful Acts of Their Armed Forces* (1957) 15–16.

[108] *American Manufacturing and Trading, Inc v. Zaire*, ICSID Case No ARB/93/1 (Award) (February 21, 1997).

[109] *Wena Hotels Ltd v. Arab Republic of Egypt*, ICSID Case No ARB/98/4 (Award on Merits) (December 8, 2000).

[110] See, eg, Treaty concerning the Reciprocal Encouragement and Protection of Investment, (United States–Turkey) (December 3, 1985) Article 2(3) ("Neither Party shall in any way impair by arbitrary or discriminatory

case depends on the facts involved; however, it is worth noting that the term "unreasonable" may give host countries grounds to defend actions taken against foreign investors. Individual investment treaties often stipulate other general treatment standards, most of which would be subsumed within the meanings of either fair and equitable treatment or full protection and security. Thus, alone or in conjunction with such basic standards of treatment, treaties may require treatment that accords with customary international law, an international minimum standard of treatment, that is not arbitrary or discriminatory, or that allows access to justice or due process.

(d) International Law

Many investment treaties provide that in no case should foreign investments be given less favorable treatment than that required by international law. Thus, this provision constitutes the minimum international standard of treatment discussed in Chapter 13. The application of this principle in individual cases is subject to a variety of interpretations, particularly with respect to issues where there is significant dispute among developing countries. One example is the efforts made by developing countries to secure a New International Economic Order, discussed in Chapter 13. A further question is whether the reference to "international law" is limited only to customary international law or whether it includes treaty provisions and general principles of law on investments.

(e) Contractual Obligations ("the Umbrella Clause")

As discussed earlier in this volume, in order to attract foreign investment, host states make various commitments and representations to foreign investors. Some of these undertakings are embodied in formal bilateral agreements such as investment accords, development contracts, public service concessions, and tax stabilization agreements, to mention only a few. Others are found in unilateral acts like foreign investment legislation, licenses, and regulatory permissions. Still others are less formal governmental actions such as the oral statements by government officials and promises about investments published by the government in press or promotional literature. Such obligations are an important part of the legal framework of any foreign investment.

The breach of state contracts and other state obligations made to investors is not ordinarily considered a breach of international law. The Permanent Court of International Justice in the *Serbian Loans case*[111] stated that "any contract which is not a contract between States in their capacity as subjects of international law is based on the domestic law of some country." More recently, in *Noble Ventures v. Romania*,[112] a case involving alleged breaches of an agreement to privatize a Romanian steel enterprise made by Romanian authorities, an ICSID tribunal recalled:

> ... the well established rule of general international law that in normal circumstances *per se* a breach of a contract by the State does not give rise to direct international responsibility on the part of the State. This derives from the clear distinction between municipal law on the one hand and international law on the other, two separate legal systems (or orders) the second of which

---

measures the management, operation, maintenance, use, enjoyment, acquisition, expansion, or disposal of investments.")

[111] (1929) PCIJ Rep Series A No 20, 41.

[112] *Noble Ventures, Inc v. Romania*, ICSID Case No ARB/01/11 (Award) (October 12, 2005).

treats the rules contained in the first as facts, as is reflected in *inter alia* Article Three of the International Law Commission's Articles on State Responsibility adopted in 2001.[113]

Even if an investor is protected by an investment treaty, usually the treatment provisions contained therein do not make contractual breaches violations of the treaty unless the state has acted so flagrantly toward its obligation that its actions constitute a denial of fair and equitable treatment, full protection and security, or another treatment standard specified in the treaty. Thus for example, many tribunals have pointed out that contractual breaches are not necessarily violations of an investment treaty.[114]

The rules above regarding the legal status of state contracts and breaches thereof do not mean that states cannot agree by treaty that state contracts and other obligations will be governed by international law and that breaches of those obligations will make states responsible under international law.[115] Such a provision would increase the costs to host states for violating their obligations to investors and thus encourage states to continue fulfilling those obligations. Accordingly, in order to protect investor–state commitments and obligations from obsolescence, many investment treaties—approximately 1,000 by some estimates[116]—contain a clause defining the treatment that the host state will give to obligations it has made to investors or investments covered by the treaty. Known commonly as an "umbrella clause," such provisions generally stipulate that: "Each Contracting Party shall observe any obligation it may have entered into with regard to the investments of investors of the other Contracting Party."[117] Similar clauses can also be found in multilateral arrangements such as the Energy Charter Treaty[118] and the ASEAN Investment Agreement.[119] The NAFTA Chapter on investments, however, contains no umbrella clause. Thus, the umbrella clause creates an exception to a well-established principle of international law concerning state contracts with, and obligations to, foreign investors.

---

[113] *Noble Ventures, Inc v. Romania*, ICSID Case No ARB/01/11 (Award) (October 12, 2005) 53.

[114] eg, *Compañía de Aguas del Aconquija SA and Vivendi Universal (formerly Compagnie Générale des Eaux) v. Argentine Republic*, ICSID Case No ARB/97/3) (Decision on Annulment) (July 3, 2002) 95, 96. ("A state may breach a treaty without breaching a contract and vice versa [. . .]")

[115] In *Noble Ventures, Inc v. Romania*, ICSID Case No ARB/01/11 (Award) (October 12, 2005) the tribunal stated:

> . . . when negotiating a bilateral investment treaty, two States may create within the scope of their mutual agreement an exception to the rules deriving from the autonomy of municipal law, on the one hand and public international law, on the other hand. In other words, two States may include in a bilateral investment treaty a provision to the effect that, in the interest of achieving the objects and goals of the treaty, the host State may incur international responsibility by reason of a breach of its contractual obligations towards the private investor of the other Party, the breach of contract being thus 'internationalized, ie assimilated to a breach of the treaty. In such a case, an international tribunal will be bound to seek to give useful effect to the provision that the parties have adopted. 54.

[116] R Dolzer and C Schreuer, *Principles of International Investment Law* (2008) 153. See also J Gill et al, "Umbrella Clauses and Bilateral Investment Treaties: A Comparative Study of the SGS Cases," 21 *J of Intl Arbitration* (2004) 397, 403 n 43 (reporting that approximately 40% of a sample drawn from *Investment Treaties* (2003) contained umbrella clauses), and UNCTAD, *Bilateral Investment Treaties 1995–2006: Trends in Investment Rulemaking* (2007) 73, stating that 40% of all BITs contain umbrella clauses.

[117] Agreement Between the Government of the United Kingdom of Great Britain and Northern Ireland and the Government of the Republic of Argentina for the Promotion and Protection of Investments (March 11, 1990).

[118] Article 10(1) of the Energy Charter Treaty in articulating the protection to be afforded to investments, states: "Each Contracting Party shall observe any obligations it has entered into with an Investor or an Investment of an Investor of a Contracting Party.

[119] Paragraph (3) of Article III, which is entitled "General Obligations," states: "Each Contracting Party shall observe any obligation arising from a particular commitment it may have entered into with regard to a specific investment of nationals or companies of the other Contracting Parties." Agreement among the Government of Brunei Darussalam, the Republic of Indonesia, Malaysia, the Republic of the Philippines, the Republic of Singapore and the Kingdom of Thailand for the Promotion and Protection of Investments (December 15, 1987).

The intention of an umbrella provision is to impose an international treaty obligation on host countries that requires them to respect obligations they have entered into regarding investments protected by the treaty. Such a provision places such obligations under the protective umbrella of international law, not just the domestic law that would otherwise normally apply exclusively. The effect of the umbrella clause is not to transform a contractual or other obligation governed by domestic law into an international obligation governed by international law. The source of the obligation, as well as its nature and scope, are delineated by the law under which it was originally made—in most cases, the law of the host country. As the Annulment Committee stated in the *CMS* case, which involved alleged breaches of obligations under Argentine law with respect to investment in natural gas transmissions by the Argentinian government: "The effect of the umbrella clause is not to transform the obligation which is relied upon into something else; the content of the obligation is unaffected, as is its proper law."[120] By virtue of the umbrella clause a host state has an international obligation to respect its obligations concerning foreign investments despite the fact that those obligations remain subject to the law under which they were originally made. The failure to respect such obligations, while remaining subject to local courts or the contractually specified dispute settlement procedures, also renders an offending state subject to the jurisdiction of investor–state arbitration or whatever other dispute settlement mechanisms are provided for by treaty.

To the extent that a contracting party has entered into obligations with an investor or investment, the contractual obligations of investment treaties require the signatory state to respect its obligations. These provisions, then, act as counter to the claim, advanced during the era of the New International Economic Order, that host countries should be able to unilaterally revise contracts that they have made with foreign investors. It may also mean that, as a result of such a provision in an investment treaty, contracts between foreign investors and host governments that are normally only subject to host country law may also be governed by international law.[121]

(f) National and/or Most-Favored-Nation Treatment

In addition to these general standards, many investment treaties contain relative standards, particularly with respect to non-discrimination in relation to both foreign and national investors. Economic and business activity is a competitive process. Economic actors constantly try to gain advantage over their competitors and to eliminate advantages that their competitors may have. In response to their perceived national interests, governments often seek through their laws, regulations, and administrative actions to: (1) assist their nationals and companies in the competitive process by taking measures that favor their interests and disfavor the interests of others; or (2) to favor certain foreign nationals and companies over other foreign nationals and companies. Government measures may thus have a discriminatory effect on the economic process.

Such discriminatory measures can impede international investment. Pursuing increased foreign investment, investment treaties often seek to remove the competitive disadvantage that may be placed on foreigners by eliminating such discriminatory treatment. Treaties do this by making nondiscrimination a standard that host countries must respect in their treatment of investors and investment from other contracting states.

---

[120] *CMS Gas Transmission Company v. Argentine Republic*, ICSID Case No ARB/01/8 (Annulment Proceeding, Decision of the Ad Hoc Committee) (September 25, 2007) 95(c).

[121] UNCTAD, *Bilateral Investment Treaties in the Mid-1990s* (1998) 56–7.

Non-discriminatory treatment has two dimensions. The first, known as national treatment, requires host states to treat foreign investors and foreign investments no less favorably than their own national investors and investments. The second, known as most-favored-nation treatment, demands that host countries treat investments and investors covered by the treaty no less favorably than other foreign investor and investments. The purpose of these treatment standards is to place all economic actors in an equal position on the assumption that this will foster competition and economic growth. Most treaties include, in some form, both of these relative treatment standards.

They thus provide for *national treatment*, which requires that a host country treat an investor or an investment, no less favorably than their own national investors or investments made by their nationals. They may also provide for *most-favored-nation treatment*, which means that a host country may not treat an investor or investment from a treaty party less favorably than its own investors or investments from any other country. National treatment allows protected foreign investors to take advantage of any benefits that a host country grants to its own nationals. Some developing countries, recognizing the disparity in financial and technological resources between their national enterprises and those of foreign companies, have resisted or sought to limit the scope of the national treatment guarantee in investment treaties. In particular, they have tried to avoid giving foreign investors benefits and subsidies designed to strengthen national industries.[122]

The application of the national treatment standard depends not only on how the standard is articulated in a treaty but also on the specific facts of the case in question. Applying national treatment standards in disputes, like those involving the fair and equitable standard, is highly fact specific and not easily amenable to a mechanistic application of treaty provisions.[123] But, unlike the fair and equitable treatment standard, tribunals in national treatment standard cases appear to have developed a more or less common, three-step analytical approach. This is particularly the case within the context of NAFTA. The first step involves identifying a group of national investors to be compared with the claimant foreign investor. The second step is to compare the relative treatment the two groups have received and evaluate whether the treatment of the claimant is less favorable that that given to the compared group of national investors. The final step is to determine whether the two are, in the words of NAFTA and similar treaties, in "like circumstances" or whether factors justifying differential treatment exist.[124] The completion of each step requires an answer to the following three questions: (1) With whom should the claimant be compared? (2) What is the nature of the difference in treatment? and (3) Is the difference in treatment justified?

Most-favored-nation treatment, on the other hand, has the effect of granting to protected foreign investors any benefit or advantage granted by the host country to investors from any other country. They thus enable such investors to take advantage of the higher standards of investor protection that may be contained in investment treaties to which the host country is a party.

Certain investment treaties, like those negotiated by the United States, combine both of these standards and require host countries to grant investors national treatment or most-favored-nation treatment, *whichever is the more favorable*.

---

[122] UNCTAD, *Bilateral Investment Treaties in the Mid-1990s* (1998) 64–5.
[123] R Dolzer and C Schreuer, *Principles of International Investment Law* (2008) 179.
[124] UNCTAD, *Investor State Dispute Settlement and Impact on Investment Rulemaking* (2007) 48.

15.7 Monetary Transfers

For any foreign investment project, the ability to repatriate income and capital, to pay foreign obligations in another currency and to purchase raw materials and spare parts from abroad are crucial to a project's success. For this reason, in investment treaty negotiations capital-exporting states have pressed for unrestricted freedom for their investors to undertake these monetary operations. Such operations are collectively referred to as "transfers."[125] Like the word "treatment," "transfer" has become a term of art in investment treaties and basically means "monetary transfers." The monetary transfer provisions of most investment treaties deal with five basic issues: (1) the general nature of the investor's rights to make monetary transfers; (2) the types of payments that are covered by the right to make transfers; (3) the currency with which the payment may be made; (4) the applicable exchange rate; and (5) the time within which the host country must allow the investor to make transfers.

Developing countries facing chronic balance-of-payments difficulties and which need to conserve foreign exchange to pay for essential goods and services are often unable or unwilling to grant foreign investors an unrestricted right to make such monetary transfers. Moreover, many developing countries have exchange-control laws to regulate the conversion and transfer of currency abroad.[126] As a result of this fundamental conflict in goals, the negotiation of treaty provisions on monetary transfers is sometimes difficult to conclude. Capital-exporting countries seek broad, unrestricted guarantees on monetary transfers while developing countries press for limited guarantees subject to a variety of exceptions. In general, investment treaties provide for broad freedom of Monetary transfers.

15.8 Expropriation and Dispossession

One of the primary functions of any investment treaty is to protect foreign investments against nationalization, expropriation, and other forms of interference with property rights by host country government. Despite opposition by some developing nations in multilateral forums, virtually all investment treaties adopt some variation of the traditional Western view of international law that a state may not expropriate an alien's property except: (1) for a public purpose, (2) in a nondiscriminatory manner, (3) upon payment of just compensation, and in most instances, (4) with provision for some form of judicial review. The various elements of the traditional rule have taken different formulations in different treaties, some more and some less protective of investor interests. Perhaps the greatest variations in treaty provisions and the most difficult negotiations arise with respect to standards of compensation. Nonetheless many, if not most, investment treaties have adopted the traditional rule, often expressed in the so-called "Hull Formula"[127] that compensation must be "prompt, adequate and effective."[128] They then proceed to define the meaning of each of these words in the particular circumstances.[129]

---

[125] M I Khalil, "Treatment of Foreign Investment in Bilateral Investment Treaties," 7 *ICSID Rev-Foreign Inv LJ* (1992) 339, 360.

[126] JW Salacuse, "Host Country Regulation and Promotion of Joint Ventures and Foreign Investment," in D N Goldsweig and R H Cummings (eds), *International Joint Ventures: A Practical Approach to Working with Foreign Investors in the US and Abroad* (1990) 107, 122–3.

[127] G H Hackworth, *Digest of International Law* (1942) 655–64.

[128] See, eg, UNCTAD, *Bilateral Investment Treaties in the Mid-1990s* (1998) 69.

[129] See, eg, Agreement for the Promotion and Reciprocal Protection of Investments (United Kingdom–Costa Rica) (September 7, 1982) Article 5.

Just as international investment law has evolved over time so, too, have the methods by which governments seek to modify or interfere with investor property rights. Whereas outright expropriation through government seizure was common until the 1980s, it has become an increasingly rare phenomenon thereafter. In the twenty-first century, governments dissatisfied with the original bargains made with foreign investors rarely send their troops to seize a factory or occupy a mine. Instead, they use their legislative and regulatory power in more subtle ways to alter the benefits flowing to the investor from the investment. Thus, a government may impose new regulations on the way the investment is operated, raise taxes on the investment substantially, or reduce the revenues flowing to the investor. The investor remains in possession of the investment, but the amount and nature of the benefits originally contemplated are significantly reduced. In legal terms, these regulatory actions diminish the nature of the investor's property rights over the investment and, if sufficiently extreme, may constitute a form of expropriation or dispossession. Such actions may rise to the level of an "indirect" expropriation, sometimes referred to as "regulatory taking."[130] They have become the most common type of intervention with foreign investments by host governments in the twenty-first century. Treaty language has evolved to cover both direct and indirect expropriations, as well as governmental measures that are equivalent to a direct or indirect expropriation. Thus, for example, NAFTA's Article 1110 is one example:

1. No Party may directly or indirectly nationalize or expropriate an investment of an investor of another Party in its territory or take a measure tantamount to nationalization or expropriation of such an investment ("expropriation"), except:
   (a) for a public purpose;
   (b) on a nondiscriminatory basis;
   (c) in accordance with due process of law and Article 1105(1); and
   (d) on payment of compensation in accordance with paragraphs 2 through 6.[131]

As will be seen, one challenge in interpreting treaty provisions on expropriation is determining whether and to what extent covered assets are protected against administrative and regulatory actions that negatively affect them, but nonetheless leave the investor in possession. This shift in governmental tactics has led to a change in the legal debate about the definition of expropriation and nationalization and also whether traditional principles of international law apply to legislative and regulatory actions that leave the investor in possession of the investment assets but diminish their freedom to control, manage, and derive benefits from it. In short, the challenge for scholars, arbitrators, and lawyers, is to determine the dividing line between investor property rights and a host government's right to reasonable regulation of investment.

Investment treaties protect "investments" from expropriation. As indicated earlier in this chapter, investment treaties define the term "investments" broadly to include both tangible and intangible assets. Thus, depending on the breadth of that definition, expropriation clauses may not only protect physical property, such as land and buildings, but also intangible forms of property, such as contractual rights, intellectual property rights, and government business concessions.

---

[130] SR Ratner, "Regulatory Takings in the Institutional Context Beyond the Fear of Fragmented International Law," 102 *AJIL* (2008) 475.
[131] North American Free Trade Agreement (December 17, 1992) (1994) 32 *ILM* 612.

Even before the advent of investment treaties, courts, and tribunals recognized that contractual rights could be subject to expropriation. In *Norwegian Shipowners' Claims,* one of the very first cases to decide the question, the United States government seized ships built for Norwegian nationals in US shipyards during World War I and also canceled ship construction contracts with Norwegian nationals. A government entity, "the Fleet Corporation," took over the ships and the contracts. In response to Norwegian claims of expropriation, the United States asserted that contractual rights could not be considered property for purposes of international law. The arbitral tribunal rejected this broad claim by reference to the domestic law of both the US and Norway. It held that "the Fleet Corporation took over the legal rights and duties of the ship owners toward the shipbuilders"[132] and that the cancellation of existing shipbuilding contracts amounted to de facto expropriation.[133] Consequently, it ordered the payment of appropriate compensation.

The *Chorzów Factory* case concerned the effect of Polish measures directed against a German company (Bayerische) that had the contractual right to manage and operate a nitrate plant, the Chorzów Factory, owned by another German company (Oberschlesische). The Permanent Court of International Justice held that both the factory owner and the company holding contractual rights to the factory were expropriated by the Polish measures: "[...] it is clear that the rights of the Bayerische to the exploitation of the factory and to the remuneration fixed by the contract for the management of the exploitation and for the use of its *patents, licences, experiments,* etc., have been directly prejudiced by the taking over of the factory by Poland."[134] The Iran–US Claims Tribunal[135] and other international tribunals have relied on and reaffirmed the *Chorzów Factory*'s holding when deciding claims of interference with rights arising under a contract and other forms of intangible property.

Following the development of investment treaties, arbitration tribunals have consistently recognized that intangible as well as tangible property may be the subject of expropriation.[136] As was stated very clearly in the *Methanex* case: "Certainly, the restrictive notion of property as a material 'thing' is obsolete and has ceded its place to a contemporary conception which includes managerial control over components of a process that is wealth producing."[137] Indeed, in contemporary practice the most prevalent types of alleged expropriations under treaties, and usually the most difficult legal questions, involve governmental measures affecting intangible rights.

---

[132] *Norwegian Shipowners' Claims (Nor v US),* (Perm Ct Arb 1922) 1 RIAA 307, 332 at 233; *The Hague Justice Portal* <http://www.haguejusticeportal.net> accessed May 8, 2009.

[133] "[...] whatever the intentions may have been, the United States took, both in fact and in law, the contracts under which the ships in question were being or were to be construed." *Norwegian Shipowners' Claims (Nor v. US),* (Perm Ct Arb 1922) 1 RIAA 307, 325.

[134] *Case Concerning Certain German Interests in Polish Upper Silesia (FRG v. Pol)* (1926) PCIJ Series A No 7 at 44; <http://www.worldcourts.com/pcij/eng/decisions/> accessed May 9, 2009.

[135] In the *Amoco Case* the tribunal determined that "[i]n spite of the fact that it is nearly sixty years old, this judgment is widely regarded as the most authoritative exposition of the principles applicable in this field, and is still valid today..." *Amoco International Finance Corp v. Iran* (1987) 15 Iran–USCTR 189, 191.

[136] *Fireman's Fund Insurance Company v. United Mexican States,* ICSID Case No ARB(AF)/02/1 (Award) (July 17, 2006) (NAFTA) 176. See also *Biloune and Marine Drive Complex Ltd v. Ghana Investments Centre and the Government of Ghana* (Award on Jurisdiction and Liability) (October 27, 1989) UNCITRAL ad hoc Tribunal 95 ILR 183, 209; *Transnational Law Digest* <http://tldb.uni-koeln.de/> accessed June 8, 2009, a non-treaty case in which the investor concluded a ten-year lease contract to renovate and manage a restaurant with an agency of the Ghana government. The Accra City Council subsequently ordered work to stop on the project and demolished the facility. In its award in favor of the claimant, the ad hoc tribunal stated: "such prevention of [an investor] from pursuing its approved project would constitute constructive expropriation of [the investor]'s contractual rights in the project [...] unless the Respondents can establish by persuasive evidence sufficient justification for these events."

[137] *Methanex v. United States,* (Final Award) (August 3, 2005) NAFTA-UNCITRAL part IV, ch D, at 7.

15.9 Operational and Other Conditions

Investment treaties sometimes provide treatment standards with respect to certain operational conditions, such as the investor's right to enter the country, employ foreign nationals, and be free of performance requirements. One of the most important conditions, of course, is the ability of the investor's employees to freely enter the host country and manage and operate the investment. Most investment treaties do not grant the investor an automatic right to enter and stay in a host country. German BITs, for example, provide that each contracting party will give "sympathetic consideration" to applications for entry.[138] Similarly, US BITs give "nationals" of contracting parties the right to enter for purposes of establishing or operating investments subject to the laws of the US.[139]

15.10 Losses from Armed Conflict or Internal Disorder

Many investment treaties also deal with investment losses due to armed conflict or internal disorder within the host country. They do not, however, normally establish an absolute right to compensation in such cases. Instead, many treaties promise that foreign investors will be treated in the same manner as nationals of the host country with respect to compensation.[140] Some also provide for most-favored-nation treatment on this question. The ICSID case of *Asian Agricultural Products Ltd v. Sri Lanka*[141] is one of the few cases that have considered this provision in detail with regards to a dispute between an injured investor and a host country government. The tribunal concluded that in addition to any specific compensatory actions taken for the benefit of other investors the provision in question would make any promised higher standard available to an injured investor. Such a different standard could come, for example, from another BIT granted to investors from other countries.

15.11 The Consequences of Treaty Violations

An important final question with respect to the various treaty standards is what are the consequences for the host country of their breach? Is the host country obligated to pay the investor compensation if it denies the investor full protection, fair and equitable treatment, or national treatment? If so, what is the standard for determining the compensation that the host state must pay? Curiously, no investment treaty specifically addresses these questions or even provides that contracting parties who breach these treatment standards are liable to compensate either the injured investor or its home state.

While one might argue that the lack of such specific provisions means that treaty standards are merely hortatory in nature, arbitral tribunals have uniformly held that states are liable to compensate investors for treaty breaches that result in their injury.[142]

---

[138] Treaty Concerning the Encouragement and Reciprocal Protection of Investments, (Federal Republic of Germany–Swaziland) (April 5, 1990) Article (3)(c).

[139] See, eg, Treaty Concerning the Encouragement and Reciprocal Protection of Investment, (United States–Sri Lanka) (September 20, 1991) Article 2(3).

[140] See, eg, Agreement for the Promotion and Reciprocal Protection of Investments (United Kingdom–Ukraine) (February 10, 1993) Article 5.

[141] *Asian Agricultural Products Ltd v. Sri Lanka*, ICSID Case No ARB/87/3 (Final Award) (June 27, 1990) (1991); 6 *ICSID Rev–Foreign Inv LJ* 526.

[142] M Weiniger, "The Standard of Compensation for Violation of the Fair and Equitable Standard," in F Ortino et al (eds), *Investment Treaty Law: Current Issues II* (2007) 197.

Tribunals have arrived at this conclusion by finding that customary international law applies to the question of liability and compensation. In particular, they have relied on *Chorzów Factory*,[143] in which the Permanent Court of International Justice stated that, according to customary international law, if a state has committed a wrong it is liable to pay reparations. The amount of such reparations must be sufficient to eliminate the consequences of the illegal act and to place the wronged party in the situation it would have been had the illegal act not taken place. For example, in the case of *MTD v. Chile*, the tribunal accepted "the classic standard announced by the Permanent Court of Justice in the *Factory at Chorzów*: compensation should 'wipe out all the consequences of the illegal act and re-establish the situation which would, in all probability, have existed if that had not been committed'."[144] Thus having determined the liability of the host state for violating a treaty treatment standard, an arbitral tribunal will next determine the compensation to be paid to the investor by comparing its actual situation after the breach with the situation it would have been in had no breach taken place. Through its decision on the amount of an award to be paid by the offending state, the tribunal will seek to place the injured investor in the same financial position it would have been had no breach occurred.

15.12 Dispute Settlement

The issues discussed above form the basic architecture of most investment treaties. A fundamental, practical question, of course, is whether countries actually respect their treaty commitments and, if not, whether an injured investor has effective legal redress against a host country's treaty violations. For foreign investors and their governments, one of the great deficiencies of customary international law has been its lack of effective and binding mechanisms to resolve investment disputes. One aim of the investment treaty movement has been to remedy this situation.

Most investment treaties provide for two distinct dispute settlement mechanisms: one for disputes between the two contracting states, and another for disputes between a host country and an aggrieved foreign investor. With respect to the former, contemporary investment treaties usually stipulate that in the event of a dispute over the interpretation or application of the treaty, the states concerned will first seek to resolve their differences through negotiation and then, if that fails, through ad hoc arbitration.

For the latter, the trend among more recent investment treaties is to provide a separate international arbitration procedure, often under the auspices of the International Centre for Settlement of Investment Disputes (ICSID), for disputes between an aggrieved foreign investor and an offending host country government. By agreeing to an investment treaty, a state often simultaneously gives the consent needed to establish ICSID or another arbitration forum for any future dispute between one contracting state and a national of another contracting state. Although the investor must first try to resolve the conflict through negotiation and may also have to exhaust remedies available locally, the investor ultimately has the power to invoke compulsory arbitration in order to secure a binding award.[145]

Granting a private party the right to bring an action against a sovereign state in an international tribunal is a revolutionary innovation that now seems to be largely taken for granted. Yet its uniqueness and power should not be overlooked. The field of international

---

[143] *Factory at Chorzów* (Merits) 1928 PCIJ Series A No 17.

[144] *MTD Equity Sdn Bhd & MTD Chile SA v. Chile*, ICSID Case No ARB/01/7 (Award) (25 May 2004) 238.

[145] See, eg, Agreement for the Liberalization, Promotion and Protection of Investment (Japan–Vietnam) (November 14, 2003) Article 13.

trade law, for example, contains no similar procedure. Violations of trade law, even though they strike at the economic interests of private parties, are resolved directly and solely by states. The World Trade Organization ("WTO") does not give a remedy to private persons injured by trade law violations.[146] It should also be noted that modern investment treaties grant aggrieved investors the right to prosecute their claims independently, without regard to the concerns and interests of their home country governments. It is this mechanism that gives important, practical significance to an investment treaty, and which truly enables investment treaties to afford protection to foreign investment. As a result of this mechanism, foreign investors are bringing increasing numbers of arbitration claims when they believe host countries have denied them protection under a treaty. In many cases, arbitral tribunals have rendered substantial awards against host countries, and it appears that host countries have generally paid them. In the event that a state fails to pay an award, the ICSID Convention requires each ICSID member state to recognize such "... award ... as binding and enforce the pecuniary obligations imposed by that award within its territories as if it were a final judgment of a court in that State."[147] Non-ICSID awards rendered under investment treaties are enforceable under the Convention on the Recognition and Enforcement of Foreign Arbitral Awards.

One effect of such awards, along with other judgments rendered against sovereign states in favor of individual private investors, is to cause host countries to take their treaty responsibilities seriously. Investment treaty provisions, their enforcement mechanisms, and the fact that arbitral tribunals hold host countries accountable serve an external discipline upon governments' behavior in their relations with foreign investors. Together, this results in a relatively effective system of foreign investment protection. It is also to be noted that decisions of arbitral tribunals, although unfortunately not always made public, tend to be lengthy, reasoned, and scholarly decisions that form part of the jurisprudence of this emerging international investment law and also solidify and give force to investment treaty provisions.

15.13 Treaty Exceptions, Amendments, and Terminations

Because of the great diversity of national policies and situations, individual states naturally seek to introduce exceptions in negotiating investment treaties in order to take into account those national policies and situations. Thus, most investment treaties have provisions that carve out exceptions to the general standards of treatment that they seek to apply to investments between the two countries. Many investment treaties contain provisions that except contracting parties from core treaty obligations under exceptional circumstances in which a country's important national interests are at stake. Such important interests include national security, the maintenance of public order, and the restoration of peace and security. For example, Article X of the bilateral investment treaty between the United States and Argentina states: "This Treaty shall not preclude the application by either Party of measures necessary for the maintenance of public order, the fulfillment of its obligations with respect to the maintenance or restoration of international peace or security, or the Protection of its own essential security interests."[148] Because of the use of

---

[146] See, eg, GT Schleyer, "Power to the People: Allowing Private Parties to Raise Claims Before the WTO Dispute Resolution System," 65 *Fordham Intl L R* (1997) 2275, 2277.

[147] Article 54, ICSID Convention.

[148] Treaty between the United States of America and the Argentine Republic Concerning the Reciprocal Encouragement and Protection of Investment (November 14, 1991). Compare the United Kingdom–Argentina BIT which does not have such broad exceptions clause. Article 7, entitled "Exception," applies only to exclude the

the term "preclude" in some treaty texts, these provisions are sometimes referred to as "nonprecluded measures provisions."[149] Many treaties, however, seek to arrive at the same result without using the term "preclude." Thus, the Energy Charter Treaty's Article 24 on Exceptions states that the Treaty's provisions are not to be construed "...to prevent any Contracting Party from taking any measure which it considers necessary..." "...for the protection of essential security interests..." and "...the maintenance of public order..." among others. Many other treaties follow this linguistic pattern.[150] Some treaties also provide exceptions to pursue other objectives, including public health, public morality, and emergency situations. It should be noted, however, that such exception clauses rarely refer specifically to *economic* crises or *economic* interests as creating a basis for justifying an exception to treaty obligations.

These general exception clauses or nonprecluded measure provisions have the justifiable goal of giving host countries the legislative and regulatory latitude to deal with threats to important national interests. On the other hand, their existence in treaties raises the risk that host countries will invoke them in unjustified circumstances in order to avoid their legal obligations and thwart the justified expectations of investors. The risk is particularly severe because of the vagueness and generality of key terms such as "protection of essential security interests." For example, can a state facing difficult economic challenges justify the expropriation of foreign investments on the grounds that such action was necessary to protect its essential security interests?

In order to provide some safeguards against abusive invocation of exception clauses, many investment treaties state conditions that must be met for a host country to legitimately invoke the clauses and avoid treaty obligations. One example is a requirement that the invoking party notify the other party of its intention to invoke the exception clause and provide pertinent information regarding the proposed measure. The treaty may also attempt to specify the conditions that must be met to legitimately allow for the exception. For example, the Korea–Japan BIT states: "The public order exceptions may be invoked only where a genuine and sufficiently serious threat is posed to one of the fundamental interests of society."[151]

Investment treaties may also contain specified exceptions that permit national legislation in areas deemed by contracting parties to be of great national importance. Two are particularly worthy of note: environmental and tax laws.

BIT's national treatment provisions to three specified situations. Agreement between the Government of the United Kingdom and Northern Ireland and the Government of the Republic of Argentina for the Promotion and Protection of Investments (December 11, 1990).

[149] WW Burke-White and A von Staden, "Investment Protection in Extra-Ordinary Times: The Interpretation and Application of Non-Precluded Measures Provisions in Bilateral Investment Treaties," 48 *Virginia J of Intl L* (2008) 307.

[150] See, eg, Article 16 of the Agreement Between the Government of the Republic of Korea and the Government of Japan for the Liberalization, Promotion, and Protection of Investment (March 22, 2002), which states:

> 1. Notwithstanding any other provisions in this Agreement other than the provisions of Article 11, each Contracting Party may: (a) take any measure which it considers necessary for the protection of its essential security interests; (i) taken in time of war, or armed conflict, or other emergency in that Contracting Party or in international relations; or (ii) relating to the implementation of national policies or international agreements respecting the non-proliferation of weapons; (b) take any measure in pursuance of its obligations under the United Nations Charter for the maintenance of international peace and security; (c) take any measure necessary to protect human, animal or plant life or health; or (d) take any measure necessary for the maintenance of public order. The public order exceptions may be invoked only where a genuine and sufficiently serious threat is posed to one of the fundamental interests of society.

[151] Agreement Between the Government of the Republic of Korea and the Government of Japan for the Liberalization, Promotion, and Protection of Investment (March 22, 2002).

With the rise in environmental concern throughout the globe, investment treaties have increasingly sought to give host countries wide latitude to legislate on matters relating to the natural environment. For instance, the US–Uruguay BIT provides: "[n]othing in this Treaty shall be construed to prevent a party from adopting, maintaining, or enforcing any measure otherwise consistent with the Treaty that it considers appropriate to ensure that investment activity in its territory is conducted in a manner sensitive to environmental concerns."[152] This particular provision would appear to be self-judging since it refers to measures that the host states "consider" appropriate. The phrase "otherwise consistent with the Treaty" would seem to mean that the measures in question would be consistent but for the fact that they were taken to assure that investments will be conducted in an environmentally sensitive manner. Investors considering a particular investment should understand the scope and force of such treaty exceptions.

No treaty is ever permanent and never changing. Thus, most international agreements, including investment treaties, contain provisions describing the process for modifying treaty provisions and, if necessary, terminating the agreement.

Investment treaties generally provide that they shall be in force for 10 or 15 years.[153] Upon the expiry of this initial period, the treaty may continue either for a fixed additional period or until it is terminated by one of the parties.[154] As a rule, a treaty may be terminated by the parties only after the end of the initial period or after the submission of advance written notice;[155] however, the termination of a treaty usually does not result in the immediate denial of treaty protection for investments made while it was in effect. Most treaty termination provisions contain a continuing effects clause which provides that investments made, acquired, or approved prior to the date of the termination of the treaty will remain in force with respect to those investments for a further period of 10, 15, or even 20 years.[156]

15.14 Conclusion

Although the more than 3,000 investment treaties concluded since the mid-twentieth century tend to cover the same issues, they differ in how they treat those issues. Some are more protective than others. For example, the BITs negotiated by the United States

---

[152] Treaty between the United States of America and the Oriental Republic of Uruguay Concerning the Encouragement and Reciprocal Protection of Investment (November 2005) Article XII, <http://tcc.export.gov/Trade_Agreements/All_Trade_Agreements/Uruguay_BIT.asp> accessed May 15, 2009.

[153] See, eg, Agreement Between the Government of the Republic of Botswana and the Government of the People's Republic of China on the Promotion and Protection of Investments, Bots–PRC, Article 14, June 12, 2000 (ten years); Agreement on Encouragement and Reciprocal Protection of Investments between the State of Eritrea and the Kingdom of the Netherlands, Eri–Neth, Article 13, April 14, 2004 (fifteen years).

[154] eg, Agreement Between the Government of the Republic of Indonesia and the Government of the People's Democratic Republic of Algeria Concerning the Promotion and Protection of Investments, Indon–Alg, Article 13, March 21, 2000, provides: "The present Agreement...shall remain force for a period of *ten years* and shall continue in force thereafter for *another period of ten years* and *so forth* unless denounced in writing by either Contracting Party one year before its expiration." (emphasis added).

[155] eg, Article 10 of the Jordan–Yemen BIT provides: "Each Contracting Party has the right to terminate this agreement at the end of its duration or at any time after the expiry of the initial ten years period by a written notice served to the other Contracting party one year prior to the intended termination date." Agreement between the Government of the Hashemite Kingdom of Jordan and the Government of the Republic of Yemen on the Mutual Promotion and Protection of Investments, Jordan-Yemen, Article 10, May 8, 1999.

[156] For example, Article 14 of the Japan-Bangladesh BIT provides: "In respect of investments and returns acquired prior to the date of termination of the present Agreement, the provisions of Articles 1 to 13 shall continue to be effective for further period of fifteen years from the date of termination of the present Agreement." Agreement between Japan and the People's Republic of Bangladesh Concerning the Promotion and Protection of Investment, Japan–Bangl, Article 14, November 10, 1998.

generally exhibit higher standards of protection than the BITs of many other countries.[157] Nonetheless, despite divergence among individual treaties, as a group investment treaties demonstrate many commonalities, including their coverage of similar issues and their use of equivalent or comparable legal concepts and vocabulary. It is these commonalities that are contributing to the creation of an international framework for investment and ultimately a global regime for international investment.[158]

---

[157] P Juillard, *L'Evolution des Sources du Droit des Investissements*, (1994) 250 *Recueil des Cours de L'Academie de Droit International* 74, 211 (asserting that the level of protection achieved by US BITs is superior to the level of protection achieved by European BITs).

[158] JW Salacuse, "The Emerging Global Regime for Investment," 51 *Harvard International Law Journal* (2010) 427–73.

PART V

CONCLUSION

16

The Interaction of the Three Legal Frameworks

16.1 In General

While the three legal frameworks for international investments are conceptually distinct and derive from different sources, they are in practice interconnected and interactive in their application to specific investment transactions. In particular, there are three legal interactions that investors, legal counsel, and government officials must understand and use in planning, managing, and protecting investments in foreign countries:

1. The national law–contractual framework interaction;
2. The national law–international law interaction; and
3. The contractual framework–international law interaction.

Together, these three interactions create a dynamic, trilateral set of processes that influence how capital flows from one country to another and the way it is used once it reaches its destination.

Let us examine each these interactions in greater depth.

16.2 The National Law–Contractual Framework Interaction

The national law, of both the home and host country, and the contractual framework of investment transactions interact in a variety of ways. First, national law creates, gives meaning to, and enforces the contractual framework for the investment transaction. Thus the various contracts that gave rise to the Dabhol Power Company in India and the Kenana Sugar Company in Sudan[1] were the products of national law of the respective host countries. The contracts relating to the international movement of the capital to finance those projects were also shaped by the national laws and regulations of countries that were the source of that capital. Moreover, investment contracts often refer to specific items of national legislation either to incorporate them into or exclude them from the investment transaction.

Contracts result from negotiations between concerned parties. National law usually controls and regulates the negotiation process, defines the scope of parties' negotiating authority, and specifies the contents of relevant contracts. For example, the laws governing the privatization of state assets often require competitive bidding as part of the negotiation process, normally designate the governmental agencies and officials that may negotiate with foreign investors on behalf of the government, and usually set out terms that must appear in any state investment contract or concession with private investors.

Even if the state is not a party to an investment transaction, national law may nonetheless require governmental approval of relevant contracts which governments consider to have a particular public interest, such as those requiring foreign exchange payments or providing for technology transfers into or out of the country concerned. In

---

[1] See Chapter 10, sections 10.5 and 10.7.

addition to regulating investment contracts, national law may also envisage the use of contracts with investors as a means to promote foreign investment. Thus, foreign investment codes and laws may empower state investment authorities to enter into contracts that grant investors a variety of incentives, such as income tax exemptions, duty-free import privileges, and government subsidized inputs like electricity and water.

More generally, the respective appropriate domains for national law and for contracts by private parties are often an important issue of governmental policy. Countries with a strong statist approach to their economies often restrict the right of private parties to undertake economic transactions on the basis of contract, while those with a more "liberal" or private sector orientation may grant considerably greater scope to the role of contract in their economies. This distinction in permitted contractual scope is often the difference between an economic system based on "public ordering" of economic transactions, in which state agencies make fundamental investment decisions, and one based on "private ordering," in which decisions on major economic transactions are left to the discretion of private companies and persons. The precise boundary between the domain of national law and the domain of contract in particular countries may shift over time. Thus, countries that have changed national policy and institutions toward state-dominated economies have tended to limit the domain of contract, while those seeking to liberalize and deregulate economic life have expanded the role they grant to contracts as devices for economic ordering.

The interaction between national law and the contractual framework is not unidirectional in the sense that it is always national law that acts upon and seeks to influence contracts. Private investors, through the device of contract, also seek to influence the nature and application of national law or at least that part of national law that affects their investments. Indeed, foreign investors commonly use contracts as part of their strategies to protect assets from potential injurious actions by host governments.[2] Thus, investors conclude agreements with host governments that provide for "stabilization clauses," which have the effect of exempting their investments from negative future changes in laws and regulations, and parties to investment transactions often enter into international arbitration clauses which enable them to avoid the jurisdiction of national courts with respect to settling disputes relating to their investments. Beyond that, investors may seek to avoid entirely the application of national law of the host country by including a choice-of-law clause in their contracts that makes applicable to the contract the law of another, usually more favorable, jurisdiction. This approach is common in international loan agreements in which lenders insist on the application of their home country law but is rarer in joint venture contracts, which are normally to be performed entirely within the host country. Thus, the joint venture contracts creating the Kenana Sugar project and the Power Purchase Agreement so fundamental to the Dabhol Power Company were governed respectively by the laws of Sudan and of India, the two host countries concerned. Moreover, in countries in which national law is not highly developed and which lack relevant legislation, investors through contracts with host states may in effect create a special legal regime for their investment projects, something that the founders of the Kenana Sugar project sought to do in its early days.

---

[2] See Chapter 7, section 7.3.

16.3 The National Law–International Law Interaction

International law is not an autonomous force driving international investment. Instead, its application in particular instances of organizing and protecting an international investment is strongly influenced by national law and national legal institutions of both host and home countries. In seeking the protection of international law with respect to investment transactions, investors, their counsel, and host country officials must engage in a process of evaluating whether an actual or proposed action or omission by a host government (usually referred to in most investment treaties as "measures") complies with relevant customary or treaty provisions of international law. In short, the application of international law to investment transactions is always a comparative process, comparing whether the government's treatment through its laws and regulations of an actual or proposed investment does or does not meet the standards required by international law.

In order to engage in that evaluation and comparison, one must thoroughly analyze and understand the relevant national law upon which such actual or proposed measure is based. For example, to determine whether an investor's alleged rights with respect to an asset have been expropriated, one must determine the nature and extent of that investor's property rights under national law in that asset. More fundamentally, governments contemplating entering into investment treaties or other international agreements affecting foreign capital must carefully analyze existing legislation to be sure that it complies with the treaty obligations they are to assume. National legal provisions that are contrary to contemplated treaty obligations do not relieve a contracting state from its international obligation to abide by those treaty commitments. If the provisions of a proposed treaty conflict with national law, three options are open to the country concerned: to reject the proposed treaty, to negotiate exceptions to the treaty so as to alleviate the conflict, or to amend national law to conform to the new treaty standards.

The interaction between national law and international law is also found in the specific references that international law makes to national law. For example, many investment treaties provide that they afford protection only to investments that are "made according to law," a reference to the national law of the host country. Thus, in order to determine whether an investment is protected by a treaty, one must first determine whether that investment was made in accordance with the requirements of a host state's national law. If the investment is determined not to have been made according to national law, the investment will not benefit from treaty protection. Similarly the application of "national treatment" or "most favored-nation-treatment" in an investment treaty requires a careful comparative analysis of the ways in which national laws treat a protected investor on the one hand and specified groups of local investors or other foreign investors on the other.

The ICSID Convention and many investment treaties apply only to persons that are "nationals" of a contracting state. To make that determination, one must refer to and analyze the nationality law of the investor's home country. Moreover, the right of an investor to invoke investor–state arbitration or other international dispute settlement process under many treaties requires the investor first "to exhaust local remedies," that is, to use available remedies under national law, at least for a fixed period of time. The application of a general or limited requirement of exhaustion of local remedies is dependent on the provisions of national law with respect to national dispute settlement processes available to the foreign investor.

Even if the applicable treaty contains no specific reference to national law, an arbitration tribunal may nonetheless invoke it to deprive an investor of the benefit of international law if that investor has violated national law in an egregious matter, for example by engaging in corrupt payments and bribery of local officials to make an investment,[3] or as stipulated in the *Tinoco* case,[4] failed to comply with the requirements of national law governing specific types of investment transactions.

States, through references to specific laws, may limit the application of the treaties they sign, for example by providing that national treatment shall not apply to investments in certain economic sectors. Indeed, the application of any relative international law standard of treatment, such as national treatment or most-favored-nation treatment, requires a comparison of the treatment granted to the aggrieved investor with the treatment granted to other investors. Such comparison requires an analysis of relevant national laws and regulations to determine whether there has been a breach of required international law treatment standards. Similarly in order to determine whether a state has complied with its treaty obligations regarding monetary transfers, one must invariably make an in-depth examination of a country's exchange control legislation.

16.4 The Contractual Framework–International Law Interaction

The contractual framework for most investments is the product of and is governed by national, not international law. Nonetheless, international law and the contractual framework interact in various ways. For example, through the process of negotiation, foreign investors in certain instances have secured agreement from host states or other investors that their investment transaction is to be governed by international law. Courts and arbitral tribunals have given effect to such contractual provisions and thereby "internationalized" the investment contract concerned. Instead of applying international law generally to an investment contract, the parties may agree that specific international law concepts, rules, and treaties will be applicable to their relationship. Thus an investment contract may provide for the application of national law but may also specify that all disputes between the parties shall be settled by arbitration under the auspices of the International Centre for Settlement of Investment Disputes in accordance with the Convention on the Settlement of Investment Disputes between States and Nationals of Other States. Indeed, through international arbitration, the interpretation and application of investment contracts become subject to international law procedures and processes.

Conversely, applicable international law may impact or invalidate provisions in certain contracts. For example, agreements between investors and governments providing for special treatment to specific investors may violate investment treaty requirements of national treatment or most-favored-nation treatment, and state contracts requiring foreign investment projects to operate in specific ways may offend prohibitions against performance requirements in investment treaties.

A further interaction between international law and an investment's contractual framework is found in investment treaties that contain an "umbrella clause," a provision that elevates obligations entered into by states with investors to the level of an international law obligation, not a purely domestic law duty that may be modified by domestic legislation.[5] Moreover, even when a treaty does not have an umbrella clause, the jurisprudence of various investor–state arbitration tribunals have held that certain breaches of contractual obligations by states have constituted breaches of other treaty standards such as "fair and equitable treatment" or "full protection and security" since in violating such obligations to

---

[3] See *World Duty Free v. The Republic of Kenya* (ICSID Case no ARB/00/7) Award, October 4, 2006.
[4] See Chapter 6, section 6.10 (c)(i).
[5] See Chapter 15, section 15.6(e).

investors a state as frustrating investor legitimate expectations in making the investment. Similarly, customary international law has determined that a government that cancels a state contract and thereby deprives an investor of valuable contractual rights may in effect have expropriated those rights and therefore is obligated to pay just compensation.

And finally, just as investors have used contracts to secure the added protection of international law, states have attempted to shape contracts to deprive investors of recourse to international law. The Calvo clauses,[6] that many Latin American countries included in their contracts with investors, are an example of this phenomenon since investors who accepted such clauses as a condition for their investment agreed not to seek diplomatic protection from their home governments, something that traditional customary international law allowed them. A modern-day version of the Calvo clause can be seen in contractual clauses whereby, as a condition for investment, foreign investors waive certain rights under investment treaties, such as the right to international investor–state arbitration to settle disputes with host governments.

---

[6] See Chapter 13, section 13.7(c).

Index